Microsoft®

Microsoft® SQL Server® 2012 Integration Services

Wee-Hyong Tok
Rakesh Parida
Matt Masson
Xiaoning Ding
Kaarthik Sivashanmugam

ISBN: 978-0-7356-6585-9

Third Printing: April 2014

Printed and bound in the United States of America.

Microsoft Press books are available through booksellers and distributors worldwide. If you need support related to this book, email Microsoft Press Book Support at mspinput@microsoft.com. Please tell us what you think of this book at *http://www.microsoft.com/learning/booksurvey.*

Acquisitions and Developmental Editor: Russell Jones

Production Editor: Melanie Yarbrough

Editorial Production: Stan Info Solutions

Technical Reviewer: boB Taylor

Copyeditor: Teresa Horton

Indexer: WordCo Indexing Services, Inc.

Cover Design: Twist Creative • Seattle

Cover Composition: ContentWorks, Inc.

Illustrator: Rebecca Demarest

[2012-10-19]

Dedicated to my wife, Juliet, and son, Nathaniel, for their love, support, and patience. And to my parents, Siak-Eng and Hwee-Tiang for shaping me into who I am today.

—Wee-Hyong Tok

I would like to dedicate this to my parents, Basanta and Sarmistha, and my soon-to-be-wife, Vijaya, for all their support and encouragement for making this happen.

—Rakesh Parida

Dedicated to my family and loving wife, whose patience and support made all this possible.

—Matt Masson

I would like to dedicate this book to my parents, ChengXian and Dezhen, my wife Yanan, my cute daughter Ruiyi, and my lovely son Ruichen. I love all of you so much.

—Xiaoning Ding

I dedicate this book to my wife, Devi, and my son, Raghav, for their love and support.

—Kaarthik Sivashanmugam

Contents at a Glance

Contents

PART II DEVELOPMENT

Chapter 4 New SSIS Designer Features 83

PART III DATABASE ADMIN

Foreword

In 1989, when we were all much younger, I had a bizarre weekend job: During the week, I was an engineer at Microrim Incorporated, the makers of R:Base—the second most popular desktop database in the world. But on Saturday mornings I would sit completely alone in our headquarters building in Redmond and rebuild the database that ran our call center. This involved getting the latest registered licenses from accounting, the up-to-date employee list from human resources, the spreadsheets from marketing that tracked our independent software vendors, and of course all of the previous phone call history from the log files, and then mashing it all together. Of course none of these systems had consistent formats or numbering schemes or storage. It took me six hours—unless I messed up a step. The process was all scripted out on a sheet of paper. There wasn't a name for it at the time, but I was building a data warehouse.

Anyone who's done this work knows in their heart the message we hear again and again from customers: Getting the right data into the right shape and to the right place at the right time is 80 percent of the effort for any data project. Data integration is the behind-the-wall plumbing that makes a beautiful fountain work flawlessly. Often the fountains get all the attention, but on the SSIS team at Microsoft, we are proud to build that plumbing.

The authors of this book are at the core of that proud team. For as long as I have known him, Kaarthik has been an ardent advocate for this simple truth: You can understand the quality of a product only if you first deeply understand the customers that use it. As the first employee for SSIS in China, Xiaoning blazed a trail. He is one of those quiet geniuses, who, when he speaks, everyone stops to listen to, because what he says will be deep and important. One of my best professional decisions was overriding my manager's advice to hire Matt. You see, he didn't quite fit our mold. Yes, he could write code well, but there was something that just didn't match our expectations. He cared way too deeply about the real world and about building end-to-end solutions to solve business problems; he wouldn't stop talking about it! We made it work. Don't tell Wee Hyong I said this, but he is probably overqualified for his job. His background as a lecturer in academia, and his history as a SQL MVP (our most valuable partners) made him a perfect candidate to be one of the public faces of SSIS. And finally, Rakesh. At the end of his first week on the job, he decided to create a community event for our customers attending a trade show that just happened to be running nearby. He coerced his teammates into helping, found a room at the convention center, and sent out the invite to our customers. In all the authors, you can see a passion for customers and solutions. You are in great hands.

The strategy for the 2012 SSIS release started with a listening tour of those customers. Their priorities were clear: Make the product easier to use and easier to manage. That sounds like a simple goal, but as I read through the chapters of this book I was astonished by just how much we accomplished toward those goals, and just how much better we've made an already great product. If you are new to SSIS, this book is a good way to dive in to solving real problems, and if you are an SSIS veteran, you will find yourself compelled by the authors' enthusiasm to go and try some of these new things. This is the best plumbing we've ever made. I'm proud of it.

When I was asked to write this foreword I was packing my office in Building 34 in Redmond. I looked out the window and I could see Building 21 across the street. Twenty-five years ago that exact same building housed the world headquarters of Microrim Incorporated. I remembered that kid alone on a Saturday. It's a small world.

Jeff Bernhardt

Group Program Manager, SQL Server Data Movement

Shanghai, China

Introduction

Microsoft SQL Server Integration Services is an enterprise-ready platform for developing data integration solutions. SQL Server Integration Services provides the ability to extract and load from and to heterogeneous data sources and destinations. In addition, it provides the ability for you to easily deploy, manage, and configure these data integration solutions. If you are a data integration developer or a database administrator looking for a data integration solution, then SQL Server Integration Services is the right tool for you.

Microsoft SQL Server 2012 Integration Services provides an organized walkthrough of Microsoft SQL Server Integration Services and the new capabilities introduced in SQL Server 2012. The text is a balanced discussion of using Integration Services to build data integration solutions, and a deep dive into Integration Services internals. It discusses how you can develop, deploy, manage, and configure Integration Services packages, with examples that will give you a great head start on building data integration solutions. Although the book does not provide exhaustive coverage of every Integration Services feature, it offers essential guidance in using the key Integration Services capabilities.

Beyond the explanatory content, each chapter includes examples, procedures, and downloadable sample projects that you can explore for yourself.

Who Should Read This Book

This book is not for rank beginners, but if you're beyond the basics, dive right in and really put SQL Server Integration Services to work! This highly organized reference packs hundreds of time-saving solutions, troubleshooting tips, and workarounds into one volume. It's all muscle and no fluff. Discover how experts perform data integration tasks—and challenge yourself to new levels of mastery.

- Gain in-depth understanding of Integration Services capabilities introduced in SQL Server 2012
- Implement Integration Services best practices and design patterns
- Master the ETL tool for data extraction, transformation, and loading
- Manage performance issues using tuning principles and techniques
- Diagnose problems and apply advanced troubleshooting features

Assumptions

This book expects that you have at least a minimal understanding of Microsoft SQL Server Integration Services and basic database concepts. This book includes examples in Transact-SQL, C#, and PowerShell. If you have not yet picked up one of those languages, you might consider reading John Sharp's *Microsoft Visual C# 2010 Step by Step* (Microsoft Press, 2010) or Itzik Ben-Gan's *Microsoft SQL Server 2012 T-SQL Fundamentals* (Microsoft Press, 2012).

With a heavy focus on database concepts, this book assumes that you have a basic understanding of relational database systems such as Microsoft SQL Server, and have had brief exposure to one of the many flavors of the query tool known as SQL. To go beyond this book and expand your knowledge of SQL and Microsoft's SQL Server database platform, other Microsoft Press books offer both complete introductions and comprehensive information on T-SQL and SQL Server.

Who Should Not Read This Book

This book does not cover basic SQL Server concepts, nor does it cover other technologies such as Analysis Services, Reporting Services, Master Data Services, and Data Quality services.

Organization of This Book

This book is divided into five sections, each of which focuses on a different aspect of Microsoft SQL Server Integration Services. Part I, "Overview" provides a quick overview of Integration Services concepts and considerations for upgrading to Microsoft SQL Server 2012 Integration Services. Part II, "Using SSIS," shows how you can leverage the new Integration Services designer features in developing data integration solutions. In addition, Part II shows how you can work with Change Data Capture, and perform data cleansing using Integration Services. Part III, "Configuration/Management and Monitoring" shows how you can configure an Integration Services project. In addition, Part III shows how you can use Transact-SQL and PowerShell with Integration Services. In addition, it provides a walkthrough of the built-in reports. The internals and advanced concepts of Integration Services take center stage in Part IV, "Deep Dive." Finally, Part V, "Troubleshooting," covers topics that show how you can monitor and troubleshoot Integration Services issues, such as package failures, identifying performance bottlenecks, and data issues.

Finding Your Best Starting Point in This Book

The different sections of *Microsoft SQL Server 2012 Integration Services* cover a wide range of concepts and walkthroughs on building data integration solutions. Depending on your needs and your existing understanding of various SQL Server Integration Services capabilities, you might wish to focus on specific areas of the book. Use the following table to determine how best to proceed through the book.

If you are	Follow these steps
New to SQL Server Integration Services	Focus on Parts I and II and on Chapters 10 and 11 in Part III, or read through the entire book in order.
Familiar with earlier releases of SQL Server Integration Services	Briefly skim Part I if you need a refresher on the core concepts. Read up on the new technologies in Parts II, III, and V and be sure to read Chapter 17 in Part IV.
Interested in using Transact-SQL or PowerShell capabilities for using SQL Server Integration Services	Chapter 12 and 13 in Part III provide a walkthrough of the concepts.
Interested in monitoring and troubleshooting SQL Server Integration Services	Read through the chapters in Part V.

Most of the book's chapters include hands-on samples that let you try out the concepts just learned. No matter which sections you choose to focus on, be sure to download and install the sample applications on your system.

Conventions and Features in This Book

This book presents information using conventions designed to make the information readable and easy to follow.

- In most cases, the book includes examples that use Transact-SQL or PowerShell. Each example consists of a series of tasks, presented as numbered steps (1, 2, and so on) listing each action you must take to complete the exercise.
- Boxed elements with labels such as "Note" provide additional information or alternative methods for completing a step successfully.

System Requirements

You will need the following hardware and software to complete the practice exercises in this book:

- .NET 3.5 Service Pack 1 is a requirement for SQL Server 2012
- SQL Server 2012 Standard Edition or higher, with SQL Server Management Studio 2012
- Computer that has a 1.4 GHz or faster processor (2 GHz or faster is recommended)
- SQL Server 2012 requires a minimum of 6 GB of available hard-disk space, and 1 GB of memory (4 GB of memory or more is recommended for optimal performance)
- Refer to *http://msdn.microsoft.com/en-us/library/ms143506.aspx* for operating system requirements for installing SQL Server 2012
- Internet connection to download software or chapter examples

Depending on your Windows configuration, you might require Local Administrator rights to install or configure SQL Server 2012 products.

Code Samples

Most of the chapters in this book include exercises that let you interactively try new material learned in the main text. All sample projects, in both their preexercise and postexercise formats, can be downloaded from the following page:

http://go.microsoft.com/FWLink/?Linkid=258311

Follow the instructions to download the SSIS_2012_examples.zip file.

> **Note** In addition to the code samples, your system should have SQL Server 2012 and SQL Server Management Studio installed.

Most of the samples require sample data from Adventure Works for SQL Server 2012. You can download the sample databases from the following page:

http://msftdbprodsamples.codeplex.com/releases/view/55330

Installing the Code Samples

Follow these steps to install the code samples on your computer so that you can use them with the exercises in this book.

1. Unzip the SSIS_2012_examples.zip file that you downloaded from the book's website (name a specific directory along with directions to create it, if necessary).

2. If prompted, review the displayed end user license agreement. If you accept the terms, select the Accept option, and then click Next.

> **Note** If the license agreement doesn't appear, you can access it from the same webpage from which you downloaded the SSIS_2012_examples .zip file.

Using the Code Samples

The folder structure created by unzipping the sample code download contains folders corresponding to each chapter. In each of the folders, you will see the code examples used in the chapter.

Acknowledgments

The authors would like to thank all the SQL Server professionals who have worked closely with the Integration Services team throughout the years to evolve the product into an enterprise-ready data integration platform, as well as all the members of the SQL Server Integration Services team for their help and contributions to this book. Specifically, the authors would like to thank Jeff Bernhardt for contributing the foreword for the book, and the editorial team at Microsoft Press and O'Reilly (Russell Jones, Melanie Yarbrough, Rani Xavier G, and Teresa Horton) for all their support of the book, from initial proposal to final completion.

Errata & Book Support

We've made every effort to ensure the accuracy of this book and its companion content. Any errors that have been reported since this book was published are listed on our Microsoft Press site:

http://go.microsoft.com/FWlink/?Linkid=258310

If you find an error that is not already listed, you can report it to us through the same page.

If you need additional support, email Microsoft Press Book Support at *mspinput@microsoft.com*.

Please note that product support for Microsoft software is not offered through the addresses above.

We Want to Hear from You

At Microsoft Press, your satisfaction is our top priority, and your feedback our most valuable asset. Please tell us what you think of this book at:

http://www.microsoft.com/learning/booksurvey

The survey is short, and we read every one of your comments and ideas. Thanks in advance for your input!

Stay in Touch

Let's keep the conversation going! We're on Twitter: *http://twitter.com/MicrosoftPress*

PART I

Overview

CHAPTER 1

SSIS Overview

In This Chapter

Enterprises depend on data integration to turn data into valuable insights and decisions. Enterprise data integration is a complicated problem due to the heterogeneity of data sources and formats, ever-increasing data volumes, and the poor quality of data. Data is typically stored in disparate systems and the result is that there are differences in data format or schema that must be resolved. The constantly decreasing costs of storage lead to increased data retention and a concomitant increase in the volume of data that needs to be processed. In turn, this results in an ever-increasing demand for scalable and high-performance data integration solutions so organizations can obtain timely insights from the collected data. The diversity of data and inconsistent duplication cause quality problems that can impact the accuracy of analytical insights and thus also affect the quality and value of the decisions. Data integration projects need to deal with these challenges and effectively consume data from a variety of sources (e.g., databases, spreadsheets, files, etc.), which requires that they clean, correlate, transform, and move the source data to the destination systems. This process is further complicated because many organizations have round-the-clock dependencies on data stores; therefore, data integration must often be frequent and integration operations must be completed as quickly as possible.

Microsoft SQL Server Integration Services (SSIS) technology addresses these challenges and provides a platform for building and managing data integration solutions. The flexible, extensible, scalable, high-performance platform and toolset in SSIS caters to enterprise demands for traditional data extract-transform-load (ETL) processes as well as other data integration needs. SSIS is a feature of Microsoft SQL Server that provides seamless interoperability with other features shipped with both SQL Server and with other Microsoft products. Typical data integration scenarios that you can address using SSIS include the following:

- Consolidating data from heterogeneous data sources
- Moving data between systems
- Loading data warehouses
- Cleaning, formatting, or standardizing data
- Identifying, capturing, and processing data changes
- Coordinating data maintenance, processing, or analysis

Some data processing scenarios require specialized technology. SSIS is not suitable for the following types of data processing:

- Processing complex business rules on data
- Coordinating, acquiring, and processing data in inter-business processes
- Processing event messages in real time
- Coordinating data communication between systems
- Building a federated view of data sources
- Unstructured data processing and integration

Common Usage Scenarios for SSIS

In this section, you'll examine some common data integration scenarios in detail and get an overview of how key SSIS features help in each of those scenarios.

Consolidation of Data from Heterogeneous Data Sources

In an organization, data is typically not contained in one system but spread all over. Different applications might have their own data stores with different schema. Similarly, different parts of the organization might have their own locally consolidated view of data, or legacy systems might be isolated, making the data available to rest of the organization at regular intervals. To make important organization-wide decisions that derive value from all this data, it is necessary to pull data from all parts of the organization, massaging and transforming it into a consistent state and shape.

The need for data consolidation also arises during organization acquisitions or mergers. Supporting connectivity to heterogeneous stores and extracting data is a key feature of any data integration software. SSIS supports connectivity to a wide range of data stores using out-of-the-box adapters and extensibility features. Source adapters read data from external sources into SSIS, whereas destination adapters write data from SSIS to external destinations.

Some of the most important built-in source and destination adapters in SSIS are the following:

- OLE DB Source and Destination

- ADO.NET Source and Destination
- ODBC Source and Destination
- Flat File Source and Destination
- Excel Source and Destination
- XML Source

> **Note** Open Database Connectivity (ODBC) source and destination components are available starting with Integration Services 2012 and are not available in earlier versions. In SQL Server 2008 and SQL Server 2008 R2, you can use ADO.NET source and destination components in SSIS to connect to ODBC data sources using the .NET ODBC Data Provider. The ADO.Net Destination component is not available in SQL Server 2005.

Other types of SSIS adapters are as follows:

- Script Source and Destination: These enable SSIS developers to author code to connect to data stores that are not supported by built-in adapters in SSIS.
- Special-purpose adapters: Most of the adapters in SSIS are general purpose, supporting any data store that can be accessed through standard interfaces; however, some of the adapters are specific to a particular data store and depend on a specific application programming interface (API). The SQL Server Destination and Dimension Processing Destination are examples of special-purpose adapters that provide connectivity to SQL Server and Analysis Server, respectively.
- Custom adapters: Using the extensibility mechanism in SSIS, customers and independent software vendors (ISVs) can build adapters that can be used to connect to data stores that do not have any built-in support in SSIS.

> **Note** Scripting in SSIS is powered by Visual Studio for Applications in SQL Server 2005 and Visual Studio Tools for Applications in SQL Server 2008 and later versions. Visual Studio for Applications and Visual Studio Tools for Applications are .NET-based script hosting technologies to embed custom experience into applications. Both of these technologies provide a runtime that executes custom code using a script engine and end-user integrated development environment (IDE) for writing and debugging custom code. Visual Studio for Applications supports VB.Net and Visual Studio Tools for Applications supports both VB.Net and C# programming.

Source and destination adapters that are not a part of SSIS installation but available for download from Microsoft.com include the following:

- Oracle Source and Destination

- Teradata Source and Destination
- SAP BI Source and Destination

> **Note** Oracle, Teradata, and SAP BW connectors are available only for advanced editions of SQL Server. See details on SQL Server editions in a later section in this chapter. Oracle and Teradata connectors are available for download at *http://www.microsoft.com/download/en/details.aspx?id=29283*. Microsoft Connector 1.1 for SAP BW is available as a part of SQL Server Feature Pack at *http://www.microsoft.com/download/en/details.aspx?id=29065*.

SSIS adapters maintain connection information to external data stores using *connection managers*. SSIS connection managers depend on technology-specific data providers or drivers for connecting to data stores. For example, OLE DB adapters use the OLE DB API and data provider to access data stores that support OLE DB. SSIS connectivity adapters are used within a *Dataflow Task,* which is powered by a data pipeline engine that facilitates high-performance data movement and transformation between sources and destinations. Figure 1-1 illustrates flow of data from source to destination through data providers or drivers.

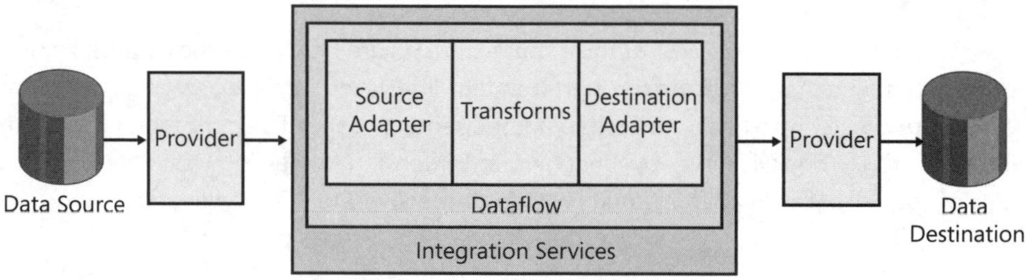

FIGURE 1-1 Representation of data flow from source to destination.

Integration Services offers several options for connecting to relational databases. OLE DB, ADO.NET, and ODBC adapters provide data store generic APIs for connecting to a wide range of databases. The only popular database connectivity option that is not supported in SSIS is Java Database Connectivity (JDBC). SSIS developers are often faced with the challenge of picking an adapter from the choices to connect to a particular data store. The factors that SSIS developers should consider when picking the connectivity options are as follows:

- Data type support
- Metadata exposed by driver or provider
- Driver or provider support in 32 and 64-bit environments
- Performance

Data Type Support

Data type support in relational databases beyond the standard ANSI SQL data types differs; each has its own type system. Data types supported by data providers and drivers provide a layer of abstraction for the type systems in data stores. Data integration tools need to ensure that they don't lose type information when reading, processing, or writing data. SSIS has its own data type system. Adapters in SSIS map external data types exposed by data providers to SSIS data types, and maintain data type fidelity during interactions with external stores. The SSIS data type system ameliorates problems when dealing with data type differences among storage systems and providers, providing a consistent basis for data processing. SSIS implicitly converts data to the equivalent types in its own data type system when reading or writing data. When that is not possible, it might be necessary to explicitly convert data to binary or string types to avoid data loss.

> **Note** See *http://msdn.microsoft.com/en-us/library/ms141036.aspx* for a comprehensive list of SSIS data types.

Metadata Exposed by Provider

SQL Server Data Tools provides the development environment in which you can build SSIS packages, which are executable units in SSIS. Design experience in SQL Server Data Tools depends on the metadata exposed by data stores through drivers or providers to guide SSIS developers in setting package properties. Such metadata is used to get a list of databases, tables, views, and metadata of columns in tables or views during package construction. If a data store does not expose a particular metadata or if the driver does not implement an interface to get some metadata from the data stores, the SSIS package development experience will be affected. Manually setting the relevant properties in SSIS packages could help in those instances.

> **Note** The Integration Services designer in SQL Server 2005, 2008, and 2008 R2 is called Business Intelligence Development Studio. In SQL Server 2012, the SSIS development environment became part of an integrated toolset named SQL Server Data Tools, which brought together database and business intelligence development into one environment.

Support in 32 and 64-Bit Environments

You can execute SSIS packages in either 32-bit or 64-bit modes. If the application is a 32-bit application, SSIS uses the 32-bit data provider.

The 32 and 64-bit versions of data providers usually have the same identifier. Once referenced using the identifier, the version of the data provider loaded during execution time will depend on the application that loads it. The data provider available to SSIS packages will depend on the bit mode under which the package is executed. For example, execution of packages inside SQL Server Data Tools is in 32-bit mode by default; hence the 32-bit provider will be used during execution in SQL Server Data Tools. Packages that successfully execute in 32-bit mode do not necessarily execute successfully in 64-bit mode (and vice versa). This is because data providers or drivers might not be available in both modes. If the 64-bit driver is not available on the executing machine, execution will fail when attempting 64-bit execution and vice versa. SSIS package developers and administrators have to keep this in mind during package development and execution.

> **Note** You can override 32-bit execution in SQL Server Data Tools by setting the value of the package property *Run64BitRuntime* to *True*. This property takes effect only within SQL Server Data Tools; it has no effect when you execute a package in SQL Server Management Studio or the DTExec utility. If the package is executed in other contexts, this property is ignored; however, there are other ways to control package execution mode in those contexts.

Performance

Several factors impact the performance of data integration operations. One of the main factors is adapter performance, which is directly related to the performance of the low-level data providers or drivers used by the adapters. Although there are general recommendations (see Table 1-1) for what adapter to use for each popular database, there is no guarantee that you will get the best performance from the recommended adapters. Adapter performance depends on several factors, such as the driver or data provider involved, and the bit mode of the drivers. We recommend that SSIS developers compare performance of different connectivity options before determining which one to use in the production environment.

TABLE 1-1 Recommended adapters for some popular data stores

Database	Recommended adapters
SQL Server	OLE DB Source and Destination
Oracle	Oracle Source and Destination
Teradata	Teradata Source and Destination
DB2	OLE DB Source and Destination
MySQL	ODBC Source and Destination
SAP BW	SAP BI Source and Destination
SAP R/3	ADO.Net Source and Destination

> **Note** Oracle and Teradata connectors are available for download at *http://www.microsoft.com/download/en/details.aspx?id=29283*. Connecting to SAP R/3 requires the Microsoft .NET Data Provider for mySAP Business Suite, which is available as part of the BizTalk Adapter Pack 2.0, available for download at *http://www.microsoft.com/download/en/detailsw.aspx?id=2755*. BizTalk is not required to install the adapter pack or to use the SAP provider. We recommend Microsoft OLE DB Provider for DB2 for connectivity to DB2 and it is available in Microsoft Host Integration Server or in the SQL Server Feature Pack.

Movement of Data Between Systems

The data integration scenario in this section covers moving data between data storage systems. Data movement can be a one-time operation during system or application migration, or it can be a recurring process that periodically moves data from one data store to another. An example of one-time movement is data migration before discontinuing an old system. Copying incremental data from a legacy system at regular intervals to a newer data store, to ensure the new system is a super set of the older one is an example of recurring data movement. These types of transfers usually involve data transformation so that the moved data conforms to the schema of the destination system. The source and destination adapters in SSIS discussed earlier in this chapter can help with connecting to the old and new systems.

You use transform components in SSIS to perform operations such as conversion, grouping, merging, sampling, sorting, distribution, or other common operations on the data that is extracted into the SSIS data pipeline. In SSIS, these transform components take data flow pipeline data as input, process it, and add the output back to the pipeline, which can be of the same shape or different than the input. Transform components can operate on data row-by-row, on a subset of rows, or on the entire data set at once. All transformations in SSIS are executed in memory, which helps with high-performance data processing and transformation. Each data transformation operation is defined on one or more columns of data in the data flow pipeline. To perform operations not supported out of the box, SSIS developers can use scripts or build custom transformations. Built-in SSIS transforms that support some of the most common data operations are as follows:

- **Aggregate** Applies aggregate functions, such as Average, Count, or Group By, to column values and copies the results to the transformation output.
- **Conditional split** Routes data rows to different outputs depending on the data content.
- **Multicast** Distributes every row from input to one or more outputs for branched processing.
- **Lookup** Performs lookups by joining data in input columns with columns in a reference dataset.
- **Merge** Combines two sorted datasets into a single dataset.
- **Sort** Sorts input data in ascending or descending order.

- **Union all** Combines multiple inputs into one output.
- **Data Conversion transform** Converts the data in an input column to a different data type.
- **Derived Column transform** Creates new column values by applying expressions to input columns.

One-time data migrations can range from simple data movement with no transformations to extremely complex movement with more than one source and heavyweight data transformation logic. Packages for complex data movement can evolve from those created for simple one-time data movement to those built from scratch by SSIS developers using SQL Server Data Tools. An employee getting data from a database table and importing it into Excel for further data analysis and processing is an example of simple one-time data movement. Such users do not necessarily have in-depth knowledge of ETL concepts or SSIS features. The Import and Export Wizard in SSIS helps such users build simple data movement solutions. This wizard constructs and uses an SSIS package behind the scenes, hiding the complexity involved in building a package. The packages created by the wizard involve source and destination adapters for the data stores participating in the movement. Figure 1-2 shows a step in the wizard for selecting tables at the source to copy to the destination. After the wizard has created a package, you can save and edit it later using the SQL Server Data Tools environment (discussed in detail later in this chapter). This capability comes in handy for SSIS developers who might have to update packages created by information workers, adding more complex transformations before making those packages available for use by the IT department. Data sources and destinations supported by the Import and Export Wizard include the following:

- Relational databases that support a .NET Framework Provider or OLE DB Provider
- Microsoft Office files: Access and Excel
- Delimited data files in plain text

You can enable simple transformation capabilities in wizard-created packages to carry out data type mapping between a source and a destination. To avoid complexity when dealing with data types, the wizard automatically maps data types of each column selected for data movement at the source to the types of destination columns, using data type mapping files that are part of the SSIS installation for this purpose. SSIS provides default mapping files in XML format for commonly used source and destination combinations. For example, the wizard uses a mapping file called DB2ToMSSql10.xml when moving data from DB2 to SQL Server 2008 or a newer version. This file maps each data type in DB2 to the corresponding types in SQL Server 2008 or later. Listing 1-1 shows a portion of this file that maps between the Timestamp data type in DB2 and the SQL Server datetime2 type.

LISTING 1-1 Data type mapping in *DB2ToMSSql10.xml*

```
<?xml version="1.0" encoding="utf-8" ?>
<dtm:DataTypeMappings
  xmlns:dtm="http://www.microsoft.com/SqlServer/Dts/DataTypeMapping.xsd"
  xmlns:xsi="http://www.w3.org/2001/XMLSchema-instance"
  SourceType="DB2OLEDB;Microsoft.HostIntegration.MsDb2Client.MsDb2Connection"
  MinSourceVersion="*"
  MaxSourceVersion="*"
```

```
  DestinationType="SQLOLEDB;SQLNCLI*;System.Data.SqlClient.SqlConnection"
  MinDestinationVersion="10.*"
  MaxDestinationVersion="*">
...
  <!-- TIMESTAMP 10.* -->
  <dtm:DataTypeMapping>
     <dtm:SourceDataType>
        <dtm:DataTypeName>TIMESTAMP</dtm:DataTypeName>
     </dtm:SourceDataType>
     <dtm:DestinationDataType>
        <dtm:NumericType>
           <dtm:DataTypeName>datetime2</dtm:DataTypeName>
           <dtm:SkipPrecision/>
           <dtm:UseSourceScale/>
        </dtm:NumericType>
     </dtm:DestinationDataType>
  </dtm:DataTypeMapping>
...
</dtm:DataTypeMappings>
```

> **Note** In SQL Server Integration Services 2012, mapping files are installed to %Program Files%\Microsoft SQL Server\110\DTS\MappingFiles by default. Users can update the default mapping files and also add mapping files to this folder to add support for more sources and destinations in the wizard. The new mapping files must conform to the published XSD schema, and map types between a unique combination of source and destination.

Different usage scenarios of Import and Export Wizard lead to different methods to launch it. For example, a SQL Server database developer or administrator who wants to import data from Microsoft Office Excel to a database could invoke the wizard from SQL Server Management Studio in the context of the destination database. This option allows you to save the package constructed by the wizard and then either execute it later or run it right away.

Another way to invoke the wizard is from SQL Server Data Tools. SSIS beginners who want to start with some basic data-moving package constructs can invoke the wizard from Solution Explorer in SQL Server Data Tools and add a package to the current solution. After adding the package, they can edit it for improvements and then save it just like any other package in the SQL Server Data Tools solution.

One-time migration scenarios often involve copying data objects and data from one instance of SQL Server to another. SSIS supports this scenario with a few tasks that you can use to transfer databases, logins, objects, stored procedures in a master database, user-defined error messages, or SQL Agent jobs between two SQL Server instances. All these transfer tasks use the SQL Management Object (SMO) connection manager to connect to the SQL Servers involved in the transfer.

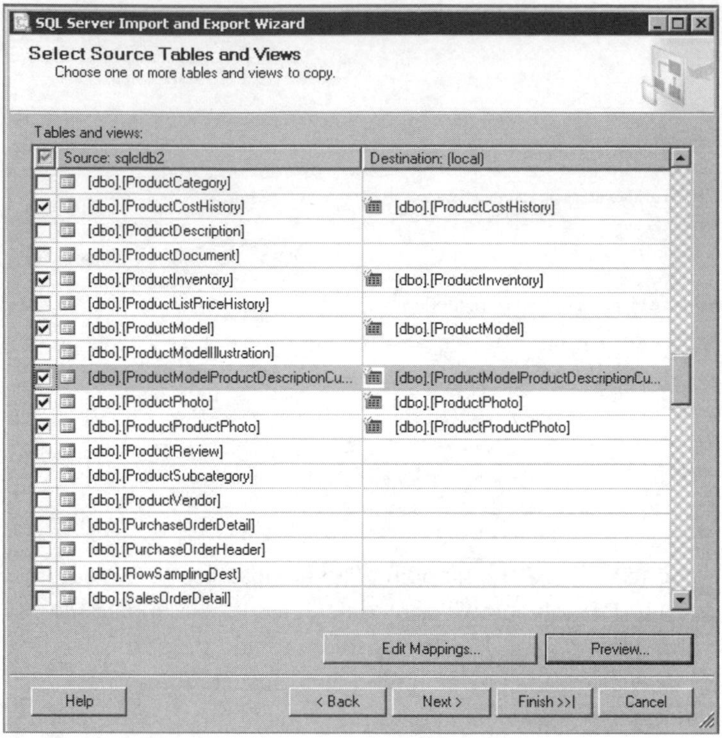

FIGURE 1-2 Make your selections in the Import and Export wizard.

You perform recurring data movements by using a SQL Server Agent job to schedule the execution of the SSIS package that performs the operation.

Loading a Data Warehouse

SSIS is a quintessential ETL tool and platform for traditional data warehouse (DW) loading. Loading DWs is the most popular use for SSIS in enterprises. In data warehousing, data is moved from operational data stores to a central location that's optimized for analysis and reporting. This type of loading can be done either incrementally or as a bulk refresh and it typically involves the following operations:

- Extract all or changed data from multiple sources
- Transform extracted data before loading at the destination
- Load dimension and fact tables at the destination
- Reference data lookup
- Key generation
- Manage historical changes

SSIS can be used effectively to implement all of these operations. Extracting data from multiple sources, transforming data, and loading tables are discussed briefly in the scenarios described earlier in this chapter. Getting changed data is discussed in the next section. This section examines other DW loading operations.

Reference data lookup involves getting data from an external reference dataset. For example, given a customer identifier, a DW loading process might need to retrieve additional data about the customer; for example, getting the customer's zip code from a customer relationship management (CRM) server that stores all customer-related information. In this case, the external dataset on the CRM server is used as the reference to add more data to the ETL pipeline. SSIS supports this step in DW processing using the Lookup Transform component. The reference dataset can be an existing table or view in a relational database, the result of a SQL query, or the Lookup Cache file. SSIS needs reference data in memory for the lookup operation. For large reference sets, the data can be preloaded into a special type of file called Lookup Cache for efficiency and high performance. The Lookup transformation uses either an OLE DB connection manager or a Lookup Cache connection manager to connect to the reference dataset. The Lookup transformation performs lookups by joining data in input columns with columns in the reference dataset. Lookup Transform can use multiple inputs for the lookup operation. Lookup inputs cannot be of certain data types like image or text. For supported string data types, the lookup operation is case sensitive and Character Map transformation has to be used explicitly to convert lookup input to upper or lowercase to match the case in the reference data. Inputs not matched in the reference data can be redirected using the Lookup transform. Connectivity from Lookup transform to relational databases is limited to OLE DB connectivity and the supported data sources are SQL Server, Oracle, and DB2. If the reference data source does not support OLE DB connectivity, a Data Flow task using any supported source adapter and Cache transform is used to create a cache file for lookup operations in another Data Flow task.

Note Lookup transform supports only exact matches when looking up the reference dataset. Fuzzy Lookup transform, discussed in the next section, supports nonexact matching on the reference data. SQL Server 2005 did not support redirection of unmatched inputs.

Generating unique keys and using them to substitute a natural primary key for dimension tables in DWs is a comment pattern. These keys are often referred to as *surrogate* or *artificial* keys and they are quite useful in making dimensional updates easier in cases where natural primary keys can change. When the natural key is an alphanumeric or composite surrogate, you use an integer key for better performance. Surrogate key generation during ETL processes is considered better than using key generation at destinations (such as using the identity key feature in SQL Server) during row inserts because referential integrity established at the destination using such destination-generated keys can break during data movement. In contrast, surrogate keys enable data portability. There is no built-in functionality in SSIS to generate keys, but it is quite easy to do. Scripting or custom extensions are popular approaches for building surrogate key generators in SSIS. Surrogate key generation typically involves getting the maximum value of the surrogate key currently used in the table of interest, and using it as a seed to assign a key to each row in the data flow pipeline, with predefined increments.

Some SSIS developers prefer to maintain the seed value within their ETL systems without having to query the database at the beginning of every ETL process.

In DWs, dimensional data can change over time. Such dimensions are commonly referred to as slowly changing dimensions (SCDs). SCD processing and managing historical changes is one of the more difficult steps in DW loading operations. There are three common types of SCDs:

- **Type 1** Old data is overwritten, and historical changes are not preserved. This type is often used with dimensional data that is no longer correct and when the historical values carry no business value.
- **Type 2** Historical changes are preserved, and a row is added for each new value. This is the most common type of change in DW dimensions. Each row (current and historical) of a dimensional value will have its own surrogate key, version number, or timestamp that can be used to get the most recent value.
- **Type 3** Create columns used to maintain current value and history. You would employ this method when changes happen only rarely, or at predefined intervals, and you need to maintain only a few of the most recent historical values.

SSIS supports this operation using the Slowly Changing Dimension transform, which coordinates the update and insertion of records in DW dimension tables. This transformation supports four types of changes:

- **Changing attribute** Supports Type 1 SCD described earlier.
- **Historical attribute** Supports Type 2 SCD described earlier.
- **Fixed attribute** Changes indicate that the column value must not change. Rows that try to change these values are redirected for further processing.
- **Inferred member** A placeholder record is created when dimension values are not yet available.

Type 3 changes are not supported in SCD transforms, but can be handled using a combination of other SSIS components. The Slowly Changing Dimension transformation has one input and up to six outputs. Each output corresponds to the update, insert, or other processing requirements of the record in the dimension table at the destination. During execution, the SCD transform identifies incoming row records with matches in a lookup table using its connection manager. After the match is found, SCD identifies the update type for each row and column, then redirects the row into the appropriate output for handling the change correctly. For example, in Type 1 dimension processing, the SCD transform outputs the row to the Changing Attributes Updates output, which is connected to OLE DB Command transform that updates the record in the dimension table using a SQL UPDATE statement.

Note The OLE DB Command transform in SSIS is a row-based component, and can significantly hurt the performance of SCD processing. The number of dimension value changes to be processed will require an equal number of calls to the database, which is obviously not an efficient approach. There are alternative approaches to design better SCD processing in SSIS, including the following:

- SQL MERGE statement for simple changes
- Custom components for large dimensions and error processing
- The SSIS Dimension Merge SCD Component, available at *http://www.codeplex.com*

Constructing and configuring steps for SCD processing can get complex during ETL design. SSIS supplies a wizard to help developers go through standard steps in SCD management. The wizard produces transformations for SCD processing in the Data Flow task and works only with dimension tables in SQL Server databases. Figure 1-3 shows the typical SSIS components involved in SCD processing. All the components shown (except the source adapter) are added by the wizard.

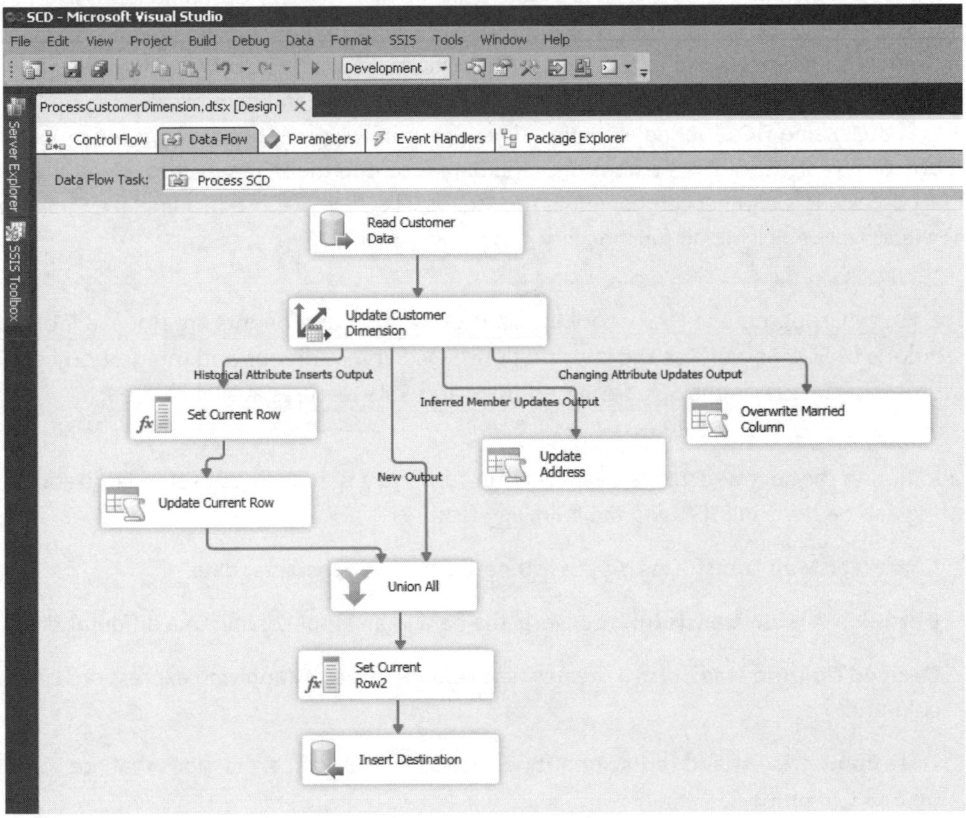

FIGURE 1-3 Slowly changing dimension processing in SSIS.

Cleaning, Formatting, or Standardization of Data

Data in organizations exist in many forms, shapes, and quality levels. Different parts of the organization might use different conventions and formats. During interbusiness transactions, data is acquired from other organizations that might use different data stores and have different data quality standards. Global organizations maintain data in different locales to serve domestic business needs in different geographical regions. Data can also get corrupted during transactions, and such data needs to be isolated during processing.

Data integration processes need to deal with these issues, gathering all the data and ensuring it's in a consistent state before processing the consolidated data in the integration environment or loading it into destinations. Most data integration tools have capabilities to help deal with dirty data, including incorrect spellings, inaccurate or invalid data, duplicates, or unexpected abbreviations.

SSIS provides some data cleansing options suitable for various customer needs, including the Fuzzy Lookup and Fuzzy Grouping transformation components that act as generic data processing operations without requiring an expert collection of domain-specific rules. Fuzzy Lookup helps in matching incoming and potentially low-quality data with a cleaned and standardized reference data set. It outputs the closest match in reference data and quality of the match. Fuzzy Grouping helps in identifying groups of rows in incoming data that are possibly referring to the same entity in a string column leading to duplicate detection in data. SSIS has Data Quality Services (DQS) Cleansing transform in SQL Server 2012. This transform is used to perform data correction and deduplication using knowledge bases built using DQS. During execution time, cleansing work happens in DQS server using the knowledge bases referenced in the transform and data is sent to the DQS server for cleansing. DQS is not a part of SSIS. It is another component in the Microsoft SQL Server product line like SSIS, providing knowledge-driven cleansing functionality.

> **Note** Fuzzy Grouping and Fuzzy Lookup transformation components are not available in all editions of SQL Server. See the later section "SQL Server Editions and Integration Services Features" for details on the SQL Server editions and SSIS features available in each.

In addition to the special-purpose cleansing transforms just described, data standardization and formatting can be done in SSIS using the following features:

- **Character Map transform** Applies string functions to character data.
- **Data Conversion transform** Converts the data in an input column to a different data type.
- **Derived Column transform** Creates new column values by applying expressions on input columns.
- **Data comparisons and replacement** Functions are used in expressions that are computed on input columns.

Cleansing and format manipulation are useful, but in most cases the nature of data has to be well understood before any type of processing happens. SSIS provides a feature called the Data Profiling task that compiles statistics on the data and can be helpful in identifying cleansing needs and minimizing data quality issues. This task is configured to compute one or more profiles. The results, which are given in XML format, can be stored in a file or in an SSIS variable. Profiling results saved to a file can be viewed in the Data Profiler Viewer. It is possible to control the workflow in SSIS packages using the results of the profiling task.

> **Note** The Data Profiling task works only with data stored in SQL Server 2000 or later versions.

Chapter 9, "Data Profiling and Cleansing Using SSIS," discusses all these data quality and cleansing capabilities in SSIS in more detail.

Identification, Capture, and Processing of Data Changes

Ever-growing volumes of data in organizations, the need for real-time reports, and a reduced batch window for data processing have all resulted in the demand for change-processing capabilities in data integration tools. Data integration processing is efficient when it can run against an incremental data set instead of the all the data available in the data stores involved. Processing data incrementally reduces the run duration of data integration processes, which in turn can help by increasing the frequency at which these processes run. Using timestamp columns, checksum, or hash-function-based solutions for change detection and capture is a common industry practice. A relatively recent and popular alternative offered by several database vendors provides the native ability to identify changed data. Data integration tools can leverage these features to identify and capture changes for incremental data processing. For example, SQL Server provides Change Data Capture (CDC) and Change Tracking (CT) features, and SSIS provides built-in and custom options to process changed data that can leverage CDC functionality when it is used.

Data integration solution developers can make use of SQL Server CDC infrastructure directly during package design. The CDC feature in SQL Server is powerful, but it is also complex, and involves considerable custom logic. For streamlined CDC processing, SSIS provides the following tasks and components:

- CDC Control task
- CDC Source
- CDC Splitter transform

> **Note** CDC and CT are available in SQL Server 2008 and later versions. The CDC processing tasks and components in SSIS are available in SQL Server 2012.

The CDC Control task is useful for controlling various stages in change data processing in SSIS packages. It requires one connection manager to the database where changes need to be identified and captured, and another (optional) connection manager to persist the state of the CDC processing operation stored in an SSIS variable. CDC processing stages managed in SSIS using this task include marking the beginning and ending of initial data load, the start of the operation, and the range of data processed. CDC Source extracts changed rows within a specified processing range. Those rows can be obtained by the control task. The source component uses database artifacts generated by SQL Server during CDC setup on the database to be observed for changes. The CDC Splitter transformation routes changed data extracted by CDC Source into three output categories—Insert, Update, and Delete—applying different processing logic to each category. Chapter 8, "Working with Change Data Capture in SSIS 2012," discusses these components in detail. As mentioned earlier, these CDC components support only SQL Server databases. SSIS supports CDC on Oracle database using a Windows service that mimics Oracle database changes in SQL Server database, enabling change processing using the CDC task and components.

Coordination of Data Maintenance, Processing, or Analysis

The Data Flow task that supports data extraction, transformation, and loading described in previous sections is executed in the context of a workflow defined in the Control Flow section of SSIS packages. Control Flow in SSIS is task oriented, and it coordinates execution of data processing tasks in the business workflow. In addition to the special-purpose Data Flow task powered by a buffer-based data processing engine, SSIS has several built-in tasks that you can use when building the control flow. These tasks, executed by the SSIS runtime engine, are useful for operations such as database administrative steps, preparation for dataflow execution, command execution on Analysis Server, and many other operations common in data integration. You can also build custom tasks using the SSIS programming model and use those as a part of the Control Flow. Execution of scripts is also possible in the Control Flow.

Three types of containers are available to host tasks. The Sequence container is used to group tasks and containers to manage them as one unit. The For Each container facilitates repeating steps in a control flow by enumerating files or objects, and the For Loop container provides another option for repeating steps in a Control Flow that uses a conditional expression. These containers can host other containers along with tasks. Tasks and containers in the Control Flow are connected by precedence constraints that determine the execution path in the workflow. Precedence constraints specify the order in which tasks and task containers are executed during runtime, or conditions that determine which part of the workflow will execute next. The simplicity of using constraints makes orchestration of steps in the SSIS workflow easy to build, debug, and manage.

SSIS includes tasks for performing database maintenance operations. These tasks are useful in building database maintenance plans in SQL Server Management Studio and also in SQL Server Data Tools along with other tasks that you can use when constructing control flow in SSIS. Figure 1-4 shows the SQL Server Management Studio designer in the process of building a database maintenance plan using SSIS maintenance tasks. Some of the popular database maintenance tasks are the following:

- **Backup Database task** Performs SQL Server database backups.
- **Rebuild Index task** Rebuilds indexes in SQL Server database tables and views.

- **Update Statistics task** Updates information about the distribution of key values for one or more sets of statistics on the specified table or view.
- **Shrink Database task** Reduces the size of SQL Server database data and log files.

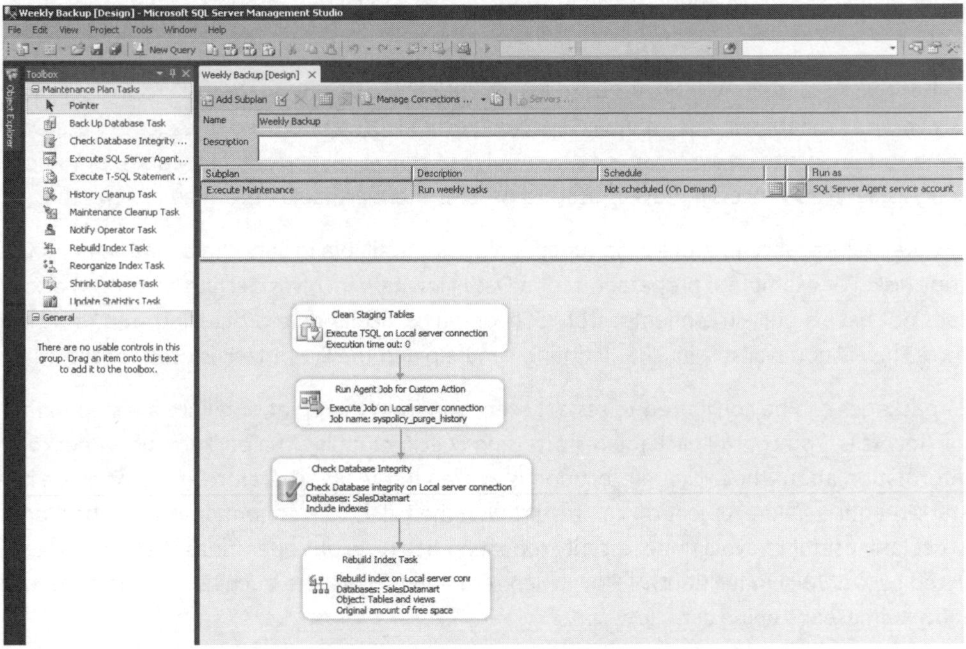

FIGURE 1-4 Database maintenance tasks in SQL Server Management Studio.

Tasks available to build Control Flow are typically used for the preparation of Data Flow task execution. For example, the Execute SQL task is used to run SQL statements on data stores. This task is used for operations like creating or truncating tables, preparing staging database, getting maximum value of an identity column in a table, executing stored procedures, or getting a count of rows in a spreadsheet. The Execute SQL task can be used with a wide range of data sources and supports several connection managers for that. Getting data files from external systems to data integration servers is a common data loading preparation step. SSIS offers a few options for this operation, and the following are the most popular:

- **File System task** Performs operations on files and directories in the file system. For example, this task can be used to get data files from a remote file share and copy them to a newly created directory in the local file system.
- **FTP task** Downloads data files from an FTP server, uploads data files to an FTP server, or manages directories on server. For example, this task can be used to get data from an FTP location for ETL processing and drop the original file from that location after download.
- **Web Service task** Executes a Web service method. For example, this task can be used to get data from a Web service that can be written to a variable or file.

If the data file obtained using one of these tasks is in XML format, you can use the XML task in SSIS to process it. This task can reformat data using XSLT, select XML nodes using XPath queries, or merge multiple XML documents. If the data file is a text or XML file and the data has to be loaded into SQL Server without any transformations, you can use the Bulk Insert task, which wraps the BULK INSERT statement in SQL Server. This provides an efficient way to copy large amounts of data to SQL Server tables or views.

SSIS has two Analysis Services tasks used for executing operations against Microsoft SQL Server Analysis Services databases. The Analysis Services Execute DDL task is used to execute Data Definition Language statements to create, drop, or alter Analysis Services mining models, cubes, or dimensions. The Analysis Services Processing task is used to process these artifacts once they are created.

Any data maintenance or processing functionality not available in SSIS can be implemented using the Script task. For example, if preparation for a Data Flow task involves getting data from a source that does not have a built-in connector from SSIS or if a particular data processing step to be included in Control Flow is not available in SSIS, scripting can help and the Script task is used for that.

SSIS packages can be configured to restart execution from the point of failure if a step in the Control Flow fails. You control package restart using checkpoint files. If a package uses checkpoint files, information about the package execution is written to the file. Therefore, if the package must be restarted after a failure, execution can restart with the failed task or container. SSIS checkpoints are particularly useful to avoid unnecessarily repeating heavyweight operations that have already completed successfully in the Control Flow when rerunning a package, such as copying a huge file, or executing a time-consuming data flow.

Administrative operations and maintenance steps often need to be executed on a regular basis and at scheduled time intervals. SQL Server Agent is used to automate execution of SSIS packages.

Evolution of SSIS

Microsoft introduced Integration Services in Microsoft SQL Server 2005. Data Transformation Services (DTS) in SQL Server 2000 can be considered a predecessor to SSIS; however, SSIS is completely different than DTS in terms of concepts, user interface, feature set, and internal architecture. The transition from a lightweight ETL tool such as DTS to a data integration platform such as SSIS was well received by SQL Server customers. Nearly instant familiarity with the design environment appealed to SSIS developers, and the scalability and performance characteristics of SSIS catered to enterprise needs. The use of SSIS in large-scale data integration projects has been growing steadily ever since its introduction. Figure 1-5 provides some details on the enhancements and features in various versions of SSIS.

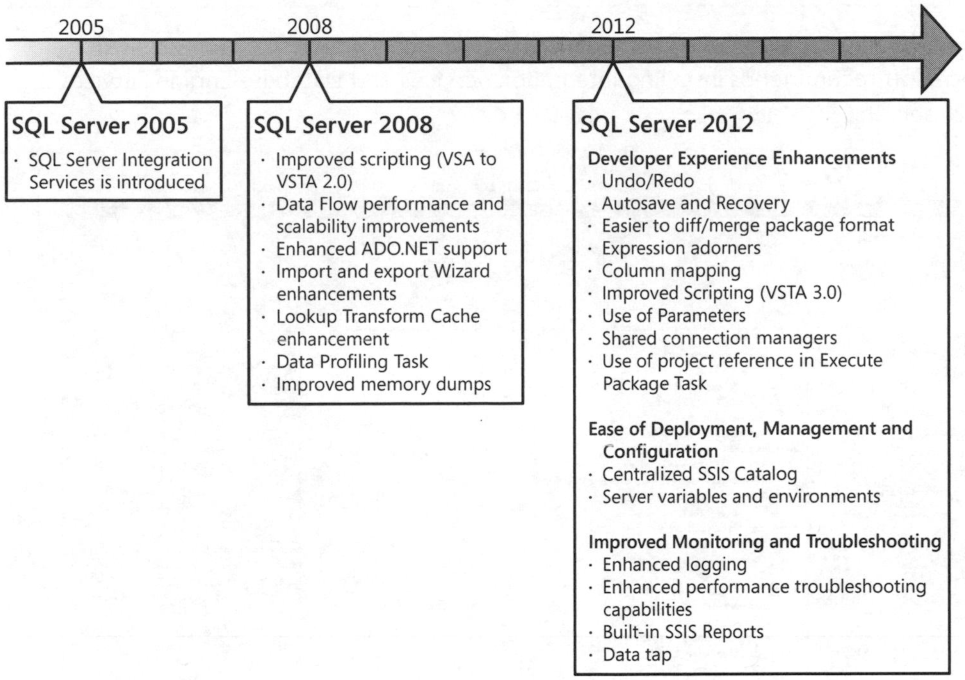

FIGURE 1-5 Evolution of SSIS.

> **Note** Details on data flow engine enhancements in different versions are covered in Chapter 15, "SSIS Engine Deep Dive."

Setting Up SSIS

You can install all SQL Server features—including SSIS—using a single setup program. The features needed to build, manage, or run SSIS solutions are spread across several SQL Server features, and must be installed appropriately. Figure 1-6 shows the feature selection screen in the SQL Server setup. The main features in SQL Server setup related to SSIS are as follows:

- Integration Services
- SQL Server Data Tools
- Database Engine Services
- Management Tools

> **Note** Setting up a dedicated server for all data integration needs is a best practice. Microsoft recommends installing Integration Services and Database Engine Services on such servers.

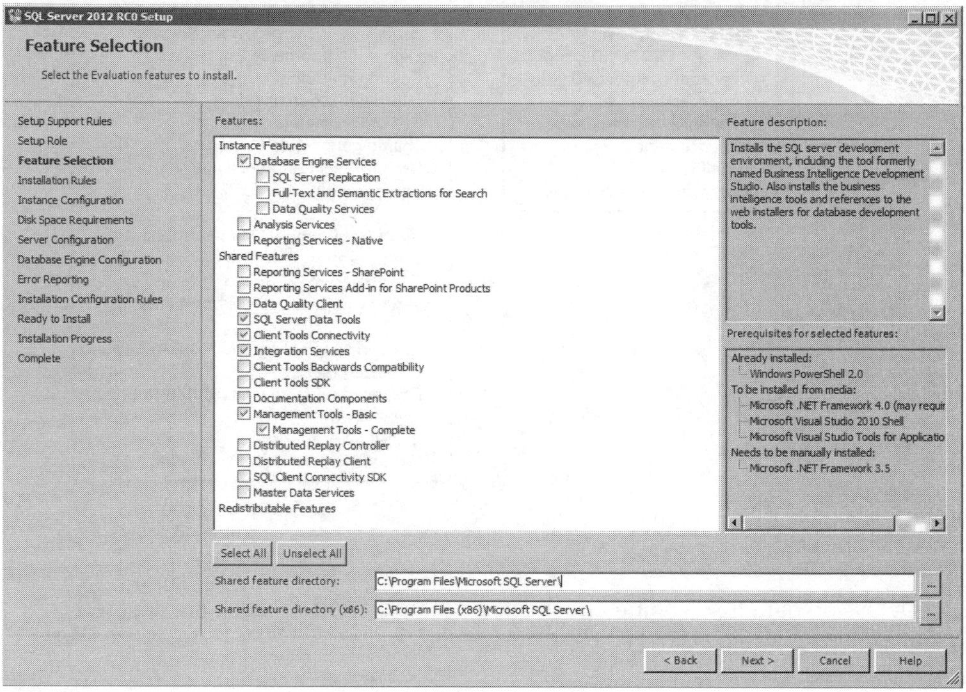

FIGURE 1-6 Feature selection screen in SQL Server Setup.

SQL Server Features Needed for Data Integration

This section takes a brief look at the features that you need to install during SQL Server setup to be able to build and run data integration solutions.

Integration Services

This feature installs the SSIS runtime, some utilities (.exe files), a Windows service named SQL Server Integration Services (followed by a version number), and various libraries (.dll files) used to enable execution of SSIS packages outside of the design environment in SQL Server Data Tools. The Windows service manages locally executed packages and packages stored in msdb in a SQL Server instance. The Integration Services feature is available under Shared Features in the SQL Server feature tree shown in Figure 1-6 because it's not SQL Server database instance specific; that is, it's a feature shared by all instances. So even if a machine has multiple database instances, you need only one copy of Integration Services on that machine. Files installed for this feature in SQL Server 2012 reside in the %Program Files%\Microsoft SQL Server\110\DTS folder. In older versions, the folder hierarchy is the same but the number indicating SQL Server version (110 in the preceding path) is different. For example, Integration Services in SQL Server 2008 has 100 in the path.

SQL Server Data Tools

The SQL Server Data Tools feature provides the development environment for building SSIS packages. This graphical design tool is an intuitive and easy-to-use environment for composing data integration activities. The designer has separate design surfaces for authoring workflow for data integration and for creating a data flow pipeline. Composition of control or data flows is simple, and involves adding built-in tasks or components into the design surface from SSIS Toolbox, then configuring and connecting them. Integration Services does not have to be installed on the same machine to develop SSIS packages using SQL Server Data Tools. However, if Integration Services is not installed, you cannot execute packages designed in SQL Server Data Tools outside of that feature on the same machine using the DTExec utility.

SQL Server Data Tools usage is not limited solely to SSIS development; instead, it is an integrated environment for building SQL Server–based business solutions involving Analysis Services, Reporting Services, or database development. SQL Server Data Tools is hosted in Microsoft Visual Studio. All these technologies support the development experience and need a design environment. Because Visual Studio is the default development environment for Microsoft technologies, it's the natural choice for SSIS development (as well as others). Visual Studio provides a familiar environment for developers, and the SQL Server Data Tools experience is well integrated with familiar Visual Studio features such as Solution Explorer, the Toolbox, the Properties pane, and the Output and Watch windows. Together, these provide a true, consistent end-to-end experience in building solutions. You can execute SSIS packages in SQL Server Data Tools and leverage other powerful capabilities, such as setting breakpoints and debugging during execution. Business Intelligence Development Studio or SQL Server Data Tools work with specific versions of Visual Studio and SSIS packages. Table 1-2 provides details on this.

TABLE 1-2 Compatibility between Visual Studio and Business Intelligence Development Studio/SQL Server Data Tools in SQL Server

SQL Server version	Name of SSIS development environment	Visual studio version for Business Intelligence Development Studio/SQL Server Data Tools
SQL Server 2005	Business Intelligence Development Studio	Visual Studio 2005 and service packs
SQL Server 2008	Business Intelligence Development Studio	Visual Studio 2008 and service packs
SQL Server 2008 R2	Business Intelligence Development Studio	Visual Studio 2008 and service packs
SQL Server 2012	SQL Server Data Tools	Visual Studio 2010 Service Pack 1+

> **Note** SSDT is a 32-bit application. It runs in WoW64 mode in AMD 64-bit processors. Business Intelligence Development Studio in SQL Server 2005, SQL Server 2008, and SQL Server 2008 R2 is not designed to run in an Itanium 64-bit architecture.

Database Engine Services

An instance of the database engine is installed as a part of this feature. Integration Services packages can be deployed to SQL Server. In SQL Server 2012, packages are deployed to the SSIS catalog, which is a database in a SQL Server instance. In previous versions of SSIS, you could deploy packages to the msdb database in SQL Server. The SSIS catalog is used for management and administration of SSIS packages. The catalog contains system database objects needed for deployment, configuration, and execution of SSIS packages in the context of a SQL Server instance. It also has database objects for monitoring or reporting execution status and troubleshooting data or performance issues. Database engine services features include SQL Server Agent, which is useful for scheduling SSIS package execution. Installing this SQL Server feature installs the components required by the Import and Export Wizard (if that is not already included in the installation through the Integration Services feature during setup). The Import and Export Wizard is included to facilitate getting data into or out of the database engine without explicitly including the Integration Services feature during SQL Server installation.

Management Tools

SQL Server Management Studio is installed as a part of this feature. SQL Server Management Studio is a popular tool among database administrators. It provides a DBA-friendly environment to manage the SSIS catalog, project folders, server variables, and project environment references in Integration Services 2012. After deploying packages to the catalog, you can configure, validate, execute, and monitor them using SQL Server Management Studio. The SSIS catalog is just a database in SQL Server with the name SSISDB, so any feature available in SQL Server Management Studio to interact with or manage a database can be used on the catalog itself. You can also use SQL Server Management Studio to interact with legacy SSIS Windows service or agent jobs that execute SSIS packages. For example, when you design a maintenance plan in SQL Server Management Studio it involves SSIS tasks.

SQL Server Editions and Integration Services Features

Several editions of SQL Server are available, and each edition is associated with a specific usage scenario. The features available in different editions correspond to the target usage scenarios. The functionality of SSIS differs among these various editions. See Table 1-3 for details.

TABLE 1-3 Integration Services features available in different editions in SQL Server 2012

Edition	Features
Express Express Tools Express Advanced Web	Import and Export Wizard Features used by the wizard (SSIS runtime, basic adapters)
Standard Business Intelligence	All SSIS functionality except the advanced features (listed in the next row)
Enterprise Evaluation Developer	Data mining model training destination adapter Dimension processing destination Partition processing adapter SAP BW adapters High-speed Oracle adapters High-speed Teradata adapters Term extraction and lookup transform Fuzzy lookup and groping transform Data mining query transform

The Business Intelligence Edition is available only in SQL Server 2012; it is not available in earlier versions. On the other hand, the Workgroup Edition is not available in SQL Server 2012, but it is available in earlier versions. The SQL Server Datacenter edition available in SQL Server 2008 R2 is not available in SQL Server 2012. If an edition is not available in SQL Server 2012, the SQL Server Installer might change the edition during the upgrade to SQL Server 2012. SQL Server Developer and Evaluation editions have restrictions on usage: The Developer edition is licensed for development purposes only, and the Evaluation edition's license is valid for only 180 days. In editions lower than Standard, the Import and Export Wizard does not allow saving packages or use of other utilities such as the Upgrade Wizard or DTExec; those are blocked. Some of the high-end editions offer flexible licensing models, which are not discussed in this book.

> **Note** See *http://www.microsoft.com/sqlserver/en/us/editions.aspx* for details about the usage scenarios for the various SQL Server editions.

Summary

This chapter described several common data integration scenarios and provided a high-level overview of the SSIS features that address the requirements for each scenario. SSIS meets most of the requirements for building and managing complex data integration solutions in enterprises. This chapter also discussed the SQL Server features needed for end-to-end SSIS solutions, and the features available in different editions of SQL Server.

CHAPTER 2

Understanding SSIS Concepts

In This Chapter

As discussed in Chapter 1, "SQL Server Integration Services Overview", Microsoft SQL Server 2012 Integration Services is a comprehensive platform for data integration applications. When the product was first released in SQL Server 7.0, however, Integration Services was only a simple extract–transform–load (ETL) utility called Data Transformation Services (DTS). Over the years Microsoft added numerous features into the product; in addition, the product architecture has been altered considerably so it can host modern data integration applications. As a result, Integration Services has become increasingly powerful, while becoming more and more complicated. Before going deeply into the discussions that you'll see later, it's important that you have a clear understanding of the different building blocks of the product.

From a user's perspective, Integration Services consists of a collection of programs and tools. Customers use those utilities to design and execute a data integration application. For example, developers usually use SQL Server Data Tools to design a package, and then run it with Dtexec.exe or server execution. When developers have some experience with extending Integration Services, such as developing a custom task, they will realize that Integration Services also provides a collection of assemblies to enable users to develop various SSIS extensions.

Actually, all those programs, tools, and extension assemblies are built on a unified underlying object model. This object model provides the skeleton of Integration Services and implements most of the functionality. All external programs or tools just interpret the user's instructions and then invoke the object model to perform work, so the object model lies at center of Integration Services.

This chapter guides you through the object model with the goal of understanding the following:

- The three main parts of the object model: control flow, data flow, and the SSIS Catalog.
- The most important objects in those three parts, and how they interact with each other.
- The new concepts introduced in SQL Server 2012, which include projects, parameters, the SSIS Catalog, environments, and references.

Control Flow

Control flow is the largest part of the object model, and also the most fundamental part. As a work flow environment, it defines the unit of jobs, how those job units cooperate each other, how they are scheduled to execute, and so on. Everything you need to do can be plugged into this work flow environment as a job unit, even some very complex operations such as data transformations. Control flow consists primarily of an execution engine and some supporting infrastructure. The engine schedules the execution order during runtime, whereas the infrastructure provides basic support for such things as containers, variables, and connection managers.

This control flow discussion starts with the most basic unit: tasks.

Tasks

Tasks are the smallest job unit in a control flow. From the perspective of the control flow engine, a task is an atomic job unit. The engine starts a task at an appropriate time and then waits for it to complete. You can implement anything you need to do as a task, such as downloading an FTP file, sending an email, creating a log file, or performing data transformations.

When you open the Toolbox window in the Package Designer, you will see there are plenty of built-in tasks. Each task is designed to meet a specific scenario, and each task has some properties you need to configure to perform the job. For example, for an Execute Process task, you need to configure the target file or folder location, select which action you want to take, and so on.

A task is not aware of other tasks in the same package. For example, you cannot write a Script task that modifies the properties of other tasks at run time—which makes it impossible to build a "self-modifying" package. There are two reasons to prohibit such behaviors: first, such package relationships are hard to understand and maintain; second, such packages are difficult or even impossible to upgrade to future SSIS versions.

Most of the built-in tasks are written in Microsoft .NET languages. Those tasks are installed in the folder %Program Files%\Microsoft SQL Server\110\DTS\Tasks by default. See Figure 2-1.

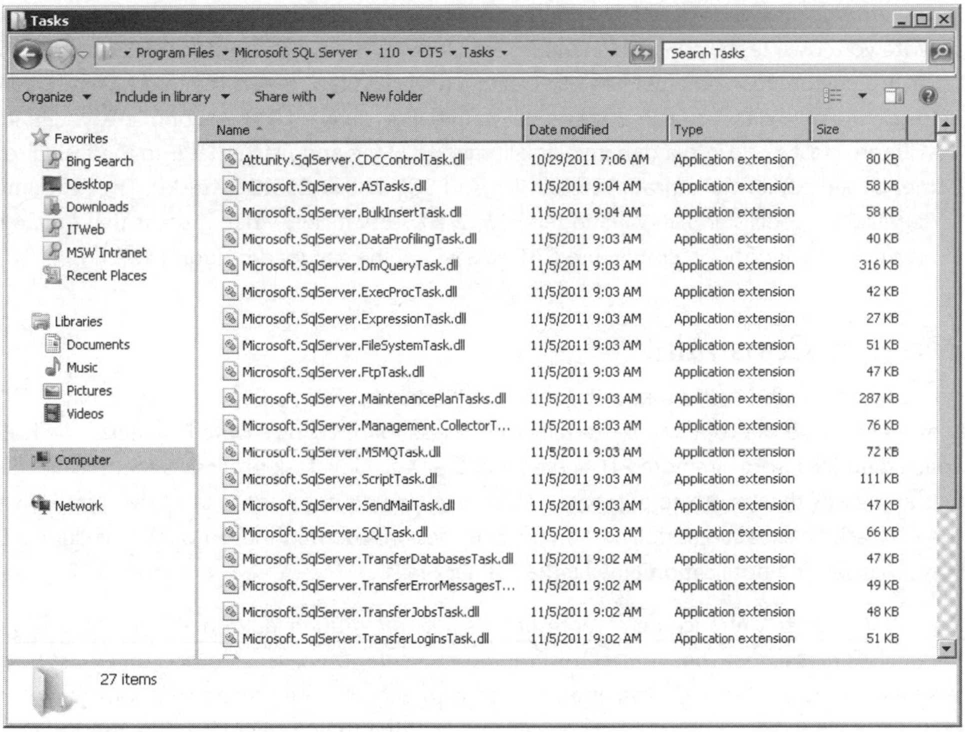

FIGURE 2-1 Managed tasks in the installation folder.

There are also several other tasks written in native languages. The Execute SQL task or Execute Package task is an example. Those native tasks are installed under the folder %Program Files%\Microsoft SQL Server\110\DTS\Binn.

For most of the common data integration scenarios you can find an appropriate built-in task. You might wonder what would happen if you want to perform a special job—for example, sending a special message to a legacy system. Basically you have two choices:

1. **Use a Script task** The stock tasks include a special task named "Script task". As mentioned in Chapter 1, the Script task is built on Visual Studio Tools for Application (VSTA). It provides an integrated development environment (IDE) that enables you to write your own code in C# or Visual Basic. The Script task gives you access to the entire package object model, including such capabilities as reading or writing variables, retrieving connection managers, or firing events. Furthermore, you can reference an external .NET assembly if that assembly is installed in the Global Assembly Cache (GAC). In most cases, the Script task itself already provides enough flexibility.

2. **Develop your own task** If even the Script task cannot fulfill your requirements, you can write your own tasks, using the standard interfaces and base classes that SSIS provides. To write a custom task, you just need to create a new class that meets the interface requirements. Inside the new class you can do essentially anything you want. When complete, you build your new task code into a dynamic-link library (DLL) file and place that into the task directory mentioned earlier (%Program Files%\Microsoft SQL Server\110\DTS\Tasks). The next time SQL Server Data Tools starts, it will find the new task automatically when it scans that folder. You also need to add the assembly into GAC so SSIS engine can load it during execution.

Precedence Constraints

Tasks must be connected each other to perform works in cooperation. For example, in many SSIS packages you can see the common pattern of an FTP task followed by a Data Flow task. The FTP task downloads data files from a remote FTP server, and the Data Flow task processes the downloaded data files and loads the result into databases. Of course, you do not want to start the Data Flow task until the FTP task finishes successfully. As an optional design, you might even want to include a Send Email task that sends a notification email if the FTP task fails.

The relationships among such tasks represent the *data integration logic*. In SSIS terminology, such logics are called *precedence constraints*. They represent a criterion or an assertion that must be met before a task can be started. Each task is associated with one or more precedence constraints. For those tasks that do not have prior tasks, you can imagine that they have an invisible precedence constraint with a criterion that is always met.

The simplest precedence constraint is just the completion state of the prior task. Each task has a state after it finishes the work. The state could be success, failure, or just completion. In the designer, a precedence constraint appears as a line from the prior task to the current task. Its color represents the required completion state of the prior task. A green line means the task will be started only when the prior task finished successfully, whereas a red line means the task will be started only when the prior task has failed. For completion, the line color is blue. You can right-click a precedence constraint line and choose Edit to switch between the different state values.

A more complex precedence constraint is based on a combination of completion states and expressions. By combining those two elements, you can express more complex requirements. For example, you could define a variable named *counter*, and specify a precedence constraint as "Start this task only when the variable *counter* is larger than five, and the prior task has finished successfully."

Furthermore, a task can have multiple precedence constraints. SSIS lets you specify those constraints combined via logical AND or logical OR. By right-clicking the precedence constraint line and selecting Edit, you can specify the specific logic in the Precedence Constraint Editor. See Figure 2-2.

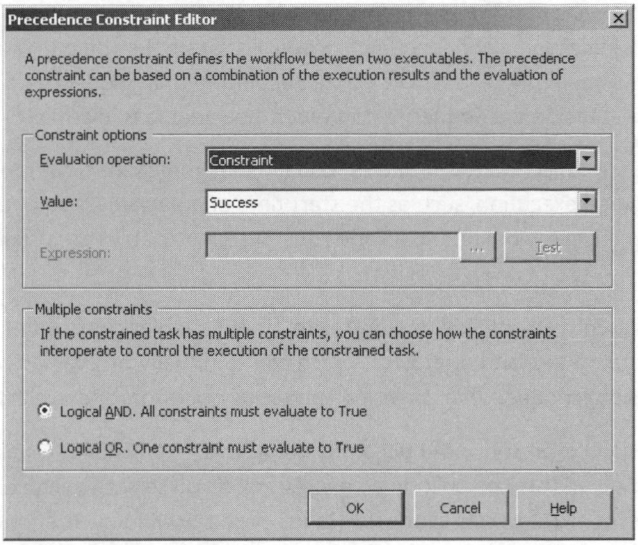

FIGURE 2-2 Precedence Constraint Editor.

Here is a simple explanation that shows how precedence constraints work. At the beginning of package execution, the control flow engine evaluates each task to see whether its precedence constraints are met. At first only those tasks that have no prior tasks are ready to execute, because their precedence constraints are always met. After those initial tasks finish, the task completion states have changed, so the engine reevaluates all the remaining tasks and starts them if their associated precedence constraints have been met. The engine keeps running this process until all executing tasks have completed, and no new tasks are ready.

Variables and Expressions

In the previous section, you saw that tasks are not aware of the existence of other tasks, which means that a task cannot update the properties of other tasks or send messages to other tasks. So the question is this: How do they communicate? After all, tasks often need to communicate with each other to finish cooperative work. For example, to process a set of downloaded files, a Data Flow task needs to know the file names retrieved by the prior FTP task.

Another question is how to customize a package so that it doesn't always run exactly the same way. For instance, suppose you have a package to process data files with a given format. Because the data file paths might change, you definitely do not want to hardcode the file paths. You need a mechanism to specify the file name when the package is started.

SSIS variables are designed to meet these two purposes. A variable is basically a memory location. It can be assigned a value either before or during package execution. To assign values before execution, you could set some command-line arguments with Dtexec.exe. To exchange information during execution, one task could write a value to a variable and another task could read it to retrieve the information.

Variables are strictly typed, which means that (for example) you cannot assign an integer to a string variable. A variable also has an initial value and a visibility scope. For example, you could define a variable in a Sequence container. Subsequently, all tasks or containers inside that Sequence container could access the variable. However, outside the Sequence container the variable is invisible.

Some variables are built in; those are called system variables. Usually they represent common facts you might need to know during package execution, such as the start time of a package. You might write that information to an auditing file every time the package runs. System variables are usually read-only values.

You can organize multiple variables into an expression along with other variables or constants. An *expression* is a series of variables, literal values, and operators, which can eventually be evaluated to a single value. SSIS has its own expression language that provides numerous operators and functions.

The relationship between variables and expressions can become complex. An expression is usually built on some variables—but a variable could also be built on an expression! If you select a variable in the designer, you will notice a property named Evaluate As Expression in the property window. That property controls whether the contents of that variable will be treated as an expression rather than a literal value.

> **Note** Be careful when defining variables on other variables or expressions, because that can sometimes introduce a circular reference, which means a variable finally references itself after several intermediate variables. Not only can circular references cause confusion, but they're also hard to debug.

Tasks reference variables or expressions through their properties. For example, in an FTP task you need to specify the file name to download. Instead of hardcoding the file name, you could define a variable and reference the variable in the property. You could also assign an expression instead of a single variable to the property. When the expression is evaluated at run time, the value is assigned to the property.

However, not all properties can accept variables or expressions. Some properties accept only literal values. Properties to which you can assign a variable or an expression are called expressionable properties. You will find a page named Expressions in most task editors that lists all the expressionable properties for that task.

Containers

As discussed earlier, tasks are the smallest building blocks in an SSIS package. A task is like a single statement in a programming language. If you have some programming experience, you will know that statements should be organized into functions or methods to give your program a clear structure. In SSIS, you manage tasks in a similar way, by organizing them into different containers so you can manage them better.

SSIS provides three different containers: a For Loop container, a Foreach Loop container, and a Sequence container.

The first two containers let you perform repeated job steps. For example, you might want to process all data files in a given folder using the same logic. The Foreach Loop container allows you to do that. First, you need to define a Data Flow task to do the data processing. Then you place that task into a Foreach Loop container and configure a Foreach file enumerator as the looping context. Each iteration of the loop maps the current file name to a variable, and the Data Flow task reads the file name from that variable.

Foreach Loop Container

In Figure 2-3, you can see that Foreach Loop container can loop on different types of objects, such as files or ADO.NET records. Each supported looping type is called a Foreach Loop enumerator, and each has specific properties you need to set. For example, you need to specify the folder location and file name filters for a Foreach file enumerator. For each different type of enumerator, you can map the various enumerated elements into variables in the Variable Mappings page, letting you then reference them in the contained tasks. Chapter 7, "Understanding SSIS Connectivity", includes an example of using a Foreach file enumerator that you might find useful.

The Foreach Loop enumerator is also extensible in SSIS. You could write your own Foreach Loop enumerator for some special use. For example, if you wanted to perform a loop based on some special object types from a legacy Enterprise Resource Planning (ERP) system, you would need a custom Foreach Loop enumerator. Figure 2-3 shows the built-in Foreach Loop enumerators.

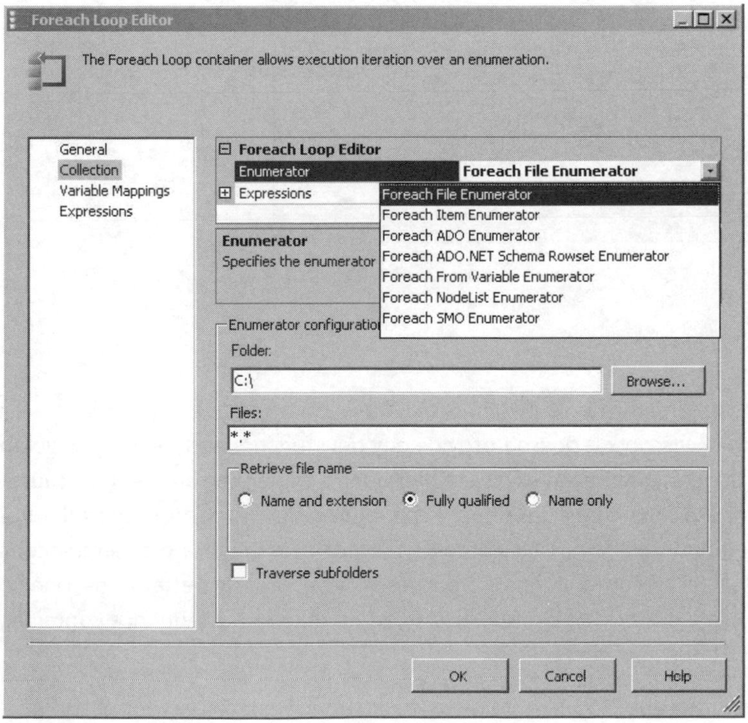

FIGURE 2-3 Foreach Loop enumerators.

For Loop Container

The For Loop container is similar to the Foreach Loop container, but it's simpler. The looping is controlled by an expression. The container keeps running until the evaluation result becomes false. Usually you will reference some variables in the expression. For example, you might define a variable to record the remaining number of emails that need to be sent. The loop runs until the remaining email number becomes zero. Figure 2-4 shows the For Loop Editor.

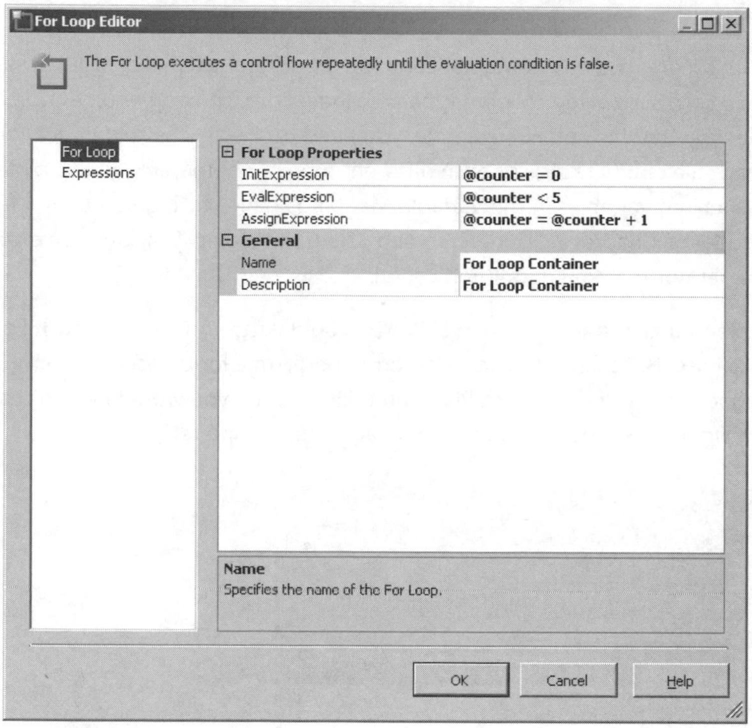

FIGURE 2-4 For Loop Editor.

Sequence Container

Compared to the first two containers, the Sequence container is less attractive at first glance. It just groups existing tasks into a new scope; it doesn't provide any new functionality, leading developers to frequently ask why this container even exists. As mentioned earlier, the answer is because it improves management. For example, three tasks might share the same property, such as the transaction settings. By grouping tasks into a Sequence container, you can set the property on the container rather than on the individual tasks. For maintenance purposes, it's obviously better to set one container property than multiple individual task properties. In addition, using a Sequence container, you can enable or disable those tasks as a whole.

There are two interesting facts about SSIS containers. The first one is that a package is also a Sequence container by itself. Of course, a package has some additional properties as the top-level object. Apart from that, though, a package is essentially just a Sequence container. The second interesting fact is that every task is wrapped by a hidden container called the Task Host. This container is designed for internal purposes. Every task needs to handle some common requirements, such as variables, connection managers, associated event handlers, and so on. The Task Host handles such common functionality, so tasks need to focus only on their own logic.

Containers can be nested. After tasks have been organized into a container, the container becomes a new job unit. You could, in turn, group that container into a larger container, containing other tasks or containers. The final structure of a package is therefore a tree where each leaf is either a task or an empty container.

Connection Managers

To design a data integration application you need to access various external data sources such as a regular relational database like Microsoft SQL Server, a flat file, or a legacy system such as your ERP system. From the previous discussions, you know that tasks do all the work in SSIS. To perform that work, a task needs a connection to those data sources. For example, an FTP task needs a connection to a specific FTP server.

In SSIS, such data connections are not implemented by tasks themselves. Instead, they are encapsulated as standalone objects called *connection managers*. This way, different tasks can share a common data connection without duplicating code. All connections are provided by their corresponding connection managers. Each connection manager only produces its own typed connection. SSIS ships with plenty of standard connection managers (see Figure 2-5).

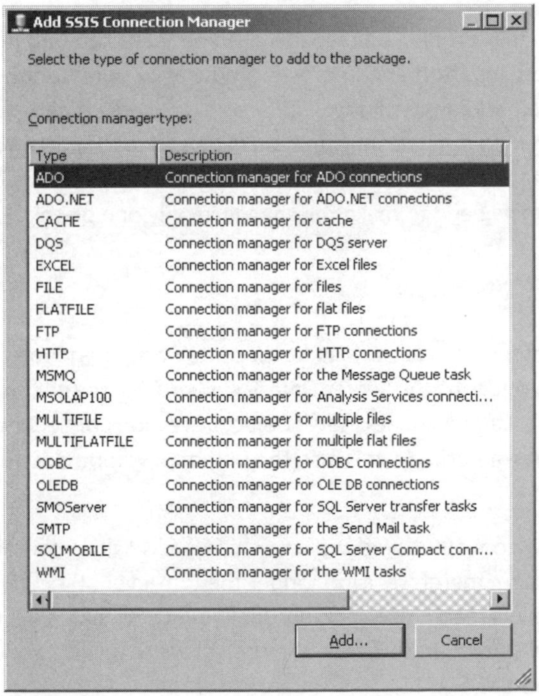

FIGURE 2-5 Connection managers.

To set up a new connection manager, you need to assign its connection properties such as address, user name, or password. Then assign the connection manager to the corresponding tasks. During run time, a task will require a connection instance from the assigned connection manager, and then perform its work on the returned connection.

Some connection managers support an important property named Retain Same Connection. If the property is set to *true*, the connection manager will always return the same connection instance even if multiple tasks require connections from it. For example, suppose you have three FTP tasks in a package and they use the same FTP connection manager. If the option is turned off (*false*), and the three tasks request an FTP connection, three instances will be established. But if you turn the option on (*true*), only one connection instance will be established, and the three tasks will share that single connection instance. In some cases doing this can improve performance and save connection resources.

An interesting thing about the connection manager is that it does not necessarily return a "real connection"; it can return any object type, depending on the implementation of that connection manager. For example the Flat File connection manager actually returns a file path string rather than an opened file handle.

As expected, connection managers are also extensible in SSIS, and it's pretty easy to develop a customized connection manager. SSIS provides standard interfaces and base classes. You just need to write your own implementation class based on those interfaces or base classes, build it into a DLL, and put the DLL into the %Program Files%\Microsoft SQL Server\110\DTS\Connections folder. The next time you start SQL Server Data Tools, your custom connection manager will appear in the list.

One important change in SQL Server 2012 is that connection managers can be shared among multiple packages. This saves a great deal of development effort and improves productivity significantly. Most ETL solutions have multiple packages, and those packages typically work against the same database or data warehouse. In previous SSIS versions you had to define connection managers for each package, but now you need to define only one connection manager, and then share it among all your packages. When something changes, such as the password, you now need to make the change in only one place.

Packages and Projects

A *package* is the SSIS object that contains all other objects, such as tasks, containers, or variables. After you create a new Integration Services solution in SQL Server Data Tools, you will see that a new package has been created in the solution. A package is the top-level object in versions of SSIS before SQL Server 2012—all your work is defined inside a package. It is also the unit of development and execution.

However, SQL Server 2012 introduces a new concept, called *project,* which is basically a container of packages and other shared items. The package, therefore, is no longer the top-level object. The term *project* is a little confusing because there is already a project in Visual Studio. For example, we always say "Create a new SSIS project in Visual Studio." In this case, the project we're talking about is not a Visual Studio project; it is a new concept in SSIS 2012.

The project concept provides a larger scope, letting you reference SSIS packages that are in the same project and information sharing among different packages. For example, a typical data warehouse ETL solution would have numerous packages. One of them would be the master control package, and the others would be child packages. The master control package calls child packages to do all the ETL work, including updating dimension tables, updating fact tables, writing logs, and so on. Usually there are some Execute Package tasks in the master control package to call those child packages. To reference the child packages, you have to specify the absolute package file path or server storage path. Using that approach, if you were to move all packages into another folder, the relationships would break, because the locations of the child packages would have changed. When you have many such cross-references, it's hard to detect such issues and fix them. In contrast, by introducing the concept of a project that can contain packages, you need to specify only the child package name instead of the absolute package path.

Furthermore, the project concept makes it easier to share information among multiple packages. In SSIS 2012, you can share connection managers and project parameters among all packages, which is very useful, because again, when changes are required, you need to make the changes in only one place rather than multiple places.

The new concept also simplifies deployment work. All the contents in an SSIS project are built into a single .ispac file after you perform the *build* command in SSDT. The build includes packages, shared connection managers, and project parameters, meaning that you can do the deployment work using only a single file.

> **Tip** The project file is actually a standard zip file. If you change the file extension from .ispac to .zip, you can easily open it and see its internal contents.

Parameters

Another new concept introduced in SQL Server 2012 is the *parameter*. There are two types of parameters: *package parameters* and *project parameters*. You can see all the package parameters on the Parameters tab in the package designer. To view all the project parameters, double-click the Project.params node in Solution Explorer.

A package parameter is like a contract between the package and its caller, for example, a parent package. A child package might require some information to perform its job, such as the name of the dimension table it should update. In previous versions of SSIS, developers usually passed that information through some external configuration, but that's not very efficient because it is an implicit way to pass information. First, it's hard to know exactly what configuration information is required to run a child package. Second, it's easy to break if something goes wrong with the external configuration. In contrast, a package parameter is an explicit way to pass the information: You can easily see what information is required when you open the package. It's also easy for SSIS to validate whether the passed parameters were assigned values at run time.

A project parameter is similar to a package parameter—it just works in a larger scope: A project parameter describes the requirements to run a project. One additional advantage is that a project parameter can be shared by all packages.

Usually you set parameter values through command-line arguments or T-SQL stored procedures when the project is executed within the SSIS Catalog. You can also set variable values through command-line arguments. Some people confuse the two terms *parameters* and *variables*, and that becomes even more confusing when you define variables or expressions based on parameter values. Here are the differences:

1. You can change variable values inside a package execution, but you cannot change parameter values.
2. From a usage perspective, you usually use parameters to define the contract between a package and its caller, whereas you use variables primarily for exchanging information inside a package.

Log Providers

The *log provider* concept is relatively simple. As its name suggests, a log provider is a storage provider to which you can write logs.

Executing an SSIS package produces a rich collection of logs (depending on your log configurations). Those logs are important for auditing or troubleshooting. You can write these logs to various places, such as disk files, databases, or Windows event logs. Log providers represent those destinations. A log provider is similar to a connection manager, but includes some special information about the logging format.

All available log providers in a package are defined on the package level, meaning you cannot define a log provider that serves only a specific container. After you define a log provider, all containers or tasks in that package have access to it. If multiple log providers are selected for a container, the logs produced by that container will be written to all those logging destinations independently.

You can view all the log providers defined in an SSIS package by selecting the SSIS | Logging menu in the package designer. Figure 2-6 shows all the built-in log provider types.

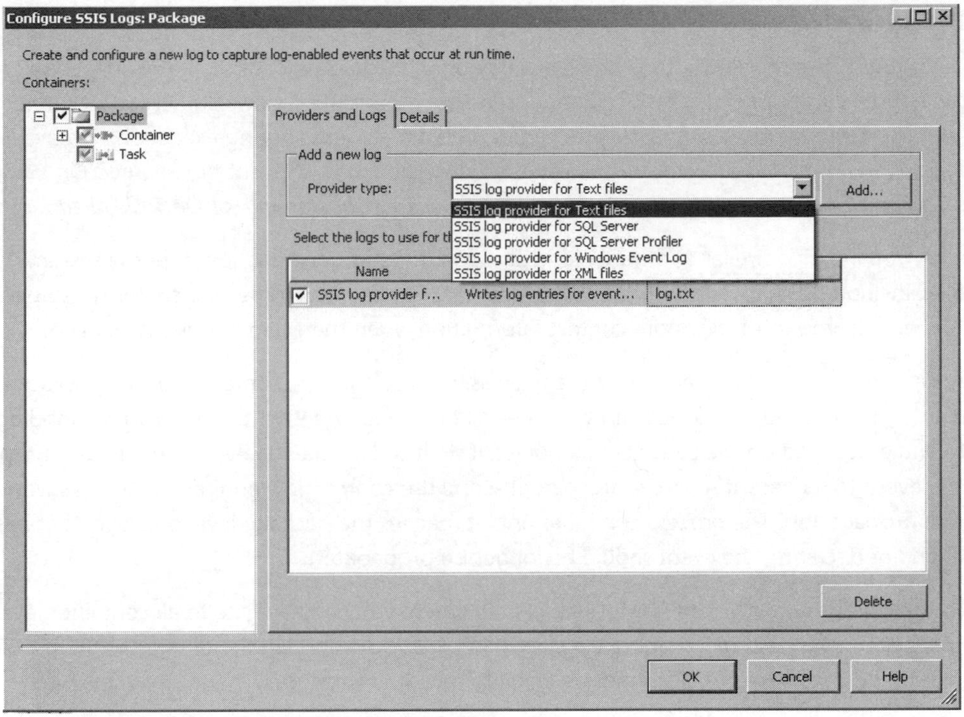

FIGURE 2-6 All built-in log provider types.

An interesting question is how a log provider works when an execution involves parent packages and child packages. SSIS adopts a great design in which all log providers are wrapped as a single log provider to child packages. It's transparent to the child package. Even if you don't define any log providers in a child package, all logs are still saved through the log providers defined in the parent package.

Most popular logging destinations have been supported by SSIS built-in log providers, such as the Text File log provider and SQL Server log provider. You can also develop your own log providers if you want to save logs to a special media.

Event Handlers

An *event handler* is a mechanism to handle events during package execution. It provides a way that you can handle some special situations besides the normal execution flow. Numerous SSIS objects, such as tasks, containers, or connection managers, could fire events during execution. The available event types are up to the object type. For example, a variable has an event type named *On Variable Value Changed*. The most common event types are *On Error, On Warning,* or *On TaskFailed*.

An event handler is similar to a standalone package that has access to some special system variables, including *Error Code, Error Description, Event Handler Start Time*, and so on. Those system variables enable you to obtain more context information when the event handler is invoked.

You can define event handlers on different levels, such as a task, a container, or the package itself. When an event is raised, the control flow engine will first check whether there is a corresponding event handler defined on the current-level object. If so, it will invoke the event handler and propagate the event to its parent scope. At the parent scope the control flow engine repeats this work to continue propagation. The process continues until it reaches the package level or a level that has an event handler declaring the event should no longer be propagated.

The package designer has an Event Handlers tab where you can navigate to all container levels and their associated event handlers. Figure 2-7 shows an *On Error* event handler defined at the package level. Internally, the event handler sends an email to an administrator.

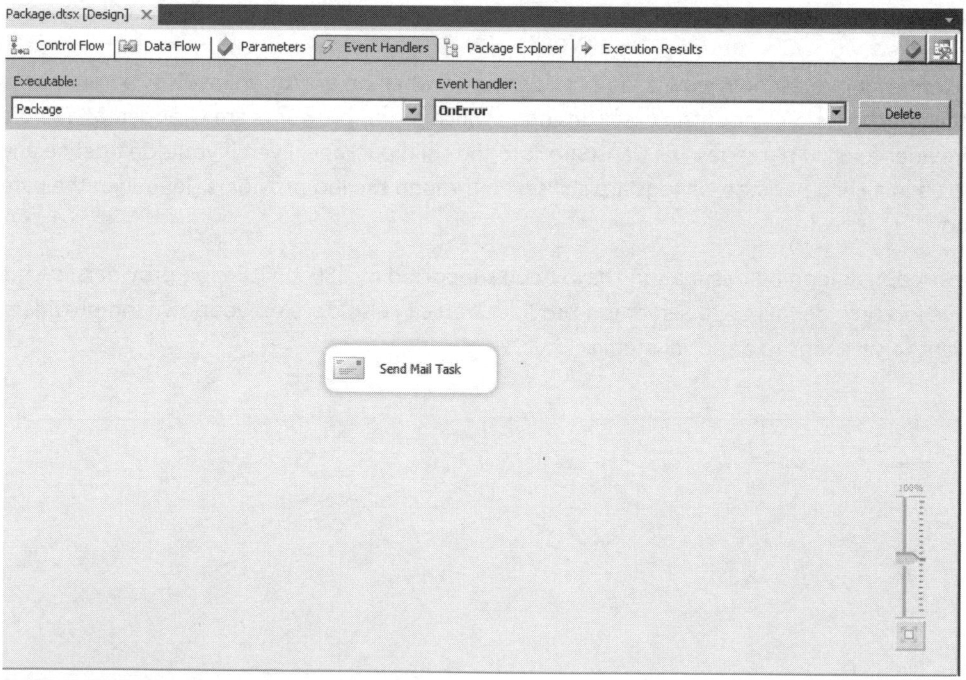

FIGURE 2-7 An event handler defined at the package level.

Data Flow

Integration Services ships with a wealth of built-in tasks, including a special task called a Data Flow task. This task provides full functionality for extracting, transforming, and loading data. The Data Flow task is the core part of a data integration application. In most cases, the other tasks are present just to do auxiliary work such as downloading files or initializing databases.

From the control flow engine perspective, a Data Flow task is a normal task with the same interfaces as any other task, but the task's complexity is nearly the same as the entire control flow. Every Data Flow task hosts a data flow instance. Inside the task, there is a data flow engine, which plans and schedules the execution of that data flow instance.

A data flow instance consists of source adapters, transform components, and destination adapters. Source adapters and destination adapters mark the boundaries of an SSIS data flow, whereas transform components between them do all the conversion work. All data comes from a source adapter, flows through some transform components, and finally ends with a destination adapter.

Source Adapters

A source adapter pulls data from external data sources, converts it to SSIS data flow formats, and then pushes it into the downstream data flow components. It will send a special data row named *end of row set* when it hits the end of the data stream, so the data flow engine knows all the data has been pulled. The logic of a source adapter is pretty straightforward. For most source adapters, the main code thread is just a loop that executes repeatedly until it hits the last row. A source adapter has zero inputs and *n* outputs.

When we talk about converting data to SSIS data flow formats, there are two primary conversions that a source adapter needs to do. First, it needs to change the shape of the data to a tabular shape. It then needs to convert the external data type system to the SSIS data type system.

The external data could be of any shape. It could be of tabular format already, such as the data from a database such as Microsoft SQL Server. It also could be hierarchical, like the data from an XML file. In either case, the source adapter has to change it to a tabular format, which is the only format that the SSIS data flow engine accepts.

All the data pushed into an SSIS data flow needs to comply with the SSIS data flow data type system, which consists of a fixed collection of data types, such as *DT_BOOL*, *DT_I4*, or *DT_WSTR*. Although SSIS natively contains most of the usual data types, there could be some special data types in the external data sources. For example, your legacy ERP system probably has a special data representation for dates and times. In such cases, the source adapter needs to convert these special representations to the equivalent SSIS data types.

SSIS already ships with many standard source adapters, such as OLE DB source adapters and ADO .NET source adapters. You can also develop your own source adapters if the existing ones do not meet your requirements.

Destination Adapters

A destination adapter works similarly to a source adapter, except that the data flows in the opposite direction; a destination adapter continues receiving data rows from upstream components until it gets an end of row set. For each data row, the destination component converts values to the format required by the external data source, and then loads the row into the external data source via its specific connection Application Programming Interfaces (APIs). A destination adapter has *n* inputs and *1* error output.

SSIS ships with more destination adapters than source adapters. In addition to popular destination adapters such as the OLE DB destination or the ADO.NET destination, SSIS also provides some special destination adapters related to Online Analysis Processing (OLAP). Those destination adapters include Data Mining Model Training, Dimension Processing, and Partition Processing. All of these require a connection to SQL Server Analysis Services. These destination adapters let you perform the most common data warehouse tasks within one package, rather than having to invoke other applications.

> **Note** Some data flow components are only available in specific SQL Server editions. For example, those destinations related to SQL Server Analysis Services are not available in SQL Server Standard or lesser versions.

Figure 2-8 shows all the built-in source adapters and destination adapters.

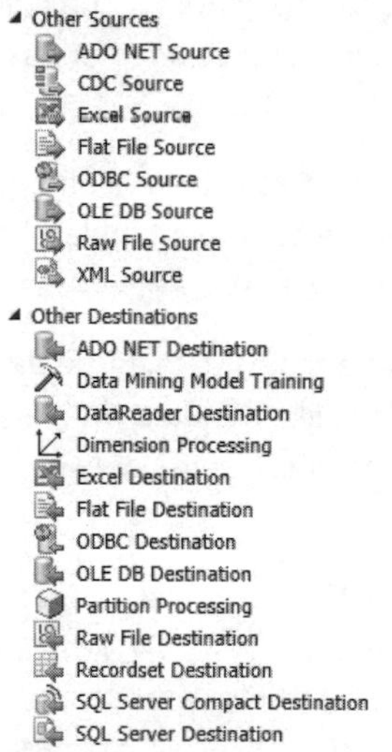

FIGURE 2-8 Source adapters and destination adapters.

Transforms

Between the source adapters and destination adapters lie the transform components. They modify the in-memory data from source adapters or derive new data according to business logic. A transform component could have *n* inputs and *n* outputs.

SSIS ships with a large number of transform components that can handle most of the common data processing scenarios, such as Conditional Split, Data Conversion, or Derived Column. Basically all those transform components can be divided into two different categories: synchronous transforms and asynchronous transforms. To understand the difference between those two types, you need to understand how the SSIS data flow processes data in memory.

After a source adapter generates a batch of data rows, the data flow engine places them into a block of memory called a *buffer*. To improve efficiency and avoid copying memory, the data flow engine does not move this buffer location during the entire data flow life cycle. After a component finishes its work, the data flow engine simply passes a pointer to the buffer to the downstream components.

A transform component must modify the buffer to perform its work. If the modification can be done in place, it's called a *synchronous* transform. On the other hand, when the component has to allocate a new buffer to hold the transform result, it's called an *asynchronous* transform.

For example, a Derived Column transform is a synchronize transform. Suppose you define a Derived Column transform that will modify the first column with a given expression; say, [column 1] = [column 1] *10. When the data flow engine passes a buffer pointer to the transform, it just modifies the contents of the first column row by row. If the original value of one cell is 10, it will overwrite it with a new value of 100. It does not need to change the buffer shape or create new buffers.

What will happen if the Derived Column transform needs to create a new column rather than modifying an existing column? This is still an in-place modification. The data flow engine will analyze the data flow layout before execution. It will notice that the Derived Column transform needs a new column and it will allocate an additional column when it creates the buffer. The column is invisible until the buffer reaches that transform. That approach avoids the memory copy overhead; even some new columns can be derived during execution.

Common synchronous transforms include Derived Column, Conditional Split, and Multicast.

On the other hand, suppose you define a transform that performs some aggregation. For example, it might group all data according to one column and sum up another column. The transform cannot do this modification in place, because even the row number has changed—where there were 10,000 rows in the original buffer, the aggregation result might contain only 10 rows. There is no way to support in-place editing in the original buffer. In such cases, the data flow engine allocates a new buffer with a new shape. The transform writes its result to the new buffer rather than modifying the existing buffer. Transforms with such behaviors are called asynchronous transforms.

Typical asynchronous transforms include Aggregation, Merge, Merge Join, and so on.

SSIS Catalog

The SSIS Catalog is a brand new element in SQL Server 2012 Integration Services. In previous versions, SSIS packages were executed in a desktop environment—customers used command-line tools such as Dtexec.exe to execute packages. In contrast, SSIS Catalog is a SQL Server application with a dedicated database named SSISDB. It provides a server-backed environment for enterprise users to develop, deploy, and manage data integration applications effectively.

Before discussing the architecture of SSIS Catalog, it's important to understand the difference between the SSIS Catalog and the existing SSIS service and MSDB database.

The existing SSIS service is a standalone Windows service—you can find it in the Windows services list when you open Control Panel. The service's executable file location is %Program Files%\Microsoft SQL Server\110\DTS\Binn\MsDtsSrvr.exe. This service runs in the background to track packages and package stores running locally. To view these running packages and manage the package stores you could connect to the service in SQL Server Management Studio by choosing the server type Integration Services. All the package store locations are saved in the configuration file %Program Files%\Microsoft SQL Server\110\DTS\Binn\MsDtsSrvr.ini.xml.

One of these package store types is the MSDB database. MSDB is a system database in SQL Server used for management purposes. SSIS defines some tables in that database to store packages. Those tables are only for storage purposes; no active service in the database does anything. There are some simple stored procedures in MSDB to help manage folders and packages, but package execution still happens on the client side. When a package is loaded from the MSDB database, its execution is no different than the execution of any other package loaded from the local file system.

Compared to the old SSIS service and MSDB database, the SSIS Catalog is a more powerful SQL application that has its own dedicated database. The SSIS Catalog consists of a set of stored procedures, views, and table-valued functions that you can use for working with projects and packages. However, when you call the stored procedure API to execute a package, that execution happens on the server side instead of the client side. The database has many public views, so you can query all deployment or execution information using any standard T-SQL tool. It also has built-in database reports to help you perform diagnosis and troubleshooting tasks. To sum up, the SSIS Catalog is a fully functional server instead of simple storage.

SSMS introduces a new node called Integration Services Catalogs to help you manage the SSIS Catalog. Figure 2-9 shows the user interface and the dedicated SSISDB database.

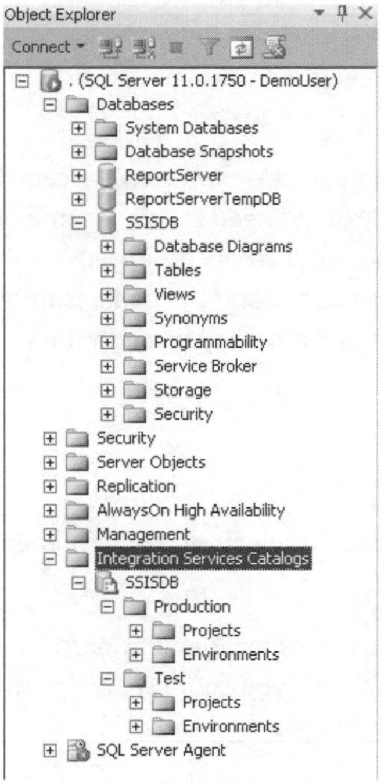

FIGURE 2-9 SSIS Catalog management interface and the dedicated database.

Overview

Figure 2-10 shows the relationship among SSIS Catalog objects. An SSIS Catalog instance has one catalog. Each catalog consists of one or more folders, and all objects are contained in a folder. You can find two types of objects in a folder: projects and environments. A project can be bound to zero or more environments. Such a binding relationship is called a *reference*.

In the following section, you'll find more information about those concepts and how they work.

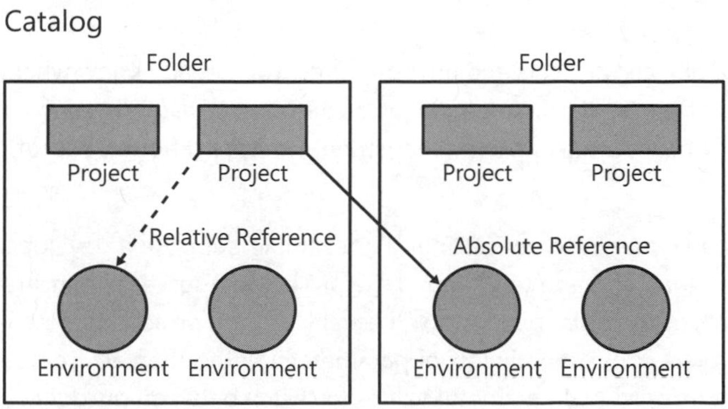

FIGURE 2-10 Object types in an SSIS Catalog.

Catalog

The catalog is the top-level object in the SSIS Catalog. All other objects are contained in a catalog. In SQL Server 2012, you can install only one SSIS catalog for each SQL Server instance.

Although catalog is the top-level object, in the SSIS Catalog object model, you won't access it too much during daily work. It's just a container to hold other objects. You do need to know some of its properties, however. Those properties are global settings that can impact all operations inside the catalog, such as the encryption algorithm. You can check all the properties and their values through the view *catalog.catalog_properties*. You can also change the value of a property through the stored procedure *catalog.configure_catalog*.

Folders

A catalog can contain many folders, and each folder can contain many projects and environments. You can query view *catalog.folders* to get the list of folders.

You can organize projects and environments into different folders for management purposes. For example, you could create a production folder and a testing folder. Then you could set different permissions on those two folders to delegate the administration work to different users.

One important thing to remember about folders is that they're based on a flat structure instead of a hierarchichal structure. In other words, you cannot create a new folder inside an existing folder. Currently, a folder has a name and a description—and no other properties.

The folder is a little special in the server security model. To simplify administrative work, only members of the ssis_admin database role and sysadmin server role can manipulate folders, which means creating folders, renaming folders, changing folder descriptions, or deleting folders. Even though an administrator can grant Modify permission on a folder to a nonadministrative user, that user still would not be able to modify the folder. See Chapter 17, "SSIS Security", for a more detailed explanation about SSIS catalog security.

Environments

A folder contains only two kinds of objects: projects and environments. You already know what a project is, but what's an environment? An environment is simply a collection of named variables. The reason for introducing such a concept is to simplify management work for different execution contexts.

It's common to execute a package under different settings. For example, suppose a developer claims that she has finished the development, and has handed the project to a server administrator. Before deploying the project to production, administrators will usually test the project against a suite of testing database servers. The project could contain lots of parameters. Without an environment, administrators would need to change individual parameter values to switch between production and testing contexts.

Using environments, administrators can instead create two different environments for those two different contexts. Those two environments have a collection of variables with same names, but each environment variable has different values. After completing the testing work, administrators simply bind the project to another environment instead of modifying the individual testing variable values. You'll find that environments can significantly improve productivity when you have lots of projects.

References

Now that we've introduced projects and environments, you might wonder how to bind them together. In the SSIS Catalog such binding is called a *reference*.

If the bound environment shares a folder with the project, the reference is called a *relative reference*. Otherwise it's called an *absolute reference*. The differentiation is important because a relative reference allows you to bind to an environment (with the same name) in the same folder.

The previous section discussed how an administrator might need to move projects between production folders and testing folders. If the reference is based on an absolute path to the target environment, however, the project will still reference the original environment even after it is moved to a new folder. In this case, a simple move operation doesn't work. Administrators would still need to adjust the reference manually.

This scenario is so common that SSIS Catalog includes an optimization for it. If the referenced environment is inside the same folder, SSIS Catalog will track the targeted environment internally based on its name instead of its absolute path. That means that when you move the project to another folder, it will automatically reference the same name environment from its new folder! Administrators can therefore create two environments with same name under a production folder and a testing folder, respectively. When a project gets put into a testing folder, it will reference the testing servers defined in the environment under the testing folder. And when the project is moved to a production folder, it will automatically reference the production server environment. That's very convenient, isn't it?

Summary

As a comprehensive platform for modern data integration applications, SSIS includes a collection of programs and tools, all of which share a unified underlying object model. Understanding these SSIS concepts is an important step toward learning and mastering the use of SSIS. This chapter reviewed the model and explained some important concepts in the model.

Conceptually, the object model can be divided into three areas: control flow, data flow, and SSIS catalog. The Control Flow provides an execution engine and capabilities so tasks can cooperate effectively. The Data Flow Task is a special task, with its own object model and execution engine. Most of the data integration work (such as data extraction, transformation, and data loading) is performed when the Data Flow Task is executed.

SSIS Catalog is a new component introduced in SQL Server 2012 that provides a server-backed environment for enterprise users to develop, deploy, and manage their data integration applications.

CHAPTER 3

Upgrading to SSIS 2012

In This Chapter

A software upgrade is a transition from an older version of software to a more recent version. Upgrading complex systems like data integration servers is a complex and daunting task to enterprise IT departments. Like any big change in an enterprise system, the upgrade process involves cost and some potential risk that existing solutions will stop functioning or behave differently. The benefits of upgrading an enterprise system typically outweigh the cost, complexity, and risk involved. However, careful analysis of the system upgrade and proper planning is necessary to mitigate the risks and reap benefits from the newer software. In this chapter, you will look into the details of upgrading to SQL Server 2012 from an earlier version from an Integration Services perspective. SQL Server 2012 Integration Services is packed with several compelling new features and substantially improves its enterprise capabilities and productivity.

What's New in SSIS 2012

New capabilities in Integration Services 2012 are geared toward improving the productivity of SSIS developers and administrators in building and managing enterprise-wide data integration solutions. Major themes and some key features that should encourage organizations to adopt SSIS or upgrade their existing solutions are the following:

- Improved package development experience
  - Ability to undo or redo changes during package development
  - Flexibility in designing components in Data Flow task enabled by improved column mapping
  - Configurable parameters in packages and projects

- Connection manager sharing across packages in a project
- Ability to compare and merge package changes

- Improved package administrative experience
  - Integration services catalog to centrally deploy, configure, and manage SSIS projects
  - Server-based execution of packages
  - Easier troubleshooting of performance and data issues
  - Better logging and flexibility in log settings

In addition to these major features, there are many other minor enhancements and fixes that will hugely improve developer productivity and management of a large number of SSIS-based solutions. Chapters in this book cover specific enhancements. Chapter 4, "New SSIS Designer Features," covers improvements to the SSIS designer; Chapter 10, "Configuration in SSIS," covers deployment and configuration of SSIS projects; and Chapters 20, "Troubleshooting SSIS Package Failures," through 23, "Troubleshooting Data Issues," cover logging and troubleshooting features.

Upgrade Considerations and Planning

A successful upgrade means an easy and error-free transition to a newer version of software with the desired end state and no unintended consequences. The key to any successful system upgrade is careful planning, execution, and validation. In other words, the system upgrade process needs to be treated like any other big project and demands consideration of risk factors, enlisting mitigation plans, making strategic and tactical decisions, securing resources, dedicating time, and so forth. The discussion in this chapter is limited to Integration Services and does not include a comprehensive upgrade review of related SQL Server features. Let's look at the upgrade planning for Integration Services.

Feature Changes in SSIS

Before SSIS installation and packages are upgraded to a more recent version, it is important to identify upgrade goals and analyze if there might be any unintended side effects to existing solutions. A thorough understanding of feature changes and mapping to business needs helps you identify upgrade goals. This involves reviewing new, deprecated, and discontinued features and breaking changes introduced in the newer version of software.

The new features listed in the previous section and the benefits of using them provide a compelling case for an upgrade to SSIS 2012 from earlier versions. During upgrade planning, you need to list the new features to be adopted as part of the upgrade process and create a roadmap for adoption of other new features. There are some discontinued features in SSIS 2012 and it is important for you to review them and determine if the upgrade would impact any existing SSIS-based solutions. In SSIS 2012, there are no breaking changes in supported functionality and no feature is marked for deprecation. Let's review the features removed in Integration Services in SQL Server 2012 and the impact to existing solutions.

Support for Data Transformation Services

Data Transformation Services (DTS) is a legacy tool. It was supported through backward compatibility in SQL Server 2005, SQL Server 2008, and SQL Server 2008 R2. It was marked for deprecation in SQL Server 2008 R2 and it is completely removed in SQL Server 2012, making the following DTS-related features unavailable after upgrade:

- DTS runtime
- Execute DTS 2000 Package task
- DTS Package Migration Wizard
- DTS Package Management in SQL Server Management Studio
- Upgrade Advisor check on DTS

All DTS packages previously executed from SSIS packages need to be migrated to SSIS packages before or after upgrading to SSIS 2012. There are several options available for DTS migration. Package Migration Wizard available in an earlier version of SSIS or a third-party tool such as DTSxChange can be used for migration.

ActiveX Script Task

ActiveX scripting is another legacy technology supported in previous versions of SSIS. Support for ActiveX scripting existed in SSIS primarily to support DTS, which used scripting to control the business logic and performing computations in packages. With the removal of DTS support in SQL Server 2012, the ActiveX script task is also removed. As a part of migrating DTS packages, ActiveX scripts controlling business logic can be rewritten using Control Flow features like containers and precedence constraints in SSIS. Computations in ActiveX scripting can be replaced with advanced .NET scripting supported by the Script task and components in SSIS.

Data Viewers

Viewers are used to display data flowing between two components in a Data Flow task. They are used during package development to troubleshoot any data issues like unexpected data or unintentional changes applied to data. When an SSIS package with data viewers is executed in Business Intelligence Development Studio/SQL Server Data Tools, data is displayed in selected formats as data flow buffers are processed. Data viewers in data flow paths have no effect when packages are executed outside of SQL Server Data Tools. Earlier versions of SSIS supported the following formats for viewing data:

- Grid
- Histogram

- Scatter plot
- Column chart

In SSIS 2012, all but Grid format are discontinued and when designing packages in SQL Server Data Tools, only Grid format is available. Data viewers in existing packages created using older versions of SSIS are not preserved during package upgrade. SSIS developers have to explicitly add Grid data viewers back to the upgraded packages.

The SQL Server Upgrade Advisor tool discussed in the "Integration Services Upgrade" section later in this chapter scans SQL Server artifacts like SSIS packages and reports issues with the upgrade caused by deprecated or discontinued features and breaking changes that would impact the scanned artifacts.

Dependencies and Tools

Integration Services is a part of the SQL Server feature set, and SSIS-based solutions usually involve other technologies like external data sources, data drivers, job schedulers, monitoring systems, and so forth. When performing an upgrade analysis of SSIS, these dependencies need to be included. For example, a dedicated SSIS-based data integration server involves not only the Integration Services SQL Server feature, but also the Database Engine Services feature and data drivers or providers to connect to external data. Upgrading Integration Services might also require the upgrade of drivers. Upgrade of the SQL Server database instance that stores packages and updates to external tools like job schedulers or monitoring systems to leverage new capabilities might also be necessary.

Upgrade Requirements

After feature changes and impacts on dependencies are understood, the next step is to look at requirements for an upgrade. SQL Server Upgrade Advisor does not help in identifying these requirements. Some of the key upgrade requirements are covered in the following sections.

Software Requirements

Every version of SQL Server has minimum version requirements in terms of supported operating systems and other software like .NET Framework or Microsoft Internet Explorer on which SQL Server features depend. Minimum software version requirements can change significantly between major releases of SQL Server. The SQL Server setup program might install or update some of the prerequisites like the .NET Framework to meet minimum requirements and other requirements like OS version need to be addressed outside of SQL Server setup. SQL Server setup will block installation or upgrade if the minimum requirements are not met. To avoid surprises during upgrade and delays in completing the upgrade process, you need to review these requirements and address them prior to launching your upgrade.

Hardware Requirements

Processor architecture support and minimum memory requirements to install or upgrade a version of SQL Server are included as hardware requirements. Not all SQL Server features or all SQL Server versions are supported in all processor architectures. For example, SQL Server 2012 does not support Itanium processors. If there are any existing assets in that architecture, they cannot be upgraded to SQL Server 2012. The SQL Server setup program blocks installation or upgrade if hardware requirements are not met.

Upgrade Duration

During the upgrade process, the upgraded server will be unavailable. Applications that depend on the system might not function properly or could have to be taken down. This downtime should be accounted for during upgrade planning.

> **Note** SQL Server installation or upgrade requirements might be dependent on the edition or the processor architecture involved. Details on upgrade support are available at *http://technet.microsoft.com/en-us/library/ms143393(SQL.110).aspx.*

Upgrade Scenarios

SQL Server upgrade often is not a simple task of upgrading a version of SQL Server installed on a machine to a newer version. The environment in which SQL Server has to be upgraded is typically complex, leading to several upgrade scenarios.

Version Upgrade Paths

SQL Server versions that can be upgraded to SQL Server 2012 are listed in Table 3-1.

TABLE 3-1 Versions supporting upgrade to SQL Server 2012

Version
SQL Server 2005
SQL Server 2008
SQL Server 2008 R2

Any server with the SQL Server features of the versions listed in Table 3-1 and service updates can be upgraded. For example, SQL Server 2008 SP2 or a higher version of service update can be upgraded to SQL Server 2012. A specific version of SQL Server installation can have more than one set of instance-specific features and only one set of instance-agnostic features (also referred as shared features) that are shared by instance-specific features. Each set of instance-specific features can be upgraded independently and when the first instance of any such feature is upgraded, all shared features of the same version are upgraded with it. SSIS is an instance-agnostic shared feature and for each version of SSIS installation only one set of Integration Services files are installed in a machine. For example, a machine can have multiple instances of SQL Server 2008 database engines belonging to the same version because Database Engine Services is an instance-specific SQL Server feature. The same machine can have only one copy of SSIS 2008 installed because Integration Services is a shared SQL Server feature. On that machine, when an instance of the database engine is upgraded to a higher version, all shared SQL Server features—including SSIS—are upgraded with it, and any nonupgraded instances would remain in the older version. There will not be any shared features in the older version.

Upgrade in Side-by-Side Installation

A server can have multiple versions of SQL Server features installed, which is commonly referred to as version side-by-side installation. Each version can have multiple sets of instance-specific features and one set of instance-agnostic features (also known as shared features). SQL Server upgrade supports upgrading a specific instance of a feature; when doing so, shared features in that version are upgraded with it. Other instances in the same version, other instance-specific features in the same version, or shared features in other versions are not affected during upgrade. For example, if there is a multiversion server with a SQL Server 2005 installation with two database instances and SSIS 2005, and a SQL Server 2008 R2 installation with three database instances and SSIS 2008 R2, only one of the versions of SSIS can be upgraded to SSIS 2012 because it is an instance-agnostic feature. However, all database instances or a specific database instance can be upgraded to SQL Server 2012. Upgrade of SSIS happens when the first database instance is upgraded. When SSIS 2008 R2 is upgraded, the machine will have a side-by-side installation of SSIS, having both SSIS 2005 and SSIS 2012.

Edition Upgrade

In addition to the two flavors of version upgrade previously described, another upgrade option is going from one edition of SQL Server to another. An edition upgrade can be combined with a version upgrade or done within the same version. For example, this type of upgrade is necessary from an SSIS perspective if a server with SQL Server 2008 Standard Edition requires the advanced SSIS adapters and transforms that are available in high-end editions like Enterprise or Business Intelligence. Such an edition upgrade can be done as a standalone upgrade in which the SSIS edition is upgraded to SQL Server 2008 Enterprise Edition without changing the version or as a part of version upgrade in which the server is upgraded to SQL Server 2012 Business Intelligence Edition.

It is necessary to understand these upgrade scenarios in detail and compare them with the needs of the organization to determine which scenario is most appropriate.

Unsupported Upgrade Scenarios

There are some unsupported SQL Server upgrade scenarios. Those from an SSIS perspective are the following:

- **Cross-platform upgrade** Upgrade from 32-bit edition to 64-bit edition is not supported.
- **Cross-version upgrade of Evaluation edition** Upgrading from a trial edition to some other edition in a higher version of SQL Server is not supported in some versions like SQL Server 2012. In those versions, edition upgrade within the same version is possible.

- **Cross-language upgrade** Transition from one localized version of SQL Server to another during upgrade is not supported.
- **Adding features during upgrade** The list of SQL Server features installed in a machine cannot be updated during upgrade process. Upgrade and feature addition or removal need to be done as two steps.

Upgrade Validation

The ultimate validation to any successful upgrade is that the upgraded system springs back to action immediately after upgrade and all existing applications that depend on it continue to work automatically or after making the changes identified during upgrade planning. In the case of SSIS upgrade, all existing packages should continue to work if all changes recommended in Upgrade Advisor are addressed. We recommend that some key packages are identified or a representative set of test packages mirroring existing production packages and execution environment is created for validating an upgrade before upgrading a production system. For example, if SQL Server Agent is used to execute packages in a 64-bit environment, then test upgrade and validation should be done in that environment. This will ensure no environment-specific issues are encountered during upgrade. The upgrade process could be interrupted in the middle due to unexpected issues or in some cases upgrading could lead to unintended consequences due to some incompatibility introduced during the upgrade or a defect in the newer version. If there are any issues during upgrade or validation, the server and artifacts might have to be restored to their original state. Hence an upgrade should always be preceded by a backup of necessary artifacts and server state. Planning should include restoration to a previous version in case of major upgrade issues.

Integration Services Upgrade

The considerations and planning discussed in the previous section are mostly applicable to the upgrade of any SQL Server feature installation. There are three major steps that need to be taken specifically for upgrading Integration Services. The first step is in analyzing SSIS packages as a part of upgrade planning. The second step is performing the upgrade of the SSIS installation and user-created SSIS packages. The third step is about taking care of post-upgrade steps.

Upgrade Advisor

SQL Server Upgrade Advisor helps with upgrade analysis during planning. Upgrade Advisor identifies feature and configuration changes that might affect successful upgrade. Upgrade Advisor for the given SQL Server version analyzes previous versions of installed SQL Server components and prepares a report containing the list of issues that need to be fixed before or after upgrade. For each identified issue, Upgrade Advisor also provides links to documentation that describes each identified issue and how to resolve it. The version of Upgrade Advisor you use should be same as that of the version targeted during the upgrade process. To perform analysis before actually upgrading an older version to SQL Server 2012, you must use SQL Server 2012 Upgrade Advisor. Upgrade Advisor includes the following tools:

- **Analysis Wizard** Used to examine SQL Server components and user-created artifacts (like packages, in the case of Integration Services).
- **Report Viewer** Used to view the reports generated by the wizard.

Upgrade Advisor is available in the Servers\redist\Upgrade Advisor folder of the SQL Server installation media, and at the Microsoft Download Center. SQL Server 2012 Upgrade Advisor analyzes instances of SQL Server 2005, SQL Server 2008, or SQL Server 2008 R2. Prerequisites for installing and running Upgrade Advisor are as follows:

- Windows Vista SP1 or SP2, Windows 7, or Windows Server 2008 R2 operating system
- Windows Installer version 4.5 or higher
- Microsoft .NET Framework 4
- Microsoft SQL Server Transact-SQL ScriptDom, a .NET Framework application programming interface (API) that provides parsing and scripting services for Transact-SQL; part of the SQL Server 2012 feature pack

Servers with previous versions of SQL Server features installed might not meet these requirements and it is not necessary to run Upgrade Advisor on the server considered for upgrade. Upgrade Advisor and its prerequisites can be installed on a development machine and connected to a remote machine with an older version of SQL Server installed to perform upgrade analysis. Some SQL Server features like Reporting Services might not support remote analysis and need Upgrade Advisor to be run locally on the machine with the feature installed. To analyze SSIS packages using the wizard, Integration Services has to be installed in the machine that runs Upgrade Advisor and packages selected for analysis must be successfully loaded by the wizard.

The first step in the Upgrade Advisor Analysis Wizard is to select the SQL Server components that need to be analyzed. After that, you provide additional component-specific parameters for analysis. Figure 3-1 shows the component selection screen. The Integration Services check box is used for analyzing SSIS packages. The Data Transformation Services check box is available but on selecting that check box you would get a warning message (Data Transformation Services is removed in SQL Server 2012) and you cannot proceed to the next steps in your upgrade analysis until you clear this check box. This reinforces the message that any DTS packages available in the server will not be analyzed.

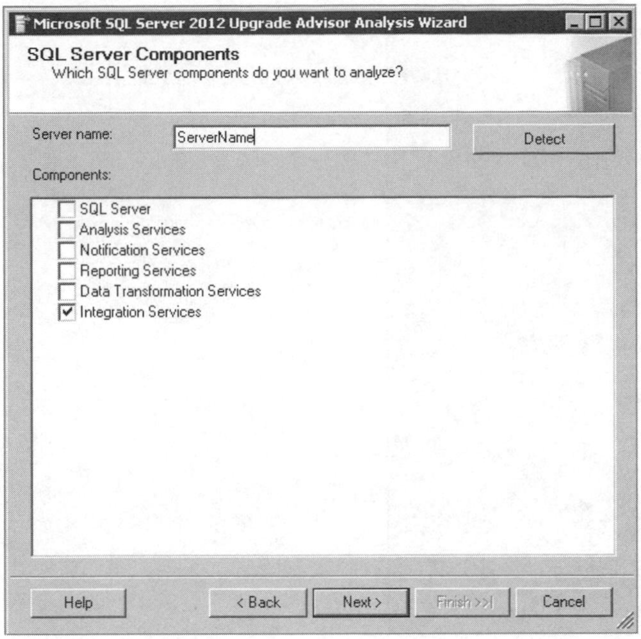

FIGURE 3-1 Component selection in the Upgrade Advisor Analysis Wizard.

Parameters required for performing an upgrade analysis on Integration Services artifacts (Figure 3-2) are as follows:

- **Analyze SSIS Packages On Server** Any SQL Server instance with SSIS packages deployed to msdb in the server selected for analysis can be specified as value for this parameter.
- **Analyze SSIS Package Files** A folder containing SSIS packages is specified for analysis. All packages in the subfolders are also included for the analysis.
- **Password For Encrypted Packages** Packages can be encrypted with a password. To load such packages for analysis, the same password used for encryption is needed.

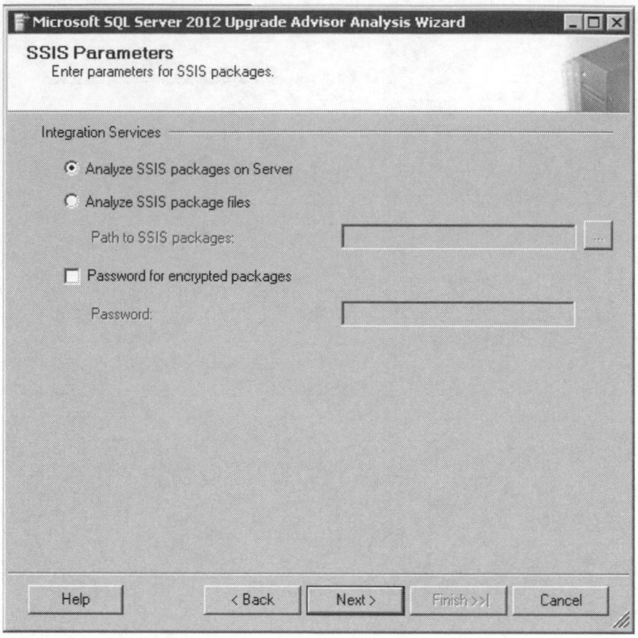

FIGURE 3-2 SSIS parameters for upgrade analysis.

There are a few restrictions when specifying parameters on the SSIS Parameters page of the Upgrade Advisor Analysis Wizard:

- The package location can be either a server or a file path and only one value can be specified for the location. If there is more than one package source or location for the packages in the server to be analyzed, upgrade analysis has to be done separately for each source and location. Because results are saved automatically for every analysis, once analysis is done on all locations, you can view upgrade analysis reports at the end of the analysis.
- The password field accepts just one value. If multiple passwords are involved, packages have to be grouped and analyzed as a group for each set of packages sharing the same password. Alternatively, packages can be modified with encryption removed to perform analysis. However, this is most likely not an option in most organizations for obvious security reasons.

Upgrade Advisor applies a few rules on packages that could be loaded successfully from the specified source location. These rules, described in Table 3-2, help in reviewing upgradability of packages.

TABLE 3-2 Rules used by Upgrade Advisor

Rule applied on	Description
Script task and components in SSIS 2005 packages	Visual Studio for Applications (VSA) is used for scripting in SSIS 2005. It is replaced with Visual Studio Tools for Applications (VSTA) in later versions. Warning is displayed to indicate script task and components will be automatically upgraded to VSTA.
Lookup transform in SSIS 2005 packages	Lookup transform is greatly enhanced after SSIS 2005 release. Warning is displayed to let users consider updating Lookup component to leverage new capabilities.
SQL Server Native Client Provider in packages of all versions	Provider name changes between versions and connection managers referencing the provider need to be updated. Warning is displayed to let users consider manually updating connection strings. It is a warning because if a manual update is not done, SSIS runtime will automatically update it before execution.
OLE DB Provider for Analysis Services in packages of all versions	Provider name changes between versions and connection managers referencing the provider need to be updated. Warning is displayed to let you consider manually updating connection strings. It is a warning because if a manual update is not done, SSIS runtime will automatically update it before execution.
Custom SSIS objects (task, data flow components, for-each enumerator, logger, and connection manager) in Integration Services 2005 packages	Names in the interfaces exposed by the SSIS API changed from 90 to 100 (IDTSxxxx90 becomes IDTSxxxx100) after Integration Services 2005 release. To accommodate this change, custom code implemented using IDTSxxxx90 interface needs to be updated with new interface names and recompiled with newer version SSIS assemblies. Custom objects implemented using Integration Services 2008 and 2008 R2 interfaces and assemblies do not need any code changes. Error reported in Upgrade Advisor to indicate recompilation is necessary for the custom object.
Execute DTS 2000 package task and ActiveX script task in packages of all versions	DTS, Execute DTS task, and ActiveX script task were deprecated in SQL Server 2008 and discontinued in SQL Server 2012. Error message is reported to indicate that these features are not supported.

Package upgrade analysis results in report warnings or errors along with a "When to fix" recommendation on each issue. If the package has any discontinued features, that will be reported as an error on analysis. All rules listed in Table 3-2 are the post-upgrade type and can be addressed during or after upgrade.

Upgrade Advisor can load only those packages developed using the same or older versions of SSIS that are installed in the machine on which Upgrade Advisor is run. For example, if SQL Server 2012 Upgrade Advisor is run on a machine with SSIS 2005 installed and the package source is a file system containing SSIS packages from SQL Server 2008 or SQL Server 2008 R2, then SSIS 2005 runtime cannot load those packages and hence they cannot be analyzed by Upgrade Advisor. Package loading and analysis would also fail if there is a package that needs a password but the password was not specified in the wizard. If a package cannot be loaded, a generic warning message (Upgrade Advisor was unable to analyze Integration Services packages) is reported to the user and more details can be found in the Upgrade Advisor log file Ssis.log at %LOCALAPPDATA%\Microsoft\SQL Server Upgrade Advisor\110\log. The error message in the log file will provide more insights into the failure. The error message snippet in the log file for password issue will look like this:

```
<Message>Loading Package C:\SSISPackages\DWL\LoadCustomers.dtsx</Message>
<Error>Failed to remove package protection with error 0xC0014037 "The package is encrypted
with a password. The password was not specified, or is not correct." This occurs in the
CPackage::LoadFromXML method.
</Error>
<Message>Failed to load package.</Message>
```

Results are saved automatically every time the wizard completes an analysis. If you run the wizard multiple times, a report is saved in XML format each time with a timestamp in the file name. The location of the reports is %HOMEPATH%\Documents\SQL Server Upgrade Advisor\110\Reports. Upgrade Advisor Report Viewer is used to view the reports generated by the wizard. Figure 3-3 shows the results of an upgrade analysis done on the following packages:

- SSIS 2008 R2 package with Execute DTS 2000 Package task
- Package that cannot be loaded by the wizard
- Package that uses SQL Server Native Client provider

Report Viewer displays the upgrade analysis report, providing details on upgrade issues and links to documentation on the issues.

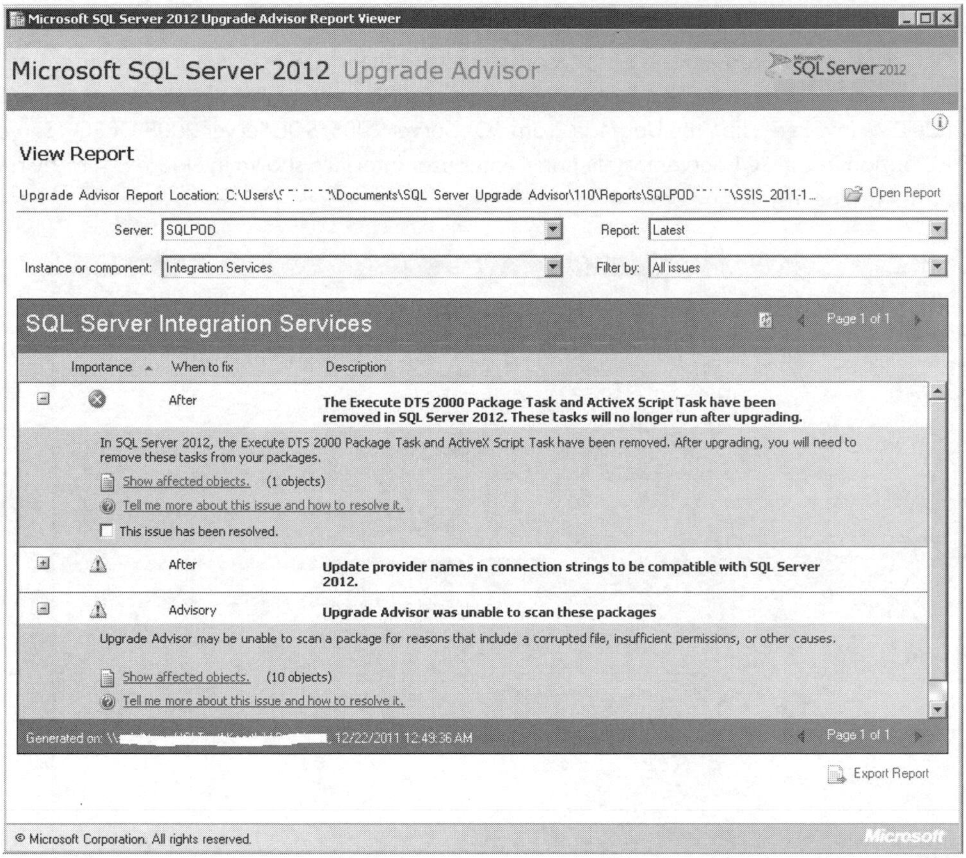

FIGURE 3-3 Report Viewer showing results of the upgrade analysis.

Performing Upgrade

After you perform an upgrade analysis on SSIS packages and draft an upgrade plan, you perform the Integration Services upgrade. This involves two steps:

- Upgrading files and objects created during SSIS installation
- Upgrading packages created by users after SSIS installation

Upgrading Installed Files and Objects

The SQL Server setup program lays out several artifacts to the install machine. To upgrade them to a higher version, you need the SQL Server setup program from the higher version. Upgrade to SQL Server 2012 is invoked using the Upgrade From SQL Server 2005, SQL Server 2008 Or SQL Server 2008 R2 option in the SQL Server Installation Center user interface shown in Figure 3-4 or by running the command-line installation option.

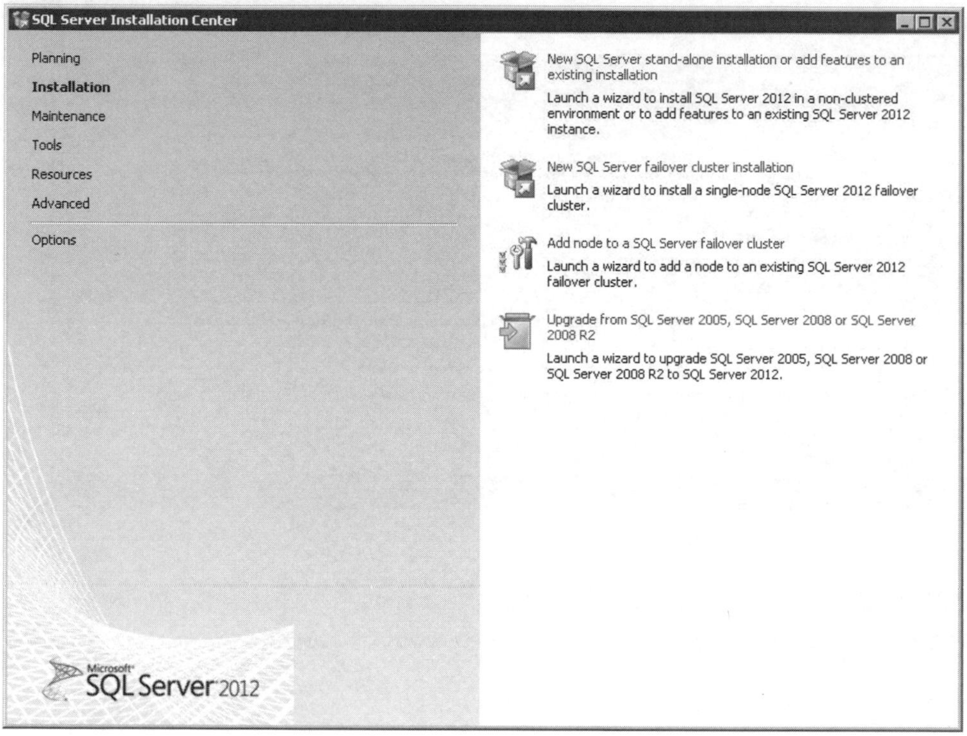

FIGURE 3-4 Installation options including upgrade.

As a part of a SQL Server 2012 upgrade, Integration Services binary files (utilities and assemblies), Windows service and its configuration file, tools that interact with SSIS (Business Intelligence Development Studio, SQL Server Management Studio), and registry entries are all upgraded to the newer version. During upgrade, newer versions of the files are placed in the machine at %ProgramFiles%\Microsoft SQL Server\110\DTS. Older version of Integration Services files are removed, as they are not necessary after upgrade for SSIS to function. Older versions of tools like SQL Server Management Studio or Business Intelligence Development Studio that interact with SSIS are not removed after upgrade but they would not work with newer version of SSIS. During SSIS 2012 upgrade, the default location of packages in the SSIS Package Store is upgraded to %ProgramFiles%\Microsoft SQL Server\110\DTS\Packages. If the SQL Server 2012 upgrade happens on a SQL Server 2005 database instance containing SSIS objects, tables and database roles in the msdb database related to SSIS are replaced with database objects reflecting the higher version. For example, SSIS packages deployed to SQL Server 2005 are stored in msdb.dbo.sysdtspackages90 table, and during upgrade this table is replaced with the msdb.dbo.sysssispackages table and rows are replicated. It should be noted that packages in each row of this new table would still be in the format supported by the older version of SSIS and need to be upgraded separately using Package Upgrade Wizard. Once a database instance is upgraded, an older version of Business Intelligence Development Studio or SQL Server Management Studio cannot interact with packages in msdb even if the package format is in an older version of SSIS.

Upgrading SSIS Projects and Packages

Integration Services projects or packages created by users are not upgraded during the SSIS version upgrade described in the previous section. SSIS project and package upgrade happens when an older version of Integration Services project with packages or a Visual Studio solution containing the project is opened in SQL Server Data Tools 2012. Solution and project files are updated by the Visual Studio Conversion Wizard and packages are upgraded by the SSIS Package Upgrade Wizard. Packages created using older versions of SSIS can also be upgraded directly without going through a project upgrade using the SSIS Package Upgrade Wizard. This wizard is useful to upgrades SSIS packages stored in the file system, SQL Server, and the SSIS package store. The first step in upgrading packages is to select the location of packages. Figure 3-5 shows the Select Source Location wizard page that is used for selecting the package location.

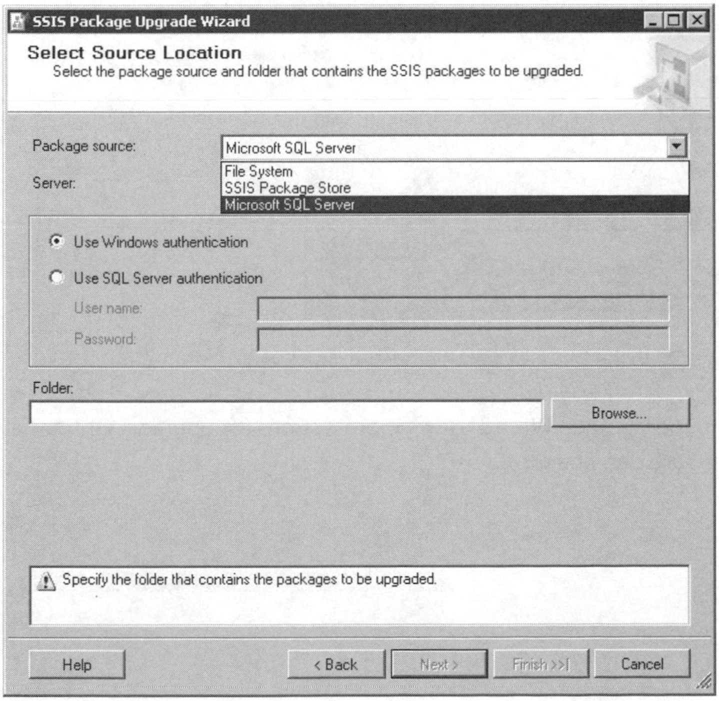

FIGURE 3-5 Package location selection in Upgrade Wizard: Step 1.

In the second step of the wizard (Figure 3-6), you select a set of packages located in the source location for upgrade. You select the packages using check boxes in the first column in the user interface. You can rename packages as a part of the upgrade process and new names are specified in the third column. Packages might need a password to be read and loaded by the Upgrade Wizard. In this step of the wizard, you specify the passwords to load the selected packages in the fourth column. In the third step, you specify the destination for saving upgraded packages. The list of destination options is the same as that of package source options, file system, SQL Server, or SSIS package store. The wizard in a particular version can connect only to the SSIS service or SQL Server of the same version for reading or writing packages.

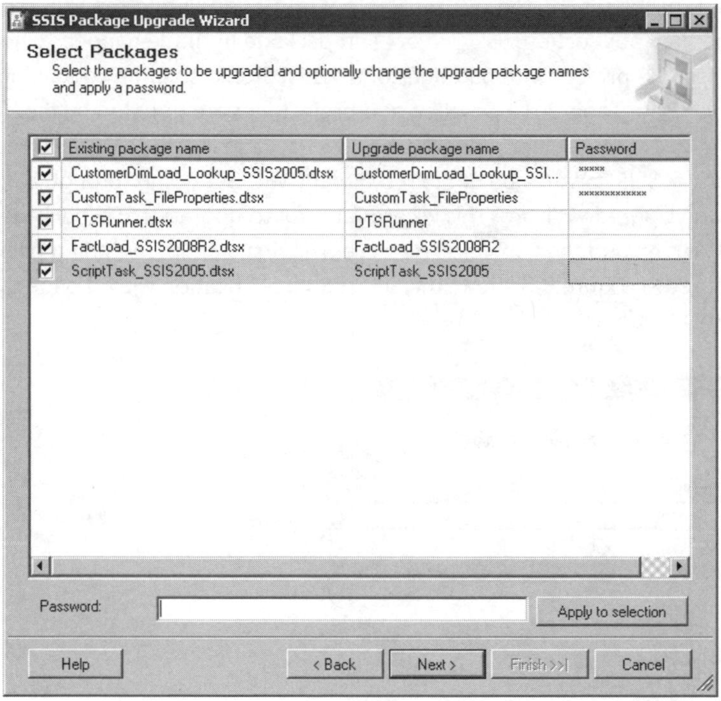

FIGURE 3-6 The Select Packages page in the SSIS Package Upgrade Wizard: Step 2.

The fourth and final step in the Upgrade Wizard allows more options for upgrade. Options available on this page of the wizard are described in Table 3-3.

TABLE 3-3 Upgrade options

Option	Comments
Update Connection String To Use New Provider Names	This option updates connection strings of the following providers ■ OLE DB Provider for Analysis Services ■ SQL Server Native Client Provider Provider name changes between versions and connection strings referencing the provider need to be updated. A new version of the provider is installed during the upgrade process. Packages designed using the old version of the provider will not work if the references are not updated and the old version of the provider is not available. An alternative is to reinstall the older version of the provider to avoid changing connection strings. This is especially useful to users who depend on behavior of the old version of the provider changed in the newer version.
Validate Upgraded Packages	If this option is used, upgraded packages are loaded into the SSIS runtime and validated before they are saved to the destination location. Packages that fail validation are not saved. This step can add a significant amount of time to the upgrade process.
Create New Package ID	The Package ID helps differentiate log entries generated by different packages. This option is used to create a new ID for each upgraded package. This option is useful if old and upgraded packages need to be differentiated in log entries.
Continue Package Upgrade Process When a Package Upgrade Fails	This option determines if the upgrade process should continue or not when an upgrade of a package fails.
Ignore Configurations	Package upgrade time can be significantly reduced using this option to skip loading configurations when loading packages for upgrade.
Backup Original Packages	This option is available only if File System is selected as the source location of the packages and the destination option is Save To Source Location. When this option is used, original packages are saved to a folder named SSISBackupFolder before the package files are overwritten.
Package Name Conflicts	This option provides three choices to deal with conflicts in package names at the destination location. In the case of name conflicts, this option directs the Upgrade Wizard to overwrite packages, add a suffix to the package name, or skip the upgrade.

Note The Ignore Configurations option is available only in Integration Services 2012.

After upgrade options are set, the package upgrade is executed. A summary of the upgrade process and individual warning and error messages and overall status are displayed to the user. Figure 3-7 shows the summary page with access to error or warning messages on individual packages.

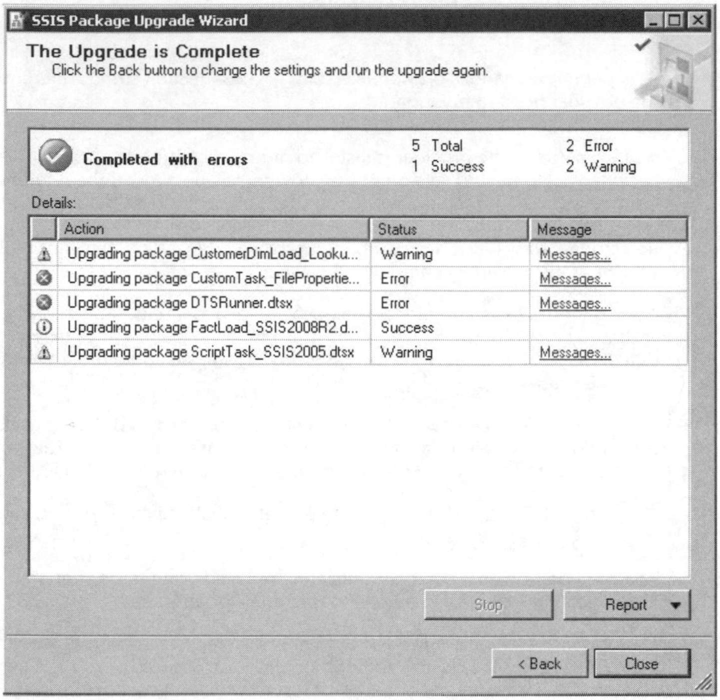

FIGURE 3-7 Upgrade Wizard summary page.

Package Upgrade Wizard Launch Options You can launch the SSIS Package Upgrade Wizard by running SSISUpgrade.exe or using SQL Server Data Tools or SQL Server Management Studio.

Upgrade Wizard Launch from SSDT You can use the Upgrade All Packages option in the SSIS Packages folder shortcut menu in an SSIS project opened in SQL Server Data Tools to launch the wizard. With this option, package source and destination properties are automatically set using the location of the project in the file system.

Upgrade Wizard Launch from SSMS By using SQL Server Management Studio, you can connect to Integration Services and then select Upgrade Packages option from the shortcut menu of a folder containing SSIS packages to launch the wizard. With this option, package source and destination properties are automatically set using the name of the folder maintained by the service.

Upgrade Failure: Common Reasons Package upgrade is a simple process of setting values of some properties in a package. Some of the common upgrade failure reasons are discussed next.

Invalid packages If a package fails to load in a version of SSIS, upgrade of that package to a newer version will fail if the Validate Upgraded Packages option is selected.

Password-protected fields If a package to be upgraded has a protection level that encrypts with a user key and the wizard is run as a different user, the upgrade will fail. If running the wizard under the same user is not an option, the package can be upgraded in SQL Server Data Tools, but protected passwords will be reset during the upgrade.

Script issues Upgrade of packages with script tasks or components will fail if there are issues with the script, such as missing assemblies, compilation errors, errors in migration from Visual Studio for Applications to Visual Studio Tools for Applications, or errors in migration from one version of Visual Studio Tools for Application to another. When Upgrade Wizard fails due to script issues, you should try upgrading using SQL Server Data Tools, which can be useful in fixing the script issues.

Package Upgrade Options Package Upgrade Wizard is the straightforward option to upgrade older versions of SSIS packages. There are few other options for performing a package upgrade.

Programmatic upgrade This option can be useful for an unattended upgrade. The Upgrade Wizard uses the same API underneath. Because the wizard needs user interface interaction, organizations that want to upgrade packages in bulk using a programmatic approach can make use of the Upgrade method in the *Microsoft.SqlServer.Dts.Runtime.Application* class. This method takes parameters that mirror the options set in the Upgrade Wizard. The return value of this method is useful to get upgrade status, details of failed and successful packages, and warnings generated during the upgrade. The signature of this method is shown in Listing 3-1.

LISTING 3-1 Signature of Upgrade method

```
public UpgradeResult Upgrade(
        IEnumerable<UpgradePackageInfo> packages,
        StorageInfo source,
        StorageInfo destination,
        BatchUpgradeOptions options,
        IDTSEvents events
)
```

In-memory upgrade in DTExec Packages created using older versions of SSIS when executed using a newer version of DTExec are upgraded at run time in memory before execution. The original package used for execution is not replaced with the upgraded version. This option can be useful before all existing older version packages are permanently upgraded and used in the production environment. However, it should be noted that runtime upgrade will affect the performance of a package, especially if it makes use of scripts. If you plan to continue using an older version of packages in the new version, we recommend that you upgrade packages up front and execute upgraded packages instead of relying on runtime upgrade.

In-line upgrade in SQL Server Data Tools When you add older version of SSIS packages to an Integration Services project in SQL Server Data Tools, package upgrade is triggered automatically and the upgraded version of the package is added to the project.

Upgrade of Visual Studio solution SSIS package upgrade is invoked as a part of upgrading an older version of Visual Studio containing an Integration Services project. Such an upgrade involves the Visual Studio solution file (.sln), Integration Services project file (.dtproj), and packages in the project. Solution and project files are updated by the Visual Studio Conversion Wizard and packages are upgraded by the SSIS Package Upgrade Wizard. A solution file upgrade results in updates to Visual Studio version and project globally unique identifier (GUID) properties. A project file upgrade results in updating the ProjectVersion XML node value indicating the version of SQL Server Data Tools that can load to a file. The upgrade might result in adding new properties to the project file as a result of new capabilities.

In-memory upgrade in Project Conversion Wizard This wizard is discussed later in this chapter. When selected for conversion, previous versions of SSIS packages are upgraded in memory before they are converted to use the new deployment model.

Changes to Package during Upgrade During the package upgrade, several changes happen in package properties, resulting in changes in the serialized version of the package in XML format. Table 3-4 discusses some changes applied to packages during an upgrade.

TABLE 3-4 Updates to package during upgrade

Change	Comments
VersionGUID property	This property is updated when an upgrade is done in SQL Server Data Tools or when the Create New Package ID option is selected in the Upgrade Wizard.
LastModifiedProductVersion property	The value of this property is set to the version of SSIS that upgraded the package.
PackageFormatVersion property	This property is updated if there is a change in the package format version during upgrade. It is an internal property used by the SSIS runtime to correctly load SSIS packages. An informational message is added to the log during the upgrade process on the change to this property. SSIS 2012 package format change are discussed in Chapter 5, "Team Development."
ExecutableType property	This property is used internally to indicate the type of executable recognized by the SSIS runtime. The SSIS package and its contents, like containers or tasks, are different executable components and each has a specific type name. Type name includes version of the executable and it changes during package upgrade. For example, the SSIS package in SQL Server 2008 R2 has SSIS.Package.2 as the executable type and it is updated to SSIS.Package.3 when the package is upgraded to SQL Server 2012. Type names are internal and can change significantly between SSIS versions. For example, the type name for SSIS packages in SQL Server 2005 is MSDTS.Package.1. The value of this property can be a full name of the assembly that contains the implementation of the executable. For example, the value of this property for Execute SQL Task in SQL Server 2005 is Microsoft.SqlServer.Dts.Tasks.ExecuteSQLTask.ExecuteSQLTask, Microsoft.SqlServer.SQLTask, Version=9.0.242.0, Culture=neutral, PublicKeyToken=89845dcd8080cc91 and it is updated to Microsoft.SqlServer.Dts.Tasks.ExecuteSQLTask.ExecuteSQLTask, Microsoft.SqlServer.SQLTask, Version=11.0.0.0, Culture=neutral, PublicKeyToken=89845dcd8080cc91 during upgrade to SQL Server 2012.

Change	Comments
Provider property	Names of SQL Server Native Client provider and OLE DB Provider for Analysis Services change between different versions of SQL Server. During package upgrade, connection strings used in connection managers are updated to use new provider names. OLE DB connection manager using SQL Server Native Client 2005 has SQLNCLI.1 in the connection string and it is upgraded to SQLNCLI11 when package is upgraded to Integration Services 2012. In SSIS 2008, OLE DB connection manager to Analysis Services database has MSOLAP.4 in the connection string and it is upgraded to MSOLAP.5 when package is upgraded to Integration Services 2012.
Upgrade of custom objects	Upgrade of custom objects from SSIS 2005 packages happens only if the mapping file is deployed at %ProgramFiles%\Microsoft SQL Server\100\DTS\UpgradeMappings folder to guide the Upgrade Wizard. The following code shows how to map custom objects implemented for SSIS 2005 to later versions for upgrade process: <ExtensionMapping tag="my custom object" oldAssemblyStrongName="MyCustomAssembly, Version=1.0.0.0, Culture=neutral, PublicKeyToken=89845dcd8080cc91" newAssemblyStrongName="MyCustomAssembly, Version=2.0.0.0, Culture=neutral, PublicKeyToken=89845dcd8080cc91"/>
Addition of new properties	If a new property is added to an SSIS package or its contents in a version, it can be added to the package during the upgrade process. For example, when upgrading an Integration Services 2005 package with a script task to a higher version, two properties, namely VSTAMajorVersion and VSTAMinorVersion, are added to the package. These properties are required by Visual Studio Tools for Applications, which is used for scripting in higher versions.
Updates to existing property values	Package upgrade might result in values of some internal properties being updated. For example, when upgrading an Integration Services 2005 package with a Script task to a later version, values of properties like Language and EntryPoint are updated to address changes needed by the scripting engine. The value of the Language property in this case is upgraded from Microsoft Visual Basic .NET to VisualBasic and the value of EntryPoint is upgraded from ScriptMain to Main.

Note Package upgrade rules are chained during the upgrade process. For example, when you upgrade an SSIS 2005 package, rules are applied to upgrade it first to SSIS 2008 and then to SSIS 2012. Connection manager reference to SQL Server Native Client provider in an SSIS 2005 package is upgraded from SQLNCLI.1 to SQLNCLI10 first and then to SQLNCLI11.

Addressing Upgrade Issues and Manual Upgrade Steps

The first recommended post-upgrade action is to address the warnings and errors raised during upgrade. There are two types of warnings. The first type is the informational warning that indicates some important action was taken during upgrade that you need to review. You should understand the potential implications of the major change that happened during the upgrade. The message given to you as a result of Script task or component upgrade involving Integration Services versions that have different scripting engines is an example of such a warning. For example, the message involving the upgrade of an SSIS 2008 Script task would look like this: Warning: Script Task: Found SQL Server Integration Services 2008 Script Task "ST_f28de6465e5e4834a00c4a07f76d879b" that requires migration! If there are no errors reported during the upgrade of a Script task, then most likely the upgrade process succeeded with package updates, but because the scripting engine used during package execution would change between the older and newer version of packages, you need to be aware of this major change. You do not have to do anything on the package but might have to plan on additional upgrade validation or just be prepared to deal with any issues that might arise during execution of the upgraded package. The second type of warning is an actionable warning, which requires SSIS package developers to take a specific action. The message given to user as a result of OLE DB Destination component upgrade from the Integration Services 2005 package to a later version like SSIS 2012 is an example of this type of warning. In this case, the default value of *FastLoadMaxInsertCommitSize* property in this component was changed from 0 to 2147483647. Because the original default value has to be updated for better results, a warning message like this is given to the user calling for an action: "The Maximum insert commit size property of the OLE DB destination "OLE DB Destination" is set to 0. This property setting can cause the running package to stop responding.

More Info For more information, see the F1 Help topic for OLE DB Destination Editor (Connection Manager Page).

Integration Services installation upgrade takes care of upgrading files and objects installed with SSIS. The Package Upgrade Wizard takes care of user-created SSIS packages. However, there are a few user-created artifacts that are not upgraded during install upgrade or package upgrade:

- **Connection strings in variables or expressions** Variables storing connection strings and expressions that build connection strings for SQL Server Native Client provider or OLE DB Provider for Analysis Services would have references to provider names and they are not updated during package upgrade. You have to manually update the provider names in the expressions and variables after package upgrade.
- **Connection strings in configurations** Provider names in configurations are not updated during package upgrade and you have to manually update them.
- **Data sources** You can create references to data stores in SQL Server Data Tools and share them in different types of projects in SQL Server Data Tools. So connection strings in data sources are not upgraded when upgrading an Integration Services project with data source. You have to manually update the data source. The connection managers generated from data sources are updated during package upgrade.
- **Connection strings in script** Package upgrade does not update provider names in connection strings referenced in Script task or component. You have to manually update the scripts.
- **SQL Agent job settings** Connection strings set on the SQL Agent Data Sources tab are not updated during the SSIS upgrade. You have to manually update these strings using the SQL Agent user interface if the SNAC provider or OLE DB provider for Analysis Services is involved.

- **References to folders in package stores** During SSIS version upgrade, the default location of the package store changes to a different location due to the version change. Default location of the package store in Integration Services 2005 is %ProgramFiles%\Microsoft SQL Server\90\DTS\Package. During the upgrade to SSIS 2012, the version changes to 110, changing the default package store location with it. References to this path in the package or script code are not updated. The only place this reference is updated is the configuration file for Integration Services Windows service at %ProgramFiles%\Microsoft SQL Server\90\DTS\Binn\MsDtsSrvr.ini, and it is done when the SSIS upgrade creates a new configuration file for the newer version of the service.

Conversion to Projects after Upgrade

In the versions prior to Integration Services 2012 and in packages from those versions upgraded to SSIS 2012, each individual package is the deployment unit and the deployment destination is msdb in a SQL Server instance or SSIS package store. In Integration Services 2012, SSIS project is the deployment unit and SSIS Catalog in a SQL Server instance is the deployment destination. Deployment to msdb or the package store is supported in SSIS 2012 for backward compatibility. If you upgrade packages from previous versions to SSIS 2012, then you can deploy them only to the older deployment destinations. The upgraded SSIS packages need to be converted using Integration Services Project Conversion to make use of new features in SSIS 2012 or deploy them to the SSIS Catalog.

Project Conversion Wizard Launch Options

There are a few options available to launch the Integration Services Project Conversion Wizard.

Command Line, Start Menu, or SQL Server Management Studio

The wizard is launched with no preset values. The wizard is launched from the command prompt by using ISProjectWizard.exe or from the Windows Start menu by selecting Microsoft SQL Server 2012 | Integration Services. You can also select Import Packages from the SQL Server Management Studio shortcut menu of the Projects node under any folder in SSIS Catalog.

SQL Server Data Tools in the Context of an Opened Project

If an Integration Services project is upgraded from a previous version or a new project created in SSIS 2012 is explicitly converted back to Package Deployment Model, it can be converted to Project Deployment Model using the conversion wizard. The Convert To Project Deployment Model selection on the shortcut menu of the project opened in SQL Server Data Tools is used for this.

The SSIS Project Conversion Wizard converts SSIS packages stored in a file system, msdb database in a SQL Server instance, or SSIS package store. The first step in converting packages is to select the location of packages. The user interface for this step looks a lot like Figure 3-5, which shows the screen to select package location in the Upgrade Wizard. In the second step of the wizard (Figure 3-8), you select a subset of packages for conversion. All selected packages have to be successfully loaded using the Integration Services 2012 runtime before the user can go the next step in the conversion. In-memory upgrade happens if the packages selected for conversion are created using an older version of SSIS. When you click Next, the wizard tries to load all selected packages. The Display Status Message column reports Ready or Error to indicate readiness to proceed to the next step. Error messages are reported for packages that cannot be loaded and they have to be excluded from the conversion. Packages might need a password to be read and loaded by the wizard. In the second step of the wizard, the password is specified for each of the packages selected for conversion. If sensitive elements in a package are encrypted with the user key, the protected information will be lost if the wizard is executed with another user profile. In those cases, the message column in the user interface displays this warning: Sensitive data lost due to incorrect user key.

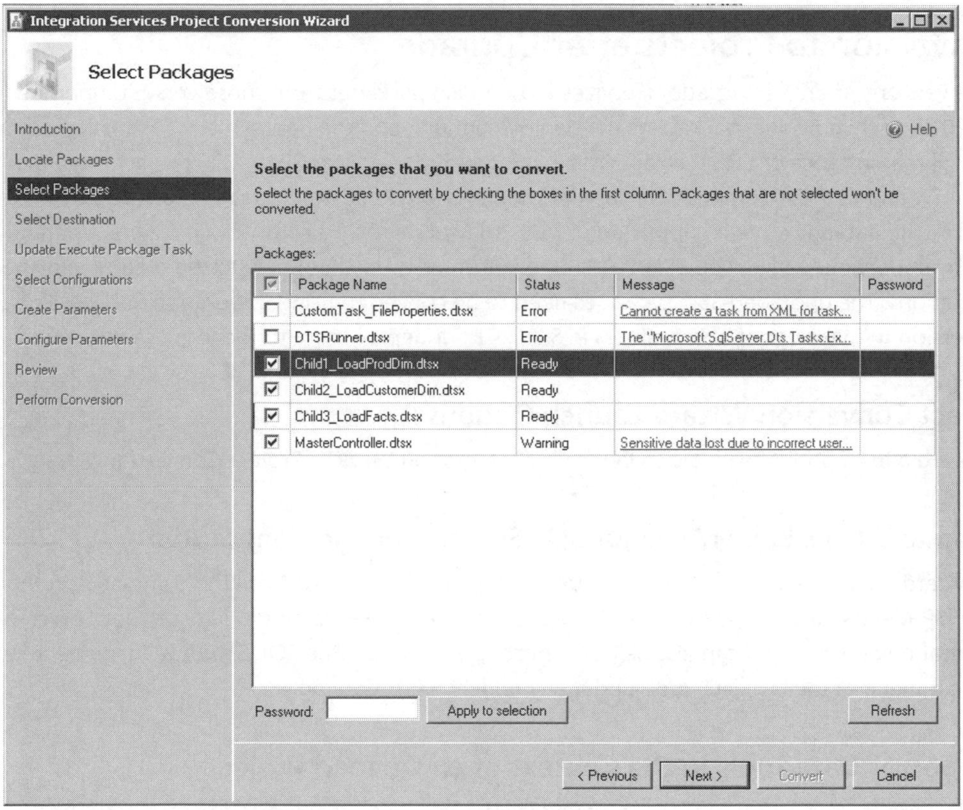

FIGURE 3-8 Package selection and loading in the Project Conversion Wizard: Step 2.

The third step of the wizard allows setting properties of the project to be created from the packages selected on the previous page (Figure 3-9). File system path to save the project, name, and description of the project are set in this step. When the wizard successfully completes, a project file (.ispac extension) is created based on the destination settings. An important setting selected for this project is Protection Level. This setting is used to define if entire packages or sensitive information in the packages that are part of the project are to be protected and how. Table 3-5 describes available protection levels. Sensitive information in the project is of the following types:

- **Passwords in connection strings**
- **Property in tasks or components** Any property of any SSIS task or component, built-in or custom developed, can be marked as sensitive during development and cannot be changed by package developers.
- **User-created parameters** SSIS package developers can mark package or project parameters created by them as sensitive.

> **Note** Step 1 (Locate Packages) and Step 2 (Select Destination) of the Project Conversion Wizard are skipped if the wizard is launched for SQL Server Data Tools. Because the wizard would be launched in the context of the opened project, location of the packages will be the file system path of the project and destination is not needed because the project file (.ispac) is not generated by the wizard. The project file is generated by building the project in SSDT.

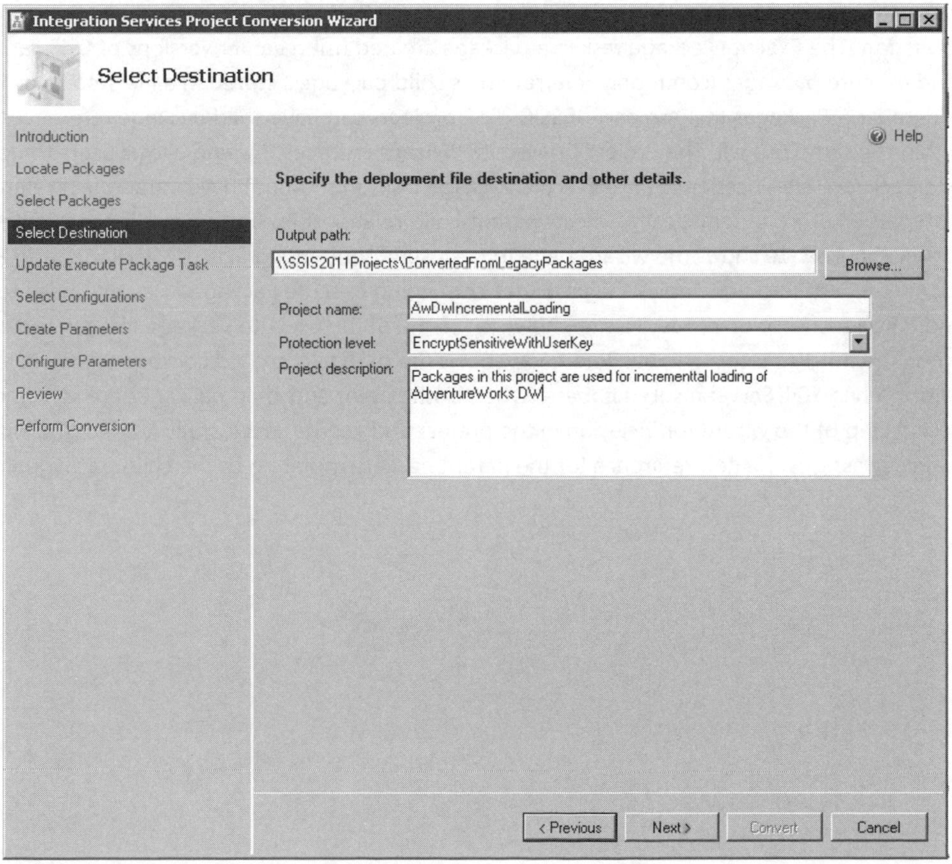

FIGURE 3-9 Destination selection page in Project Conversion Wizard: Step 3.

TABLE 3-5 Description of protection levels

Protection level	Description
DontSaveSensitive	Sensitive properties are not saved as a part of the project, making the property values unavailable to anyone accessing the project or its contents.
EncryptSenstiveWithUserKey	Sensitive properties are saved as a part of the project but encrypted using a key representing the current user's Windows OS logon credentials. The encrypted property values are available only to the same user with the same Windows user profile. Other users or user profiles cannot access the project or the contents.
EncryptSensitiveWithPassword	Sensitive properties are saved as a part of the project but protected using a password. To access the project or its contents, the same password is needed.
EncryptAllWithUserKey	Entire project, including the contents of all files that are part of the project, are protected using the user key.
EncryptAllWithPassword	Entire project, including the contents of all files that are part of the project, are protected using a password.

Note The Microsoft Data Protection API (DPAPI) that provides operating system-level data protection services is used in protecting projects and the contents.

The fourth step in the conversion helps updating Execute Package tasks in the packages selected for conversion. The Execute Package task in a package created using earlier versions of SSIS can reference and execute packages (commonly referred to as child packages) stored in a file system or SQL Server database. Packages that are part of SSIS 2012 projects can have child package references limited within the same project. The Project Conversion Wizard enforces this and allows users to update the child package references or remove Execute Package tasks that cannot have intraproject references. In this step, the wizard automatically detects parent-child relationships among packages selected for conversion. Figure 3-10 shows the wizard page that is used for updating Execute Package tasks. The first column, Parent Package, shows the packages containing Execute Package tasks that have to be updated. The second column, Task Name, shows the name of the Execute Package tasks in the parent packages. The third column, Original Reference, shows the path to the child package stored in a file system or path in SQL Server msdb database. When both parent and child packages are selected in the second step of the wizard for inclusion in the project and can be successfully loaded, the wizard automatically assigns the new reference for the parent package pointing to the child package in the same project, which is shown in Figure 3-10 as the fourth column. In the cases when a child package reference cannot be assigned, the wizard leaves the reference empty, allowing the user to set it. Execute Package tasks in a parent package that do not have any child package reference assigned cannot be included in the project, and the wizard does not allow you to move to the next step until a reference is assigned or the parent package is excluded.

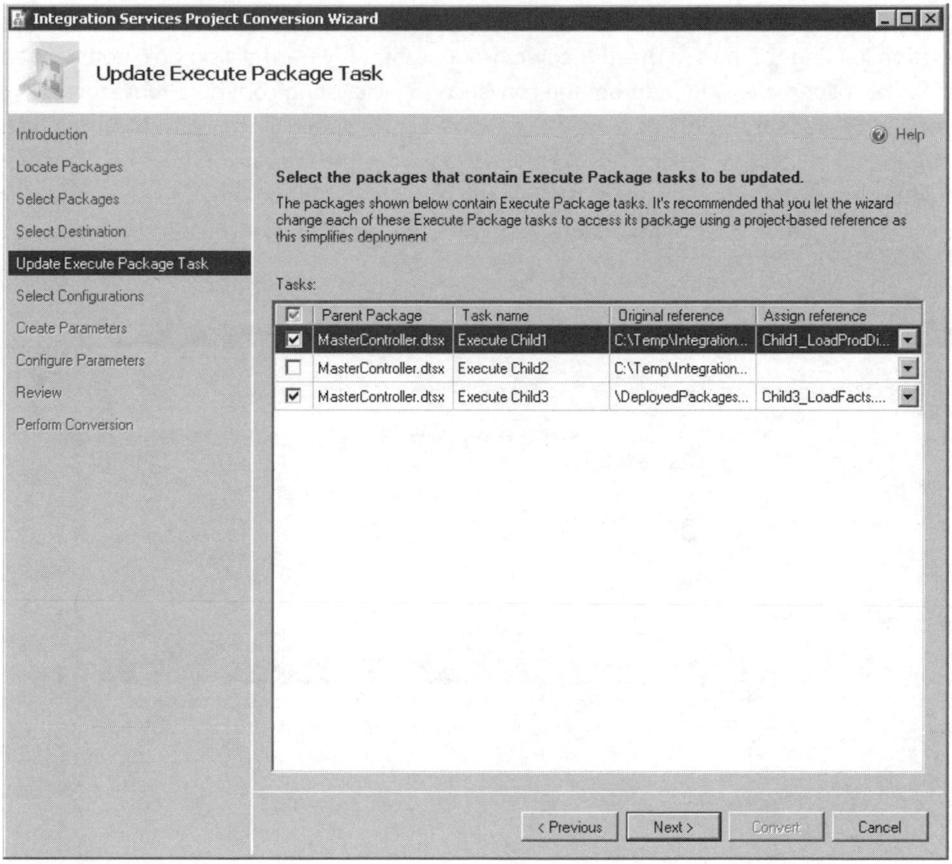

FIGURE 3-10 Updating Execute Package tasks in the Project Conversion Wizard: Step 4.

The fifth step in the conversion is to select the configurations that need to be converted to package or project parameters that are supported in Integration Services 2012. The configurations referenced by the packages selected for conversion are loaded by the wizard. Figure 3-11 shows this page of the wizard. The dialog box has five columns. The first column is to pick the configurations to be included in the conversion. The second column, Package, shows the names of the packages that have the configuration references. The third column, Type, shows the type of configuration, and the fourth column, Configuration String, shows details on the configuration reference. The status of configuration loading is shown in the fifth column, Status, of this wizard dialog box. Configurations that cannot be loaded are excluded from the conversion. Any existing configurations stored in a file system or SQL Server not referenced by any of the packages included in the conversion can be added to the conversion process by clicking Add Configuration. Once the conversion from configurations to parameters happens there is no need to retain the configurations and they can be removed from the project using the Remove Configurations From All Packages After Conversion check box on this wizard page.

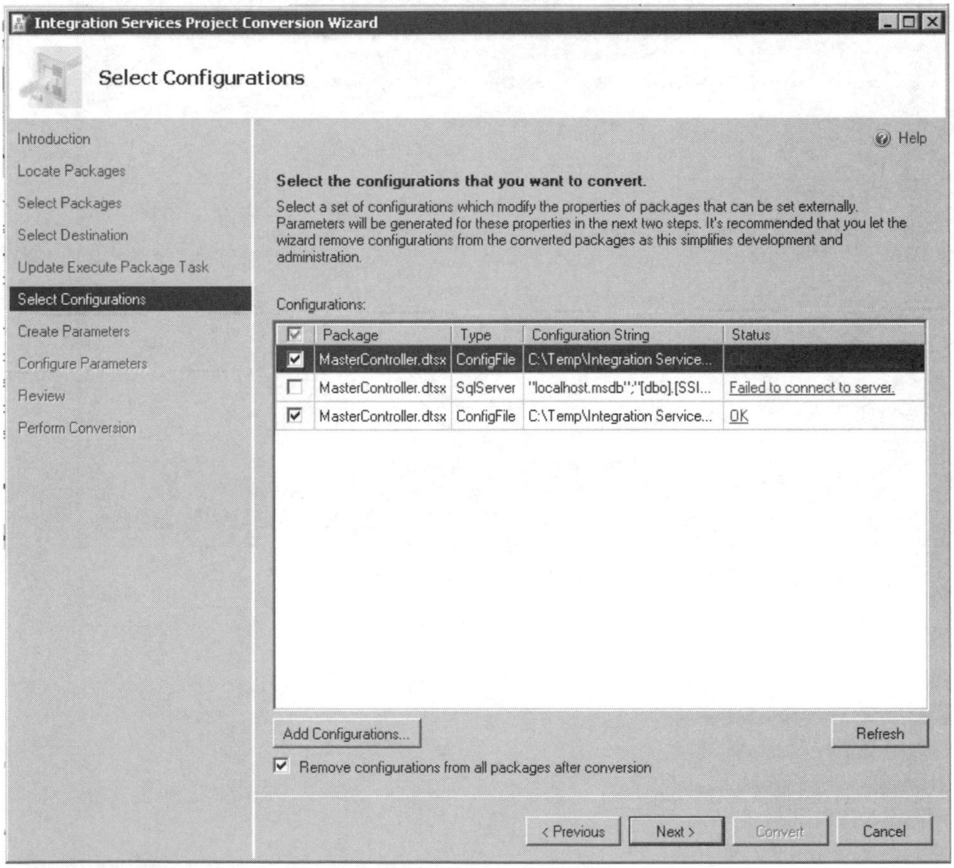

FIGURE 3-11 Configuration selection during project conversion: Step 5.

Note The sixth page of the Project Conversion Wizard is Create Parameters (Figure 3-12). The wizard reads the properties in the selected packages set by configurations and creates parameters to set values of configured properties replacing configurations. The second column shows the names of the packages that reference configurations and the third column is used to set the names of the parameters created in this step. Scope of the parameters created in this step can be set to package or project in the fourth column. The property set by the parameter selected and the data type of the property are shown at the bottom of the page. The wizard detects sensitive properties in packages and automatically creates sensitive parameters for them.

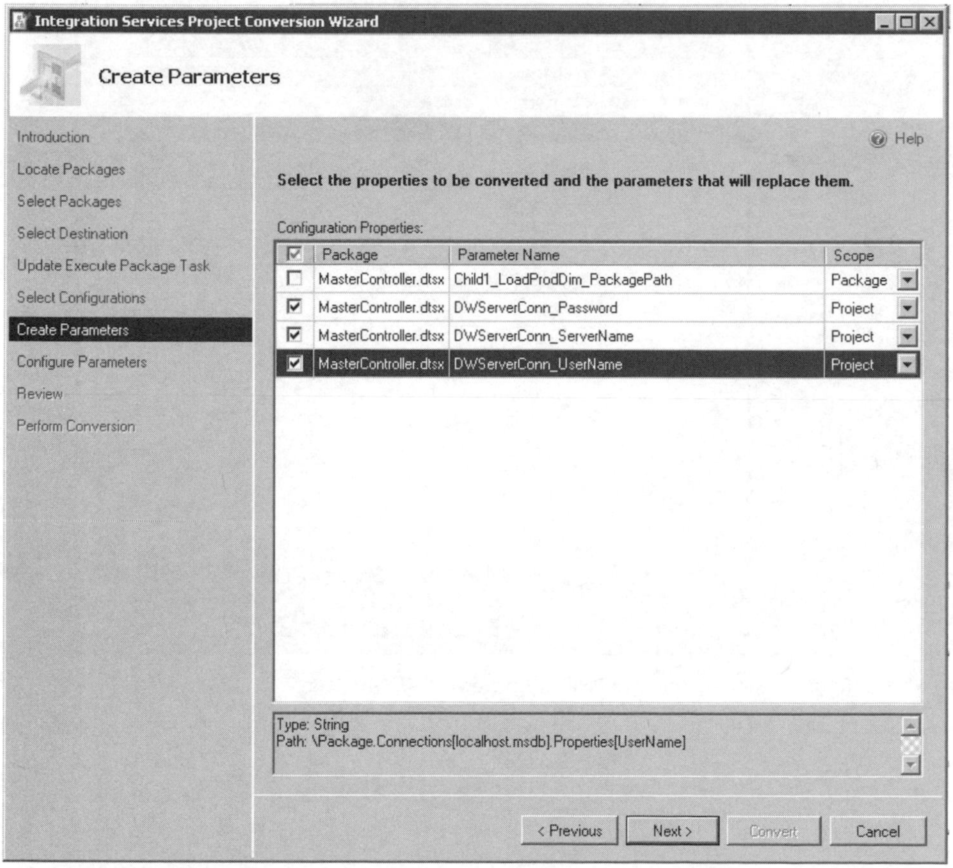

FIGURE 3-12 Create Parameters page in the Project Conversion Wizard: Step 6.

The next step in the conversion is to configure the parameters created. The default values of the parameters are set in this step. Figure 3-13 shows this wizard page. The values of sensitive properties are protected and not shown in plain text. The ellipses button at the end of each row can be used to open the Set Parameter Details dialog box (Figure 3-14) to set the description and required properties for the selected parameter.

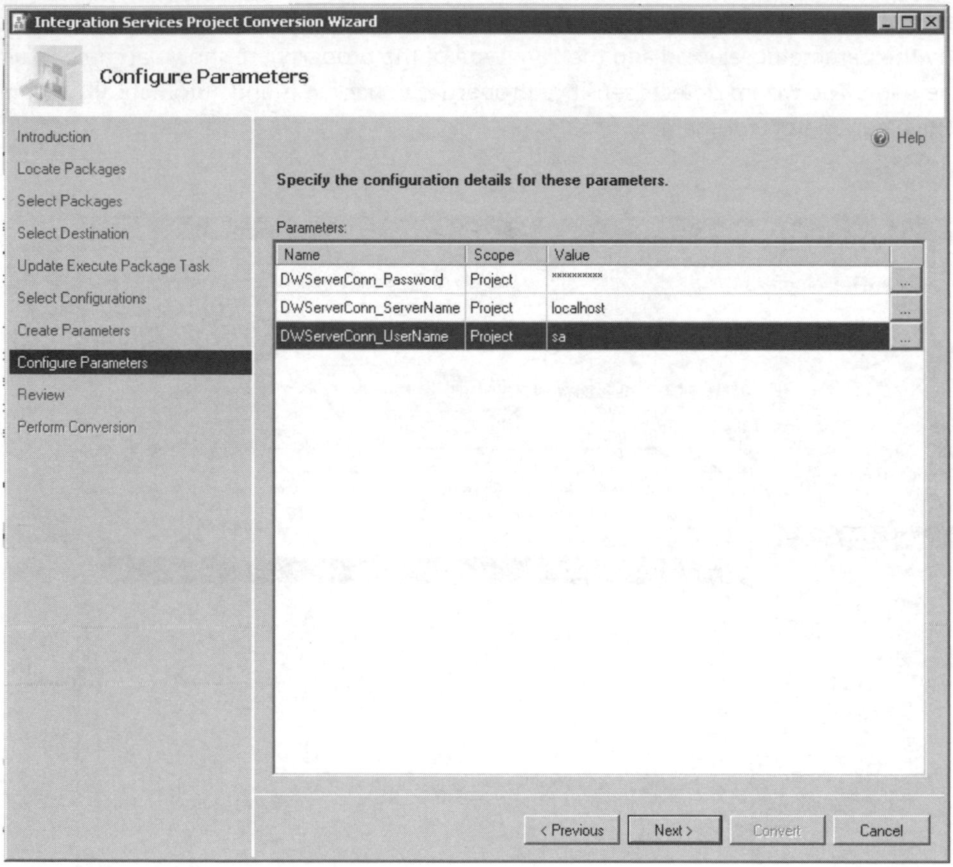

FIGURE 3-13 Configure Parameters page in Project Conversion Wizard: Step 7.

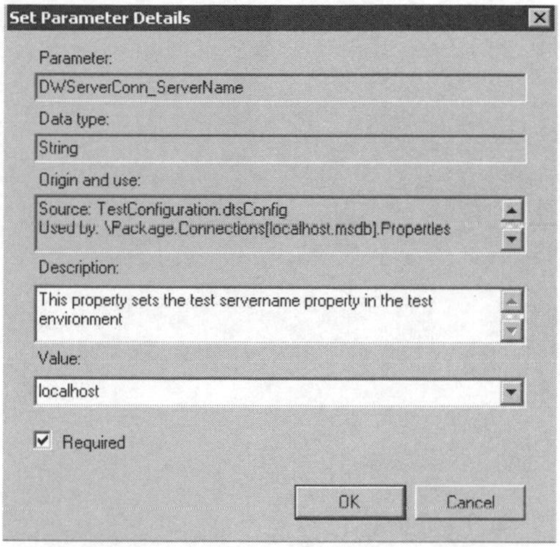

FIGURE 3-14 Set Parameter Details dialog box.

The wizard finally displays the project conversion settings done using the wizard for review before letting the user perform the conversion. On the last page of the wizard, status of conversion of each package is displayed and a detailed report of the steps executed during project conversion can be saved for later use by clicking Save Report.

Summary

Upgrading Integration Services requires proper planning. Understanding how SQL Server feature upgrade and SSIS package upgrade works will you with your planning. Wizards are available to perform upgrade analysis, package upgrade, and conversion of upgraded packages to the project deployment model. SSIS 2012 has several new capabilities that justify the costs involved in upgrading.

PART II

Development

CHAPTER 4

New SSIS Designer Features

In This Chapter

The Integration Services Designer

Visual Studio

The first thing you'll notice when starting a new SSIS project in SQL Server 2012 is that SQL Server Data Tools (formerly Business Intelligence Development Studio) has been upgraded to Microsoft Visual Studio 2010 SP1. Along with the upgrade comes an updated look and feel (shown in Figure 4-1): You'll find many small visual improvements, such as an updated color scheme, new icons, and rounded corners on the tasks and transforms.

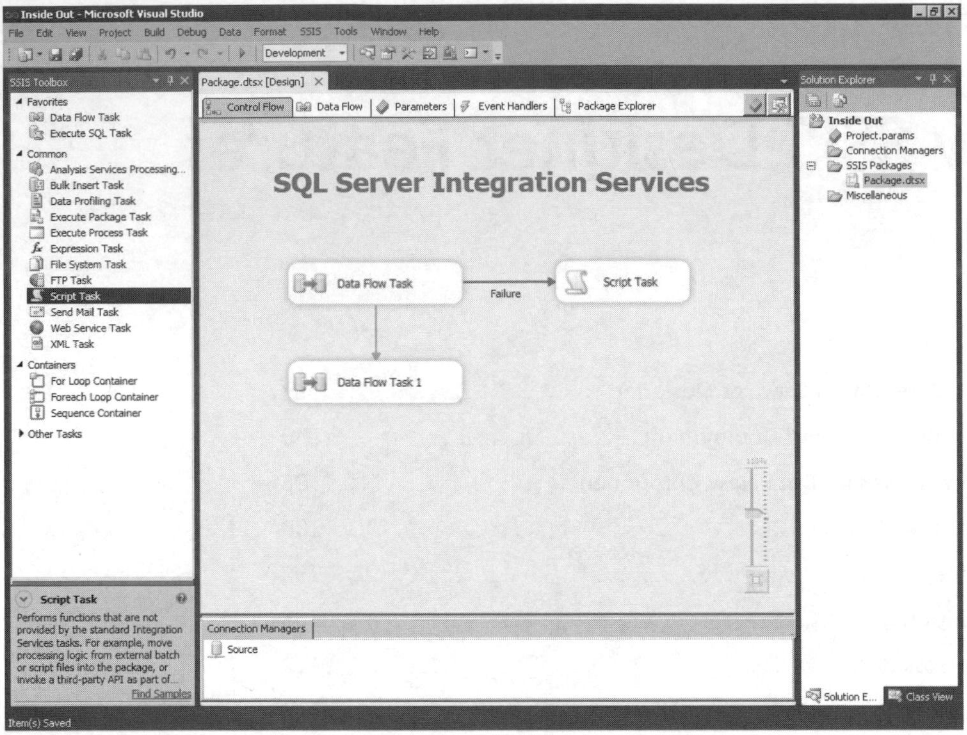

FIGURE 4-1 The SQL Server 2012 designer for Integration Services.

> **Note** Changes were made to way the SSIS Visual Studio project is packaged, so that Microsoft will be able to release an update for SQL Server Data Tools that supports new versions of Visual Studio without waiting for a new release of SQL Server.

Undo and Redo

Perhaps the biggest usability feature missing from previous versions of the product is undo and redo functionality. You can undo most operations within the designer by pressing Ctrl+Z or clicking the Undo button. You can redo changes with Ctrl+Y, or by clicking the Redo button on the toolbar.

Getting Started Window

The Getting Started (SSIS) window (Figure 4-2) appears when creating new SSIS projects. It provides a live feed from Microsoft.com, displaying SSIS news, as well as links to tutorial videos and samples. If the window has been closed, you can open it by clicking the SSIS menu and selecting Getting Started.

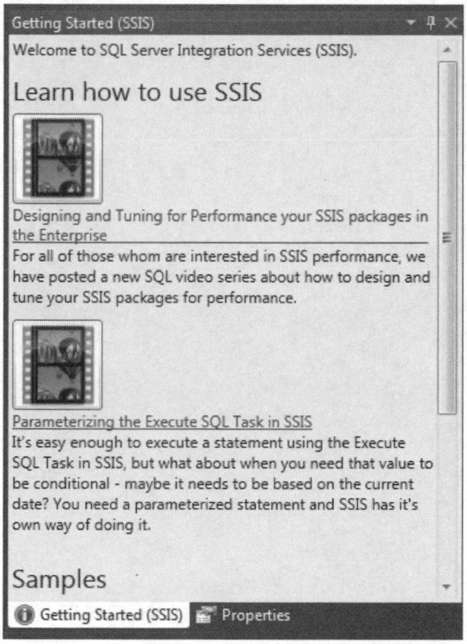

FIGURE 4-2 The Getting Started window.

Toolbox

SSIS now has its own toolbox window. The SQL 2012 toolbox includes significant performance improvements over previous versions, and will automatically display third-party tasks and components installed on your development machine. Items in the toolbox are divided into different categories (which change depending on whether you are looking at the Control Flow or the Data Flow designer). The bottom area of the toolbox displays the name and description of the currently selected item. Most toolbox items will also display in this area a help button and a Find Samples link that will bring up samples that demonstrate how the item can be used within an SSIS package. You can display the toolbox from the SSIS menu by selecting SSIS Toolbox, or by clicking the new SSIS Toolbox button in the upper-right corner of the designer area.

Tasks in the Control Flow toolbox (Figure 4-3) are divided into four categories: Favorites, Common, Containers, and Other Tasks. The Favorites section displays the two most commonly used tasks by default, the Data Flow Task and the Execute SQL Task.

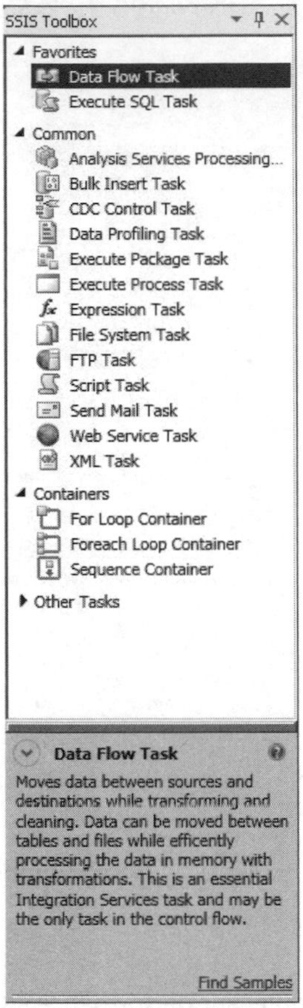

FIGURE 4-3 The toolbox for the Control Flow.

Components in the Data Flow toolbox (Figure 4-4) are divided into five categories: Favorites, Common, Other Transforms, Other Sources, and Other Destinations. The Favorites category contains the new Source and Destination Assistants, which are described later in this chapter.

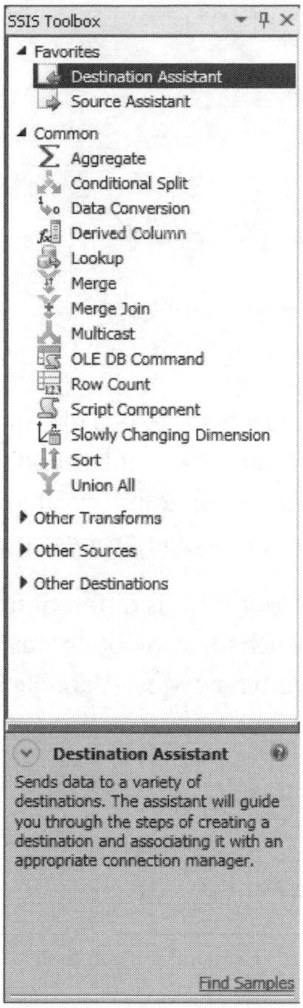

FIGURE 4-4 The toolbox for the Data Flow.

Toolbox items can be moved between categories by right-clicking the item name, and selecting one of the Move To options. The shortcut menu also gives you the Refresh1 Toolbox option, which will look for newly installed third-party tasks and components, and the Reset Toolbox Defaults option, which moves the tasks back to their default categories.

Variables Window

Many usability improvements have been made to the SSIS Variables window (Figure 4-5). It now appears at the bottom of the designer by default, and like most Visual Studio tool windows, it can be docked to any location within the designer. You can display the Variables window from the SSIS Menu by selecting Variables, or by clicking the new Variables button in the top right corner of the designer window.

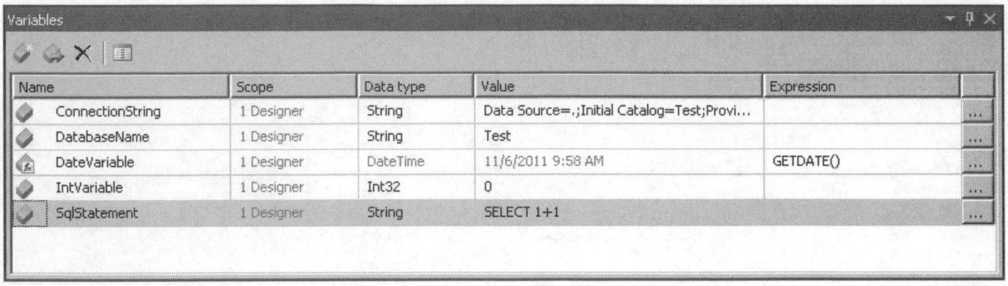

FIGURE 4-5 The SSIS Variables window.

The Variables window shows the default value of a variable. If the variable is set to evaluate using an expression, the expression is displayed in the final column, and the value cannot be modified directly. Clicking the ellipsis button at the end of the row will open the Expression Builder dialog box. Setting a new expression on a variable will automatically set its *EvaluateAsExpression* property to *True*.

In SQL Server 2012, new variables are always created at the Package scope. This is different from previous versions, where the variable would be created in the scope of whichever task or container was currently selected in the designer. The Variables window also contains a new Move Variable button, which allows you to move a variable to a new scope (Figure 4-6).

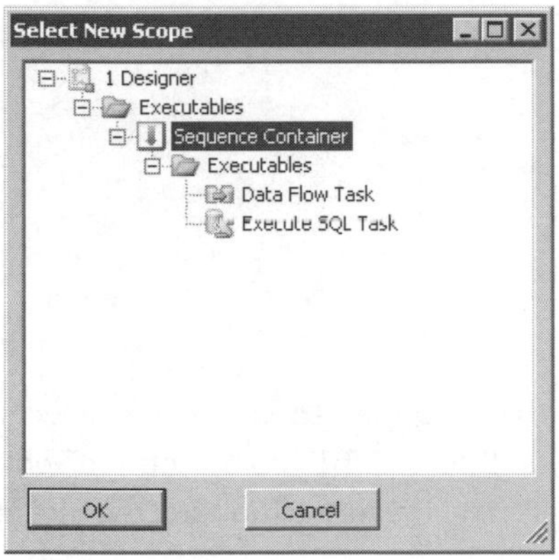

FIGURE 4-6 The Move Variable button allows you to change a variable's scope.

Zoom Control

Both the Control Flow and Data Flow designer surfaces contain a new zoom control in the lower-right corner. This control allows you to easily resize the designer view in (up to 5x size increase) and out (up to 10 percent of the original size). The bottom of the control has a Fit View To Window button that will automatically resize your view so that all package contents fit on one screen.

Autosave and Recovery

SSIS projects now make use of the AutoRecover functionality provided by Visual Studio. This feature allows you to recover your work if SQL Server Data Tools shuts down unexpectedly (due to power failure, crash, or misbehaving third-party add-on). When Visual Studio restarts after an unexpected shutdown, you will be prompted to recover any unsaved changes to your SSIS packages. You can control the AutoRecover settings on the Tools | Options... | Environment | AutoRecover preferences page.

Status Icons

Previous versions of SSIS used colors (green, yellow, and red) to indicate the status of tasks and components while the package was running. The same colors are used in SQL Server 2012, but instead of changing the background color of the task or component, a status icon is displayed in the upper-right corner of the box (Figure 4-7).

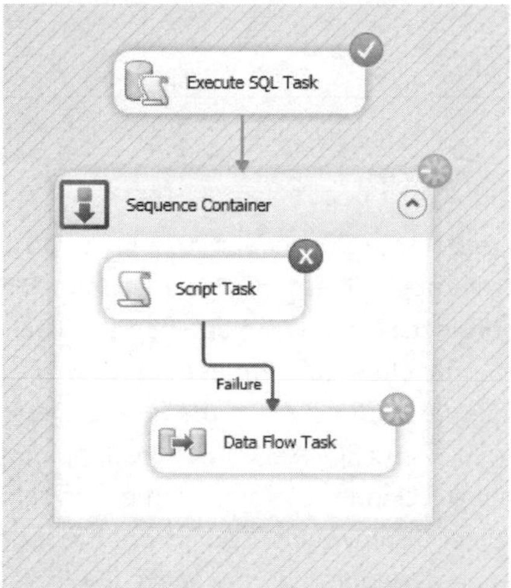

FIGURE 4-7 Status is used to indicate progress instead of changing the background color of the box.

> **Note** Using status icons instead of colors is one of the many accessibility changes that was made for SSIS in SQL Server 2012. Although many people might miss the flashing green and red box colors used in previous versions, not everyone was able to enjoy them, as perception of red and green are affected by the most common form of colorblindness.

Annotations

A number of improvements were made to package annotations, including the following:

- Annotations are persisted in plain text in the package (.dtsx) file. Previous versions of the product had the annotation text encoded in a way that made it very difficult to extract for documentation purposes.
- The annotation window automatically grows as you type.
- Annotations now accept new lines; just press Enter.
- You can easily change the font style, size, and color of an annotation block by right-clicking the annotation block and selecting Set Annotation Text Font.
- You can create a new annotation by clicking the design surface and starting to type.

Configuration and Deployment

Solution Explorer Changes

The Solution Explorer window has been updated for SSIS projects in SQL Server 2012 to support the introduction of the Project Deployment Model. Two different deployment models are supported in this version of SSIS. Figure 4-8 shows a solution with two projects; the top project (named File Based) is in the Package Deployment Model, whereas the bottom project (named Project Based) is in the Project Deployment Model. New projects created in SQL Server 2012 will be in the Project Deployment Model by default. Existing projects from SQL Server 2005 and SQL Server 2008 will open in the Package Deployment Model. You can switch models by right-clicking the project name, and selecting Convert To Package Deployment Model or Convert To Project Deployment Model from the shortcut menu. The nodes that appear under a project will change depending on the active deployment model for that project.

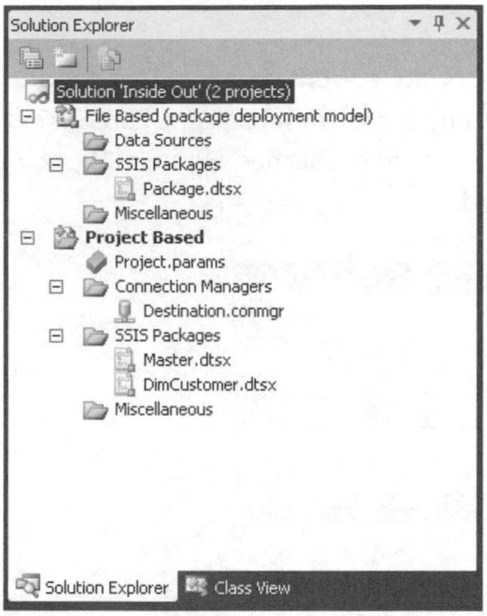

FIGURE 4-8 The SQL Server 2012 Solution Explorer window.

Project Parameters

The Project.params node is a file that stores any project-level parameters. This node will appear for only projects in the Project Deployment Model. Double-clicking this node opens the parameter designer (Figure 4-9).

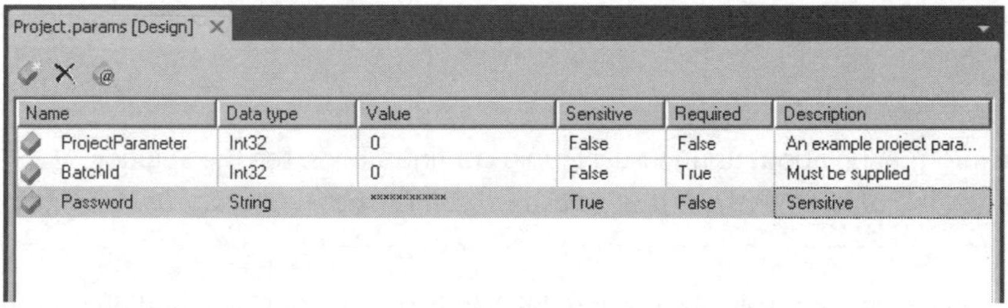

Project.params [Design]
Name
Data type
Value
Sensitive
Required
Description
ProjectParameter
Int32
0
False
False
An example project para...
BatchId
Int32
0
False
True
Must be supplied
Password
String
True
False
Sensitive

FIGURE 4-9 The designer for project-level parameters.

Connection Managers

SQL Server 2012 allows you to create connection managers at the project level, which get shared among all packages within the project. Each shared connection manager appears as a node under the Connection Managers folder, and is stored in a separate file (with a .conmgr extension). Shared connection managers are available only when using the Project Deployment Model. Shared connection managers replace the use of Data Source (.ds) files from previous versions of the product; the Data Sources folder is shown only when using the Package Deployment Model.

Parameter Tab

Clicking the Parameters tab opens the parameter designer for the current package. This designer allows you to view, create, and edit the parameters exposed by the current package. Parameters function a lot like read-only variables, and they have many of the same properties. Figure 4-10 shows the package parameter designer, with three parameters defined.

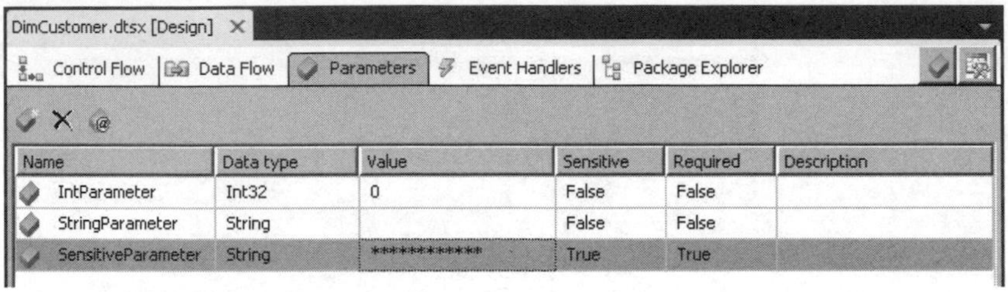

FIGURE 4-10 The package parameter designer.

Visual Studio Configurations

Visual Studio allows a project to contain multiple configurations. In most types of Visual Studio projects, configurations are used to define different build properties (*Debug* vs. *Release*), or settings that affect the way the application runs on a certain platform. SSIS supports the use of Visual Studio configurations in SQL Server 2012, allowing you to externalize your parameter values for different environments. SSIS projects contain a single Development configuration by default. Configurations can be managed by right-clicking the project name in Solution Explorer, selecting Properties, and clicking Configuration Manager.

> **Note** For more information about using Visual Studio configurations, see the Solution Configuration entry in Books Online at *http://msdn.microsoft.com/en-us/library/bb166577.aspx*.

You can externalize a parameter value by clicking the Add Parameter to Configuration button in the parameter designer (Figure 4-11), which opens the Manage Parameter Values dialog box (Figure 4-12). When this is launched from the package parameter designer, you will be able to externalize parameters declared at the package level. Launching the user interface from the project parameter designer allows you to configure project-level parameters.

FIGURE 4-11 The Add Parameter to Configuration button is found in the parameter designer.

The Manage Parameter Values dialog box will show the list of parameters with values that are currently stored within a Visual Studio configuration, with a column for each configuration in the project. To externalize a parameter, click Add and select the parameter from the list. Figure 4-12 shows a package with a single externalized parameter value (*SourceDirectory*). The project has two configurations defined: Monthly and Daily. The current configuration (also known as the active configuration) will be indicated in the column header. In this example, the user has set different values for each configuration. The Monthly configuration (which might represent settings to use for a monthly run of the SSIS package) has a value of C:\InputFiles\Monthly. The Daily configuration (which might represent settings to use for daily runs of the package) has a value of C:\InputFiles\Daily. Clicking Sync will copy the value of the active configuration to all other configurations in the project.

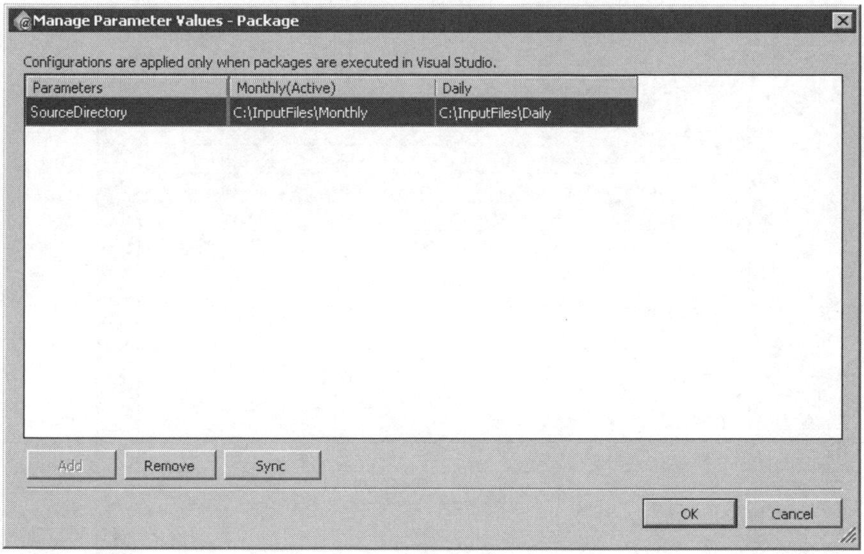

FIGURE 4-12 The Manage Parameter Values dialog box.

> **Note** Parameter configurations are stored within the Visual Studio project file (.dtproj). To save any changes made in the Manage Parameter Values dialog box, you must save the project.

Project Compilation

When using the Project Deployment Model, building an SSIS project produces a project deployment file (.ispac) that contains the packages, shared connection managers, and parameter information for the project. The default values for parameters within the project are taken from the active Visual Studio configuration.

Deployment Wizard

The Integration Services Deployment Wizard (Figure 4-13) is used to deploy project files (.ispac) to an SSIS Catalog. It can also be used to move projects between different SSIS Catalog instances. The wizard can be launched by double-clicking a project file (.ispac), or by running ISDeploymentWizard.exe from the command line. When using the Project Deployment Model, you can also launch the wizard by right-clicking the project in Solution Explorer and selecting Deploy.

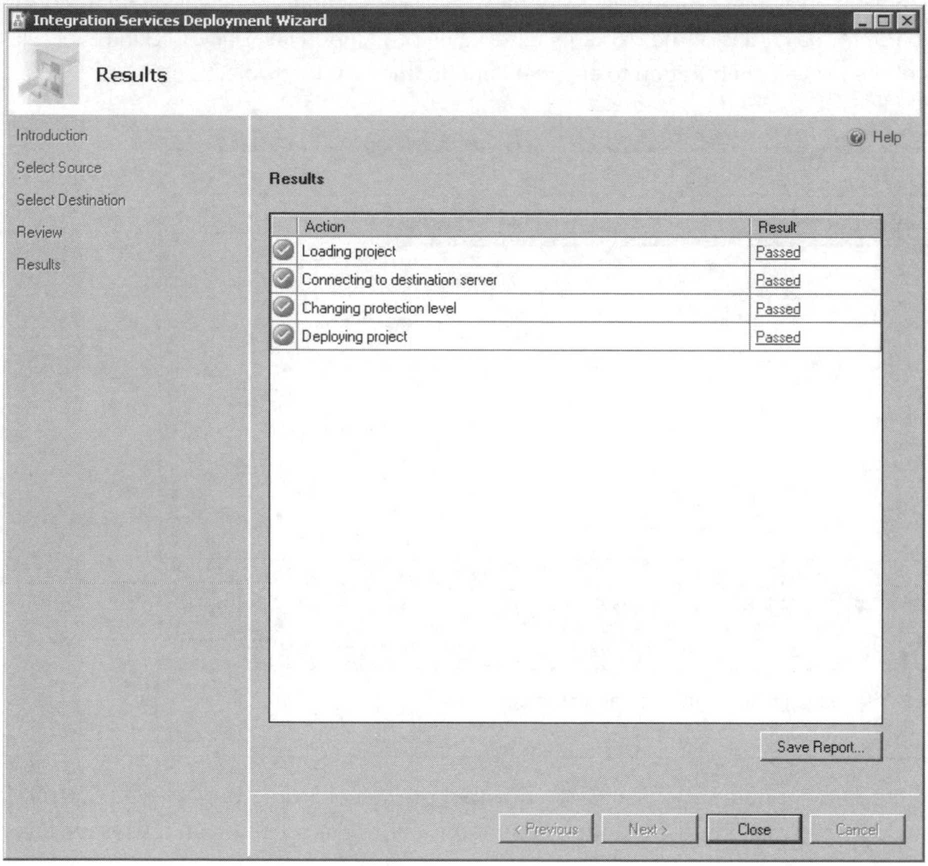

FIGURE 4-13 The Integration Services Deployment Wizard.

Project Conversion Wizard

The Project Conversion Wizard (Figure 4-14) is used to convert SSIS projects in the Package Deployment Model to the Project Deployment Model. One of the main uses of the wizard is to migrate projects created in previous versions of SSIS, so they can take advantage of the new features and functionality in SQL Server 2012.

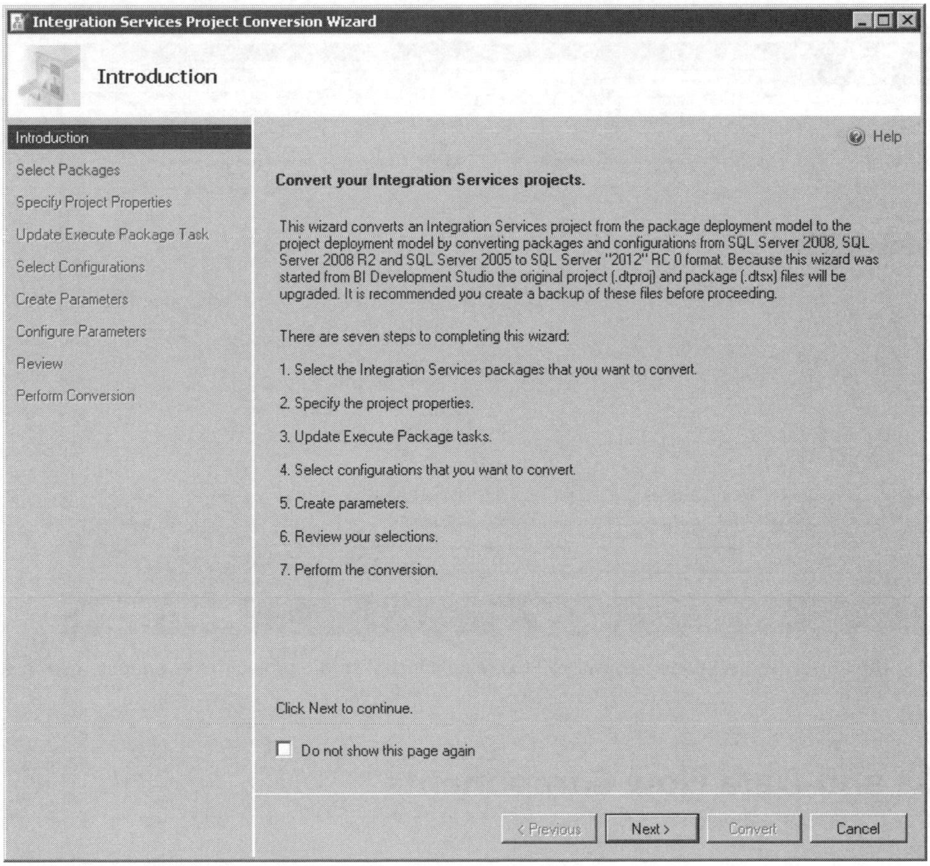

FIGURE 4-14 The Integration Services Project Conversion Wizard.

Import Project Wizard

The Import Project Wizard allows you to create a new SSIS Visual Studio project (.dtproj) from an existing project deployment file (.ispac), or a project in an SSIS Catalog. The wizard can be launched by selecting Integration Services Import Project Wizard when creating a new project in Visual Studio (Figure 4-15). This process is helpful for editing an existing project if you don't have the original source files available.

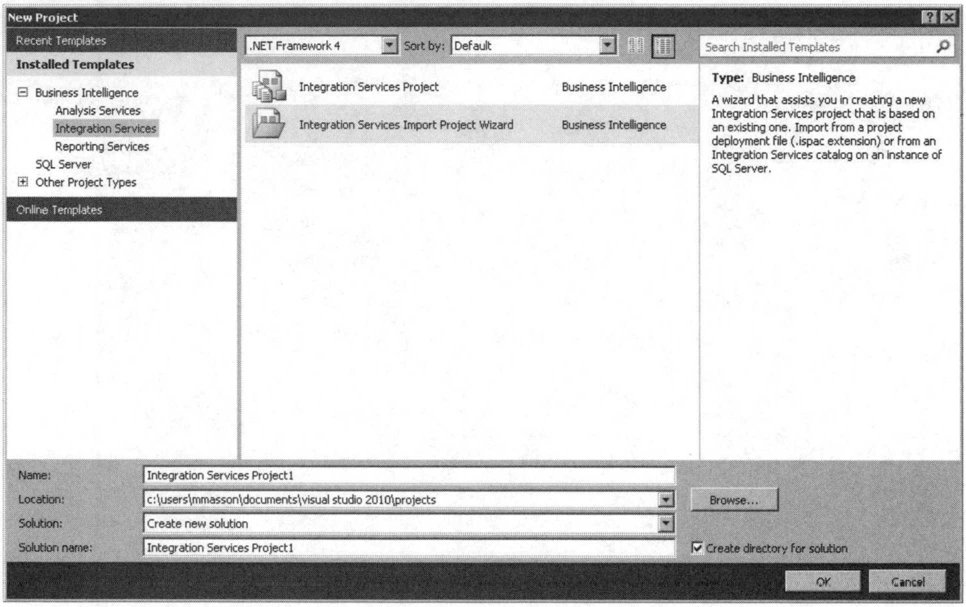

FIGURE 4-15 The Import Project Wizard allows you to create a Visual Studio project from a deployment file.

New Tasks and Data Flow Components

Change Data Capture

SQL Server 2012 introduces a new set of components that make it easier to perform Change Data Capture (CDC) with SQL Server and Oracle. The components include a CDC Control task, a CDC Source component, and a CDC Splitter transformation.

> **Note** More information about the CDC functionality in SQL Server 2012 can be found in Chapter 8, "Working with Change Data Capture."

CDC Control Task

The CDC Control task (Figure 4-16) is used to set and track the state of your CDC operations.

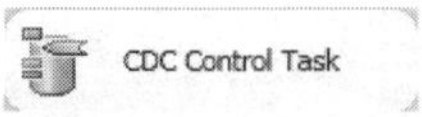

FIGURE 4-16 The CDC Control task.

You'll typically use this task to mark start and end dates for your CDC process, or to retrieve the next range of dates to process. The task will store all of the state information needed by the CDC Source component in a variable. You can also persist the state information in a database table to maintain state across package executions. Figure 4-17 shows the CDC Control Task Editor user interface.

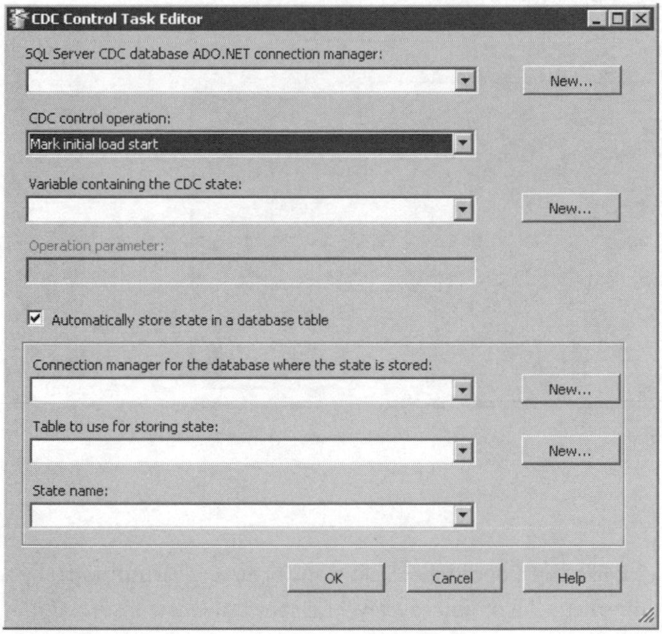

FIGURE 4-17 The editor for the CDC Control task.

CDC Source

The new CDC Source Data Flow component (Figure 4-18) is used to retrieve changed rows from a CDC-enabled table. The CDC Source works with both SQL Server and Oracle sources.

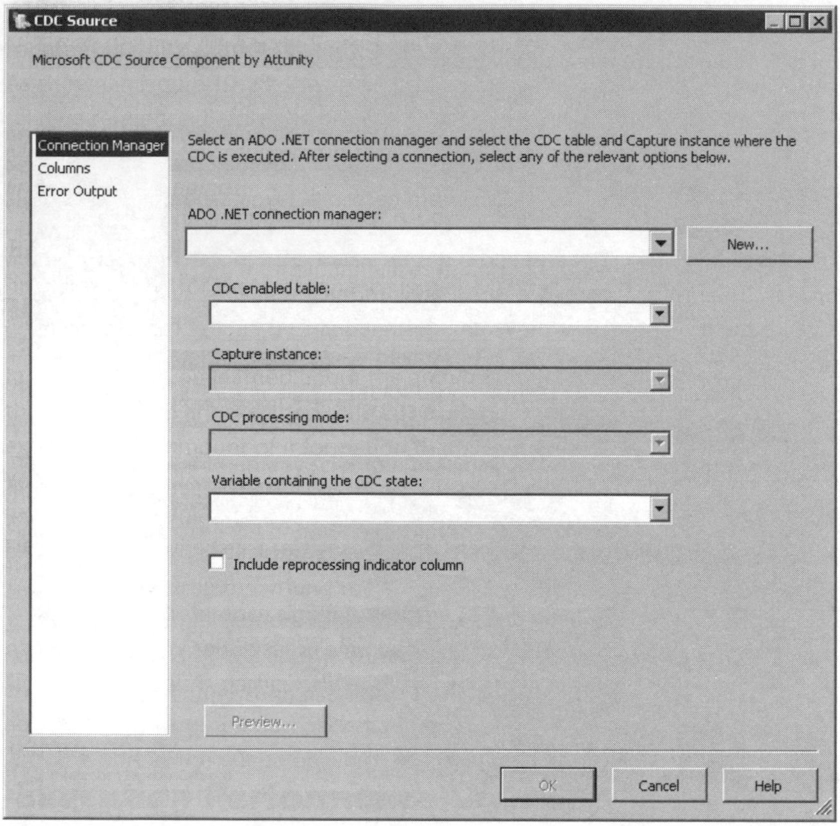

FIGURE 4-18 The CDC Source component.

CDC Splitter

The CDC Splitter transform works a lot like the Conditional Split transform. It will automatically split rows coming from a CDC Source component. Incoming rows will be sent down the Insert, Update, or Delete paths, based on the CDC operation type of the row (Figure 4-19).

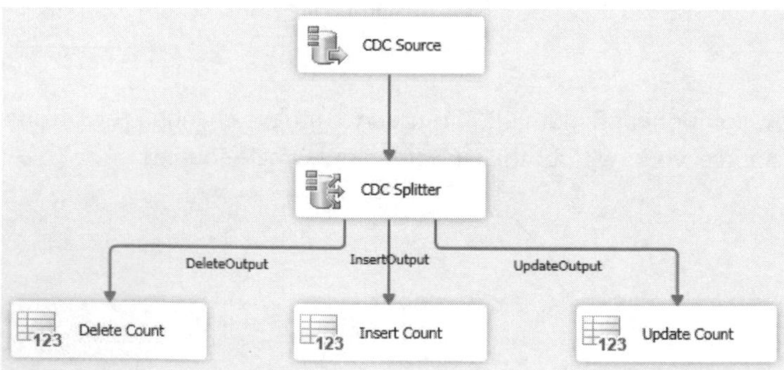

FIGURE 4-19 The CDC Splitter transform processes rows from the CDC Source component.

Expression Task

The Expression task (see Figure 4-20) can be used to explicitly set a variable value using an SSIS expression.

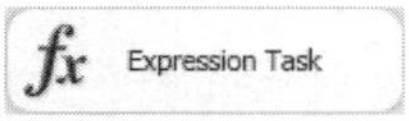

FIGURE 4-20 The Expression task.

The task gives you control over when a value is applied to a variable, and can be used as an alternative to setting the variable's *EvaluateAsExpression* property to *True*. Unlike expressions set directly on the variable (using *EvaluateAsExpression*), the Expression task evaluates only at runtime, not design time. This means that the variable value saved within the package file (.dtsx) is not modified by the Expression task. Figure 4-21 provides an example of an expression being set on the *User::FilePath* variable. Note the syntax is slightly different from regular SSIS property expressions in that it includes the name of the variable to which you are assigning the value.

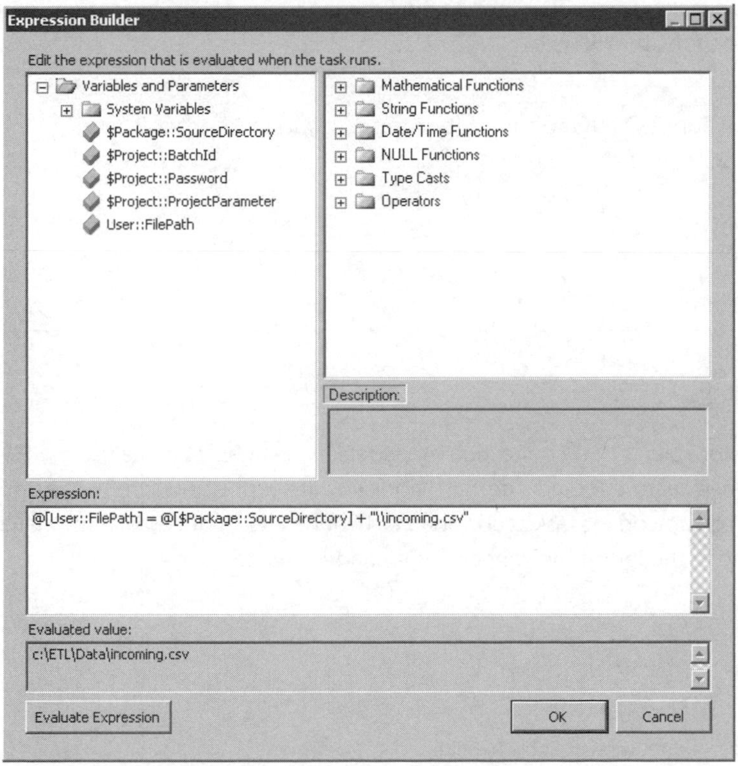

FIGURE 4-21 The Expression task uses the same Expression Builder control as SSIS property expressions.

DQS Cleansing Transform

The DQS Cleansing transform allows you to cleanse data within your data flow using Data Quality Services, a new product in SQL Server 2012. This transform allows you to add one or more columns to domains within a DQS Knowledge Base. At runtime, incoming data will be sent to the DQS server for cleansing.

> **Note** More information about Data Quality Services and the DQS Cleansing transform can be found in Chapter 9, "Data Cleansing Using SSIS."

ODBC Source and Destination

SQL Server 2008 supported Open Database Connectivity (ODBC) through ADO.NET, but compatibility and performance with certain ODBC providers was not optimal. SSIS has increased its support for ODBC in SQL Server 2012 by providing new Source and Destination components in the Data Flow. Both Source and Destination make use of ODBC connection managers, and the Destination component supports Bulk Insert for most providers.

> **Note** More information about ODBC connectivity can be found in Chapter 7, "Understanding SSIS Connectivity."

Control Flow

Expression Adorners

There is now a visual indicator when tasks, connection managers, and variables make use of SSIS property expressions. This new feature (called Adorners) adds a white expression icon to the upper-left corner of the object's regular icon for tasks and variables (Figure 4-22). For connection managers, the expression icon is added to the left of the connection manager's name.

FIGURE 4-22 Tasks with property expressions are now highlighted in the designer.

Connection Managers

The Connection Managers view in the designer window (Figure 4-23) has had a few visual updates in SQL Server 2012. Icons have been updated to show the different connection manager types, and an expression icon is shown for connection managers that use expression properties. Shared connection managers, which are declared at the project level, appear with a (project) prefix before their name.

FIGURE 4-23 The new Connection Managers view in the SSIS designer window.

Connection managers can be individually taken offline. This is much like the Work Offline mode, which can be set at the SSIS project level. When a connection manager is offline, all calls to it are essentially short-circuited and return right away. This is useful when a server is offline, as it prevents long waits while connections timeout. A connection manager's connectivity status is validated when a package is opened. If the connection cannot be established, the connection manager is automatically placed in Offline mode. You can put a connection manager online by right-clicking it and selecting Test Connectivity from the shortcut menu. To force a connection manager into an offline state, right-click it and select Work Offline.

Execute SQL Task

The Execute SQL task has a new property called *TypeConversionMode*. This property controls whether the Execute SQL task attempts to perform data type conversion at runtime. For example, imagine the query for the Execute SQL task returns a value of "101" as a VARCHAR(10) data type—a string—and you are assigning it to a package variable with an Int32 data type—a number. In SQL Server 2012, the Execute Package task attempts to convert the value to the package variable type when the *TypeConversionMode* is set to *Allowed*. If the *TypeConversionMode* is set to *None*, strict data type matching is enforced, and you get an error at runtime, the same behavior you'd get in previous versions of SSIS. Packages upgraded from earlier versions of SSIS will have a default *TypeConversionMode* of *None* to preserve compatibility. New Execute SQL tasks will have a default value of *Allowed*.

Note The Execute SQL task uses the .NET Framework to perform the data type conversion. If the conversion is invalid, or there is potential data loss, you will get an error at runtime. For more information about the data type conversion rules, see the *Convert.ChangeType* method entry in Books Online: *http://msdn.microsoft.com/en-us/library/ttf5d382.aspx.*

Connection Assistants

The Source Assistant and Destination Assistant are new Data Flow toolbox items in SQL Server 2012. Dragging them onto the designer will open a wizard that guides you through the process of adding a new source or destination component to your data flow. The first page of the wizard (Figure 4-24) asks you what type of data source you'd like to be connecting to: SQL Server, Excel, or Flat File. After you select the data source type, the wizard automatically determines the best connection manager and source or destination component for you. For example, when you select SQL Server, the wizard will pick the OLE DB provider. You are given the option to create a new connection manager or reuse an existing one. When the wizard completes, it adds a new Source or Destination component to your Data Flow that you can then connect to other transforms.

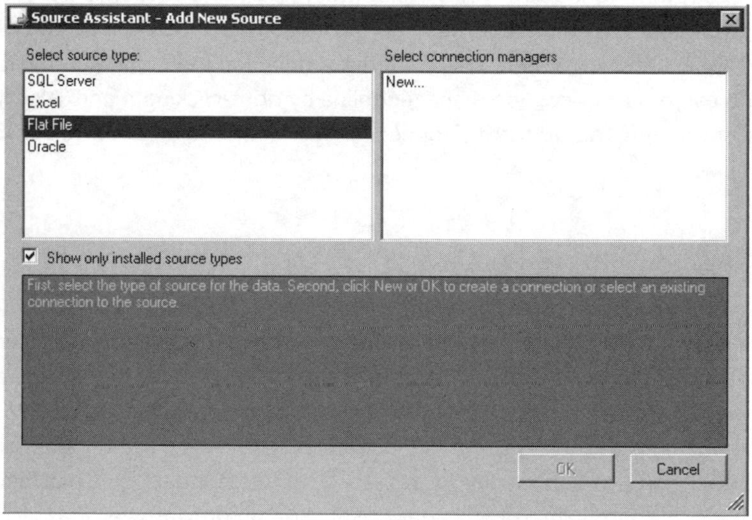

FIGURE 4-24 The first page of the Data Flow Source Assistant Wizard.

> **Note** The Connection Assistant Wizard will display only the 32-bit providers installed on your system. It will not find or recognize any 64-bit providers you have installed.

The Connection Assistant user interface includes a check box that allows the wizard to automatically filter out data sources for which it can't find providers on your system. If you clear this check box, all data sources will be displayed. If you select a data source with no provider installed, a message will be displayed with a hint as to where you can download the preferred provider.

> **Note** The connection assistants are configured through the Connectivity.xml file located under the *<Visual Studio Root>\Common7\IDE\PrivateAssemblies* folder. You can modify this file to add new connectivity options, as well as change the default provider for each data source.

Improved Column Mapping

A number of usability improvements have been made to the column mapping functionality in the SSIS Data Flow. Data Flow components are now much smarter about the way they map incoming columns. Most will automatically match columns based on name and data type instead of relying on Lineage IDs like they did in previous releases. This means that you can connect a new source component to an existing set of transformations, and SSIS will automatically resolve the column mappings, assuming that all of the expected columns exist. If SSIS is unable to resolve all of the expected column mappings, an error icon is displayed on the path with the missing columns (Figure 4-25).

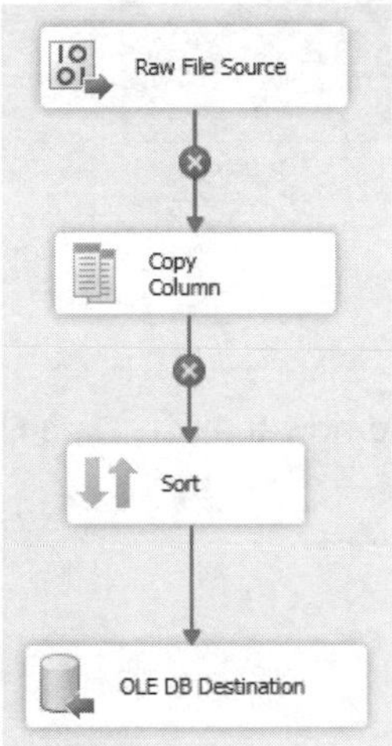

FIGURE 4-25 Error icons are displayed on the Data Flow paths when there are missing columns.

Double-clicking the error icons (or right-clicking the path and selecting Resolve References from the shortcut menu) opens the new Resolve References dialog box (Figure 4-26). This dialog box lets you map output columns to input columns, as well as delete columns that are no longer required. The dialog box has a lot of useful functionality, such as filtering capabilities, automatic mapping based on name and data type, and importing and exporting the column mappings to and from Excel. Resolving column references with this dialog box will fix all column mappings for an entire execution tree.

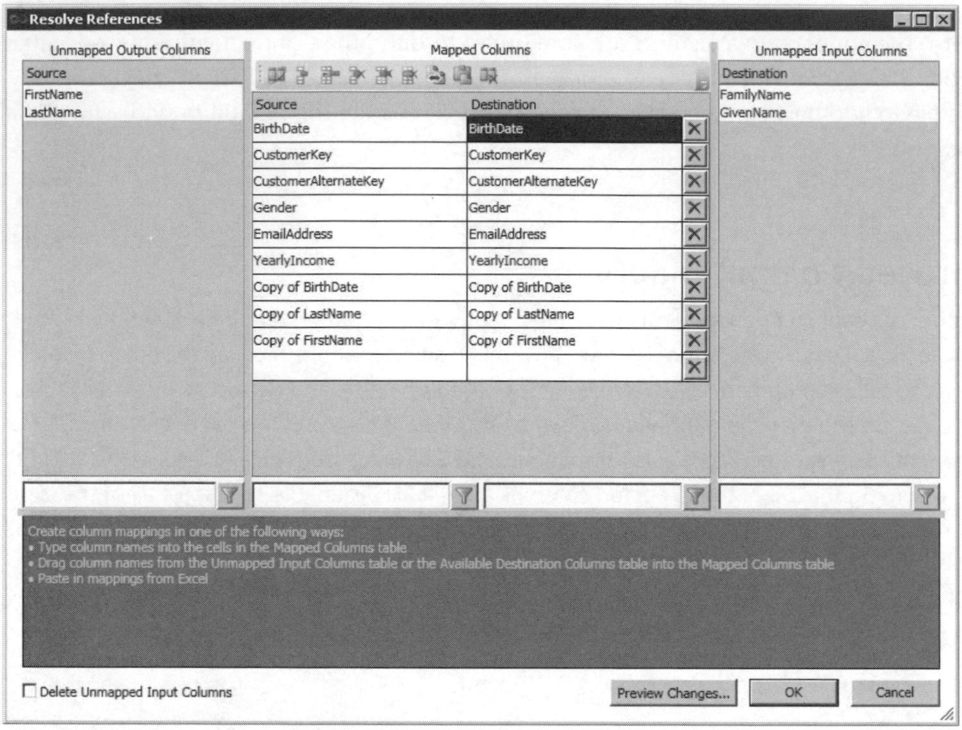

FIGURE 4-26 The Resolve References dialog box.

> **Note** For more information about Lineage IDs, execution trees, and how the SSIS Data Flow does its column mapping, see Chapter 15, "SSIS Engine Deep-Dive."

Editing Components in an Error State

Previous versions of SSIS did not allow you to open up the editor for a Data Flow component if it was in an error state. You would need to resolve any column mapping errors, or you would be limited to using only the Advanced Editor. Data Flow components remember their metadata in SQL Server 2012, which allows you to edit them even if they are in an error state.

Grouping

SQL Server 2012 allows you to group together one or more objects in the Data Flow. Creating a group in the Data Flow is similar to adding a Sequence container in the Control Flow, except it exists only within the designer. Groups do not affect the way the Data Flow actually runs. Groups can be expanded and collapsed, and are a useful way to hide portions of very complicated Data Flows. Figure 4-27 shows a Data Flow with a group that isolates some of the processing logic. This group could be collapsed to hide the transforms inside.

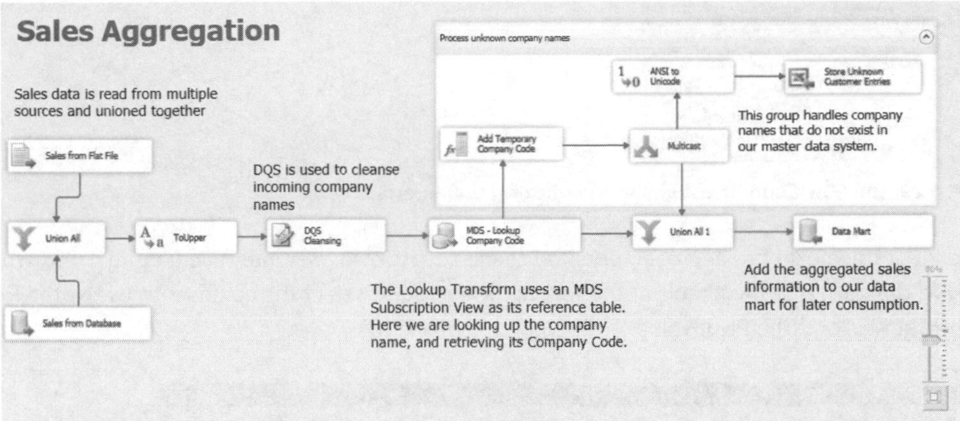

FIGURE 4-27 Complicated Data Flow with a group.

Simplified Data Viewers

Data viewers have been simplified in SQL Server 2012. There is only one type of viewer now, the Grid View. To add a data viewer, right-click the path on which you want to see the data and select Enable Data Viewer. Figure 4-28 shows the icon that indicates an active data viewer. You can configure which columns are displayed by double-clicking the path, and selecting the Data Viewer tab.

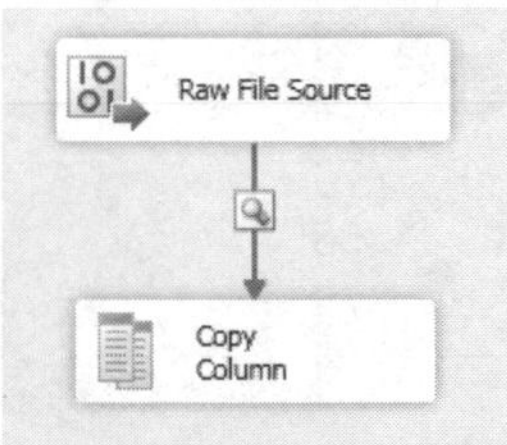

FIGURE 4-28 Data viewers are indicated with an icon on the Data Flow path.

> **Note** All columns in the path are displayed by default when a data viewer is first added. If you change the incoming columns after a viewer has been created, you will need to manually add the new columns to the data viewer for them to be displayed.

Row Count and Pivot Transform User Interfaces

A simple user interface has been added for the Row Count transform (Figure 4-29). The interface has a simple drop-down control and allows you to select any Int32 or Int64 package variables.

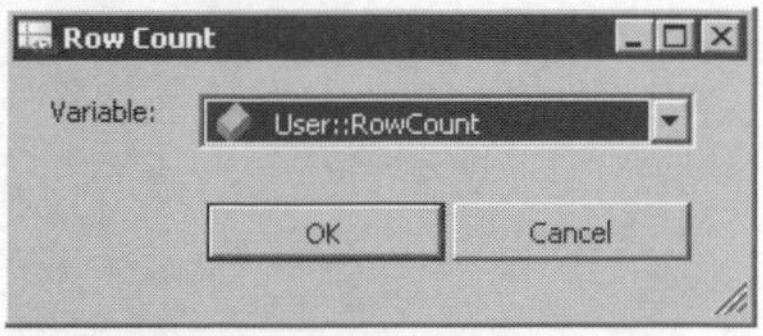

FIGURE 4-29 The Row Count transform now has its own user interface.

The Pivot transform has also been updated to include its own user interface (Figure 4-30), which displays a diagram of a pivot table at the top, allowing you to select the columns to use as the Pivot Key, the Set Key, and the Pivot Value.

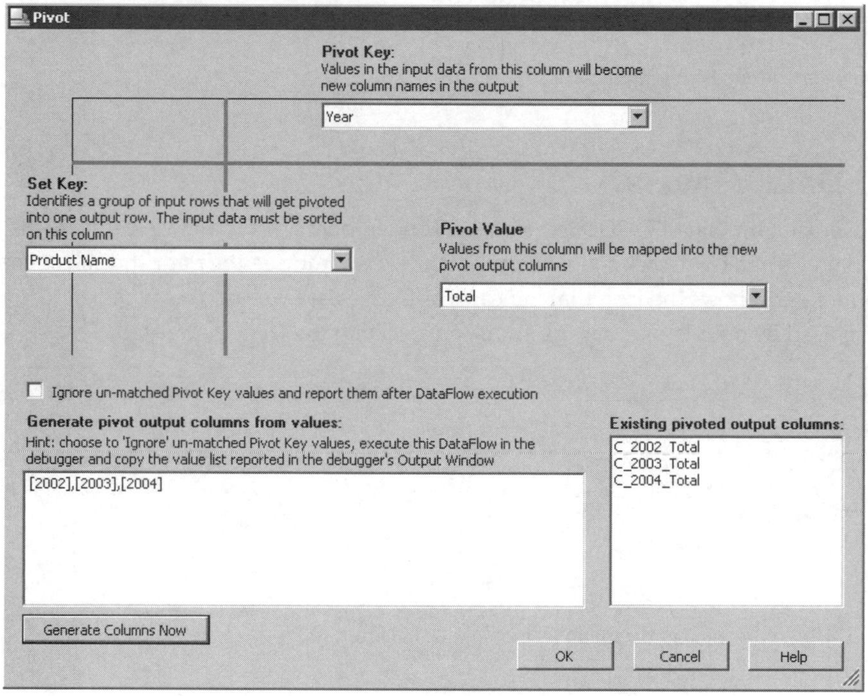

FIGURE 4-30 The Pivot transform now has its own user interface.

Flat File Source Changes

A couple of improvements were made to the Flat File Source parser: It can now support ragged-right delimited files and embedded qualifiers.

Ragged-Right Delimited Files

Ragged-right delimited files can have rows with a varying number of columns. The columns will always appear in the same order, but certain rows will be missing one or more of their trailing columns. These missing columns are meant to be interpreted as *NULL* values. Listing 4-1 shows an example of this file format. Notice that each row has a *Key* and *AlternateKey* value, but the *SubCategoryKey* and *WeightMeasureCode* fields are optional. The second data row is missing the final field (*WeightMeasure Code*), and the third data row is missing both the final two fields (*SubCategoryKey* and *WeightMeasure Code*).

LISTING 4-1 The ragged-right delimited file format

```
Key,AlternateKey,SubCategoryKey,WeightMeasureCode
211,FT-R92R-F8,14,LB
212,HL-U509-R,31
184,RM-R600
426,FR-M63B-40,12,LB
```

The Flat File Source parser in previous versions of SSIS would not look for row delimiters until it had seen the expected number of columns. Table 4-1 shows how the sample data set would be interpreted in SQL Server 2005 and SQL Server 2008. Notice that the entry for the third data row (key 184) is parsed as a single column.

TABLE 4-1 Results from the ragged-right delimited file in previous versions of SSIS.

Key	AlternateKey	SubCategoryKey	WeightMeasureCode
211	FT-R92R-F8	14	LB
212	HL-U509-R	31	184,RM-R600
426	FR-M63B-40	12	LB

The SSIS Flat File Source now fully supports the ragged-right delimited file format. Table 4-2 shows what the data set looks like when parsed in SQL Server 2012.

TABLE 4-2 Results from the ragged-right delimited file when parsed correctly.

Key	AlternateKey	SubCategoryKey	WeightMeasureCode
211	FT-R92R-F8	14	LB
212	HL-U509-R	31	
184	RM-R600		
426	FR-M63B-40	12	LB

Note The new parsing behavior to support ragged-right delimited files is enabled by default, but can be disabled by setting the *AlwaysCheckForRowDelimiters* property on the Flat File Connection Manager to False. If you do not need this functionality, disabling it might give you a slight performance bonus when working with large flat files.

Embedded Qualifiers

If a field value in a flat file contains the column delimiter (for example, a comma or tab), you can use a qualifier mark when the field value starts and ends. This is typically an apostrophe (') or double quote (") character. To use the qualifying character as a literal within the string, you would typically "escape" it by doubling the character. Listing 4-2 shows a sample data set that uses double quote characters as a text qualifier. The first data row contains a double quote literal character, which is escaped using a second double quote character.

LISTING 4-2 A data set that uses embedded qualifiers

```
Key,AlternateKey,EnglishDescription
396,HS-3479,"High-quality 1"" thread-less headset, with a grease port"
252,FR-R92R-56,"Our lightest and best quality aluminum frame"
261,FR-R38B-62,"The LL Frame provides a safe, comfortable ride"
```

Although text qualifiers were supported, the Flat File Source did not support embedded qualifiers in previous versions of SQL Server. In fact, it was unable to parse data sets like the one in Listing 4-2, and would return an error while parsing the first data row due to the lack of a delimiter immediately after the double quote qualifier. Table 4-3 shows how the Flat File Source correctly interprets embedded qualifiers in SQL Server 2012.

TABLE 4-3 Results from the data containing embedded qualifiers when parsed in SQL Server 2012.

Key	AlternateKey	WeightMeasureCode
396	HS-3479	High-quality 1" thread-less headset, with a grease port
252	FR-R92R-56	Our lightest and best quality aluminum frame
261	FR-R38B-62	The LL Frame provides a safe, comfortable ride

Scripting

Visual Studio Tools for Applications

SSIS uses Visual Studio Tools for Applications to provide support for its .NET scripting functionality. Visual Studio Tools for Applications provides an integrated development environment (IDE), allowing users to embed VB.NET and C# code within their SSIS packages. SQL Server 2012 contains a new version of Visual Studio Tools for Applications (3.0), which is based on the Visual Studio 2010 shell, and fully supports .NET 4.

In SQL Server 2008, Visual Studio Tools for Applications was used both at design time (when the script is created) and at runtime (when the package is run). A number of changes were made in SQL Server 2012 that allow SSIS to fully embed the script and execute the .NET assembly inline without the need to spin up the Visual Studio Tools for Applications runtime. This improvement leads to some minor performance benefits, and also allows the product to support a much requested feature: Script component debugging.

Script Component Debugging

The Script task has always supported debugging, but users were limited to using message boxes and log messages to debug their Script components. Script component debugging is now supported in SQL Server 2012, allowing you to set breakpoints and walk through your code within the Visual Studio Tools for Applications designer. Figure 4-31 shows the debugging of a Script component source.

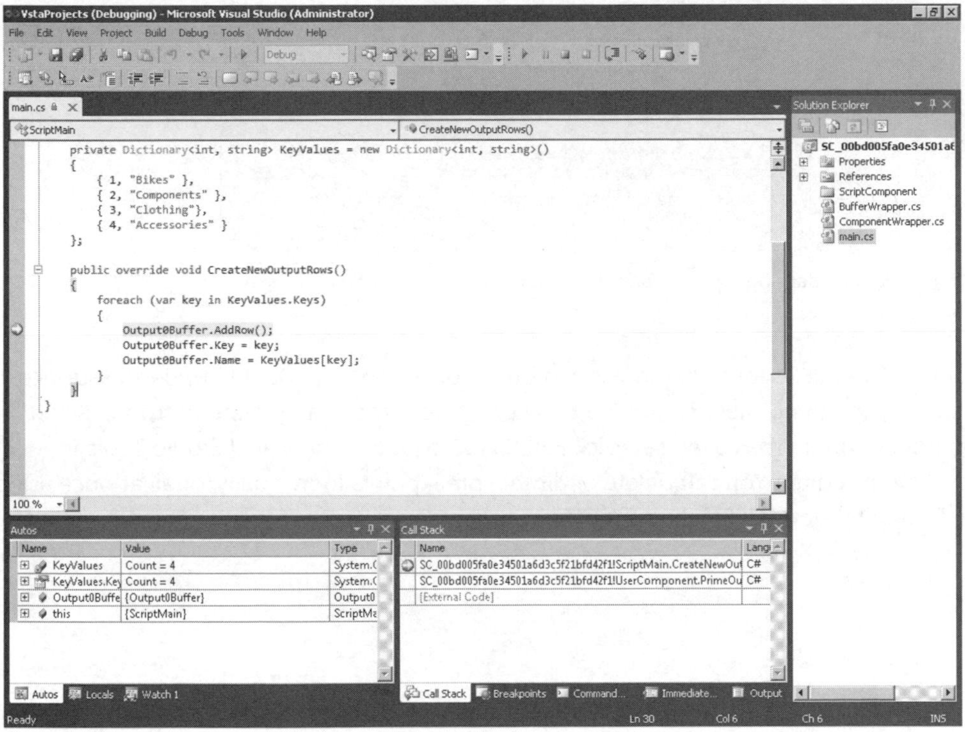

FIGURE 4-31 Debugging a Script component.

To enable debugging, your project must be set to run in 32-bit mode within the Visual Studio designer. This is done by opening the properties for your SSIS project and setting the *Run64BitRuntime* property on the Configuration Properties | Debugging tab to False (Figure 4-32). Because Visual Studio is a 32-bit application, debugging doesn't work when the package runs in a 64-bit mode. This same limitation exists for debugging the Script task as well.

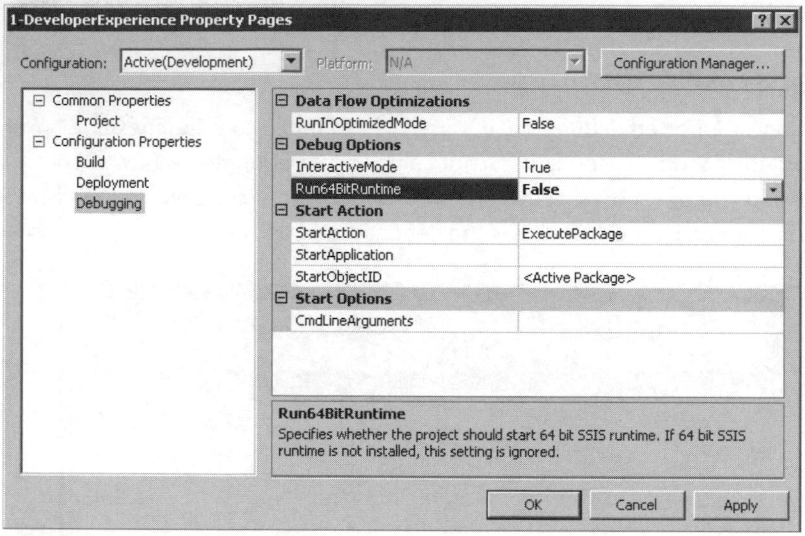

FIGURE 4-32 Enable debugging by setting the project's *Run64BitRuntime* to *False*.

> **Note** Unlike the Script task, there is no visual indicator on the Data Flow design surface when a Script component contains a breakpoint. To remove a breakpoint from a Script component after it has been set, click Edit Script to launch the Visual Studio Tools for Applications editor. You can delete or disable breakpoints individually, or all at once using the Debug | Delete All Breakpoints menu option.

.NET 4 Framework Support

New Script tasks and Script components will target .NET Framework 4 by default. The target framework can be changed in the script project's properties dialog box from within the Visual Studio Tools for Applications designer (Figure 4-33).

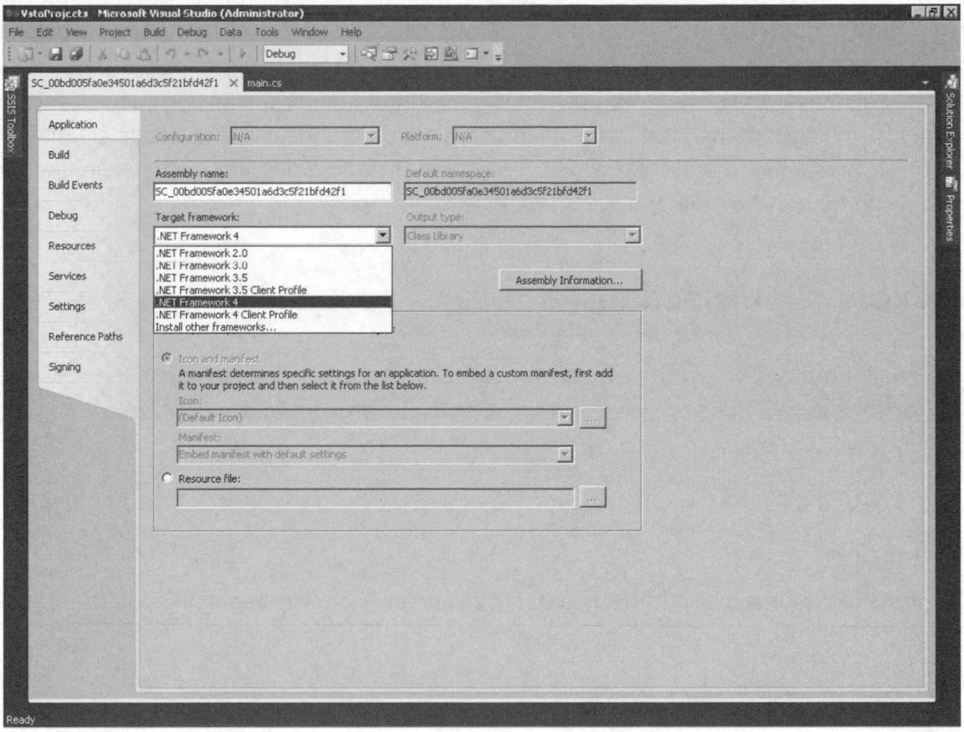

FIGURE 4-33 Enable debugging by setting the project's *Run64BitRuntime* to *False*.

Removal of the Character Limit

SQL Server 2012 has removed the 4,000-character limit in SSIS expressions that existed in previous versions of the product. This limit affected users in two ways; the physical length of the expression string had to be fewer than 4,000 characters, and strings created by the expression would be truncated if they went over the limit. It was possible to set a string greater than 4,000 characters in length to a variable using a Script task, but this workaround is no longer needed. The character limit is gone from all of the places that use the SSIS expression engine, including property expressions, the Derived Column transform, and the Conditional Split transform.

New Expression Functions

> **Note** For examples on how to use the new SSIS expression functions, please see the Functions entry in Books Online: *http://msdn.microsoft.com/en-us/library/ms141671(v=SQL.110).aspx.*

LEFT Function

The *LEFT* function returns the specified number of characters from the beginning of a string.

```
LEFT ( <string>, <number> )
```

This is similar to the *RIGHT* function, which returns characters from the end of the string. In previous versions of SSIS, you'd accomplish this with the *SUBSTRING* function, starting at the first character.

REPLACENULL Function

The *REPLACENULL* function returns the value of the second expression argument if the first expression argument evaluates to *NULL*.

```
REPLACENULL ( <expression_1>, <expression_2> )
```

If the first expression argument is not *NULL*, then it is returned instead. This function is useful for substituting a *NULL* value with a default value in a Derived Column transform. *REPLACENULL* provides an alternate, easier to use syntax than performing a *NULL* check with the Conditional (? :) operator.

> **Note** The *REPLACENULL* function works with most data types (everything except the LOB types—DT_IMAGE, DT_TEXT, and DT_NTEXT), but both expressions should evaluate to the same data type. If there is a data type mismatch between the arguments, the function will attempt to cast the value of the second expression to the data type of the first. If the cast cannot be done, the expression will return an error.

TOKEN Function

The *TOKEN* function splits the given string (first argument) into a set of tokens using the delimiters (second argument), and returns the specified occurrence (third argument).

```
TOKEN ( <string>, <delimiters>, <occurrence> )
```

Note that the occurrence index starts at 1, and not 0. To get the first token occurrence in the string, you'd use a value of 1. If the specified occurrence is higher than the number of actual tokens in the string, the function returns an empty string. You can use the *TOKENCOUNT* function to determine how many tokens exist in the string. The delimiter argument is a string containing one or more characters. Each character in the string is treated as a separate delimiter.

> **Note** The underlying implementation of the TOKEN and TOKENCOUNT functions is based on the strtok C++ function. For more information on how the function determines how to split the string into tokens, see the entry in Books Online: *http://msdn.microsoft.com/en-us/library/2c8d19sb.aspx*.

TOKENCOUNT Function

The *TOKENCOUNT* function splits a string the same way that the *TOKEN* function does.

```
TOKENCOUNT ( <string>, <delimiters> )
```

Instead of returning individual tokens from the string, it returns the total number of tokens within that string. It can be used to easily determine the value to use to retrieve the last token in a string. For example, when splitting a file path, *TOKENCOUNT* can be used to determine the occurrence value to use to return the file name.

Summary

This chapter provided an overview of the new features and productivity enhancements in the Integration Services designer for SQL Server Data Tools. It explored the new tasks and Data Flow components, and some of the long-awaited features like Undo and Script component debugging. Many of the topics introduced here are further explorer in later chapters of the book.

CHAPTER 5

Team Development

In This Chapter

Improvements in SQL Server 2012

This section describes some important changes that were made to SQL Server Integration Services in SQL Server 2012 to improve the overall team development experience for SSIS users.

Package Format Changes

SQL Server Integration Services packages are XML files with a .dtsx file extension. In previous versions of the product, this XML was verbose with very little formatting, which made it difficult to read without loading it in the SSIS designer. Significant changes were made to the SSIS package format in SQL Server 2012 to make the package XML easier to read and easier to "diff" (compare two versions of the file and tell exactly what has changed). These changes were targeted to improve the user experience when using SSIS with source control systems, a core component of most best practices associated with the software development lifecycle. The new package format makes it easier to diff and merge two versions of a package, so it is easier for multiple developers to work on the same packages.

The package format in SQL Server 2012 includes the following improvements:

- **Formatted output** The package XML is now formatted so that each line contains a single element or attribute (also known as pretty printing).
- **Less verbose** The XML is more concise. Task properties are now represented as simple attributes, instead of spanning multiple elements.
- **Readable annotations** Package annotations are stored in clear text instead of encoded blocks, making it easier for utilities to extract them for documentation.

- **Reference IDs** The unique values used to identify objects in the Data Flow (Lineage IDs) and other parts of the package (such as connection managers) are no longer persisted to the package file. This makes it possible to merge Data Flow changes between multiple versions of a package.
- **Alphabetical sorting** Objects are sorted alphabetically. This ensures that they stay in a (relatively) static location, and makes them easier to diff.
- **Default property values are not persisted** Most tasks and Data Flow components will only persist property values that have been changed from their default.
- **Collections** Objects that can appear more than once (variables, connection managers, event handlers, and so on) are now contained within a parent element, making the XML easier to parse with automated utilities.
- **Layout information** The layout information used by the SSIS designer used to appear as encoded blocks of XML in multiple places in the file. All layout information is now contained within a single CDATA tag at the end of the file, making it easier to distinguish layout changes (which can usually be ignored or overwritten) and actual extract-transform-load (ETL) logic changes in the package.

> **Note** After a package has been upgraded to SQL Server 2012 format, it cannot be downgraded or used with previous versions of SSIS. Details about the file format used for SSIS packages in SQL Server 2008 R2 is available in Books Online at *http://msdn.microsoft.com/en-us/library/gg587140.aspx*.

Visual Studio Configurations

As described in Chapter 4, "New SSIS Designer Features," SSIS now supports the use of Visual Studio configurations as a way of externalizing parameter values. This feature is very helpful for team development, as it allows developers to add configurations for their environments. For example, Elton and Elliot are ETL developers working on the same project. Most of their packages use a *SourceDirectory* parameter to locate the flat files used by their data flows. Elton uses the *D:\Test\Data* directory on his development machine, and Elliot has his files in *C:\ETL*. By creating separate Visual Studio configurations and adding the *SourceDirectory* parameter to them, the two developers can easily switch to the configuration that is appropriate for their environment without modifying individual values within the packages.

Visual Studio configurations can also be used to control the default parameter values that will be put into the project deployment file (.ispac). When the project is compiled, the values from the active configuration will be used as the default parameter values. This allows you to create separate project deployment files targeted for specific environments (for example, test, integration, or production).

> **Note** Changing the active configuration will change the default parameter values, as well as any properties using these parameters in an expression. This will change the underlying values in the XML of the package file (.dtsx). These changes will cause the package to be checked out if it is currently under source control.

Using Source Control Management with SSIS

Using a source control system for version management is a best practice of the application development lifecycle. SSIS package files should be managed in the same way as source code files from other Visual Studio project types (like C# or VB.NET).

This section describes how to use SSIS with a source control and build management system using Visual Studio. We use Visual Studio Team Foundation Server 2010 as our example, but many of the same principles will apply when using an alternative source control system. More information about Visual Studio Team Foundation Server can be found at *http://www.microsoft.com/visualstudio/en-us/products/2010-editions/team-foundation-server/overview.*

> **Note** The default installation of the SSIS designer (SQL Server Data Tools) provides you with a Visual Studio 2012 shell, but does not include a source control plug-in. To integrate with your source control system, you will need to install an add-in for Visual Studio. To enable integration with Team Foundation Server, you should install Microsoft Visual Studio Team Explorer 2010. It is available as a free download from Microsoft.com at *http://www.microsoft.com/download/en/details.aspx?displaylang=en&id=329.*

Connecting to Team Foundation Server

Before you can start using SSIS with Team Foundation Server, you will need to connect to the server and create a new Team Foundation Server project (or workspace). You will need to perform these steps whenever you are connecting to a new Team Foundation Server server.

1. Open SQL Server Data Tools.
2. From the top menu, select View | Team Explorer.
3. In the Team Explorer view, click Add Server.

   Enter the Team Foundation Server server information in the Add Team Foundation Server dialog box (Figure 5-1), and click OK.

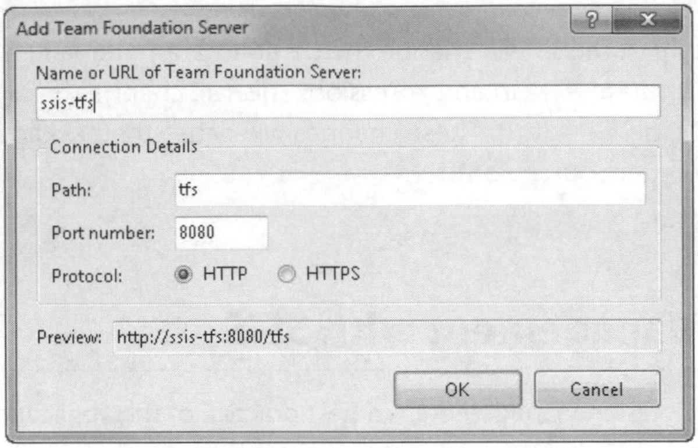

FIGURE 5-1 Add Team Foundation Server dialog box.

4. Select the new server in the Connect To Team Project dialog box, and select the appropriate Team Project Collection (see Figure 5-2).

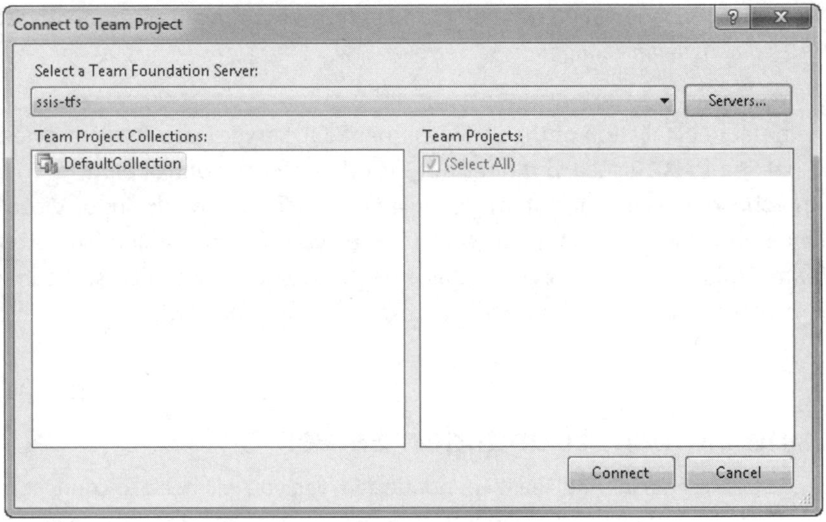

FIGURE 5-2 Connect To Team Project dialog box.

5. Click Connect.

Once connected, the Team Explorer view will show all Team Foundation Server projects on the server. If no projects are available, you can create a new project with the following steps.

1. In the Team Explorer view, right-click the Team Foundation Server Server Collection name and click New Team Project (Figure 5-3).

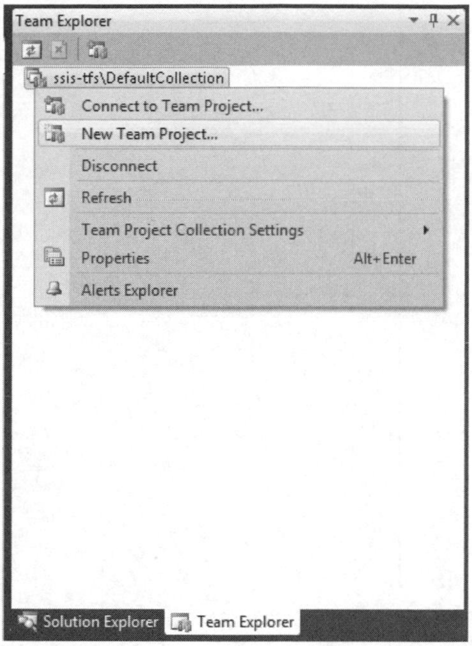

FIGURE 5-3 Creating a new team project in Team Foundation Server in the Team Explorer view.

2. Enter a name and description for your project (for example, **Data Warehouse Project**), and click Next.

3. Select a Process Template for your project. The process template controls work item types, reports, queries, and process guidance for your project. The template you select will depend on your team or organization's process and practices relating to application development. You might choose to create a custom template, or download one from the Team Foundation Server community sites. For this example, we will use one of the default templates that ship with Team Foundation Server 2010: MSF for Agile Software Development v5.0. Once you have made your selection, click Next.

4. Next you're provided with the option to create a new source control folder or a branch from an existing folder. If this is your first Team Foundation Server project, select Create an Empty Source Control Folder.

5. Click Finish to create the project.

6. After the project is created, you will see it listed in the Team Explorer view (Figure 5-4). The items you find under the project node will depend on the process template that was selected in Step 3, but typically include Work Items, Builds, and Source Control.

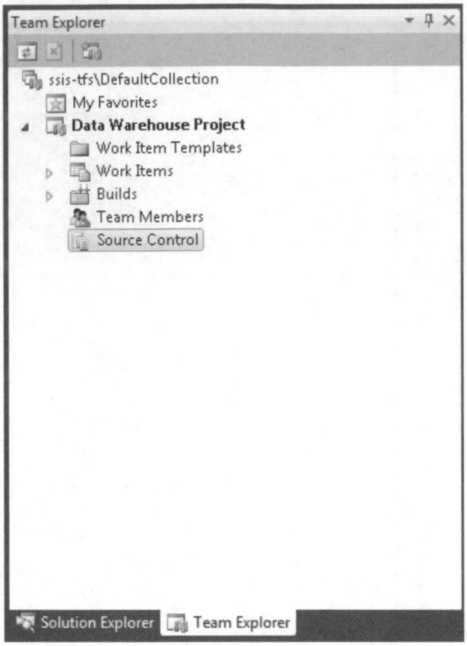

FIGURE 5-4 Projects in the Team Explorer view.

Adding an SSIS Project to Team Foundation Server

You can see the SSIS projects (as well as other source code) that are part of your selected Team Foundation Server project by double-clicking the Source Control node in the Team Explorer view. This will open the Source Control Explorer view (Figure 5-5).

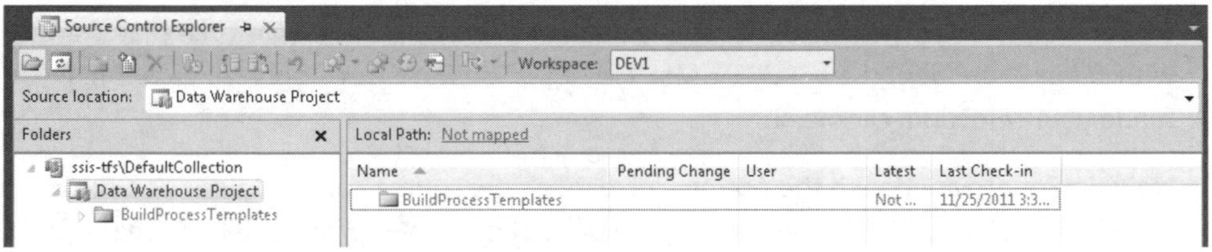

FIGURE 5-5 The Source Code Explorer window shows you the source code in your Team Foundation Server project.

You can use the following steps to add a new SSIS project to Team Foundation Server.

1. Create or open an existing SSIS project.
2. Right-click the project in the Solution Explorer view, and select Add Solution to Source Control (Figure 5-6).

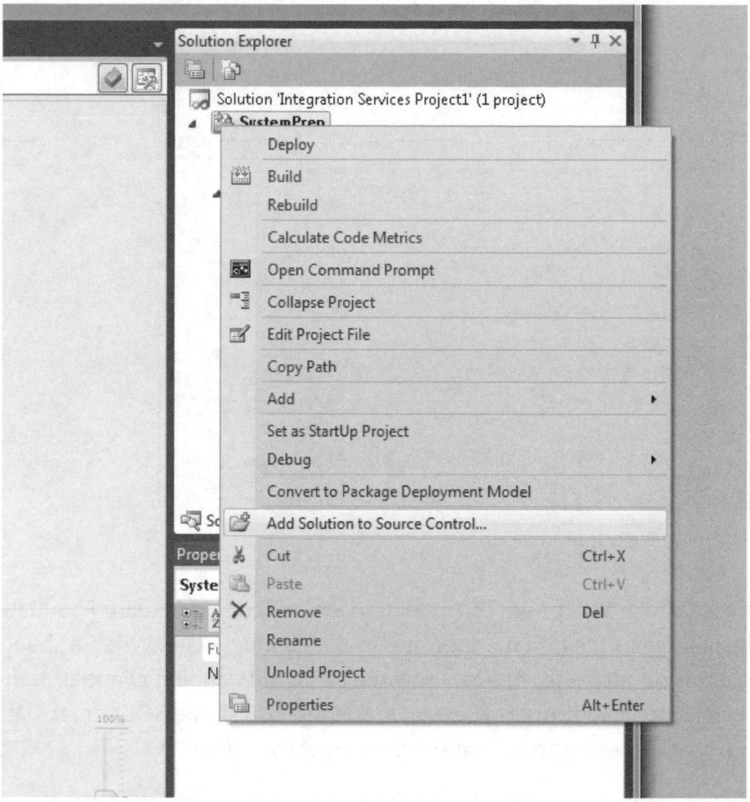

FIGURE 5-6 Adding a solution to source control.

3. In this step you add a new top-level folder to the Team Foundation Server project. You use this folder to store the current SSIS project, and any additional projects you add in the future. Click Make New Folder to create a new top-level folder, and enter a name (for this example use **SSIS**). Enter a folder name for the solution (for this example use the name **SystemPrep**). Figure 5-7 shows how the completed dialog box looks.

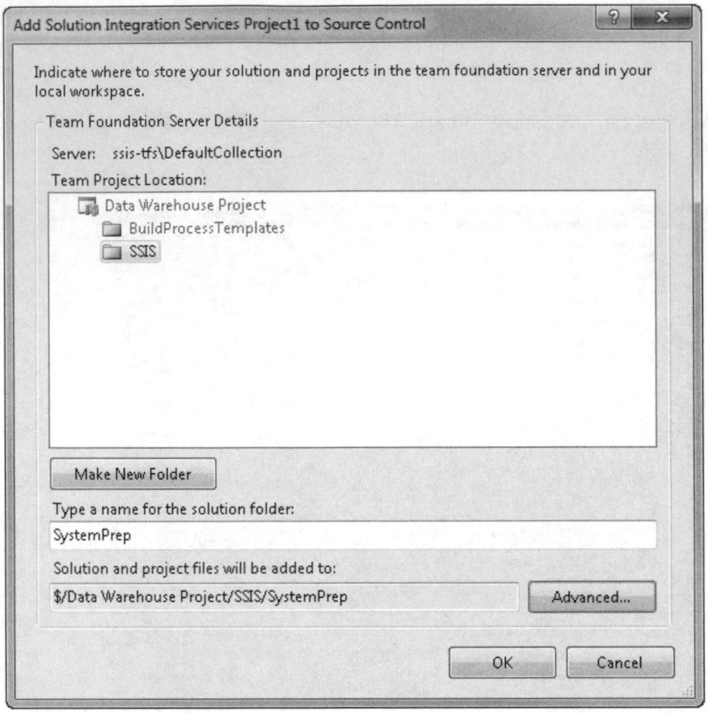

FIGURE 5-7 Naming the solution folder.

4. After you click OK, the SSIS project and solution are added to the Team Foundation Server source control. When a file is first added, it is in the Pending state. When a change is pending, it is still local to your machine. You can view the list of outstanding changes in the Pending Changes view (accessible from the View menu). Figure 5-8 shows SQL Server Data Tools with the Pending Changes view showing at the bottom of the screen.

5. To commit your changes, click Check In in the Pending Changes view. Once you check in, other users will be able to sync and view your changes.

Table 5-1 shows a list of file extensions of the files that make up an SSIS project. All of the files contain XML documents.

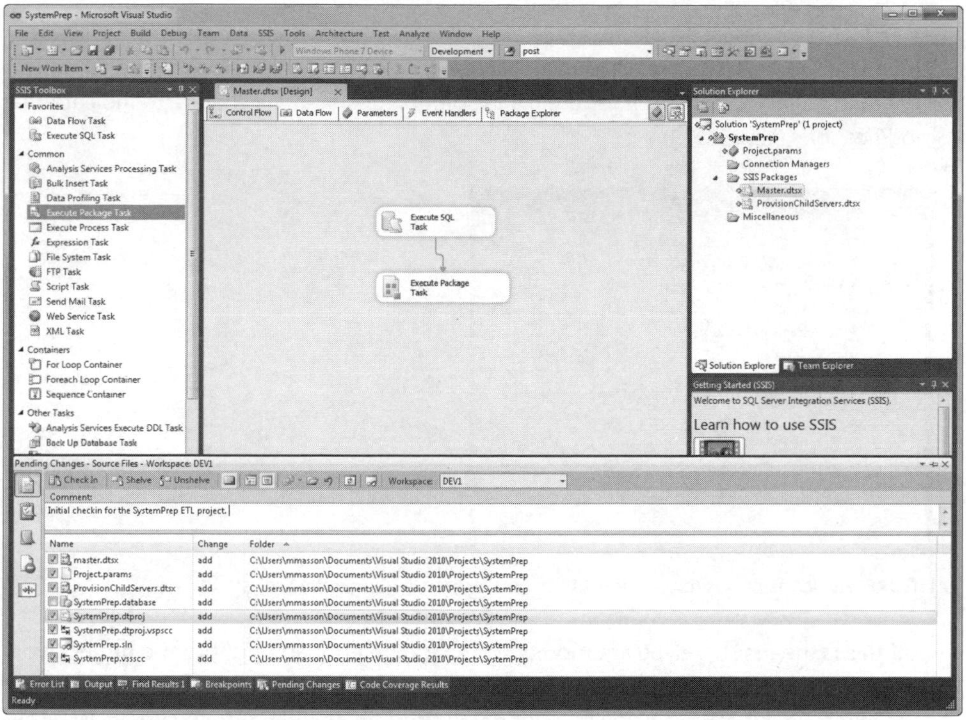

FIGURE 5-8 The Pending Changes view shows changes before they are committed.

TABLE 5-1 File extensions for an SSIS project

File extension	Description
.dtsx	SSIS package files. A project will typically contain multiple .dtsx files.
.params	This file stores the project parameters. There will be only one per project.
.dtproj	This is the Visual Studio project file. It contains the list of files for the project, deployment settings, and a cache of parameter and connection manager values that will be exposed when deployed to the SSIS Catalog.
.dtproj.user	This is a part of the Visual Studio project, and contains user-specific information. SSIS uses this file to cache information related to sensitive parameters. It should not be included as part of your Team Foundation Server project, as each user will have his or her own version of this file.
.conmgr	This is a shared connection manager file. Each shared connection manager added to your SSIS project will have its own .conmgr file.
.sln	The Visual Studio solution file.
.dtproj.vspscc	This file is automatically generated and used by Team Foundation Server.
.vssscc	This file is automatically generated and used by Team Foundation Server.
.database	This file is automatically created by SQL Server BI projects in Visual Studio, and is not actually used by SSIS.

Change Management

When you modify and save a file under source control, it will be "checked out" and placed in the list of pending changes. The icon for the file in Solution Explorer will change to indicate that it is open for modifications (Figure 5-9).

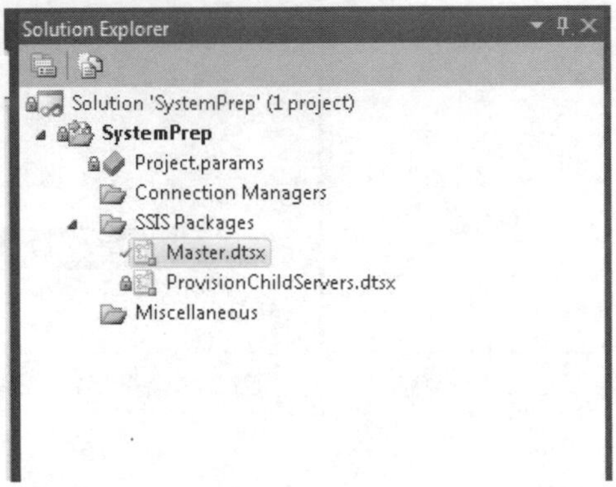

FIGURE 5-9 Icons are used to differentiate files in the pending changes list.

If this is the first time you are modifying a package after adding it to the project, you might receive a warning that the character encoding has changed (Figure 5-10). In some environments, SSIS packages might be initially created with your default system encoding (for example, Windows-1252). When the package is modified in the designer and then saved, the encoding will be switched to UTF-8. To eliminate this warning, you can change the expected file encoding in Team Foundation Server.

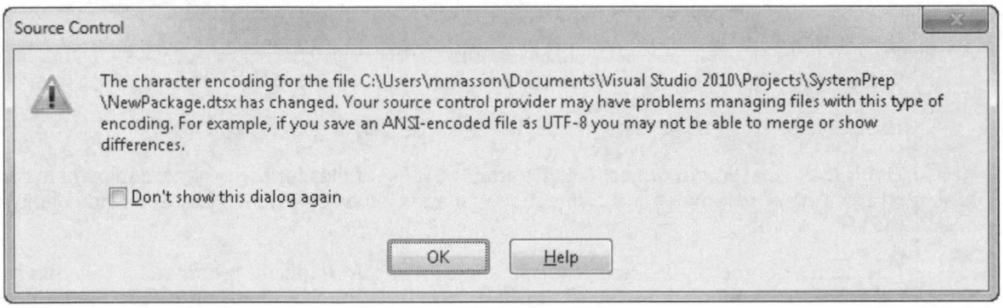

FIGURE 5-10 Visual Studio warning message shown for SSIS packages under source control.

To change the encoding for a file that is already in Team Foundation Server, perform the following steps:

1. Launch the Source Code Explorer.
2. Right-click the package file, and select Properties.
3. Click Set Encoding... (Figure 5-11).

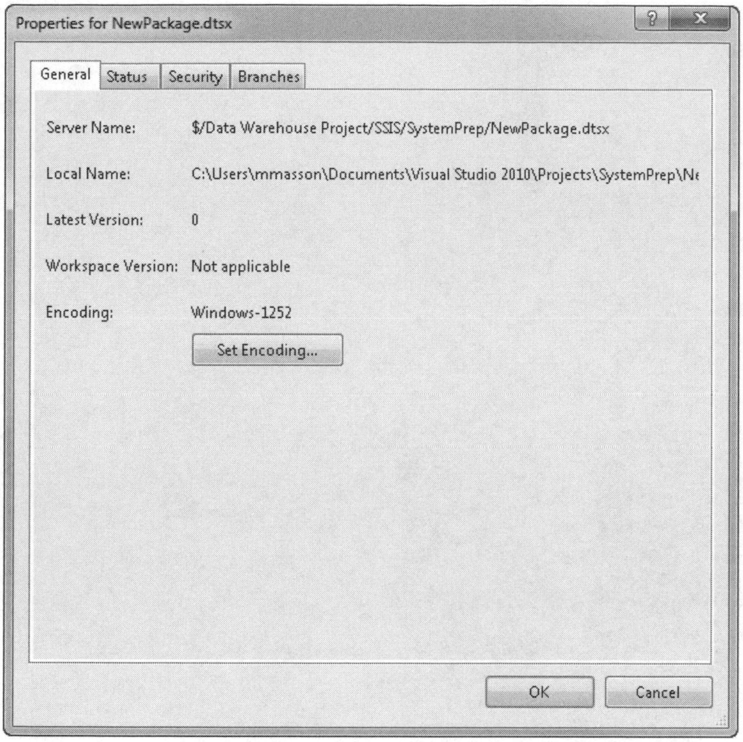

FIGURE 5-11 The Properties dialog box displays the current file encoding.

4. Select an encoding value from the drop-down list, or click Detect to have it automatically set to the new file encoding (for example, UTF-8).

5. Click OK to save the file encoding changes.

Now you will no longer see the warning when saving the file.

When you are done modifying your package files, you can submit the changes from Pending Changes. You can view the change history of a file by right-clicking the file and selecting View History (Figure 5-12). The History dialog box (Figure 5-13) shows the full path to the file, and all changes that have been made to the file (including the changeset that initially added it to Team Foundation Server). This information is extremely useful when working in a team environment, as it allows you to see when a file was changed, who made the change, and why it was changed.

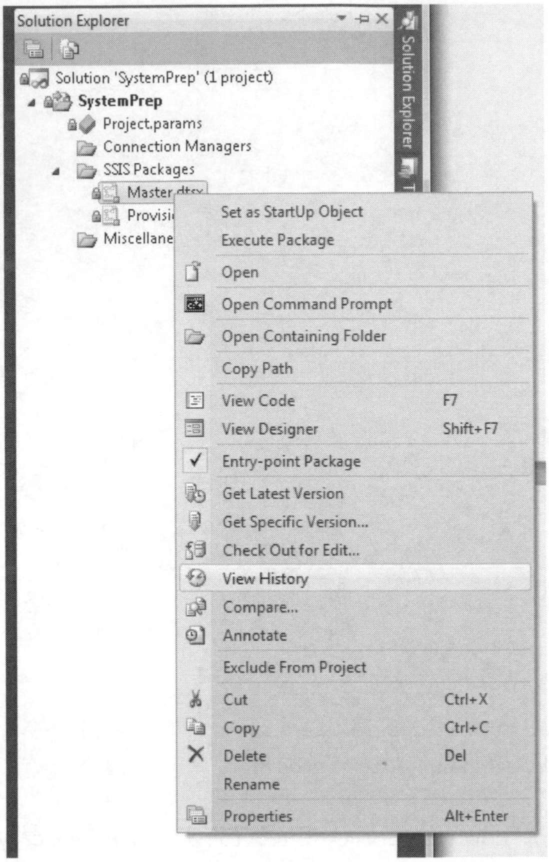

FIGURE 5-12 You can select the View History option from the Solution Explorer shortcut menu.

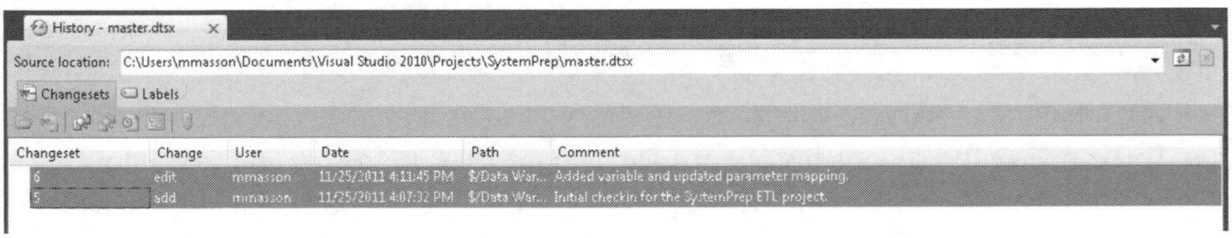

FIGURE 5-13 The History tab shows all changes to the file back to its initial check-in.

To see the differences between two revisions of the file, select two of the changes in the History tab, right-click, and select Compare from the shortcut menu. This will launch the Team Foundation Server diff utility, and will show the package XML changes between the selected versions. Figure 5-14 shows a diff of two packages. Changed lines are highlighted in blue, newly added lines appear in green, and removed lines appear in red. The first set of changes show that the *VersionBuild* and *VersionGUID* values have changed. These are two special package properties that will change every time you save a package, and can safely be ignored. The next change shows that a package variable named *Variable* was renamed to *NewVariable*, and the Execute Package task had a new parameter binding added to it.

FIGURE 5-14 Viewing the differences between two changes of a file.

Changes to the SSIS Visual Studio Project File

Certain changes you make during development will cause the Visual Studio project file (.dtproj) to be modified. These changes include the following:

- Adding or removing packages, shared connection managers, or project parameters
- Modifying package parameters
- Modifying package connection managers

Each type of change will modify the .dtproj file in a different way, but they do share one change in common: Each change to the project file will update the *PasswordVerifier* property. This field is used internally by SSIS to determine when it needs to refresh encrypted values.

As an example, let's look at what happens when you add a package to your project. When you create a new package, the package file (.dtsx) is created and added to source control. Entries for it are added to the Visual Studio project file, much like when you add any sort of source file to a .NET language project, such as C# or VB.NET. Figure 5-15 shows the Pending Changes view after you've added a new package to your project. Figure 5-16 shows the actual XML changes being made to the Visual Studio project file.

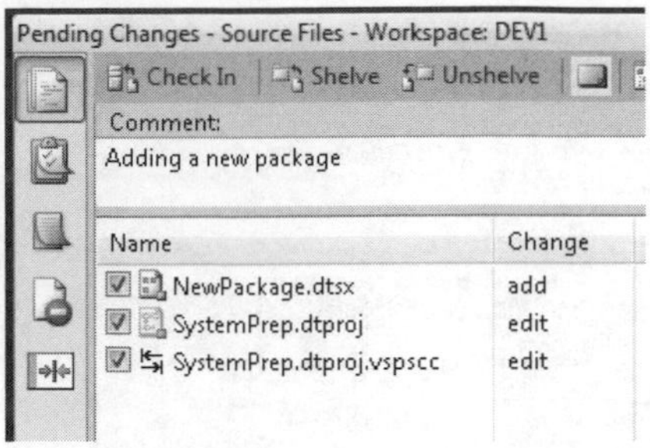

FIGURE 5-15 Adding a package modifies the Visual Studio project file.

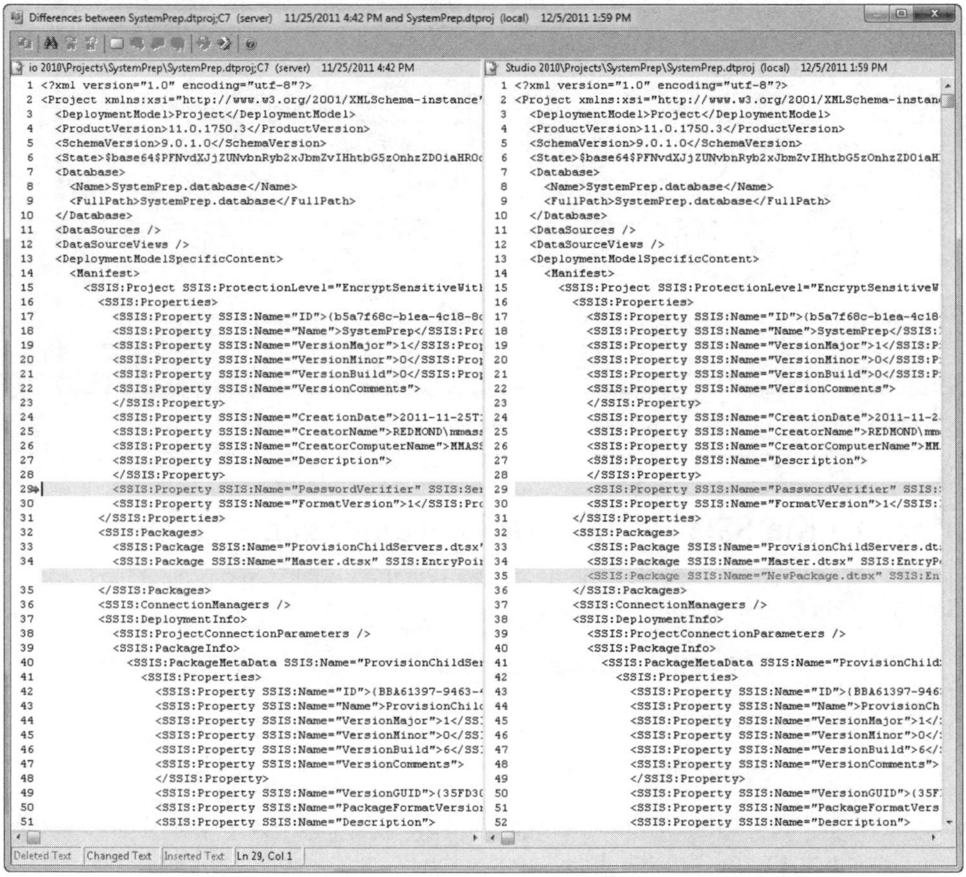

FIGURE 5-16 Changes to the Visual Studio Project file (.dtproj) when adding a new package.

If you open the .dtproj file in an XML editor, you will see that it contains entries for all parameters within the SSIS project, including Project Parameters, Package Parameters, and the parameters that are automatically generated for connection manager properties. When the SSIS project is compiled into the project deployment file (.ispac), this information is used to create a project manifest that gets embedded in the deployment file. The SSIS runtime uses this file to quickly identify all parameters, avoiding the need to open each package individually. This causes the .dtproj file to be changed frequently—it will be checked out of source control anytime a parameter or connection manager is added, removed, or modified.

Best Practices

The final part of this chapter covers some high-level best practices to keep in mind when doing team development with SSIS. Specifically, we cover the following:

- Using small, simple packages
- One developer per package
- Consistent naming conventions

Using Small, Simple Packages

Limiting the number of tasks that a package contains keeps it simple, and will typically reduce the frequency with which it needs to change. Having no more than one Data Flow task per package is a good way to divide the workload across multiple package files (although this doesn't always make sense for performance reasons). For example, when loading a data warehouse, you might wish to load each dimension with a separate package.

One Developer Per Package

When planning a data integration solution, it is common to break the ETL portion into a set of distinct operations. Typically, you will be able to map each operation to a single package. Many teams will then divide up the packages among their developers, trying to reduce the amount of overlap between them. Ideally, each package has a single owner, and will have only one person working on it at a time. If you find you have multiple people working on a package simultaneously, it might be an indicator that you should divide up the work across more than one package (see the previous tip about keeping packages simple).

Consistent Naming Conventions

Defining a consistent set of naming conventions for your team can be a big help. You can identify a task or component in the user interface by its icon, but it's sometimes harder to know exactly what you're looking at when diffing the package XML and all you have is a transform name like Modify Data. The new format in SQL Server 2012 does make it easier to identify the current object when you're looking, but many teams find that using an identifying prefix for the names of their tasks and transforms (such as DFT for Data Flow task) simplifies the process. The conventions you use will be up to your team; sticking to them is the most important thing.

See Also *SQL Server MVP Jamie Thomson's blog is a fantastic resource for SSIS users. Jamie was one of the early pioneers of SSIS team development, and has some great blog posts about his experiences as a consultant. Although the original content was written for SQL Server 2005, much of his advice still applies in SQL Server 2012, especially when using the Package Deployment Model. You can find his list of best practices and common naming conventions here:* http://sqlblog.com/blogs/jamie_thomson/archive/2012/01/29/suggested-best-practises-and-naming-conventions.aspx.

Summary

This chapter examined team development practices with SSIS. You saw how to use SSIS with a source control system (using Visual Studio Team Foundation Server 2010 as an example), and exactly how the files that make up your project change as you develop your ETL solution. This chapter also explored some of the features of the new package XML format in SQL Server 2012. Finally, you saw some generalized best practices to use when working with SSIS in a team environment.

CHAPTER 6

Developing an SSIS Solution

In This Chapter

SSIS Project Deployment Models

When developing an SSIS Project in SQL Server 2012, you can use either the Package Deployment Model or the Project Deployment Model. The Project Deployment Model determines the set of SSIS features that you can use when working with SSIS projects. The Project Deployment Model is the default deployment model when a new Integration Services project is created. When you upgrade from an existing SSIS project, the project will use the Package Deployment Model. Using SQL Server Data Tools, you can convert from the Package Deployment Model to the Project Deployment Model (or vice versa).

Package Deployment Model

The Package Deployment Model is introduced in SSIS 2012 to maintain backward compatibility with earlier versions of SSIS. When working with this deployment model, SSIS packages are managed as individual files on the file system (with a *.dtsx* extension). The SSIS packages can be deployed to all the SSIS package locations prior to SSIS 2012. These package locations include the file system, SQL Server (stored in the system database, *msdb*), or the SSIS Package Store. In addition, when you build the project, you can choose to configure the build process to produce the deployment utility for deployment of SSIS packages. Figure 6-1 shows an example of an SSIS project using the Package Deployment Model.

FIGURE 6-1 SSIS project using the Package Deployment Model.

Converting from Package to Project Deployment Model

SSIS 2012 introduces new capabilities that are available in the Project Deployment Model. To make use of these new capabilities, you might consider converting the SSIS project to use the Project Deployment Model. To do this, perform the following steps:

1. Right-click the project.
2. Select Convert to Project Deployment Model.

   This launches the Project Conversion Wizard, which performs a premigration assessment of all the SSIS packages and provides suggestions on how you can make use of the new SSIS 2012 capabilities.
3. Select the packages that will be migrated.
4. Specify the properties for the project.
5. If any of the packages uses the Execute Package task, the Project Conversion Wizard can help you make changes to the Execute Package task such that it references packages in the same project.
6. In the Select Configurations step, the wizard scans for existing configurations that are used. You can add additional configurations that are used at runtime.
7. In the Create Parameters step, you can create parameters for the packages and map them to a common package.
8. In the Configure Parameters step, you can configure the parameters that are used.
9. Review the summary provided.

10. Click Migration.

11. Congratulations! You have successfully performed the conversion from the Package to the Project Deployment Model.

Project Deployment Model

The Project Deployment Model allows you to use the new features that are introduced in SSIS 2012, including the ability to use parameters and shared connection managers. When using this deployment model, SSIS configurations are not available. When an SSIS project is built using the Project Deployment Model (Figure 6-2), all the SSIS packages in the project are bundled into a single file, called a project deployment file (with an .ispac extension). One of the advantages of having a single project deployment file is that it allows the extract-transform-load (ETL) developer to easily hand off the file to the administrator, without worrying that certain dependent SSIS packages that need to be deployed to the server are missing. During deployment of the SSIS project to an SSIS Catalog, the project deployment file is the unit of deployment. When a new Integration Services project is created using SQL Server Data Tools, the Project Deployment Model is the default model used.

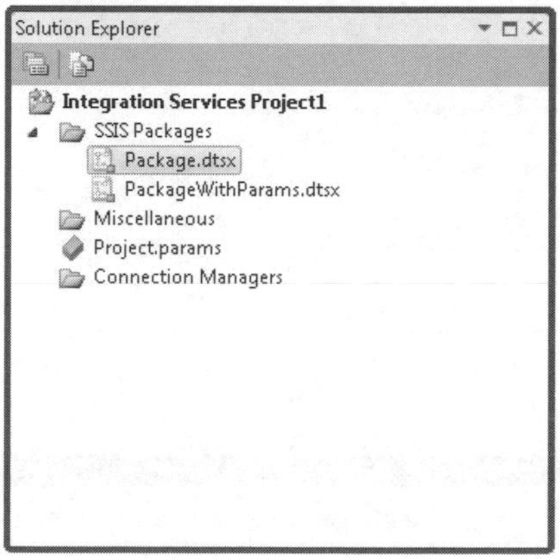

FIGURE 6-2 SSIS project using the Project Deployment Model.

Prior to SSIS 2012, SSIS configurations were commonly used for configuring the behavior of the package by specifying values for property paths in a package. Different types of SSIS configurations are supported, including XML Configuration files (with a .dtsConfig extension), configurations that are stored in a SQL Server table, registry entry, and environment variable. In addition, you can also make use of configurations that are available in a parent package variable. When you use the Project Deployment Model in SSIS 2012, you will not be able to make use of SSIS configurations in a package. The Package Configurations option is not available if you started from a new Integration Services project. However, if you have converted a project from the Package to the Project Deployment Model and have not removed all the configurations, this option allows you to continue using SSIS configurations. Once you are ready to start using parameters for configuring packages, you can remove the SSIS configuration references that are in the packages.

Converting from Project to Package Deployment Model

If you want to convert an SSIS project from the Project Deployment Model to the Package Deployment Model, each of the SSIS packages in the project cannot make use of features that are not available in the Package Deployment Model. One of the common issues that prevent a successful conversion to the Package Deployment Model is the use of parameters in the project or packages. The use of parameters is a new feature introduced in SSIS 2012, and is available only in the Project Deployment Model.

To convert from the Project Deployment Model to the Package Deployment Model, perform the following steps:

1. Right-click the project and choose Convert to Package Deployment Model (Figure 6-3).

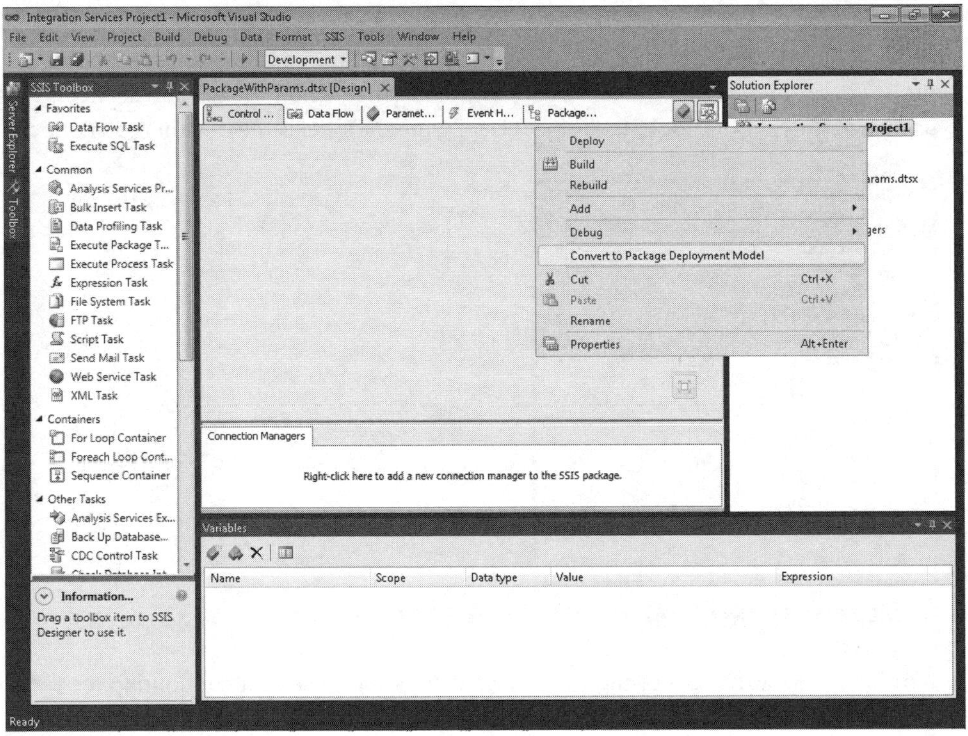

FIGURE 6-3 Convert to Package Deployment Model.

2. An information message will be shown. Click OK to proceed.

   This starts the compatibility check for each of the packages in the project. If there are packages that are using features that are only available in the Project Deployment Model, conversion will fail (see Figure 6-4).

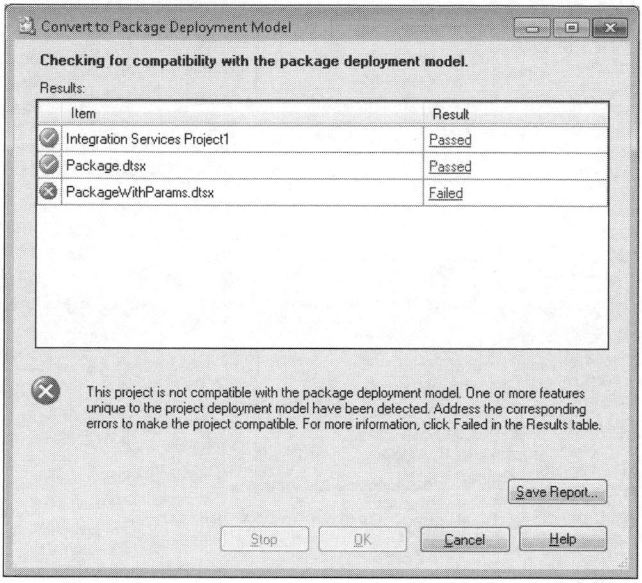

FIGURE 6-4 Conversion failed due to a package using parameters.

3. When conversion fails, click Cancel. The project will remain in the Project Deployment Model. In this example, the conversion failed due to the package *PackageWithParams.dtsx*, which is using parameters.

4. For illustration purposes, remove *PackageWithParams.dtsx* from the project and try the conversion again. Another alternative is to identify the parts (for example, expressions) of the packages that are using parameters, and modify them so they do not use parameters.

5. Once you have made the changes, right-click the project and choose Convert To Package Deployment Model, then click OK.

6. Click OK again. The project has been successfully converted to the Package Deployment Model (see Figure 6-5).

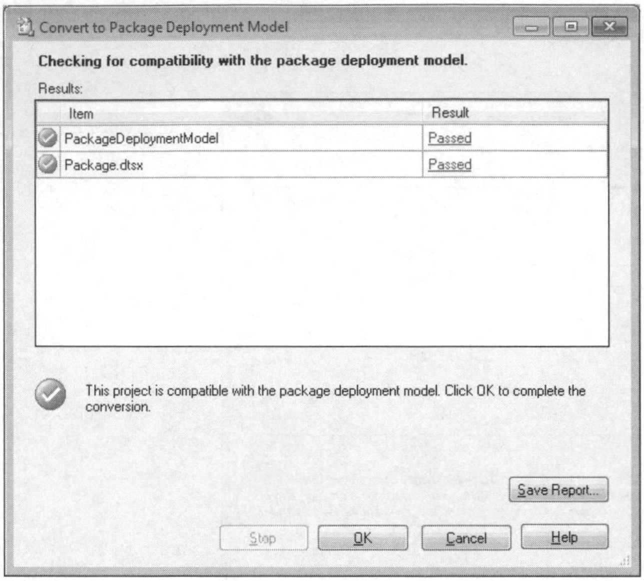

FIGURE 6-5 Successful conversion to the Package Deployment Model.

Develop an Integration Services Project

In Chapter 1, "SSIS Overview," you learned about the different scenarios in which Integration Services can play an important role. In this section, you learn how you can make use of SQL Server Data Tools to develop an Integration Services project.

Creating an SSIS Project

This section shows you how to develop an Integration Services project that contains multiple packages that uses these tasks. To create a new Integration Services project, follow these steps:

1. Launch SQL Server Data Tools.

2. Select File | New Project.

3. Choose the Business Intelligence Template (see Figure 6-6).

4. Select the Integration Services Project, and name it **MyFirstSSISProject**.

5. Click OK.

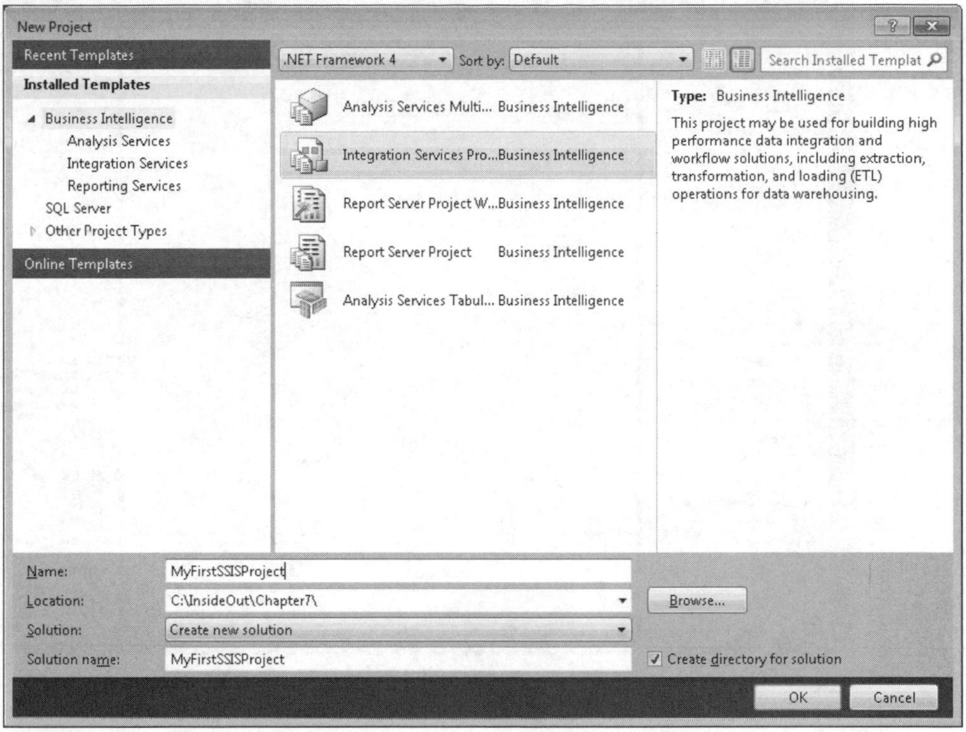

FIGURE 6-6 New Integration Services project.

6. After the SSIS project is created, you will see the SSIS design environment, shown in Figure 6-7. This will be the design environment that you work with when developing an SSIS project.

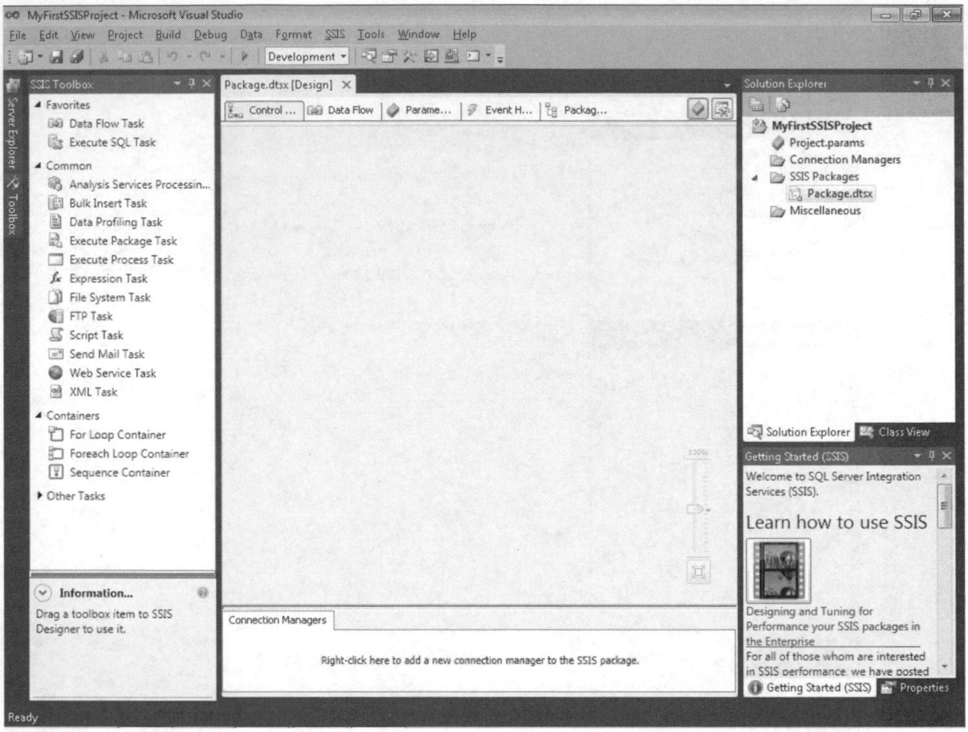

FIGURE 6-7 SSIS design environment.

7. In Solution Explorer, you will see the following:

- **Project.params** Clicking this allows you to create project parameters.
- **Connection Managers** This folder contains shared connection managers that can be used by all the packages in the project.
- **SSIS Packages** A default package called *Package.dtsx* is created.
- **Miscellaneous** You can include miscellaneous documents in this folder.

8. If you are a new user or unfamiliar with how to use a task or component, the Getting Started (SSIS) videos can help. You can see this in Figure 6-7 in the lower-right corner.

Note The SSIS design environment will look different in previous versions of SSIS. In SQL Server 2005, SQL Server 2008, and SQL Server 2008 R2, the design environment is provided by Business Intelligence Development Studio. Significant changes have been made in SSIS 2012. Chapter 4, "New SSIS Designer Features," provides details on the designer improvements made in SSIS 2012.

9. In Solution Explorer, right-click the Connection Managers folder, and select New Connection Manager (Figure 6-8). This creates a shared connection manager, which allows you to reuse the same connection manager in different packages, without having to create a new connection manager that accesses the same data sources or destination for each package.

10. Select OLEDB – Connection Manager For OLE DB Connections and click Add.

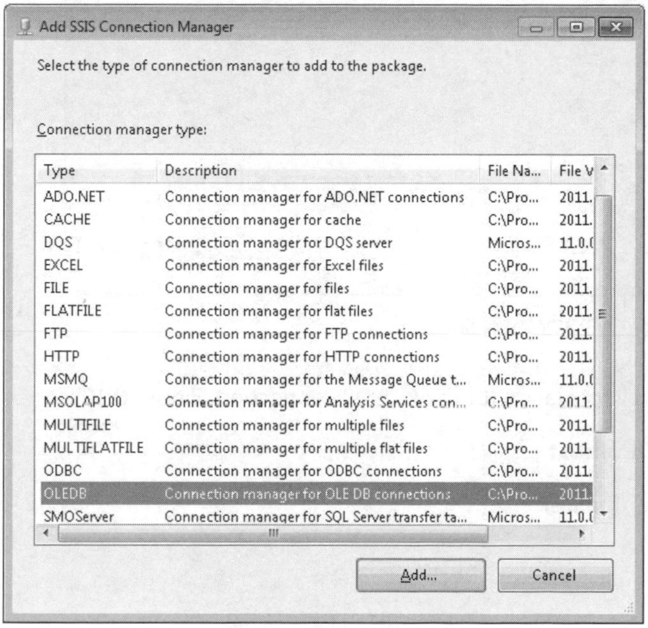

FIGURE 6-8 Adding a new connection manager.

11. After selecting the OLE DB Manager, you will need to configure the OLE DB connection. Click New (Figure 6-9).

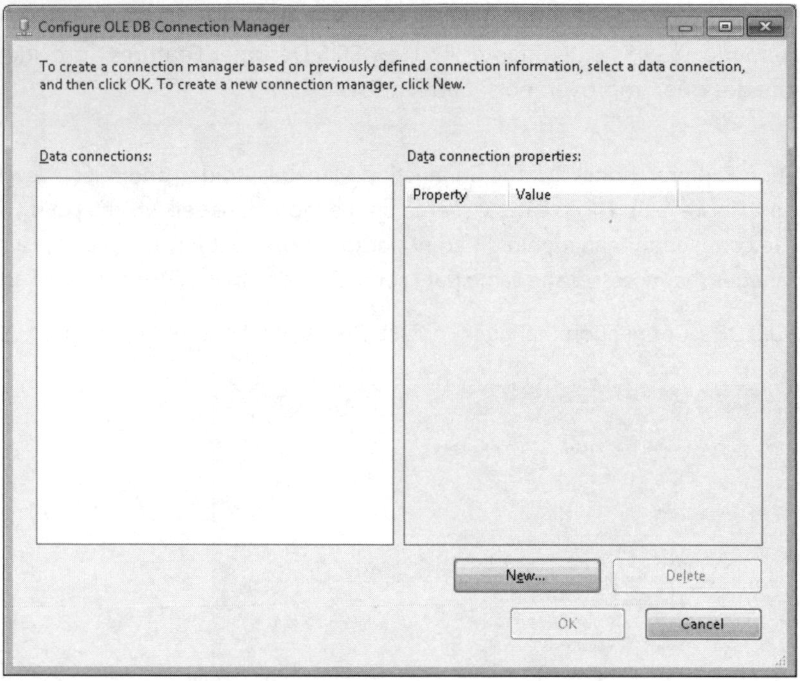

FIGURE 6-9 Creating an OLE DB connection.

12. Specify the following information for the OLE DB connection (Figure 6-10):

- **Server Name localhost**
- **Database Name master**

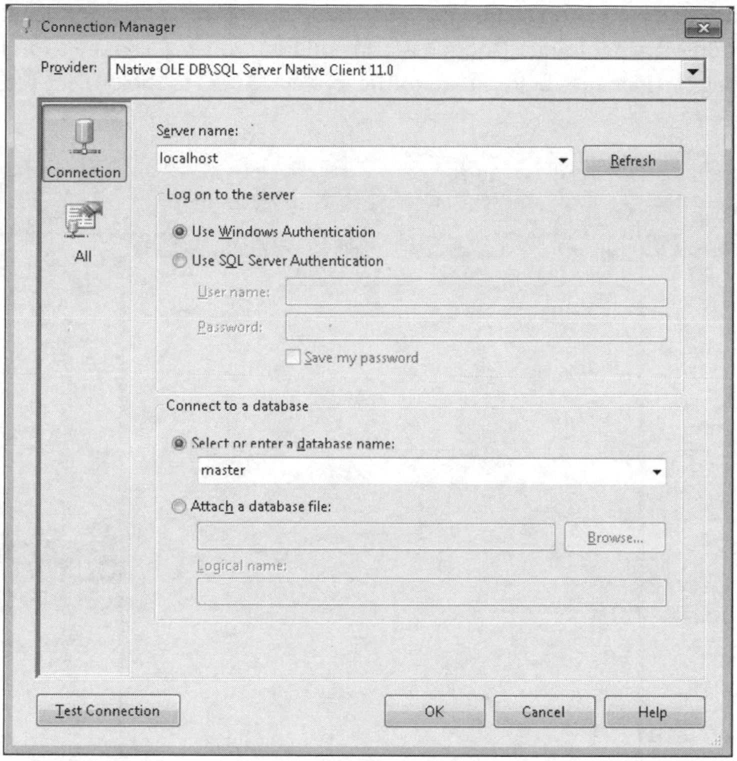

FIGURE 6-10 Information for the OLE DB connection.

13. Click OK in the Connection Manager dialog box.
14. Click OK in the Configure OLE DB Connection Manager dialog box.

15. You will notice that a new connection manager, *localhost.master.conmgr*, has been created in the Connection Manager folder (Figure 6-11). In addition, you will also see a *(project) localhost master* connection manager being created. The *(project)* refers to the project-scoped connection manager.

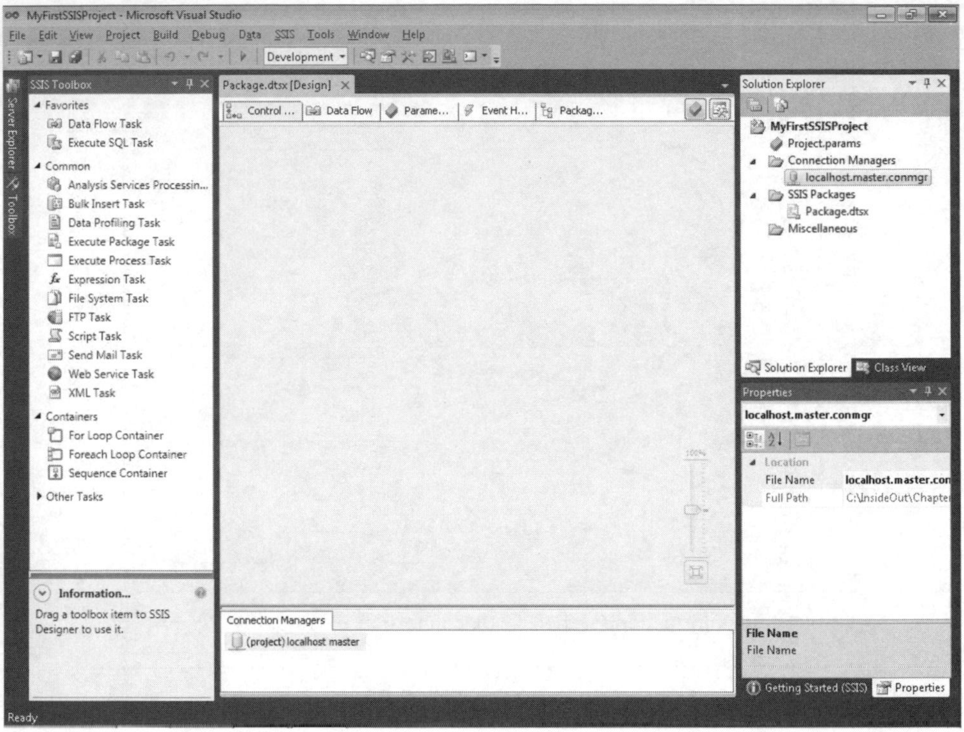

FIGURE 6-11 New shared connection manager created.

16. From the SSIS toolbox, drag the Execute SQL task into the Control Flow.

17. Double-click Execute SQL task.

18. In the Execute SQL Task Editor, specify **localhost.master** as the connection (Figure 6-12).

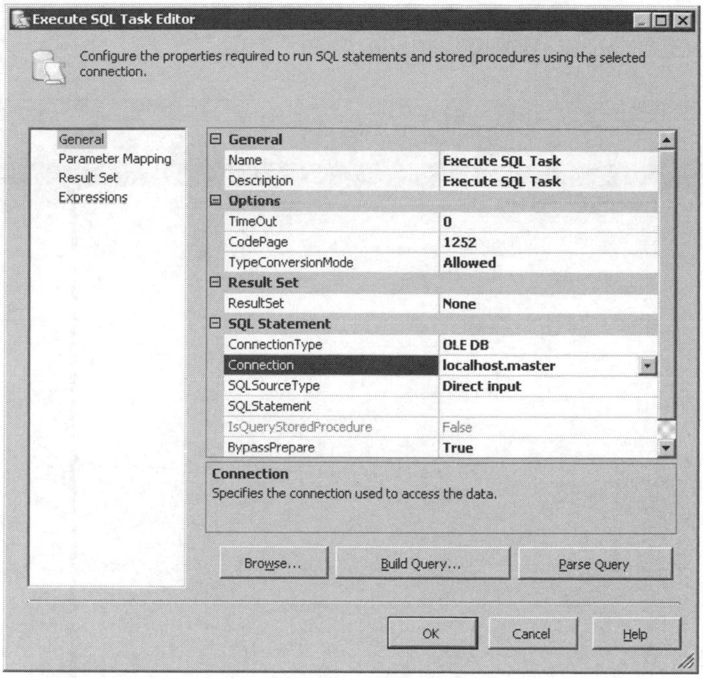

FIGURE 6-12 Specify the connection using the Execute SQL Task Editor.

In this example, we use the Execute SQL task to create a database called EnterpriseDataWarehouse.

> **Note** In most scenarios, the databases will have been created. For purpose of illustration, we are creating the database so that the example can be self-contained.

19. Enter the following text for SQL Statement:

```
IF NOT EXISTS (SELECT name FROM sys.databases
                     WHERE name = N'EnterpriseDataWarehouse')
BEGIN
CREATE DATABASE [EnterpriseDataWarehouse]
END
```

20. Click OK.

21. Right-click the Execute SQL Task, and choose Execute Task. This executes the task that creates the EnterpriseDataWarehouse database (Figure 6-13).

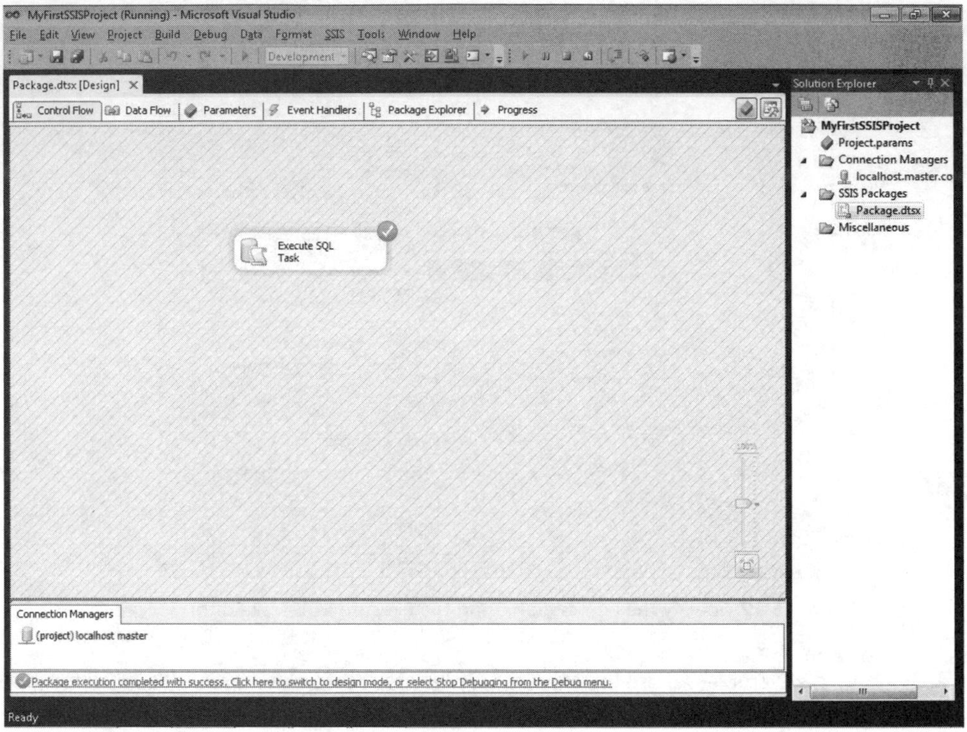

FIGURE 6-13 Execute SQL task (successful execution).

22. Drag a second Execute SQL task in the Control Flow.

23. Rename the Execute SQL task **Create Call Record Table**.

24. Right-click Connection Managers and create a new OLE DB Connection Manager (Figure 6-14):

   - **Server Name localhost**
   - **Database Name EnterpriseDataWarehouse**

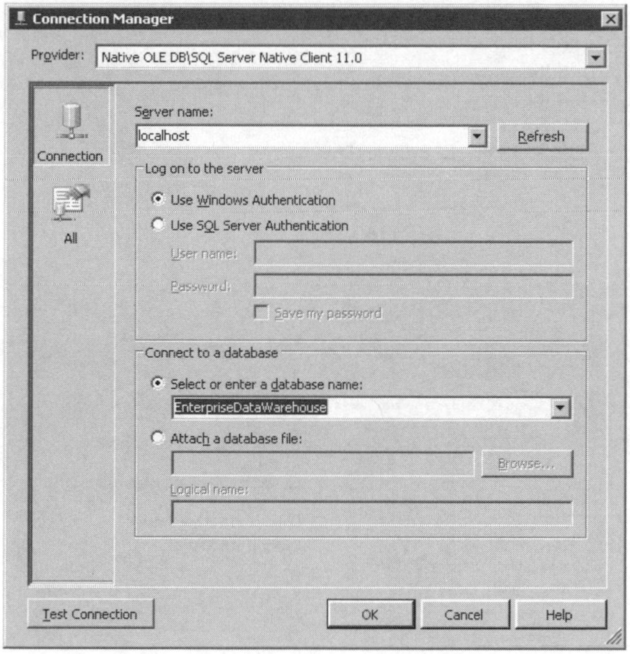

FIGURE 6-14 Creating a new OLE DB connection to the EnterpriseDataWarehouse database.

25. In the Execute SQL Task Editor, specify ***localhost.EnterpriseDataWarehouse*** as the connection (Figure 6-15). Enter the following text for SQL Statement:

```
IF NOT EXISTS (SELECT * FROM sys.objects WHERE
object_id = OBJECT_ID(N'[dbo].[CallRecords]') AND type in (N'U'))
BEGIN
CREATE TABLE [dbo].[CallRecords](
[id] [int] IDENTITY(1,1) NOT NULL,
[caller_no] [varchar](50) NULL,
[callee_no] [varchar](50) NULL,
[duration_secs] [int] NULL,
CONSTRAINT [PK_CallRecords] PRIMARY KEY CLUSTERED
(
[id] ASC
)
)
END
```

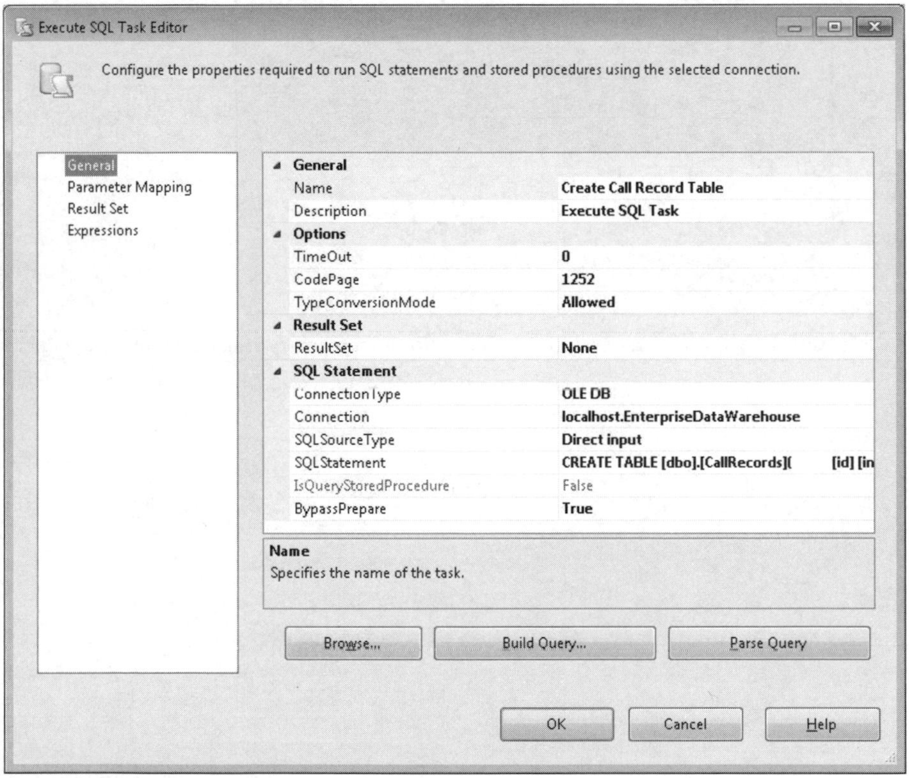

FIGURE 6-15 Specify the connection using the Execute SQL Task Editor.

26. Click OK.

27. Click the first Execute SQL task, and connect the precedence constraint to the second Execute SQL task, called Create Call Record Table. Figure 6-16 shows a package with two Execute SQL tasks.

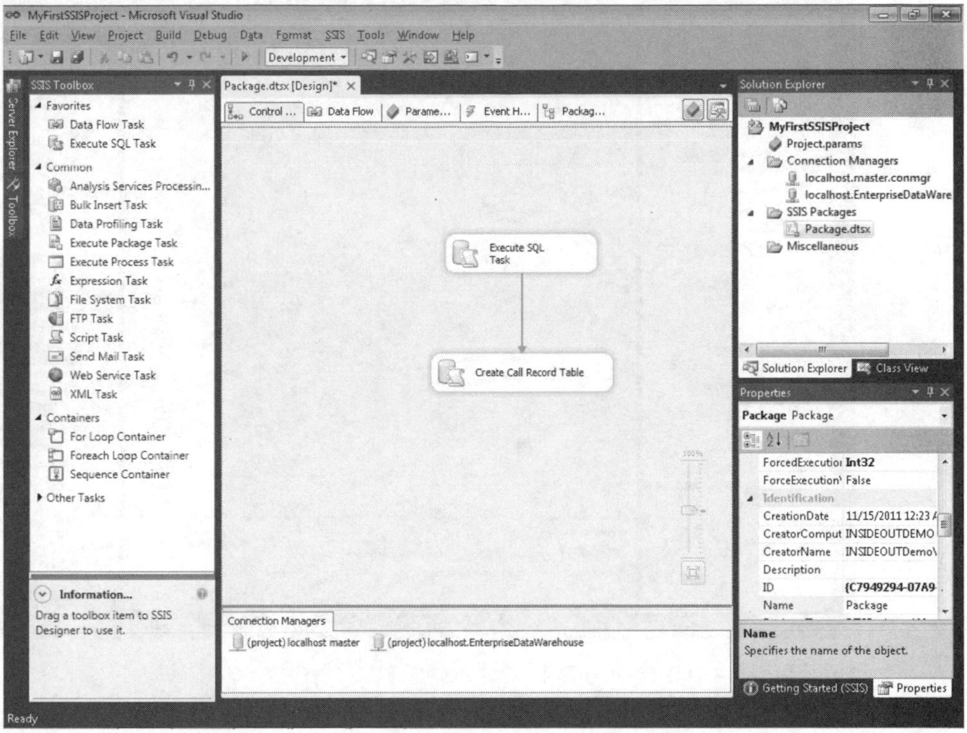

FIGURE 6-16 SSIS package to prepare the EnterpriseDataWarehouse database.

Designing an Integration Services Data Flow

In this section, you learn how to use build an SSIS package that uses the ForEach container and Data Flow task to load data from multiple text files to a SQL Server database. These text files are found in the SampleData directory. The new package is added to the SSIS project that you started working on in the previous section.

1. Right-click SSIS Packages.

2. Select New SSIS Package.

3. After the package has been created, rename it **MyDataFlow.dtsx**.

4. After the OLE DB Connection has been created, you are ready to start working on the Data Flow task. To do this, drag a Data Flow task onto the Control Flow (Figure 6-17).

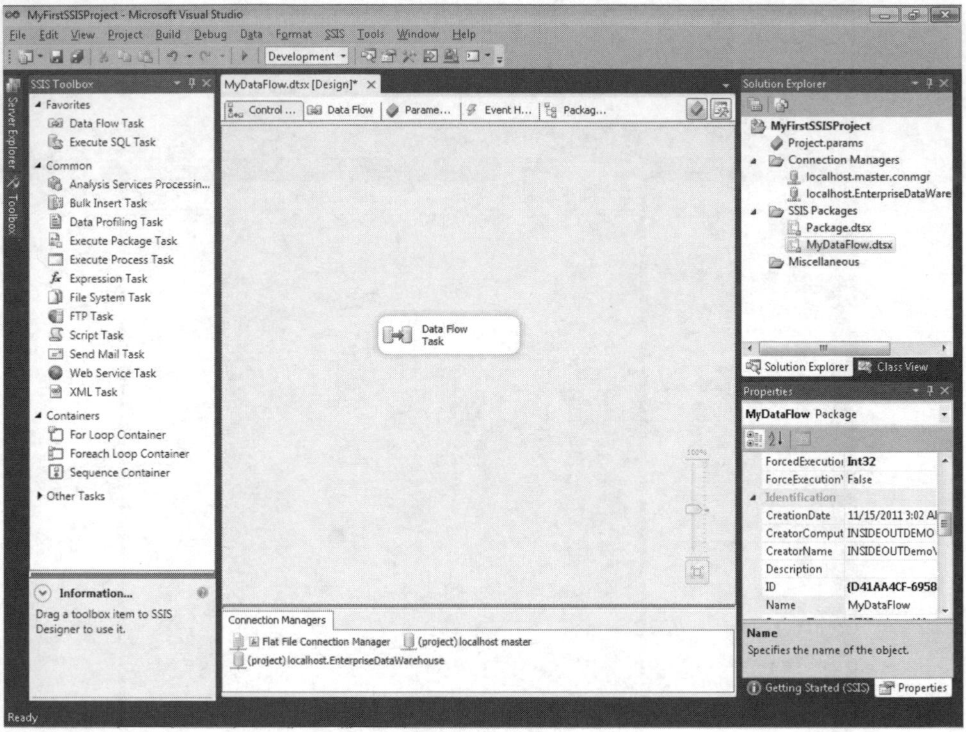

FIGURE 6-17 SSIS package with a Data Flow task.

5. Double-click the Data Flow task, and then click the Source Assistant (Figure 6-18), and select the following:

   - Types: Flat File
   - Connection Managers: New…

6. Click OK.

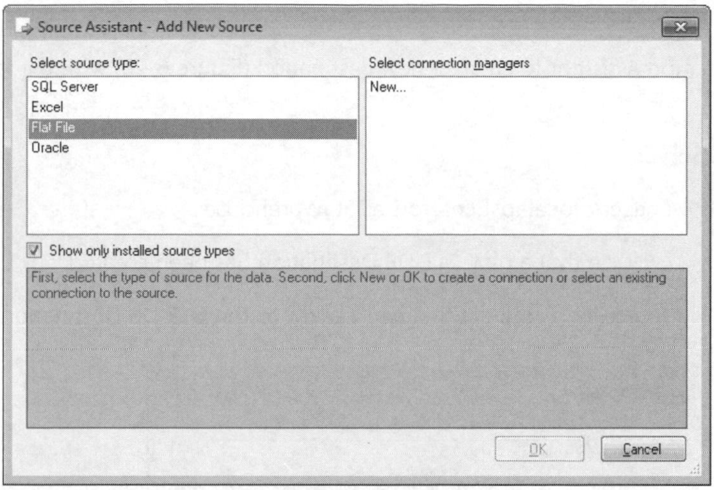

FIGURE 6-18 Creating a new data source using the Source Assistant.

7. You will be prompted to provide more information on the file to be used as the Flat File source. Select the *cdr-1.txt* file in the Chapter 6 *SampleData* directory (Figure 6-19).

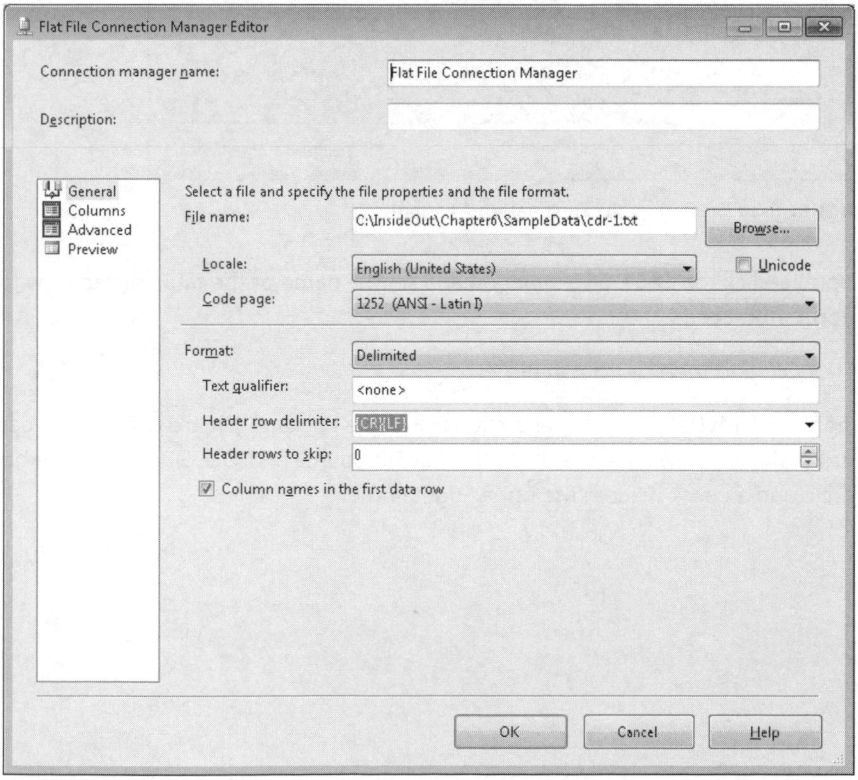

FIGURE 6-19 Setting up the Flat File source.

8. Click Columns and then click OK.

9. Use the Destination Assistant to create a new destination (Figure 6-20) with the following settings:

   - Types: SQL Server
   - Connection Managers: localhost.EnterpriseDataWarehouse

10. Click OK, and you will see that a new OLE DB Destination has been created.

11. Click the Flat File source, and connect the green arrow to the OLE DB Destination.

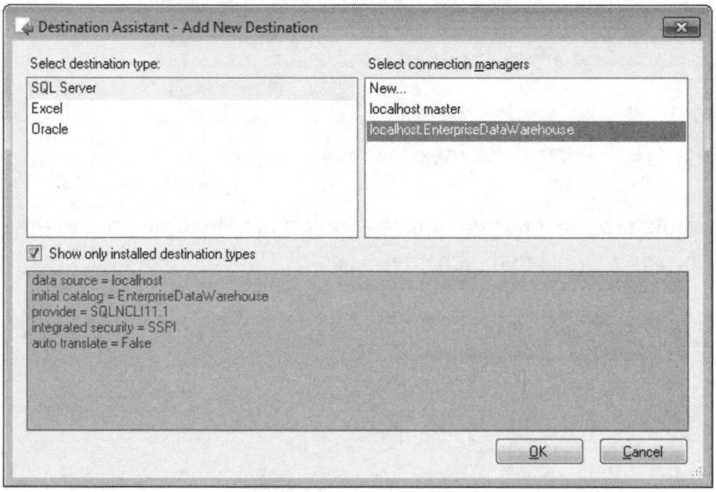

FIGURE 6-20 Setting up the Destination Assistant.

12. Double-click the OLE DB Destination and set the name of the table or the view to **dbo.CallRecords.**

13. Click OK, and then click Save All.

14. Right-click MyDataFlow.dtsx and choose Execute Package (Figure 6-21). If the package runs successfully, you will see that both the Flat File source and OLE DB destination have a green circle and a check mark at the upper-right corner.

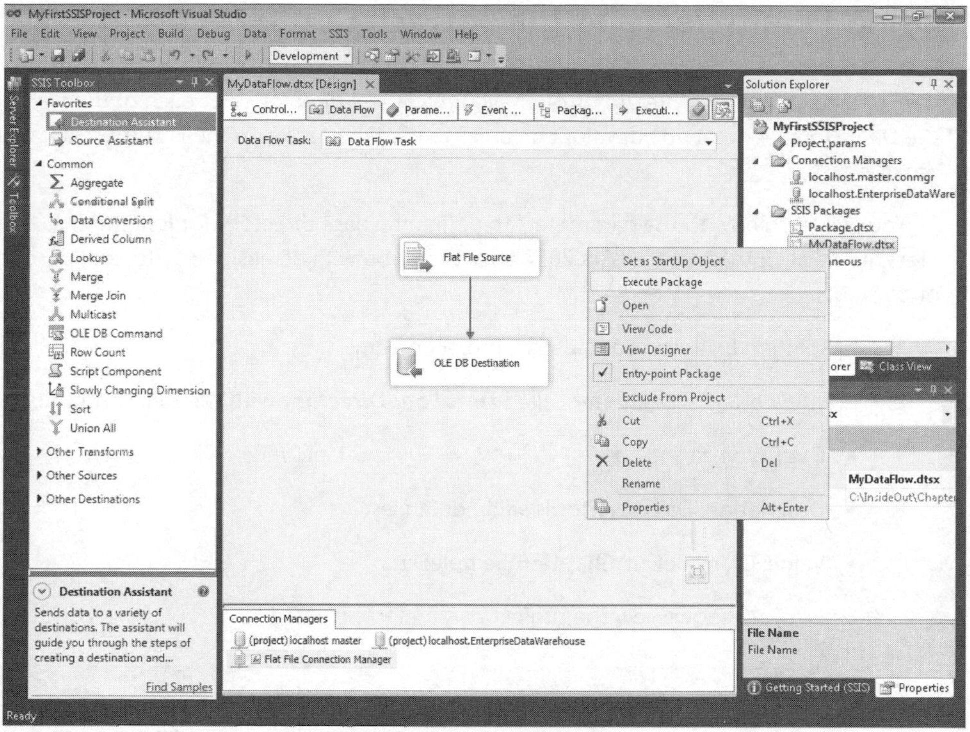

FIGURE 6-21 Execute a package in SQL Server Data Tools.

> **Tip** You will notice that there is an *Entry-Point Package menu selection.* A common SSIS package design pattern is to make use of a parent package to control the execution of several child packages. The ability to mark a package as an entry-point package is provided to enable SSIS developers to indicate that a package is a parent package. This provides valuable information to the administrator of the SSIS Catalog and enables the administrator to determine the correct set of packages to execute on the server.

Congratulations! You have just successfully designed a simple data flow, and executed the package that contains the data flow.

In the next section, you learn how to expand this example to use the sample Data Flow task to load several files (in a user-specified directory) to the database.

Using Parameters and the ForEach Container

This section shows how to use of the ForEach container available in SSIS. In this section, you use the ForEach container to iterate through all the files in a directory. For each of the files, you will use the Data Flow task that you developed earlier to load the data into the EnterpriseDataWarehouse database.

You will learn how to use parameters to define the base directory for loading the data files. Parameters are newly introduced in SSIS 2012 to provide you with an easier way to configure an SSIS project or package.

1. In Solution Explorer, double-click project.params.
2. Create a project parameter called ***DataLoadDirectory*** with the following values:
   - Data Type: String
   - Description: Directory for loading data files
   - Value: C:\InsideOut\Chapter6\SampleData

   Figure 6-22 shows how the project parameter is created.

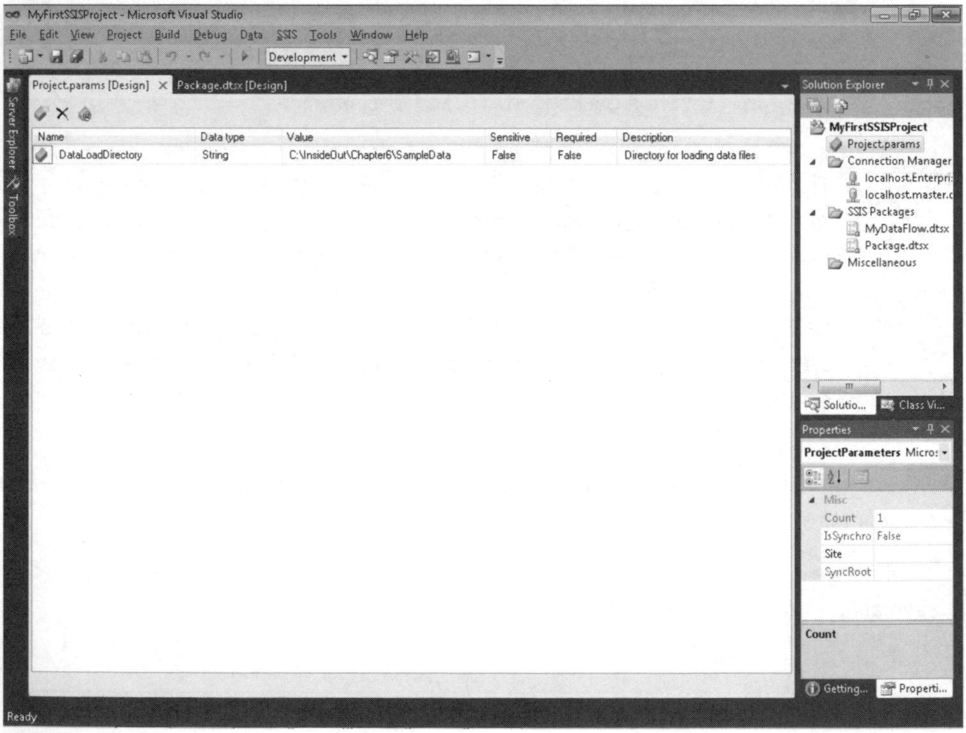

FIGURE 6-22 Creating a project parameter: *DataLoadDirectory*.

Tip Project parameters can be used by all the packages in the project.

3. Click the package MyDataFlow.dtsx.
4. Next, create a package variable by clicking the Variables icon (Figure 6-23).

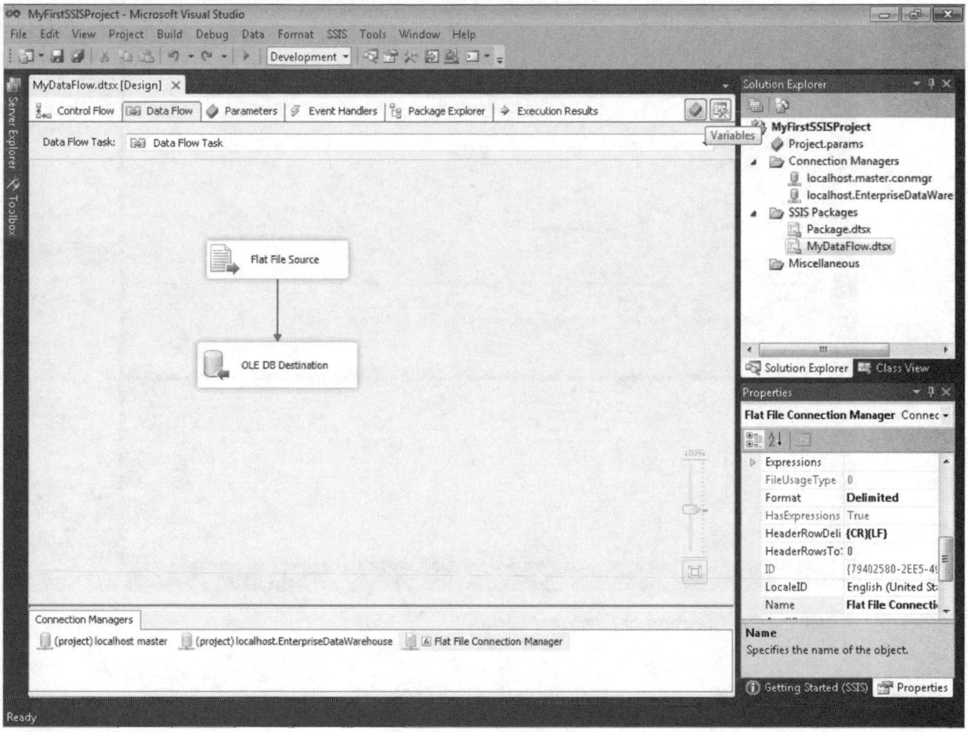

FIGURE 6-23 Using variables.

5. Create a variable called *Filename* (Data Type: String; Figure 6-24). You will use this variable to store the file name used by the ForEach container.

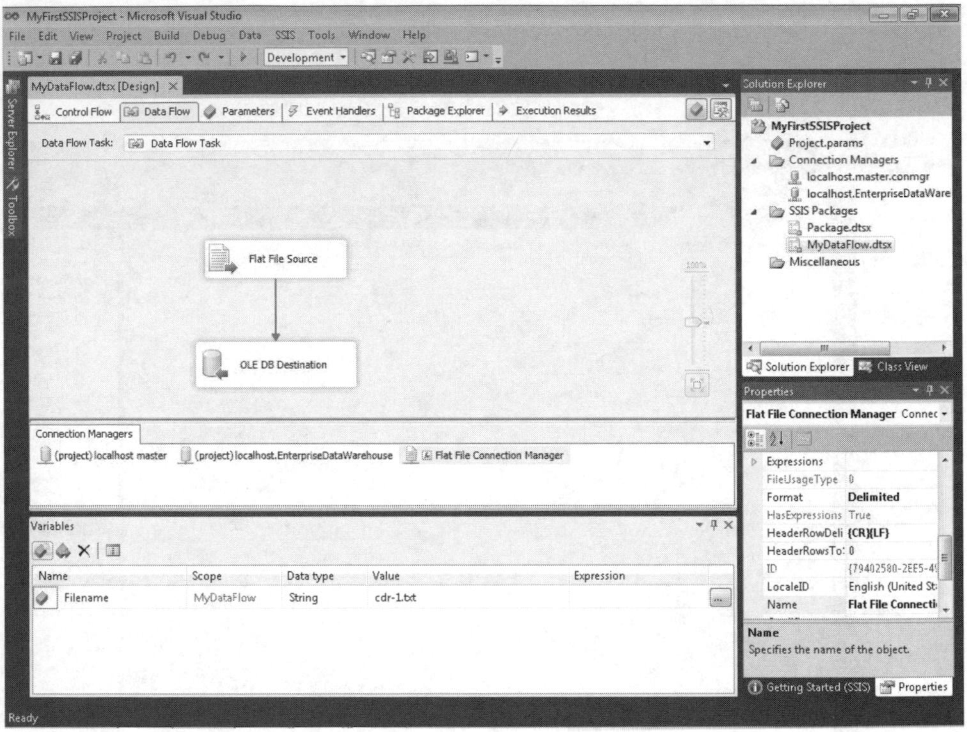

FIGURE 6-24 Creation of *Filename* variable.

6. Drag the ForEach container into the Control Flow.

7. Drag the Data Flow task into the ForEach container.

8. Next, to configure the ForEach container to iterate through all the files in the directory, double-click the ForEach container. Use the ForEachFile enumerator and configure the enumerator as follows (Figure 6-25):

   - Folder: *C:\InsideOut\Chapter6\SampleData*
   - Files: *.txt

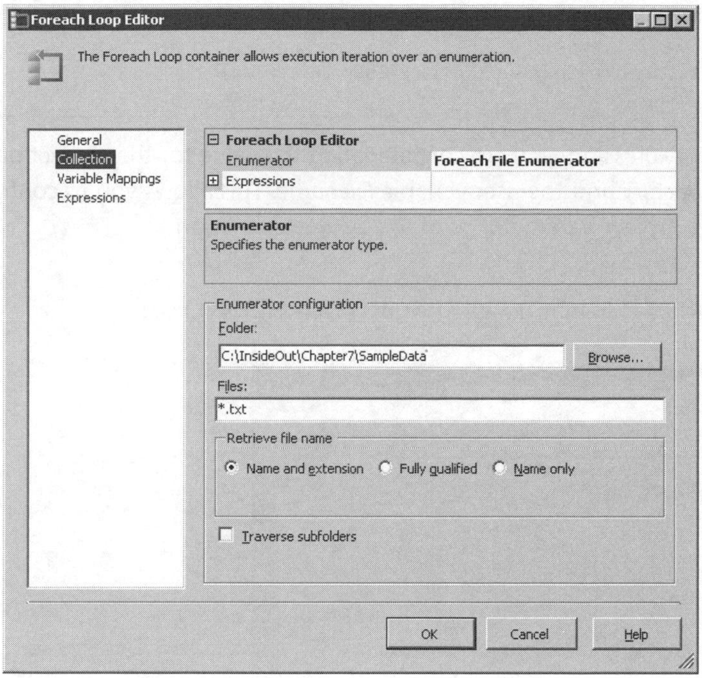

FIGURE 6-25 ForEach enumerator.

9. Click Variables Mapping, and choose the variable *User::Filename*, with Index 0.
10. Click OK.
11. In Connection Manager, click the Flat File connection manager. In the Properties dialog box for the Flat File connection manager, click Expressions.
12. From the Property drop-down list, select the *ConnectionString* property, and then click the ellipsis button.

13. In the Expressions dialog box, use the following expression (Figure 6-26):

```
@[$Project::DataLoadDirectory]+ "\\" +  @[User::Filename]
```

> **Note** In this expression, you are concatenating the value for the project parameter *DataLoadDirectory* and the user variable *Filename*. This allows you to configure the value for the project parameter prior to package execution.

14. Click Evaluate Expression to make sure that the expression is correct.

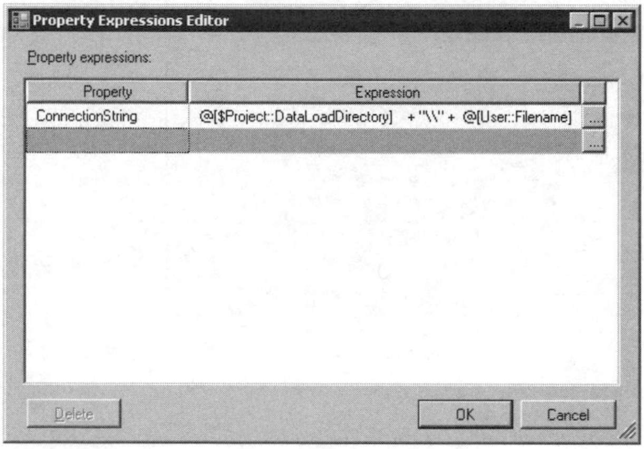

FIGURE 6-26 Property Expressions Editor: Setting the expression for the Flat File connection manager.

In this section, you have learned the following:

- How to make use of project parameters for configuring a project.
- How to make use of a variable to store the filename provided by the ForEach file enumerator.
- How to use the ForEach container to iterate through all the text files in a directory and load them into the database.

Using the Execute Package Task

The Execute Package task is used to invoke the execution of other packages. In earlier versions of SSIS, the Execute Package task provides the ability to execute packages that have been deployed to the package locations SQL Server and file system. When packages are deployed to a production server, the SSIS developer or administrator will have to make sure that the parent and child packages are all deployed correctly. In short, all packages that are used in Execute Package task in parent packages will have to be accessible by the parent package. Otherwise, the execution of a parent package will fail.

In SSIS 2012, when a parent package references packages that are deployed to SQL Server or file system, we refer to these references as external references. SSIS 2012 provides you with the ability to execute packages that are in the same project, called Project Reference. This helps solve the problem of missing child packages because the SSIS project (and all the packages that it contains) are deployed as a single deployment unit, the SSIS project deployment file (.ispac extension).

In this section, you learn how to use the Execute Package task and use project references to refer to packages in the same project. To do this, follow these steps:

1. Create a new SSIS package, ParentPackage.dtsx.
2. Drag two Execute Package tasks to the Control Flow.
3. Name the two Execute Package tasks **Preparation** and **Load CDR Files**.
4. Connect the green arrow for the Execute Package task Preparation to the other Execute Package task.
5. Double-click the Execute Package task Preparation (Figure 6-27).
6. Click Package. You will notice the default ReferenceType is Project Reference.
7. From the PackageNameFromProjectReference drop-down list, select Package.dtsx. Click OK.

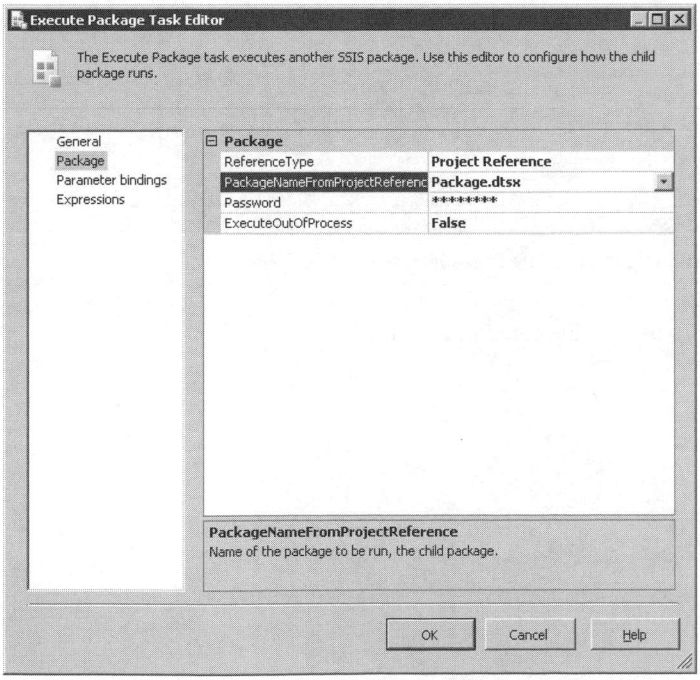

FIGURE 6-27 Setting up the Execute Package task Preparation.

8. Double-click the Execute Package task Load CDR File (Figure 6-28).

9. Click Package. You will notice the default ReferenceType is Project Reference.

10. From the PackageNameFromProjectReference drop-down list, select MyDataFlow.dtsx. Click OK.

11. Right-click Parent Package and select Execute Package.

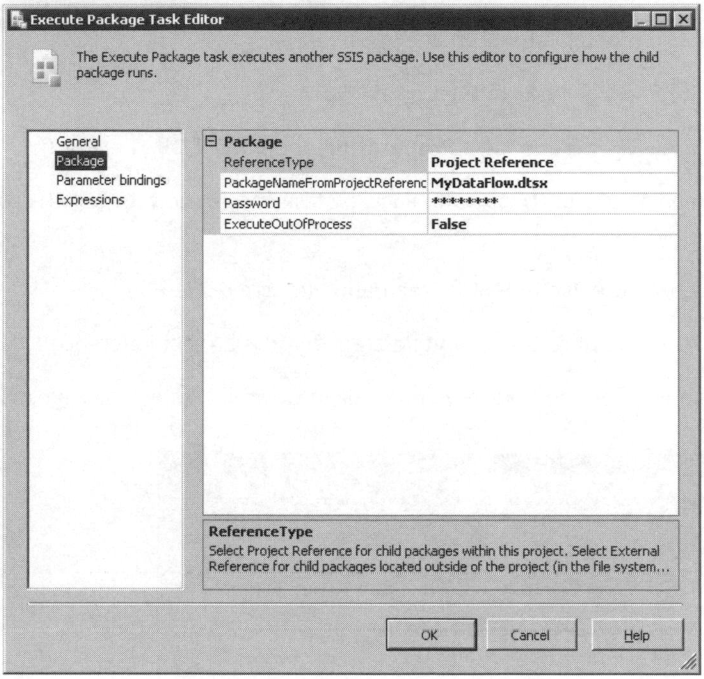

FIGURE 6-28 Setting up the Execute Package Task Load CDR File.

You have seen how to use the Execute Package Task.

Building and Deploying an Integration Services Project

After you have completed development of the SSIS project, you can build the project. In SSIS 2012, this produces an SSIS project deployment file (.ispac extension), which contains all the packages that you have developed and a manifest file, which contains metadata for the project and packages.

You can find out more about the properties of the project by right-clicking the project and choosing Properties. Figure 6-29 shows the project properties that you can modify.

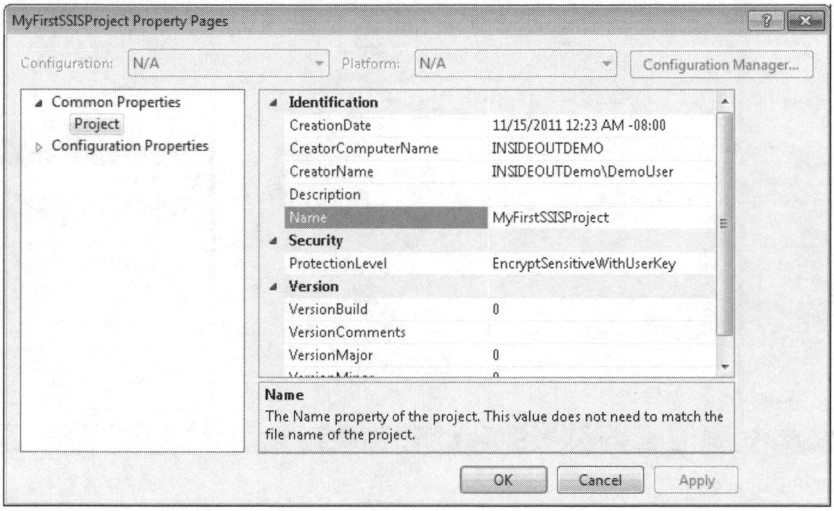

FIGURE 6-29 Project properties.

In SSIS 2012, the unit of deployment to the SSIS Catalog is the project deployment file. Using SQL Server Data Tools, after the project is built, you can use the Integration Services Deployment Wizard to deploy the project to the SSIS Catalog. To do this in SQL Server Data Tools, follow these steps:

1. Right-click the SSIS project and choose Build (Figure 6-30).
2. After the project has been built successfully, choose Deploy. This launches the Integration Services Deployment Wizard, which will guide you through the steps of deploying the project to the SSIS Catalog (see Figure 6-30).

> **Note** In earlier versions of SSIS, when you build an SSIS project in Business Intelligence Development Studio, and you have chosen to create the Deployment Utility, the deployment manifest will be created.

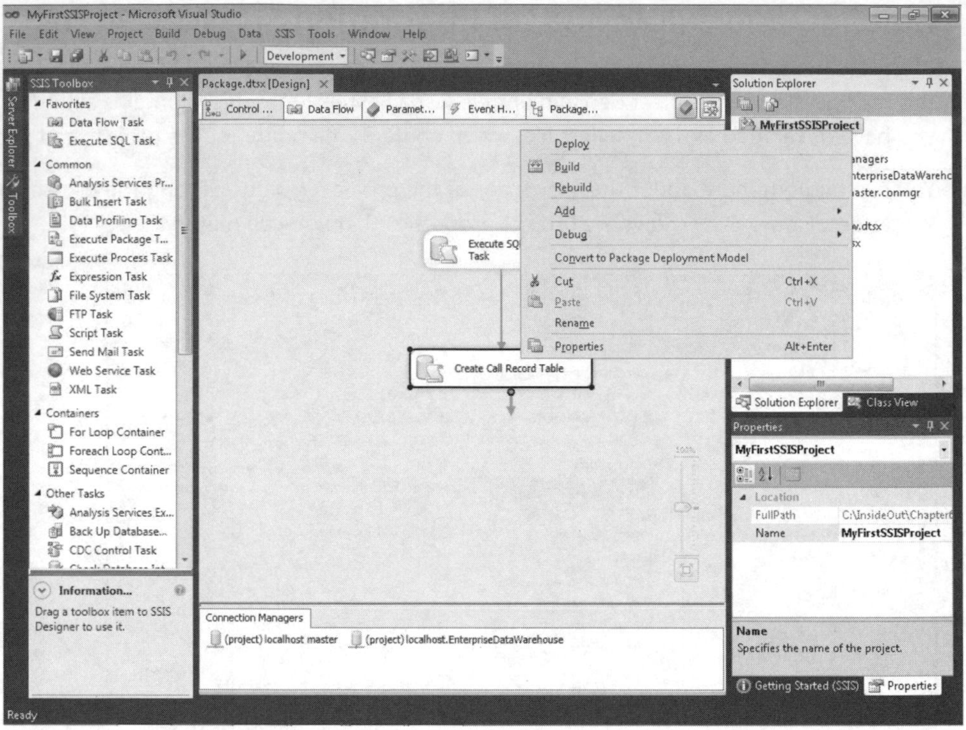

FIGURE 6-30 Building an SSIS project.

Summary

In this chapter, you gained essential skills that can help you develop an SSIS project. You learned how to use parameters, variables, and the Execute Package task to invoke the execution of packages in the same project. In addition, you also learned how to build the project and deploy it to the server.

CHAPTER 7

Understanding SSIS Connectivity

In This Chapter

SSIS is used as a universal platform for performing extract-transform-load (ETL) operations for data sourced from heterogeneous data sources. This is because SSIS doesn't centrally own or manage any specific connectivity option or technology. Rather, because it uses an extensible object model, SSIS can be easily extended to support a specific connectivity technology or data vendor. This flexibility has resulted in SSIS being interoperable with a multitude of available connectivity options. However, with such a large number of options, it can be difficult to make the correct connectivity choice between your data source and its respective destination. Understanding the various connectivity options will help you to choose an appropriate option for your scenario.

Previous Connectivity Options in SSIS

As you know already, SSIS supports all the major existing connectivity technologies for connecting to data sources. An easy way to discover all the connectivity options is to check out the available connection manager types, which are bundled with SSIS. Figure 7-1 shows the various connection manager types for which you can create a connection using the Add SSIS Connection Manager dialog box that appears when you choose to create a new connection.

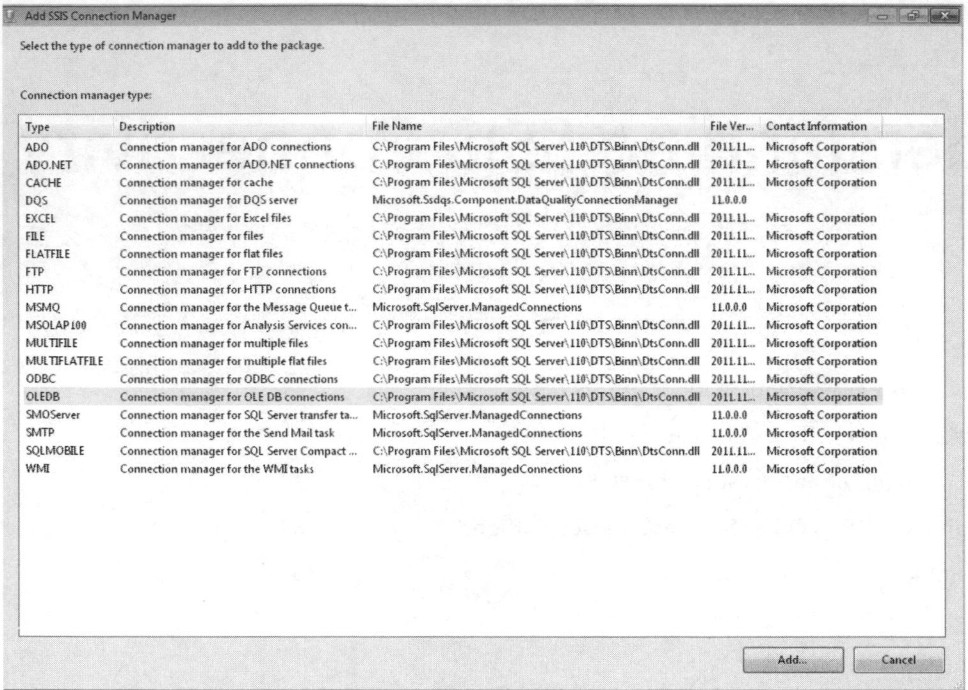

FIGURE 7-1 Types of connection managers available in SSIS.

Each type of connection manager in SSIS can connect using a different connectivity technology. Based on the technology it can also define its unique characteristics, which can optimize a connection.

Providers for Connectivity Technology

Some of the connection technologies will require installation on the system. For instance, choosing an OLE DB connection manager will let you choose all the OLE DB data providers that are installed in your system, as shown in Figure 7-2. In Figure 7-2, you can see that there are several OLE DB providers preinstalled with SSIS. In most cases, you will be able to get a custom provider from a specific data source vendor's website. Some of these providers might define several custom properties, which could help the provider optimize the connectivity to the data source. Hence, choosing a correct data provider along with the connectivity technology will help you optimize your connection.

You will notice a similar behavior with the other database connection technologies, such as Open Database Connectivity (ODBC) and ADO.NET. The ADO.NET provider dialog box displays a list of ADO.NET 2.0 data providers. However, with the ADO.NET OLE DB bridge provider, you can choose the OLE DB providers installed on your system with an ADO.NET connection manager.

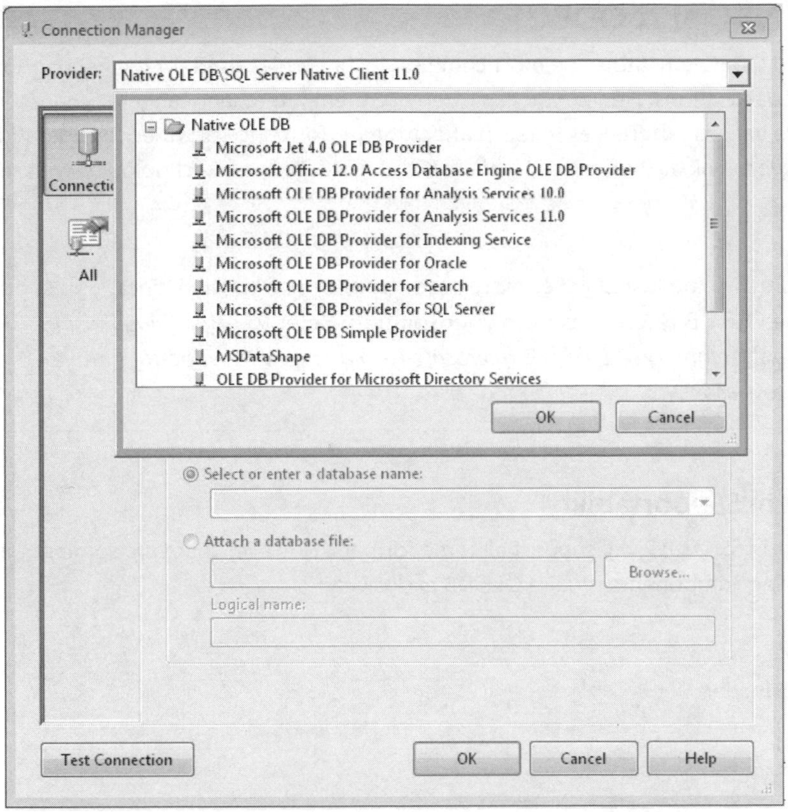

FIGURE 7-2 Types of OLE DB providers available preinstalled with SSIS.

Similarly, the ODBC connection manager uses the ADO.NET ODBC bridge provider. However, you will have to build a connection string using the ODBC control panel. This can be done by selecting the Use Connection String and pressing Build. This will invoke the ODBC control panel, which will display the available ODBC providers on your system.

> **Tip** ODBC has become a very popular connectivity technology. With more vendors adopting it as their technology of choice, you have better chances of finding an optimized provider with ODBC compared to the other technologies.

All providers will define a standard set of properties, which are displayed on the All tab of a Connection Manager dialog box. Some providers implement several custom properties to optimize the connections. These are defined in the Advanced property group.

OLE DB, ADO.NET, and ODBC

OLE DB, ADO.NET, and ODBC constitute the most common technologies used for connecting to most database sources and destinations. Hence, you can often use them interchangeably for your scenario. However, they do have various differences that can affect the performance or other considerations in your scenario. Let's have a look at the various facets that differentiate these technologies with respect to SSIS.

> **Note** SQL Server 2012 is the last SQL Server release to support OLE DB. Hence, you should proactively remove OLE DB references from your solution. Refer to *http://blogs.msdn.com/b/sqlnativeclient/archive/2011/08/29/microsoft-is-aligning-with-odbc-for-native-relational-data-access.aspx.*

Task and Transform Supportability

Most SSIS components in SSIS 2012 will support all three formats. However there are some notable exceptions. The following components require OLE DB exclusively:

- Bulk Insert task
- SQL Server destination
- Lookup
- Fuzzy lookup
- Fuzzy grouping
- Slowly changing dimensions
- Term extraction
- Term lookup

The OLE DB command, which was exclusive to OLE DB, now supports ADO.NET and ODBC connections. Other tasks and transforms will support all the previously mentioned connection technologies.

Performance

There are many online examples of performance comparisons between OLE DB, which is a native technology, and other managed technologies such as ADO.NET and ODBC. However, such a comparison should be extremely subjective to the environment. In Chapter 21, "SSIS Performance Best Practices," you will learn how to improve the overall performance of your package by making changes to your design. Changing the connection technology of your source or destination can be one such change.

The performance of your solution is more dependent on the provider than the provider technology that you use. For instance, a provider might work in a more optimal way than others connecting to the same database. It might not all be because of the connection technology, but the way a provider connects to the database. For instance, the Oracle connectors from Attunity generally prove faster than the inbox OLE DB connectors for Oracle. Both of them can further be optimized using optimized querying, calibrating correct batch sizes of rows, and avoiding string data types as described in the MSDN study at *http://blogs.msdn.com/sqlperf/archive/2009/08/14/using-ssis-to-get-data-out-of-oracle-a-big-surprise.aspx*.

However, you might find that there may be some cases where OLE DB can perform better than some other connection technologies because OLE DB is a native technology. ADO.NET and ODBC are written in managed code, providing benefits such as better abstraction and extensibility. This can result in a performance overhead in comparison to OLE DB, which is a Connection Object Model (COM)-based native technology.

To conclude, performance is highly subjective to the connectivity scenario that you have. You should perform the following steps to choose a provider with the correct connection technology:

1. Start by comparing performance using the different connectivity technologies that are feasible for you.
2. Use the performance measurement strategy described in Chapter 21 to benchmark performance across different providers.
3. Optimize the selected provider using strategies such as avoiding string to numeric data type conversion, calibrating batch sizes, and so on.
4. Iterate over the process multiple times until you achieve satisfactory performance levels.

Database Vendor Support

Each database vendor might release its own connectors respective to each technology. These connectors can vary in performance, supporting advanced options, data types, and so on. They can also be aligned to a specific database version. If you are using a specific database as a source and destination, you can usually find the different connectors offered by the database vendor.

See Also *See* http://social.technet.microsoft.com/wiki/contents/articles/ssis-and-data-sources.aspx *for a detailed list of connectors by various database vendors.*

New Connectivity Options in SSIS 2012

SSIS 2012 includes several additions with respect to connectivity. New ODBC support has been added for SSIS 2012 with the ODBC Source and Destination. These new components can use the ODBC connections to perform their respective operations. The following sections will give you an in-depth understanding of the components and the advanced features they incorporate. To leverage their complete benefits, however, you must understand the ODBC connection technology and its features.

Introducing ODBC

ODBC is a database application programming interface (API) based on the Call Level Interface (CLI) API definition, which is a standard defined by organizations such as X/Open and ISO/CA. It is a standard defined by Microsoft to access heterogeneous sources of data. Its standards ensure that it is independent of any specific database vendor and can be used for retrieving data from most data sources.

ODBC relies on maximum interoperability; that is, it can access different types of data sources with similar source code. It uses the concept of drivers where each driver acts as an interface for a type of database. Instead of making calls directly to the databases, ODBC applications can use these drivers to abstract database vendor-specific implementations.

ODBC and Database Vendors

ODBC with respect to SSIS has several benefits. Primarily, with OLE DB's deprecation, ODBC is becoming the de facto technology for most database vendors. Hence, most vendors are implementing ODBC connectivity drivers for connecting to their databases. As you know, ODBC provides a simple interface to implement complex properties such as mentioning specific database names or optimizing the way data is retrieved. You will learn in the next section how the ODBC source and destination can use these benefits to define properties such as row-wise parameter binding and so on.

ODBC Drivers

One of the advantages of ODBC is the number of available drivers to connect to a single type of data source. For instance, to connect to a SQL Server, by default you can use any one of three drivers installed on your system as shown in Figure 7-3.

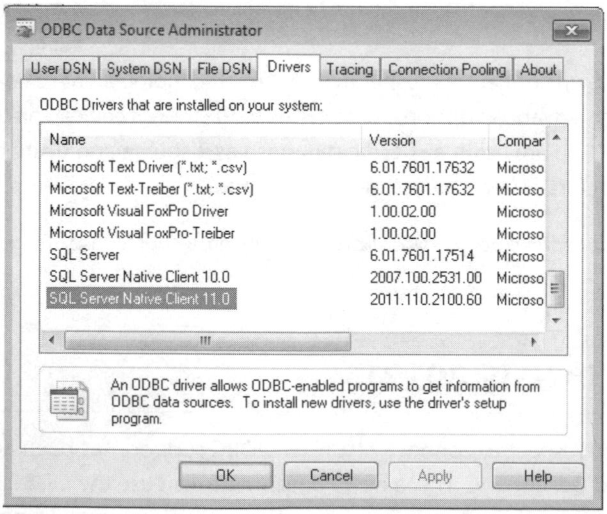

FIGURE 7-3 ODBC drivers.

The advantage of having multiple drivers is each of those drivers might be implemented in a different way; that is, a particular driver could implement some optimization that might enable faster data transfers. Other drivers could provide better error tracing or support for rare data types. Thus, you should choose a driver that best supports your requirement or specific features you might be looking for.

For instance, if you are looking for asynchronous execution of some ODBC methods when connecting to SQL Server, you will have to choose SQL Server native client 11.0 as described at *http://msdn.microsoft.com/en-us/library/cc280510(v=SQL.110).aspx.*

ODBC Tracing

ODBC connections have the added benefit of verbose logging. The ODBC driver manager has tracing capabilities that allow it to record any method calls made by any application into a log file. Understanding ODBC tracing will help you diagnose issues with the ODBC source and destination in SSIS.

See Also *Refer to the following link to understand the procedure to enable ODBC tracing:* http://support.microsoft.com/kb/274551.

In Figure 7-4, you can first see how you can enable an ODBC trace. In Listing 7-1, you can see a snippet of trace log recording some of the functions called by the ODBC source in the trace log that was created when we created a Data Flow task with a simple ODBC source and destination and executed them.

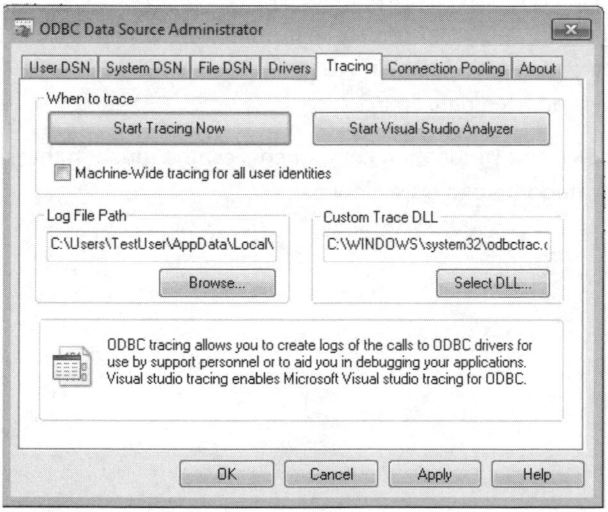

FIGURE 7-4 Enabling ODBC tracing.

LISTING 7-1 Snippet from ODBC trace for an SSIS ODBC source

```
DtsDebugHost    1018-13c0   ENTER SQLAllocHandle
          SQLSMALLINT                 1 <SQL_HANDLE_ENV>
          SQLHANDLE             0x0000000000000000
          SQLHANDLE *           0x000000000277D4E0

DtsDebugHost    1018-13c0   EXIT  SQLAllocHandle  with return code 0 (SQL_SUCCESS)
          SQLSMALLINT                 1 <SQL_HANDLE_ENV>
          SQLHANDLE             0x0000000000000000
          SQLHANDLE *           0x000000000277D4E0 ( 0x00000000002CBFE0)

DtsDebugHost    1018-13c0   ENTER SQLSetEnvAttr
          SQLHENV               0x00000000002CBFE0
          SQLINTEGER                 200 <SQL_ATTR_ODBC_VERSION>
          SQLPOINTER                 3 <SQL_OV_ODBC3>
          SQLINTEGER                   0

DtsDebugHost    1018-13c0   EXIT  SQLSetEnvAttr  with return code 0 (SQL_SUCCESS)
          SQLHENV               0x00000000002CBFE0
          SQLINTEGER                 200 <SQL_ATTR_ODBC_VERSION>
          SQLPOINTER                 3 <SQL_OV_ODBC3>
          SQLINTEGER                   0
```

ODBC Components for SSIS

This section looks at the new ODBC components introduced with SSIS 2012.

The ODBC Source and Destination are high-performance data integration components capable of using ODBC connections for acquiring and inserting data in a Data Flow task. They can be used to perform bulk copy operations for ODBC-supported data sources.

As shown in Figure 7-5, the ODBC Source and Destination components can be found in the SSIS toolbox in the sources and destinations categories of a Data Flow pane.

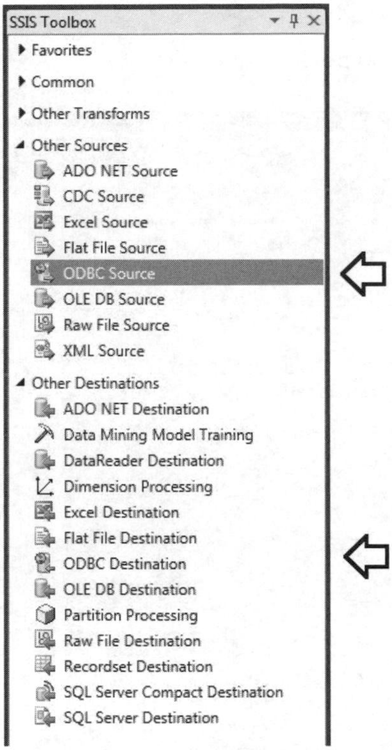

FIGURE 7-5 ODBC Source and Destination in SSIS Toolbox.

Now you will learn how you can use each of these components in our Data Flow task.

ODBC Source

The ODBC Source is a Data Flow source component that uses an ODBC connection that specifies the provider to be used. The source of the component can be a table, view, or SQL statement. The source would have data output columns that can be mapped to downstream transformations or destinations.

Basic Setup of ODBC Source

In Figure 7-6, you can see the ODBC Source basic editor dialog box.

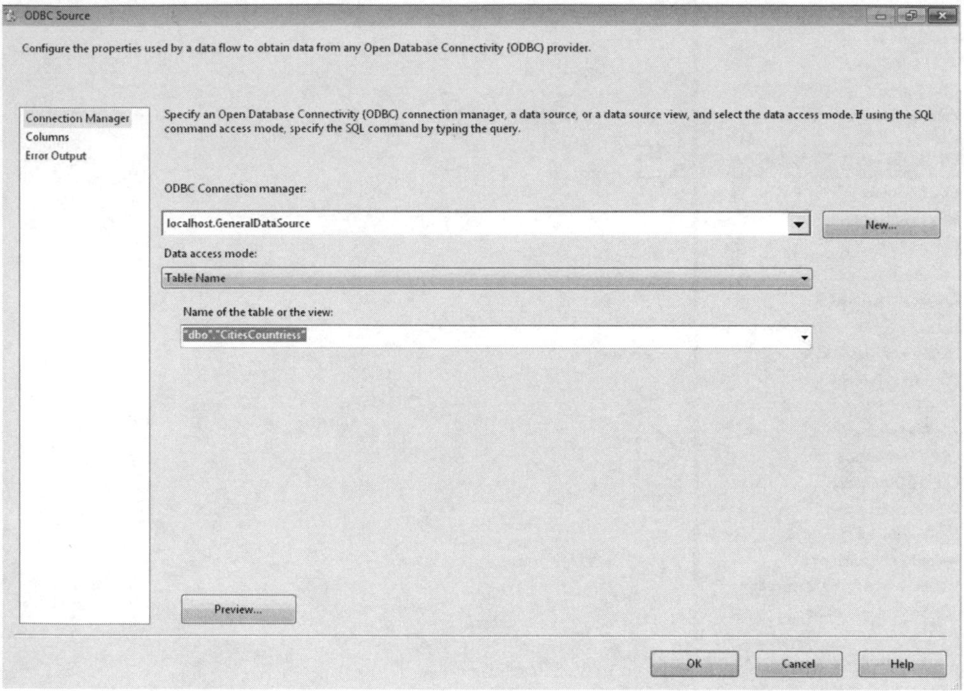

FIGURE 7-6 ODBC Source basic editor dialog box.

- **Connection Manager** You have to create an ODBC connection manager to use with the component. The ODBC connection manager can use any ODBC-supported driver installed on the system.
- **Data Access Mode** This defines the type of data source for the component. You can retrieve data from a table, view, or a SQL statement that returns a valid result set. You can use the Parse Query button to check the syntactical correctness of the SQL statement.

Note The ODBC Source component doesn't let you pass parameters to the SQL statement. Hence, if you need to use stored procedures, you will have to use procedures that don't require a parameter.

After the connection manager, data access mode, and data source (table or SQL statement) are correctly configured, you will be able to map the input columns in the Columns section of the dialog box.

- **Error Output** The ODBC Source component uses the standard SSIS error output model. Thus using the Error Output pane, you can configure redirection of rows on occurrence of errors such as invalid data conversion or truncation. Similar to the standard error output of a component, it will redirect the row data as well as the *ErrorCode and ErrorColumn.*

Bulk Fetch Logic

Before taking on the advanced properties of the ODBC component, you should understand how the component implements the bulk fetching capabilities.

The ODBC source can retrieve data from a data source in the following two ways:

- **Batch (default)** When you use the Batch option, the component will try to use the most efficient fetch method based on the ODBC provider being used. Using this property will result in the component (in the case of most modern ODBC providers) using the *SQLFetchScroll* function to retrieve data in batches of rows. However, if the provider doesn't support the function, then the component defaults to the next option available, Row by row.

See Also *For more information about SQLFetchScroll, refer to* http://msdn.microsoft.com/en-us/library/windows/desktop/ms714682(v=vs.85).aspx.

- **Row by row** When you use the Row by row option, the component will retrieve a single row at a time from the database using the *SQLFetch* function of ODBC.

In the next section, you will see how you can advise the ODBC Source component to use one of these two techniques for retrieving your data.

Advanced ODBC Source

ODBC Source has several advanced properties that let you customize the way you can access your data. You can configure these properties using the Custom Properties tab of the Advanced Editor of the component. Figure 7-7 shows the Custom Properties tab as well as the advanced properties.

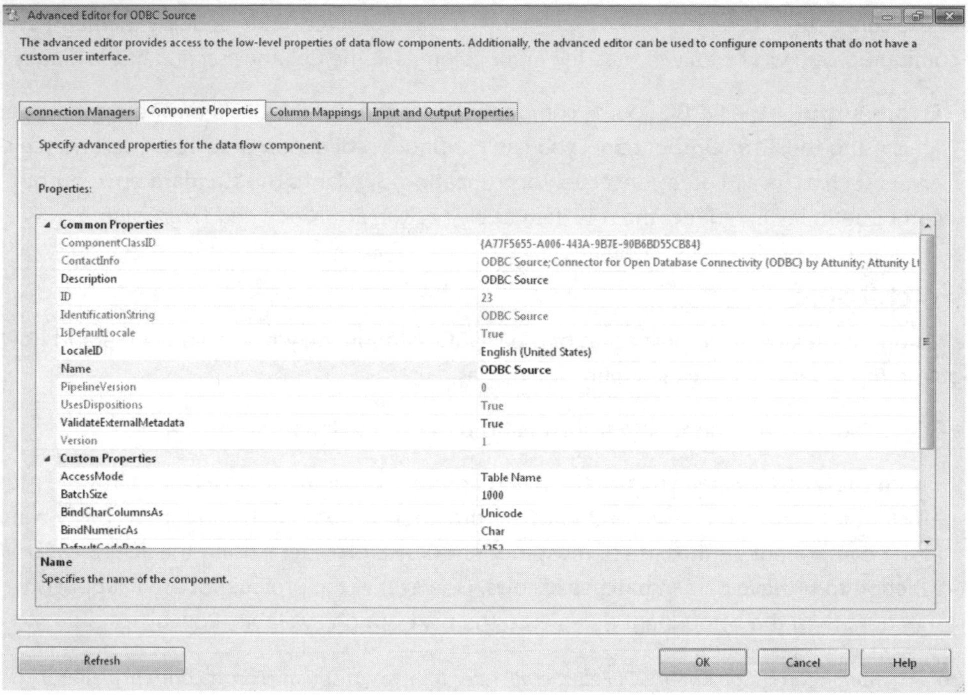

FIGURE 7-7 Advanced Editor of an ODBC Source component.

Here's a brief explanation of each of those properties.

- **AccessMode, SqlCommand, StatementTimeout, TableName** The *AccessMode* property similar to the Access Mode property from the basic setup. If Table is selected, the *TableName* property will be used to get the table or the view to be used in the query. If *SQL Command* is selected, the SqlCommand property value would be used as a query. The *StatementTimeout* property's value is used to define the timeout in seconds on the ODBC statements issued to the database. The value 0 uses the value defined in the ODBC data source.

- **BatchSize and FetchMethod** You can use the *FetchMethod* property to advise the ODBC Source component to use the Bulk Fetch logic to retrieve your data. As you know from the previous section, you can set the property's value either to Batch, which will use the bulk fetch capabilities of the provider, or Row by row, which fetches a single row at a time.

  If you have selected the *FetchMethod* as Batch and the provider supports the bulk fetching capabilities, then you can use the *BatchSize* property to advise the component about the number of records it should fit in a single batch. The component determines if the provider is capable of batch retrieval and defaults to 1 if it is not (or the *FetchMethod* uses Row by row).

- **BindNumericsAs** The component uses the value of this property to determine how it handles columns having types SQL_TYPE_NUMERIC or SQL_TYPE_DECIMAL. You can direct the component by choosing one of the following two options:
  - **Char** When this option is selected, the component would treat all the columns with the preceding types as strings. Thus, they would be converted into the standard ODBC character type SQL_C_CHAR. The component would make a direct data binding, which doesn't require conversion of the columns. This can result in performance gains depending on the amount of data you are retrieving. This is the default option.

    Using this option is useful when you are retrieving a large amount of data. In this case, you could retrieve all the numeric data into string columns at the destination and create a post-processing task for converting the string data into the respective numeric data. Hence, you can offload the expensive operation of data type conversion on to the database server.
  - **Numeric** When this option is selected, the component attempts to convert all the above numeric types of data from the data source into standard ODBC numeric type SQL_C_NUMERIC. This could result in performance overhead as the component has to perform data conversion on the retrieved numeric data. To do so, internally it calls the *SQLGetData* function individually for each numeric column and row, thus resulting in a performance overhead.

    You should use this option in the case of limited amounts of records. You should also choose this option if you think that the data conversion in SSIS is quicker than converting it at the destination database server.
- **BindCharColumnsAs** You can use this property to direct the component on how it should handle Unicode string data. This property is used by the component when the recordset has columns of the multibyte string types such as SQL_CHAR, SQL_VARCHAR, and SQL_LONGVARCHAR (CHAR columns).

  The possible options are the following:
  - **Unicode** When this option is selected, the component binds the CHAR columns with the preceding data types as ODBC wide string types (SQL_C_WCHAR). This binding can be performed for most ODBC 3.x providers as well as for several ODBC 2.x providers that support binding CHAR columns as wide strings.

    The advantage of this option is that (with the *ExposeCharColumnsAsUnicode* property set to *True*) you are not required to specify the actual code page for conversion when the columns get mapped to the Data Transformation Services (DTS) type DT_WSTR.
  - **ANSI** When this option is selected, the component binds the CHAR columns as regular strings (SQL_C_CHAR). The component code page must be set to match the code page of the data returned by the provider.

- **ExposeCharColumnsAsUnicode** Using this Boolean property, you can direct the component on how it will map the CHAR columns defined from the previous property to their equivalent DTS data type. If it is selected to be *False*, CHAR columns are mapped as multibyte strings (DT_STR). If it is selected to be *True*, the CHAR columns are mapped as wide strings (DT_WSTR).

ODBC Destination

The ODBC Destination is a Data Flow Destination component that uses an ODBC connection that specifies the provider to be used. The destination of the component can be defined as a table or a view. The destination would have data input columns that can be mapped to upstream transformations or sources.

Basic Setup of ODBC Destination

In Figure 7-8, you can see the ODBC Destination basic editor dialog box.

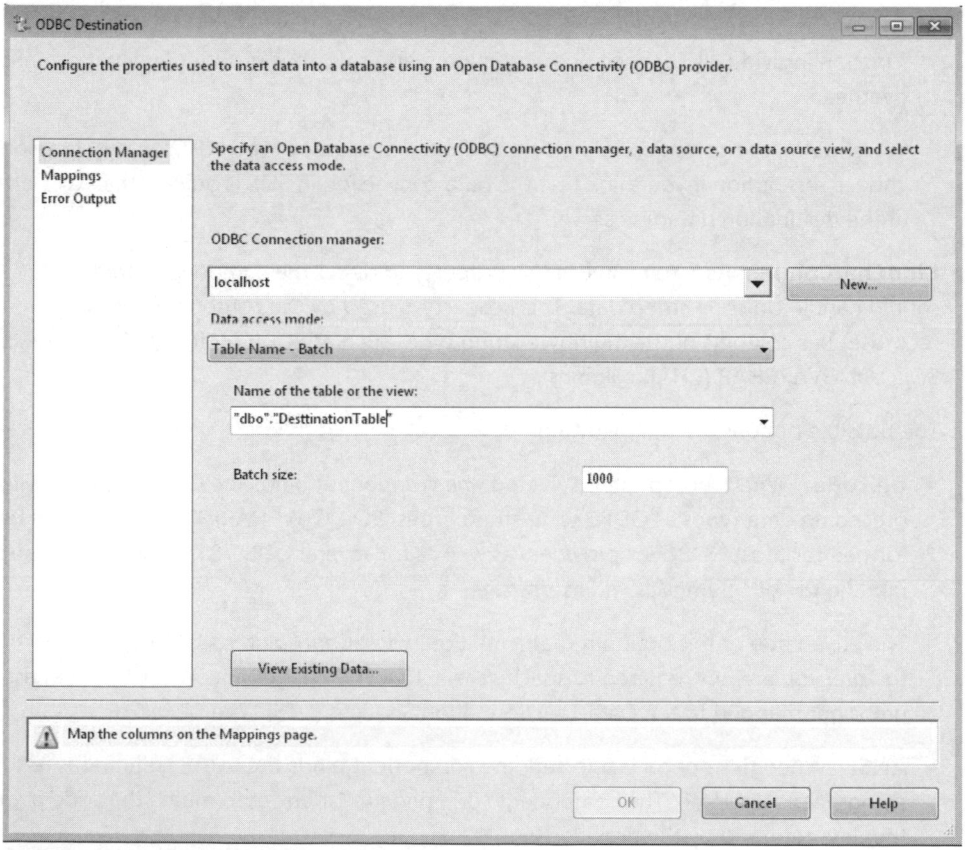

FIGURE 7-8 ODBC Destination basic editor dialog box.

- **Connection Manager** You have to create an ODBC connection manager to use with the component. The ODBC connection manager can use any ODBC-supported driver installed on the system.
- **Data Access Mode** This defines the way data would be inserted into the destination table or the view. The two possible options are Batch or Row by row. Check the following section on the bulk insert logic that this component uses to understand more about these options.
- **Batch Size** As you can see in Figure 7-8, the ODBC destination property lets you define a Batch Size property. The value mentioned is used to determine the number of records to be inserted in a single batch when you choose the Batch data access method for inserting data into your destination.
- **Error Output** The ODBC Destination component uses the standard SSIS error output model. Thus using the Error Output pane, you can configure redirection of rows on occurrence of errors such as invalid data conversion or truncation. Similar to the standard error output of a component, it will redirect the row data as well as the *ErrorCode* and *ErrorColumn*.

Bulk Insert Logic

Before understanding the advanced properties of the ODBC component, you should understand how the component implements the bulk insert capabilities.

The ODBC Destination can insert data into a destination in the following two ways:

- **Batch (default)** When you use the Batch option, the component will try to use the most efficient insertion method based on the ODBC provider being used. Using this property will result in the component (in the case of most modern ODBC providers) preparing an INSERT statement with parameters. Then, using row-wise array parameter binding where array size is determined by the *BatchSize* parameter, it would prepare the final ODBC INSERT statement. However, if the provider doesn't support the function, then the component defaults to the next option available, Row by row.
- **Row by row** With this option, the component would prepare an ODBC INSERT statement with parameters and use the *SQLExecute* ODBC function to insert rows one at a time.

Now you'll see how you can further tune the ODBC Destination component using the advanced editor.

Advanced ODBC Destination

ODBC Destination has several advanced properties that let you customize the way you can insert your data. These properties can be configured using the Custom Properties tab of the Advanced Editor of the component. Figure 7-9 shows you the Custom Properties tab as well as the advanced properties.

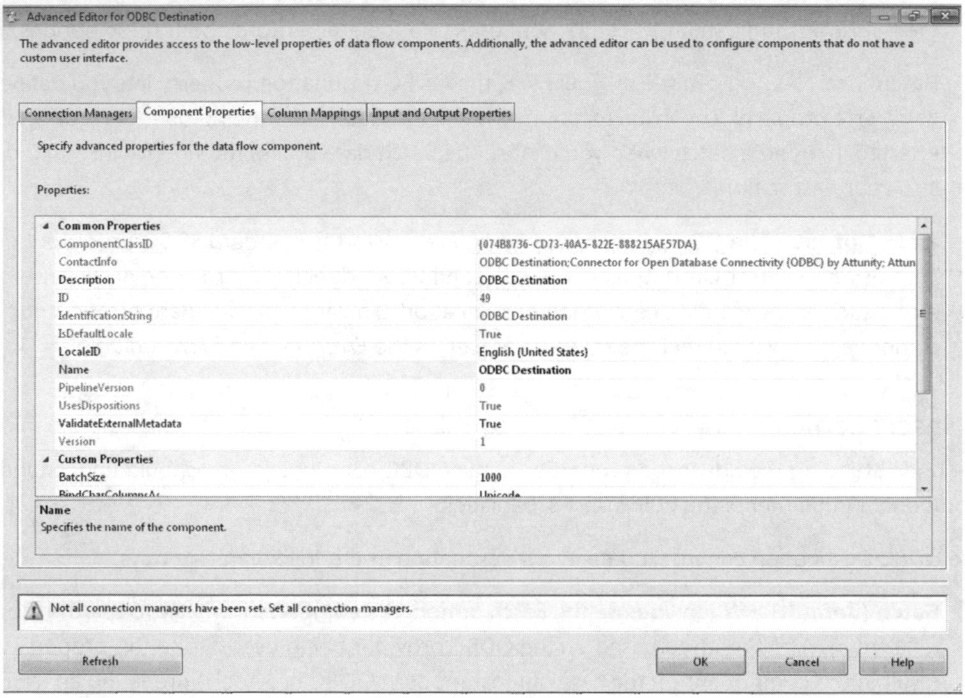

FIGURE 7-9 Advanced Editor of an ODBC Destination component.

Now let's look at each of those properties:

- **StatementTimeout, TableName** The *TableName* property is used to determine the table or the view where data is to be inserted. The *StatementTimeout* property's value is used to define the timeout in seconds on the ODBC statements issued to the database. The value 0 uses the value defined in the ODBC data source.

- **BatchSize and InsertMethod** You can use the InsertMethod property to advise the ODBC Source component to use the Bulk Insert logic to insert your data. As you know from the previous section, you can set the property's value either to Batch, which will use the bulk insert capabilities of the provider, or Row by row, which inserts a single row at a time.

  If you have selected the *InsertMethod* as Batch and the provider supports the bulk inserting capabilities, then you can use the *BatchSize* property to advise the component about the number of records it should fit in a single batch. The component determines if the provider is capable of batch retrieval and defaults to 1 in case it is not (or the *InsertMethod* uses Row by row).

- **TransactionSize** The *TransactionSize* property determines the number of INSERT statements to be issued in a single transaction. The default value is 0, which signifies that the component will work in autocommit mode (commit after each statement).

> **Note** The ODBC connection manager doesn't support distributed transactions (SupportsDTCTransactions defaults to False). Also, if you set the RetainSame Connection property of the connection manager to True, the TransactionSize property should be set to the default value (that is, 0) because it will not be able to support the transaction over multiple components.

- **BindNumericsAs** The component uses the value to this property to determine how it handles columns having types SQL_TYPE_NUMERIC or SQL_TYPE_DECIMAL. This property is the same as the *BindNumericAs* property described in the ODBC Source component.

  Thus, using the default option Char, you can ask the component to bind the columns as strings. Because the data binding is direct and intermediate conversion and validation are not required for each numeric column, the overall performance is faster.

- **BindCharColumnsAs** You can use this property to direct the component on how it should handle Unicode string data. This property is used by the component when the recordset has columns of the multibyte string types such as SQL_CHAR, SQL_VARCHAR, and SQL_LONGVARCHAR (CHAR columns). The property is similar to the *BindCharColumnsAs* property of the ODBC Source component.
- **LobChunkSize** Using this property you can specify the size of the chunk used for Large Object (LOB) columns when using a table with LOB data. A chunk can be described as one or more memory blocks to store LOB data. This property will be used by the ODBC destination component to define LOB chunk size for adapters that support this property. For instance, Oracle can support the LOB chunk size as a connection property.

Connectivity Considerations for SSIS

64-Bit and SSIS

Most users of SSIS use 64-bit systems to maintain their SQL Server environment. Such 64-bit installations need some special considerations with respect to SSIS. In the following section, you will learn more about these considerations and how you can use 64-bit or 32-bit versions of your adapters to connect to external data sources.

64-Bit Processors and WOW64

There are different varieties of 64-bit architectures available for processors. The most common ones are the x86-64, which AMD processors define as AMD64 and Intel defines as EMT64, or the IA64, which are used in the Intel Itanium series of processors.

> **Note** SQL Server 2012 requires an x86-64 installation of Windows Server and no longer supports IA64 installs. Check *http://msdn.microsoft.com/en-us/library/ms143506(v=sql.110).aspx.*

Because application compilations depend on the underlying processor architecture, there might be effects on functionality based on the type of processor on which the application is running. However, Windows (Windows XP and later) allows you to execute 32-bit applications (applications compiled on x86 compilers) on 64-bit processors. The x86-64 architecture includes the hardware-level support for 32-bit instructions. Hence, WOW64 efficiently switches between the 32-bit and 64-bit modes. On the IA64 processor, the WOW64 translates the 32-bit instructions into their 64-bit equivalents, thus enabling the execution of a 32-bit application.

See Also *To learn more about WOW64 and its other considerations check out this MSDN article:* http://msdn.microsoft.com/en-us/library/aa384249(v=VS.85).aspx.

SSIS, as does any other Windows application, has dependencies based on the system architecture that is used to execute it. In the next few sections, you will learn how you can configure SSIS to execute on different kind of environments and how it affects your connectivity.

> **Tip** Execute DTS2000 Packages task, which is deprecated in SSIS 2012, is a 32-bit-only task and required a 32-bit runtime to execute. Similarly, some adapters might be 32-bit only, which will require a 32-bit runtime to execute.

SSIS Tools on 64-Bit Architecture

Although the WOW64 application allows you to execute 32-bit applications on 64-bit systems, a single process will not be able to handle code that is compiled in two different architectures. SSIS invokes a number of dynamic-link libraries (DLLs) during execution. For instance, for loading a connectivity adapter, SSIS will load the respective DLL. However, as mentioned earlier, a 64-bit application cannot load a 32-bit DLL or vice versa. This limits SSIS and its various tools available to interoperate between the previously mentioned architectures. Table 7-1 shows the SSIS tools and the various architectures on which they can operate.

TABLE 7-1 SSIS tools and processor architectures

Tool	64-bit	32-bit
SQL Server Data Tools	No	Yes
DTExec	Yes	Yes
DTExecUI	Yes	Yes
SSIS catalog	Yes	Yes
SSIS packages on SQL Agent	Yes	Yes

As you can see in Table 7-1, some of the tools are not available for a given architecture. In the next section, you explore which SSIS configuration options you can use with different tools to enable executions on 32-bit or 64-bit architectures.

When you install SSIS using the SQL Server setup on a 64-bit machine, only the 64-bit runtime and tools are installed. If you are required to execute packages in 32-bit mode, you will have to select the additional options to install the 32-bit runtime and tools. For example, on a 64-bit computer running an x86-64 operating system, you must select Management Tools Complete – SQL Server Data Tools to install SQL Server Data Tools. This is because SQL Server Data Tools has only a 32-bit installation, as elaborated in the next sections.

SQL Server Data Tools

The SQL Server Data Tools application is compiled on a 32-bit architecture. Thus, it can invoke only 32-bit compiled DLLs, so you have to install the 32-bit adapters if you want to use them during design time. You will not be able to use 64-bit adapters even if you have them installed at design time. That is why most vendors provide you both architecture varieties of their adapters. Thus, you must install both adapters even if you might want to use just the 64-bit adapter. For instance, if you have installed a 64-bit Oracle connectivity adapter, you must install the 32-bit adapter to configure its properties during design time on SQL Server Data Tools.

However, in some cases although you want to design your package using the 32-bit adapter, you might actually want your package to use the 64-bit adapter during actual execution. You can do this using the *Run64BitRuntime* property of the SSIS project. The property can be found in the Configuration Properties | Debugging section of the Property pages. Setting this property to *True* will make sure that your package is executed in 64-bit mode both during development and later executions.

In Figure 7-10, you can see how to set the *Run64BitRuntime* property of the project.

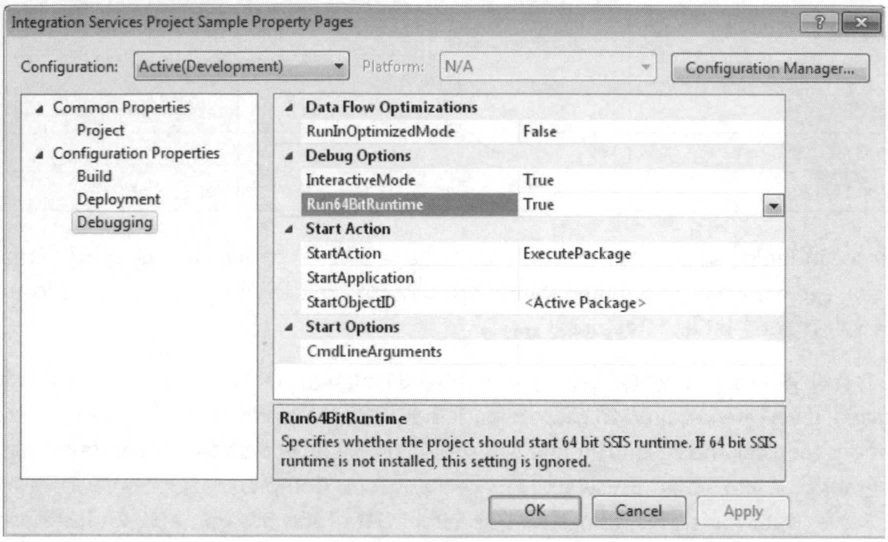

FIGURE 7-10 *Run64BitRuntime* property of a project.

> **Note** *Run64BitRuntime* defaults to *True* when SSIS is installed on a 64-bit computer.

As with SQL Server Data Tools, there are similar properties for other tools and systems where you can execute an SSIS package as discussed in the following sections.

SSIS Catalog and Package Execution Tools

In the SSIS Catalog, you can choose to execute your packages using the Execute Package dialog box or using T-SQL or the SSIS Management Model. Let's look at how you can configure your action to execute the package using a 64-bit runtime.

In Figure 7-11, you can see the 32-Bit Runtime check box. Selecting this check box will ensure that your package is executed using the 32-bit runtime and all DLLs loaded are 32-bit versions.

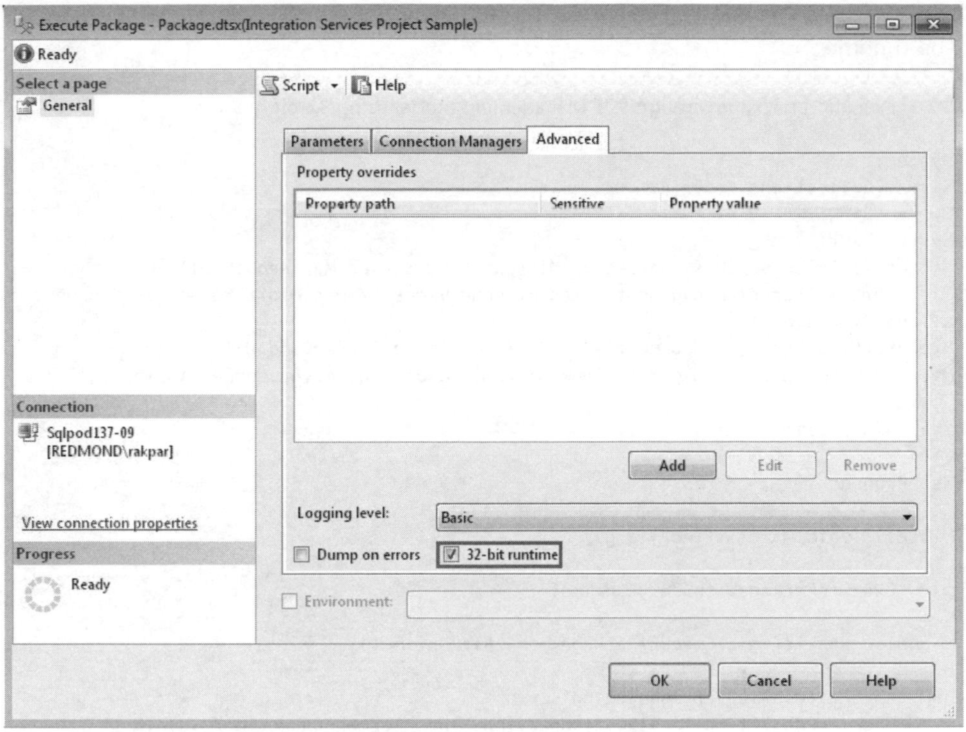

FIGURE 7-11 32-bit runtime in the Execute Package dialog box.

Listing 7-2 shows you how you can execute a package using the T-SQL API with specifying the 32-bit runtime to *true*.

LISTING 7-2 T-SQL API for executing a package using 32-bit runtime

```
   DECLARE @execution_id bigint

EXEC [SSISDB].[catalog].[create_execution]
@package_name=N'Package.dtsx'
,@execution_id=@execution_id OUTPUT
,@folder_name=N'Folder'
,@project_name=N'Integration Services Project Sample'
,@use32bitruntime=True -- Sets the parameter for using the 32-bit runtime
,@reference_id=Null

DECLARE @var0 smallint = 1

EXEC [SSISDB].[catalog].[set_execution_parameter_value]
@execution_id
,@object_type=50
,@parameter_name=N'LOGGING_LEVEL'
,@parameter_value=@var0

EXEC [SSISDB].[catalog].[start_execution] @execution_id
GO
```

Listing 7-3 shows you how you can execute a package using the SSIS Management Model using the 32-bit runtime.

LISTING 7-3 Executing package through SSIS Management Model using 32-bit runtime

```
using System;
using System.Collections.Generic;
using System.Linq;
using System.Text;
using Microsoft.SqlServer.Dts.Runtime; //Microsoft.SqlServer.ManagedDTS.dll
using Microsoft.SqlServer.Management.IntegrationServices; //Microsoft.SqlServer.Management.
IntegrationServices.dll
using Microsoft.SqlServer.Management.Smo; //Microsoft.SqlServer.Smo.dll
using Microsoft.SqlServer.Management.Common; //Microsoft.SqlServer.ConnectionInfo.dll

namespace SSISSamples
{
    class Program
    {
        static void Main(string[] args)
        {
           ExecutePackageWith32BitRuntime();
        }
        public static void ExecutePackageWith32BitRuntime()
        {
            //Create a server connection
            ServerConnection localhostconnection = new ServerConnection("localhost");
            Server localhost = new Server(localhostconnection);
            IntegrationServices iscatalog = new IntegrationServices(localhost);
            //Get the package
            CatalogFolder folder = iscatalog.Catalogs["SSISDB"].Folders["Folder"];
            ProjectInfo proj = folder.Projects["Integration Services Project Sample"];
            Microsoft.SqlServer.Management.IntegrationServices.PackageInfo pkg = proj.
            Packages["Package.dtsx"];
            pkg.Execute(true, null); //public long Execute(bool use32RuntimeOn64,
            EnvironmentReference reference);
        }

    }
}
```

Figure 7-12 shows how you can configure SQL Agent to use the 32-bit runtime to execute a package.

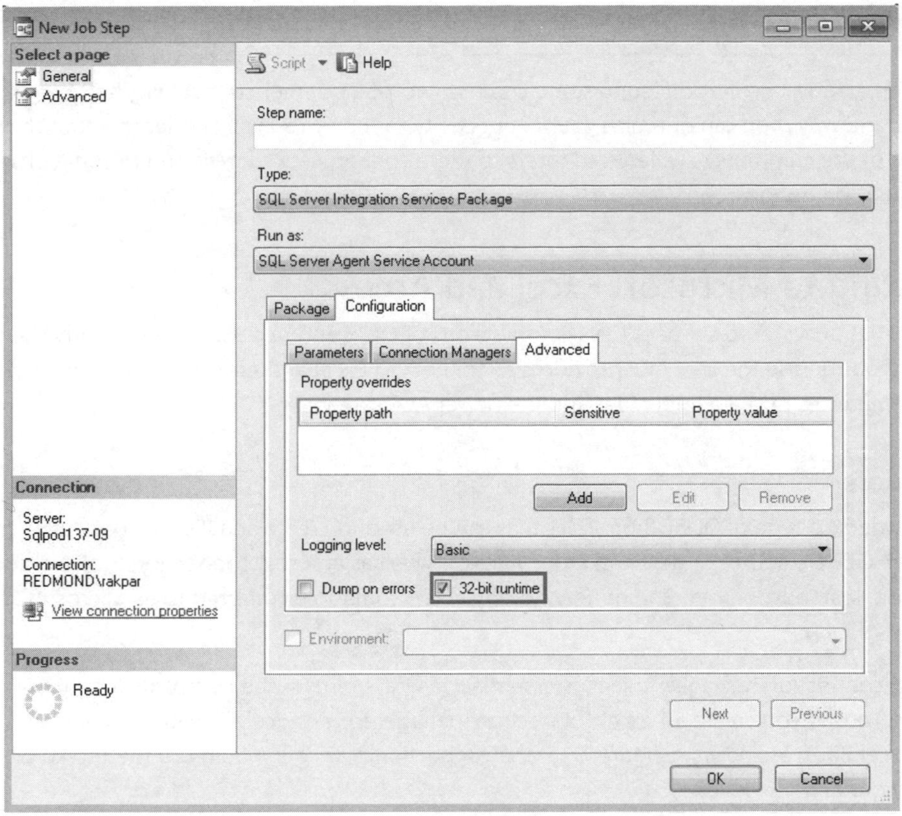

FIGURE 7-12 Executing a package using 32-bit runtime on SQL Agent.

When you install SQL Server Integration Services, both the 32-bit and 64-bit versions of DTExec and DTExecUI are installed on your computer. They are usually installed in the following locations:

- **For 64 bit** <*drive*>:\Program Files\Microsoft SQL Server\110\DTS\Binn
- **For 32 bit** <*drive*>:\Program Files (x86)\Microsoft SQL Server\110\DTS\Binn

You can invoke the respective DTExec or DTExecUI to execute the package in either 32-bit or 64-bit format.

Connectivity to Other Sources and Destinations

In this section, you will be introduced to some common non-SQL Server connectivity sources and destinations and ways you can optimize your connectivity to them. You will also learn about the various nuances of the commonly available adapters to these connectivity sources and destinations and their configuration options.

Connecting to Microsoft Excel and Access

SSIS uses the Jet provider to connect to various versions of Excel and Access. However, with Microsoft Office 2007 you can use the new ACE providers to connect to Excel and Access. The following section explores the nuances of the primitive Jet and the newer ACE providers.

Jet Providers

The Jet provider is a type of OLE DB provider that can be used to create an OLE DB connection manager with the OLE DB source or destination for Access as well as an Excel connection for Excel source or destination. It stands for Joint Engine Technology and is sometimes referred to as Microsoft Jet Engine.

The Excel connection manager, in fact, is essentially a wrapper over the Microsoft Jet 4.0 OLE DB provider. Thus, if you create an Excel connection manager for an Excel file with versions prior to Microsoft Excel 2007, as shown in Figure 7-13, the connection manager would use the Jet 4.0 OLE DB provider to connect.

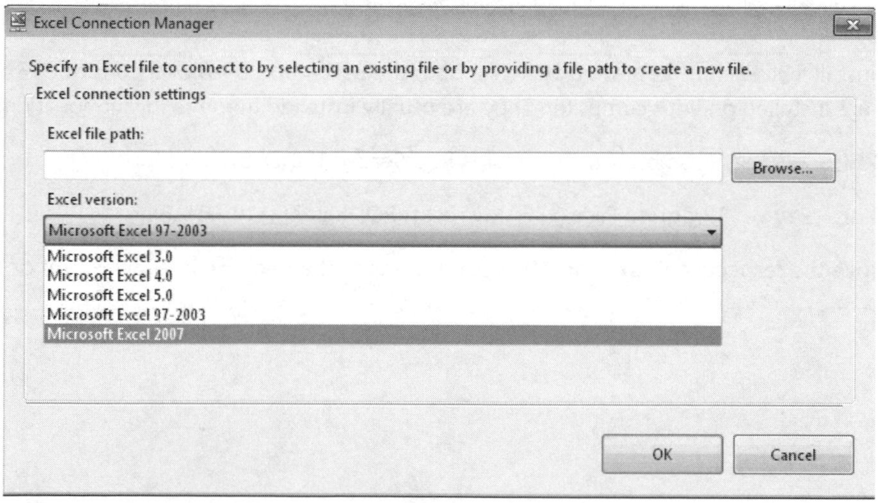

FIGURE 7-13 Excel versions that use the Jet 4.0 OLE DB provider.

Similarly, you can use the Jet 4.0 OLE DB provider to connect to Microsoft Access data files, as shown in Figure 7-14.

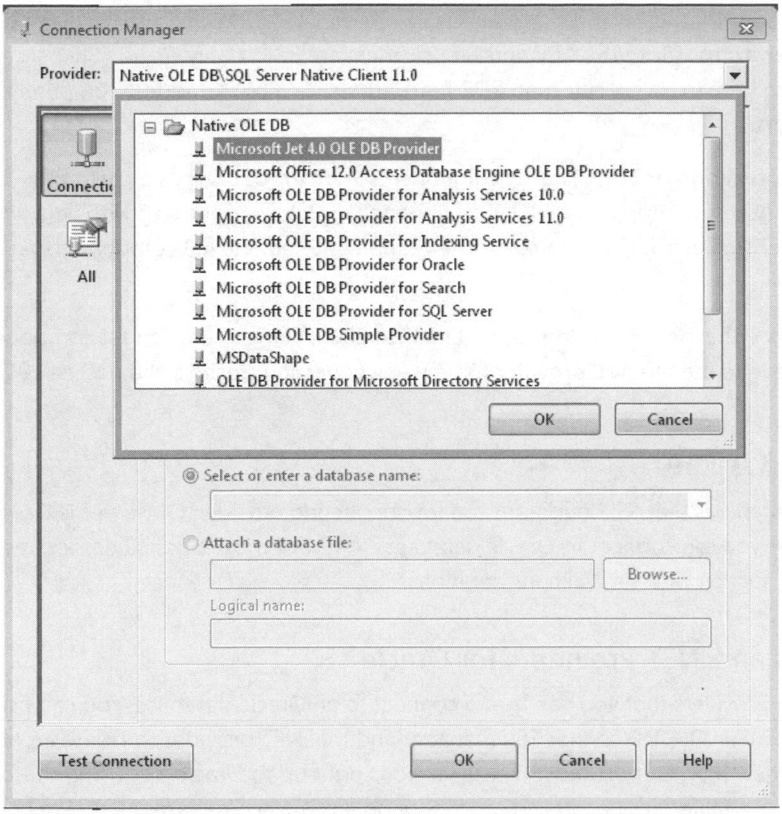

FIGURE 7-14 OLE DB connection manager with Jet 4.0 OLE DB provider to connect to Access.

See Also *For more about Microsoft Jet providers, see* http://msdn.microsoft.com/en-us/library/windows/desktop/ms681754(v=vs.85).aspx.

ACE Providers

Microsoft Office 2007 and later versions use the ACE providers for connectivity. Thus, for connecting to Microsoft Office 2007 files, you have to use the ACE providers provided in SSIS. If, as in Figure 7-13, you choose a Microsoft Excel 2007 file, it will default to use the ACE provider with a connection string such as Provider=Microsoft.ACE.OLEDB.12.0;Data Source=C:\Book2.xlsx;Extended Properties="Excel 12.0 XML;HDR=YES";

The ACE provider supports only the Microsoft Office 2007 data and cannot be used with previous versions.

Other Considerations for ACE and Jet

Now let's look at some other considerations that you must understand when choosing a correct provider for your scenario.

- **32-bit considerations** Both the ACE and Jet providers are 32-bit only. Thus, SSIS packages containing them have to be executed on a 32-bit runtime in WOW64 mode or on purely 32-bit computers.
- **Functional deprecation of Jet** The Jet components were introduced as a part of the Microsoft Data Access Components (MDAC) components. However, starting with version 2.6, MDAC no longer supports Jet components. The Jet database engine 4.0 components are now deprecated.
- **Office versions** Thus, for all versions up until Office 2005, you can use the Jet components, whereas you have to use the ACE provider for any newer version starting with Office 2007.

Connecting to Oracle

One of the common databases that SSIS packages use for connecting outside SQL Server is Oracle. There are multiple ways you can connect to Oracle databases. A few of those possibilities are mentioned in the following section with several considerations.

Microsoft OLE DB and .NET Providers for Oracle

These are the standard providers that you can use to connect to an Oracle database. You can use the OLE DB provider to create an OLE DB connection manager and the .NET provider to create an ADO .NET connection manager. They support most Oracle versions right up to Oracle 11i. Using these providers, you can query a table, view, or stored procedure on an Oracle database. As shown in Figure 7-15, you can create either an OLE DB or ADO.NET connection manager using the providers installed.

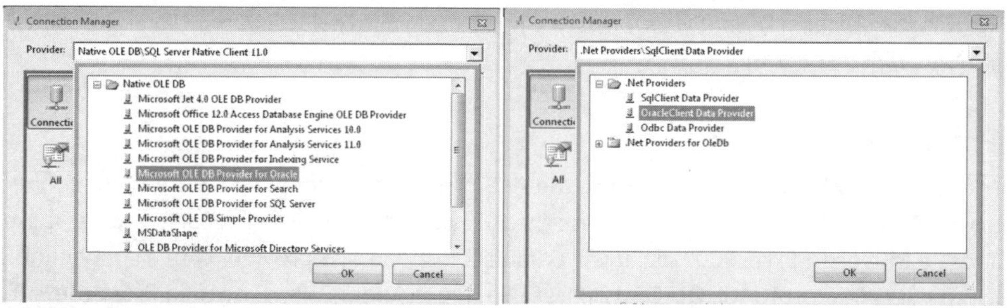

FIGURE 7-15 Microsoft OLE DB and ADO.NET providers for Oracle.

The advantage of these providers is they are extremely simple to use with the most basic of configurations required. They are also installed along with SSIS out of the box and hence are certified by Microsoft. However, the OLE DB provider lacks 64-bit support. Also, both these providers do not support any high-performance or bulk data loading techniques.

Oracle OLE DB Provider

The Oracle OLE DB provider can be used to create OLE DB and ADO.NET connection managers. There are both 32-bit and 64-bit versions of this adapter available. You can choose the Oracle database version-specific driver download from the Oracle downloads website. In addition to connection to Oracle tables, views, and stored procedures, they can also be used to perform custom Oracle connectivity features or implementation of Oracle-specific methods of querying. They also incorporate Oracle high-performance connectivity, resulting in faster data retrieval.

See Also *See more about ODAC components at* http://www.oracle.com/technetwork/topics/dotnet/tech-info/odac-112-r4-ds-1444666.pdf.

You can install these components by either downloading the ODAC components or the Oracle client for a specific Oracle database version. Once installed, you can use them while creating a connection manager as shown in Figure 7-16.

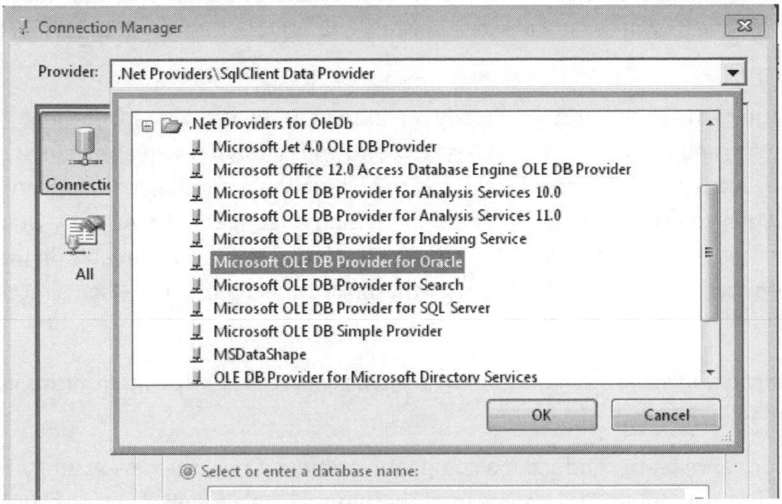

FIGURE 7-16 Oracle OLE DB providers for SSIS.

This provider is useful to perform high-performance data loading. However, it is known to have issues with data type mapping between SSIS and Oracle data types. For instance, using the NUMBER column from Oracle would result in the truncation of all decimal places as it gets mapped to a DT_I4 data type in SSIS.

ODBC Connections

With the ODBC source and destinations in SSIS 2012, you can also use ODBC to connect to Oracle data sources. You can create an ODBC data source for the Oracle database using the several available options. You can use either the Microsoft ODBC for Oracle or Oracle's own ODBC driver. Microsoft's ODBC driver comes standard in Microsoft Data Access Components, and the Oracle ODBC driver is installed as a part of the ODAC installations. You can choose to create an ODBC data source using the ODBC data source administrator.

The Microsoft ODBC driver for Oracle is ODBC 2.5 compliant and supports only 32-bit executions. It has support through Oracle 7.x and only limited support for Oracle 8 and later. Hence, it might not support a lot of the newer data types such as Unicode data types, BLOBS, CLOBS, and so on.

Attunity Connectors for Oracle

Attunity has provided connectors for SSIS to connect to Oracle. These connectors are available through Microsoft downloads, and they support Oracle database versions 9.X and later. These connectors use Oracle's OCI client interface with its array binding techniques. They also use the concept of direct path APIs, providing significantly better performance compared to the previous connectors.

See Also *To understand more about Oracle's direct path technology, refer to* http://docs.oracle.com/cd/B28359_01/appdev.111/b28395/oci13obn.htm.

The Attunity connectors are installed as separate components. These include various source and destination components as well as a different type of connection manager. Thus, packages that use OLE DB or ADO.NET components will require a redesign when you replace them with the Attunity connectors.

The biggest advantage of the connectors, as already mentioned, is the use of the OCI client interface with array binding and use of direct path APIs to perform fast loads. In an array binding load scenario, the data is loaded into Oracle tables in batches where the entire batch is inserted in the same transaction. When you choose to perform fast load using direct path, the Attunity Oracle destination component uses the OCI direct path protocol for loading into the Oracle table. In most cases, this would perform better than Microsoft's out-of-the-box connectors, as they lack direct loading capabilities.

See Also *For more information regarding Attunity's fast loading techniques refer to* http://msdn.microsoft.com/en-us/library/ee470675(v=sql.100).aspx.

The SQL Server performance team conducted a comparative study of how the new Attunity connectors measure up against the regular SSIS connectors. They immediately found a performance improvement by just using the Attunity connectors. They also performed various tuning and optimization steps such as the following:

- Creating batches of row sizes and adjusting the number of rows in a batch to find an optimal size
- Avoiding type conversion of numeric data types by converting them to strings

The preceding tuning techniques are not proprietary to the Attunity components; you can use them with other components as generic performance tuning techniques.

Note You can find the detailed study here: *http://blogs.msdn.com/b/sqlperf/archive/2009/08/14/using-ssis-to-get-data-out-of-oracle-a-big-surprise.aspx.*

The Attunity connectors for Oracle version 1.2 are available for all SSIS versions earlier than SSIS 2012. For SSIS 2012, you will have to install the Attunity connectors for Oracle version 2.0. They can be downloaded from the Microsoft Download Center at *http://www.microsoft.com/en-us/download/details.aspx?id=29283*.

In addition to the existing features, the Attunity connectors for Oracle version 2.0 will have support for LOB data types. Here's the resultant mapping when you use the LOB data types.

- CLOB gets mapped to DT_TEXT.
- NCLOB gets mapped to DT_NTEXT.
- BLOB gets mapped to DT_NTEXT.

LOBs are supported by the source component and the destination component in the Array Load mode only. LOB data types are not supported in the FastLoad direct path mode.

You cannot install the Attunity connectors for Oracle version 1.2 and later on an IA64 machine; you must use these connectors only on an x86 or an x64 machine.

Creating Custom Components

In rare cases, you might find that the available connection managers or source or destination components are insufficient for your scenario. You might have a data source that has special connectivity requirements or you might be aware of some optimization technique that is not implemented in already available connectivity components. This scenario requires you to create your own custom components.

You can create custom components such as a source or a destination or even a connection manager using the SSIS design time and runtime API. Let's take a product sample, for instance. For this scenario, we need to store the dataset output from a source or transformation into an XML file or a runtime variable that can later be used as an XML source. The custom component product sample can be found at *http://msftisprodsamples.codeplex.com/*. Let's look at the *DataSetDestination* product sample as an example of creating a custom destination component.

In the sample, all the columns apart from ones with type *DT_BYTES* and *DT_IMAGE* are converted into their respective types. You now have a special requirement where you need to cast *DT_GUID* columns into strings and store them in the variable or the XML file. Let us see how we can modify this existing sample to do that.

The most important methods in the destination component are the ones that are executed when it processes the input data. This is done in the *ProcessInput* method in the *DataSetDest.cs* for our sample. Listing 7-4 shows how two methods—*ProcessInput,* which is an overridden method, and *GetDataTable,* which is a method of this component—are modified to make the destination component store GUIDs as strings. Check for the comment *//Cast GUIDS to strings*, which denote the code changes from the original version. For all of the code changes, check the modified *DataSetDest.cs* in the companion content for this chapter.

LISTING 7-4 Modifying the *DataSetDestination* component

```
#region ProcessInput
/// <summary>
/// Add the rows from the input buffer to the the DataSet.
/// </summary>
/// <param name="inputID">The ID of the IDTSInput100</param>
/// <param name="buffer">The PipelineBuffer containing the records to process</param>
public override void ProcessInput(int inputID, PipelineBuffer buffer)
{
    if (buffer == null)
    {
        throw new ArgumentNullException("buffer");
    }

    if (!buffer.EndOfRowset)
    {
        while (buffer.NextRow() == true)
        {
            // IDTSInput100 input = ComponentMetaData.InputCollection.
            GetObjectByID(inputID);
            DataRow row = this.runtimeDataTable.NewRow();
            for (int x = 0; x < this.columnInfos.Length; x++)
            {
                ColumnInfo ci = (ColumnInfo)this.columnInfos[x];
                if (!buffer.IsNull(ci.bufferIndex))
                {
                    BufferColumn bc = buffer.GetColumnInfo(ci.bufferIndex);
                    if (bc.DataType == DataType.DT_GUID)
                    {
                        //Cast GUIDs to strings
                        row[ci.Name] = buffer.GetGuid(ci.bufferIndex).ToString();
                    }
                    if (bc.DataType == DataType.DT_BYTES)
                    {
                        row[ci.Name] = buffer.GetBytes(ci.bufferIndex);
                    }
                    else if (bc.DataType == DataType.DT_IMAGE)
                    {
                        byte[] bytes = new byte[buffer.GetBlobLength(ci.bufferIndex)];
                        bytes = buffer.GetBlobData(ci.bufferIndex, 0, bytes.Length);
                        row[ci.Name] = bytes;
                    }
                    else
                    {
                        row[ci.Name] = buffer[ci.bufferIndex];
                    }
                }
            }

            // Add the row to the DataTable
            this.runtimeDataTable.Rows.Add(row);
        }
    }
}
#endregion
```

As a result of the change in logic in *ProcessInput*, all the values in the *DT_GUID* columns in the input buffer will be converted into strings, which will be stored in the result dataset.

Similarly, you can make changes to the way you create your datasets in your custom source component, or map special properties in your custom connection managers.

Using Script Components

In the previous section, you saw how to create a custom component as a destination to handle some custom logic. You can perform a similar action using a script component as a destination. To understand more about using a script component as a source, transformation, or a destination, see *http://msdn.microsoft.com/en-us/library/ms135939.aspx.*

The following example creates a script component as a source. The input is the table *Human resources.Department* but with the *ModifiedDate* column data typecast into a string.

You can create the script component as a source, and then add a new ADO.NET connection manager as *AdventureWorks* for this example. You can then create columns with the correct data type mapping for the table, with *ModifiedDate* becoming a *DT_STR* as shown in Figure 7-17.

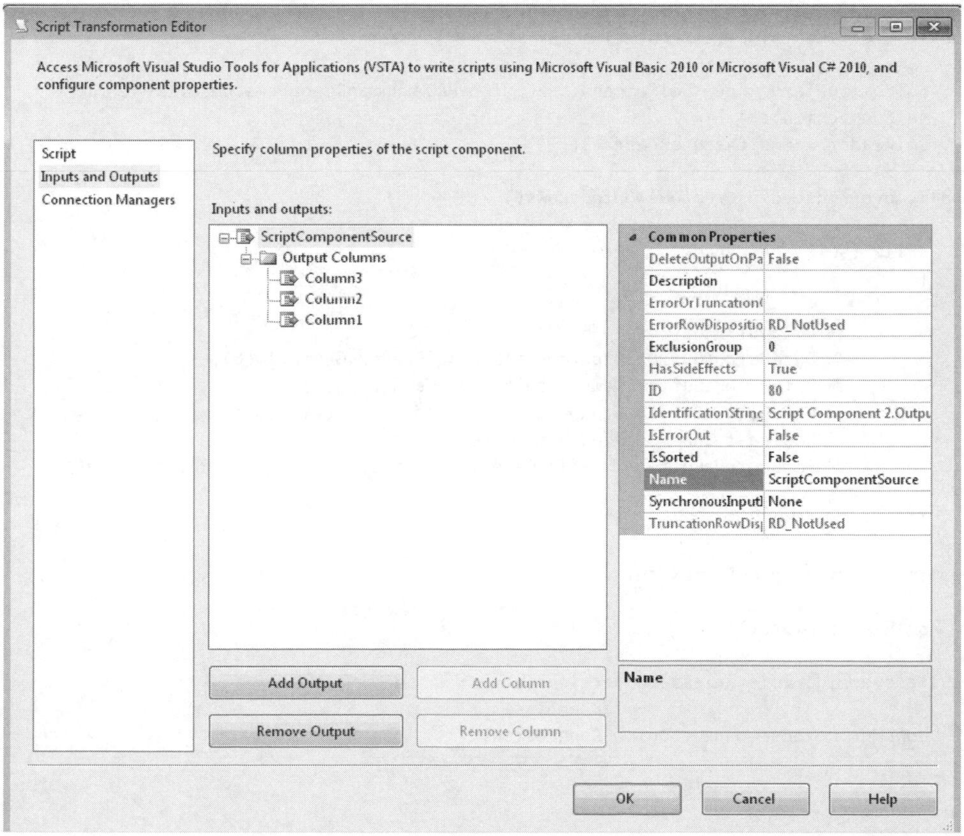

FIGURE 7-17 Script transformation as a source sample.

Next, you need to edit the script for this component. You have to override the *CreateNewOutputRows* to introduce a typecast to string as shown in Listing 7-5. Here's an overview of how the code for the script component will look.

LISTING 7-5 Script component used as custom source

```
#region Namespaces
using System;
using System.Data;
using System.Data.SqlClient;
using Microsoft.SqlServer.Dts.Pipeline.Wrapper;
using Microsoft.SqlServer.Dts.Runtime.Wrapper;
#endregion
[Microsoft.SqlServer.Dts.Pipeline.SSISScriptComponentEntryPointAttribute]
public class ScriptMain : UserComponent
{
    IDTSConnectionManager100 connMgr;
    SqlConnection sqlConnection;
    SqlDataReader sqlReader;
    public override void AcquireConnections(object Transcation)
    {
        connMgr = this.Connections.AdventureWorksADONET;
        sqlConnection = (SqlConnection)connMgr.AcquireConnection(null);
    }
    public override void PreExecute()
    {
        SqlCommand cmd = new SqlCommand("SELECT * FROM HumanResources.Department",
        sqlConnection);
        sqlReader = cmd.ExecuteReader();
    }
    public override void CreateNewOutputRows()
    {
        while (sqlReader.Read())
        {
            {
                MyDataOutputBuffer.AddRow();
                MyDataOutputBuffer.DepartmentID = sqlReader.GetInt16(0);
                MyDataOutputBuffer.Name = sqlReader.GetString(1);
                MyDataOutputBuffer.GroupName = sqlReader.GetString(2);
                //Now cast the Modified date into a string
                MyDataOutputBuffer.ModifiedDate = sqlReader.GetDateTime(3).ToString();
            }
        }
    }
    public override void PostExecute()
    {
        sqlReader.Close();
    }
    public override void ReleaseConnections()
    {
        connMgr.ReleaseConnection(sqlConnection);
    }
}
```

You can find the complete package solution (Integration Services Project Sample) and the preceding listing in the companion content for this chapter.

Summary

This chapter illuminated some of the common problems people encounter when solving connectivity issues with SSIS. You saw how to choose the right connection technology for your project, and were introduced to new connection technology in SSIS 2012, such as ODBC having its own Source and Destination components. You also learned about other aspects, such as how 64-bit or 32-bit process architecture can affect your implementations. This chapter also provided more information about connecting to data sources such as Excel, Access, and Oracle. Some of the newer connectors to Oracle were introduced. Finally, you saw how to create custom components as sources and destinations and saw an example of creating a script component as a custom source.

CHAPTER 8

Working with Change Data Capture in SSIS 2012

In This Chapter

Change data capture (CDC) and using the change data has become a common and important operation in most data warehousing scenarios. Integrating the process of creating and consuming change data in extract-transform-load (ETL) processes is a common requirement. SSIS and SQL Server enable you to easily create and consume such change data. This chapter introduces various CDC techniques in SQL Server and how you can use SSIS to consume the change data. It also introduces you to the new CDC components for Oracle database systems.

CDC in SQL Server

CDC is the process of capturing change data in your tables. The types of changes that can be captured include *INSERTS, UPDATES,* and *DELETES.* The CDC features in SQL Server were introduced with SQL Server 2008. You can use SQL Server to capture the inserted, updated, or deleted data from your SQL Server tables into a type of tables called the *Change* tables. The *Change* tables are created by SQL Server mirroring the tables for which you are capturing the change data along with some metadata columns that would provide more information, such as the type of the change, date and time information, and so on. To learn more about CDC in SQL Server refer to *http://msdn.microsoft.com/en-us/library/cc645937.aspx.*

Tip CDC in SQL Server is available for only the Developer, Enterprise, and Evaluation editions.

Now, you'll learn to set up a simple CDC operation in SQL Server.

Using CDC in SQL Server

Setting up CDC in SQL Server involves the following two steps:

1. Enable your database for CDC.
2. Enable a table on the CDC-enabled database for CDC.

Listing 8-1 shows how you can enable CDC using Transact-SQL (T-SQL).

LISTING 8-1 Enabling CDC on your database

```
--1.       Enable your database for CDC
USE AdventureWorks2012
GO
EXEC sys.sp_cdc_enable_db
GO
--2.       Enable a table on the CDC enabled database for CDC
USE AdventureWorks2012
GO
/* Create if CDC filegroup does not exist*/
ALTER DATABASE [AdventureWorks2012] ADD FILEGROUP [AdventureWorks2012_CT]
GO
EXEC sys.sp_cdc_enable_table
@source_schema = N'HumanResources',
@source_name   = N'Employee',
@role_name     = N'CDCRole',
@filegroup_name = N'AdventureWorks2012_CT',
@supports_net_changes = 1
GO
```

The code in Listing 8-1 will enable the table *HumanResources.Employee* for CDC and there would be a new CDC agent job created that will start capturing the changes to the table. For a complete description of all the parameters involved in the *sys.sp_cdc_enable_table* stored procedure, refer to the MSDN link *http://msdn.microsoft.com/en-us/library/bb522475.aspx*.

Enabling the CDC on the table also creates a few related functions that can be used to capture the changes on the table.

The function *cdc.fn_cdc_get_all_changes_HumanResources_Employee* is created to get a snapshot of all the changes for a row between two Logical Sequence Number (LSN) intervals. The function *cdc.fn_cdc_get_net_changes_HumanResources_Employee* will capture the net change for each row in the specified LSN range. An LSN is defined as a log sequence number that is a unique identifier for every record in the SQL Server transaction log.

You can use the preceding functions as shown in Listing 8-2.

LISTING 8-2 Querying change data from CDC-enabled tables

```
USE [AdventureWorks2012]
GO
--Define the LSN range
DECLARE @from_lsn binary(10), @to_lsn binary(10)
SET @from_lsn =
   sys.fn_cdc_get_min_lsn('HumanResources_Employee')
SET @to_lsn   = sys.fn_cdc_get_max_lsn()
-- Get all the changes for the table
SELECT * FROM cdc.fn_cdc_get_all_changes_HumanResources_Employee
  (@from_lsn, @to_lsn, N'all')
-- Get all the net changes for the table
SELECT * FROM cdc.fn_cdc_get_net_changes_HumanResources_Employee
  (@from_lsn, @to_lsn, N'all')
```

You can also query the change data directly from the CT tables that are created for a CDC-enabled table. Because you enabled the CDC for the *HumanResources.Employee*, you can now expect a system table named *cdc.HumanResource_.Employee_CT* table to be created. The CT table would have all the columns from the original table along with some metadata columns. For a complete description of all the metadata columns, refer to *http://msdn.microsoft.com/en-us/library/bb500305.aspx*.

You will use the preceding functions as well as the CT table in later sections in this chapter where you learn how SSIS uses the functions just discussed and other CDC functions to consume change data from SQL Server CT tables.

CDC Scenarios in ETLs

Before exploring how SSIS can consume CDC data, you should understand the various scenarios in which you need to consume changed data from SQL Server in your ETL process.

Enabling CDC on a table is important if you want to track the changes to each record in that table. Some of the scenarios where you would do so would be the following:

- **Change data for dimensions** A dimension table such as an Employee master table where you need to track every record to sync changes between tables.
- **Change data between table references** A table containing records that, when changed, trigger another action such as a tables in master–child relationships.
- **Trimming down amount of data processed** Consuming only certain types of changes from an upstream table to be processed and inserted into a downstream table.

Let's take the first scenario as an example. You now have to sync the changes in the *Human Resources.Employee* table between a source and a destination database. You can use the workflow illustrated in Figure 8-1 to perform that action.

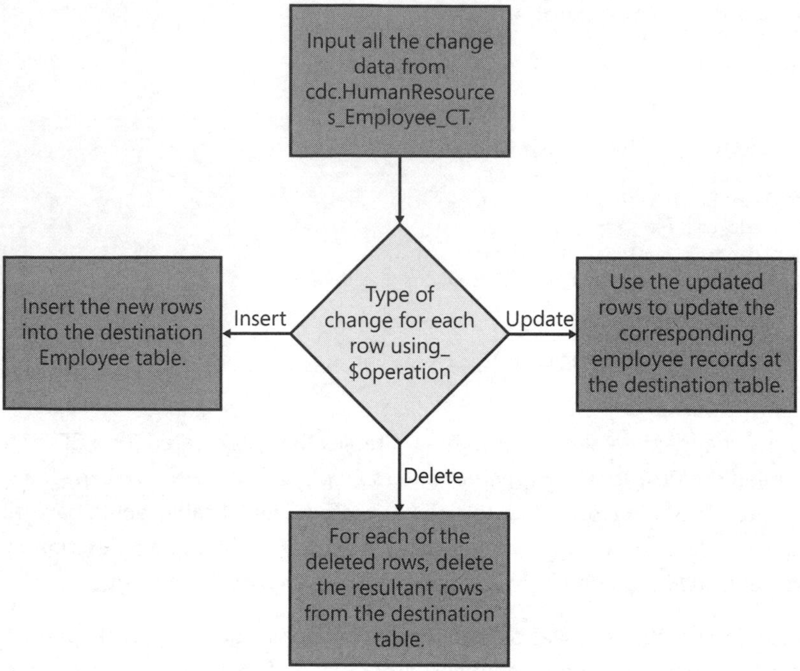

FIGURE 8-1 Flowchart to consume change data for a dimension.

In some of the following sections about the new SSIS components in SQL Server 2012, you will learn how you can use SSIS to represent the previous flowchart in a Data Flow task.

Stages in CDC

Figure 8-1 shows a common scenario that consumed changes from a table, but you have to perform a few operations on the source and the target tables before consuming the changes. Here's a bit more discussion about those operations.

Initial Data Loading

Before you start syncing changes between the source and target tables, you must make sure that the source and the target tables are identical. For example, take the *HumanResources.Employee* table. This example syncs changes from the *HumanResources.Employee* table in source database (Database A) to destination database (Database B). Before the start of the CDC operation, the table in Database A has five rows. After syncing the CDC changes from the table in Database A to Database B, Database B should have an identical copy of the table in Database A. Therefore, we create an initial copy of the table from Database A to Database B. You can see the process in Figure 8-2.

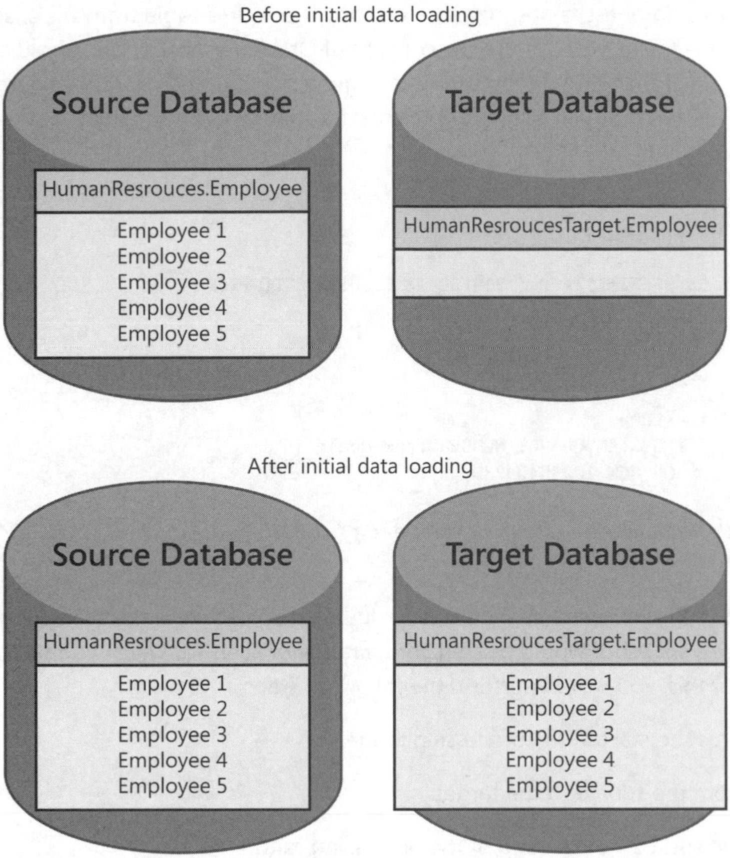

FIGURE 8-2 Initial data loading for CDC.

After the target table is loaded with initial data from the source, you can start the process of consuming the changes from the source table and applying them to the destination table.

The operation of initial data loading is also dependent on the state of the source database. If there is no activity in the source database, you can easily copy the source table. However, if there are ongoing inserts, updates, or deletes on the source table, you must ensure that you capture a state (a start and end LSN) of the source table, and replicate that in the target table. Any changes after that state should be considered CDC changes and consumed accordingly. You can perform this type of initial data load by capturing a snapshot of the data.

In SQL Server, you can take a database snapshot and then copy the source table from the snapshot to populate the target table. In Oracle, you can use the concept of Oracle flashback, where you can query using a System Change Number (SCN) or timestamps to get a specific state from the source table. For example, you can use the query in Listing 8-3 to create a snapshot of the table.

LISTING 8-3 Using Oracle flashback query

```
--Flashback query using Timestamp

SQL> SELECT * FROM EMPLOYEE AS OF TIMESTAMP ('21-FEB-12 8:50:58','DD-MON-YY

HH24: MI: SS');

--Flashback query using SCN
--Get the SCN number for a timestamp
SQL> select DBMS_FLASHBACK. GET_SYSTEM_CHANGE_NUMBER from dual;
SQL> SELECT * FROM EMPLOYEE AS OF SCN 10280403230;
```

See Also *For more about Oracle flashback, see* http://docs.oracle.com/cd/B28359_01/appdev.111/b28424/adfns_flashback.htm.

As you already know, in SQL Server, every change is recorded with an LSN in the database log, so another technique to capture a snapshot would be to record a range of LSNs for which you take a snapshot of the database. For this, you would perform the following steps:

1. Record the start LSN as the start of the processing range.
2. Bulk load the data from the source to the target.
3. Record the LSN as the end LSN or the end of the processing range.

In the next section, you learn how the new components in SSIS let you perform such initial data loading activities.

Syncing CDC Changes

After the initial snapshot is synced between the source and the target tables, you can start syncing the CDC changes between source and the target table. In our earlier example in the "Initial Data Loading" section, we were syncing changes between a source and target table. A CDC change on the source table can either be an *INSERT, UPDATE,* or *DELETE*. Thus, you need to consume these changes from the respective _CT table and perform operations that make the required modifications on the target table. In Figure 8-3, the two arrows show the operations based on the CDC changes to the source table.

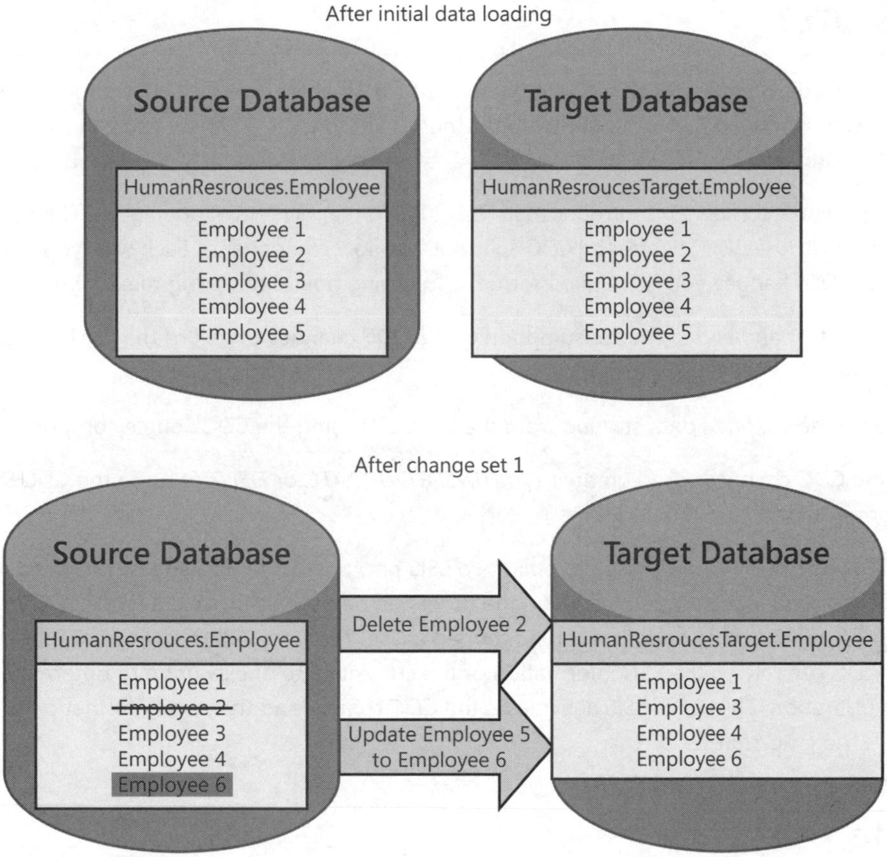

FIGURE 8-3 Syncing changes using CDC.

Some of the solutions you can create to sync changes using CDC are the following:

- Use an SSIS package with custom CDC implementation, such as one where you enable SQL Server CDC on the table, read the changes from the _CT table, and use a *MERGE* statement in an Execute SQL task to consume the changes and *upsert* them in the target table.
- Use an SSIS package on a CDC-enabled table and use the new CDC components introduced in SQL Server 2012 described in the next section.

> **Note** SQL Server replication can also be used to sync changes between tables. However, SQL Server replication's target scenarios mostly involve real-time data sync instead of enabling consumption of changes in an ETL scenario.

CDC in SSIS 2012

You were introduced to the new CDC task and components in Chapter 4, "New SSIS Designer Features." In this section you learn in more depth about those components and how you can use them in common CDC scenarios.

There are three new components introduced in SSIS 2012 for handling CDC operations. They are the CDC Control task, the CDC Source, and CDC Splitter Data Flow components. Each time you have to process a set of CDC changes, you need to perform the following operations using these components:

1. Mark the start and end of the consumption of the CDC changes to record the start and end LSNs using the CDC Control task.
2. Consume the changed data starting from the start LSN using the CDC Source component.
3. Split the CDC changes based on their type (*INSERT*, *UPDATE*, or *DELETE*) using the CDC Splitter component.

For each CDC operation you will have to build two SSIS packages. One package can be used to perform the initial data loading operations and the other can be used to process a set of CDC changes. Execution of either of these packages can be termed a *CDC run*. The SSIS tasks and components involved in a CDC run rely on the LSN information or the current state of execution to determine the next stage of operation. This set of SSIS activities is the *CDC context* and the state information of the CDC context is the *CDC state*.

CDC State

As you learned from previous sections, the SSIS CDC components and tasks use the CDC state of a CDC context to determine the parameters of their execution. Before learning how the tasks and components use the CDC state, let's understand what the various CDC states are.

CDC State String

A CDC state is basically a string in the following format:

<state-name>/CS/<cs-lsn>/[CE/<ce-lsn>/][IR/<ir-start>/<ir-end>/]TS/<timestamp>/ER/<short-error-text>

Table 8-1 describes the tokens in this string.

TABLE 8-1 Description of tokens in a CDC state string

Term	Description
<state-name>	The name of the current CDC state. You will learn more about the various CDC states in the next section.
CS	Marks the current processing range start point (Current Start).
<cs-lsn>	The last LSN processed in the previous CDC run.
CE	Signifies the current processing range end point (Current End). The presence of the CE component in the CDC state is an indication that either a CDC package is currently processing or that a CDC package failed before fully processing its CDC processing range (with the mentioned end point).
<ce-lsn>	Signifies the last LSN to be processed in the current CDC run. It is always assumed that the LSN to be processed is the maximum LSN currently available from the SQL Server LSN table.
IR	Marks the initial processing range.
<ir-start>	Signifies an LSN of a change just before initial load began.
<ir-end>	Signifies an LSN of a change just after initial load ended.
TS	Marks the last CDC state update timestamp.
<timestamp>	A decimal representation of the 64-bit *System.DateTime.UtcNow* property.
ER	It is mentioned in the state when the last CDC operation has failed.
<short-error-text>	It is mentioned when there is an error and ER is present in the string. This is a small description of the error that has occurred.

The LSNs or SCNs (in the case of Oracle databases) are encoded as a hexadecimal string of up to 20 digits. They represent the LSN value in a Binary(10) data type.

> **Tip** An example of a CDC state is *ILSTART/IR/0x0000162B158700000000//TS/2011-08-07T17:10:43.0031645/*, signifying the start of the initial loading from the mentioned LSN value.

Types of CDC States

The various types of states in which a CDC context can exist in are described in Table 8-2.

TABLE 8-2 Types of CDC states

States	Description
0 - (INITIAL)	This is the initial state before any package was run on the current CDC group. This is also the state when the CDC state is empty.
ILSTART (Initial Load Started)	This is the state when you perform the initial loading in your package.
ILEND (Initial Load Ended)	This is the state when the initial loading is completed successfully.
ILUPDATE (Initial Load Update)	This is the state when you are processing the initial range of CDC changes (the first processing after the initial loading of data).
TFEND (CDC change processing Update Ended)	This is the state of the CDC context when the previous CDC run has completed successfully and the CDC context is ready to process the next CDC change data range.
TFSTART (CDC change processing Ended)	This is the state of the CDC context when you are processing the range of data after the initial data loading and processing of the initial processing range has completed. It either indicates that a regular CDC run has started but hasn't finished yet or the CDC run finished in an error or incorrect state.
TFREDO (Reprocessing Trickle-Feed Updates)	This state is used when the previous run didn't finish cleanly and the CDC run is being repeated.
ERROR	The CDC group is in an error state.

You can use the information from the CDC state to determine the current state and its details about your CDC context. In the next section on the CDC Control task, you learn more about how the CDC Control task is used to transition between the different states just mentioned.

Storing a CDC State

The CDC state of a CDC context can also be stored in the following ways:

- You can opt not to persist the CDC state after a package has completed execution. In such a case, any future CDC run will not be able to use the CDC information. However, there can be occasions where you don't need to store the state, such as one where you just need to perform the initial load and CDC processing range once and there would be no future executions on that table.
- You can opt to store your CDC state in a SQL Server database. This will ensure that any future CDC run will be able to start from the end LSN of the previous run and thus, it would process the new CDC changes. This is useful in scenarios where you will need to continuously process CDC changes between source and target tables.

In a SQL Server database, you can create the *cdc_states* table either by yourself or using the CDC Control task. The script of the table will look like Listing 8-4.

LISTING 8-4 *Create* statement for *cdc_states* table

```
CREATE TABLE [dbo].[cdc_states](
   [name] [nvarchar](1000) NULL,
   [state] [nvarchar](256) NULL
) ON [PRIMARY]

GO

CREATE UNIQUE NONCLUSTERED INDEX [cdc_states_name] ON [dbo].[cdc_states]
(
   [name] ASC
) WITH (PAD_INDEX  = OFF) ON [PRIMARY]
GO
```

Now, let's learn how this component works to perform the CDC scenarios that you learned before.

CDC Control Task

As you have already seen, changes to a table can be identified by an LSN from the log. These LSNs are useful when you want to consume the CDC changes from a table and you need to mark the range of LSNs for which you want to consume the changes. This set of LSNs for which you consume the CDC changes and process them is called the CDC processing range. The first processing range following an initial data loading activity is called an initial processing range.

The CDC Control task helps you maintain the CDC processing range, which will help you determine the rows to be processed in a CDC operation. Basically you can think of the CDC Control task as a gatekeeper that records the start and the end LSN for processing the changes on a CDC-enabled table.

Now that you have basic knowledge of a CDC run, let's understand how we can use the CDC Control task.

Configuring a CDC Control Task

The basic editor of a CDC Control task is shown in Figure 8-4.

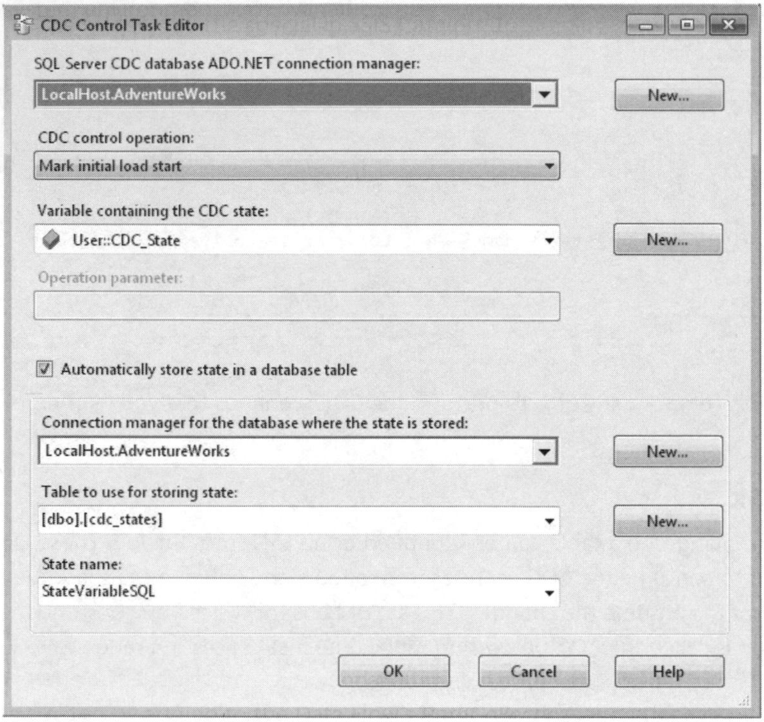

FIGURE 8-4 CDC Control Task Editor.

Now we can explore all the properties of the CDC Control Task Editor.

- **SQL Server CDC Database ADO .NET Connection Manager** This is the connection manager for the database containing the CDC tables.
- **CDC Control Operation** This is the type of CDC control operation to be executed in the next steps of the package. The various types of operations are discussed in the next section.
- **Variable Containing The CDC State** A *DT_STR* variable has to be created for storing the CDC state string during the package execution.
- **SQL Server LSN/snapshot database name** If reading from a snapshot database for initial loading, you should mention the snapshot database name here. If no snapshot database is being used, you can mention an LSN after which changes will be consumed. This is enabled only when you use the *MarkCDCStart* operation.
- **Automatically Store State In A Database Table** Selecting this check box would ensure that the CDC state (stored in the variable chosen in the Variable Containing The State drop-down list box) after modification is automatically stored to the database and table mentioned in the next steps.

- **Connection Manager For The Database Where The State Is Stored** Defines the ADO .NET connection information for the SQL Server database containing the state table.
- **Table To Use For Storing State** The table used for storing the states in the SQL Server database.
- **State Name** Each state table can store multiple state values, so you can use a state name to identify a particular state value.

Now you'll explore the operations that you can define in the CDC Control task.

CDC Control Task Operations

The CDC Control task is available on the Control Flow SSIS toolbox. Once you have a Control task in your package, you can use it to perform the operations shown in Table 8-3.

TABLE 8-3 Overview of the CDC Control task operations

Operation	Details	Corresponding CDC State
MarkInitialLoadStart	Used to signify that you are starting to perform an initial loading operation.	ILSTART
MarkInitialLoadEnd	Used to signify that you have completed an initial loading operation.	ILEND
GetProcessingRange	Will get the processing range for which the CDC changes will be consumed in the current package execution.	If you are processing the range for the first time after the initial load, the CDC state is set to ILUPDATE. For any future CDC runs after the initial processing range the state is set to TFSTART.
MarkProcessedRange	Updates the CDC processing range to record the completion of consumption of a processing range after a package execution.	TFEND
MarkCdcStart	Record a specific LSN or a SCN (Oracle) as the start LSN for the next *GetProcessingRange* operation.	The CDC state is unchanged but the LSN in the CDC state string is updated with the value specified by thtfe *MarkCDCStart* operation.
ResetCDCState	Record the current start LSN to the maximum LSN from the SQL Server LSN records	The CDC state is unchanged but the LSN in the CDC state string is updated with the value from the maximum LSN.

Here is some additional information about these SSIS operations.

- ***MarkInitialLoadStart*** As you have already seen, before consuming the CDC changes of a table, you will have to create an initial snapshot of the table and sync it with the target table. This Control task operation is used at the start of such an initial load package. It records the current LSN before it starts to read the source tables and load the target tables.

  For SQL Server, the current LSN can be calculated using the *sys.fn_cdc_get_max_lsn* system function. The CDC Control task actually invokes a procedure called *sys.sp_replincrementlsn*.

> **Note** The *sys.sp_replincrementlsn* stored procedure requires the caller to have the Execute permission on the stored procedure as the stored procedure itself requires the *db_owner* role.

- ***MarkInitialLoadEnd*** You can use this operation at the end of an initial load CDC run to record the current LSN from the source database once the initial load package completes reading data from the source tables.

  The values for the current LSN are calculated again by invoking the *sys.sp_replincrementlsn* stored procedure.

- ***MarkCDCStart*** This operation is used to denote the start of the CDC processing using a start LSN or a snapshot database for CDC processing. It is used in the case where you have no changes on the source database or you are loading from a snapshot. It is not exactly initial loading but it's an alternative to creating a package with *MarkInitialLoadStart/End* because you have static source databases.

  > **Note** You should use *MarkInitialLoadStart/End* for active databases where CDC changes are concurrently happening.

  The *OperationParameter* property of the CDC Control task is enabled. You can use it to denote if you are loading using a specific LSN (SQL Server) or SCN (Oracle) or using a snapshot database. If it is empty then the LSN would be calculated as from the value from the previous *MarkLoadInitialEnd*.

  Once you have marked the CDC state using the *MarkCDCStart*, the next set of CDC changes would be consumed from the LSN that was marked using the operation. This operation will update the *CS* component of the CDC state and NULL out the *IR* and *CE* components.

- ***GetProcessingRange*** The *GetProcessingRange* operations let you define a processing range on your source table for which you want to consume the CDC changes. The CDC processing range is determined on the basis of the current state of the SQL Server CDC instance as well as the current values in your CDC state.

Let's use the following terms as references in the table:

IS LSN from the CDC state after initial loading was started but didn't finish cleanly (*Mark ProcessedRange* wasn't called). Otherwise, an SSIS package invoked in parallel is persisting its IS value in the CDC state.

IE Current LSN at the end of an initial loading package.

min LSN from *sys.fn_cdc_get_min_lsn(cdc_instance).*

max LSN from *sys.fn_cdc_get_max_lsn().*

CS Start LSN for the processing range being determined in each case.

CE End LSN for the processing range being determined.

In Case 1, max has not yet reached IS (SQL Server CDC capture instance was suspended or slow).

In this image:
- o CS = max (Calculation: min(is, max)).
- o CE = max (Calculation: min(ie, max)).
  Each CDC Source data flow will not process any rows until max is not greater than IS.
- o MarkProcessedRange will set the CDC status to the original IR/<IS>/<IE>/.

In Case 2, max is between IS and IE.

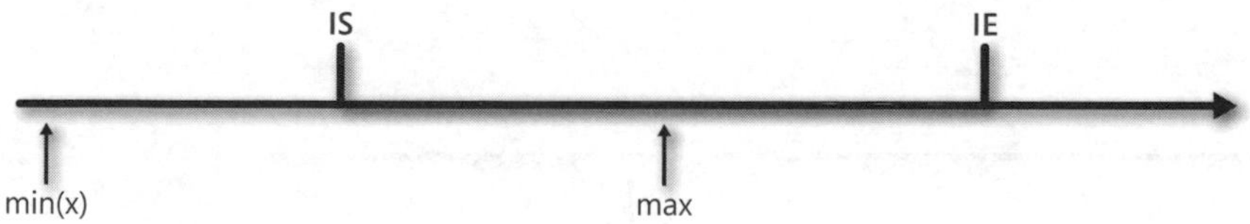

In this image:
- o CS = IS (Calculation: min(is, max)).
  CDC Source Data Flow for instance x will process data with LSNs starting from max(IS, min(x)).
- o CE = max (Calculation: min(ie, max)).
- o MarkProcessedRange will update the CDC status to modified IR as in IR/<max>/<IE>/ advancing the initial range forward.

In Case 3, max is higher than IE.

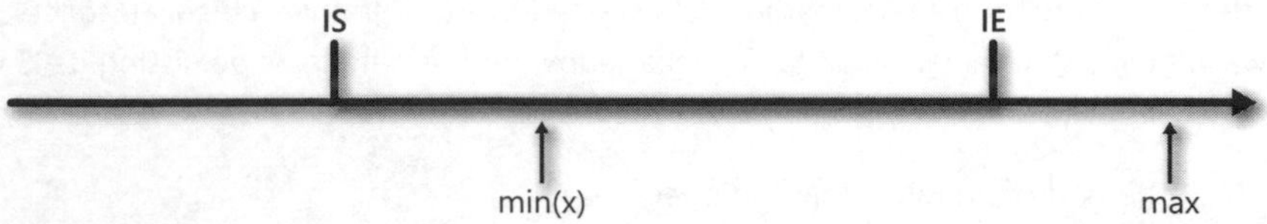

In this image:

- o CS = IS (Calculation: min(is, max)).
- o CE = IE (Calculation: min(ie, max)).
- o MarkProcessedRange will set the CDC state to a new marked start position for the next run as in CS/<ie>/ getting rid of the initial range indication.

In Case 4, max has not yet reached CS (SQL Server CDC capture job was suspended or slow but this is not an initial loading scenario).

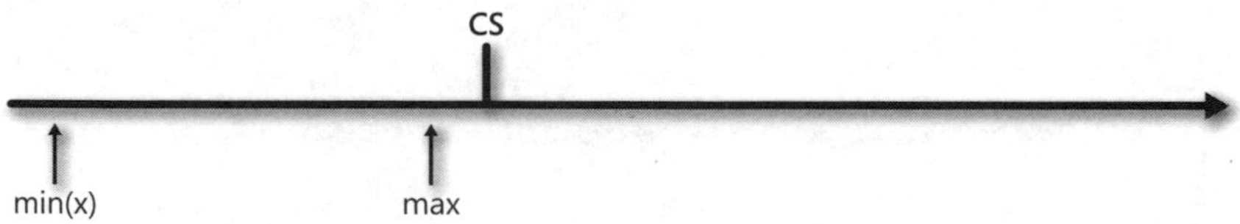

In this image:

- o CS = max (Calculation: min(cs, max)).
- o CE = max.
- o Each CDC Source Data Flow will return without doing anything as there are no available CDC changes in the database after CS.
- o MarkProcessedRange will revert to the original CS/<cs>/. The next time the package processes and it contains changes after CS (that is, max > CS) then Case 5 will be used.

In Case 5, max is higher than CS.

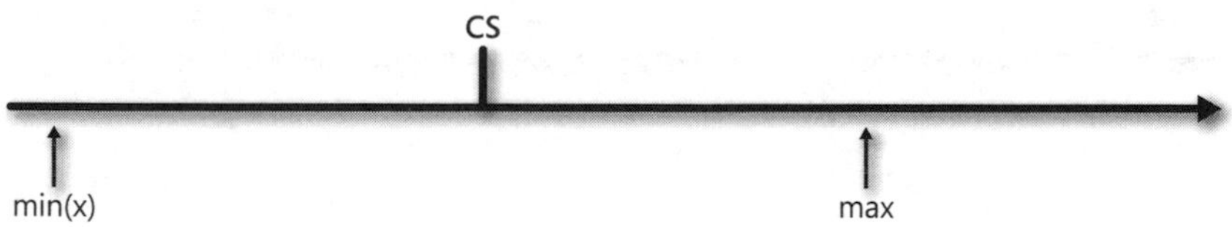

In this image:

- o CS = CS (Calculation: min(CS, max)).
- o CE = max.
  Each CDC Source Data Flow will return without doing anything (NOP).
- o MarkProcessedRange will switch to a new marked start position for the next run as in CS/<max>/.

- *MarkProcessedRange* You can use the *MarkProcessedRange* operation after each CDC run to mark the successful completion of the run. It will mark the CDC state with the last handled LSN with a *CSstate* (which will be used by the next *GetProcessingRange* operation).

Figure 8-5 shows sample containers where an initial loading was done, followed by a *GetProcessing Range* operation.

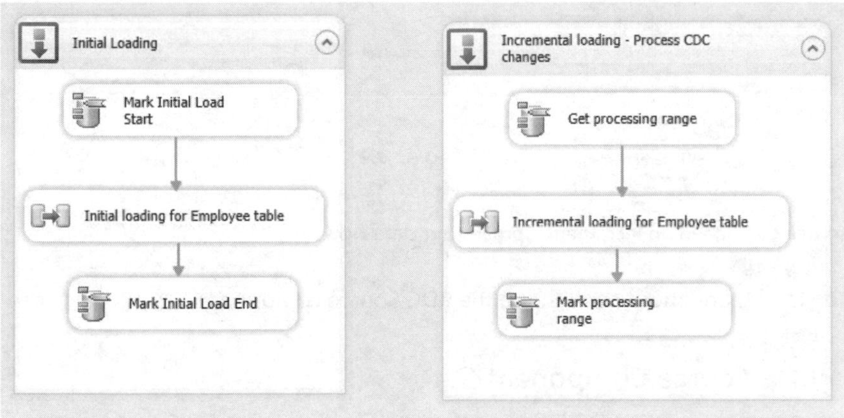

FIGURE 8-5 Use of initial loading and processing of CDC changes in an SSIS package.

You can find the example of the use of the CDC Control task in the Integration Services Project Sample SSIS project sample in the code samples for this chapter. The project contains two projects, one for initial loading and the other for incremental processing of CDC changes as shown in Figure 8-5.

Data Flow Component: CDC Source

The CDC Source Data Flow component is used for reading the changed rows within a processing range from a SQL Server CDC instance. It has two outputs, one for the changed rows retrieved and another error output. You can configure the CDC Source Data Flow component to either read all the changes or only the net changes in rows from a CDC instance for a given processing range. For instance, you would be using the CDC Source Data Flow component in the Incremental loading for Employee table Data Flow task as shown in Figure 8-5.

Figure 8-6 shows you how the Incremental loading for Employee table Data Flow task shown in Figure 8-5 uses a CDC Source Data Flow component to consume the changed data from a CDC instance of a SQL Server table.

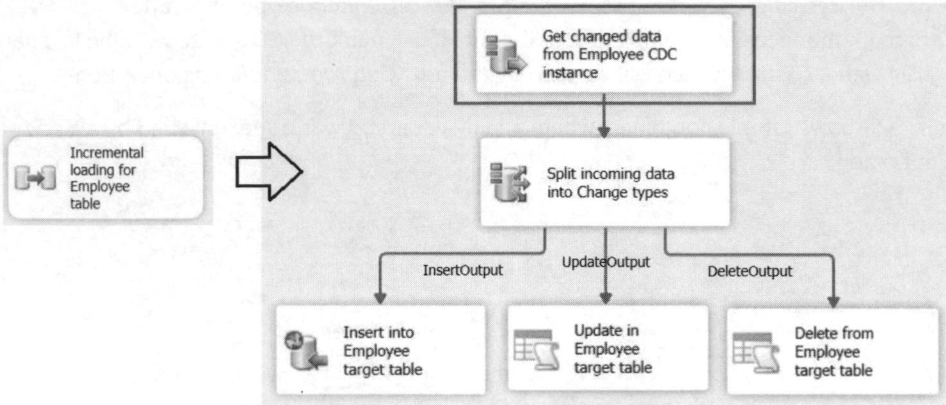

FIGURE 8-6 CDC Source component in incremental processing Data Flow task.

Now let's understand more about configuring the CDC Source component.

Configuring a CDC Source Component

Let us look at the basic editor for the CDC Source task, shown in Figure 8-7, to discover its properties.

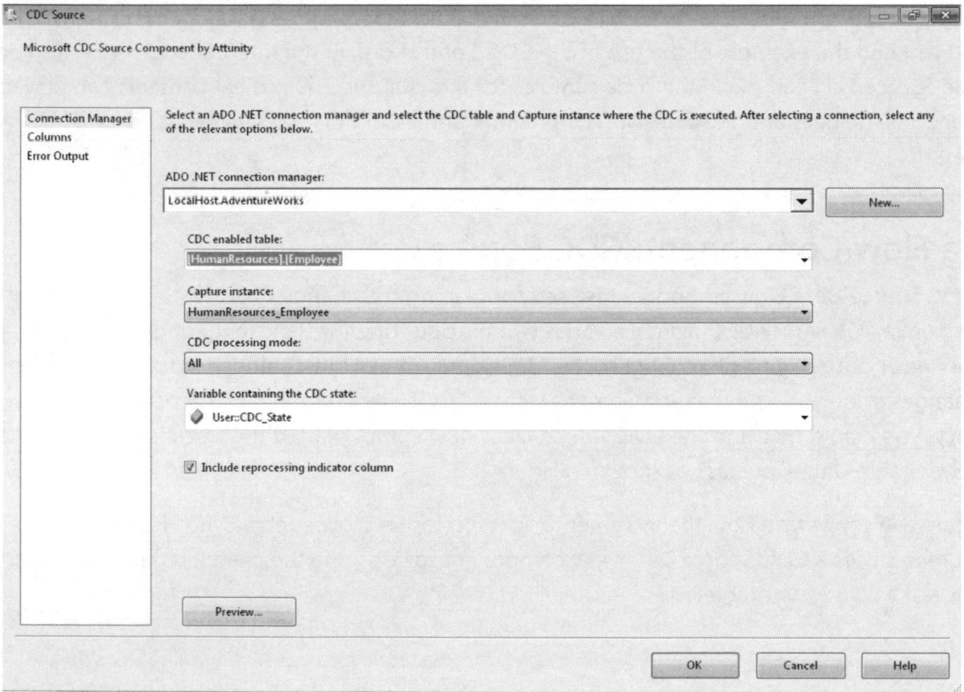

FIGURE 8-7 Basic editor of CDC Source component.

The following list describes all the properties of the CDC Source component:

- **ADO .NET Connection Manager** This property is used to provide the connection manager for connecting to the SQL Server CDC database where you can find the change tables.
- **CDC Enabled Table** This is the name of the table for which you are capturing the CDC changes.
- **Capture Instance** This signifies the CDC capture instance for the SQL Server table mentioned in CDC Enabled Table. Because a table can have multiple CDC instances, the drop-down list would provide you with all the active CDC capture instances available on the table.
- **CDC Processing Mode** You can use the CDC processing mode to configure the CDC Source component to retrieve either the net changes or all changes on a table. You can also configure it to add an update indicator column that can be used to mark columns that have been updated. The different options that you can set for the CDC processing mode are listed in Table 8-4.

TABLE 8-4 CDC processing modes

Mode	Description
All	Return all the changes for the table.
All with Old Values	Return all the changes for the table including old values for the rows that were deleted or updated.
Net	Return only the net changes for the table.
Net with Update Mask	Return only the net changes with an additional output column named *_$<column_name>_Changed* for every column that was updated. This value is based on the *_$update_mask* column in the change table.
Net with Merge	Returns only the net changes after merging changes (inserts/updates or deletes) on a single row from the change table.

The next section explains more about the *All*, *Net* techniques introduced earlier.

- **Variable Containing The CDC State** This signifies the variable containing the CDC state for the current CDC run. This value would have already been configured by the CDC Control task preceding this Data Flow task.
- **Include Reprocessing Indicator Column** In some cases you might have to perform some special action if you are reprocessing the same set of changes; for instance, the previous CDC run to process the changes has failed and your CDC target table might be in an inconsistent state (only a subset of the changes might have been applied). In this case, you need only to consume the changes that were not consumed in the target table. Thus, in this run you need an indicator specifying that this is a rerun of the same processing range so that you can handle the changes differently. For instance, for updating your target table you could use the T-SQL statement in Listing 8-5 in the Update Employee target table from Figure 8-6.

LISTING 8-5 T-SQL for OLE DB command for updating using reprocessing indicator

```
DECLARE @reprocessingid VARCHAR(5)
SELECT @reprocessingid = ?
IF @reprocessingid LIKE 'True'
BEGIN
   --Ignore the row
END
ELSE
BEGIN
   --Regular processing
UPDATE [HumanResources].[Employee_CDCTarget]
   SET [BusinessEntityID] = ?
      ,[NationalIDNumber] = ?
      ,[LoginID] = ?
      ,[OrganizationNode] = ?
      ,[JobTitle] = ?
      ,[BirthDate] = ?
      ,[MaritalStatus] = ?
      ,[Gender] = ?
      ,[HireDate] = ?
      ,[SalariedFlag] = ?
      ,[VacationHours] = ?
      ,[SickLeaveHours] = ?
      ,[CurrentFlag] = ?
      ,[rowguid] = ?
      ,[ModifiedDate] = ?
 WHERE BusinessEntityID = ?

 END
```

Selecting this check box would add a *_$reprocessing* column to the output. The column would be *true* for each data row processed during the initial processing range (initial data loading) or reprocessing a specific processing range after failure. For any other case it will use the value *false*.

Net vs. All Changes

As you saw earlier, you can configure the *CDC Processing Mode* property of the component to determine if all or the net changes are produced. Now let us learn more about how the component uses the CDC functions to determine the all or the net changes from a CDC change table.

When you set the processing mode to Net changes, you are asking the CDC Source component to get the final state of each row. If a single row has multiple modifications to it, such as *EmployeeID* 12 was inserted with login name *Employee12* in one change and in another change the login name was updated to *Employee12_1,* then the final value of that row (that is, *Employee12_1*) will be retrieved when Net changes is used. Internally the CDC component would issue the T-SQL statements shown in Listing 8-6.

LISTING 8-6 T-SQL for *Net* changes

```
DECLARE @from _lsn binary(10), @to_lsn binary(10)
SELECT @from _lsn = <processing-range-start-lsn>
SELECT @to_lsn = <processing-range-end-lsn>
SELECT * FROM cdc.fn_cdc_get_net_changes_<capture-instance>(@from_lsn, @to_lsn, ‘all’)
```

> **Note** To consume changes using the Net option, you must have a primary key on the source table.

The *all* parameter would change to *all with mask* based on how you configure the CDC processing mode.

Similarly, when you select All options for the CDC processing mode, all the changes for a given row would be retrieved from the change table. Thus, from the previous example, you would retrieve both the rows having login name *Employee12* and *Employee12_1*. The component will issue the T-SQL statement in Listing 8-7 to retrieve all the changes.

LISTING 8-7 T-SQL for *All* changes

```
DECLARE @from_lsn binary(10), @to_lsn binary(10)
SELECT @from_lsn = <processing-range-start-lsn>
SELECT @to_lsn = <processing-range-end-lsn>
SELECT * FROM cdc.fn_cdc_get_all_changes_<capture-instance>(@from_lsn, @to_lsn, ‘all’)
```

The *all* parameter would change to *all upload old* if you set the CDC processing mode to *All with old values*.

A minimum LSN value in the preceding listings is calculated by calling the function *sys.fn_cdc_get_min_lsn(‘<capture-instance>’)*. If the *start-lsn* element of the processing range is missing in the CDC state string, the *@from_lsn* will be set to the minimum LSN calculated before. If the *start-lsn* of the processing range is retrieved correctly, the *@from_lsn* will be set to the maximum of the *start-lsn* and the minimum LSN values. The *@to_lsn* will be calculated from the *end-lsn* element of the state. If the *end-lsn* element is missing in the CDC state string, an error will be reported.

> **Tip** To learn more about consuming net or all changes using SQL Server CDC refer to *http://technet.microsoft.com/en-us/library/bb895288(v=SQL.100).aspx.*

CDC Splitter Component

The CDC Splitter component uses the output from the CDC Source component to split the output into three outputs (insert/update or delete) based on the type of the change for each row received from the CDC Source component. The CDC Splitter component is a synchronous Data Flow component.

Types of Changes

The Splitter component uses the _$operation column from the CDC source and uses the standard values from SQL Server CDC to determine the type of change in the incoming changed row. Based on how you configure your Source component, you can have the possible values in Table 8-5 for the _$operation column.

TABLE 8-5 Types of values for _$operation column

Value	Type	Description
1	Delete	Will always get mapped to the delete output
2	Insert	Will always get mapped to the insert output
3, 4, 5	Types of updates	Will always get mapped to the update output

See Also *To understand more about how the _$operation column value is determined refer to* http://technet.microsoft.com/en-us/library/bb510627.aspx *for all changes and* http://technet.microsoft.com/en-us/library/bb522511.aspx *for net changes.*

Using the Splitter Component

You can just drag the Splitter component and start using it. It has no properties to be configured. It will always have the CDC source as its input component and it will have three outputs based on type of change (insert, update, or delete) in the incoming data.

The component also has an error output. Any row with an _$operation value other than the values mentioned in Table 8-5 will be redirected to this error output. Because the _$operation value will always be generated from the SQL Server function in the preceding CDC Source component, you can safely assume that the value would always be between 1 and 5 so this error output can be safely ignored.

You can see the splitter component in use in Figure 8-8.

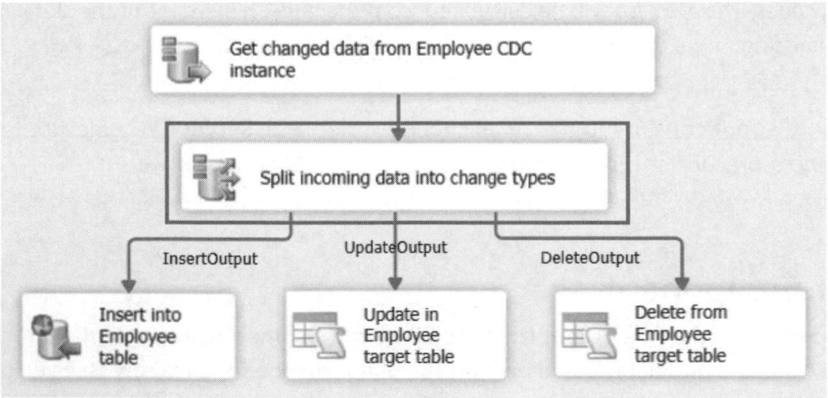

FIGURE 8-8 Splitter component in use.

As you can see in Figure 8-8, it will have three outputs that will stream the change rows according to the type of change mentioned in the _*$operation* column.

Using a CDC Splitter is useful when you are using it to consume net changes from the CDC Source. This would imply that the Splitter component would get only one change for each row and the change stream can be processed in any order. Because the Splitter component doesn't perform any operation to order the stream of changes, processing all changes from the CDC source could produce inconsistent results. For instance, if a set of changes contain an INSERT followed by a DELETE, when split by operation into different Data Flows, it can have the DELETE applied before the INSERT because it doesn't assume any order.

CDC for Oracle

CDC for SQL Server was introduced in SQL Server 2008. It has proven valuable for users who wanted an out-of-the-box solution for tracking data changes on their tables. However, for Oracle databases, we don't have a known out-of-the-box solution that can help you track changes on your data in tables. With SQL Server 2012, you will be able to use the CDC for Oracle features to use the SQL Server CDC infrastructure to track changes for your Oracle tables. Fundamentally, you are still using the SQL Server CDC to perform the CDC functionality but the CDC tracking is performed on mirror tables, which are mirrored off your original Oracle tables. Any changes in your original Oracle table would be captured in the mirror tables and tracked using SQL Server CDC. In addition, using this feature, any solutions that were built to consume SQL Server CDC implementations can in turn consume CDC data from Oracle databases as well.

In the following sections, you will learn more about how you can set up and configure CDC for Oracle. You will also learn about operating and troubleshooting the CDC scenarios and how you can use the CDC components in SSIS that you learned about in the previous section on Oracle tables using the CDC for Oracle features.

Introduction

CDC for Oracle consists of a set of components. These components essentially perform the following functionalities:

- Create mirror tables of the Oracle tables on a SQL Server database.
- Continuously monitor the source Oracle tables and copy transaction data from the source Oracle tables into the SQL Server tables using a CDC for Oracle service.
- Enable SQL Server CDC to capture changes from the mirrored tables.

In Figure 8-9, you can see an overview of the whole process just described. Figure 8-9 describes a scenario where you have a table called *HumanResources.Employee* on your Oracle database. You want to capture the changes on that table. To do so, use the CDC for Oracle features available in SQL Server 2012 as shown in the illustration.

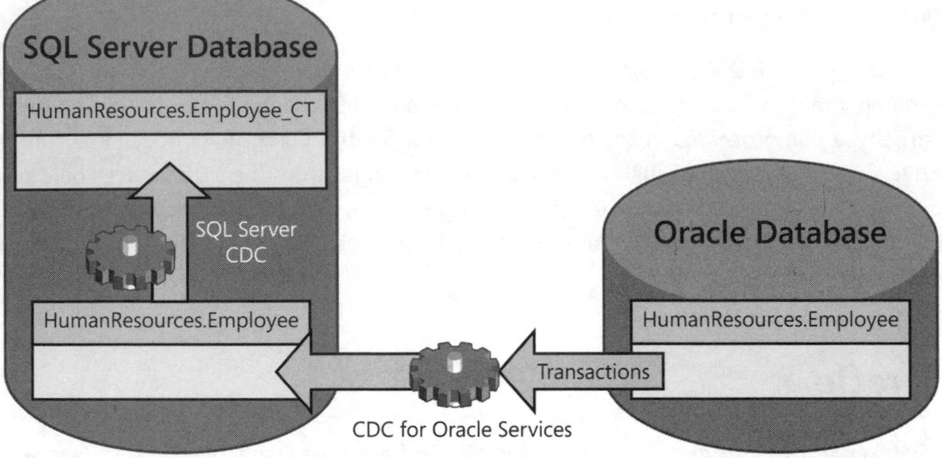

FIGURE 8-9 How CDC for Oracle Service works.

Let's see how a record originating from the Oracle table would be captured in a SQL Server CDC in the following steps:

1. An Oracle service was created with an Oracle CDC instance monitoring the *HumanResources.Employee* table in the Oracle database. It creates a replica of *HumanResources.Employee* from the Oracle database on a SQL Server database with the same name, *HumanResources.Employee*. It has also enabled SQL Server CDC on that replica, creating a *HumanResources.Employee_CT* table. However, you should note that only the schema of the table is replicated and not the data. You will still have to perform the initial replication of data yourself.
2. A new row is inserted into the *HumanResources.Employee* table in the Oracle database.
3. Oracle log miner captures the change and records a transaction.
4. The Oracle service captures the transaction using the Oracle log records from the Oracle log miner.
5. The Oracle service replicates the transaction on the SQL Server database and inserts the row into the *HumanResources.Employee* table in the SQL Server database.
6. SQL Server CDC captures that change in the *HumanResources.Employee* table in the SQL Server database and records the change in the *HumanResources.Employee_CT* table in the CDC schema.

Thus, these six steps show how a record originating from the Oracle database was change tracked in a SQL Server database.

Now let us look at the various components involved in setting up and operating the scenario described in Figure 8-9.

Components for Creating CDC for Oracle

As you saw earlier, you need the following major functionalities to capture change data from your Oracle tables:

- A component that helps you create a mirror table from your Oracle source table on your SQL Server database.
- A service that continuously monitors the transactions performed on the source Oracle table and replicates the transactions on the mirrored SQL Server table.
- A table that tracks the status of your change tracking as well as the status of the transaction copy operations that your service is performing.

> **Note** SQL Server mirroring or replication technologies are not intended here.

In SQL Server 2012, you receive the following components that help you perform the functionalities already listed.

CDC Service Configuration MMC

The CDC Service Configuration Microsoft Management Console (MMC) snap-in helps you create, update, or delete Oracle CDC services on your local machine. These Oracle CDC services essentially are Windows services that will be running on your local system.

Installation

The CDC Service Configuration MMC can be installed using its MSI installer. Note that it is not installed by default. The MSI installer named *AttunityOracleCdcService.msi* can be found in your installation media in the folder *\Tools\AttunityCDCOracle*. In the folder you will find x64 or x86 folders that correspond to the different processor architectures. Within the x86 or x64 folder, you can find folders for various locales, including 1033, which corresponds to English (US). Thus, to install the English (US) x64 version, you must go to the *\Tools\AttunityCDCOracle\x64\1033* folder.

Once installed, you would find a shortcut created under the Start menu: Start | Program | Attunity | Change Data Capture for Oracle | CDC Service Configuration.

> **Note** You must install the same bit version of the MSI as the Oracle client installation you have on the local system. Thus, if you have installed the x86 version of Oracle client then you must also install the x86 version of the Oracle CDC service.

Using the CDC Service Configuration MMC

Now let's look at how we can use the MMC to perform the different functionalities it provides. There are primarily two actions:

- **Prepare SQL Server** Before creating a service, you will have to prepare a SQL Server instance. Preparing a SQL Server instance creates a database called MSXDBCDC on the instance. The CDC services use that database for storing their transactional information. You will learn more about MSXDBCDC in forthcoming sections. You can prepare the SQL Server instance by using the *Prepare SQL Server Instance* action in the MMC.

- **Create a new CDC service** One of the fundamental parts of the scenario as detailed earlier was a service that continuously monitors the source Oracle database. The CDC Service Configuration MMC will help you create such a service, as shown in Figure 8-10.

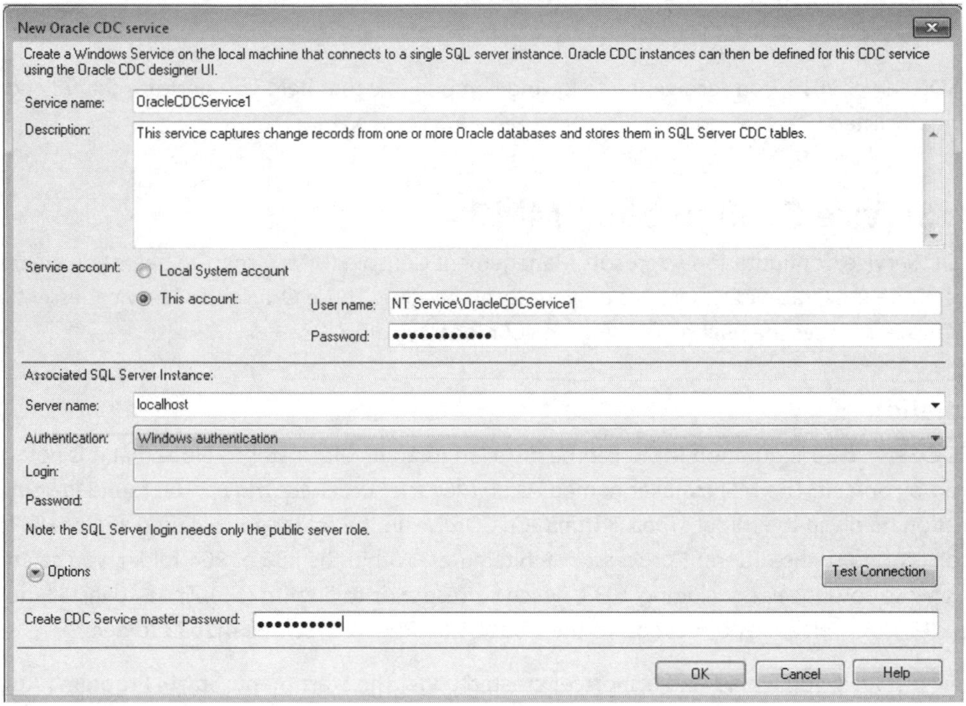

FIGURE 8-10 New Oracle CDC service.

Let's learn more about some of the fields in Figure 8-10.

- **Service Name** This is the name of the Windows service that would be created on your local system.

- **Service Account** This is the system account that will be used to run the Windows service created.

- **Associated SQL Server Instance** This is the SQL Server instance where the metadata, such as transaction progress, would be stored in a database called MSXDBCDC. Note that you have to prepare the SQL Server instance before associating it here using the Prepare SQL Server Instance action.
- **Create CDC Service Master Password** This password is used to create an asymmetric key on your associated SQL Server instance. The key will be used to encrypt the credentials required to connect to the source Oracle database's log mining infrastructure to extract transactions.

What Happens When a Service Is Created?

As you learned earlier, one of the components that you require in the end-to-end flow that consumes the change data from a source Oracle table would be a service that continuously monitors the transactions on the source Oracle database. The service also replicates those transactions on the destination mirrored SQL Server database.

When you use the Oracle CDC service MMC to create a service, it performs the following actions:

- Creates a Windows service using the configuration options mentioned on your local system
- Registers the Windows service with the Windows Service Control Manager on the local system
- Creates the registry entry HKLM\Software\Microsoft\XDBCDCSVC\<*cdc-service-name*>

The registry entry contains the following values:

- **SqlConnectString (REG_BINARY)** Contains the encrypted value for the SQL Server to connect to for the service.
- **SqlUsername (REG_BINARY)** Contains the encrypted value for the SQL Server login's username used to connect to the SQL Server mentioned earlier. This is used only when using the SQL Server authentication.
- **SqlPassword (REG_BINARY)** Contains the encrypted value for the SQL Server login's password used to connect to the SQL Server mentioned earlier. This is used only when using the SQL Server authentication.
- **AsymmetricKeyPassword (REG_BINARY)** Password to encrypt the log mining credentials for the source Oracle database.

All password values are stored as binary values that represent the encrypted value using Data Protection API (DPAPI) with the machine profile.

Oracle CDC Designer MMC

The Oracle CDC Designer MMC snap-in helps you create and manage CDC instances on a SQL Server instance.

Installation

The CDC Service Designer MMC can be installed using its MSI installer. Note that it is not installed by default. The MSI installer named *AttunityOracleCdcDesigner.msi* can be found in your installation media under the folder *\Tools\AttunityCDCOracle*. In this folder, you will find x64 or x86 folders that correspond to the different processor architectures. Within the x86 or x64 folder you would find folders for various locales including 1033, which corresponds to English (US).

Thus, to install the English (US) x64 version you must go to the *\Tools\AttunityCDCOracle\x64\1033* folder.

Once installed, you will find a shortcut created under the Start menu: Start | Program | Attunity | Change Data Capture for Oracle | CDC Designer.

Oracle CDC Instance

Before learning how the CDC designer works, it is important to understand the concept of an Oracle CDC instance.

An Oracle CDC instance is defined as an object that contains the following configuration information:

- The source Oracle database connection information.
- Credentials and properties to connect to the source Oracle databases.
- Source tables for which you need to capture CDC. You can even configure the instance to capture only a subset of the columns of each table.
- Mirror SQL Server database containing the mirror tables for the source tables or columns defined in the previous step.

Once created, the CDC instance configuration information is stored in a table called *cdc.xdbcdc_config* and the CDC state of the instance is stored in the *cdc.xdbcdc_state* table. These tables are stored in the SQL Server database created for the instance.

Therefore, using an Oracle CDC instance you can define the set of objects and information required for syncing changes from a source Oracle database. Now, let's learn how you can use the CDC designer to create an Oracle CDC instance. Let's call it a CDC instance for simplicity.

Using the CDC Designer

Let's step through the CDC designer and learn how we can create a CDC instance using the CDC Designer MMC.

As mentioned before, the CDC Designer MMC, once installed, can be found through the Start menu at All Programs | Change Data Capture for Oracle by Attunity | Oracle CDC Designer Configuration. It will invoke an MMC that you can use to create a CDC instance.

The first screen will ask you to connect to a SQL Server instance. Note that the CDC Designer MMC will retrieve all the CDC services you have configured on the SQL Server instance you connect to. These are the same CDC services that you created in the previous section using the CDC Service Configuration MMC.

Once connected, the CDC Designer will list all the available services on the SQL Server instance chosen, as shown in Figure 8-11.

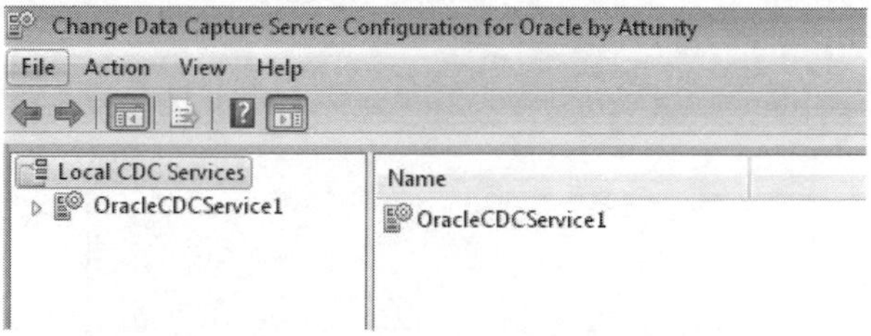

FIGURE 8-11 CDC services available on a SQL Server instance displayed in the CDC Designer.

You can now create a CDC instance using one of the available CDC services. Let's use the CDC service OracleCDCService1 as shown in Figure 8-11.

You can create a new CDC instance by right-clicking the service and choosing New Oracle CDC Instance as shown in Figure 8-12. This option launches the Create Oracle CDC Instance Wizard.

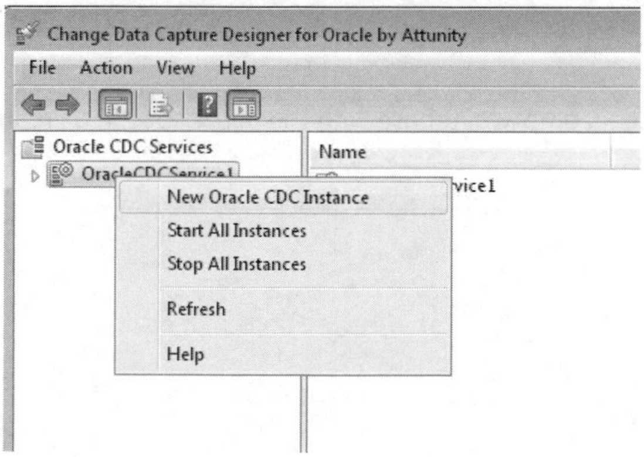

FIGURE 8-12 Creating a new Oracle CDC instance using the CDC Designer.

Create Oracle CDC Instance Wizard

Let's step through the Create Oracle CDC Instance Wizard. The first screen of the wizard requires you to input a name for the CDC instance to be created. As you know already, a CDC instance is also associated with a SQL Server database that will be created to contain the mirror tables of the source Oracle tables. The CDC service enables SQL Server CDC on the database and the mirror tables created. This screen also informs you of the database that will be created. Note that the name of the database defaults to the name of the instance. Now, let's create a new Oracle CDC instance by stating its name and creating the associated SQL Server database, as shown in Figure 8-13.

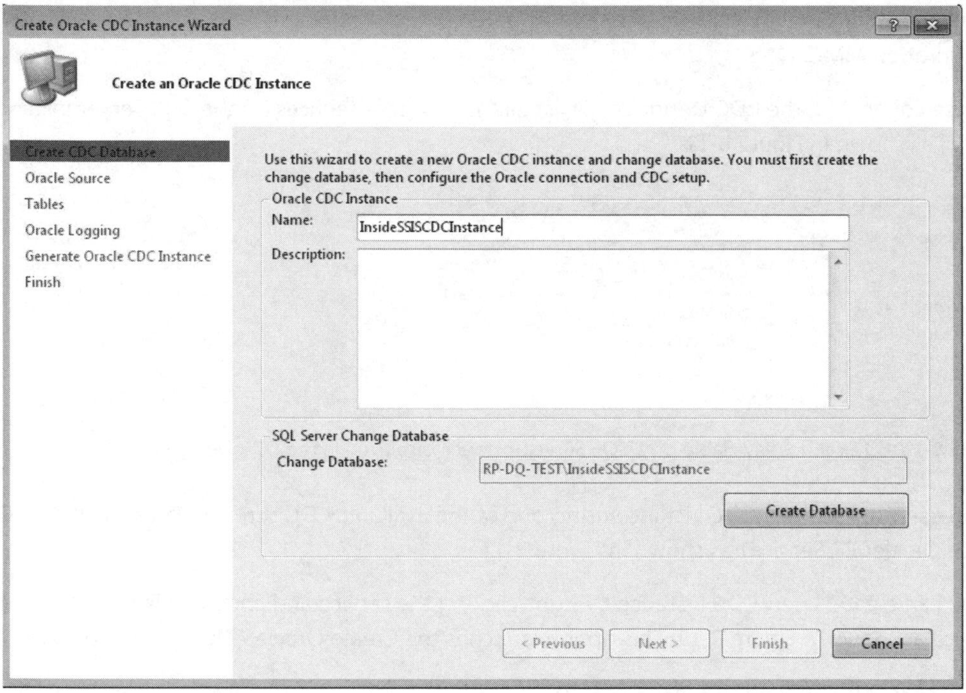

FIGURE 8-13 Create Oracle CDC Instance Wizard: Create CDC Database screen.

Once you click Create Database, you notice an empty database with the name specified created on the chosen SQL Server instance.

On the next screen, you have to provide the connection properties to connect to the source Oracle database. The source Oracle database is the database containing the Oracle tables for which you want to execute the CDC functionality. As shown in Figure 8-14, you will have to provide the Oracle connection string in the format *host[:port][/service name]*. You will also have to provide the credentials of an Oracle user that will be used for the following:

- Reading the Oracle redo logs (the user must have required privileges for reading the redo logs).
- Reading the source tables' metadata (the user must have privileges to read the tables).

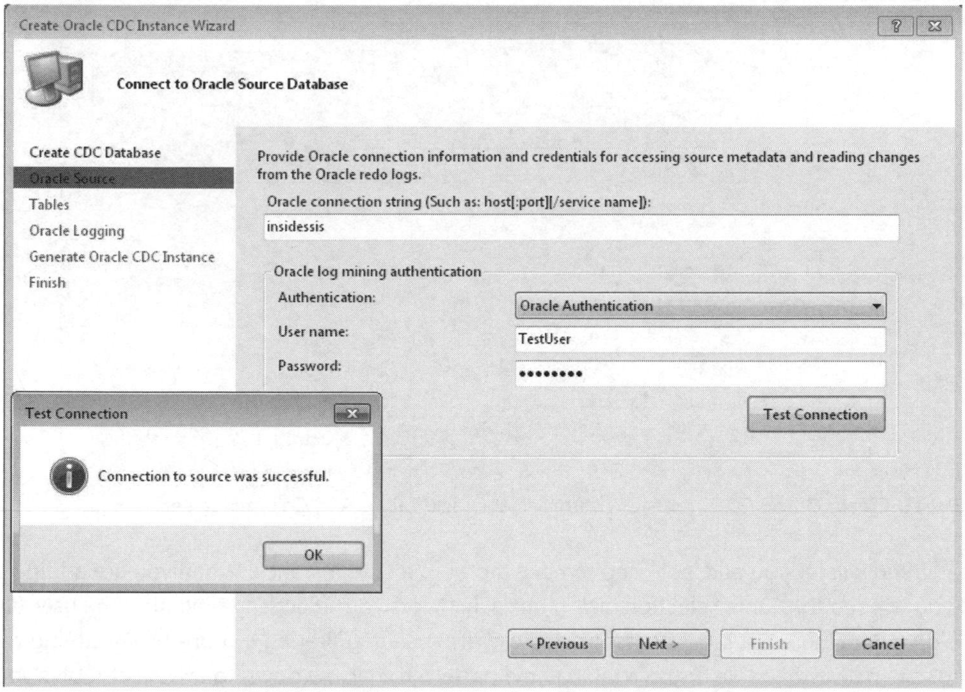

FIGURE 8-14 Create Oracle CDC Instance Wizard: Connect To Oracle Source Database screen.

Once connected to the Oracle source database, you can select the tables that you want to enable CDC for on the Select Oracle Tables and Columns screen shown in Figure 8-15.

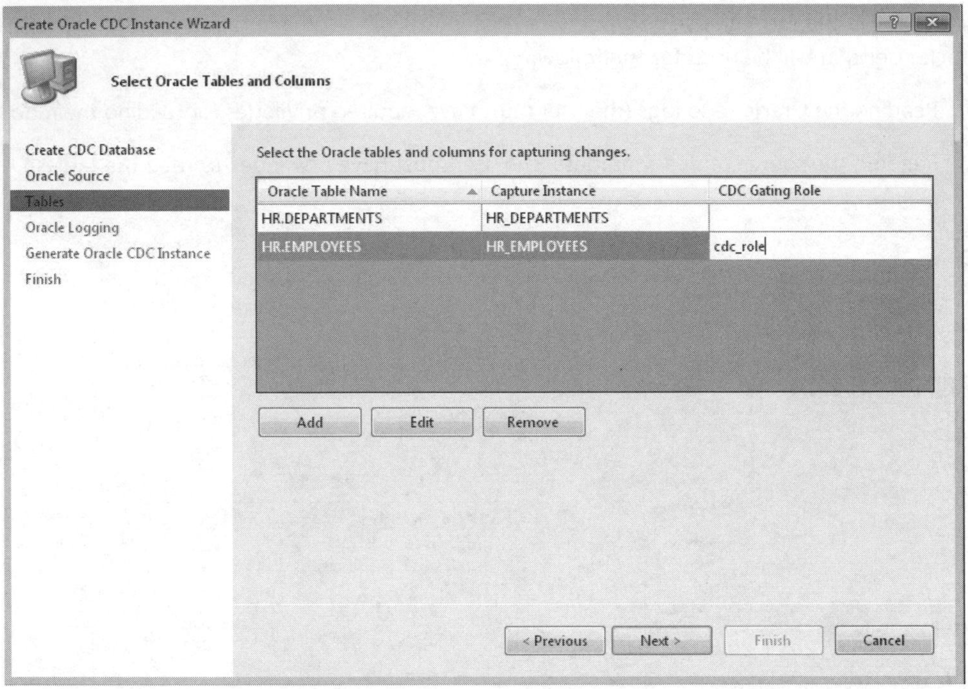

FIGURE 8-15 Create Oracle CDC Instance Wizard: Select Oracle Tables And Columns screen.

The screen will let you add, edit, and remove tables in a CDC instance. When you are adding a table, you will see the Table Selection dialog box, which lets you select any table that the user (Oracle user selected in Figure 8-14) has access to. You can also use the filtering options by specifying the specific schema for the table or use a table name pattern to narrow down to the exact tables you require as shown in Figure 8-16.

> **Tip** If you have a large number of Oracle tables, filtering based on schema and name can help you navigate through the window much more efficiently. Without the filtering, the dialog box will try to list all the tables to which the user has access and will slow down or freeze.

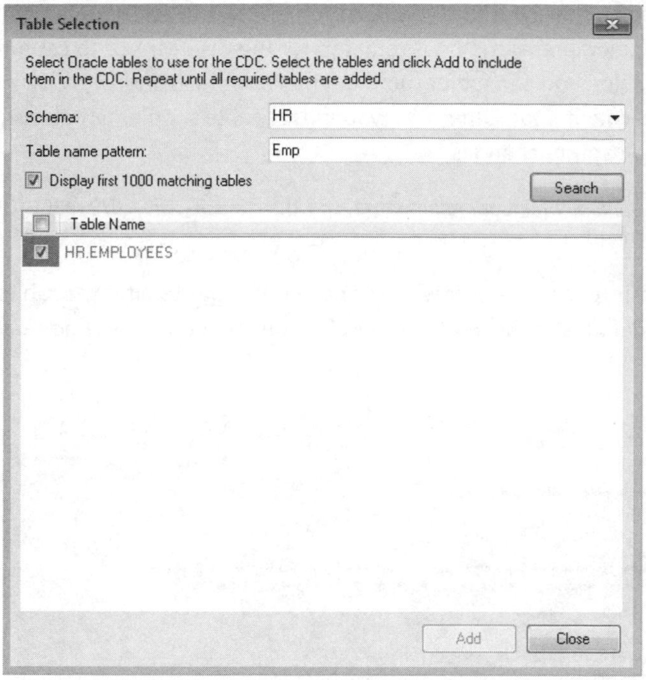

FIGURE 8-16 Table selection dialog box.

The Edit window lets you select the exact columns that you want to include for the selected table. It will also allow you to define a CDC security role for the table. Note that if the CDC role doesn't exist, the designer would create a new CDC security role. Let's edit the *HR.Employees* table selected as shown in Figure 8-17.

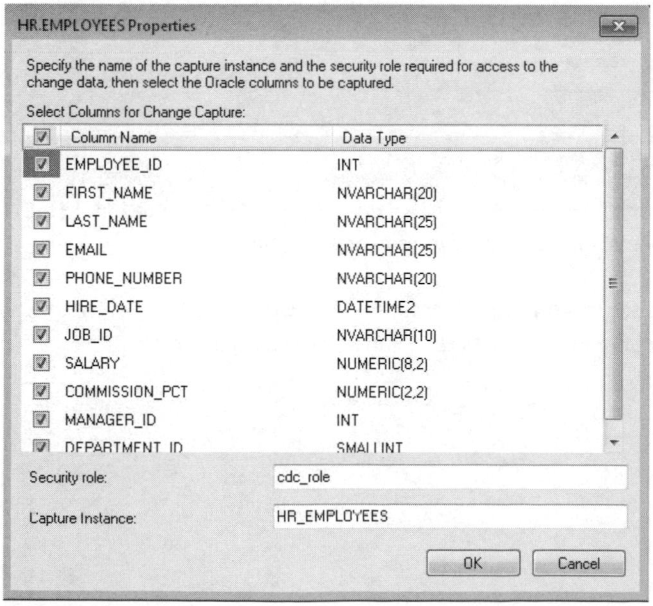

FIGURE 8-17 Table Properties dialog box.

The next wizard screen will show you the script that you must run on your Oracle source database to enable supplemental logging. Supplemental logging is required for the CDC service to capture the logs or the changes on the source tables. You can either run the script from the window by clicking Run Script or you can save it and execute it later. Either way, you must enable supplemental logging before starting your CDC instance to capture changes.

See Also *To learn more about Oracle supplemental logging, refer to* http://docs.oracle.com/cd/B19306_01/server.102/b14215/logminer.htm#i1021068.

When you click Run Script, you can specify the user who will have privileges to alter the tables used in the CDC instance. The user defaults to the user specified for connecting to the Oracle database as shown in Figure 8-18.

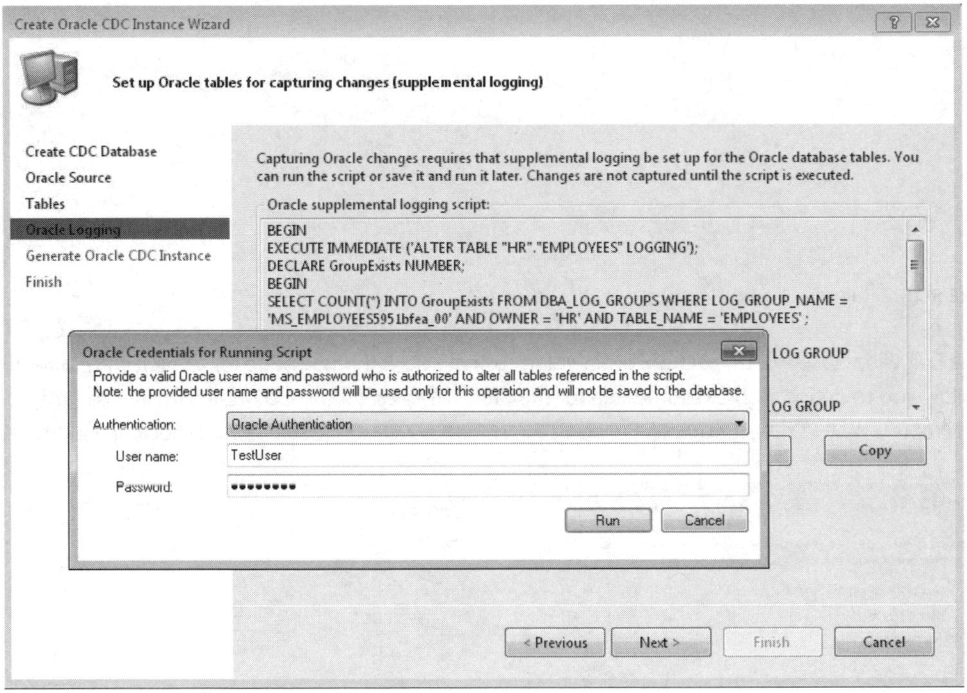

FIGURE 8-18 Create Oracle CDC Instance Wizard: Enabling supplemental logging.

You have now completed all the steps required to configure your CDC instance. On the next screen you can execute all the steps to set up your Oracle CDC instance, as shown in Figure 8-19.

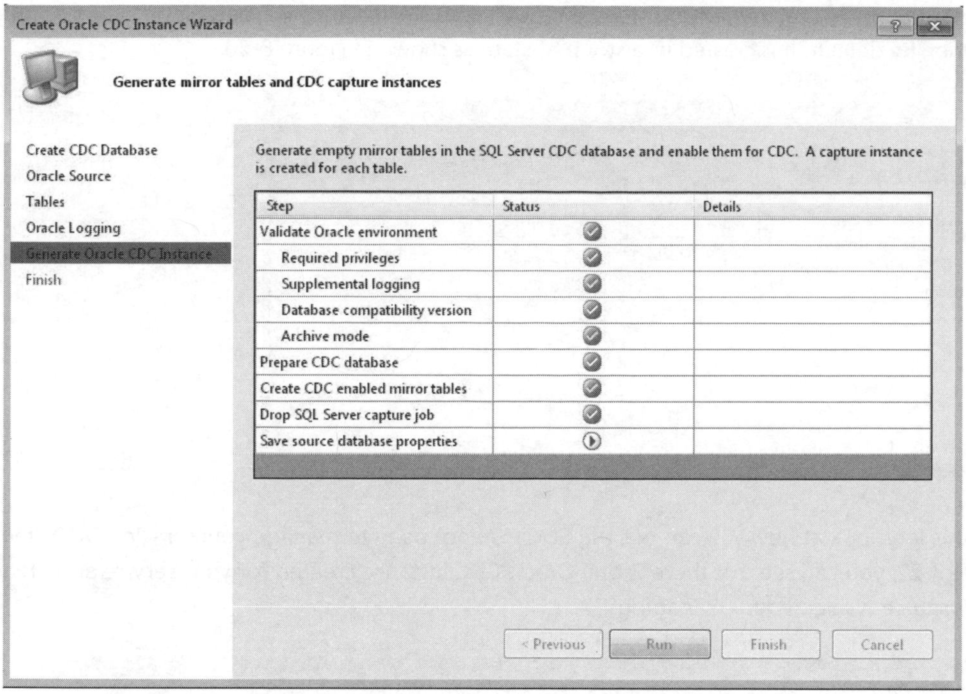

FIGURE 8-19 Create Oracle CDC Instance Wizard: Execute the setup steps.

> **Tip** One of the steps that the wizard performs is to check if archive mode is enabled on your database. This mode is disabled by default. You can enable it by using a user with SYSDBA privileges and running the command in Listing 8-8.

LISTING 8-8 Steps for enabling archive mode on an Oracle database

```
CONNECT / AS SYSDBA
STARTUP MOUNT;
ALTER DATABASE ARCHIVELOG;
ALTER DATABASE OPEN;
```

Once you have executed all the steps, a new Oracle CDC instance is created and available on your designer. By default, it is created in a stopped state as shown in Figure 8-20.

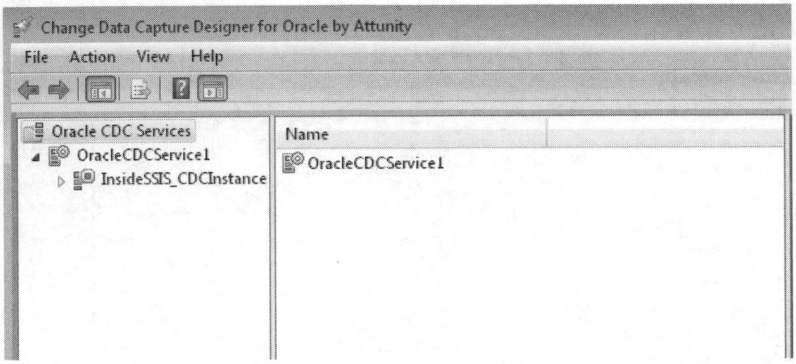

FIGURE 8-20 New CDC Instance created for a CDC service using the CDC Designer.

Now, let's look at how you can use the CDC instance pane to manage your Oracle CDC instance. In Figure 8-21, you can see that there is one Oracle CDC instance created for your service and *InsideSSIS CDCInstance* is selected for managing.

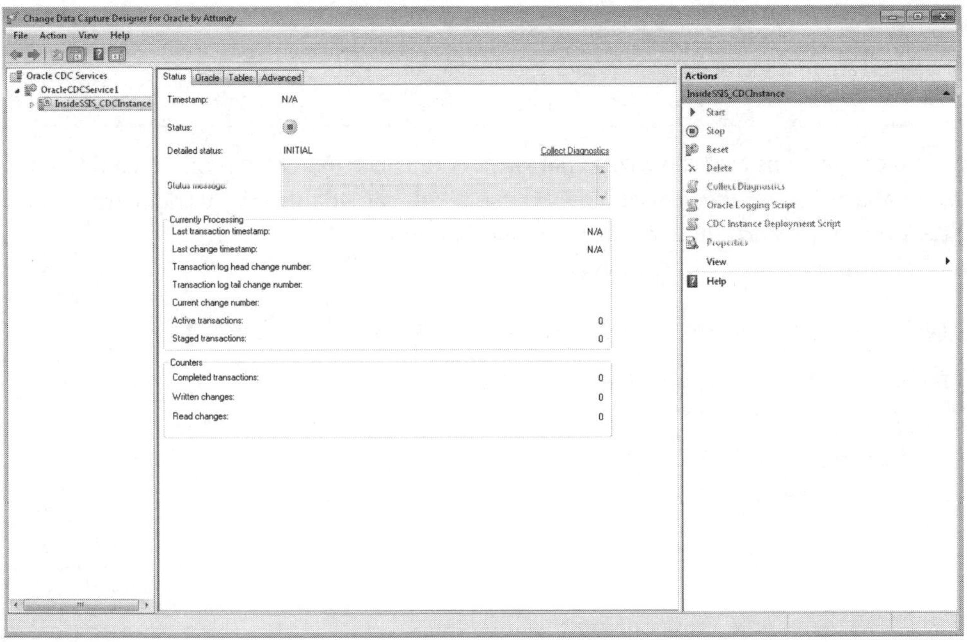

FIGURE 8-21 Managing a CDC instance using the Designer MMC.

You can see in Figure 8-21 that the screen for managing the CDC instance has several actions available, as listed in Table 8-6.

TABLE 8-6 Actions available for a CDC instance

Action	Description
Start	Starts the CDC instance. Once the CDC instance is started, it starts reading the logs and capturing changes using the Oracle LogMiner facility. It then orders all the Oracle transactions in order of their transaction commit. It then writes those changes to the mirrored SQL Server table.
Stop	Stops the CDC instance. Note that when you stop an instance, the changes captured until that time are committed to the destination SQL Server tables. No new changes are captured.
Reset	Resets the CDC instance to its initial or empty state. Note that this action is only available when your CDC instance is in a stopped state. When you reset your instance, all changes captured in the change tables and the CDC instance internal state are deleted. When you start the instance the next time, changes and transactions are captured from that time onward (the time when you start again).
Delete	Deletes the instance and the associated SQL Server tables and databases. This action is available when an instance is stopped.
Collect Diagnostics	Collects the diagnostics information from the *xdbcdc_trace* table and saves it to a file.
Oracle Logging Script	This allows you to regenerate the Oracle supplemental logging script that you must execute on your source Oracle tables before you start the instance.
CoraclDC Instance Deployment Script	This script can be used to re-create the SQL Server database and tables associated with the CDC instance.

Now let's look at the other properties you can see on the screen. The center pane describes the various properties of the CDC instance for a given timestamp. For instance, let's take the example of Figure 8-22 where the CDC instance is in a processing state and the properties have some values associated with them.

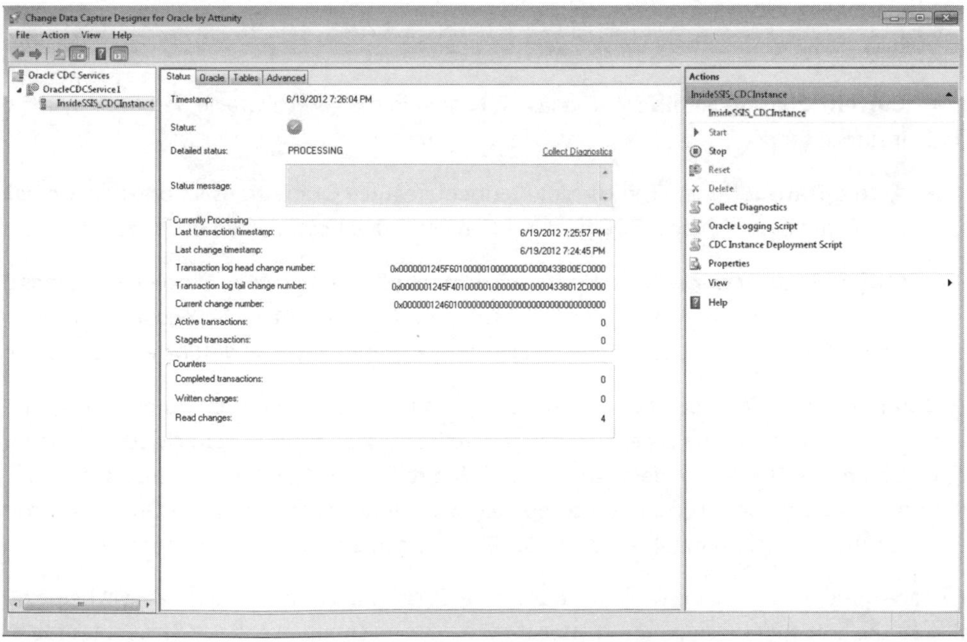

FIGURE 8-22 CDC instance processing changes.

Let's review some of those important properties, described as follows:

- **Status** It describes the current status of the CDC instance. It can be Running, Stopped, Error, or Paused. Running and Stopped are its ideal states. The CDC instance can be in an Error state if the CDC instance is not running because the CDC instance couldn't be in Running state after multiple retries. It can be in the Paused state when the CDC instance is running but the processing is suspended because of an error. The help file for the designer describes the statuses in more detail.

  The status message is also associated with a *Detailed Status* message that can describe the error if the CDC instance is in an *Error* or *Paused* state. It also lists the *Timestamp* for the UTC time when the CDC state of the CDC instance was last read from the state table.

- **Currently Processing** The Currently Processing section contains information about the transactions that the Oracle CDC instance is currently processing. Let's learn more about some of those properties:

  - **Last Transaction Timestamp** This describes the local timestamp at the SQL Server of the last transaction written to the change tables.
  - **Last Change Timestamp** This describes the local timestamp of the most recent change seen by the Oracle CDC Instance in the source Oracle database transaction logs.
  - **Transaction Log Head Change Number** This denotes the most recent SCN that was read from the Oracle transaction log.
  - **Transaction Log Tail Change Number** This denotes the SCN to which the Oracle CDC instance will reposition in the event of a restart or any other type of failure (including cluster failover).
  - **Current Change Number** The last SCN seen in the source Oracle database by the CDC instance service.
  - **Active Transactions** The current number of source Oracle transactions that are being processed by the Oracle CDC instance that are not yet committed or rolled back.
  - **Staged Transactions** This denotes the current number of source Oracle transactions that are staged to the *cdc.xdbcdc_staged_transactions* table. This is an intermediate table where the transactions are recorded before being actually committed to the destination SQL Server table.

- **Counters** The Counters section describes the number of changes being read and written by the CDC instance. In this case, the changes are being read from the Oracle source tables and written to the SQL Server destination tables. It also lists the number of completed transactions. A transaction is considered completed when it has been read from Oracle and committed to the SQL Server database. A transaction can contain multiple changes.

There are three other tabs available for the Oracle CDC instance. The Oracle tab will help you reconfigure the credentials required to connect to the Oracle source database. The Tables tab allows you to edit the tables and columns selected for the CDC instance. The Advanced tab allows you to set the properties for a CDC instance. For the list of all the properties that can be configured, you can check out the *cdc.xdbcdc_config* table for an instance.

MSXDBCDC Database

When you prepare a SQL Server for the first time to create a CDC service on it, a database called MSXDBCDC is created on the SQL server. There is always one MSXDBCDC database per SQL Server instance, which implies that you will use MSXDBCDC for storing all the CDC services on the database. Thus, whenever you are connecting to a database for creating a service, you are in turn using the MSXDBCDC database to store the metadata about the service.

The MSXDBCDC can be created using the Oracle CDC Service Configuration MMC snap-in, which can either create this database (after the user connects to SQL Server as sysadmin) or can produce a T-SQL script for creating the MSXDBCDC database manually by a SQL Server sysadmin (possibly after inspection). Once the MSXDBCDC database is created, new Oracle CDC services can be created and new Oracle CDC instances can be defined for those services. The owner of this database is the same identity with which the Oracle CDC service connects to the SQL Server instance.

Most actions you perform on the MMC have some resultant insert, update, or delete operation on a table in the MSXDBCDC database. Most of these actions can also be directly performed on the database without interacting with the MMC. Let's learn more about the tables and stored procedures available in the database and their functionalities.

Tables in MSXDBCDC

The MSXDBCDC database contains certain tables that contain the metadata for all the CDC services associated with the SQL Server instance. Table 8-7 lists the tables and their descriptions.

TABLE 8-7 Tables in the MSXDBCDC database

Table	Description
dbo.xdbcdc_trace	This table stores tracing information produced by the Oracle CDC services.
dbo.xdbcdc_databases	This table contains the names of Oracle CDC databases in the current SQL Server instance. The Oracle CDC service uses this table to determine which instances to start or stop and which instances need to be reconfigured.
dbo.xdbcdc_services	This table lists the name of the CDC services that are associated with the SQL Server instance. This table is used by the CDC Service Configuration MMC to determine the list of CDC services in a SQL Server instance to which it can connect.

Stored Procedures in MSXDBCDC

The database also contains several stored procedures. These stored procedures represent several actions that you can also execute through the MMCs. However, a DBA or a developer might choose to use these procedures directly to perform administrative actions on a CDC service or an instance. Let's understand some of these procedures.

dbo.xdbcdc_reset_db(dbname) This stored procedure is used for clearing the data contents of an Oracle CDC instance. You can use this procedure in the following cases:

1. You want to restart the change capture from the current timestamp, ignoring the previous changes. You can do this when you perform database recovery for the source Oracle database or the Oracle database was idle for a long period of time.
2. You realize the current CDC state for the instance is corrupted and you want to reset the CDC state.

When you invoke the procedure, it internally performs the following steps:

- Stop the CDC instance (if it was active).
- Truncate the *_CT* tables, the *cdc.lsn_time_mapping* table, and the *cdc.ddl_history* system tables.
- Clear the *cdc.xdbcdc_state* table.
- Clear the *start_lsn* column of all *cdc.change_table* rows.

This procedure requires the caller to be a member of the *db_owner* fixed database role of the CDC database that is being reset.

dbo.xdbcdc_enable_db(*dbname,svcname*) This procedure is used to initialize a database. The initialization of the database involves the following steps:

- Create the various *cdc.xdbcdc_** tables in the database (if they do not exist).
- Add an entry for the given CDC database in the *MSXDBCDC.xdbcdc_databases* table.
- Add a user *cdc_service* for the login name mentioned in the *cdc_service_sql_user* column from the *MSXDBCDC.xdbcdc_services* table as a member of the *db_owner* of the CDC database.

This procedure requires the caller to be a member of the sysadmin fixed server role of the SQL Server instance.

dbo.xdbcdc_disable_db(*dbname*) This procedure removes the CDC database from the *MSXDBCDC.xdbcdc_databases* table. This procedure also requires the caller to be a member of the sysadmin fixed user role of the SQL Server instance.

dbo.xdbcdc_add_service(*servicename,sqluser*) This stored procedure adds an entry for the service in the *MSXDBCDC.xdbcdc_services* table and increments the *ref_count* column of that table. The *ref_count* column denotes the number of services with the same name of the same SQL Server instance. This procedure requires the caller to be a member of the db_owner fixed database role of the MSXDBCDC database or to be a member of either the sysadmin or serveradmin fixed server roles of the SQL Server instance.

dbo.xdbcdc_remove_service(*servicename*) This stored procedure decrements the *ref_count* column in the row for the service name in the *MSXDBCDC.xdbcdc_services* table. When the *ref_count* drops to zero, it also deletes that row denoting all services with that name have been removed from the SQL Server instance. This procedure requires the caller to be a member of the db_owner fixed database role of the MSXDBCDC database or to be a member of either the sysadmin or serveradmin fixed server roles of the SQL Server instance.

dbo.xdbcdc_start(*dbname*) This procedure starts the service associated with the database name provided. This procedure requires the caller to be a member of the db_owner fixed database role of the CDC database or to be a member of either sysadmin or serveradmin fixed server roles of the SQL Server instance.

dbo.xdbcdc_stop(*dbname*) This procedure will stop the service associated with the database name provided. This procedure requires the caller to be a member of the db_owner fixed database role of the CDC database or to be a member of either the sysadmin or serveradmin fixed server roles of the SQL Server instance.

dbo.xdbcdc_update_config(*dbname*) This is an internal stored procedure that updates the configuration version of a database to the current timestamp. This procedure requires the caller to be a member of the db_owner fixed database role of the CDC database or to be a member of either the sysadmin or serveradmin fixed server roles of the SQL Server instance.

Thus, you can use some of these procedures to directly modify your CDC services and instances without using the MMCs.

Oracle CDC Service Executable (xdbcdcsvc.exe)

One of the great things about the Oracle CDC service is the multiple ways you can create and administer the services. You have already created services using the MMCs and the T-SQL stored procedures. Now, let us see how we can create and administer services using the executable *xdbcdcsvc.exe.*

Installation

The executable is installed along with the other components when you install the Oracle CDC Service Configuration MMC. Once installed, the respective executable (x64 or x86 depending on the MSI you installed) can be found in the path *<<installation folder>>\Change Data Capture for Oracle by Attunity\xdbcdcsvc.exe*

Commands

The *xdbcdcsvc.exe* file provides multiple commands to perform administrative tasks on your Oracle CDC services. These commands usually act as parameters to *xdbcdcsvc.exe* at the command prompt. Based on additional parameters, they will usually perform an administrative task. Let's learn more about those commands.

Config command You can use the *config* command to update the configuration of an existing Oracle CDC service. You can also use specific parameters to update only specific components of the service configuration such as the connection string of the SQL Server to connect to. This command must be executed by a machine administrator. Listing 8-9 shows you the syntax of the command.

LISTING 8-9 Syntax of <config>

```
xdbcdcsvc.exe config command
xdbcdcsvc.exe config <cdc-service-name>
[connect= <sql-server-connection-string>]
   [key= <asym-key-password>]
   [svcacct= <windows-account> <windows-password>]
   [sqlacct= <sql-username> <sql-password>]
Sample usage:
Xdbcdcsvc.exe config OracleCDCService1 connect= "server=localhost;trusted_connection=Yes;" key=
InsideSSIS svcacct= TestUser InsideSSIS2012
```

where

- **cdc-service-name (required)** The CDC service name to update.
- **sql-server-connection-string** This is the connect string to update. See the next section, "Create command," for usage notes.
- **asym-key-password** This is the asymmetric key password to update.
- **windows-account, windows-password** This is the Windows service account credentials to update.
- **sql-username, sql-password** This is the SQL Server authentication credentials to update. If the sqlacct= option is specified without an empty username ("") and an empty password, the Oracle CDC service will connect to the SQL Server instance using Windows authentication using the specified service account.

Create command You can use the *create* command to create a new Oracle CDC service from the command line. The command must be executed by a machine administrator. Listing 8-10 shows you the syntax and the usage of the *create* command.

LISTING 8-10 Syntax of <create>

```
xdbcdcsvc.exe create command
xdbcdcsvc.exe create <cdc-service-name>
[connect= <sql-server-connection-string>]
   [key= <asym-key-password>]
   [svcacct= <windows-account> <windows-password>]
   [sqlacct= <sql-username> <sql-password>]
Sample usage:
Xdbcdcsvc.exe create OracleCDCService1 connect= "server=localhost;trusted_connection=Yes;" key=
InsideSSIS sqlacct= SQLTestUser SQLInsideSSIS2012
```

where

- **cdc-service-name (required)** The name with which the CDC service is to be created. If a service with the same name exists, then the *xdbcdcsvc.exe* executable returns an error. You should avoid long service names, as the service names are used at multiple places including registry keys. You cannot use the characters "\" and "/" in the service names.

- **sql-server-connection-string** This is the connect string to update and to use for connecting to the SQL Server instance with which the Oracle CDC service will be associated. If the connect string contains spaces or quotes, it must be quoted. Embedded quotes are escaped by doubling the quotes.
- **asym-key-password** This is a password with which the service will guard the asymmetric key it uses for storing the source database log mining credentials.
- **windows-account, windows-password** This specifies the Windows account and password with which the Oracle CDC service will be registered.
- **sql-username, sql-password** This specifies that the Oracle CDC service will connect to the SQL Server instance using SQL Server authentication. If omitted, the Oracle CDC service will connect to the SQL Server instance using Windows Authentication.

The preceding parameters are sufficient for creating a service. Once created, you can always reconfigure the service using the *config* command.

> **Tip** For using parameter values with one or more spaces or even double quotes, you must place them between double quotes at the command line. For instance, for using a password like *Hello World*, you should use *"Hello World"*.

Delete command As you might have inferred already, creating an Oracle CDC service does the following things:

- Creates a Windows service on your local system
- Creates Windows registry key entries for storing key and connection information

For deleting a service you can use *sc delete,* which is the Windows Service Manager API for deleting a service. However, using the Windows Service Manager API will cause orphan registry entries that are not deleted using the service manager, which just deletes the service. You must use the *delete* command for *xdbcdcsvc.exe* to delete the service. This makes sure that it deletes the Windows service and clears the related registry keys. Listing 8-11 shows you the syntax and usage of the *delete* command.

LISTING 8-11 Syntax of <delete>

```
xdbcdcsvc.exe delete command
xdbcdcsvc.exe delete <cdc-service-name>
Sample usage:
Xdbcdcsvc.exe delete OracleCDCService1
```

where

- **cdc-service-name (required)** The name of the Oracle CDC service to be deleted

Help command You can always use the *help* command to list the options available for use with *xdbcdcsvc.exe,* as shown in Listing 8-12.

LISTING 8-12 Syntax of <help>

```
xdbcdcsvc.exe help command
xdbcdcsvc.exe help
or
xdbcdcsvc.exe /?
```

Data Type Handling

Oracle and SQL Server conform to some ANSI standards, but not all their data types have one-to-one mappings. As a part of an Oracle CDC service instance setup, mirror tables are created inside the SQL Server CDC database. These mirror tables are created with the goal of replicating the schema of the original Oracle tables but with SQL Server column data types. Table 8-8 tells you more about the mapping used when creating these mirror tables. The user does have some control over those mirror tables because he or she will be able to change the default data type mapping from Oracle to SQL Server. However, it still has to conform to values in Table 8-8.

TABLE 8-8 Data type mapping between Oracle and SQL Server

Oracle Type	SQL Type	Comments
BFILE	Ignored	BFILE is not supported in an Oracle CDC instance.
BINARY_FLOAT	REAL	
BINARY_DOUBLE	FLOAT	
BLOB	VARBINARY(MAX)	No change data will be captured and only a change indication would be recorded.
CHAR	NVARCHAR	Length same as in Oracle.
CLOB	VARCHAR(MAX)	No change data will be captured and only a change indication would be recorded.
DATE	DATETIME2	Scale will be trimmed to 0.
FLOAT([1-24])	REAL	
FLOAT([25-53])	FLOAT	
FLOAT([54-126])	FLOAT	
INTERVAL YEAR [(1-9)] TO MONTH	VARCHAR(13)	
INTERVAL DAY [(1-9)] TO SECOND [(1-9)]	VARCHAR(29)	
LONG	VARCHAR(MAX)	No change data will be captured and only a change indication would be recorded.
LONG RAW	VARBINARY(MAX)	No change data will be captured and only a change indication would be recorded.
NCHAR	NVARCHAR	Length is retained the same as in Oracle data type for the column.

Oracle Type	SQL Type	Comments
NCLOB	NVARCHAR(MAX)	No change data will be captured and only a change indication would be recorded.
NUMBER	FLOAT	
NUMBER(1 - 4,0)	SMALLINT	
NUMBER(5 - 9,0)	INT	
NUMBER(10 - 18,0)	BIGINT	
NUMBER(19 - 38,0)	NUMERIC(P, 0)	Precision same as in Oracle data type for the column.
NUMBER(P, S) 1 =< S =< P	NUMERIC(P, S)	Precision and scale retained the same as the Oracle data type for the column.
NUMBER(P, S) S < 0	FLOAT	
NUMBER(P, S) S > P	FLOAT	
NVARCHAR2	NVARCHAR	Length is retained the same as in Oracle data type for the column.
RAW	VARBINARY	Length is retained the same as in Oracle data type for the column.
REAL	FLOAT	
REF	Ignored	
ROWID	Ignored	
TIMESTAMP([0-7])	DATETIME2([0-7])	Scale is retained the same as in Oracle data type for the column.
TIMESTAMP([8-9])	DATETIME2(7)	
TIMESTAMP WITH TIME ZONE	VARCHAR(37)	
TIMESTAMP WITH LOCAL TIME ZONE	VARCHAR(37)	
UROWID	Ignored	
User defined	Unsupportable	Oracle CDC instance cannot capture a table with this data type.
VARCHAR2	NVARCHAR	Length is retained the same as in Oracle data type for the column.
VARRAY	Unsupportable	Oracle CDC instance cannot capture a table with this data type.
VIRTUAL	Unsupportable	Oracle CDC instance cannot capture a table with this data type.
XMLTYPE	NVARCHAR(MAX)	No change data will be captured and only a change indication would be recorded.

Tip You can also create data type mapping for data types that can be internally type casted such as most data types can be type casted to *CHAR, VARCHAR, NCHAR,* and *NVARCHAR.*

SSIS CDC Components

Once you have created the mirror tables on SQL Server that are being replicated with the transactions from the source Oracle databases, they behave just like any other SQL Server tables. The Oracle CDC service also enables SQL Server CDC on these mirror tables resulting in the CT tables. Now you can use the CDC components of SSIS 2012 to consume changes from these tables just as you would consume changes from any other table.

Let's recap the steps you performed to start capturing CDC data from your source Oracle tables.

1. Enable Oracle CDC service and create a CDC instance. This creates mirror tables on the SQL Server database.
2. Enable SQL Server CDC on the mirror tables.
3. Use CDC components in SSIS to capture changes from the SQL Server *_CT* tables created from the mirror tables.

Summary

This chapter introduced the new CDC features in SQL Server 2012. Using these features, you can perform CDC in your SSIS packages using the CDC Control task, CDC Source, and CDC Splitter components. You also learned how you can use SQL Server CDC to track changes on your Oracle tables using the new features introduced in SQL Server 2012. Using the MMCs, you can create the Oracle CDC services and the Oracle CDC instances that will help you create mirror tables on SQL Server using the source Oracle tables. The Oracle CDC instance also enables CDC on the mirror tables and the service replicates all the transactions from the source Oracle tables on to the destination SQL server tables. The Oracle CDC instance setup enables CDC on the mirror SQL Server tables, resulting in change tracking of those tables. Thus, you effectively enabled change tracking on the original Oracle tables.

CHAPTER 9

Data Cleansing Using SSIS

In This Chapter

SQL Server Integration Services provides great support for handling data quality. It offers a rich set of built-in functionality and seamless interoperability with other data quality features in SQL Server and partner solutions. You can perform comprehensive data quality management integrated with data integration processes using the profiling and cleansing capabilities available in SSIS. This is especially useful in integration scenarios involving multiple data stores with duplicate, inconsistent, or incorrect data. Let's look at the data profiling and cleansing capabilities in SSIS.

Data Profiling Task

You use the Data Profiling task in SSIS to analyze and understand the nature of data in a table or view in a SQL Server database. The profile of the data analyzed is written to a file or an SSIS variable in XML format. Data profiling can be performed as an independent step outside of data integration to help you understand the nature of the data before designing data cleaning solutions, or can be done as a part of data integration to control the data processing logic. When performed within a data integration process, you use the XML result of the profiling step to determine what to do with the data before loading it to the destination or to determine whether to skip loading when the data quality is not acceptable and no cleaning solution is in place.

This task uses the ADO.NET connection manager to connect to a SQL Server instance used for profiling. It can profile data available in SQL Server 2000 and newer versions. If you need to profile data available somewhere else, you need to load it into a SQL Server database for profiling. The types of profiling operations (also known as *profiling requests*) supported by this task are listed in Table 9-1.

TABLE 9-1 Profile types and uses

Profile	Use
Candidate Key	Analyze whether a column or set of columns is appropriate to serve as a key for the selected dataset. Integer, string, and datetime data types are supported.
Column Length Distribution	Compute minimum and maximum lengths of values in string columns and percentage of rows in each distinct length value.
Column Null Ratio	Compute percentage of null values in columns of any data types.
Column Pattern	Derive regular expressions representing values of string columns.
Column Statistics	Compute statistics such as minimum, maximum, average, and standard deviation for numeric columns, and minimum and maximum for datetime columns.
Column Value Distribution	Compute distinct values and percentage of rows with each value.
Functional Dependency	Analyze the extent to which the values in dependent columns depend on the values in the determinant columns.
Value Inclusion	Compute the overlap in the values between two sets of columns.

Profiling operation names that start with "column" analyze one column per profiling request. The other three profiling operations can analyze multiple columns or relationships between columns and datasets. In a data profiling task, you can execute each of these types of profiling operations on the same or on different datasets. When profiling is limited to one dataset, you can use the Quick Profile button in the Data Profiling Task Editor (Figure 9-1) to launch the editor for profiling on one table or view.

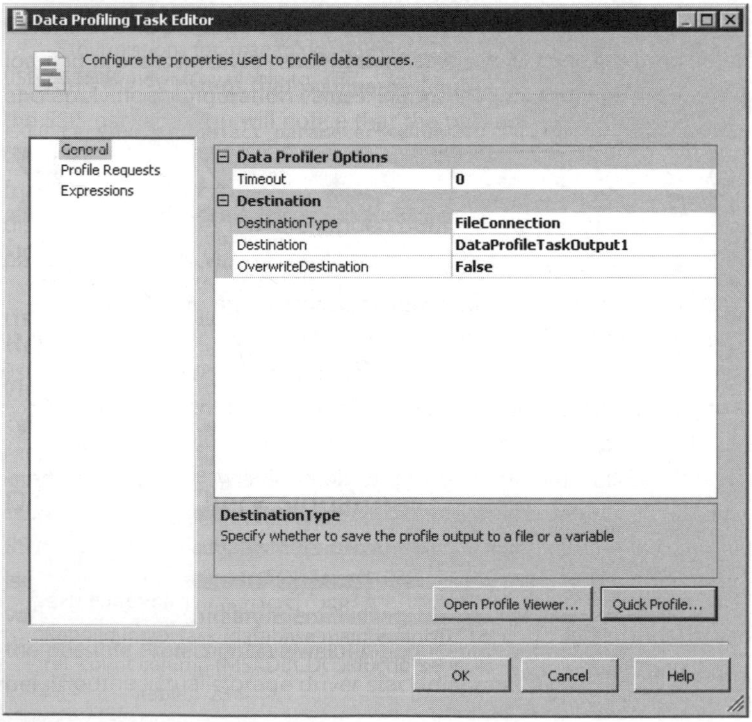

FIGURE 9-1 Data Profiling Task Editor.

Configuring profiling on a single table or view is a simple step that you take by specifying a connection manager and the name of the table or view. The common profiling options are selected automatically, and the configuration uses the default settings available for different profiling operations. For example, functional dependency profiling is not a common operation, so it is not included by default in the quick profile editor. After you exit from the quick profile editor and confirm the changes, the task is configured with the default settings. You can go to the Profile Requests page in the task editor and edit those settings. Figure 9-2 shows the editor for configuring a quick profile.

If your profiling involves multiple datasets or advanced settings, then Quick Profiling might not be sufficient; instead, you'll need to use the standard features in the task editor. If the task has been configured using Quick Profiling, you can use the Profile Requests page of the task editor to update the settings. Each profile request has the following properties:

- **Connection Manager** Name of the SSIS ADO.NET connection manager to connect to the SQL Server database containing the data to be profiled.
- **Table or View** Name of the table or view to use for profiling.
- **Columns** Names columns from the table or view to include in profiling. "*" is used to specify all columns.
- **Special properties** Profiling requests might have properties specific to the profiling operation involved. For example, Column Null Ratio request does not have any special property. Candidate Key request has three special properties namely, *ThresholdSetting*, *KeyStrength-Threshold*, and *MaxNumberOfViolations*.

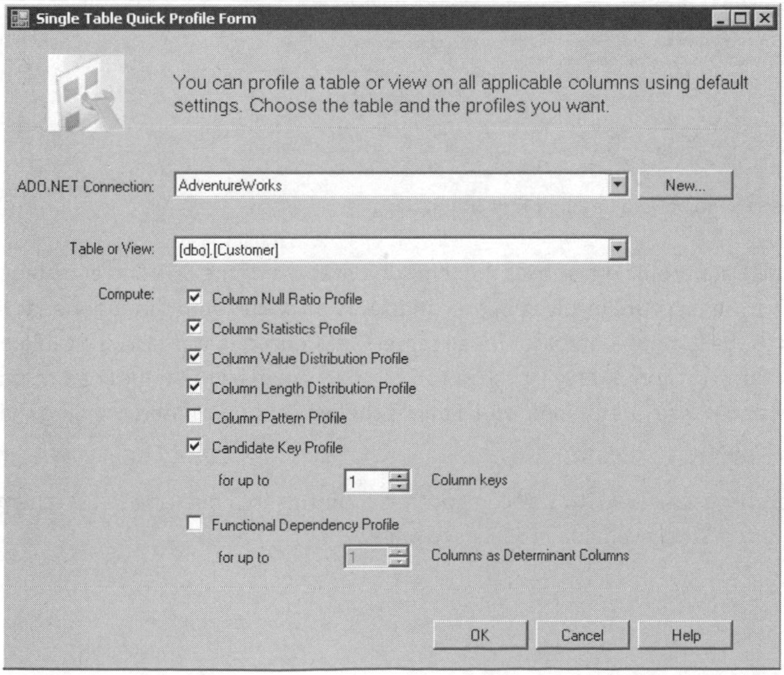

FIGURE 9-2 Quick Profile Form.

Figure 9-3 shows the Profile Requests page in the Data Profiling Task Editor. Viewing the filter option in the user interface helps in filtering the profile requests displayed. Each profile request has an identifier; the *Request ID* property of the profile stores this identifier. You can edit this property value to create a more meaningful identifier. The bottom half of the page displays the properties of the selected request.

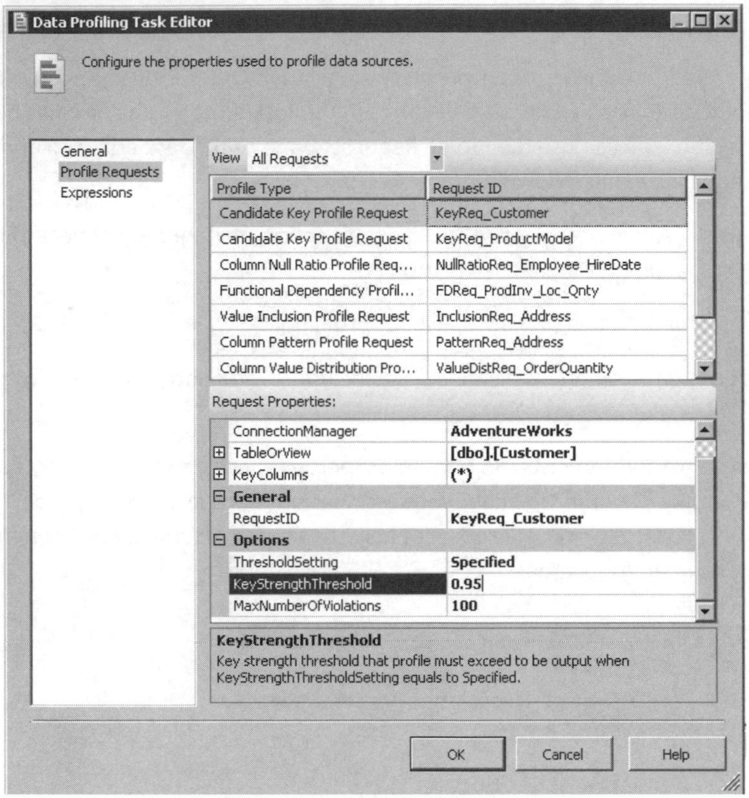

FIGURE 9-3 Profile Requests page in Data Profiling Task Editor.

During execution, the Data Profiling task uses the tempdb database of the SQL Server instance involved in profiling. The user account involved in executing SSIS packages with this task needs Read and Write permissions to the tempdb databases for all servers referenced in this task. If a table or view is empty, the task does not compute any of the profiles on it. When all the values of a column referenced in a profile request are *null*, Column Null Ratio is the only column-based profiling that can be performed on that column.

The output of the profiling task is an XML document that conforms to a published XSD schema. You can save the output to a string variable in SSIS or to a file.

Warning The output might contain sensitive metadata information about the table, view, or the columns processed. If you request profiling on sensitive data values, the output could also contain sensitive values from the dataset processed. Take appropriate precautions when persisting or using the profiling result. If you save the result to the file system, you should use file access control for protection.

You use the Data Profile Viewer to view data profiles saved to files. You can launch the viewer using either of the following options:

- Run DataProfileViewer.exe from the command line or from the Start menu by selecting Microsoft SQL Server, then Integration Services.
- In the task editor, click Open Profile Viewer.

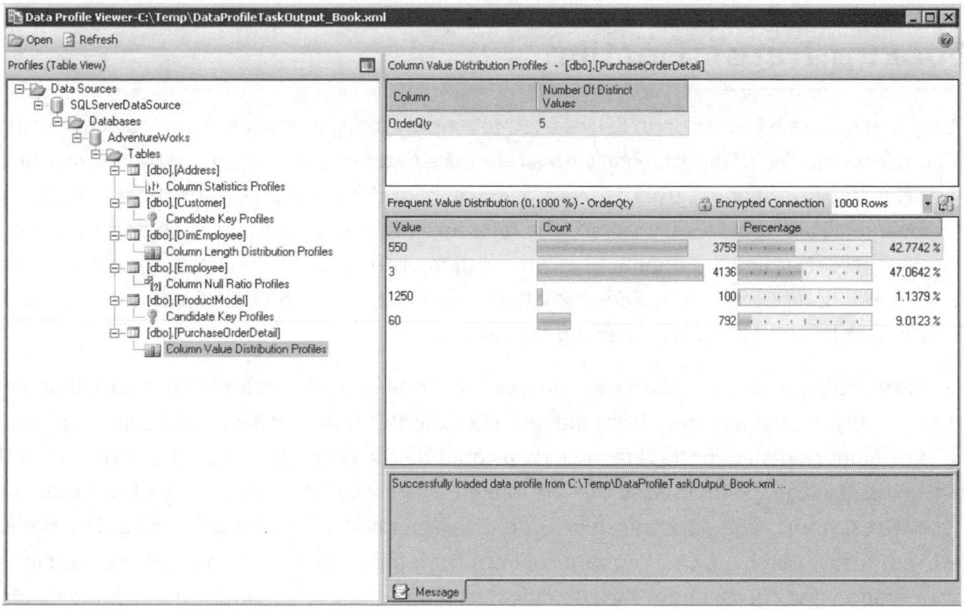

FIGURE 9-4 Data Profile Task Viewer.

The viewer loads the result of data profiling saved to XML output and displays computed profiles. Using the Profiles pane, you can explore profiles and select a profile for review. Results are displayed in the Results pane on the right side of the viewer, which includes a details section and drill-down section for showing detailed results and rows associated with the profile results in the dataset, respectively. Figure 9-4 shows results of profiling done on tables in a SQL Server database. Column value distribution profiling results are shown. The table profiled had five distinct values, with two values (550 and 3) amounting to 90 percent of the row values. By clicking one of the values in the details section, you can fetch the rows in the table containing that value in the data source. These rows are displayed in the drill-down pane at the bottom of the screen (not shown in Figure 9-4). Profile results like this can provide deep insights on the nature of data that can influence design and optimization of data processing steps or control the logical flow during execution.

> **Note** The drill-down option in the Results pane should be exercised carefully. It sends real-time queries to the data sources to fetch live data. This can hurt the performance of the data source. If drill-down is executed on an aged profiling result, the data fetched by the queries sent to the data sources could be different than the values originally involved during profiling. Windows Authentication is used to connect to the data source during drill-down. The current user running the viewer needs access to the data source for drill-down operation to succeed. Connection managers in SSIS packages with the Data Profiling task originally involved for profiling are not used during the drill-down step.

Fuzzy Lookup Transformation

The Fuzzy Lookup transformation in SSIS is used to employ fuzzy matching techniques to compare an incoming row in the Data Flow pipeline with a reference dataset and find one or more exact or close matches. This transformation is useful to improve quality of data that is corrupt, incorrectly formatted, misspelled, abbreviated, or truncated. The reference dataset is typically clean and standardized, and it is used to determine the quality of incoming data or to clean it. The reference dataset needs to be available in a database in a SQL Server 2000 or newer instance and OLE DB connection manager is used to connect to the database containing the reference data.

The Fuzzy Lookup transformation has one input and one output. Input contains data that might be dirty and output can have data from the reference dataset that matches with looked-up input values. The values matched in the reference data could be the clean or standardized version of the input value used in the lookup operation. The lookup match operation can be exact or fuzzy. Any data type that supports comparison can be used with exact matching and only string data types can be used with fuzzy matching. One or more columns from the transformation input are used in the lookup operation and the values in the columns selected for lookup are matched with the column values' reference data. The lookup operation produces matched values and similarity and confidence scores for the match. These scores can be used to determine if matched data can be considered for the cleansing operation. Fuzzy Lookup is often used in conjunction with the Lookup transformation that supports exact match and provides better performance for exact match in comparison with the Fuzzy Lookup. Unmatched data rows from the Lookup transformation are sent to Fuzzy Lookup for nonexact match. Output of Fuzzy Lookup is sent to conditional Split transformation to redirect high-confidence rows with high-similarity matches to cleansing; other rows are sent for manual review. Figure 9-5 shows the package that performs these steps.

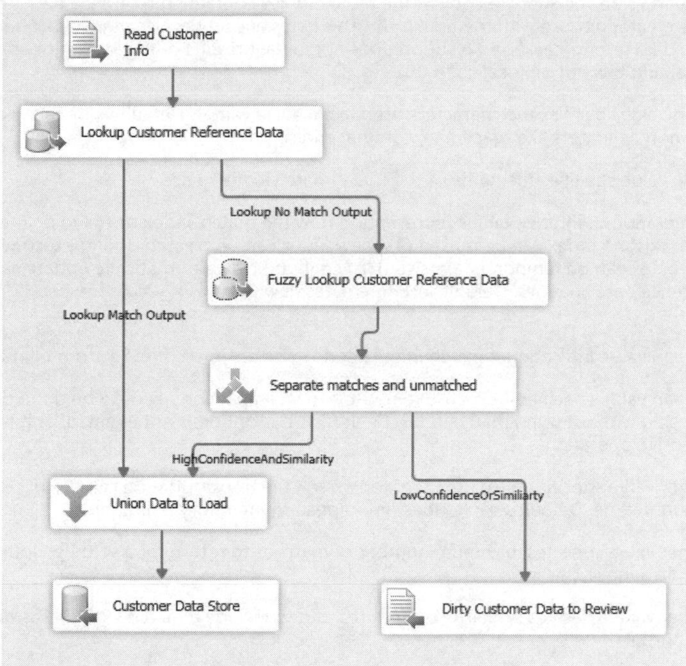

FIGURE 9-5 Using Fuzzy Lookup with other Data Flow components.

> **Note** The Fuzzy Lookup transformation creates tables and indexes in the *tempdb* database of the SQL Server instance containing reference data. The user executing an SSIS package with this transformation needs Read and Write privileges in this database for successful completion of the Fuzzy Lookup operation.

Properties of the Fuzzy Lookup transformation include settings to control the fuzzy matching operation. Properties of the transformation are described in Table 9-2.

TABLE 9-2 Fuzzy Lookup transformation properties

Property	Description
ReferenceTable	String value sets the name of the table or view containing reference data.
CopyReferenceTable	Boolean value specifies if a copy of the table or view containing reference data needs to be created for use with the transform. This helps ensure data change in reference table data during package execution does not impact results of the lookup operation. By default, this option is set to *true*.
Delimiters	String value specifies the characters used to tokenize values. Default value includes common delimiters like space, tab, comma, and so on.
MatchIndexName	String value specifies the name of the fuzzy-match index to use.
MatchIndexOptions	Enumeration of integer values representing how the match-index needs to be managed. Existing index can be reused or a new index can be created during execution. New index can be temporary, persisted, or configured to automatically update as reference data changes. Default setting creates new index every time the package is executed.
DropExistingMatchIndex	Boolean value indicating if match index needs to be dropped if reuse is not enabled.
Exhaustive	Boolean value specifies if exhaustive row-by-row comparison needs to be done during matching without using match index. By default this option is not enabled, as it is an expensive operation.
MaxMemoryUsage	Integer value specifies maximum memory in MB the transformation can use during execution time. Default setting does not impose any memory limitation.
MaxOutputMatchesPerInput	Integer value specifies maximum number of matches to return for a value on lookup. Default value is 1.
MinSimilarity	Integer value specifies similarity score threshold to include a match in the transformation output.
WarmCaches	Boolean value for performance optimization property. It is enabled by default to load reference table and match index into memory before execution of the transformation.

Note You need to use the Advanced Editor of the transformation to set the values for the *Exhaustive* and *MaxMemoryUsage* properties and any value more than 100 for the *MaxOutputMatchesPerInput* property.

Configuring Fuzzy Lookup transformation involves setting these properties and creating a lookup relationship between columns in input and reference data. Figure 9-6 shows the Create Relationships editor launched using the Edit Mappings option from the shortcut menu in the Columns tab of the transformation editor. This user interface allows you to set the mapping type, comparison flags to use during lookup, a minimum similarity score for each mapping, and the name of the output column containing matched reference data. When you specify more than one column for fuzzy matching, values in all those columns need to be sufficiently similar per the fuzzy matching settings for lookup to succeed. Having exact match mappings in the lookup operation helps in getting better results on the fuzzy match mappings, because identification of duplicates in the columns specified for fuzzy match is then narrowed down to the rows with identical values in the columns specified for the exact match.

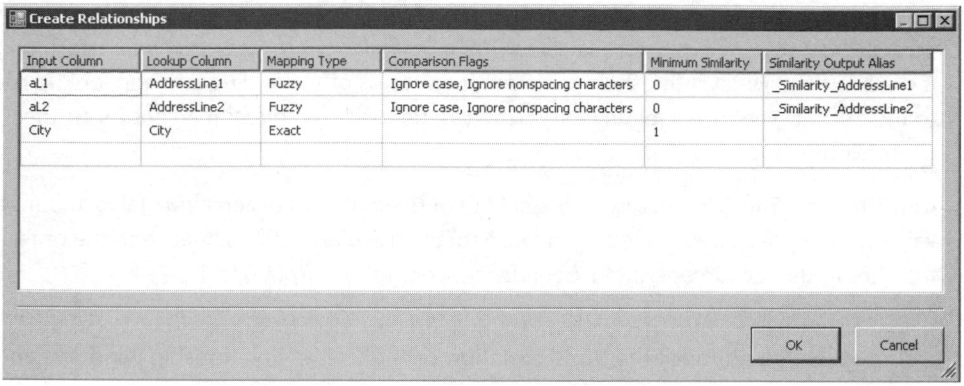

FIGURE 9-6 Create Relationships editor to configure lookup settings.

> **Note** Comparison Flags options available for matching are also available in other SSIS transformations, namely Sort, Aggregate, and Fuzzy grouping. These options are used to control comparison of string values. The comparison flags available in SSIS are listed in Table 9-3.

TABLE 9-3 Comparison flags and description

Flag	Description
Ignore case	Specifies whether the comparison is case sensitive
Ignore kana type	Specifies whether the comparison distinguishes between the two types of Japanese kana characters, hiragana and katakana
Ignore character width	Specifies whether the comparison distinguishes between a single-byte character and the same character when it is represented as a double-byte character
Ignore nonspacing characters	Specifies whether the comparison distinguishes between spacing characters and diacritics
Ignore symbols	Specifies whether the comparison distinguishes between letter characters and symbols such as white-space characters, punctuation, currency symbols, and mathematical symbols
Sort punctuation as symbols	Specifies whether the comparison sorts all punctuation symbols (except the hyphen and apostrophe) before the alphanumeric characters

The transformation produces one output row for each input row. Output of the transformation includes pass-through columns from input, columns included from the matched reference data, and the following columns:

- **Column-level similarity score** This is a measure of mathematical similarity between the values in input columns and matched values from the columns in the reference dataset. The similarity score ranges from 0 to 1, with 1 indicating an exact match. The similarity score for each column mapped for lookup needs to be greater than the threshold defined in the *MinSimilarity* property of the mapping for the lookup to succeed and add rows to the transformation output.

- **Row-level similarity score** This is a measure of overall similarity for each matched row across all columns selected for matching. The *MinSimilarity* property of the transformation is used as the row-level threshold to determine success of the lookup and add lookup rows to the output. The row-level similarity score can be used to redirect matches for further processing.

- **Confidence** This is a measure of the quality of the match between input value and matched value from a reference dataset. Confidence for a particular match is relative to the other matches in the lookup operation. Confidence score ranges from 0 to 1.

> **Note** The advanced editor of the transformation or the Create Relationship window can be used to update default names (_Similarity, _Confidence, and _Similarity_<*input column name*>) used for the output columns.

Minimum similarity threshold is available on each column mapped and the similarity score is computed for each column match. The overall similarity across all columns matched needs to meet the respective thresholds for a successful lookup. Good matches involve high similarity and confidence scores. High similarity does not mean high confidence or vice versa. For example, during lookup if there are several high-similarity matches, confidence will likely be low because it is a measure relative to all other matches.

> **Note** Threshold for column and row level similarity depends on the nature of the data and processing involved. The recommended practice is to play with different values and observe the results to narrow down the threshold that is appropriate for the data involved.

Fuzzy Lookup transformation does not involve special domain-specific rules or complex scripts to perform matching. Fuzzy matching in the transformation uses a domain-independent distance function involving the following parameters:

- **Edit distance** Defines the minimum number of edit operations required to convert a given string to another string with which it is compared. Allowed edit operations are insertion, deletion, or replacement of characters in the given string.

- **Number of tokens** Represents the count of tokens in string values. A token is the sequence of characters representing a semantic unit involved in match operation. Delimiters are specified in Fuzzy Lookup transform to tokenize the data for performing lookup.

- **Token order** Represents the sequence of tokens in string values.

- **Relative token frequency** Describes frequency of token occurrences in the data.

During execution time, the following operations are performed by a Fuzzy Lookup transformation with default settings.

1. Reference table or view is copied to a temporary table in the tempdb database of the same SQL Server instance.

2. Key column of integer data type is added to the newly created temporary table and index is built on the key column.

3. Match index on the new table is built.

4. Tokenized values from the reference data, the occurrences, and substrings are stored in the match index.

5. Match index is used during lookup operation and match is determined using tokens and substrings shared by the values that are compared.

6. Matches are retrieved from the reference data and thorough comparison is performed before adding the match to the transformation output.

> **Note** Fuzzy Lookup transformation is an asynchronous and blocking component in SSIS Data Flow and it produces output only after all rows are processed. This characteristic plays a huge role in the performance of the transformation and resource consumption during execution. The size of the temporary table and index created by the Fuzzy Lookup component is dependent on the size of the reference dataset and tokens in the reference data. Use of this transform can involve heavy use of disk space and memory. Settings like *MaxMemoryUsage* and *WarmCaches* need to be used appropriately to handle that. The match index needs to be reused where possible to speed up package execution. Referencing a remote server in the lookup operation can add significant overhead caused by the heavy usage of the network for the interaction between the transformation and the server. Referencing a SQL Server instance in *localhost* can potentially lead to memory contention between SQL Server and the process executing Fuzzy Lookup transformation.

Fuzzy Grouping Transformation

The Fuzzy Grouping transformation in SSIS is used to employ fuzzy matching techniques to identify duplicates in the incoming rows in the Data Flow pipeline and select the canonical value that can be used to eliminate the duplicates. This transformation is useful to improve quality of data that contain duplicate values caused by data corruption, incorrect formatting, misspelling, abbreviation, or truncation. This transformation uses the Fuzzy Lookup transform internally to perform grouping.

The Fuzzy Grouping transformation has one input and one output. Input contains data that might be dirty in terms of duplicate entries and output contains input rows grouped using the settings specified in the transformation. The values added to output could be the standardized version of the input value used in the grouping operation. The grouping operation can be exact or fuzzy. Any data type that supports comparison can be used with exact matching and fuzzy matching is supported only on string data types. One or more columns from the transformation input are used to identify rows that are likely duplicates. The grouping operation also results in a similarity score for each duplicate entry identified. These scores can be used to determine if the results of grouping operation can be used for the cleansing operation. This transformation uses an OLE DB connection manager to a SQL Server database that is used to create temporary tables and indexes. SQL Server 2000 or a newer version should be used for this purpose.

Properties of the Fuzzy Grouping transformation include settings to control the fuzzy matching operation. Properties of the transformation are described in Table 9-4. Because fuzzy lookup is used internally, important properties it needs are exposed as properties of the Fuzzy Grouping transformation.

TABLE 9-4 Fuzzy Grouping transformation properties

Property	Description
Delimiters	String value specifies the characters used to tokenize values for grouping. Default value includes common delimiters like space, tab, comma, and so on.
Exhaustive	Boolean value specifies if exhaustive row-by-row comparison needs to be done during matching without using match index. By default this option is not enabled, as it is an expensive operation.
MaxMemoryUsage	Integer value specifies maximum memory in MB the transformation can use during execution time. Default setting does not impose any memory limitation.
MinSimilarity	Integer value specifies minimum similarity score to determine if a value is duplicate of another.

Note You need to use the advanced editor of the transformation to set the values for the *Exhaustive* and *MaxMemoryUsage* properties.

Configuration of the Fuzzy Grouping transformation involves setting these properties and identifying columns to use in grouping and matching types for each column. Figure 9-7 shows the Columns tab in the Fuzzy Grouping Transformation Editor used for selecting the columns and configuring the grouping operation. It allows setting matching types, similarity threshold for filtering matching results, comparison flags to use during matching, and the significance of leading or trailing numerals during comparison. The Numerals column in the user interface shown in Figure 9-7 is used to specify if leading numerals, trailing numerals, neither, or both are significant and need to be included in the matching operation. Figure 9-7 also shows the multiselect option window in setting the comparison flag properties for the mappings. If more than one column is specified for fuzzy matching, then values in all of those columns need to be sufficiently similar per settings for grouping to succeed. Having exact match mappings in the grouping operation help in getting better results on the fuzzy match mappings because identifying duplicates in the columns specified for the fuzzy match are narrowed down to the rows with identical values in the columns specified for exact match.

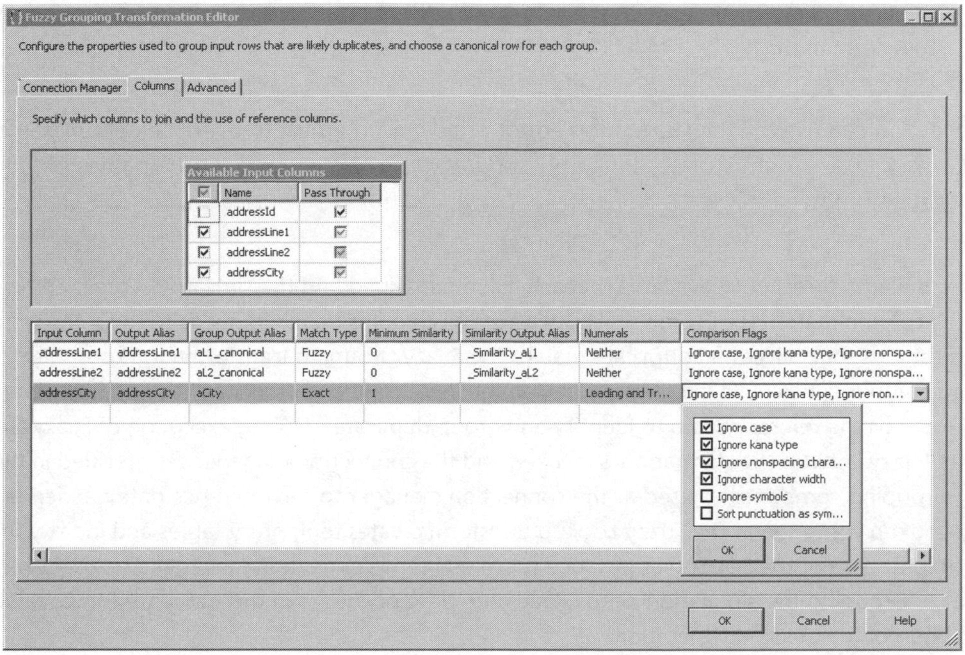

FIGURE 9-7 Column selection in Fuzzy Grouping Transformation Editor.

The transformation produces one output row for each input row. Output of the transformation includes pass-through columns from input and the following columns:

- **Row identifier** A unique integer value is assigned to each input row and it is used to reference rows when assigning duplicates.
- **Column-level similarity score** This is a measure of mathematical similarity between the values in input columns and match result identified as duplicates. The similarity score ranges from 0 to 1, with 1 indicating an exact match. The similarity score for each column selected for grouping needs to be greater than the threshold defined in the *MinSimilarity* property of the mapping for a grouping to succeed and add a duplicate entry to the transformation output.
- **Row-level similarity score** This is a measure of overall similarity for each matched row across all columns selected for grouping. The *MinSimilarity* property of the transformation is used as the row-level threshold to determine the success of duplicate matching and add rows to the output. This score can be used to redirect matches for further processing.
- **Duplicate identifier** This groups the rows that are duplicates of a canonical row and the identifier of the canonical row is used as the value of this column in every duplicate row.
- **Canonical value columns** An output column containing the canonical value of the corresponding input column used in the grouping operation is added to the transformation output. If multiple columns are used in the grouping operation, multiple canonical value columns are added to the transformation output. The column values from the canonical row used as the

duplicate identifier are used as the values of the canonical value columns in the output of the transformation.

Note You can use the transformation editor or advanced editor to override default names (like _key_in, key_out, _score, _Similarity_<*input column name*>) and set the names of the output columns.

The similarity threshold is available on each column mapped and the similarity score is computed for each column match. The overall similarity across all columns matched needs to meet the respective thresholds for a successful duplicate match. The Fuzzy Grouping transformation uses the Fuzzy Lookup component to build the match index on the input rows and essentially does a fuzzy lookup using input as the reference data to identify and group duplicates. During execution of Fuzzy Grouping, the Fuzzy Lookup transformation is invoked and the connection manager set specified in the Fuzzy Grouping component is used as the connection manager to the reference data needed by the Fuzzy Lookup component. The Fuzzy Lookup transform creates temporary tables and indexes in the tempdb database of the SQL Server instance specified in the connection manager. The user executing the Fuzzy Grouping transformation needs Read and Write privileges in this database for successful completion of the grouping operation.

Note The Fuzzy Grouping transformation is an asynchronous and blocking component in the SSIS Data Flow and it produces output only after all rows are processed. This characteristic plays a huge role in the performance of the transformation and resource consumption during execution. Performance of this transformation can greatly improve if the connection manager references a SQL Server instance in the machine that is executing the transformation.

See Also *More details on the Fuzzy Lookup and Fuzzy Grouping transformations and the performance considerations are available in the whitepaper from Microsoft at* v.

Data Quality Services Cleansing Transform

Data Quality Services (DQS) is a feature introduced in SQL Server 2012. This knowledge-driven data quality solution is used for performing data quality tasks such as correction, enrichment, standardization, and deduplication. SSIS 2012 has a new transformation component called the DQS Cleansing transformation in the advanced editions of SQL Server. This component is used to leverage DQS cleansing capabilities as a part of the data integration done using SSIS. Unlike the Fuzzy Lookup and Fuzzy Grouping transformations, this transformation depends on a domain-specific knowledge base (KB) for the data quality operations. KBs are built and maintained outside of SSIS using DQS functionality. Knowledge bases maintain knowledge about the data in that domain like good values, bad values, relations between values, validation rules, and so on. KBs can also involve third-party reference data services and datasets available at trusted public domains like Windows Azure Marketplace or directly from premium commercial content providers. Reference data can be imported into KBs or they can be configured to use external knowledge by mapping reference data service to KB domains that are used during the cleansing operation.

> **Note** The DQS Cleansing transform is installed with SSIS features during SQL Server installation. This transform needs a DQS server to implement cleansing functionality and it is not installed with SSIS.

Configuration of the DQS Cleansing transformation involves providing a DQS server name, selecting a KB from the server, specifying domains from the KB to use for cleansing different columns and settings to control the transformation output. The DQS Cleansing transform has a special connection manager called DQS cleansing connection manager that just stores the name of the DQS server. The server is a SQL Server 2012 instance containing different DQS KBs that are used for the cleansing operation. After you set the connection manager, you can select a KB in the DQS server for the cleansing operation. Figure 9-8 shows the Connection Manager tab in the DQS Cleansing Transformation Editor. It shows the use of a KB named DQS Data that is available as a part of the DQS feature in SQL Server. Each DQS Cleansing transform can have a reference to one KB. Each KB can have one or more domains that are used during cleansing. For example, the DQS Data KB contains different domains like US – State, US – Counties, Country/Region, and so on, to help with address cleansing. Each domain specializes in a particular category of data and can be used for cleansing data in that category. For example, the US – State domain in the DQS Data KB is used to identify invalid U.S. state names and correct them. The data the transformation receives as input is sent to the DQS server and the cleansed data received back from the server is added to the output of the transformation. The domains in KBs are data type aware and the domains assigned to columns need to be of compatible data types.

> **Note** You should use a KB in the DQS Cleansing transformation only if it contains sufficient knowledge for the cleansing operation. The DQS Cleansing transformation performs batch cleansing operations. We recommend that you perform interactive cleansing using the Data Quality Services Client utility installed as a part of DQS to understand the effectiveness of the KB in cleansing the data of interest before performing the batch operation in SSIS using this transform.

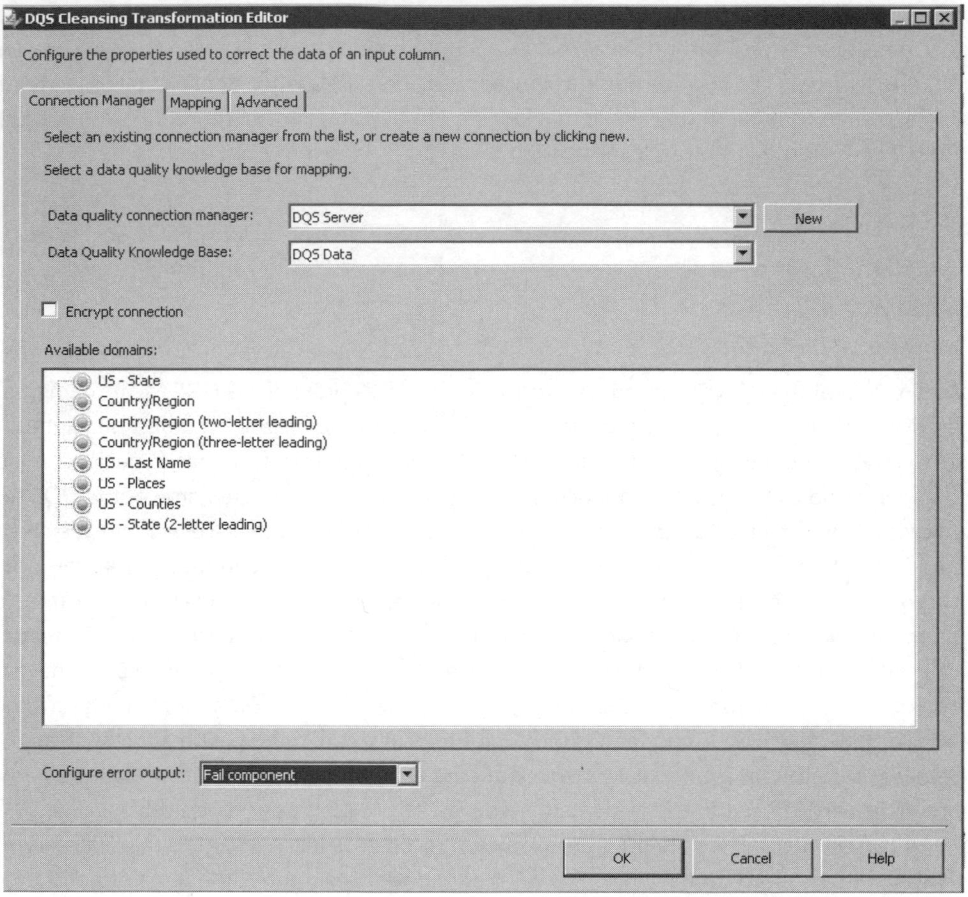

FIGURE 9-8 Connection Manager tab in the DQS Cleansing Transformation Editor.

The DQS Cleansing transformation has one input and one output. The input contains data that could be dirty in terms of duplicate or inaccurate values and the output contains the results of cleansing done in the DQS server. You select columns in the transformation input that need to be cleansed and map them to domains in the DQS KB associated with the transformation. Figure 9-9 shows the Mapping tab in the DQS Cleansing Transformation Editor. This user interface is used to select columns and assign domains to each column. It is also used to set the names of the output columns.

> **Note** DQS has two types of domains, single and composite. Single domains are mapped to individual input columns in the DQS transformation, each representing an entity to be validated and cleansed using the KB. In the case of composite domains, DQS parses the data from individual columns into multiple domains that make up the composite.

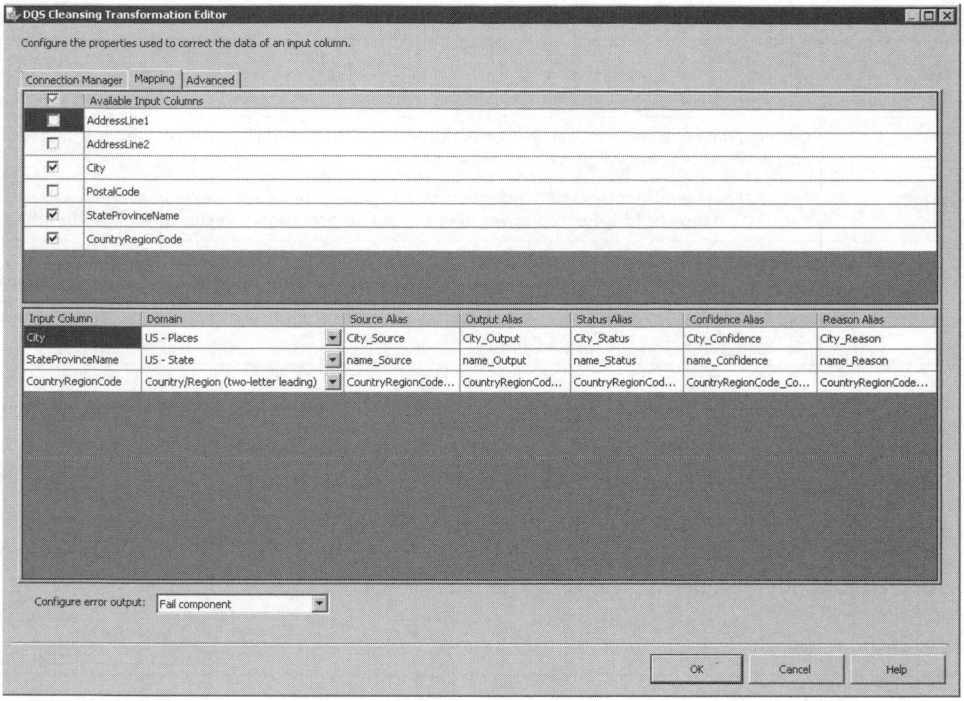

FIGURE 9-9 Mapping tab in the DQS Cleansing Transform Editor.

The transformation produces one output row for each input row. Output of the transformation includes columns from input and the following columns:

- **Cleansed columns** Data from the input columns selected for cleansing are sent to the server and the corrected data is added to the output. In Figure 9-9, the Source Alias column in the user interface is used to set the names of the transformation output columns containing original data and the Output Alias column is used to set the name of the transformation output column containing the result of the cleansing operation. The result of cleansing can be different than the original value if cleansing happened or the same value if it could not be cleansed by DQS. If the Standardize Output check box is selected on the Advanced tab shown in Figure 9-10, the cleansed value will be the standardized value in the domain. Standardization in the domain is controlled in the DQS server and cannot be done using SSIS.
- **Column-level cleansing status** Results of the correction operation for each column selected for cleansing are available in the transformation output. Names of the columns containing status are set using the Status Alias column in the user interface shown in Figure 9-9. Possible status values and their use are described in Table 9-5.

TABLE 9-5 DQS cleansing status

Status	Description
Correct	Original data is correct and not modified.
Corrected	Original data was incorrect and a correction value with a confidence level higher than the auto-correction threshold value is identified.
Auto Suggest	Original data was incorrect and a correction value with confidence level higher than the auto-suggestion threshold value but lower than the auto-correction threshold value is identified.
New	Original data is consistent with domain rules and could be a valid value not available in the KB or a correction value with a confidence level lower than the auto-suggestion threshold is identified.
Invalid	Original data is invalid in the domain, failed any domain rule, or DQS server is unable to determine the validity of the original data.

- **Column-level output reason** The reason for the result of correction operation on input values in each column selected for cleansing is added to the output. Names of the columns containing reasons are set using the Reason Alias column shown in Figure 9-9. Possible status values and their uses are described in Table 9-6. The option to add column-level reasons to the transformation output is available on the Advanced tab in the DQS Cleansing Transformation Editor under Enable Field Level Columns as shown in Figure 9-10.

TABLE 9-6 Output reason

Reason	Description
Domain Value	Value considered for cleansing is a valid domain value. Corresponding cleansing status message is Correct.
DQS Cleansing	Value considered for cleansing was corrected or a correction value was suggested by DQS. Corresponding cleansing status messages are Corrected or Auto Suggest.
New Value	Value considered for cleansing is probably a new value to be considered for adding to the domain. Corresponding cleansing status message is New.

- **Column-level confidence score** This is a measure of confidence on the correction or suggestion from the DQS server. The score ranges from 0 to 1, and is available only for the rows with status of Corrected or Auto Suggest and with the reason DQS Cleansing. The option to add a column-level score to the transformation output is available on the Advanced tab in the DQS Cleansing Transformation Editor under Enable Field Level Columns as shown in Figure 9-10.
- **Row-level cleansing status** This is an overall status aggregating all column-level cleansing status messages. A Conditional Split transformation is typically used to split different types of output rows to appropriately process them in the SSIS Data Flow pipeline. For example, you can send rows with a status of New or Invalid to a destination for manual review and updating KBs.

- **Information from reference data services** Third-party services mapped to KB domains involved in the transformation can return extra information during cleansing. For example, address cleansing might return Latitude and Longitude information as a part of cleansing. Additional cleansing data and its schema are available in _Additional Data and _Additional Data Schema columns in the output. These columns are not included in output by default but you can add them to the output using the options on the Advanced tab of the DQS Cleansing Transformation Editor.

> **Note** Auto-suggestion and auto-correction threshold values cannot be set in the DQS Cleansing transformation. It is done using the Data Quality Services Client, which is part of the DQS installation.

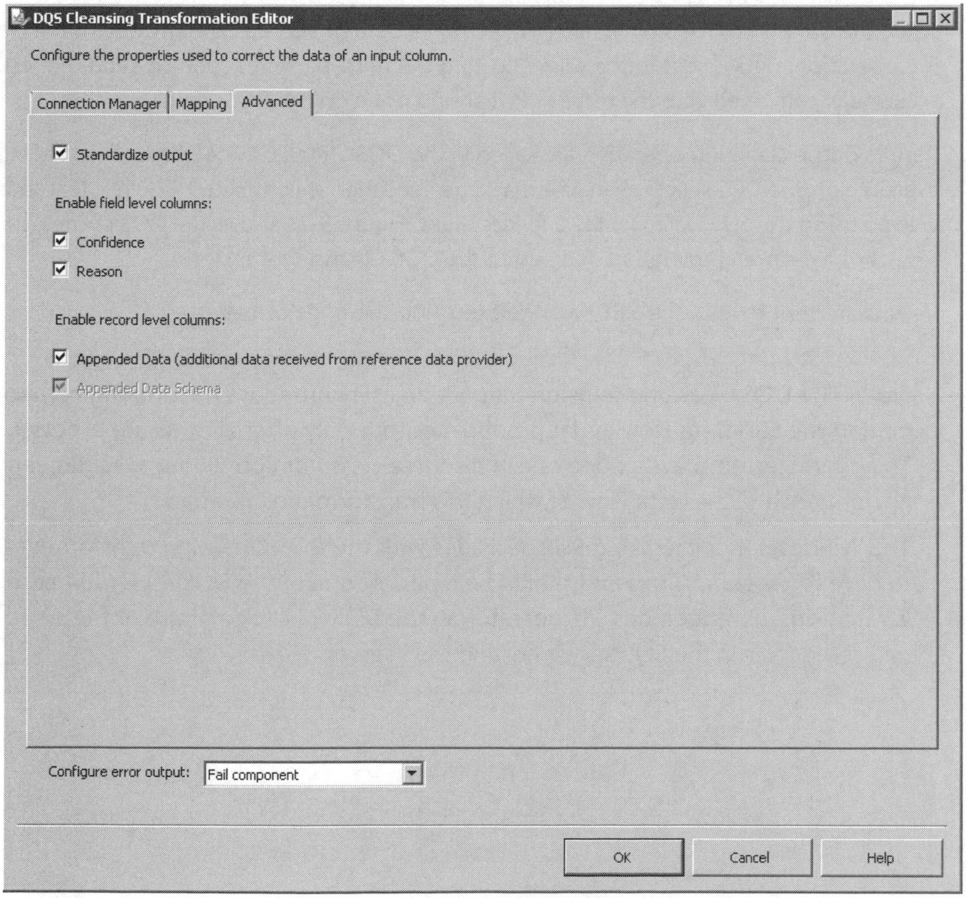

FIGURE 9-10 Advanced Tab of the DQS Cleansing Transformation Editor.

During execution of the DQS Cleansing transformation, the following operations are performed:

1. A data quality project of type "cleansing" is created on the DQS server. The format of the project name is Package.DQS Cleansing_<*timestamp*>_{*packageguid*}. This project will be accessible even after the execution of the package containing the transformation is completed. Several SQL Server objects like tables, views, stored procedures, functions, and so on, are created in the DQS_PROJECTS database on the DQS server. These objects are created for each data quality project saved to the DQS server.
2. The data to be processed is sent to the DQS server as batches of 1,000 rows to perform cleansing using the data quality project saved in the previous step.
3. Cleansing operations are performed in the DQS server. DQS functionality and KBs available in the DQS_MAIN database are used for cleansing. The DQS_STAGING_DATA database is used to stage the data for processing. If external reference data or services are involved in the cleansing operation, data is sent to the server hosting the third-party functionality and the result received is combined with the results of cleansing done on the DQS server.
4. Results of the cleansing operation are saved in the DQS_PROJECTS database. The results are available on the DQS server even after package execution is completed. The results can be viewed using the SQL Data Quality Services client. Figure 9-11 shows the DQS client displaying results of a cleansing operation done using the DQS Cleansing transform.
5. Results are sent back to the SSIS package executing the transformation.

> **Note** The DQS Cleansing transformation is an asynchronous and blocking component in the SSIS Data Flow and it produces output only after all rows are processed. This characteristic plays a huge role in resource consumption during execution and performance of the Data Flow of which this transformation is a part.
>
> The Windows user executing SSIS packages with the DQS Cleansing transform needs to have login permissions and should be a part of one of the DQS roles (dqs_administrator, dqs_kb_editor, dqs_kb_operator) in the DQS_MAIN database or the sysadmin server role in the SQL Server hosting DQS server.

FIGURE 9-11 Review of cleansing results in the SQL Data Quality Services client.

Summary

SSIS supports assessing and improving quality of data that it processes. Different types of data quality components, built-in capabilities to leverage external functionality and domain-independent to domain-specific, address most of the needs in data quality management as a part of the data integration done in SSIS. In addition to these special-purpose data quality components, SSIS has other components (like Data Conversion, Character Map, or Derived Column transformations and data comparison or replacement functions) that can be used for cleaning or standardizing data.

PART III

Database Admin

CHAPTER 10

Configuration in SSIS

In This Chapter

Chapter 2, "SSIS Concepts," introduced the concept of configurations for SSIS packages and projects. This chapter provides a detailed analysis of configurations for SSIS and explores new features in SQL Server 2012.

Configurations provide runtime values for package and project properties, as well as variable values during SSIS package execution. As introduced in Chapter 7, "Understanding SSIS Connectivity," SSIS packages can be designed to have runtime values for various properties within the packages. The concept of configurations enables this behavior, providing SSIS packages and projects with values supplied to them during execution.

The process of creating package configurations in SSIS has a certain flow to it. You start by creating packages in the development environment. In this phase, you create the flow logic within the package and define the various actions and behavior of the package under differing circumstances. In most cases your package has several properties with values that depend on the execution environment or the development phase that the package is in. These are the properties you would like to make configurable. The values of these configurable properties can then be modified during their execution.

This chapter dives deep into configuring SSIS packages and projects, starting with the basics of configuring SSIS packages. Next, it looks at how you can create configurations using new features in SQL Server 2012. The chapter then reviews the various options available in SSIS prior to SQL Server 2012. Finally, it lists some of the best practices for configuring SSIS packages and projects. To understand the best practices, you first need to understand how and when you would need to configure your packages and projects.

Configuration Basics

You probably already have a basic understanding of why you should be using configurations. This section contains an in-depth exploration of the development lifecycle for an SSIS package or project with respect to configurations.

> **Tip** For a quick refresher on configuration options in SSIS, refer to this MSDN article about SSIS package configurations: *http://msdn.microsoft.com/en-us/library/ms141682.aspx.*

How Configurations Are Applied

Before you can understand how to use configurations, it is important to understand how configurations are applied.

Configurations are essentially key–value pairs. In such a pair, the *key* defines the property path of the property that needs to be configured and the *value* holds the value that needs to be applied. The execution utility, which can be dtexec, SQL Agent, or SSIS Server, can then use this property path to apply the configured value to the property. It then executes the package with that value.

Property Path

A property path defines the location of the property within the package component hierarchy. An example of a property path is as follows:

```
\Package.Variables[User::VariableToBeConfigured].Properties[Value]
```

The preceding XML sample defines the property path of the *Value* property of the variable *VariableToBeConfigured* (which you can see at the end). That is preceded by *\Package.Variables[User ::VariableToBeConfigured]* which is its package path. You can obtain package paths easily in the SQL Server Data Tools window on the Properties tab as shown in Figure 10-1.

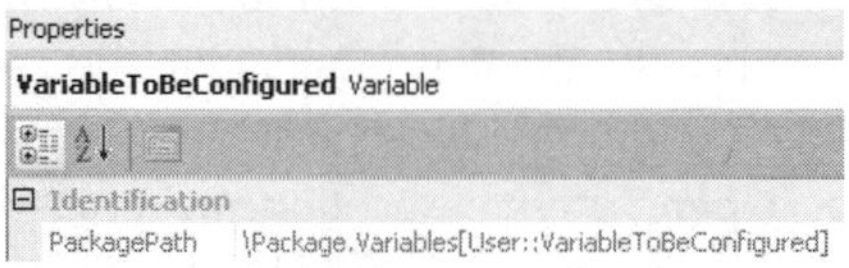

FIGURE 10-1 Package path from the Properties tab for a variable.

What to Configure

Often, SSIS developers face the dilemma of choosing which of the various package attributes require configuration. The following set of questions should help you choose the properties that require configurability.

- Is the property's value based on the current execution environment? For example, you might configure the server name property of a connection manager to hold the development environment server name during developing the package. This might require a new value in a different execution environment, such as a production environment.
- Have you designed the execution flow within a package to be based on a condition that requires an external value? For example, your control flow path might have a conditional expression on it. This expression might depend on a variable value that needs to be provided before the package execution.
- Does your package have tasks or components that might require an override of their property's default value defined during development? For example, you might be required to change the SQL statement in your Execute SQL task during package execution.

If you answered "yes" to any of these questions, you have a good requirement for adding a configuration for the respective property. Often it is difficult to identify all the properties in the package or a project that should be ideally configured. It can also be described as a skill that a developer grows over time. The earlier the properties to be configured are identified, however, the easier it becomes to develop the actual package.

It is also important to note that you will not be able to configure the metadata of Data Flow components that can affect the definition of a flow. They can be the columns, column names, data types, and other nonexpressionable properties within a Data Flow.

Changes in SSIS 2012

There are several changes in the way you create configurations for your packages and projects. You can use the new features like configuring using parameters in SSIS 2012. However, to use all the new features, you will have to convert your project containing the target packages to the Project Deployment Model. The Project Conversion Wizard is an easy way to convert your packages from the package to Project Deployment Model. This also means that you can retain the old configuration models by keeping your SSIS project in a Package Deployment Model. We discuss these features in more depth in the following sections.

Configuration in SSIS 2012

In SSIS 2012, the method for storing and executing packages has changed. With the new server model, packages are now being stored on the SSIS Catalog. They can now be configured and executed on the server itself. Therefore, the techniques and best practices to configure packages on SSIS 2012 will also change accordingly. In SSIS 2012, the following new features are introduced to make it easier to configure SSIS packages:

- Package and project parameters
- SSIS environments

Parameters

As we have already seen, a basic configuration model helps you to provide runtime values to your package execution environment. SSIS 2012 makes this configuration model much more intuitive with the new concept of parameters.

Parameters are runtime arguments for a package or a project that are created during the package design and can then be provided a value during the execution of the respective package or project. The values of the parameters can be predetermined or easily configured while executing the package. Parameters are also the only way to configure packages and projects in the new Project Deployment Model. Hence, if you intend to use the new SSIS 2012 project model and deploy your packages to the SSIS Catalog, then parameters are the primary configuration model that SSIS offers out of the box. An easy way to visualize parameters at this stage is to see them as specially annotated SSIS variables. You can create a parameter and use it in exactly the same way you could create SSIS variables in earlier versions.

There are two types of parameters that you can create: project and package parameters. As the name suggests, the scope and functionality of each type of parameter differs slightly.

Project Parameters

Project parameters are created for a given SSIS project. They can then be used in any of the packages within the project. Each project parameter can be configured once for the project and the new configured value can be used when any package from the project is executed. We discuss project parameters further in later sections.

Package Parameters

Package parameters are created for individual packages and are only available to the package for which they have been created. The parameter can be configured and the configured value can be used by the package during execution.

We discuss how to create and execute packages and projects with parameters in more detail in the following sections.

Creating Package Parameters

As discussed before, parameters are created during design time. This means you should be creating the parameters for a package or a project in SQL Server Data Tools when you are designing them. SQL Server Data Tools has new dialog boxes and options that enable you to work with parameters. You will be able to create parameters for projects and packages that are in the Project Deployment Model. An easy way to know if your project is ready for creating parameters is to check the annotation on the project in the Solution Explorer, as shown in Figures 10-2 and 10-3. Note that the Project Deployment Model is the default model chosen for new projects created in SSIS 2012.

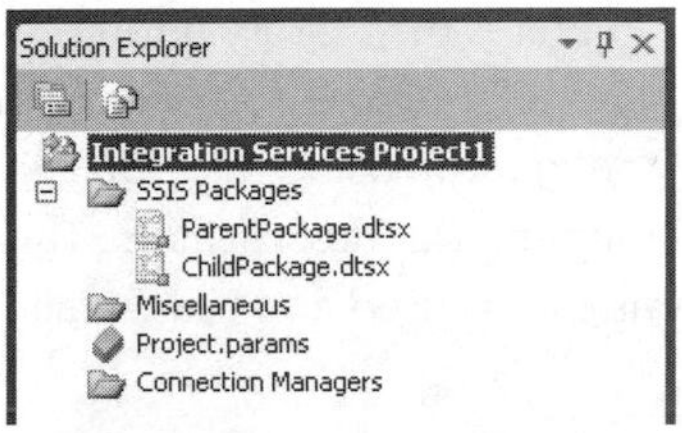

FIGURE 10-2 SSIS project in the Project Deployment Model.

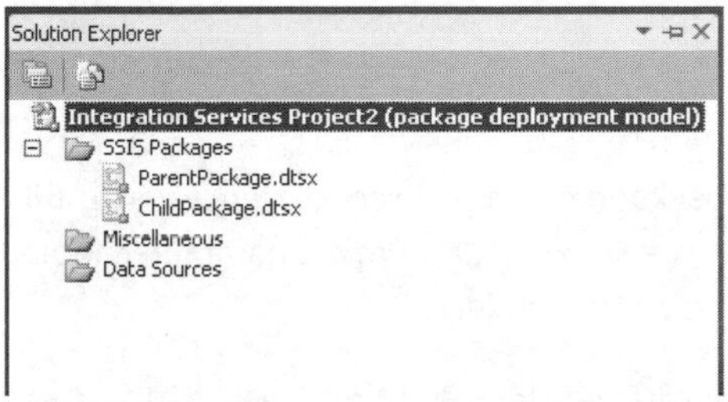

FIGURE 10-3 SSIS project in the Package Deployment Model.

Once your project is in the Project Deployment Model, your project and packages can use parameters. Package parameters can be created in SQL Server Data Tools using the Parameters tab on a package design surface, as shown in Figure 10-4.

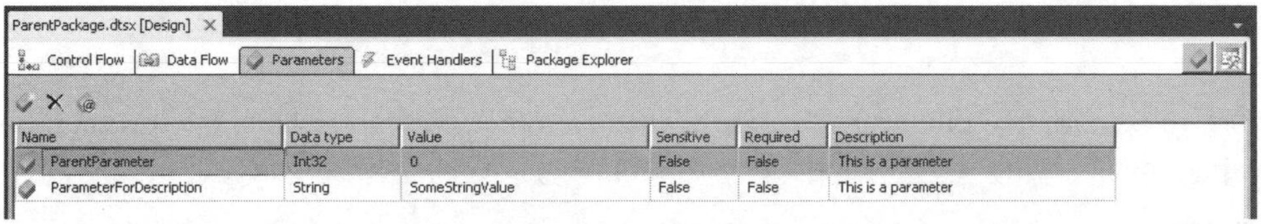

FIGURE 10-4 Parameters tab on the package design surface.

A new parameter can be created on the tab by clicking a new row in the grid or by using the Add Parameter button provided on the tab. There are also Delete Parameter and Add Parameter to Configuration buttons. The Add Parameter to Configuration button is used to create a parameter with a value that can be configured along with Visual Studio configurations. You can find more details about it in Chapter 5, "Team Development."

A parameter has several properties. Some of the special properties of a parameter are as follows:

- **Sensitive** Defines whether the parameter contains sensitive data. If true, all sensitivity rules of sensitive SSIS variables such as masking of value field are applied to the parameter. Thus, you can create a sensitive parameter such as a password parameter by flagging its Sensitive property to be true.

- **Required** Defines whether providing a value to the parameter is mandatory during execution. If *true*, you will have to define a value for the parameter before each execution. If *false*, the default value is used during execution (if not configured). Using this, you can decide at design time that a parameter should always be configured during execution. This will help you avoid instances where the default value of a parameter is used and causes failures in execution.

> **Tip** You use a different value of the *ServerName* parameter during development and it requires a new value in the production server. This is a case for creating the required parameter.

- **Scope** Defines whether the parameter is a package or project scope. Hence, using this property you can distinguish whether a parameter is a *Package* or a *Project* parameter. Note that this property is automatically configured and is not editable.
- **Data Type** As we have discussed, parameters are specially annotated SSIS variables. They follow the same data type considerations as variables. You can configure a parameter to hold a value of any type of a generic SSIS data type.

> **Note** Although SSIS variables support *Char, DBNull*, and *Object*, SSIS parameters do not. An easy way to represent *Char* is to use *Int16* to represent the ASCII equivalent of the character.

Figure 10-5 shows the properties that are available for each parameter. Note the scope property for the parameter saying it is package scope, thus making it a *Package Parameter*.

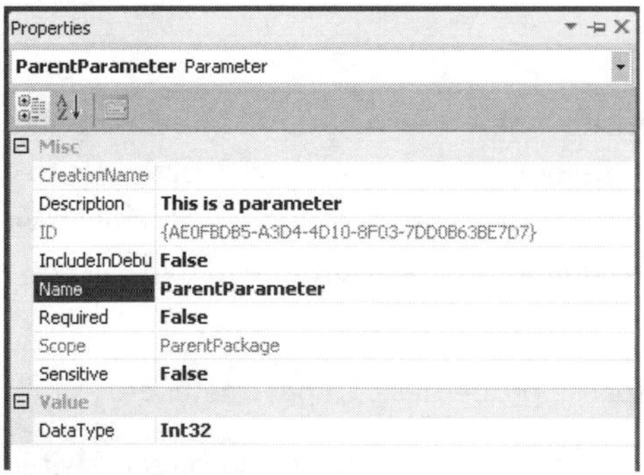

FIGURE 10-5 Properties of a parameter.

Creating Project Parameters

Project parameters, as the name suggests, are created at the scope of the project. Once created, a project parameter can be used in any of the packages within the project. A project parameter can be created in SQL Server Data Tools using the *Project.params* window of a project. As shown in Figure 10-6, the *Project.params* window is available in the Solution Explorer.

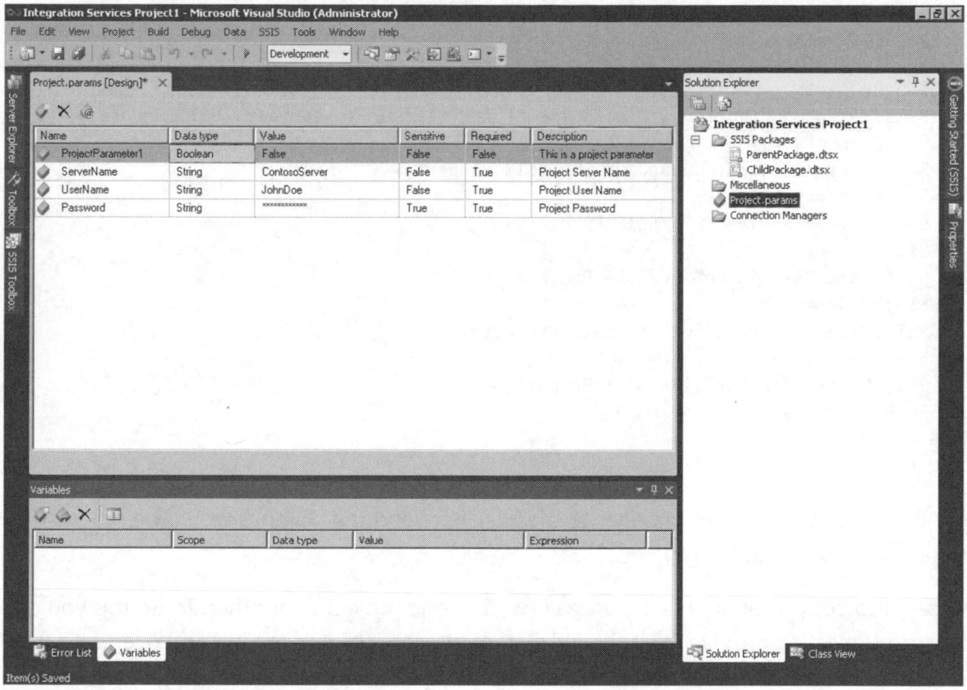

FIGURE 10-6 *Project.params* window.

You can create the project parameters in the exact same manner that you created the package parameters. Figure 10-6 shows four project parameters created for which *Pasword* is a *sensitive parameter* and *ServerName1* is a *required parameter.*

More About *Project.params*

Project parameters provide the ability to share the parameter across packages. You can create a set of project parameters and use them for multiple projects. This is done by using the *Project.params* file.

Each SSIS project in the Project Deployment Model has a *Project.params* file associated with it. The file is the code behind of the *Project.params* window (shown in Figure 10-6) of a project in SQL Server Data Tools. It is located in the same directory in the file system as the project and packages themselves. Each *Project.params* file contains all the project parameters defined for the project. So, if I create a *Project Parameter* called *ServerName1* that is a required *String* parameter with value *myServer*, my *Project.params* file will contain the code shown in Listing 10-1.

LISTING 10-1 Parameter definition in *Project.params*

```
<?xml version="1.0"?>
<SSIS:Parameters xmlns:SSIS="www.microsoft.com/SqlServer/SSIS">
  <SSIS:Parameter
    SSIS:Name="ServerName1">
    <SSIS:Properties>
      <SSIS:Property
        SSIS:Name="ID">{8eeddea1-d3da-4ba3-99da-500d219c6fb1}</SSIS:Property>
      <SSIS:Property
        SSIS:Name="CreationName"></SSIS:Property>
      <SSIS:Property
        SSIS:Name="Description">This is the central server to connect</SSIS:Property>
      <SSIS:Property
        SSIS:Name="IncludeInDebugDump">0</SSIS:Property>
      <SSIS:Property
        SSIS:Name="Required">0</SSIS:Property>
      <SSIS:Property
        SSIS:Name="Sensitive">0</SSIS:Property>
      <SSIS:Property
        SSIS:Name="Value">myServer</SSIS:Property>
      <SSIS:Property
        SSIS:Name="DataType">18</SSIS:Property>
    </SSIS:Properties>
  </SSIS:Parameter>
</SSIS:Parameters>
```

Note that you can make any changes to the XML here and the changes would be reflected for the parameter in the package design.

You can also copy a set of *project parameters* from one project to another. To do this you can simply copy the *Project.params* file from the file system directory of one project and overwrite the *Project.params* file in the file system directory of the target project. The destination project will be able to use the copied project parameters and they can be used in the packages for the destination project.

> **Note** The IDs of the parameters might be regenerated when copied to a destination project.

> **Tip** Copying the *Project.params* file is a great way to make parameter templates that contain the basic parameters for any SSIS project in your enterprise.

API for Creating Parameters

SSIS application programming interfaces (APIs) provided in the SSIS object model can also be utilized for creating project and package parameters. Sample code to create projects with project parameters is shown in Listing 10-2.

LISTING 10-2 Creating project parameters using an API

```
//Reference required for Microsoft.SqlServer.Dts.Runtime library
public void CreateProjectWithParameters()
{
    //Define a project
    Project myProject = Project.CreateProject();
    //Define a package
    Package myPackage = new Package();
    myPackage.Name = "myPackage";
    //Add package to the project
    myProject.PackageItems.Add(myPackage,"myPackage.dtsx");
    //Add a new Project Parameter
    Parameter paramServerName1 = myProject.Parameters.Add("ServerName1", TypeCode.String);
    paramServerName1.Value = "myServer";
    //Make it a required parameter
    paramServerName1.Required = true;
    //Save the project to disk
    string projectFileName = "myProject.ispac";
    myProject.SaveTo(projectFileName);
}
```

Thus, we can use *Parameter paramServerName1 = myProject.Parameters.Add("ServerName1", TypeCode.String);* to create the parameter for the project and add it to the parameter collections of the project.

> **Tip** In Listing 10-2, note that we didn't initialize all the properties of the parameter like *Sensitive*. In such a case the default value of the property would be used. For instance the parameter in Listing 10-2 would be a nonsensitive parameter.

You can similarly create parameters for your package, the only difference being that you would add parameters to your package's parameter collection instead of the project's parameter collection as shown in Listing 10-3.

LISTING 10-3 Creating package parameters

```
//Reference required for Microsoft.SqlServer.Dts.Runtime library

public void CreatePackageWithParameters()
{
    //Define a project
    Project myProject = Project.CreateProject();
    //Define a package
    Package myPackage = new Package();
    myPackage.Name = "myPackage";
    //Add package to the project
    myProject.PackageItems.Add(myPackage, "myPackage.dtsx");
    //Add a new Project Parameter
    Parameter paramPackageServerName1 = myPackage.Parameters.Add("PackageServerName1",
TypeCode.String);
    paramPackageServerName1.Value = "myPackageServer";
    //Make it a required parameter
    paramPackageServerName1.Required = true;
    //Save the project to disk
    string projectFileName = "myProject.ispac";
    myProject.SaveTo(projectFileName);
}
```

Now we can use the projects created to deploy them to an SSIS Catalog and execute them in the Catalog.

***See Also** More about deployment can be found in Chapter 7 and executing on a Catalog is covered in Chapter 11, "Running SSIS Packages."*

Using Parameters

As defined earlier, you can use parameters as runtime arguments for your package or project execution. In the following sections, you'll see various usage patterns of parameters and how are they are especially beneficial in the server storage and execution model of SSIS in SQL Server 2012.

Parameters in Expressions and Property Paths

One of the most common uses of configurations was to configure the value of a property in a package with a value provided by the configuration model at run time. In SSIS versions before SQL Server 2012, you could accomplish this by mapping a configuration item to a property path in the package. The SSIS runtime would then take care of assigning the value mentioned in the configuration item to the mapped property path. Such a mapping when created through the Package Configuration Wizard in a package deployment format would look like Figure 10-7.

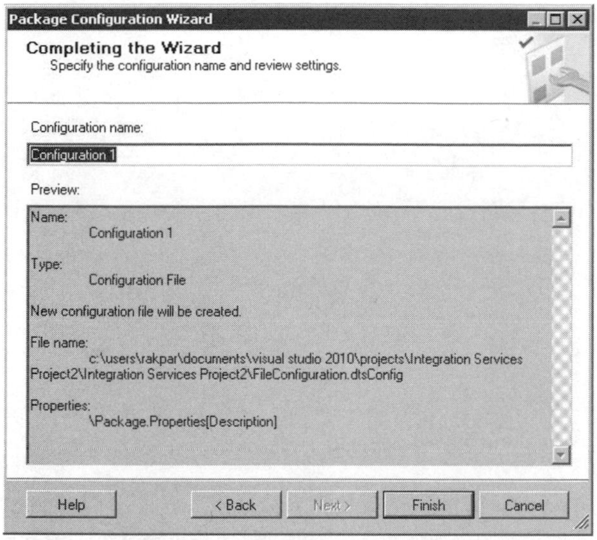

FIGURE 10-7 Configuration item mapped to a property path.

In a second way, you can also create a configuration for a variable value and then use the variable value for either assigning to a property of the package or for controlling the behavior of the package. So, in addition to creating a configuration for the variable item as shown in Figure 10-8, you would also create an expression assigning the variable value to the required property path as shown in Figure 10-9.

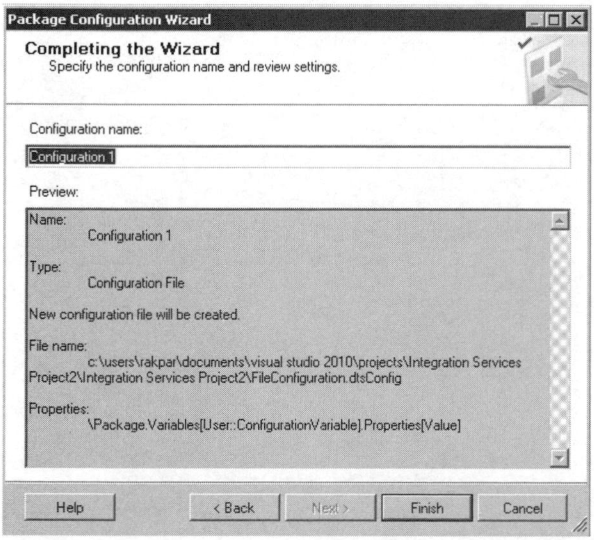

FIGURE 10-8 Configuration item mapped to a variable value.

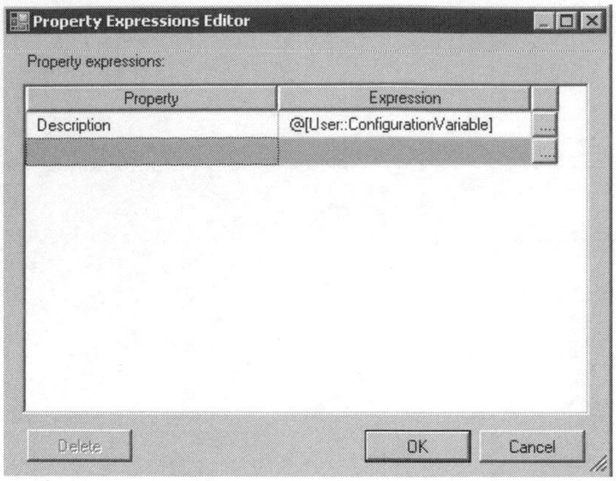

FIGURE 10-9 Variable value assigned to a property using an expression.

The way parameters are used is extremely similar to the second method just described. Instead of creating a configuration item that gets assigned to a variable and that variable being assigned to the property path, you can create a parameter that can be used to assign a value to the property path using an expression.

To do this, you must create a parameter using one of the methods described in the previous sections. After you create the parameter, you can the assign the parameter value to the required property path using an expression, as you had done with the variable value before. The new Expression Builder in SQL Server 2012 will allow you to use the parameters in the configurations, as shown in Figure 10-10.

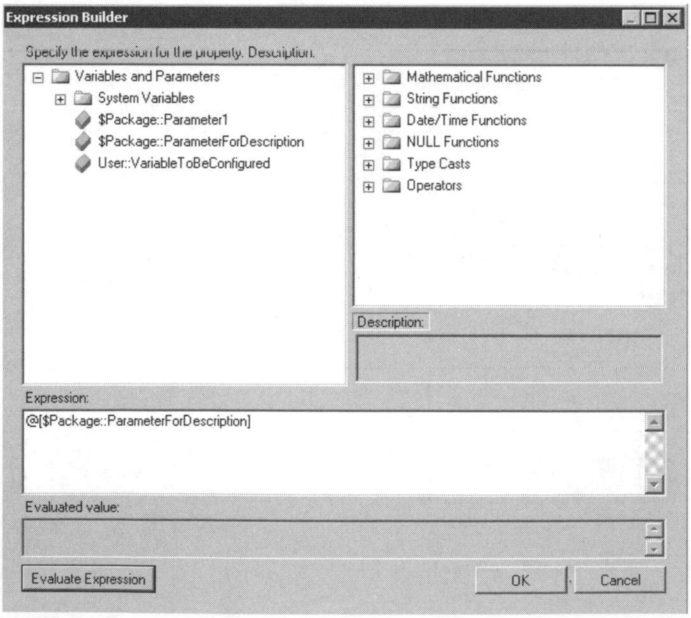

FIGURE 10-10 New Expression Builder for SQL Server 2012 showing parameters.

> **Note** You can see how the parameters in Figure 10-10 are annotated by *$Package* where *$* signifies that it is a parameter and *Package* signifies the scope of the parameter.

Thus, the new expression would use the value of the parameter that can be provided during run-time and the property mapped would get the runtime value by evaluating the expression.

Parameters and Execute Package Tasks

Another common use of the configurations was to pass values between parent and child package execution scenarios. In a Package Deployment Model, where you can still create configurations, you will create a child package with a parent package configuration as shown in Figure 10-11.

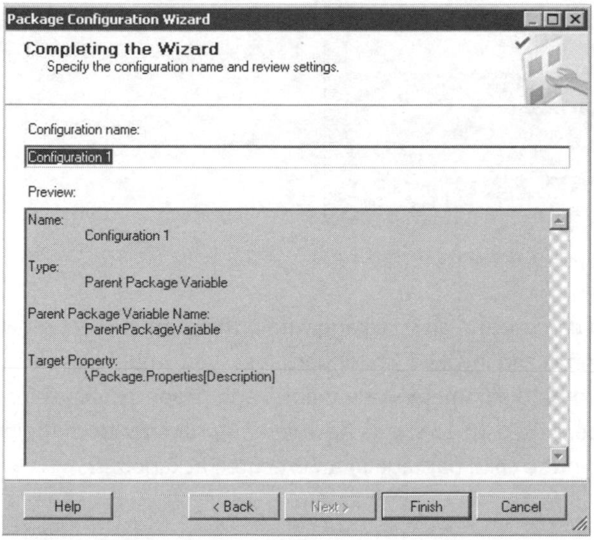

FIGURE 10-11 Parent package variable configuration in Package Deployment Model.

The *Execute Package task* in the parent package would refer to the child package and the variable value from the parent package would be used to assign the value to the mapped property in the child package when it is executed.

Using parameters in the Project Deployment Model is similar to what was described earlier. To do that, you need to understand how to create parameter Bindings in an Execute Package task.

In the Project Deployment Model, a package would be able to execute any other package in the same project using the Execute Package task. As shown in Figure 10-12, in the new task, you refer to a package in the same project. This is signified in the *ReferenceType* attribute, which states that the reference made is of the type *Project Reference.*

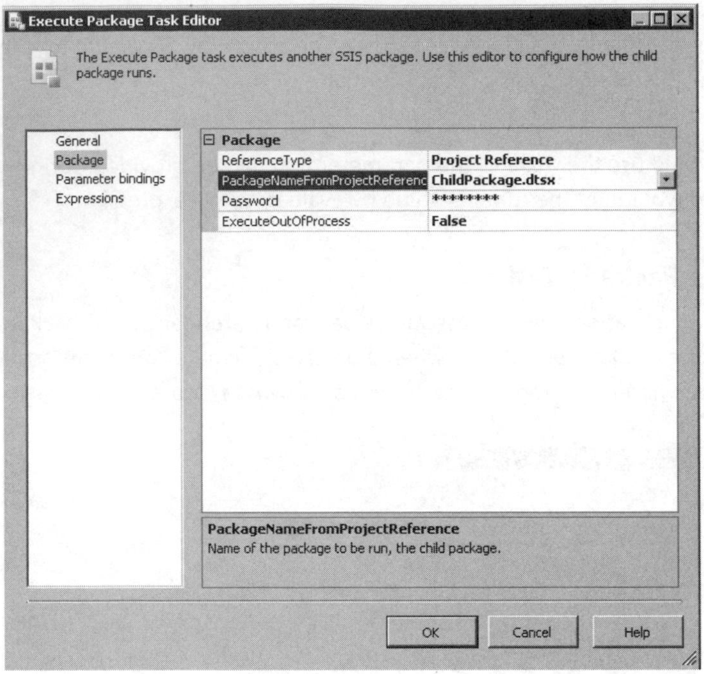

FIGURE 10-12 Execute Package task using a project reference.

Now, using the project reference, you can execute any package within the same project. However, to pass values between the invoking (parent) and invoked (child) packages, you would use parameter bindings. Parameter bindings allow you to bind parameters or variables and property values from the parent to parameters in the child package. Figure 10-13 shows how *ParentParameter* from the parent package is bound to the *ChildParameter* in the child package in an Execute Package task.

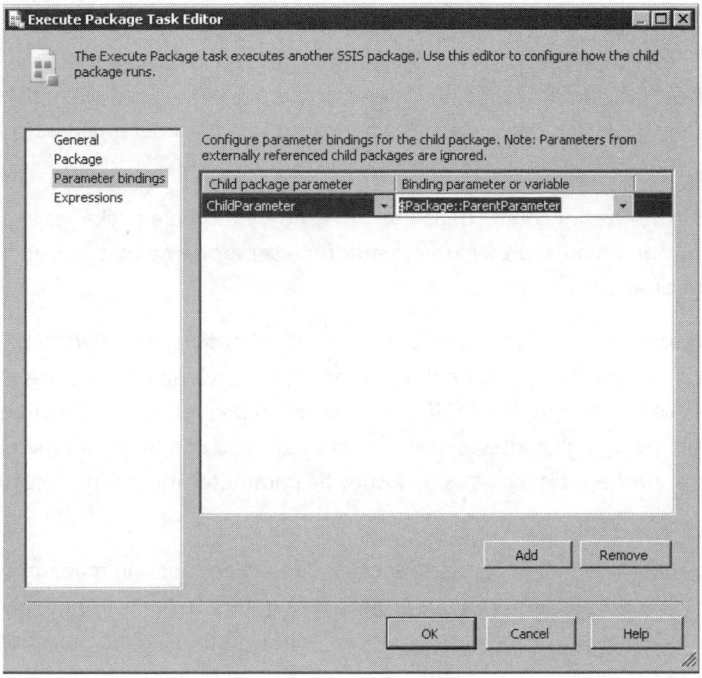

FIGURE 10-13 Execute Package task using parameter bindings.

> **Note** Parameter bindings follow the same rules as any other variable value assignment where the type of value being assigned and the type of the parameter should be identical for the assignment to occur. For instance a *String* value would only be assigned to a parameter of type *String*.

When the parent package is executed and when it eventually executes the Execute Package task, the value would be passed to the child package's parameter using the parameter bindings. The child package then uses the new value assigned to the parameter throughout its execution.

Use of Project Parameters

As defined earlier, project parameters are scoped at the project level and are available to all the packages within the project. Thus, you should define parameters to be project scoped when they are going to be shared between packages. Common instances where a project parameter can be created include the following:

- Connection strings and attributes of connections that are used by multiple packages in a project. For instance, you can create a project parameter for a server name that is used by multiple packages in the project.
- SSIS package template parameters such as *ErrorCode* or *ErrorDescription* that need to be used in multiple packages in a project. SSIS package development has matured in many instances, where developers like to create templates of SSIS packages using best practices. Creating project parameters would help you create such templates where you can have parameters that can be used in all the packages, such as using a specific parameter for storing a custom *ErrorCode*.
- Parameters used in project connection managers. Because project connection managers are available to all packages in a project, you can use project parameters to have a single parameter value assignment at the project scope rather than assigning values to the connection manager in each package.

Differences between Parameters and Variables

You have already seen where parameters are used in instances in which you were using variables before such as the following:

1. Using variables' values in expressions assigned to property values.
2. Using configurations assigned to variable values and then using the runtime values to determine package execution logic such as evaluating a condition in a precedence constraint.

In SQL Server 2012, you would use parameters to perform these actions. You might now ask what the fundamental differences between a variable and parameter are. Why and where should you be using a parameter versus a variable?

One of the major differences is how parameters are used by the SSIS engine. You might have already noted that parameters are considered replacements for configurations in the Project Deployment Model. Thus, they are entities that the engine exposes while configuring, validating, or executing a package. The next section, which describes server execution, includes special dialog boxes and methods that can be used to configure parameters. In comparison, the only way to configure variables would be to use the */SET* option to override the property value of the variable.

One of the other advantages of using parameters is that you can define their scope. You can define if you want a shared parameter that needs to be executed across packages by defining it as a project parameter or define it as a package parameter that is scoped to it package. Again, you might not be able to do the same with variables.

Configuring Parameters on the SSIS Catalog

In this section you learn how packages and projects are configured, validated, and executed on the new SSIS Catalog.

> **Tip** SSIS Catalog package execution is described in detail in Chapter 16, "SSIS Catalog Deep Dive."

Configuring, Validating, and Executing Packages and Projects

Once you have created your packages and projects, you can then deploy your project to the SSIS Catalog. To learn more about deploying SSIS packages, see Chapter 6, "Developing a SSIS Solution."

When a project is deployed to an SSIS Catalog, all the packages, associated project parameters, and project connection managers are also deployed to the SSIS Catalog. A package on the Catalog can be executed in multiple ways, such as using SQL Server Management Studio or SQL Server Agent and other methods. We discuss all the options and how to configure your packages and projects in each of those options in the following sections.

Configuration Through SSMS

Once your project is successfully deployed to the Catalog, you can then configure, validate, and execute the packages within that project using various dialog boxes available through SQL Server Management Studio.

Configuring and Validating Packages

You might have created parameters for configuring values. Your packages might also have connection managers and other objects that were created on a different system. After deployment, one of the first actions you will perform is to configure your packages and projects with the new values for the current system and validate that the packages do not return an error with the new values.

To configure a package, you can right-click a package and select Configure. The Configure dialog box lists all the available parameters that can now be assigned a value, as shown in Figure 10-14. It also lists all the connection managers in the package where you can change the various properties of the connection, as shown in Figure 10-15.

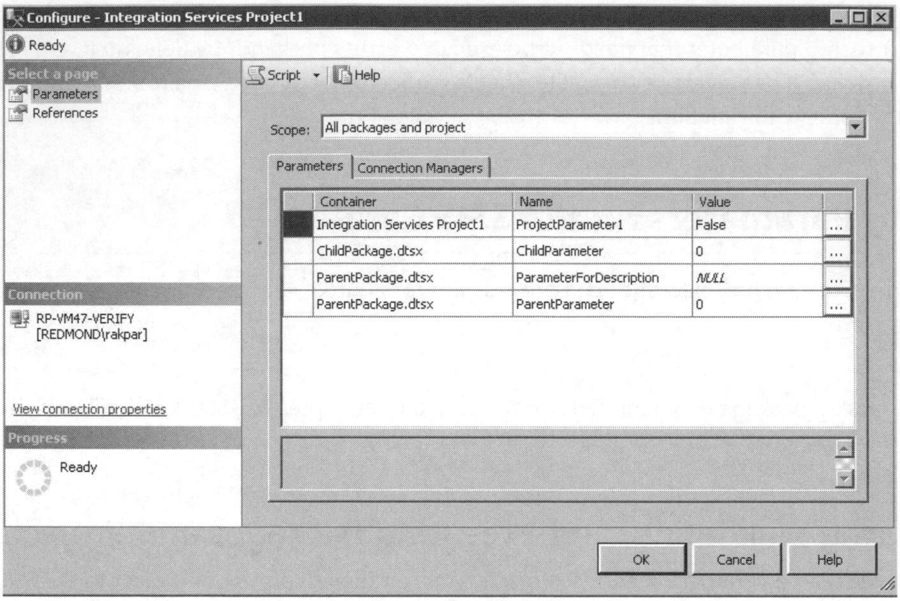

FIGURE 10-14 Configuring parameters using SQL Server Management Studio.

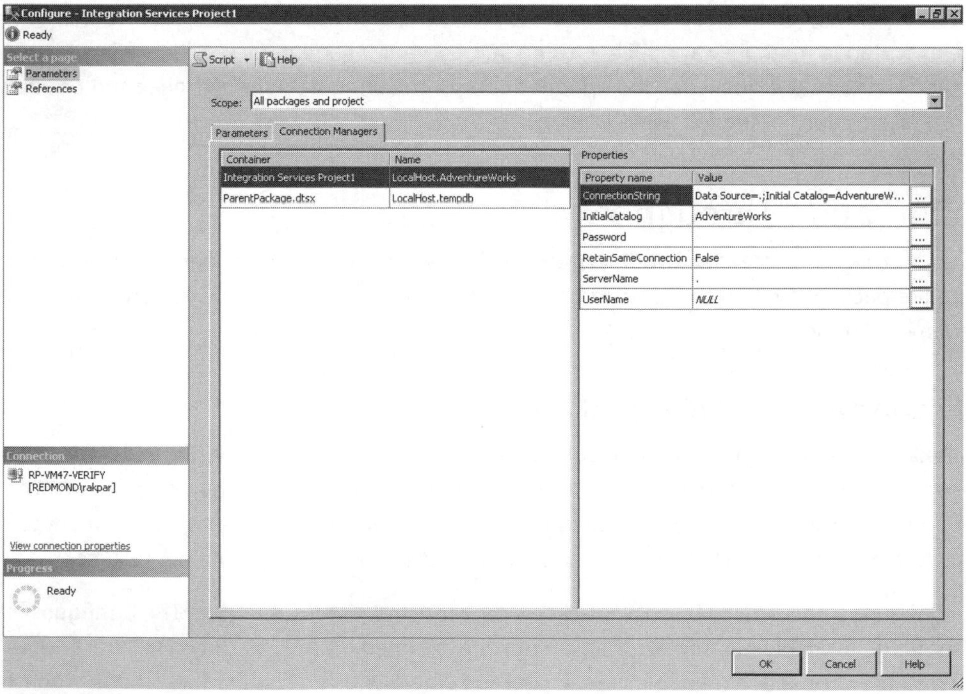

FIGURE 10-15 Configuring connection managers using SQL Server Management Studio.

From both these figures, notice that in the Configure dialog box, you can change the scope of the configuration to show all parameters from the all packages and projects to select a particular project or package and show its parameters and connection managers. It also has a References section in which you can use environments to assign parameter values. Environments are discussed further in the following sections.

Once you have configured the required parameters and connection strings for the packages, you are now ready to validate your package execution. Validating your package will ensure that the package execution doesn't fail due to improperly configured package or project parameters or connection managers.

See Also *See* http://www.sqlis.com/post/What-is-Validation.aspx *for a detailed explanation of SSIS validation.*

You can validate an entire project or just a package. When validating a project, the engine iteratively validates each package within the project. While validating, you also have an option to mention if the package or the project needs to execute using 32-bit runtime. Once selected, that option ensures that the SSIS engine loads the 32-bit version of all related components, such as connection adapters and so on.

See Also *More about SSIS 32-bit and 64-bit can be found at* http://msdn.microsoft.com/en-us/library/ms141766(v=SQL.105).aspx.

As shown in Figure 10-16, you can also see all the configured values for the package and project parameters and connection managers that will be used when their validation occurs.

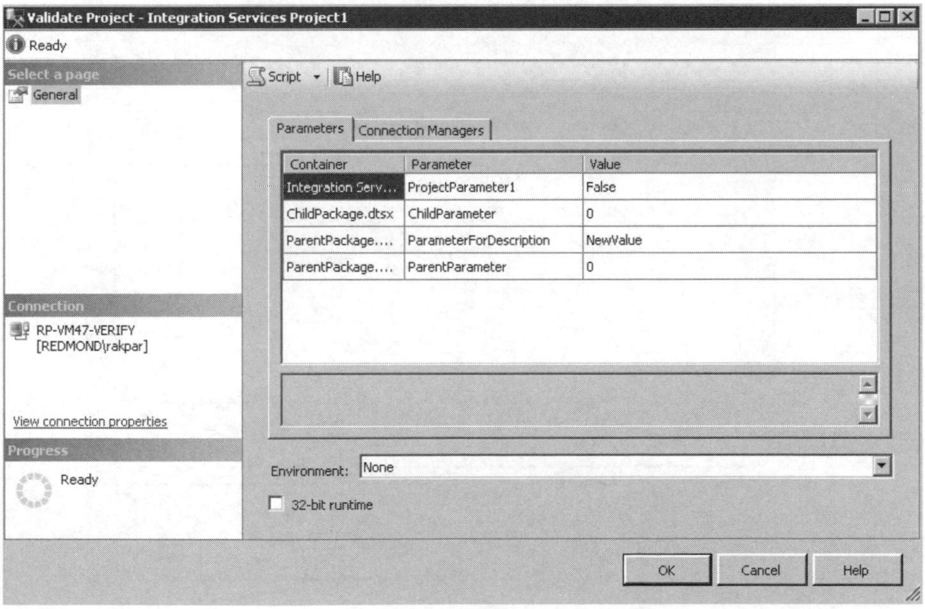

FIGURE 10-16 Validate Project dialog box using SQL Server Management Studio.

In Figure 10-16, you can see that the parameter *ParameterForDescription* shows the new configured value *NewValue,* which was provided using the Configure dialog box shown in Figure 10-14. When you click OK, it will use the new value to validate the package.

After you click OK, you are then presented a report about the validation. This report describes all the validation steps that were performed and reports any errors caused during validation. In the case of errors in the report, you can reconfigure and revalidate the packages or project with new values.

See Also *SSIS Catalog reports are discussed in detail in Chapter 14, "SSIS Reports."*

Executing with Configured Values

Once you have configured and validated your package and project with the new values for parameters and connection managers, you are now ready to execute your package. A more detailed explanation about package execution on the SSIS Catalog is mentioned in Chapter 16.

When you execute your package using the Execute dialog box, it will display all the parameters and connection managers with values that you have configured using the Configure dialog box. Note that you also have an option to override that value with a new value during execution. In Figure 10-17, you can see the highlighted value that was provided in the Execute dialog box.

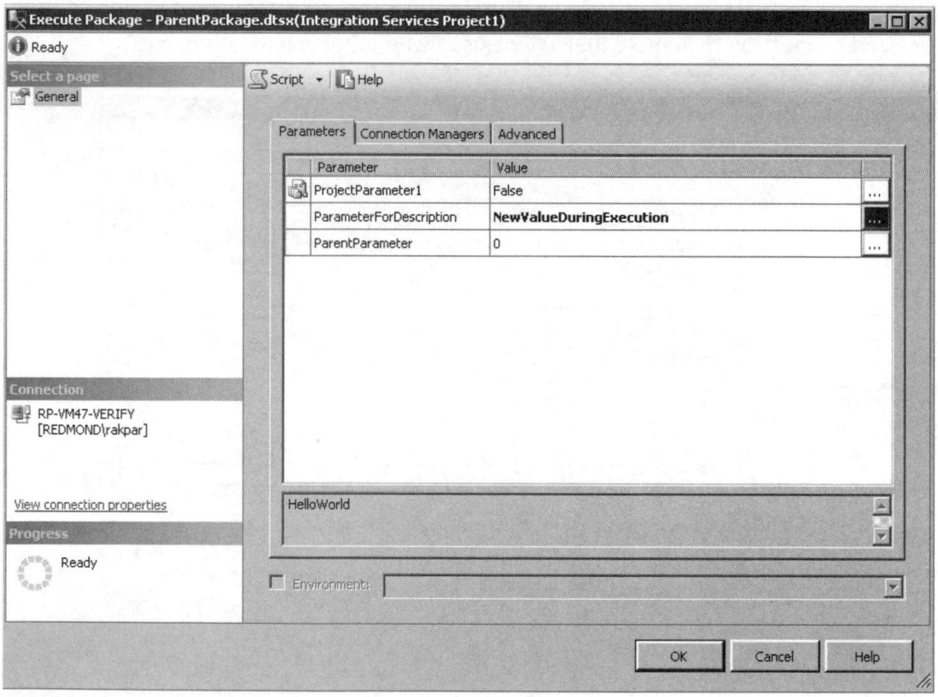

FIGURE 10-17 Execute dialog box with a new override value.

Note that apart from the Parameters and Connection Managers tabs, there is also an Advanced tab. On the Advanced tab, you can provide property overrides. Property overrides are similar to the */Set Value* option in the previous versions of SSIS. A sample property override is shown in Figure 10-18.

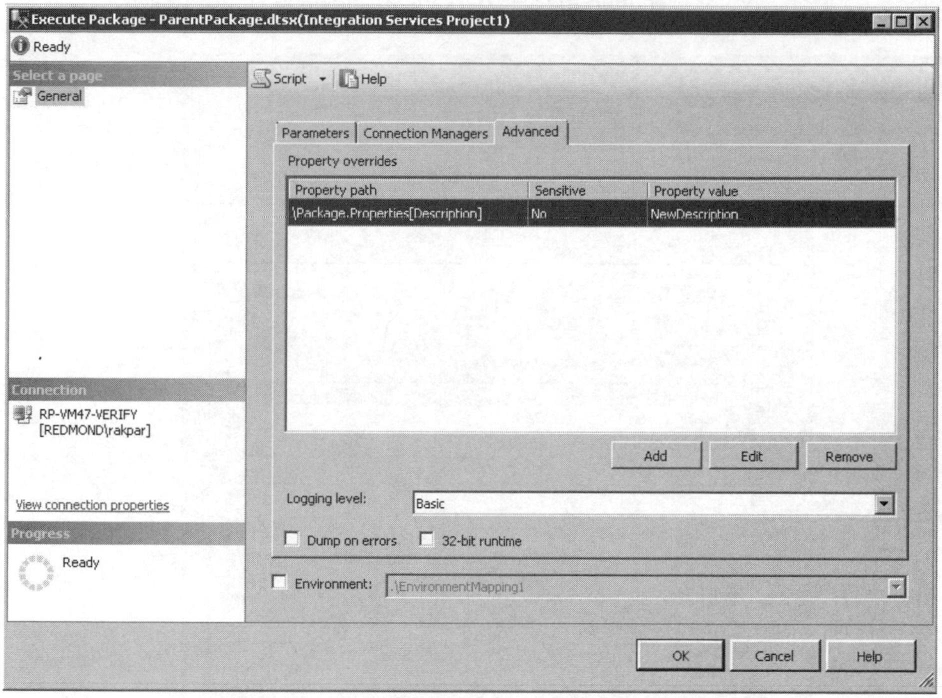

FIGURE 10-18 Property overrides using the Advanced tab.

Using the Advanced tab, you can also indicate if you want to have a 32-bit execution of the package. As during validation, a 32-bit runtime option means that the 32-bit version of all related components like connection adapters would be loaded by the engine.

The Advanced tab also has options for enabling the logging level and dump on errors. The logging level describes the extent of package execution logging, and dump on errors ensures that it creates an SSIS dump when an error occurs during package execution.

See Also *You can find out more about SSIS logging and dump on errors in Chapter 18, "SSIS Logging," and Chapter 19, "Automating SSIS."*

Configuration Using SQL Agent, DTExec, and T-SQL

You learn more about executing packages in Chapter 11. This section provides an overview of configuring packages and projects using these tools.

SQL Agent and Configuration

If you are executing your package through SQLAgent, you will have an option to configure your package parameters, connection managers, and property overrides on the Configuration tab when you are creating a new job step for executing the SSIS package as shown in Figure 10-19.

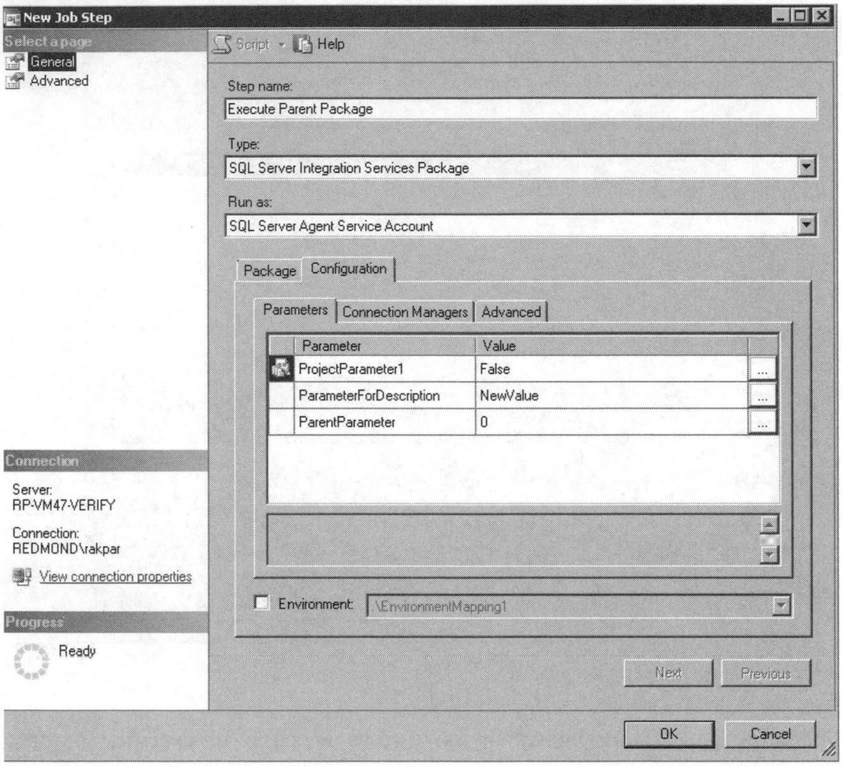

FIGURE 10-19 Configuring SSIS packages using SQL Agent job step.

Any configured value for the package will be shown here. However, you have the option to override the value during execution.

DTExec and Configuration

DTExec.exe would be able to execute a package with the preconfigured value in the Catalog. You can also configure the value of a parameter using the */Parameter* option as shown in Listing 10-4.

LISTING 10-4 Configuring and executing packages using DTExec.exe

```
dtexec /Server "localhost" /ISServer "\SSISDB\MyProjectFolder\Integration Services
Project1\ParentPackage.dtsx" /Parameter "$Package::ParentParameter(Int32);2" /Par
"$Package::ParameterForDescription(String);HelloWorld"
```

In Listing 10-4, you can see the use of the */Parameter* option, which is in the format of *[$Package::|$Project::|$ServerOption::]parameter_name[(data_type)];literal_value*. You can provide multiple parameters to configure the parameters defined in the package.

Configuring Using T-SQL Stored Procedures

As with all other operations like execution and validation, you can also configure packages stored on the Catalog using Transact-SQL (T-SQL) stored procedures.

You need to use the *[SSISDB].[catalog].[set_object_parameter_value]* stored procedure on the SSISDB database on the same server as the SSIS Catalog containing the package to set a parameter value. Listing 10-5 shows a use of the procedure to set a value for a parameter.

LISTING 10-5 T-SQL stored procedure to configure values

```
DECLARE @var int = 2
EXEC [SSISDB].[catalog].[set_object_parameter_value]
@object_type=30
, @parameter_name=N'ParentParameter'
, @object_name=N'ParentPackage.dtsx'
, @folder_name=N'MyProjectFolder'
, @project_name=N'Integration Services Project1'
, @value_type=V //Set value by Value or by Reference (R)
, @parameter_value=@var
GO
```

You can also use other stored procedures to set values during execution (*catalog. set_execution_ parameter_value*) and override values during execution (*catalog.set_execution_property_override_value*)

SSIS Environments

You saw in the earlier section on configuration using SQL Server Management Studio that you had a tab named References. This tab is used to assign SSIS environment references to package configurations.

SSIS Environments can be simply defined as a grouping of key–value pairs. Each key–value pair can represent a variable and its respective value. In Figure 10-20, you can see such a pair where the variable is *ParentParameter* and the value is *1*.

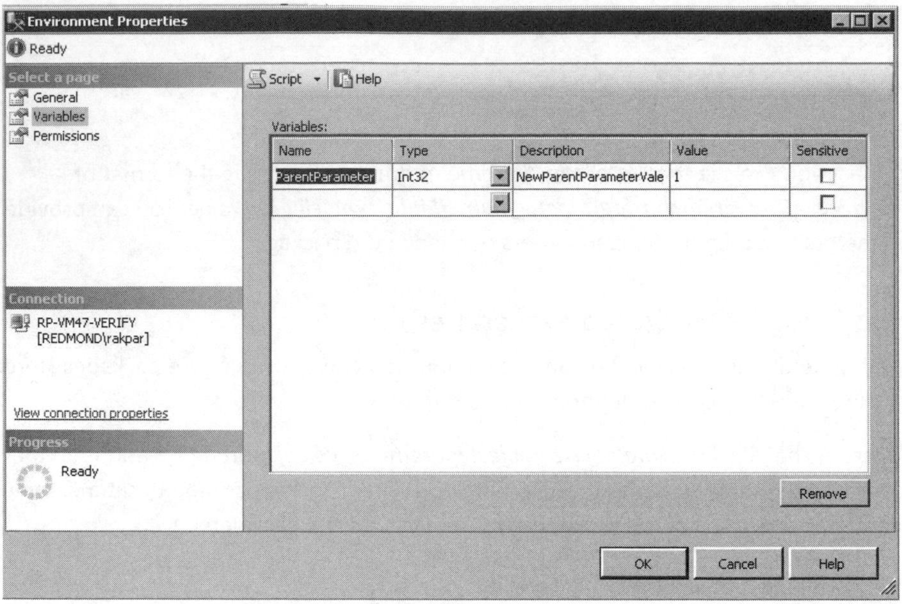

FIGURE 10-20 Variables and values in an environment.

When an environment is assigned to a package, the engine uses the variables defined in the environment and maps them to the parameters defined in the package. This mapping can be done in the Set Parameter Value dialog box while assigning a value to a parameter. After assignment of the value to be mapped to the SSIS environment server variable, your Execute or Configure dialog box Parameters tab could look like the one shown in Figure 10-21.

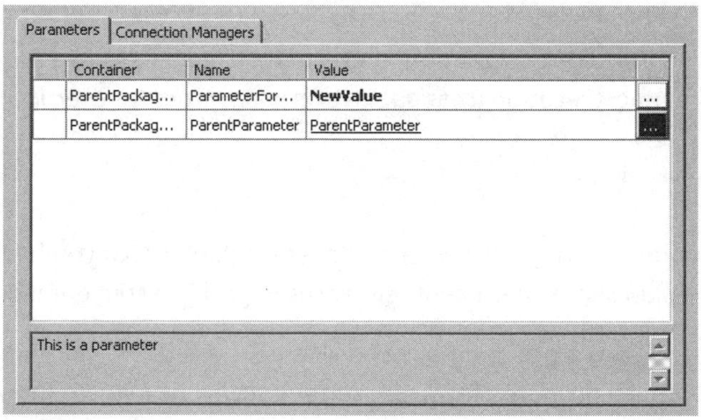

FIGURE 10-21 Parameter value mapped to SSIS environment server variable.

A server environment name should be unique under the same folder. The access of the environment is controlled by SSIS_Admin or anyone with manage_objects SSIS role permission, so you can only view the environments for which you have permission. You learn more about SSIS row-level security in Chapter 17, "SSIS Security."

Using T-SQL, you can use the stored procedures to perform operations on environments shown in Table 10-1.

TABLE 10-1 Stored procedures for operations on environments

Stored Procedure	Operation
catalog.create_environment	Create a new environment. Environments created are stored in the *catalog.internal.environments* table.
catalog.create_environment_reference	Assign an environment reference to a project or package. Environment references are stored in the *catalog.internal.environment_references* table.
catalog.create_environment_variable	Create a new variable within the environment. Environment variables are stored in the *catalog.internal.environment_references* table.
catalog.delete_environment	Deletes an existing environment.
catalog.delete_environment_reference	Deletes an existing environment reference.
catalog.delete_environment_variable	Deletes an existing variable from an environment.

Relative and Absolute References

References can be assigned to a project in two different ways: relative and absolute. They can be differentiated by the way an environment is assigned in a reference, as shown in Figure 10-22.

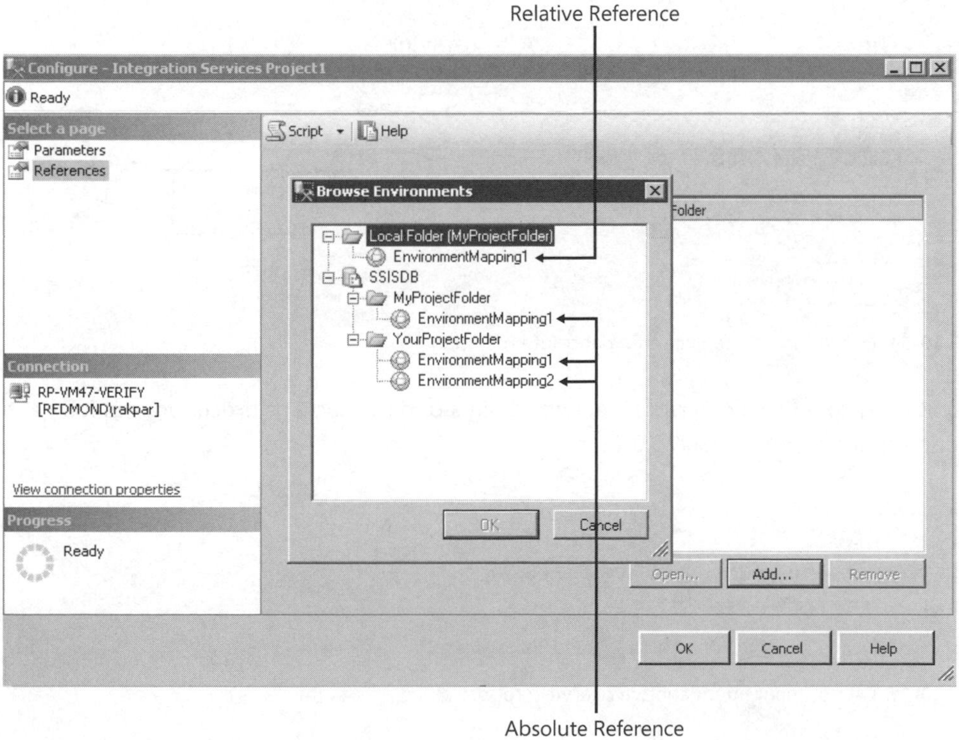

FIGURE 10-22 Relative vs. absolute reference.

A relative reference signifies that the SSIS project in the Catalog always refers to the environment in its local folder based on the name of the environment to which it was assigned. As shown in Figure 10-23, the project refers to environment *EnvironmentMapping1* using the relative reference. Before the project was moved from the folder *MyProjectFolder,* it referred to *MyProjectFolder.EnvironmentMapping1*. After the project was moved it refers to *YourProjectFolder.EnvironmentMapping1*.

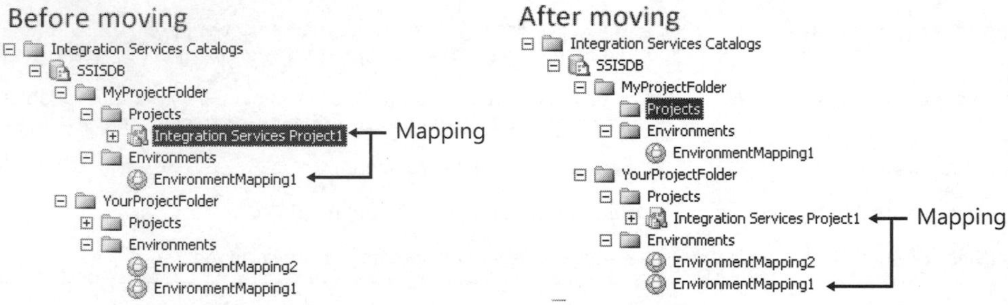

FIGURE 10-23 Environment reference using relative reference.

An absolute reference signifies that the SSIS project refers to the ID of an environment and not the name, so it refers to the same environment irrespective of which folder it is located in, as shown in Figure 10-24. This is particularly useful when moving projects across folder boundaries.

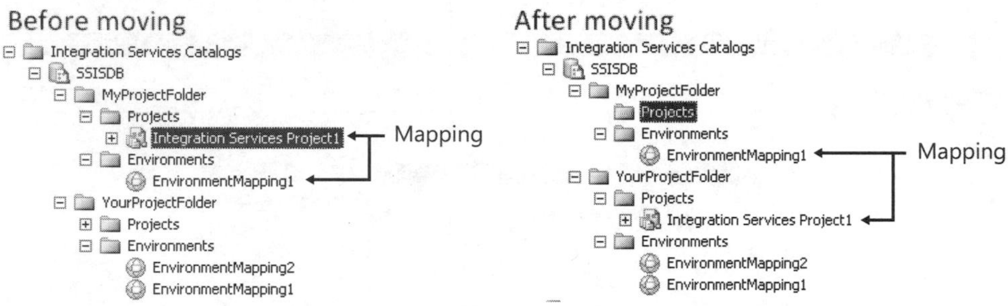

FIGURE 10-24 Environment reference using absolute mapping.

An easy way to find which environment was assigned to the package execution is to look at the execution report, shown in Figure 10-25.

Execution Information

Operation ID	14 (Execution)
Name	YourProjectFolder\Integration Services Project1\ParentPackage.dtsx
Environment	MyProjectFolder\EnvironmentMapping1
Status	Succeeded

FIGURE 10-25 Environment information in overview report.

Evaluation Order of Parameters

Parameters are evaluated in the same order that configuration models before SSIS 2012 used. The values of parameters are assigned in the following order:

1. Project is loaded.
2. Package is loaded.
3. Values for project parameters configured are applied to the corresponding package properties.
4. Values for the package parameters configured are applied to the corresponding package properties.
5. Any override values supplied are applied to the package properties.
6. The package is executed.
7. Parent package parameters are applied when the Execute Package task is invoked.

After the evaluation order is applied, the engine always uses a single value for each parameter.

> **Tip** You will find this order useful when you are trying to debug a package that has multiple parameters assigned to the same property. You can then find the exact cause of the error by understanding the how the value of the property is evaluated.

Package Deployment Model and Backward Compatibility

Before SQL Server 2012, there were multiple ways to configure your packages. The primary ways you could configure the value of the property were as follows:

- Defining package configurations during development of the package.
- Using the */SET* option while using dtexec to execute the package. You would provide the property path and the new value as parameters to the */SET* option.
- Using the indirect configuration where a property value is calculated using an expression using another configured value; for instance, a variable value that is configured using package configurations.

SSIS projects in SQL Server 2012 whether upgraded from previous versions or created in SQL Server 2012 have the option of using the previous configuration model to assign runtime values to properties within a package. This can be done by using the legacy deployment model.

Package Deployment Model

As we already introduced, an SSIS project is a collection of SSIS packages. We can define an SSIS project to work with the old configuration model using the pre–SQL Server 2012 options of using package configurations. When a project is using package configurations, it is defined to be using the Package Deployment Model. This can be done by converting an SSIS project to a Package Deployment Model as shown in Figure 10-26. Note that the Project Deployment Model is the default option for all new SSIS projects created in SQL Server 2012.

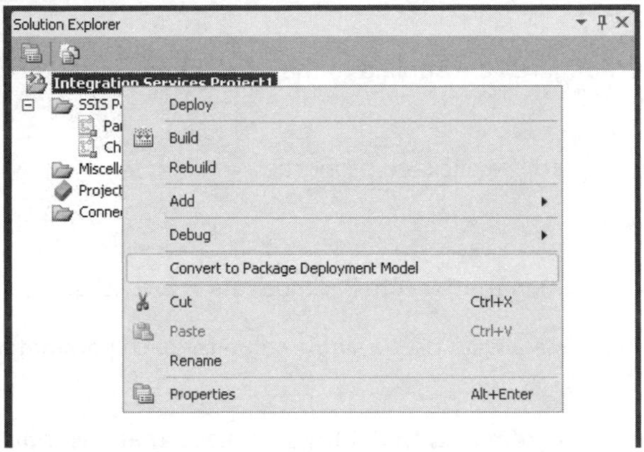

FIGURE 10-26 Package Deployment Model for SSIS project.

Note that conversion to the Package Deployment Model will fail if your project has the following elements, which are new in SQL Server 2012:

- **Project or package parameters** These have to be deleted or converted into individual package variables.
- **Project connection managers** These have to be deleted or converted back to package connection managers.

Once the project has been successfully converted into a Package Deployment Model you can then use package configurations to configure your package. You should also notice that the package configurations are a new item on the SSIS menu shown in Figure 10-27.

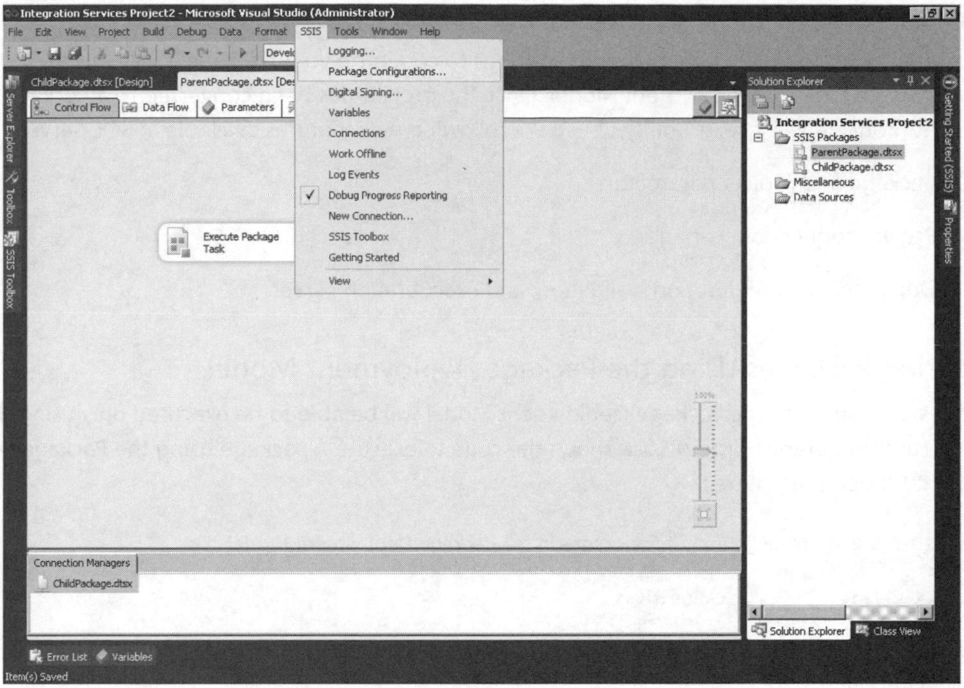

FIGURE 10-27 Package Configurations menu item.

You will also have to select the Enable Package Configurations check box when creating new package configurations. The new package configurations created will work in the exact same way that package configurations used to work in previous versions of SSIS. For more details, check Books Online for SSIS package configurations.

The packages can now be configured with the following options that were available in the earlier versions of SSIS:

- XML Configuration File
- Environment Variable
- Registry Entry
- Parent Package Variable
- SQL Server Configurations

All configuration application rules and the order of their application logic from previous versions of SSIS are applied to the packages executing under the Package Deployment Model.

Limitations of the Package Deployment Model

Although it is great to use all the preceding options to configure your package, there are a few limitations of using a Package Deployment Model. Once the project has been converted to a Package Deployment Model, it will lose its ability to use the following new features available in SQL Server 2012:

- Package and project parameters
- Project connection managers
- Deployment, configuration, validation, and execution on server

Executing Packages Using the Package Deployment Model

Packages created using the Package Deployment Model will be able to be executed only using dtexec and the runtime libraries. Listing 10-6 shows the code to execute a package using the Package Deployment Model using dtexec.

LISTING 10-6 Using dtexec to execute packages in the Package Deployment Model

```
C:\> DTEXEC /FILE "\"C:\Package.dtsx\""
```

You can also use the DTS runtime to execute the packages using the Package Deployment Model as shown in Listing 10-7.

LISTING 10-7 Using the runtime API to execute packages in the Package Deployment Model

```
//Reference required for Microsoft.SqlServer.Dts.Runtime library

public DTSExecResult ExecutePackageWithConfigurations()
{
    //Define a package
    Package pkgWithConfig = new Package();
    //Enable the configurations
    pkgWithConfig.EnableConfigurations = true;
    //Add a variable to be configured
    pkgWithConfig.Variables.Add("VariableToBeConfigured", false, "user", "HelloWorld");
    //Add a new configuration to the package
    Configuration newPkgConfig = pkgWithConfig.Configurations.Add();
    newPkgConfig.Name = "XMLFileConfig";
    newPkgConfig.ConfigurationType = DTSConfigurationType.ConfigFile;
    newPkgConfig.ConfigurationString = @"C:\myDTSConfigFile.dtsConfig";
    newPkgConfig.PackagePath =
"\\Package.Variables[User::VariableToBeConfigured].Properties[Value]";
    DTSExecResult result = pkgWithConfig.Execute();
    pkgWithConfig.Dispose();
    return result;
}
```

Best Practices for Configuring SSIS

In this section we look at various best practices in configuring SSIS packages and projects in enterprise production environments. You should also note that the following is not an exhaustive list. In fact, you can come up with your own best practices based on your experiences with the product.

Best Practices with Package Deployment Model

There are various best practices for configuring SSIS packages built with the Package Deployment Model. As discussed earlier, you can create new packages as well as store pre–SQL Server 2012 packages in projects that are in the Package Deployment Model. You will then have to use the traditional SSIS configuration model to create configurations for the packages in the project. This method was introduced to you in the section "Configuration Basics" at the start of this chapter.

Package Templates

One of the more common ways to incorporate basic best practices into your package design is to use package templates. Creating package templates is useful not just for creating configuration-related best practices, but also for incorporating practices related to logging, variable creations, and so forth.

> **Note** A package template is not a different type of package or object in SSIS. It is just a sample package that you can make multiple copies of. The copied packages will retain all the objects that were present in the initial package.

The goal of creating a package template is to create a template that embodies all the required configuration options. Any subsequent package created with that package template will then inherently have those configuration options. The primary configuration options that you should be thinking about are as follows:

- Any common configuration that is used by multiple packages. Common examples are central server names, user names, passwords, and file paths for files such as log files.
- Any variables or properties that are being used in auditing or configuration frameworks you might be using.
- Any configuration item that you might want all child packages to have.
- Best practices of using common values for properties such as *CheckpointFileName, BlobTempStoragePath, BufferTempStoragePath,* and so on.

> **Tip** Package templates can be used not only for configurations, but also for other features like logging and auditing, error handling, and so on.

SQL Server Configurations

One of the best practices for configurations is to use SQL Server configurations to configure your packages. The advantages of SQL Server configurations are as follows:

1. It provides central management of your configured properties. You don't have to maintain multiple copies of XML configuration files and handle the manageability of those files.
2. You will have a single connection string instead of having issues with file paths (absolute or relative) given for the XML configuration file.
3. You will have a structured way to modify configured values in the table. You can use all the facilities SQL Server provides, such as Change Data Capture and so forth for change tracking. It is quite difficult to implement such solutions for XML configuration files.

Indirect Configurations Using Environment Variables

A common problem users face while configuring SSIS packages is locating their configuration files or tables. As you already know, you can have multiple configuration types. Of these, in most cases you have to mention the connection string or a file path for the actual configuration item. As for an XML file configuration, you have to mention the file path of the XML file. In the case of SQL Server configuration, you will mention the connection string for the SQL Server database. In most cases where the preceding configurations are used, you will have to change the file path or the configuration string when you move your package between systems. It will thus result in you having to modify the package or have a file or a SQL Server database using the exact same file path or connection string, respectively, in each system to which the package is moved.

The solution to this problem is to use *indirect configurations,* which store the location of the configuration. When you use environment variables to store your configurations' path, you can easily configure each path or connection string on a system by modifying an environment variable. Thus, each time you move your package to a new system, you can create a new environment variable in the system. You can set the connection string or the path in the environment variable and SSIS will use it to find its configuration. You can create the indirect configuration in the Package Configuration Wizard as shown in Figure 10-28.

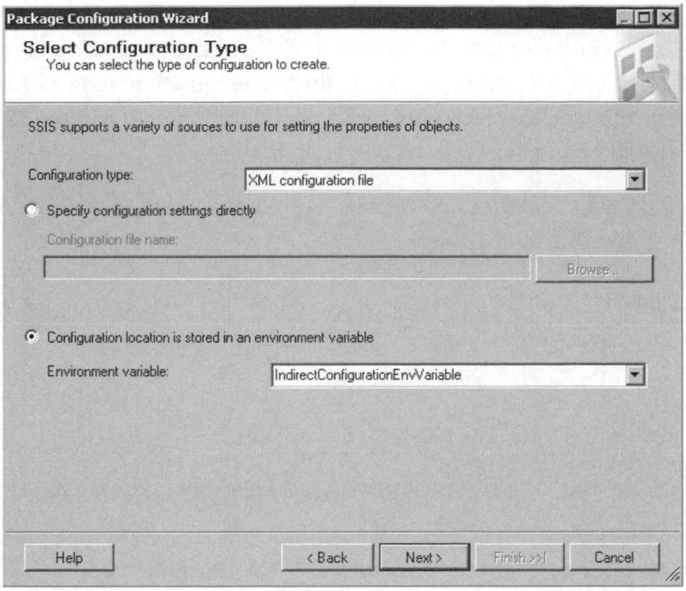

FIGURE 10-28 Using indirect configurations.

As shown in Figure 10-28, you will now need to create and set the environment variable *IndirectConfigurationEnvVariable* to have the file path of the XML configuration file. The advantage here is the package is no longer dependent on the file path of the XML configuration file with respect to the system on which it is getting executed.

Overriding Configurations

You might find in several cases that you have missed a configuration. Unfortunately you might have realized this only after your packages have reached production systems. In several cases, you might have to follow several guidelines with moving code binaries and packages between development and production systems. This could slow down the whole process of adding the missed configuration to the package. You can easily fix these using runtime arguments, though.

Now for some background on how SSIS evaluates configurations. You might already know that SSIS has an order in which it evaluates configurations. In that order SSIS loads configuration files or items and applies them to the defined property paths. However, these configuration files or items are not bound to a package. In other words, you can add or modify a configuration item and the SSIS package would pick up the new configuration item when it is executed.

For instance, you might have a package that uses an XML file configuration. Within the XML file configuration you have the items shown in Listing 10-8.

LISTING 10-8 Package XML file configuration

```
<?xml version="1.0"?>
<DTSConfiguration>
   <DTSConfigurationHeading>
            <DTSConfigurationFileInfo GeneratedBy="REDMOND\rakpar"
GeneratedFromPackageName="ParentPackage"
GeneratedFromPackageID="{9BDB7AB4-CE84-457F-B6B1-3A5BBE9029E4}" GeneratedDate="11/18/2011
2:54:51 PM"/>
   </DTSConfigurationHeading>
   <Configuration ConfiguredType="Property" Path="\Package.Properties[Description]"
ValueType="String">
            <ConfiguredValue>HelloWorld</ConfiguredValue>
   </Configuration>
</DTSConfiguration>
```

If you want to add a new configuration without changing the package, you can simply add a new *<Configuration>* item to the preceding XML and have the respective property path configured using the new XML file when the package is executed. Now if you use the XML file with the code shown in Listing 10-9, you would notice that the package uses *ForcedExecutionValue* as mentioned in the configuration.

LISTING 10-9 Package XML file configuration

```
<?xml version="1.0"?>
<DTSConfiguration>
   <DTSConfigurationHeading>
            <DTSConfigurationFileInfo GeneratedBy="REDMOND\rakpar"
GeneratedFromPackageName="ParentPackage"
GeneratedFromPackageID="{9BDB7AB4-CE84-457F-B6B1-3A5BBE9029E4}" GeneratedDate="11/18/2011
3:03:12 PM"/>
   </DTSConfigurationHeading>
   <Configuration ConfiguredType="Property" Path="\Package.Properties[Description]"
ValueType="String">
            <ConfiguredValue>HelloWorld</ConfiguredValue>
   </Configuration>
   <Configuration ConfiguredType="Property" Path="\Package.Properties[ForcedExecutionValue]"
ValueType="Int32">
            <ConfiguredValue>1</ConfiguredValue>
   </Configuration>
</DTSConfiguration>
```

You can also do the thing if you are using dtexec, which allows you to mention a property path and provide a value for it during runtime. So effectively you can use the *Set* parameter to modify the *ForcedExecutionValue* property within the package when it is executed as shown in Listing 10-10.

LISTING 10-10 DTExec using the */SET* option

```
C:\>dtexec.exe /FILE "\"C:\Integration Services Project1\ParentPackage.dtsx\"" /SET
"\"=\"\"\Package.Properties[ForcedExecutionValue]\"";1
```

Best Practices with Project Deployment Model

As discussed before, there are several features introduced in SSIS in SQL Server 2012 that made best practices with respect to configuring packages as a standard feature that you can use. We briefly discuss them in this section.

Project Parameters and Project Connection Managers

In the Project Deployment Model you can create project parameters and project connection managers. You should be using either one of them if you have multiple packages using connections with same connection strings or parameters with the same value in the same project.

You should also use them when you prescribe all the child packages and the projects to use them. You can thus map the use of the project parameters and project connection managers to the package templates. For instance, for my SSIS project I have the following objects that will be common to any package that I create:

- Logging server
- Logging user name and password
- Log file location
- Checkpoint file name

Figure 10-29 shows how you would create a project with appropriate project parameters and project connection managers for the preceding objects.

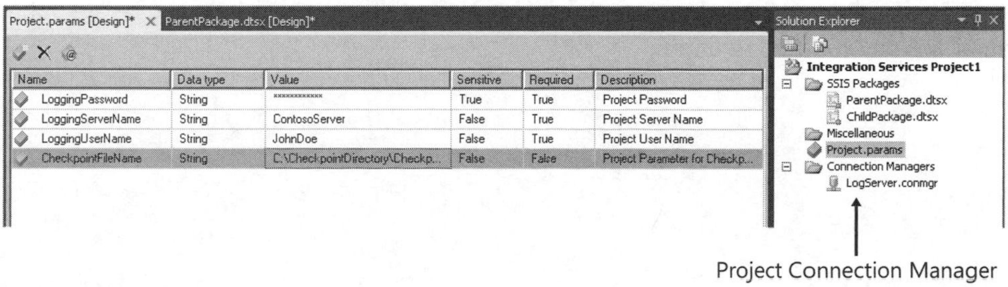

FIGURE 10-29 Project parameters and connection managers.

You have to then use the project parameter in your individual packages. For instance, you can create an expression for the *CheckpointFileName* to use the parameter you just created, as shown in Figure 10-30.

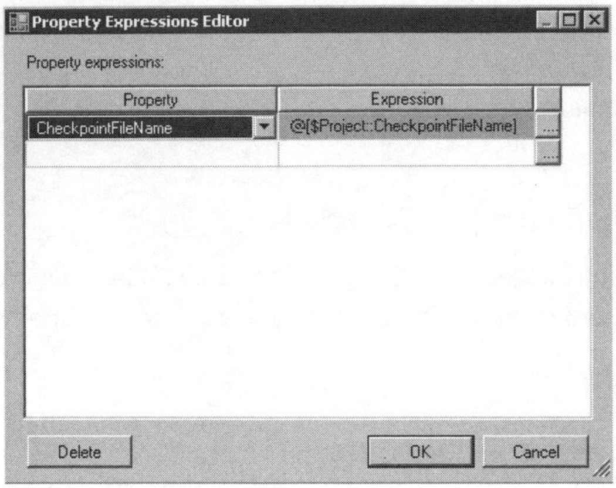

FIGURE 10-30 Using project parameters.

Thus, using the project parameters you can configure all the similar properties from the child packages.

The advantages of the project parameters and shared connection managers are similar to the advantages described in the package templates sections. You will have to configure them only once for the project and the new configured value will be used when any of the packages in the project are executed. Hence, using project parameters and connection managers for creating such common objects not only helps you to create them once and use them in any package in the project, but also helps you to configure once and all packages use the configured value.

Summary

Optimal configuration of SSIS packages and projects requires a good understanding of how configiurations work with SSIS. This chapter covered how SSIS processes configurations. The various new options available in SQL Server 2012 will ease the processing of configuring and executing SSIS packages. These, along with the best practices of implementing them, will help you create optimal configurations for your SSIS solutions.

CHAPTER 11

Running SSIS Packages

In This Chapter

Ways to Run SSIS Packages

Although there are lots of ways to run an SSIS package, without a doubt, dtexec is still the most frequently used method. It is also the basis for some other approaches (such as SQL Agent, which is introduced later in this chapter, which calls dtexec to do its work). It's important to clearly understand the capability of the tool.

The dtexec utility is a command-line tool; the executable file is named *dtexec.exe*. The utility has both 32-bit and 64-bit versions. By default the 64-bit version is installed as *%Program Files%\Microsoft SQL Server\110\DTS\Binn\dtexec.exe*, and the 32-bit binary is installed as *%Program Files(x86)%\Microsoft SQL Server\110\DTS\Binn\dtexec.exe*.

Usually the 64-bit version binary provides better performance, because SSIS can then use more memory. It's important to note that the 64-bit version of dtexec will try to load 64-bit drivers. For instance, if your SSIS package has a Data Flow that accesses an Oracle database, you must install the 64-bit Oracle database driver to make the package work.

See Also *You can refer to* http://msdn.microsoft.com/en-us/library/ms141766.aspx *for more discussions related to SSIS 32-bit and 64-bit versions.*

Sometimes users are not sure about which version they are executing. They simply open a command window and type **dtexec**, but they are unaware if that launches the 32-bit version or the 64-bit version. Which version executes usually depends on the folder order in the operating system environment *PATH* variable. You could type **where dtexec** to see which binary the operating system finds. Of course, a simpler way is to run dtexec with option */?* and check the printed version information (see Figure 11-1).

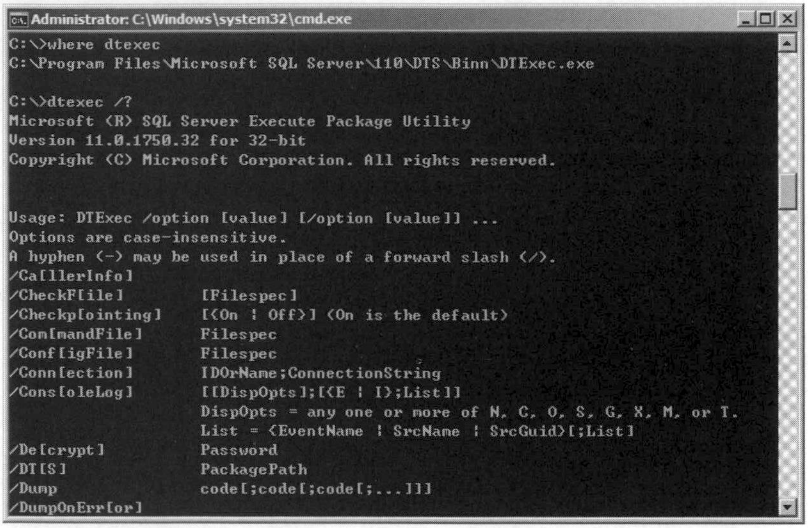

FIGURE 11-1 Check the version information printed by dtexec.

In Figure 11-1, you can see that the dtexec utility supports a long list of options. This section does not exhaustively detail those options; instead, it focuses on topics that are most frequently asked about and the new options added in SQL Server 2012. Those new options were added primarily to support two new features: the Project Deployment Model and the SSIS Catalog.

Table 11-1 shows all the new options in SSIS 2012.

TABLE 11-1 New dtexec options in SSIS 2012

Option Name	Description
/IS[Server]	Execute a package stored in an SSIS Catalog
/Par[ameter]	Set one or more parameter values, including both project parameters and project parameters
/Proj[ect]	Execute a package in Project Deployment Model
/Pack[age]	Specify the package to be used in an execution; it is supposed to be used with */Project*
/Env[Reference]	Reference the specified environment

Package Locations

You could store SSIS packages in different locations. SSIS supports the following location types:

- File system
- MSDB database in SQL Server
- Package Store
- SSIS Catalog

File System

It's very simple to run a package on a file system if the package does not belong to any project. Just use the option */File* or its short form */f* to specify the absolute file path of the package, as shown in Listing 11-1.

LISTING 11-1 Execute a package on a file system

```
C:\>dtexec /file d:\Demo\DemoPackage.dtsx
```

However, you can't execute a package in that way if the package is in the Project Deployment Model, which is the default case in SSIS 2012. Dtexec will throw an error if the package references any project-related objects, which could be a project parameter, an Execute Package task with project references, and so on. To execute an individual package in a project, you must specify both the project deployment file and the package name. These are specified by the new option */Project* and */Package*. Listing 11-2 shows an example.

LISTING 11-2 Execute a package in the Project Deployment Model

```
C:\>dtexec /project D:\Demo\DemoPackage\bin\Development\DemoPackage.ispac /package package.dtsx
```

MSDB Database

The msdb database is a system database in SQL Server. It contains all required entities for database management purposes, such as the definition of SQL Agent jobs. SSIS defines some tables and stored procedures in the database so users can save their packages. Some SQL Server tasks such as the maintenance plans also use SSIS internally. The msdb database is where they store the required SSIS packages.

You can manage folders and packages in msdb in SQL Server Management Studio. To do that, just connect to Integration Services in the SQL Server Management Studio connection window. The SQL Server Management Studio user interface enables you to create, rename, or delete a folder. You can also manipulate packages by importing, deleting, or running them. Figure 11-2 shows a demo package in the msdb database.

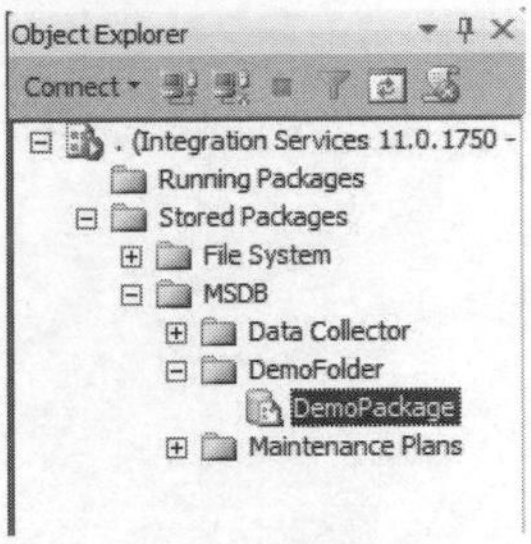

FIGURE 11-2 A demo package in the msdb database.

Remember msdb is just a different storage type; it does not affect executions. After the package is loaded from the msdb database, its execution is the same as the execution of packages loaded from the file system. The package is still running on your local machine. It's not the same as the package execution on the SSIS Catalog, which is introduced later in this chapter. Packages on the SSIS Catalog are executed remotely on the server machine.

To execute a package in the msdb database, you have to provide the SQL Server address, connection credential, package folder name, and package name. If your server instance supports SQL Server Authentication mode, you can use the */Username* and */Password* options on the command line. If those two options are omitted, dtexec will use Windows Authentication mode and the current user's credential. Windows Authentication mode is recommended for security purposes.

Listing 11-3 shows how to execute a package named DemoPackage that is stored in the folder *DemoFolder*. It uses Windows Authentication mode. Listing 11-4 shows the command to execute the same package with SQL Server Authentication mode.

LISTING 11-3 Run a package in msdb with Windows Authentication

```
C:\>dtexec /SQL "\DemoFolder\DemoPackage"
```

LISTING 11-4 Run a package in msdb with SQL Server Authentication

```
C:\>dtexec /SQL "\DemoFolder\DemoPackage" /User "DemoUser" /Password "DemoPassword"
```

Package Store

The SSIS package store is a file system location maintained by the SSIS Service, a stand-alone Windows service to maintain package store and package executions on a local machine. You can also manage those folders and packages via SQL Server Management Studio. Figure 11-3 shows a demo package in the package store.

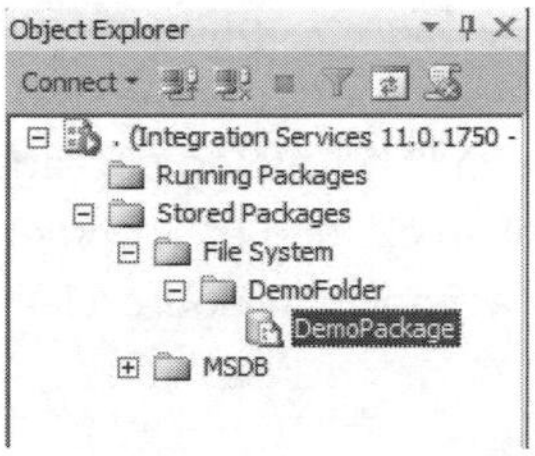

FIGURE 11-3 A demo package in the package store.

> **Note** The location of the package store and all folders is defined in the configuration file *%Program Files%\Microsoft SQL Server\110\DTS\Binn\MsDtsSrvr.ini.xml*. However, you are not supposed to modify this file manually.

To access a package in the package store, you need to specify the option */DTS* with the folder name and package name. It is slightly different than the msdb database because it supports only the Windows Authentication mode. You can use the */DTS* option in conjunction with the */Server* option. If you omit the */Server* option, the default local instance of the SSIS Service is assumed. Listing 11-5 shows the command to run a demo package in the local package store.

LISTING 11-5 Run a demo package in the local package store

```
C:\>dtexec /DTS "\File System\DemoFolder\DemoPackage"
```

SSIS Catalog

SSIS Catalog is a new component introduced in SQL Server 2012. The detailed information and its management user interface will be introduced in subsequent sections. Here we just briefly show how to run a package in SSIS Catalog with dtexec.

If you have a demo package in SSIS Catalog, you can use the new added option */ISServer* to execute the package. A full path to the package is required, as shown in Listing 11-6. In this case the execution does not reference any environment.

LISTING 11-6 Run a package in SSIS Catalog without environment reference

```
C:\>dtexec /ISServer \SSISDB\DemoFolder\DemoProject\DemoPackage.dtsx
```

If your execution needs to reference an environment, you can use the */ISServer* option in conjunction with another new option, */EnvReference*. The tricky part is that you need to specify the environment ID instead of the environment path. Listing 11-7 shows how to run an SSIS Catalog package with reference to an environment with ID 1. You can find the identifier of an existing environment by clicking the Property shortcut menu in SQL Server Management Studio, as shown in Figure 11-4.

LISTING 11-7 Run a package in SSIS Catalog with environment reference

```
C:\>dtexec /ISServer \SSISDB\DemoFolder\DemoProject\DemoPackage.dtsx /EnvReference 1
```

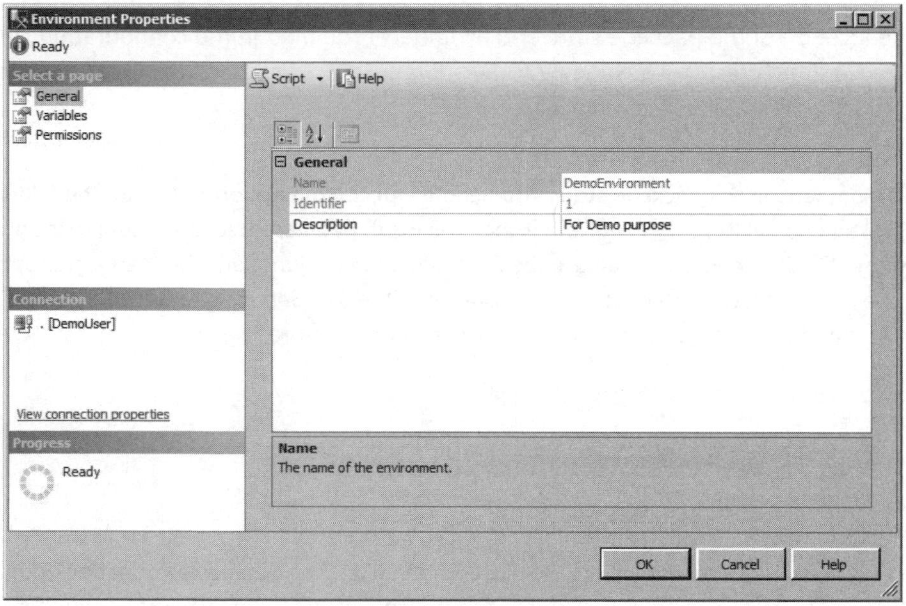

FIGURE 11-4 Find the identifier of an existing environment.

> **Note** Usually you should execute packages in SSIS Catalog through SQL Server Management Studio or T-SQL scripts, thus you could leverage the power of the SSIS Catalog server. The new added option */ISServer* is mainly for SQL Agent, which will call dtexec to execute packages in SSIS Catalog.

Configuring Packages

There are several ways to configure a package execution. Configurations and variables are the traditional mechanisms for SSIS to run under different conditions. In SQL Server 2012, another mechanism called *parameters* is introduced. A project or a package could have some parameters, either required or optional. It's like a contract between the package and its caller.

Dtexec provides the following options that allow you to specify the configuration or parameter values:

- ***SET*** Overrides the value of a given package object identified by its property path
- ***ConfigFile*** Specifies a runtime configuration file
- ***Parameter*** Specifies values for project parameters or package parameters

SET

This option allows you to override the configuration of a given package object. The object could be a variable, property, container, or log provider for each enumerator or connection within a package. The object is identified by its package path, which is unique inside a package.

When the */SET* option is specified, it sets the specified property path to the value given. Multiple */SET* options can be specified together. When the option is used with */ISSERVER*, an optional prefix *$Sensitive::* can be specified to indicate that the property should be considered sensitive on the server.

Listing 11-8 shows how to override a variable value before executing it.

LISTING 11-8 Override the value of a variable

```
C:\>dtexec /File d:\Demo\DemoPackage.dtsx /set \Package.Variables[DemoVariable].Value; DemoValue
```

ConfigFile

This option is straightforward. It allows you to set a runtime XML configuration file, which could be different from the configuration files that were specified at design time. Notice, though, you cannot use the option to replace configured values that you also specified at design time with other configurations. A sample command is shown in Listing 11-9.

LISTING 11-9 Set an XML configuration file

```
C:\>dtexec /File d:\Demo\DemoPackage.dtsx /ConfigFile d:\Demo\DemoConfig.dtsconfig
```

Parameter

This option allows you to specify literal values for parameters. Because there could be both project parameters and package parameters, the syntax of this option is a little complex: *Par[ameter] [$Package::|$Project::|$ServerOption::]parameter_name[(data_type)];literal_value*.

Multiple parameter options can be specified. Different prefixes (*$Package::*, *$Project::*, and *$ServerOption::*) are used to indicate the type of parameter. If none of them is specified, the default parameter type is package. For nonstring parameter values, the data type should be specified in parentheses following the parameter name.

Listing 11-10 is an example of executing a package that is provided with a string value *DemoValue* for the project parameter *DemoProjectParameter*. Notice you don't have to specify the data types because the parameter value type is string.

LISTING 11-10 Set value on a project parameter

```
C:\dtexec /isserver "\SSISDB\DemoFolder\DemoProject\DemoPackage.dtsx" /server "." /parameter
$Project::DemoProjectParameter;DemoValue
```

Listing 11-11 appends an integer value 99 for the package parameter *DemoPackageParameter*. This time you need to specify the data type because it's not a string.

LISTING 11-11 Set values on a project parameter and a package parameter

```
C:\dtexec /isserver "\SSISDB\DemoFolder\DemoProject\DemoPackage.dtsx" /server "." /parameter
$Project::DemoProjectParameter;DemoValue /parameter DemoPackageParameter(int32);99
```

Error Dumps

During execution, SSIS might throw some warnings or errors. Dtexec provides the following options to dump errors for troubleshooting:

- ***WarnAsError*** Treat every warning as an error.
- ***Dump*** Dump the specified errors by a list of error IDs.
- ***DumpOnError*** Dump any error in the package execution.

Listing 11-12 generates a dump file when a DTS_E_EXECPROCTASK_FILENOTINPATH error (ID 0xC0029154) happens.

LISTING 11-12 Dump the given error

```
C:\>dtexec /file d:\Demo\DemoPackage.dtsx /Dump 0xC0029154
```

The code in Listing 11-13 will dump any errors, including warnings.

LISTING 11-13 Dump any errors and warnings

```
C:\>dtexec /file d:\Demo\DemoPackage.dtsx /WarnAsError /DumpOnError
```

The dumped files are put into the folder *%Program Files%\Microsoft SQL Server\110\Shared\ErrorDumps*. Every dump actually contains two files. The file with an .mdmp extension is a binary file that contains the memory snapshot. It requires a special tool such as WinDBG to view the file contents. The other file with extension .tmp is a plain text file and you can open it with a regular text reader such as Windows Notepad. It saves the values of some important class members when the error happens.

You can choose to apply the */Dump* option to all packages that the dtexec utility runs so you don't have to specify it every time. To do that, just add a *DumpOnCodes* REG_SZ value to the HKEY_LOCAL_MACHINE\SOFTWARE\Microsoft\Microsoft SQL Server\110\SSIS\Setup\DtsPath registry key. The data value in *DumpOnCodes* specifies the error code or codes that will trigger the system to create debug dump files. Multiple error codes must be separated by a semicolon. If you add a *DumpOnCodes* value to the registry key and also use the */Dump* option, the system will create debug dump files that are based on both settings.

Note With the tool dtutil.exe and */Dump* option, you could generate a dump file any time when the package is executing. It would not stop the execution. Check the following link to see how it works: *http://msdn.microsoft.com/en-us/library/ms162820.aspx*.

Logging Options

Logging is important for SSIS because it can help users with troubleshooting or auditing. Usually people specify the logging options and log providers in the package designer, shown in Figure 11-5.

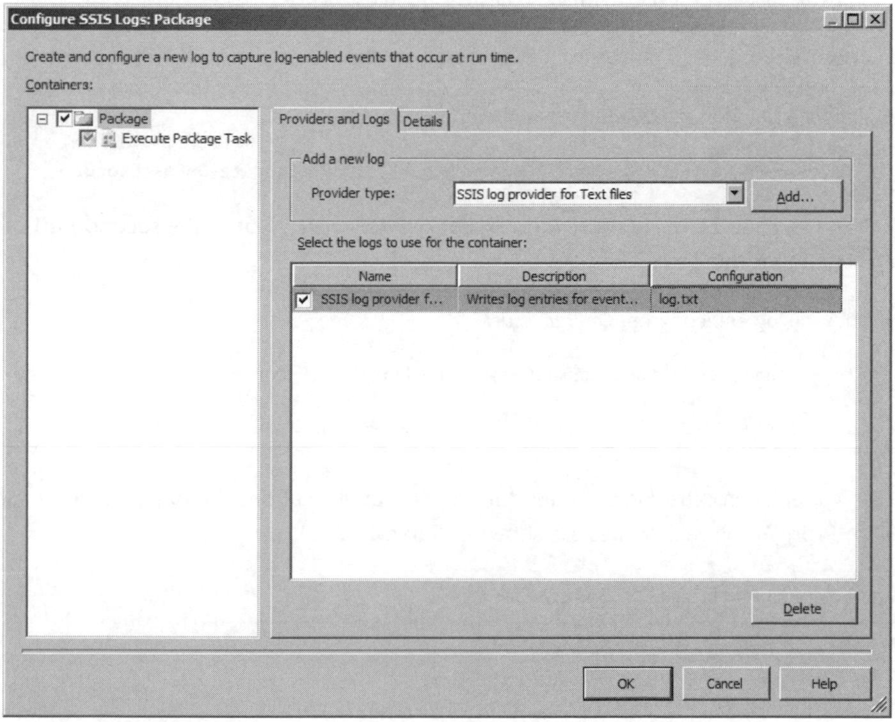

FIGURE 11-5 The Providers And Logs tab in the package designer.

However, dtexec also provides the ability to dynamically specify the logging options before execution. It primarily involves three options:

- ***ConsoleLog*** This option can filter logs and print them in the command window.
- ***Logger*** This option can specify the given logger providers.
- ***Vlog*** This option writes all events to the log providers.

Let's go through those options one by one.

ConsoleLog

This option enables you to dynamically specify the log entries that should be displayed in the console window. It uses a complex presentation format so it's a little tricky to figure out how it works. The full format of *ConsoleLog* is *Cons[oleLog] [[DisplayOptions];{E | I}; src_name_or_guid [src_name_or_guid[...]]]*. It contains three parts. First it decides which fields of a log entry should be displayed, such as "NC" means "name" and "computer".

For example, Listing 11-14 shows all fields of one log entry type, *OnPreExecute*.

LISTING 11-14 Show all fields of *OnPreExecute* log entries in the console window

```
C:\>dtexec /file d:\Demo\DemoPackage.dtsx /ConsoleLog NCOSGXMT;I;OnPreExecute
```

The command in Listing 11-15 shows only the "message" and "time" fields of two log entry types.

LISTING 11-15 Show partial fields of *OnPreExecute* log entries

```
C:\>dtexec /file d:\Demo\DemoPackage.dtsx /ConsoleLog MT;I;OnPreExecute;OnPostExecute
```

The command in Listing 11-16 shows all logs except *OnPreExecute*. Notice the second part of the option value is changed from I to E.

LISTING 11-16 Show all log entries except *OnPreExecute*

```
C:\>dtexec /file d:\Demo\DemoPackage.dtsx /ConsoleLog NCOSGXMT;E;OnPreExecute
```

Logger

This option just appends an extra log provider during package execution. The log provider is specified by its class ID or ProgID. The valid values are shown in Table 11-2.

TABLE 11-2 Valid class ID and ProgID of log provider types

Log Provider Type	ProgID and Class ID
Text file	DTS.LogProviderTextFile.3 {03E07F2D-EA22-440B-8DE9-B56A22F0E9FF }
SQL Profiler	DTS.LogProviderSQLProfiler.3 {601D0CD1-672E-4F07-BA58-BFF7B5CE0060}
SQL Server	DTS.LogProviderSQLServer.3 {1E4F606D-382A-4812-8E08-C5D5A04FFE98}
Windows event logger	DTS.LogProviderEventLog.3 {9BD4455F-7B98-4280-9AA9-932EC8B411D9}
XML file	DTS.LogProviderXMLFile.3 {9D1392C1-01C0-4148-A258-F20AF6E4EA3E }

Listing 11-17 shows a sample command.

LISTING 11-17 Append an extra text file log provider

```
C:\>dtexec /file d:\Demo\DemoPackage.dtsx /Logger DTS.LogProviderTextFile.1
```

VLog

This option enables you to write all SSIS package events to the log providers that were enabled when the package was designed. Additionally, it can write all those events to a text file if you specify a file name, so it's very useful for quick troubleshooting. You can see all the events even if the original package does not enable any logging options.

Listing 11-18 shows a sample command.

LISTING 11-18 Write all events to a log provider

```
C:\>dtexec /file d:\Demo\DemoPackage.dtsx /VLog d:\demo\log.txt
```

Running Packages in the SSIS Catalog

In this section we focus on how to run packages in the SSIS Catalog. As introduced earlier, the SSIS Catalog is a brand new component introduced in SQL Server 2012. It provides a server-backed environment for enterprise users to develop, deploy, and manage their data integration applications.

Only SSIS projects with the Project Deployment Model can be deployed to an SSIS Catalog; you can't leverage the power of the SSIS Catalog if your project is in the legacy Package Deployment Model. After a project is deployed, the SSIS Catalog will do some validations, break it into different pieces, and then save each piece into database tables. Refer to Chapter 16, "SSIS Catalog Deep Dive," for more details on the SSIS Catalog.

To run a package in the SSIS Catalog, you basically have two options: the new user interface introduced in SQL Server Management Studio or T-SQL programming. In this section you are guided through those two approaches. No matter which approach you use, you can watch the execution progress through reports and views. You can also stop an execution through the stored procedure application programming interfaces (APIs) provided by SSIS Catalog.

One important thing you need to realize is that the package is executed on SSIS Catalog; it is not related to your client machine. Therefore, if there are some file references in your package, it must use the file path on the server machine instead of your client machine.

> **Note** SSIS Catalog does not leverage dtexec.exe to execute packages. Instead, it uses a new execution host named ISServerExec.exe. This host is optimized for the server execution environment and it also has 32-bit and 64-bit versions.

In SQL Server 2012 a new node named Integration Services Catalogs has been added in SQL Server Management Studio. This new user interface makes it very easy to configure, validate, and execute an SSIS package in the SSIS Catalog.

Prepare Executions

Before running an SSIS package, you can use the new features in SQL Server Management Studio to configure the package. To configure a package, just select the package node in SQL Server Management Studio and select Configure on the shortcut menu. This opens a dialog box to help you configure its parameters, references, and connection managers, as shown in Figure 11-6.

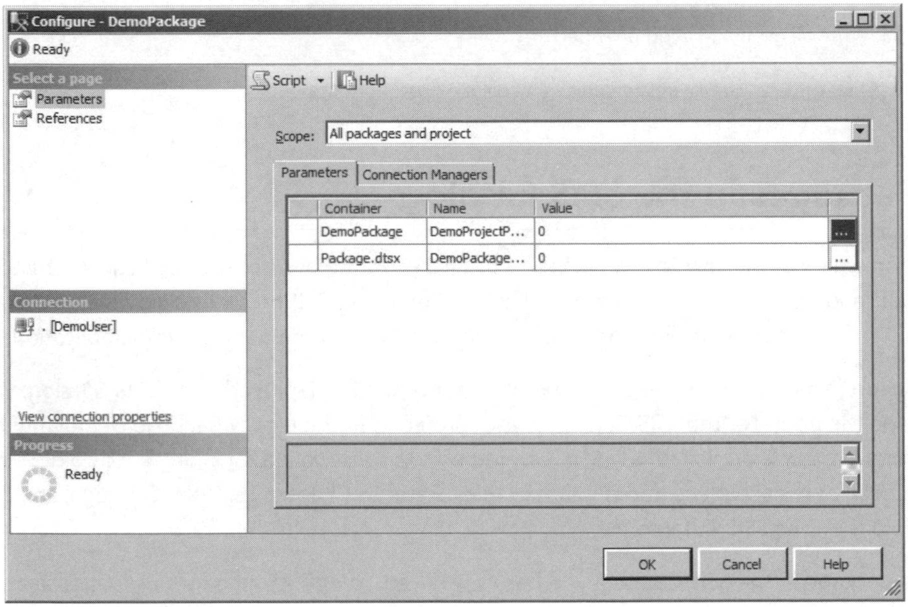

FIGURE 11-6 Configure an SSIS package in SQL Server Management Studio.

There are two pages in the dialog box, which you can switch in the left pane. Because there could be lots of project parameters and package parameters in a project, this page provides a drop-down list box to help you narrow the scope. You can choose to only show parameters in the following scopes:

- All packages and project
- Entry-point package and project
- Current project
- Current package

For each parameter, click the associated ellipsis button (...) to edit its value. Basically you have three choices in the dialog box: specify a literal value, use the default value, or map it to an environment variable (see Figure 11-7).

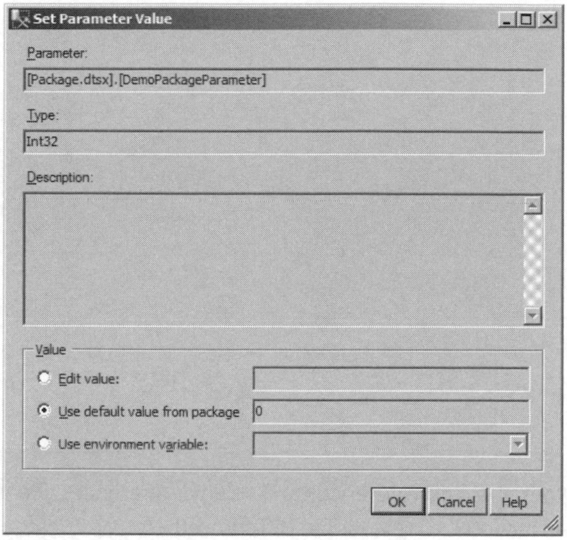

FIGURE 11-7 Edit the values of a parameter.

The second page helps you manage the environments referenced by this project. It shows a list of references that have been bound to the current project, shown in Figure 11-8.

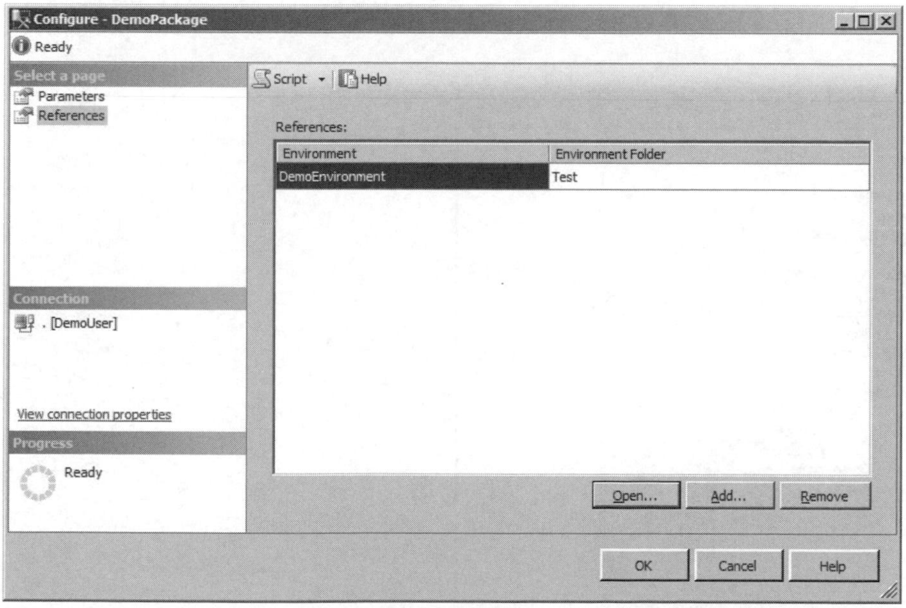

FIGURE 11-8 Manage the referenced environments.

You can add or remove an environment reference here. You can also click Open to jump to the detailed information window of the environment. It's very easy to browse the available environments and reference one of them, as shown in Figure 11-9.

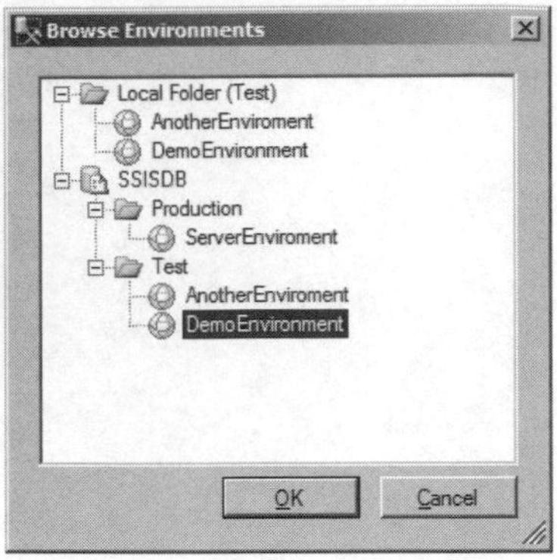

FIGURE 11-9 Browse the available environments.

> **Note** SSIS Catalog behaves differently with absolute references and relative references. Please refer to Chapter 2, "Understanding SSIS Concepts," to review the difference between them.

Starting SSIS Package Executions

Similar to package configuration, to execute a package just locate the package node in SQL Server Management Studio and select Execute from the shortcut menu (see Figure 11-10).

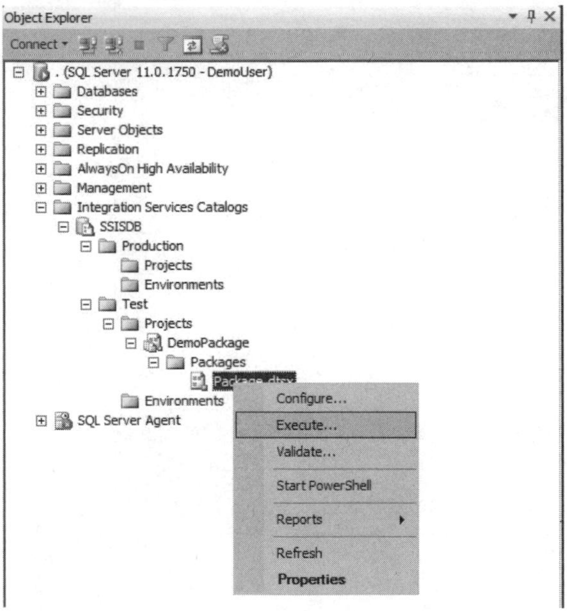

FIGURE 11-10 Run an SSIS package in SQL Server Management Studio.

After you select the menu item, a new dialog box is launched to help you configure the package before the execution starts. Compared to the Configure dialog box, this Execute dialog box provides more options. Usually it's flexible enough to cover most requirements.

There are three tabs in the dialog box. The first tab, Parameters, allows you to assign the environment reference and configure the values of parameters, including both project parameters and package parameters (see Figure 11-11).

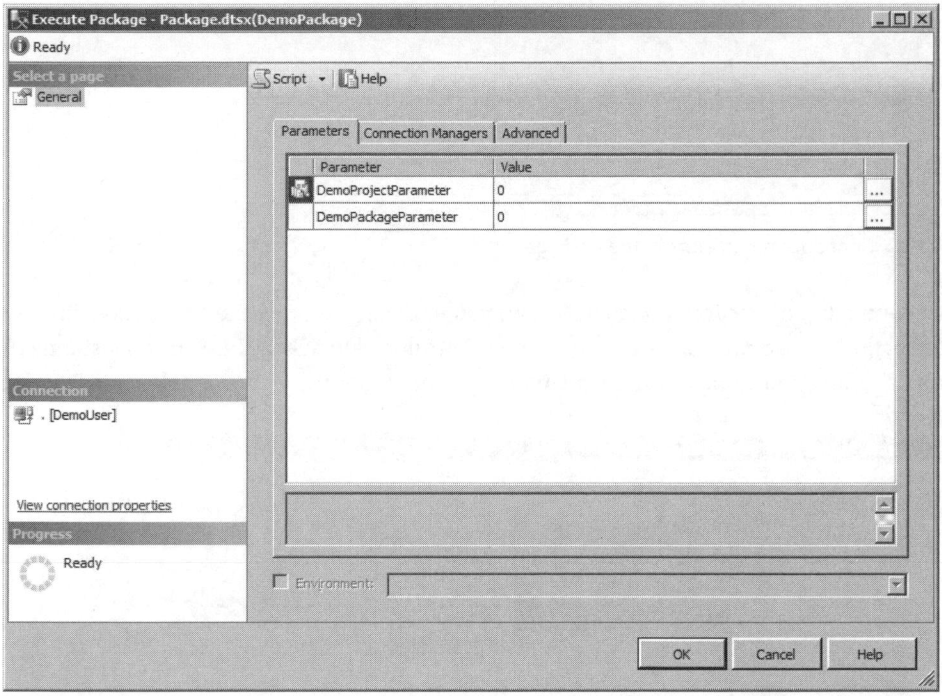

FIGURE 11-11 Configure parameters in the package.

A project can be bound to multiple environments, but it can use only one reference in one execution, so on this tab there is an Environment check box and a list of available environments. You can select the check box and pick one environment from the list.

All visible parameters are shown in a data grid. There is a demo project parameter and a package parameter defined in the demo package, so you can see there are two items in the grid in Figure 11-11. There is a special icon before each project parameter to indicate it's a shared project parameter. You can specify the values for each parameter by clicking the ellipsis button (...) in the grid. Different from the Configure dialog box, here you can assign only a literal value to the parameter (see Figure 11-12).

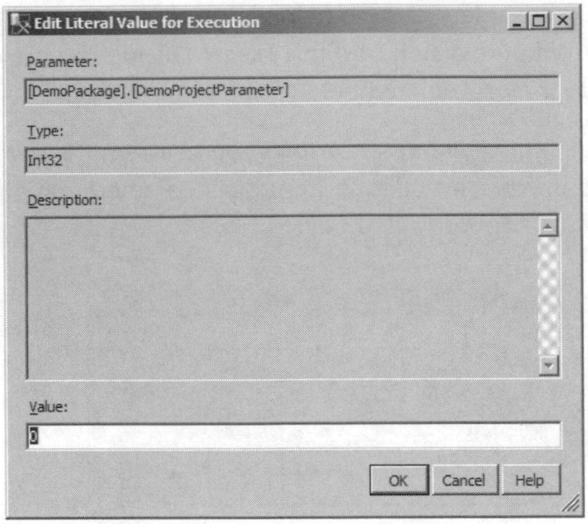

FIGURE 11-12 Configure parameters in the package.

The second tab, Connection Managers, allows you to directly modify the connection strings of each connection manager. It's a very useful feature introduced in SSIS 2012. You can instantly override the value of connection strings without creating any configuration files or variables (see Figure 11-13).

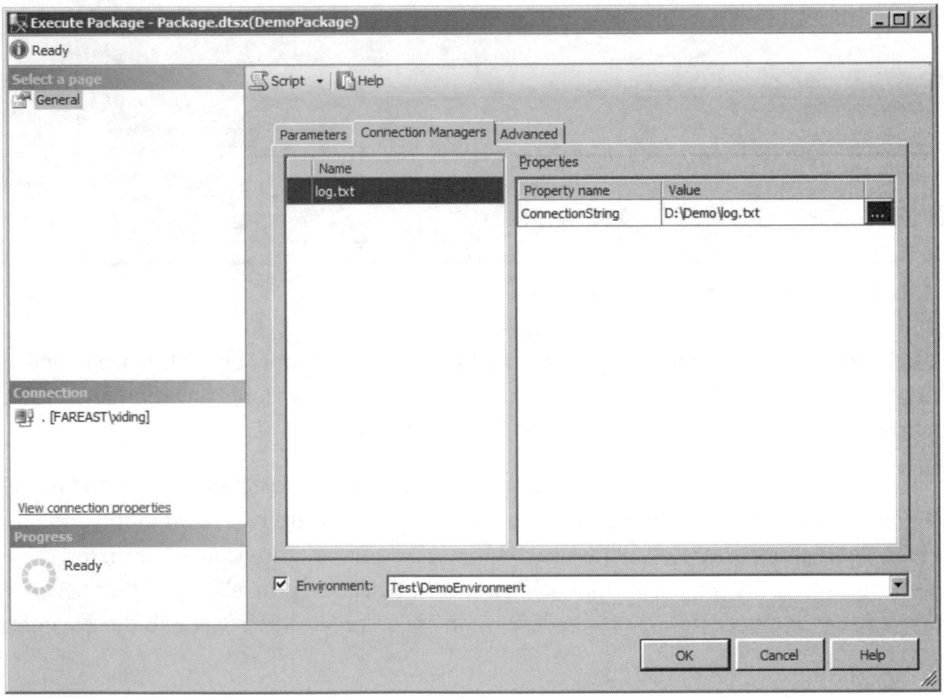

FIGURE 11-13 Configure parameters in the package.

The Advanced tab shows some advanced options that usually you don't need to change (see Figure 11-14).

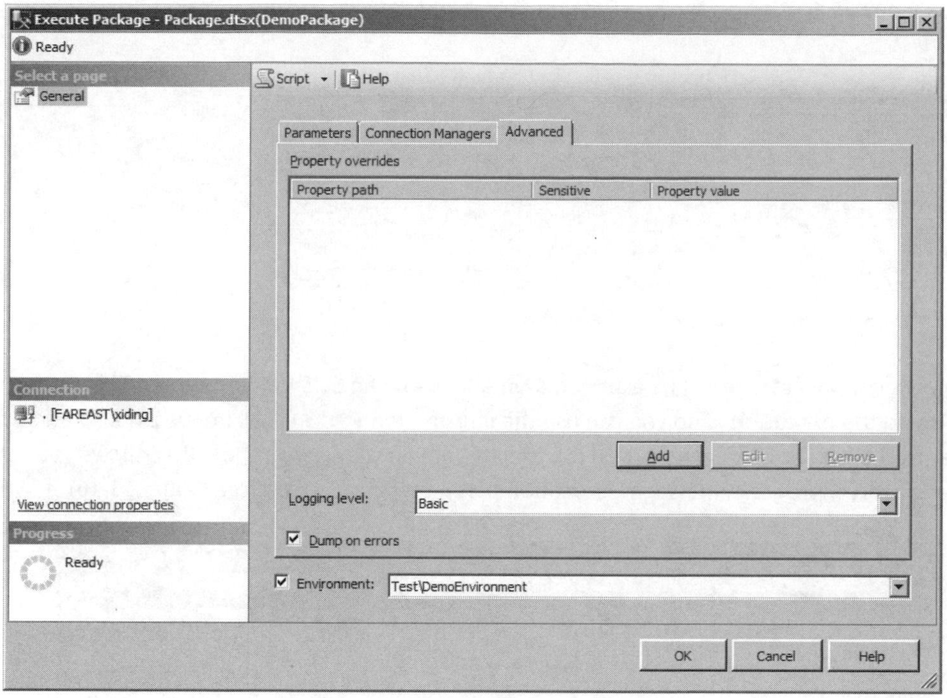

FIGURE 11-14 The Advanced tab of the Execute Package dialog box.

It includes the following options:

- **Property Overrides** Uses a literal value to overwrite the property of a given object
- **Logging Level** Indicates which level should be used to filter the logs of this execution
- **Dump On Errors** Indicates whether errors should be dumped

View Executions

After you finish all the configurations in the preceding section, click OK in the dialog box. This launches a new execution on the SSIS Catalog server and you see a prompt dialog box, shown in Figure 11-15.

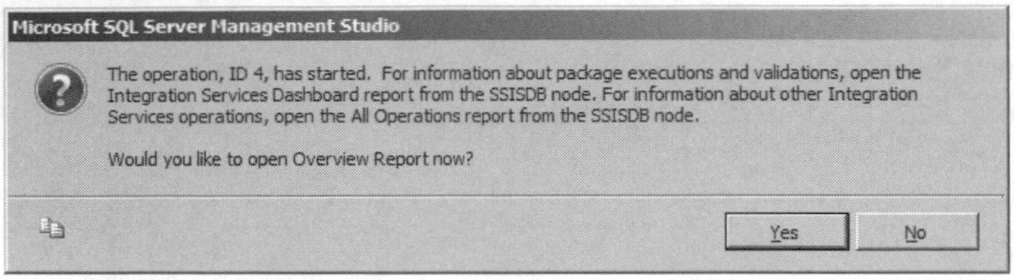

FIGURE 11-15 The prompt dialog box of an execution.

Every execution instance will be assigned a unique ID by the SSIS Catalog server. This dialog box tells you the execution ID so you can use the information to do T-SQL queries. It also asks you whether to show the overview report on the execution. This is a useful report that allows you to check the overall status, progress, messages, execution parameters, and so on (see Figure 11-16).

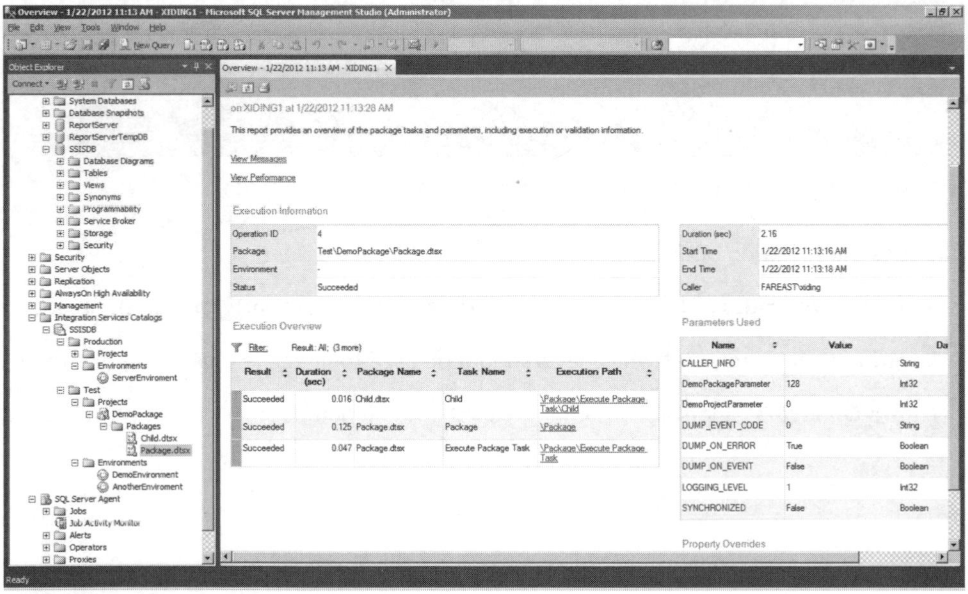

FIGURE 11-16 The status report of an execution.

Executions with T-SQL

Besides the SQL Server Management Studio user interface you could also validate or execute packages through the T-SQL APIs provided by the SSIS Catalog. Compared to the previous approach, it's more efficient because the user interface operations are also mapped to T-SQL invocations ultimately.

SSIS Catalog provides the stored procedures and views related to executions listed in Table 11-3.

TABLE 11-3 APIs and views related to package execution

Object Type	Object Name	Comments
Stored Procedure	*Catalog.create_execution*	Create an execution instance. It could be started by a later invocation.
Stored Procedure	*Catalog.create_execution_dump*	Dynamically create a dump file on an ongoing execution. It would not stop the execution.
Stored Procedure	*Catalog. set_execution_ parameter_value*	Set the execution parameter value.
Stored Procedure	*Catalog. set_execution_ property_override_value*	Override a property path value of an execution.
Stored Procedure	*Catalog. start_execution*	Start an execution.
Stored Procedure	*Catalog. stop_operation*	Stop an execution.
Views	*Catalog.executions*	The status of an execution.
Views	*Catalog.operation_messages*	You can check all messages related to an execution.

Listing 11-19 shows a simple T-SQL script to launch an execution and print its execution ID. The script assumes a project named DemoProject has been deployed into folder *DemoFolder.*

LISTING 11-19 Launch an execution and print its execution ID

```
USE SSISDB
   DECLARE @execution_id bigint

EXEC catalog.create_execution
           @folder_name=N'DemoFolder',
           @project_name=N'DemoProject',

           @package_name=N'DemoPackage.dtsx',
           @reference_id=Null,

           @execution_id=@execution_id OUTPUT

EXEC catalog.start_execution @execution_id

PRINT @execution_id
```

Listing 11-20 shows another T-SQL query to view the result of an execution with execution ID 5.

LISTING 11-20 Query the execution result

```
USE SSISDB

SELECT * FROM catalog.executions WHERE execution_id=5
```

Please refer to Chapter 12, "SSIS T-SQL Magic," for more detailed examples.

Running Packages from SQL Agent

SQL Server Agent is an important tool for database administrators. It's used for running jobs on schedule or on occurrence of some events. Essentially SQL Server Agent is a Windows service running in the background, and all the job and schedule information is stored in the SQL Server database. A typical use of SQL Agent is to run an SSIS package every night to incrementally update the data warehouse.

Every SQL Agent job consists of one or multiple job steps, and every job step is an instance of a given job type. Different job types accomplish different work, such as running a T-SQL query or executing an operating system command. SQL Agent supports a rich set of job types. As a data integration tool, SSIS has good integration with SQL Agent. One of the job step types in SQL Agent is SQL Server Integration Services Package. By creating a new step of that type you can call an SSIS package on different locations, such as a file system or package store.

Because SSIS Catalog is added in SQL Server 2012, accordingly SQL Agent adds support for SSIS Catalog. In other words, now in SQL Agent you can execute a package from the following places:

- SQL Server msdb database
- File system
- SSIS package store
- SSIS Catalog

As an example, we introduce how to execute an SSIS package from the SSIS Catalog. It's similar to other cases.

Create an SSIS Job Step

To create a new SQL Agent job, just expand the SQL Server Agent node in SQL Server Management Studio, right-click the Jobs node, and choose New Jobs from the shortcut menu (see Figure 11-17).

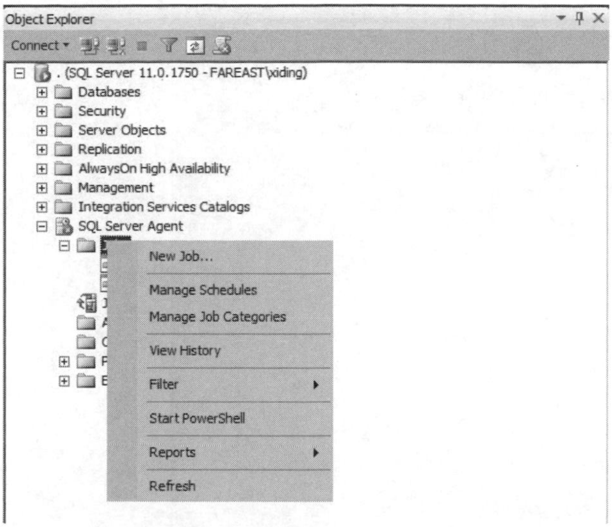

FIGURE 11-17 Create a new SQL Agent Job.

> **Note** By default, the SQL Server Agent service is stopped, so you will probably get an error message when you try to expand the node in SQL Server Management Studio. To start the service, right-click the SQL Server Agent node and select Start.

In the job definition window, specify a job name and then go to the Steps page. On that page, you can see the step list of the current job. Of course, it's empty at first. Click New to create a new job step, as shown in Figure 11-18.

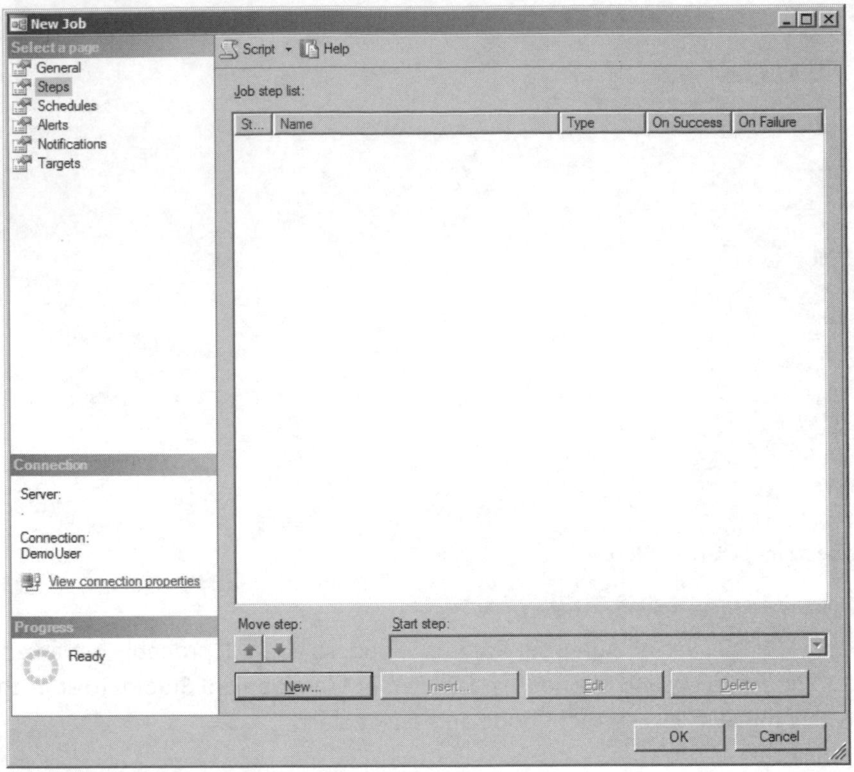

FIGURE 11-18 Create a new job step.

Execute Packages from the SSIS Catalog

By default, the new job step type is Transact SQL (T-SQL) so there are lots of options related to T-SQL. Choose SQL Server Integration Services Package from the drop-down list and you will notice the dialog box layout changes. Now it shows some configuration options specific to SSIS. The first option is the Run As drop-down box, which lists the available credentials that the current job can use. Make sure SSIS Catalog is selected in the Package Source drop-down box, then specify the connection information for the SSIS Catalog and choose the package path (see Figure 11-19).

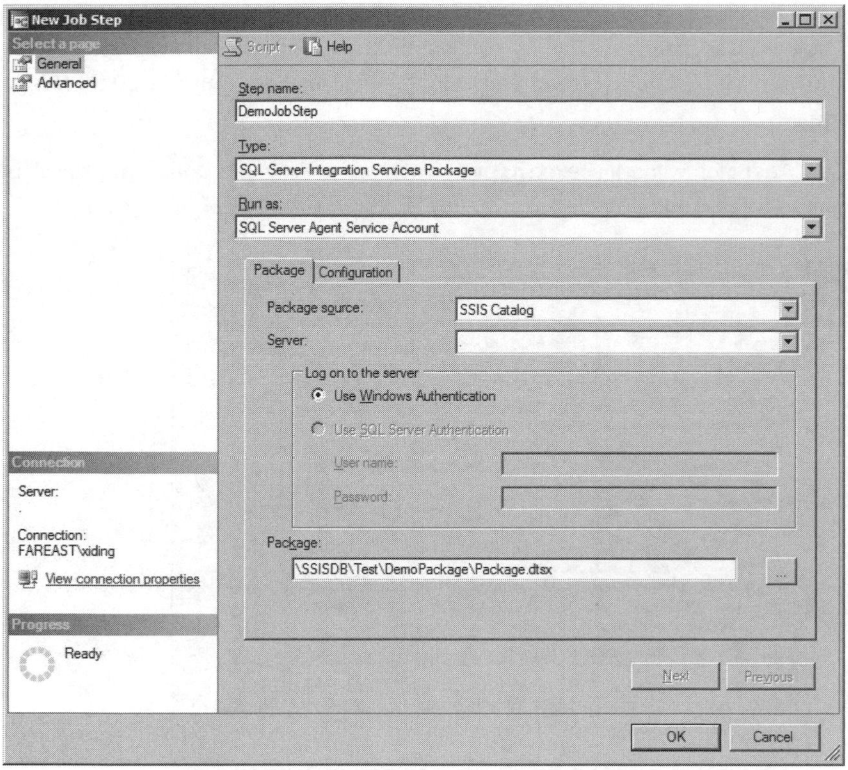

FIGURE 11-19 Specify the package information.

When the job is triggered, SQL Agent will use the specified credential to connect to the SSIS Catalog and execute the package.

> **Note** The default credential is SQL Agent account, which does not have permissions to execute SSIS Catalog objects, so your job will fail when it tries to connect to the SSIS Catalog and execute packages. You need to define your own SQL Agent proxy account. Refer to the following link for the detailed instructions: *http://msdn.microsoft.com/en-us/library/ms189064.aspx*.

After the package location and connection credentials are specified, you can do some configurations on the package, such as parameter values, connection strings, and so on. It's pretty similar to the configuration window in SSIS Catalog you saw earlier in this chapter. See Figure 11-20 for the sample configuration page.

Internally an SQL Agent job will call dtexec to perform its work. All your configurations will be converted to command-line arguments and sent to dtexec at run time.

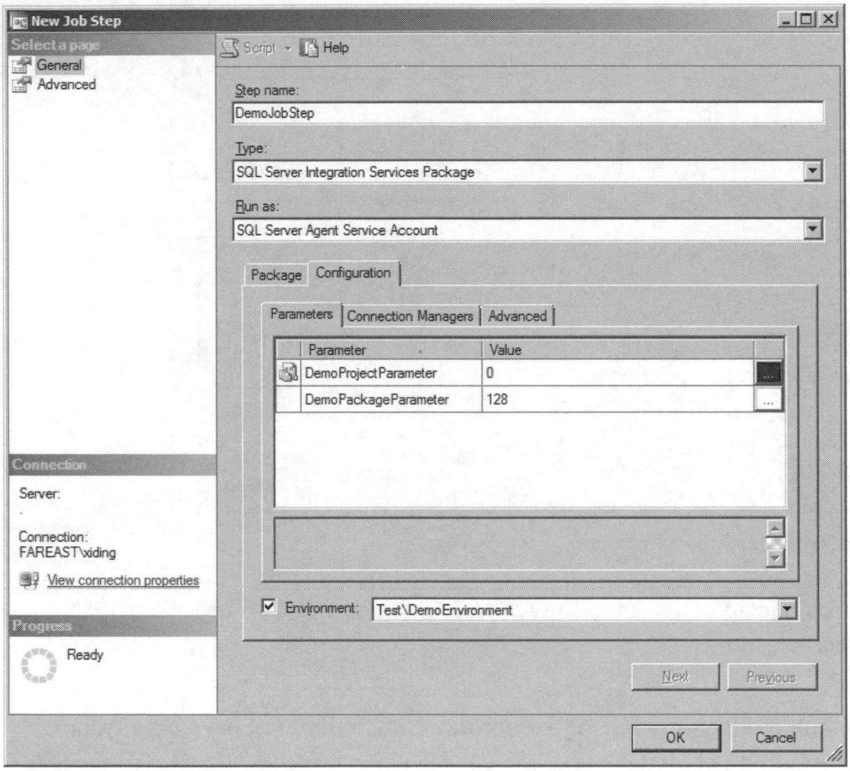

FIGURE 11-20 Configure the package.

After all those configurations are done, click OK to save the job definition into the database. To test whether it works correctly, just find the job item in the Jobs list and select Start Job At Step... from the shortcut menu.

Running Packages via PowerShell

PowerShell is a new Windows command-line shell to help administrators perform manageability tasks. As a scripting platform built on the .NET Framework, it's very extensible because it can leverage lots of .NET assemblies. SQL Server PowerShell was first introduced in SQL Server 2008, but SSIS integration was not provided until SQL Server 2012. Now you can manage SSIS Catalog objects in PowerShell, which includes folders, projects, environments, and more. Of course you can also start and stop executions.

Refer to Chapter 13, "SSIS PowerShell Magic," to see how to run SSIS packages via PowerShell integration.

Creating and Running SSIS Packages Programmatically

As SSIS provides a very flexible approach, you can write your own application to develop a package or run an existing package. SSIS provides lots of extension assemblies so you can integrate SSIS with your custom applications.

To develop such an application, you need to add references to some assemblies and use the namespaces accordingly. Table 11-4 provides a list of the primarily involved assemblies.

TABLE 11-4 Primary assemblies and namespaces

Assembly Name	Namespace	Comments
Microsoft.SQLServer. ManagedDTS.dll	*Microsoft.SqlServer.Dts.Runtime*	This assembly contains the most commonly used interfaces and classes.
Microsoft.SQLServer. DTSRuntimeWrap.dll	*Microsoft.SqlServer.Dts.Runtime. Wrapper*	Reference this assembly if you need access some control flow Interop classes or interfaces.
Microsoft.SQLServer. DTSPipelineWrap.dll	*Microsoft.SqlServer.Dts.Pipeline. Wrapper*	Reference this assembly if you need access the Data Flow specific classes or interfaces.

Listing 11-21 shows a complete C# program that creates and runs an SSIS package on the fly. This sample package contains a Data Flow task, which in turn contains an OLE DB source and a flat file destination. The source component will read all SSIS Catalog properties from view *[catalog].[catalog_properties]* and then the destination component will write them into a text file.

To build this program successfully, you need to reference all three assemblies listed in Table 11-4.

LISTING 11-21 Create a sample package and run it

```
   using System;
using System.IO;
using Microsoft.SqlServer.Dts.Runtime;
using Microsoft.SqlServer.Dts.Pipeline.Wrapper;
using wrap = Microsoft.SqlServer.Dts.Runtime.Wrapper;

class Program
{

/// <summary>
/// The entry point
/// </summary>
static void Main(string[] args)
{
   CreateAndRunSamplePackage();
}

   /// <summary>
/// Create a sample package, run it, and print the execution result
/// </summary>
public static void CreateAndRunSamplePackage()
{
    using (Project project = Project.CreateProject())
    {
        Package package = CreateSamplePackage();
        project.PackageItems.Add(package, "package1.dtsx");

        //run the package
        DTSExecResult result = project.PackageItems[0].Package.Execute(null, null, null, null,
null);
        Console.WriteLine("Execution result: " + result);
     }
}

/// <summary>
/// Create a sample package with a data flow
/// </summary>
private static Package CreateSamplePackage()
{
    const string OututFileName = @"d:\OutputData.txt";
    const string OleDBConnectionString = @"Provider=SQLNCLI11;Integrated Security=SSPI;Persist
Security Info=False;Initial Catalog=ssisdb;Data Source=(local);Auto Translate=False;";
    const string ViewName = @"[catalog].[catalog_properties]";

    Package package = new Package();

    //add connection managers
    ConnectionManager oleDBConnection = AddOleDBConnectionManager(package,
OleDBConnectionString);
    ConnectionManager fileConnection = AddFlatFileConnectionManager(package, OututFileName);

    //add data flow task
    TaskHost th = package.Executables.Add("STOCK:PipelineTask") as TaskHost;
```

```
    th.Name = "DataFlow";
    MainPipe dataFlow = th.InnerObject as MainPipe;

    //add data flow components
    IDTSComponentMetaData100 oledbSource = AddOLEDBSource(package, dataFlow, oleDBConnection,
ViewName);
    IDTSComponentMetaData100 flatfileDestination =
        AddFlatFileDestination(package, dataFlow, oledbSource.OutputCollection[0],
fileConnection);

    return package;
}

/// <summary>
/// Add an OLE DB connection manager into the package
/// </summary>
private static ConnectionManager AddOleDBConnectionManager(Package package, string
connectionString)
{
    ConnectionManager oleDBConnection = package.Connections.Add("OLEDB");

    oleDBConnection.Name = "OLEDBConnection";
    oleDBConnection.ConnectionString = connectionString;

    return oleDBConnection;
}

/// <summary>
/// Add a flat file connection manager into the package
/// </summary>
private static ConnectionManager AddFlatFileConnectionManager(Package package, string fileName)
{
    ConnectionManager fileConnection = package.Connections.Add("FLATFILE");

    fileConnection.Properties["ConnectionString"].SetValue(fileConnection, fileName);
    fileConnection.Properties["Format"].SetValue(fileConnection, "Delimited");
    fileConnection.Properties["DataRowsToSkip"].SetValue(fileConnection, 0);
    fileConnection.Properties["ColumnNamesInFirstDataRow"].SetValue(fileConnection, false);
    fileConnection.Properties["Name"].SetValue(fileConnection, "FlatFileConnection");
    fileConnection.Properties["RowDelimiter"].SetValue(fileConnection, "\r\n");
    fileConnection.Properties["TextQualifier"].SetValue(fileConnection, "\"");

    return fileConnection;
}

/// <summary>
/// Create an OLE DB Source that reads the given table or view
/// </summary>
private static IDTSComponentMetaData100 AddOLEDBSource(Package package, MainPipe dataFlow,
    ConnectionManager oleDBConnection, string tableOrViewName)
{
    //create and initialize the component
    IDTSComponentMetaData100 oledbSource = dataFlow.ComponentMetaDataCollection.New();
    oledbSource.ComponentClassID = "DTSAdapter.OLEDBSource";
    oledbSource.Name = "OLEDBSource";

    CManagedComponentWrapper componentWrapper = oledbSource.Instantiate();
```

```
    componentWrapper.ProvideComponentProperties();

    //bind the connection manager
    oledbSource.RuntimeConnectionCollection[0].ConnectionManagerID = oleDBConnection.ID;
    oledbSource.RuntimeConnectionCollection[0].ConnectionManager
        = DtsConvert.GetExtendedInterface(oleDBConnection);

    //set custom component properties
    componentWrapper.SetComponentProperty("OpenRowset", tableOrViewName);
    componentWrapper.SetComponentProperty("AccessMode", 0);

    //acquire Connections and reinitialize the component
    componentWrapper.AcquireConnections(null);
    componentWrapper.ReinitializeMetaData();
    componentWrapper.ReleaseConnections();

    return oledbSource;
}

/// <summary>
/// Add a flat file destination, and connect it to the given source output
/// </summary>
private static IDTSComponentMetaData100 AddFlatFileDestination(Package package, MainPipe
dataFlow,
    IDTSOutput100 sourceOutput, ConnectionManager fileConnection)
{
    // Add the component to the dataFlow metadata collection
    IDTSComponentMetaData100 flatfileDestination = dataFlow.ComponentMetaDataCollection.New();
    flatfileDestination.ComponentClassID = "DTSAdapter.FlatFileDestination";
    flatfileDestination.Name = "FlatFileDestination";

    CManagedComponentWrapper componentWrapper = flatfileDestination.Instantiate();
    componentWrapper.ProvideComponentProperties();

    //bind the connection manager
    flatfileDestination.RuntimeConnectionCollection[0].ConnectionManagerID
        = fileConnection.ID;
    flatfileDestination.RuntimeConnectionCollection[0].ConnectionManager
        = DtsConvert.GetExtendedInterface(fileConnection);

    //connect the component to source component
    dataFlow.PathCollection.New().AttachPathAndPropagateNotifications(sourceOutput,
        flatfileDestination.InputCollection[0]);

    // Add columns to the FlatFileConnectionManager
    AddColumnsToConnectionManager(package, flatfileDestination,fileConnection);

    // Acquire the connection, reinitialize the metadata,
    // map the columns, then release the connection.
    componentWrapper.AcquireConnections(null);
    componentWrapper.ReinitializeMetaData();
    MapFlatFileDestinationColumns(flatfileDestination, componentWrapper);
    componentWrapper.ReleaseConnections();

    return flatfileDestination;
}
```

```
/// <summary>
/// Add all input columns in the destination component to the associated connection manager
/// </summary>
private static void AddColumnsToConnectionManager(Package package, IDTSComponentMetaData100
fileDestination,
    ConnectionManager fileConnection)
{
    wrap.IDTSConnectionManagerFlatFile100 ff = fileConnection.InnerObject as wrap.
IDTSConnectionManagerFlatFile100;

    IDTSVirtualInputColumnCollection100 virtualInputColumns =
        fileDestination.InputCollection[0].GetVirtualInput().VirtualInputColumnCollection;

    //add all columns with the required format
    for (int columnIndex = 0; columnIndex < virtualInputColumns.Count; columnIndex++)
    {
        wrap.IDTSConnectionManagerFlatFileColumn100 col = ff.Columns.Add();
        if (columnIndex == virtualInputColumns.Count - 1)
        {
            col.ColumnDelimiter = "\r\n";
        }
        else
        {
            col.ColumnDelimiter = @",";
        }

        col.ColumnType = "Delimited";
        col.DataType = virtualInputColumns[columnIndex].DataType;
        col.DataPrecision = virtualInputColumns[columnIndex].Precision;
        col.DataScale = virtualInputColumns[columnIndex].Scale;
        wrap.IDTSName100 name = col as wrap.IDTSName100;
        name.Name = virtualInputColumns[columnIndex].Name;
    }
}

/// <summary>
/// Use all input columns and map them to the external columns
/// </summary>
private static void MapFlatFileDestinationColumns(IDTSComponentMetaData100 flatfileDestination,
    CManagedComponentWrapper componentWrapper)
{
    //find and use all input columns
    IDTSVirtualInput100 virtualInput = flatfileDestination.InputCollection[0].GetVirtualInput();
    foreach (IDTSVirtualInputColumn100 column in virtualInput.VirtualInputColumnCollection)
    {
        componentWrapper.SetUsageType(flatfileDestination.InputCollection[0].ID,
            virtualInput, column.LineageID, DTSUsageType.UT_READONLY);
    }

    //find the corresponding external metadata column.

    foreach (IDTSInputColumn100 inputColumn
in flatfileDestination.InputCollection[0].InputColumnCollection)
    {
        IDTSExternalMetadataColumn100 externalColumn =
            flatfileDestination.InputCollection[0].ExternalMetadataColumnCollection[inputColumn.
Name];
```

```
            componentWrapper.MapInputColumn(flatfileDestination.InputCollection[0].ID, inputColumn.
ID, externalColumn.ID);
        }
    }
}
```

Summary

In this chapter we discussed various approaches to execute an SSIS package. The approaches introduced include dtexec, SSIS Catalog, SQL Agent, PowerShell, and running SSIS packages programmatically. Among those approaches, dtexec utility is most often used. We gave a detailed introduction and focused on the new options. These new options are for SSIS projects that use the Project Deployment Model and are deployed to the SSIS Catalog. We also discussed some common topics in dtexec, such as configuration, logging, and error dumps. Then we showed how to configure and run SSIS packages that have been deployed to the SSIS Catalog from SQL Server Management Studio. In addition, we discussed how to access packages and projects from SQL Agent. Finally, we showed how to create and run an SSIS package programmatically. This provides a flexible approach for integrating SSIS with your custom applications.

CHAPTER 12

SSIS T-SQL Magic

In This Chapter

Overview of SSIS Stored Procedures and Views

SSIS 2012 introduces new views, stored procedures and table-value functions that provide powerful capabilities and a rich set of information for a database administrator. These views and stored procedures are available in the user database, called SSISDB, in a SQL Server instance.

Users should take advantage of the stored procedures, table-value function, and views in SSISDB that are using the *catalog* schema. All database users of SSISDB can access these stored procedures, table-value functions, and views. When invoking the stored procedures, some of the operations (for example, creation of a folder in the SSIS Catalog, changing properties of the SSIS Catalog) can only be performed if you are an *sa*, a member of the *sysadmin* or *ssis_admin* role. Information that is presented in the views is protected by row-level security, and you can only access information for the SSIS securables to which you have been granted permissions. (Refer to Chapter 17, "SSIS Security," for information on SSIS security.)

In this chapter, you will learn the T-SQL magic that can be used to deploy, configure, and manage the projects and packages that have been deployed to the SSIS Catalog. By using T-SQL, you gain additional flexibility in being able to script and automate commonly performed administrative tasks on the SSIS Catalog. This chapter provides you with an in-depth understanding of working with the

SSIS Catalog, and how you can make use of the stored procedures and views available in the SSIS Catalog to interact with the following SSIS objects:

- SSIS Catalog
- Folders
- Projects and packages
- Environment and environment variables

Integration Services Catalog

SSIS 2012 introduces the concept of an Integration Services catalog, which functions as a container for SSIS projects. After SSIS has been installed, a database administrator creates the SSIS Catalog on a SQL Server instance using either SQL Server Management Studio or PowerShell scripts.

SSIS Catalog Properties

The SSIS Catalog properties are used in various SSIS operations (Figure 12-1). Most of the SSIS Catalog properties (except *SCHEMA_BUILD* and *SCHEMA_VERSION*) can be modified to change the behavior of SSIS operations. The properties *SCHEMA_BUILD* and *SCHEMA_VERSION* are read-only properties used internally by SSIS to check the build number and version number for the SSIS Catalog.

property_name	property_value
ENCRYPTION_ALGORITHM	AES_256
MAX_PROJECT_VERSIONS	10
OPERATION_CLEANUP_ENABLED	TRUE
RETENTION_WINDOW	365
SCHEMA_BUILD	11.0.1750.32
SCHEMA_VERSION	2
SERVER_LOGGING_LEVEL	1
VERSION_CLEANUP_ENABLED	TRUE

FIGURE 12-1 SSIS Catalog properties.

- ***ENCRYPTION_ALGORITHM*** The encryption algorithm used to encrypt the SSIS projects that are deployed to the SSIS Catalog, and the values of parameters that have been marked as sensitive.
- ***VERSION_CLEANUP_ENABLED*** Determines whether the older version of each SSIS project is removed. If the value is set to *TRUE*, the maximum versions for a project will be maintained at *MAX_PROJECT_VERSIONS*. This is maintained by a SQL Server Agent job. The valid values for the property are *TRUE and FALSE*.
- ***MAX_PROJECT_VERSIONS*** The maximum number of versions that are maintained for each project.

- ***OPERATION_CLEANUP_ENABLED*** Determines whether the operation and execution logs are removed from the SSIS Catalog when it is no longer in the retention window. If the value is set to *TRUE*, a SQL Server Agent job ensures that the operation records in the SSIS Catalog are within the *RETENTION_WINDOW*. The valid values for the property are *TRUE* and *FALSE*.

- ***RETENTION_WINDOW*** The number of days for which operation and execution logs are retained in the SSIS Catalog.

- ***SERVER_LOGGING_LEVEL*** The logging level for the server. When an execution is started, the logging level of the execution will be set to the value of the *SERVER_LOGGING_LEVEL* Catalog property. The valid values are 0 (None), 1 (Basic), 2 (Performance), and 3 (Verbose).

- ***SCHEMA_BUILD*** Build number for the SSIS Catalog (read-only).

- ***SCHEMA_VERSION*** Version number for the SSIS Catalog (read-only).

Querying the SSIS Catalog Properties

The view *catalog.catalog_properties* shows the SSIS Catalog properties that are currently used by SSIS. Listing 12-1 shows a T-SQL snippet that retrieves information about the values for each of the SSIS Catalog properties.

LISTING 12-1 T-SQL query for finding about the Catalog properties

```
use SSISDB

SELECT *
FROM catalog.catalog_properties
ORDER BY property_name
```

Setting SSIS Catalog Properties

The stored procedure *catalog.configure_catalog* is used to modify the properties of the SSIS Catalog. You will need to be a member of the database role *ssis_admin* or a member of the server role *sysadmin* to configure the SSIS Catalog. Otherwise the stored procedure will fail and return an error message. Listing 12-2 shows the T-SQL snippet that can be used to make changes to the catalog property *MAX_PROJECT_VERSIONS*, such that the maximum number of project versions that are maintained per project is 20.

LISTING 12-2 Using *catalog.configure_catalog* to change the *MAX_PROJECT_VERSIONS* property

```
USE SSISDB
EXEC catalog.configure_catalog 'MAX_PROJECT_VERSIONS', '20'
```

You can verify that the catalog properties have been modified successfully by checking the return code of the stored procedure or querying the view *catalog.catalog_properties*.

In addition, if you are making changes to the *ENCRYPTION_ALGORITHM* catalog property, it requires that the database SSISDB is in single-user mode. When the encryption algorithm is changed, all the projects and sensitive values that are stored in the SSIS Catalog will need to be decrypted using the old encryption algorithm, and then reencrypted using the new encryption algorithm. Therefore, it is important that there are no other users using the database when these operations are being executed. The valid values for encryption algorithms are *TRIPLE_DES_3KEY*, *AES_128*, *AES_192*, and *AES_256*. *AES_256* is the default encryption algorithm used when the SSIS Catalog is created.

SSIS Projects and Packages

SSIS 2012 introduces new capabilities that make it easier to deploy, configure, and manage projects and packages that have been deployed to the SSIS Catalog. Whenever you use tools such as the Deployment Wizard or SQL Server Management Studio, this issues T-SQL queries to the SSIS Catalog. This is good news, because it means you can write your own T-SQL scripts for various operations. Most important, besides the rich set of stored procedures and table-value functions that are already available in SSISDB, you can compose higher level stored procedures for tasks that are useful to your organization.

Deploy an SSIS Project to the SSIS Catalog

To deploy an SSIS project to the SSIS Catalog, you make use of the stored procedure *catalog.deploy_project*. To make use of *catalog.deploy_project*, you need to provide the values for the following three parameters:

- **Folder Name** Name of the folder to which to deploy the SSIS project
- **Project Name** Name of the project
- **Project Binary** The binary stream for the project

In addition, if you want to obtain the operation identifier for the deploy project operation, you can pass an additional out parameter when invoking *catalog.deploy_project*. Before the project is deployed, you will need to create the folder. You can use the T-SQL query given in Listing 12-3.

LISTING 12-3 Creating a folder

```
USE SSISDB
EXEC CATALOG.CREATE_FOLDER 'Chapter12'
```

After the folder is created, you can deploy the SSIS project deployment file for MyFirstSSISProject, in *C:\InsideOut\Chapter12\Code\MyFirstSSISProject.ispac*, to the folder. Listing 12-4 shows the T-SQL query that can be used to deploy an SSIS project, called MyFirstSSISProject, to a folder called *Chapter12* in the SSIS Catalog.

The identifier for the operation is returned via the *@OpID* parameter. In the T-SQL query, you will also notice that the BULK rowset provider for OPENROWSET is used to read the bytes from the project deployment file, and store it in the *varbinary(max)* variable *@ProjectBinary*. Listing 12-5 shows the T-SQL query that can be used to verify the status of the project deployment. A value of 7 shows a successful project deployment.

LISTING 12-4 Deploy an SSIS project to the SSIS Catalog

```
USE SSISDB

DECLARE @ProjectBinary as varbinary(max)
DECLARE @OpID as bigint

SET @ProjectBinary = (SELECT *
 FROM OPENROWSET(BULK 'C:\InsideOut\Chapter12\Code\MyFirstSSISProject.ispac',
 SINGLE_BLOB) as BinaryData)

EXEC catalog.deploy_project 'Chapter12','MyFirstSSISProject',
   @ProjectBinary, @OpID out
```

LISTING 12-5 Verifying the status of the project deployment

```
SELECT object_name, start_time, end_time, status
FROM catalog.operations
WHERE operation_id = @OpID
```

Learning About the SSIS Projects Deployed to the SSIS Catalog

Information for all the SSIS projects that have been deployed to the SSIS Catalog can be found in the view *catalog.projects*. The information in this view includes the following:

- **Project ID** Unique identifier for the project.
- **Folder ID** Unique identifier for the folder to which the project is deployed.
- **Name** Name of the project.
- **Description** Description of the project.
- **Project Format Version** Version of the project format. In SQL Server 2012, the value is 1.
- **Deployed By SID** The security identifier (SID) for the user who deployed the project.
- **Deployed By Name** The name of the user who deployed the project.
- **Last Deployed Time** The last deployed date and time for the project.
- **Created Time** The date and time when the project is first created.
- **Object Version LSN** Whenever a project with the same name is deployed to the same folder, the object version LSN is incremented by one.
- **Validation Status and Last Validation Time** These columns are not used in SQL Server 2012.

It is important to note that row-level security is enforced on the view *catalog.projects*. Consequently, you can see only the projects that you have deployed to the SSIS Catalog and projects that you have been explicitly given Read permission on. Members of the database role *ssis_admin* or server role *sysadmin* will be able to see all the projects that have been deployed to the SSIS Catalog.

Listing 12-6 shows the T-SQL query used to obtain the information for all projects deployed to the folder *Chapter12* in the SSIS Catalog. In the query, you will also notice that we are joining with another very useful view, *catalog.folders*, which provides information for all the folders that have been created in the SSIS Catalog.

LISTING 12-6 Obtaining information for projects that have been deployed to a specific folder

```
   USE SSISDB

SELECT p.name,object_version_lsn, p.deployed_by_name, p.last_deployed_time
FROM catalog.projects p, catalog.folders f
WHERE f.name = 'Chapter12'
and p.folder_id = f.folder_id
```

You can also find information for the packages that are in each project using the *catalog.packages* view, and metadata about each package. Listing 12-7 shows how you can query the view to find out about all the packages for the SSIS project MyFirstSSISProject. In the T-SQL, you will also notice that we are including a column called *entry_point*. This column is used to indicate a package has been marked as an entry-point package by the SSIS developer during design time. By default, all packages are entry-point packages unless the SSIS developer makes changes to it. The concept of having an entry point is useful in scenarios where you have a set of parent and child packages. To indicate to an administrator that only the parent packages should be executed, the SSIS developer can use SQL Server Data Tools to make these changes.

LISTING 12-7 Obtaining information on packages in a project

```
USE SSISDB

SELECT p.package_id, p.entry_point, p.name, p.description
FROM catalog.packages p, catalog.projects proj, catalog.folders f
WHERE p.project_id = proj.project_id
and proj.folder_id = f.folder_id
and proj.name = 'MyFirstSSISProject'
and f.name = 'Chapter12'
```

Configuring SSIS Projects

In Chapter 10, "Configuration in SSIS", you learned how to make use of SQL Server Management Studio to configure SSIS projects and packages that have been deployed to the SSIS Catalog. In this section, you learn to use T-SQL for configuring SSIS projects and packages.

Learning About the Parameters for a Project

After your SSIS projects have been deployed to the SSIS Catalog, you can find out about the parameters for a project by querying the view *catalog.object_parameters*. This view provides information about the parameters for projects and packages that have been deployed to the SSIS Catalog.

In this view, the *object_type* column allows you to figure out whether a parameter is a project parameter (object type = 20) or a package parameter (object type = 30). The *object_name* column can refer to the name of a project or package. The *value_type* column is used to specify whether the value used by the package during execution is a literal value (value type = V) or referencing an SSIS environment variable (value type = R). If any of the parameters references an SSIS environment variable, you will need to specify the environment to be used during package execution. The *value_set* column is used to specify whether the user has explicitly set a value for the parameter, and the valid values are 0 and 1. The *design_default_value* refers to the value specified during package design; it cannot be changed using T-SQL.

If the projects and packages that you have deployed to the SSIS Catalog make use of connection managers (either project-scoped or package-scoped), you will also notice that the name of the parameter is prefixed with "CM:". In SSIS 2012, these connection-manager-related parameters are automatically generated when you deploy an SSIS project to the SSIS Catalog. This allows you to configure the value for properties of the connection manager, even though you have not explicitly declared them as parameters during the package design. Most important, when packages fail, the value specified for these connection managers can help in troubleshooting causes of failures of connections to data sources. Figure 12-2 shows some of the columns in the *catalog.object_parameters* view.

Results | Messages

	parameter_id	project_id	object_type	object_name	parameter_name	data_type	required	sensitive
62	194	4	30	MyDataFlow.dtsx	CM.Flat File Connection Manager.AlwaysCheckForRo...	Boolean	0	0
63	195	4	30	MyDataFlow.dtsx	CM.Flat File Connection Manager.CodePage	Int32	0	0
64	196	4	30	MyDataFlow.dtsx	CM.Flat File Connection Manager.ColumnNamesInFirst...	Boolean	0	0
65	197	4	30	MyDataFlow.dtsx	CM.Flat File Connection Manager.DataRowsToSkip	Int32	0	0
66	198	4	30	MyDataFlow.dtsx	CM.Flat File Connection Manager.Format	String	0	0
67	199	4	30	MyDataFlow.dtsx	CM.Flat File Connection Manager.HeaderRowDelimiter	String	0	0
68	200	4	30	MyDataFlow.dtsx	CM.Flat File Connection Manager.HeaderRowsToSkip	Int32	0	0
69	201	4	30	MyDataFlow.dtsx	CM.Flat File Connection Manager.LocaleID	Int32	0	0
70	202	4	30	MyDataFlow.dtsx	CM.Flat File Connection Manager.RowDelimiter	String	0	0
71	203	4	30	MyDataFlow.dtsx,	CM.Flat File Connection Manager.TextQualifier	String	0	0
72	204	4	30	MyDataFlow.dtsx	CM.Flat File Connection Manager.Unicode	Boolean	0	0

FIGURE 12-2 Columns in the *catalog.object_parameters* view.

Listing 12-8 shows how you can obtain the parameters for the project MyFirstSSISProject, which has been deployed to the folder *Chapter12*. To obtain the name of the project and the folder, the *catalog.projects* and *catalog.folders* views are also used in the query.

LISTING 12-8 Obtaining information about the project and package parameters

```
USE SSISDB

SELECT object_type, object_name, parameter_name, data_type, [required],
            sensitive, design_default_value, value_type, value_set
FROM catalog.object_parameters p, catalog.projects proj, catalog.folders f
WHERE p.project_id = proj.project_id
 and proj.folder_id = f.folder_id
 and proj.name = 'MyFirstSSISProject'
 and f.name = 'Chapter12'
ORDER BY parameter_name
```

Setting the Value of a Parameter

To configure the value of project and package parameters, you can make use of the stored procedure *catalog.set_object_parameter_value*. Listing 12-9 shows how you can set the value of the parameter *DataLoadDirectory* for the SSIS Project MyFirstSSISProject, which has been deployed to the *Chapter12* folder. In the T-SQL query, you will also notice that we specified that the value type is *V*. This means that the set value is referring to a literal value. If you are configuring the project such that it refers to an SSIS environment variable, the value type will be *R* and the parameter value will contain the name of the SSIS environment variable. When referenced values are used, the name of the SSIS environment is not required. The SSIS environment is also provided as the execution context during package execution.

LISTING 12-9 Setting parameter value

```
USE SSISDB

EXEC catalog.set_object_parameter_value
   @object_type=20,
   @parameter_name=N'DataLoadDirectory',
   @object_name=N'MyFirstSSISProject',
   @folder_name=N'Chapter12',
   @project_name=N'MyFirstSSISProject',
   @value_type=V,
   @parameter_value= N'C:\InsideOut\Chapter12\SampleData'
```

Note When the value of a parameter is set, the stored procedure will check that the data type for the value specified is compatible for the data type of the parameter. If it is not compatible, the stored procedure will fail.

Managing SSIS Projects in the SSIS Catalog

After the SSIS projects have been deployed to the SSIS Catalog, you can make use of the stored procedures in SSISDB for managing the projects. In this section, you will learn about the stored procedures for performing common operations in the SSIS Catalog, including the following:

- Deleting a project
- Moving a project to another folder
- Restoring a project to an earlier version

Deleting SSIS Projects

To delete a project, you can make use of the stored procedure *catalog.delete_project*. Deleting a project will delete the project references to environments. Listing 12-10 shows how you can delete a project, called MyFirstSSISProject, from the folder *Chapter12*.

LISTING 12-10 Deleting a project

```
EXEC [SSISDB].[catalog].[delete_project]
          @project_name=N'MyFirstSSISProject',
          @folder_name=N'Chapter12'
```

> **Tip** If you need help figuring out the different T-SQL scripts that can be used for different operations in the SSIS Catalog, you can use the Script functionality in SQL Server Management Studio to start. For example, the T-SQL given in Listing 12-10 is generated by right-clicking the project MyFirstSSISProject and selecting Delete. In the Delete Object dialog box, click Script, which generates the corresponding T-SQL script.

Moving SSIS Projects

To move a project to another folder, you can make use of the stored procedure *catalog.move_project*. Listing 12-11 shows how you can move the project MyFirstSSISProject from the *Chapter12* folder to the *Production* folder. The names of the source folder, project name, and destination folder are prefixed by N to ensure that Unicode strings can also be specified.

LISTING 12-11 Moving a project to another folder

```
USE SSISDB

EXEC [SSISDB].[catalog].[create_folder] 'Production'

EXEC [SSISDB].[catalog].[move_project]
 @source_folder=N'Chapter12',
 @project_name=N'MyFirstSSISProject',
 @destination_folder=N'Production'
```

Restoring an SSIS Project to an Earlier Version

Whenever an SSIS project is deployed to the SSIS Catalog, the older version of the SSIS project is archived. The newly deployed SSIS project will be used whenever the packages in the project are executed. Sometimes during an execution of packages from the newly deployed project, you might notice that the packages are not performing as expected. For example, the following scenario might sound familiar: "My packages used to be working for the last six months. I'm not sure why they suddenly failed during last night's scheduled execution." After a careful investigation, you might have noticed that the project has been changed, and the change might have been causing the packages to fail. While the fix is being investigated, you might want to execute the packages that belong to the older version.

Listing 12-12 shows the T-SQL query that can be used to find out the current Logical Sequence Number (LSN) for the current project, MyFirstSSISProject, which has been deployed to the *Chapter12* folder. In addition, you can obtain information about all the versions of the project by querying the *catalog.object_versions* view. Listing 12-13 shows the T-SQL query that can be used to find out about the versions for the project, ordered by the created time. The *created_time* value corresponds to the time at which the specific version of the project is deployed.

LISTING 12-12 Object LSN for the current deployed project

```
USE SSISDB

SELECT p.name,object_version_lsn, p.deployed_by_name, p.last_deployed_time
FROM catalog.projects p, catalog.folders f
WHERE p.name = ‘MyFirstSSISProject’ and f.name = ‘Chapter12’
and p.folder_id = f.folder_id
```

LISTING 12-13 Information about all the versions for the project

```
USE SSISDB

SELECT v.object_version_lsn, v.created_by, v.object_name,
 CONVERT(nvarchar(30), v.created_time, 109) as created_time,v.description
FROM catalog.object_versions v, catalog.projects p, catalog.folders f
WHERE p.project_id = v.object_id
and p.name = ‘MyFirstSSISProject’ and f.name = ‘Chapter12’
and p.folder_id = f.folder_id
ORDER BY created_time desc
```

Note The number of older SSIS projects that are stored depends on the value for the *MAX_PROJECT_VERSIONS* catalog property.

Once you have gathered all the information for the project, you can find out the version of the project, where the package has been executing successfully in the past. Listing 12-14 shows how you can do that by querying the *catalog.executions* view. Specifically, you might want to know instances of package executions that have successfully executed in the past (that is, status = 7). This will help you make a decision on the version of the project to be restored.

LISTING 12-14 Information about all past executions

```
USE SSISDB

SELECT e.execution_id,e.package_name, e.start_time, e.status, e.project_lsn, e.executed_as_name
FROM catalog.executions e
WHERE folder_name = 'Chapter12' and
project_name = 'MyFirstSSISProject'
```

Once you have figured out the exact object LSN to be restored, you can invoke the stored procedure *catalog.restore_project*. You will need to provide the name of the folder, the name of the project, and the version of the LSN to which you want to restore. If you specify a wrong object version LSN, you will get an error message indicating that the object version does not match the project ID or you do not have sufficient permissions. Listing 12-15 shows how you can restore the SSIS project MyFirstSSISProject that is in the *Chapter12* folder to an earlier version, with object_version_lsn = 8.

LISTING 12-15 Restoring the project

```
EXEC catalog.restore_project @folder_name ='Chapter12',
@project_name='MyFirstSSISProject',
@object_version_lsn = 8
```

Note The Object Version LSN is a globally increasing sequence number that applies to each project deployment. Hence, for the same project, you might not get consecutive LSNs. If you want to obtain a continuous range of version numbers for the project, you can make use of the SQL Server function *DENSE_RANK*.

Running SSIS Packages in the SSIS Catalog

In SSIS 2012, you can make use of T-SQL scripts to configure and execute packages that are deployed to the SSIS Catalog. In addition, you can monitor and stop the execution of the packages using T-SQL. We cover how to make use of stored procedures, views, and table-value functions for monitoring and troubleshooting performance and data issues in Chapter 22, "Troubleshooting SSIS Performance Issues," and Chapter 23, "Troubleshooting Data Issues."

A key difference between SSIS 2012 and earlier versions (SQL Server 2005, SQL Server 2008, and SQL Server 2008 R2) is that in SSIS 2012, when you make use of T-SQL, SSIS Management Object Model (MOM), and PowerShell to execute packages, these packages run on the server in which the SSIS Catalog has been deployed. In earlier versions, when you invoke dtexec to run packages, these packages run locally on the machine where dtexec is invoked.

Starting and Stopping SSIS Package Execution

The stored procedures *catalog.create_excecution* and *catalog.start_execution* are used when starting the execution of packages deployed to the SSIS Catalog. When using T-SQL to start an execution, the following steps are often used:

1. Create an execution.
2. Set the values of parameters for the package.
3. Set property overrides (if needed).
4. Start the execution.

By default, when an execution is started using *catalog.start_execution*, it executes asynchronously. The package continues to run in the background as a process that executes in the security context of the user who invoked the stored procedure *catalog.start_execution*. Listing 12-16 shows Steps 1, 2, and 4 of starting package execution.

From the T-SQL code snippet, you can also observe that we are setting the *reference_id* as NULL because for this specific execution, we are not referencing any SSIS environment value. This is covered in the section "SSIS Environments" later in this chapter.

LISTING 12-16 Creating and starting package execution

```
USE SSISDB

DECLARE @execution_id bigint

EXEC catalog.create_execution
          @folder_name=N'Chapter12',
          @project_name=N'MyFirstSSISProject',
          @package_name=N'MyDataFlow.dtsx',
          @reference_id=Null,
          @execution_id=@execution_id OUTPUT


DECLARE @dirName sql_variant = N'C:\InsideOut\Chapter12\SampleData'

EXEC catalog.set_execution_parameter_value
          @execution_id,
          @object_type=20,
          @parameter_name=N'DataLoadDirectory',
          @parameter_value=@dirName

EXEC catalog.start_execution @execution_id
```

Property Overrides

In earlier versions of SSIS, property paths in SSIS configuration files are commonly used to set the value for specific properties of components in the package. The concept of parameters is introduced in SSIS 2012 to make it easier to configure projects and packages (refer to Chapter 10). As parameters need to be added explicitly to a package at design time, you might be faced with a situation where you need to modify specific values for properties in the package, for which the mapping between the property and parameter has not been established. Property overrides are introduced in in SSIS 2012 to allow you to make the changes to the values of the properties prior to execution.

Given an execution identifier, the stored procedure *catlog.set_execution_property_override_value* can be used for setting up property overrides. Depending on the sensitivity of the value used in property overrides, you can mark it as a sensitive value. All sensitive values are stored in an encrypted form in the SSIS Catalog. Listing 12-17 shows how you can create a property override. It relies on the T-SQL query given in Listing 12-16, and makes use of the *@execution_id*.

LISTING 12-17 Using property overrides

```
USE SSISDB

EXEC catalog.set_execution_property_override_value
          @execution_id,
          @property_path=N'\Package.Variables[User::Filename].Value',
          @property_value=N'cdr-yyy.txt',
          @sensitive=False
```

> **Note** Property overrides can only be set before the package execution starts. After the package has started execution, you will get this error message: "The property cannot be overridden after the execution has been started."

Discovering Package Execution Details

After a package has started or completed execution, you can find out more about the parameter values that are specified for the package execution by querying the *catalog.execution_parameter_values* view. In this view, you will see the values used for a specific package execution.

Listing 12-18 shows a T-SQL query to retrieve the parameter values for the package execution with execution identifier 30. From the view, you will observe parameters with different object types. The object type is used to differentiate between the different types of parameters: project parameters (20), package parameters (30), and execution-specific parameters (50). The execution-specific parameters, added automatically to each package execution, control the behavior of the execution. These parameters include the following:

- ***CALLER_INFO*** This is used mainly by SQL Agent to provide additional information that the package execution is invoked within SQL Agent.
- ***DUMP_EVENT_CODE*** This defines the list of SSIS event codes that will cause a dump to occur. The format is similar to the /Dump option used in dtexec.
- ***DUMP_ON_ERROR*** When set to *True*, this causes an execution to dump when an OnError occurs. This is similar to the /DumpOnError used in dtexec.
- ***DUMP_ON_EVENT*** When set to *True*, this causes an execution to dump when any of the events specified in *DUMP_EVENT_CODE* occurs.

- ***LOGGING_LEVEL*** This sets the logging level for the execution to None (0), Basic (1), Performance (2), or Verbose (3). By default, if this is not set, it defaults to the server logging level.
- ***SYNCHRONIZED*** Determines whether the package execution is synchronous or asynchronous. By default, this is set to *False* (that is, all package executions execute asynchronously, and the stored procedure catalog.start_execution returns immediately).

LISTING 12-18 Details about package execution

```
USE SSISDB

SELECT object_type, sensitive, parameter_name,
parameter_value, parameter_data_type
FROM catalog.execution_parameter_values
WHERE execution_id = 30
ORDER BY object_type, parameter_name
```

Setting the Logging Level for a Package Execution

SSIS 2012 introduces the ability to automatically log the SSIS events that are generated during SSIS package execution. These SSIS events might include information, warning, error, and custom events that are produced when an SSIS package executes. To control the amount of information that is logged, you can set the value for the logging level. In an earlier section, you learned how to set the server-wide logging level, which affects all package execution.

Prior to starting the package execution, you can also set the logging level for that specific package execution if you need more details to be captured. To set the value for the *LOGGING_LEVEL* parameter, you make use of the same stored procedure used for setting parameter values: *catalog.set_execution_parameter_value*. Listing 12-19 shows how you can change the logging level for an execution to the Performance logging level (with a value of 2).

LISTING 12-19 Setting the logging level

```
USE SSISDB

DECLARE @execution_id bigint

EXEC catalog.create_execution
          @folder_name=N'Chapter12',
          @project_name=N'MyFirstSSISProject',
          @package_name=N'MyDataFlow.dtsx',
          @reference_id=Null,
          @execution_id=@execution_id OUTPUT

SELECT @execution_id

EXEC catalog.set_execution_parameter_value
          @execution_id,
          @object_type=50,
          @parameter_name=N'LOGGING_LEVEL',
          @parameter_value=2

EXEC catalog.start_execution @execution_id
```

Asynchronous vs. Synchronous Executions

By default, all package executions are asynchronous. Earlier you learned about the different execution-specific parameters. The *SYNCHRONIZED* parameter is used to determine whether a package execution is asynchronous or synchronous. All SQL Agent job steps that execute SSIS packages that have been deployed to the SSIS Catalog execute synchronously. If you look at the execution parameters for the package executions invoked by SQL Agent, you will notice that the value for the synchronized parameter has been set to *True*. This is done by SQL Agent implicitly.

To set the value for the parameter, you make use of the same stored procedure used for setting parameter values: *catalog.set_execution_parameter_value*. Listing 12-20 shows how you can set up a synchronous execution.

LISTING 12-20 Setting a package execution to be synchronous

```
USE SSISDB

DECLARE @execution_id bigint

EXEC catalog.create_execution
@folder_name=N'Chapter12', @project_name=N'MyFirstSSISProject',
@package_name=N'MyDataFlow.dtsx',@reference_id=Null,
@execution_id=@execution_id OUTPUT

SELECT @execution_id

EXEC catalog.set_execution_parameter_value @execution_id,
@object_type=50, @parameter_name=N'SYNCHRONIZED', @parameter_value=1

EXEC catalog.start_execution @execution_id
```

Stopping Package Execution To stop package execution, you can make use of the stored procedure *catalog.stop_operation*. Besides stopping package execution, the stored procedure can also be used to stop the execution of other asynchronous operations (for example, project and package validation). In Listing 12-21, we show how to make use of *catalog.stop_operation* to stop the execution of the package execution, with an execution identifier of 30.

LISTING 12-21 Stopping package execution

```
USE SSISDB

EXEC catalog.stop_operation 30
```

SSIS Environments

SSIS environments are containers for SSIS environment variables. In this section, you learn how to make use of T-SQL to create SSIS environments and environment variables that can be used during package execution. You also learn how to create an environment reference for a project.

Creating SSIS Environments

To create a new SSIS environment, you make use of the stored procedure *catalog.create_environment*. In Listing 12-22, you will see how you can create two environments: Staging and Production in the folder *Chapter12*.

LISTING 12-22 Creating two SSIS environments: Staging and Production

```
USE SSISDB

EXEC catalog.create_environment
          @folder_name=N'Chapter12',
          @environment_name=N'Staging',
          @environment_description=N'Staging environment'

EXEC catalog.create_environment
          @folder_name=N'Chapter12',
          @environment_name=N'Production',
          @environment_description=N'Production environment'
```

> **Note** When creating a new SSIS environment in a folder, the operation might fail with the following error message: "The environment '<EnvName>' already exists or you have not been granted the appropriate permissions to create it." However, when you query *catalog.environments*, you might not see any environment with the name that you have specified. This is because row-level security is enforced on the view *catalog.environments*, and this is causing you to be unable to see all the environments.

Creating SSIS Environment Variables

After the environment is created, you can create SSIS environment variables using the stored procedure *catalog.create_environment_variable*. Listing 12-23 shows how you can create the variable, *DataDir*, in each of the environments.

LISTING 12-23 Creating environment variables

```
USE SSISDB

EXEC catalog.create_environment_variable
          @folder_name=N'Chapter12',
          @environment_name=N'Production',
          @variable_name=N'DataDir',
          @description=N'Absolute path for the data directory',
          @value= N'C:\InsideOut\Chapter12\SampleData',
          @sensitive=False,
          @data_type=N'String'
```

```
EXEC catalog.create_environment_variable
          @folder_name=N'Chapter12',
          @environment_name=N'Staging',
          @variable_name=N'DataDir',
          @description=N'Absolute path for the data directory',
          @value= N'C:\InsideOut\Chapter12\SampleData',
          @sensitive=False,
          @data_type=N'String'
```

Configuring SSIS Projects Using SSIS Environments

In Chapter 2, "SSIS Concepts," you learned about the differences between relative and absolute environment references. In this section, you learn how to make use of T-SQL to define them.

Creating Project References to SSIS Environments

To create project references to an SSIS environment, you make use of the stored procedure *catalog.create_environment_reference*. In Listing 12-24, we created two project references to the Staging and Production environment, respectively. In addition, notice that we set the reference type to be R, which indicates that these environment references are relative. When you move the project to a new folder, the project references will point to the same named environments in that folder.

> **Note** If the new folder does not have the same name environment, you will see an error message ("The specified object with name 'Production' does not exist. It might have been removed. Make sure it exists and try again.") when you try to open the environment using the SQL Server Management Studio user interface.

LISTING 12-24 Creating relative project references to SSIS environments

```
USE SSISDB

DECLARE @reference_id bigint

EXEC catalog.create_environment_reference
 @folder_name=N'Chapter12',
 @project_name=N'MyFirstSSISProject',
 @environment_name=N'Staging',
 @reference_type='R',
 @reference_id=@reference_id OUTPUT

 EXEC catalog.create_environment_reference
 @folder_name=N'Chapter12',
 @project_name=N'MyFirstSSISProject',
 @environment_name=N'Production',
 @reference_type='R',
 @reference_id=@reference_id OUTPUT
```

To create absolute project references to environment, you can set the reference to be A. Listing 12-25 shows how you can create absolute SSIS environment references. In the T-SQL, notice that for absolute project references, you will need to specify the folder in which the environment is located. In this example, the environment is in the folder *Chapter12*.

LISTING 12-25 Creating absolute project references to SSIS environments

```
USE SSISDB

DECLARE @reference_id bigint

EXEC catalog.create_environment_reference
 @folder_name=N'Chapter12',
 @project_name=N'MyFirstSSISProject',
 @environment_folder_name=N'Chapter12',
 @environment_name=N'Staging',
 @reference_type='A',
 @reference_id=@reference_id OUTPUT

 EXEC catalog.create_environment_reference
 @folder_name=N'Chapter12',
 @project_name=N'MyFirstSSISProject',
 @environment_folder_name=N'Chapter12',
 @environment_name=N'Production',
 @reference_type='A',
 @reference_id=@reference_id OUTPUT
```

Configuring SSIS Projects Using Reference Values

Earlier in this chapter, you learned how to set the value for parameters using literal values. Listing 12-26 shows how you can set the value for the parameter *DataLoadDirectory* as a referenced value. To indicate that it is a referenced value, the value type is specified as R.

LISTING 12-26 Using reference values

```
USE SSISDB

EXEC catalog.set_object_parameter_value
          @object_type=20,
          @folder_name=N'Chapter12',
          @project_name=N'MyFirstSSISProject',
          @parameter_name=N'DataLoadDirectory',
          @object_name=N'MyFirstSSISProject',
          @value_type='R',
          @parameter_value=N'DataDir'
```

> **Note** When the value for a parameter is set as a referenced value, the name of the SSIS environment is not included because the specific environment used is only determined prior to package execution.

Package Execution Using SSIS Environments

To specify an environment to be used for execution, you will need to pass in the identifier for the project reference to the environment. To find out about the identifier value for each of the project references, you need to query the *catalog.environment_references* view, as shown in Listing 12-27.

LISTING 12-27 Obtaining the identifier value for project references

```
USE SSISDB

SELECT [reference_id]
 ,[reference_type]
 ,[environment_folder_name]
 ,[environment_name]
 FROM catalog.environment_references r, catalog.projects p
 WHERE r.project_id = p.project_id
 and p.name = 'MyFirstSSISProject'
```

Once you have obtained the identifier value for the project reference, you can use it when invoking *catalog.create_execution.* In Listing 12-28, you will notice that we specified a value of 2 for the SSIS environment. Prior to package execution, the referenced value for the specified environment variable will be resolved, and the package execution is started.

LISTING 12-28 Package execution using project references

```
USE SSISDB

DECLARE @execution_id bigint

EXEC catalog.create_execution
   @folder_name=N'Chapter12',
   @project_name=N'MyFirstSSISProject',
   @package_name=N'MyDataFlow.dtsx',
   @use32bitruntime=False,
   @reference_id=2,
   @execution_id=@execution_id OUTPUT

EXEC [SSISDB].[catalog].[start_execution] @execution_id
```

Managing SSIS Environment and Environment Variables

In this section, you learn how to manage the SSIS environment and environment variables. To obtain rich information about the SSIS environments that have been created, and the environment variables that are contained by each of the environments, you can use the *catalog.environment* and *catalog.environment_variables* view. Listing 12-29 shows how you can use these two views to find out about the SSIS environments and environments that are created in the folder *Chapter12.*

LISTING 12-29 Getting information about SSIS environment and environment variables

```
USE SSISDB

SELECT e.environment_id, e.name, e.created_by_name, e.description
FROM catalog.environments e , catalog.folders f
WHERE e.folder_id = f.folder_id
and f.name = 'Chapter12'

SELECT e.name as env_name,ev.variable_id, ev.name, ev.value, ev.type, ev.sensitive,
ev.description
FROM catalog.environment_variables ev, catalog.environments e , catalog.folders f
WHERE e.folder_id = f.folder_id
and f.name = 'Chapter12'
and ev.environment_id = e.environment_id
```

After creating an environment, you might need to delete the environment. To delete an environment, you can make use of the stored procedure *catalog.delete_environment*. Listing 12-30 shows how you can delete the Staging environment from the *Chapter12* folder.

LISTING 12-30 Deleting an SSIS environment

```
USE SSISDB

EXEC catalog.delete_environment 'Chapter12', 'Staging'
```

You can also move an SSIS environment between different folders in the SSIS Catalog. The stored procedure *catalog.move_environment* can be used to perform this operation. Listing 12-31 shows how you can move the Production environment from the *Chapter12* folder to *Chapter12DestFolder*.

LISTING 12-31 Moving an SSIS environment to another folder

```
USE SSISDB

EXEC catalog.move_environment
           'Chapter12',
           'Production',
           'Chapter12DestFolder'
```

Note When SSIS environments are deleted, or moved from one folder to another, it might cause the project references to be broken. You can use T-SQL queries to find out which are the broken project references and then fix them.

Summary

In this chapter, you learned how to make use of the public views and stored procedures that are introduced in SSIS 2012 to deploy, configure, and execute packages that have been deployed to the SSIS Catalog. The public views provide a rich set of information to a database administrator, opening up new possibilities for administration of SSIS projects and packages.

CHAPTER 13

SSIS PowerShell Magic

In This Chapter

Chapter 12, "SSIS T-SQL Magic," introduced you to the various Transact-SQL (T-SQL) options for managing the new SSIS Catalog introduced with SSIS 2012. Improving manageability for database administrators was one of the key improvements in SSIS 2012. As part of those improvements, one new feature was the integration of SSIS with PowerShell.

PowerShell Refresher

PowerShell is a Windows command-line shell that enables administrators to perform manageability tasks. It has a command shell prompt as well as a scripting environment that can be used to create PowerShell scripts. It is largely a scripting platform built on the Microsoft .NET Framework. Using its Component Object Model (COM) and Windows Management Instrumentation (WMI) compatibilities, you can perform local and remote Windows system administration tasks.

The following are the primary building blocks of PowerShell:

- **Cmdlets** Built-in PowerShell commands that can be used in a PowerShell script.
- **Providers** PowerShell objects that let you access data sources like SQL Server databases, SSIS Catalogs, and generic Windows-based data stores like the file system or the registry.
- **PowerShell scripts** Scripts containing PowerShell functions, cmdlets, and executables. Scripts are suffixed by .ps1.
- **PowerShell functions** Block of PowerShell code that can be encapsulated and called once or multiple times using the name of the block.

A PowerShell script can be as simple as a few lines of code to perform a complex operation as shown in Listing 13-1, which displays if a given folder exists on the local system.

LISTING 13-1 A simple PowerShell script

```
#PowerShell script to check if folder exists
$ssisFolderPath = “C:\\InsideSSIS”
If ([System.IO.Directory]::Exists($ssisFolderPath))
{
   Write-Host “Folder exists”
}
Else
{
   Write-Host “Folder does not exist”
}
```

See Also *More information about PowerShell scripting is available at* http://technet.microsoft.com/en-us/library/bb978526.aspx.

PowerShell and SQL Server

PowerShell support was introduced for SQL Server with SQL Server 2008. It lets database administrators perform complex operations that would involve complex T-SQL scripting to be done with simple PowerShell scripts.

SQL Server 2008 also introduced the following enhancements for operating with PowerShell:

- **SQL Server Provider** A provider you can use to build paths similar to system paths where a drive is equivalent to a SQL Server management object and the nodes are based on the SQL Server object model.
- **sqlps** This is a PowerShell mini shell that is an abstraction over the PowerShell environment. It is integrated into SQL Server Data Tools as well as the SQL Server Agent. A session created with it will have all the SQL Server PowerShell snap-ins loaded and registered.
- **Other cmdlets** Various cmdlets were also introduced to enable execution of a SQL Server action (for example, *Invoke-Sqlcmd*, which is used to execute *SQLCMD* scripts).

You can directly start a PowerShell session by right-clicking an object and selecting Start PowerShell in the SQL Server Data Tools Object Explorer pane shown in Figure 13-1. The *sqlps* session started will have all the required SQL Server PowerShell snap-ins loaded and registered. This will also default to the path of the object that was used to open the window, as shown in Figure 13-2.

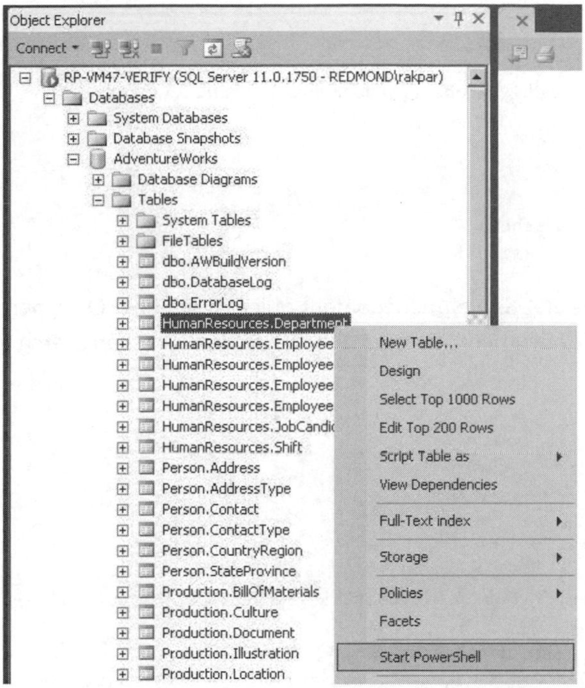

FIGURE 13-1 Start PowerShell option on SQL Server Data Tools.

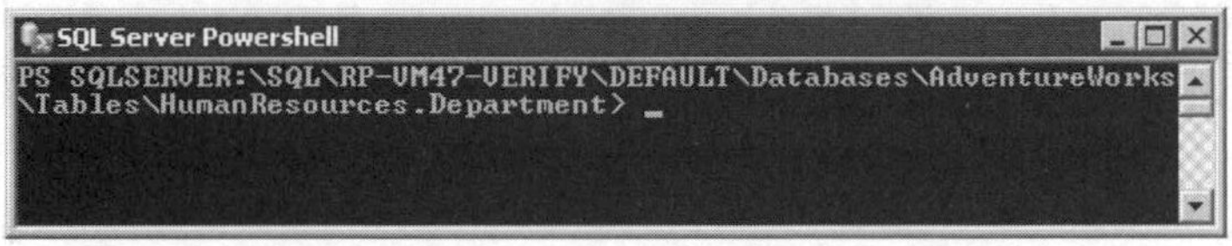

FIGURE 13-2 SQL Server PowerShell window.

After starting a session with *sqlps* or from a PowerShell session where a SQL Server provider is registered, you can address SQL Server nodes just like file system paths, as shown in Listing 13-2.

> **Note** This example and subsequent listings assume that you have installed the AdventureWorks2012 database on your default instance of the local server. It can be installed from *http://msftdbprodsamples.codeplex.com/releases/view/55330.*

LISTING 13-2 Usage of SQL Server Provider in PowerShell

```
#Set the location to the tables node
Set-Location SQLSERVER:\SQL\localhost\DEFAULT\Databases\AdventureWorks2012\Tables

#Get all the tables in the database
Get-Childitem

#Get all the tables within the purchasing schema
Get-ChildItem | where {$_.Schema -eq "Purchasing"}
```

Within an *sqlps* session you can use the SQL Server management object model (SMO) to perform administrative operations on a SQL Server object. In Listing 13-3, we show how you can search for a table in a database.

LISTING 13-3 Using SMO with PowerShell

```
$server="Localhost"
$dbname="AdventureWorks2012"
$tbname="VendorContact"
#Load the SMO assembly
[System.Reflection.Assembly]::LoadWithPartialName("Microsoft.SqlServer.SMO") | out-null

#Access the server using SMO and look up its databases
$SMOserver = New-Object ('Microsoft.SqlServer.Management.Smo.Server') -argumentlist $server
$db = $SMOserver.databases[$dbname]
    foreach($test in $db.Tables)
    {
        if($test.Name -eq $tbname)
        {
            Write-Host $test.Name " table is found"
        }
    }
```

Note that access to the SQL Server using PowerShell is not limited to the SQL Server provider. You can also write a small client access application similar to an ADO .NET database access application using PowerShell as shown in Listing 13-4.

LISTING 13-4 Using PowerShell to query a SQL Server table

```
#Create a new sql connection
$newSQLConn = New-Object System.Data.SqlClient.SqlConnection
$newSQLConn.ConnectionString = "Data Source=.;Database=AdventureWorks2012;Integrated
Security='True'"

#Create a new sqlcmd
$cmdText = "SELECT * FROM HumanResources.Employee"
$sqlCmd = New-Object System.Data.SqlClient.SqlCommand($cmdText,$newSQLConn)
#Open the connection and execute the command
$newSQLConn.Open()
$dataReader = $sqlCmd.ExecuteReader()
```

```
#Read the content of the data reader
while($dataReader.Read())
{
$emdID = $dataReader["EmployeeID"].ToString()
Write-Host "$emdID"
}
$newSQLConn.Close()
```

You will use some of these concepts when you begin working with the SSIS objects in the next sections.

Managing SSIS with PowerShell

As you have seen in previous chapters, the SSIS Catalog can contain multiple SSIS objects. These objects require multiple administrative actions to be configured appropriately and include deployment to the SSIS Catalog on a server, and managing projects, packages, environments, folders, and so on for a catalog. The next sections show how you can use PowerShell to perform administrative operations on your SSIS Catalog. You will also see how to use PowerShell to query your catalog views and execute T-SQL statements on those views.

SSIS Management Object Model

As you saw in Chapter 10, "Configuration in SSIS," and Chapter 11, "Running SSIS Packages," there are quite a few ways to configure SSIS objects. One of the most common ways is to use the Management Object Model. The following section provides a quick refresher of the object model basics.

The primary namespace containing the rich set of managed application programming interfaces (APIs) for the object model is *Microsoft.SqlServer.Management.IntegrationServices.* These managed APIs represent a wrapper over the T-SQL APIs provided for managing the SSIS objects. A quick review of performing some of the operations such as creating a catalog and a folder using the management model is shown in Listing 13-5. (Note that you can create a connection using the code in Listing 13-4, which is required in Listing 13-5.)

LISTING 13-5 SSIS Management Object Model management API usage

```
// Create an IntegrationServices instance using an SMO server connection.
// Here SMO = Microsoft.SqlServer.Management.Smo; connection is a ServerConnection.
SMO.Server server = new SMO.Server(connection);
IntegrationServices isserver = new IntegrationServices(server);

//Create a catalog under isserver, specify the password.
Catalog catalog = new Catalog(isserver, "SSISDB", "password");
catalog.Create();

//Create a folder under catalog, with folder description
CatalogFolder folder = new CatalogFolder(catalog, "folder1", "Description of folder1.");
folder.Create();
```

```
//Create an environment under folder1
EnvironmentInfo environment = new EnvironmentInfo(folder, "environment1", "Description of
environment");
environment.Create();
```

Similarly, the SSIS Management Object Model can be also used to perform other operations, such as deploying a project; configuring, validating, and executing a package; and monitoring an execution. For an in-depth analysis of these operations, refer to Chapters 10 and 11.

In the next section, you'll learn how we use the same SSIS Management Object Model along with PowerShell to manage SSIS objects.

PowerShell with SSIS Management Object Model

Using PowerShell with the SSIS Management Object Model is very similar to using the managed API to perform the same action. As you know already, PowerShell acts as a .NET abstraction over a managed interface. Hence, we can use any API that is available in the managed interface using PowerShell.

As you saw in the previous section, the managed interface that is required for using the SSIS Management Object Model is *Microsoft.SqlServer.Management.IntegrationServices*. If SSIS is installed on your system, then you would be able to find *Microsoft.SqlServer.Management.IntegrationServices.dll* registered on your system. Using reflection, we have to load the assembly so that we can use the managed API that has been defined in the assembly as shown in Listing 13-6.

LISTING 13-6 Loading the SSIS Management Object Model assembly

```
# Load the IntegrationServices Assembly
[Reflection.Assembly]::LoadWithPartialName("Microsoft.SqlServer.Management.IntegrationServices")
```

Once the assembly is loaded, you can then use the namespace *Microsoft.SqlServer.Management.IntegrationServices* and use the managed API. In the following sections, you will see several administrative operations executed using PowerShell.

Creating or Dropping an SSIS Catalog

Listing 13-7 shows you how to create and drop an SSIS Catalog using PowerShell. Listing 13-7 assumes that you have a localhost SQL Server instance with the AdventureWorks2012 database available on the instance.

LISTING 13-7 Creating and dropping SSIS Catalogs

```
# Load the IntegrationServices Assembly
[Reflection.Assembly]::LoadWithPartialName("Microsoft.SqlServer.Management.IntegrationServices")

# Store the IntegrationServices Assembly namespace to avoid typing it every time
$ISNamespace = "Microsoft.SqlServer.Management.IntegrationServices.IntegrationServices"

Write-Host "Connecting to server ..."
```

```
# Create a connection to the server
$sqlConnectionString = "Data Source=localhost;Initial Catalog=master;Integrated Security=SSPI;"
$sqlConnection = New-Object System.Data.SqlClient.SqlConnection $sqlConnectionString

# Create the Integration Services object
$integrationServices = New-Object $ISNamespace $sqlConnection

Write-Host "Removing previous catalog ..."

# Drop the existing catalog if it exists
if ($integrationServices.Catalogs.Count -gt 0) { $integrationServices.Catalogs["SSISDB"].
Drop() }

Write-Host "Creating new SSISDB Catalog ..."

# Provision a new SSIS Catalog
$catalog = New-Object $ISNamespace".Catalog" ($integrationServices, "SSISDB", "Denali2012")
$catalog.Create()
```

Creating and Dropping Folders

Listing 13-8 shows you how you can manage folders on your SSIS Catalog.

LISTING 13-8 Managing folders and environments using PowerShell

```
# Load the IntegrationServices Assembly
[Reflection.Assembly]::LoadWithPartialName("Microsoft.SqlServer.Management.IntegrationServices")
# Store the IntegrationServices Assembly namespace to avoid typing it every time
$ISNamespace = "Microsoft.SqlServer.Management.IntegrationServices"

Write-Host "Connecting to server ..."

# Create a connection to the server
$sqlConnectionString = "Data Source=localhost;Initial Catalog=master;Integrated Security=SSPI;"
$sqlConnection = New-Object System.Data.SqlClient.SqlConnection $sqlConnectionString

# Create the Integration Services object
$integrationServices = New-Object $ISNamespace".IntegrationServices" $sqlConnection

# Get the existing SSIS Catalog
$catalog = $integrationServices.Catalogs["SSISDB"]

Write-Host "Creating Folder ..."

#Drop a folder if exists
if ($catalog.Folders["Folder"]) { $catalog.Folders["Folder"].Drop() }

# Create a new folder
$folder = New-Object $ISNamespace".CatalogFolder" ($catalog, "Folder", "Some description")
$folder.Create()
```

All the listings in the following section use Listing 13-8 as the precedence for creating a folder.

Deploying and Managing Projects

Listing 13-9 shows how you can deploy and manage your project. Note that this listing is a continuation of Listing 13-8. It assumes that the folder is already created using the code in Listing 13-8.

LISTING 13-9 Deploying and managing projects

```
Write-Host "Deploying PowerShellDemo project ..."

# Read the project file into a byte array
[byte[]] $projectFile = [System.IO.File]::ReadAllBytes("C:\Demos\PowerShellDemo.ispac")

# deploy it to the folder
$folder.DeployProject("Integration Services Project1", $projectFile)

#Get the project
$project = $folder.Projects["Integration Services Project1"]

#Display the properties of the project
Write-Host $project.Name " was deployed with"
Write-Host "Description: " $project.Description
Write-Host "ProjectID: " $project.ProjectID
/*Output
Deploying PowerShellDemo project ...

Id            : 117
OperationType : 101
CreatedTime   : 12/23/2011 2:47:18 PM +00:00
ObjectType    : 20
ObjectId      : 4
ObjectName    : Integration Services Project1
Status        : Success
CallerName    : rakpar
StartTime     : 12/23/2011 2:47:18 PM +00:00
EndTime       : 12/23/2011 2:47:19 PM +00:00
StoppedByName :
Messages      : {}
Parent        : Catalog[@Name='SSISDB']
Completed     : True
IdentityKey   : Operation[@Id='117']
Urn           : IntegrationServices[@Name='RP-VM47-VERIFY']/Catalog[@Name='SSISDB']/Operation[@
Id='117']
Properties    : {Name=Id/Type=System.Int64/Writable=True/Value=117, Name=OperationType/
                Type=System.Int16/Writable=False/Value=101, Name=CreatedTime/Type=System.
                Nullable`1[System.DateTimeOffset]/Writable=False/Value=12/23/2011 2:47:18 PM,
                Name=ObjectType/Type=System.Nullable`1[System.Int16]/Writable=False/Value=20...}
Metadata      : Microsoft.SqlServer.Management.Sdk.Sfc.Metadata.SfcMetadataDiscovery

Integration Services Project1  was deployed with
Description:  Some description
ProjectID:  4
*/
```

As you can see from Listing 13-9, the project was successfully deployed and the project properties as well as the operation details were displayed on the console after the successful deployment.

Create Environments and Environment Variables

Listing 13-10 shows you how to create environments and environment variables.

LISTING 13-10 Creating environments and environment variables with PowerShell

```
Write-Host "Creating a new environment..."

#Drop an environment if already exists
if ($folder.Environments["NewEnv"]) { $folder.Environments["NewEnv"].Drop() }

#Create an environment
$env = New-Object $ISNamespace".EnvironmentInfo" ($folder, "NewEnv", "New Environment")
$env.Create()

WriteHost "Create an environment variable..."

#Creating an environment variable of type Int32
$parType = "Int32"
$env.Variables.Add("var1", "Int32" , 1, $false, "Some description")
$env.Alter()
```

Creating Package Executions with Parameters and References

Listing 13-11 shows how to create package parameters and package executions.

LISTING 13-11 Creating package executions and parameters

```
# Read the project file, and deploy it to the folder
Write-Host "Deploying ExecutionDemo project ..."
[byte[]] $projectFile = [System.IO.File]::ReadAllBytes("C:\Demos\PowerShellDemo.ispac")
$folder.DeployProject("PowerShellDemo", $projectFile)

#we can specify the value of parameters to be either constants or
# to take the value from  environment variables

$package = $project.Packages["DemoPackage.dtsx"]

# setting value of parameter to constant
$package.Parameters["Servername"].Set(

[Microsoft.SqlServer.Management.IntegrationServices.ParameterInfo+ParameterValueType]::Literal,
"TestServer");
$package.Alter()

# binding value of another parameter to value of an env variable

# creating an environment
$environment = New-Object $ISNamespace".EnvironmentInfo" ($folder, "Env1", "Env1 Desc.")
$environment.Create()

# adding variable to our environment
$environment.Variables.Add("Variable1", [System.TypeCode]::Int32, "10", "false", "Desc.")
$environment.Alter()
```

```
# making project refer to this environment
$project = $folder.Projects[$SSISProjectName]
$project.References.Add($SSISEnv, $folder.Name)
$project.Alter()

# making package parameter refer to this  environment variable
$package.Parameters["CoolParam"].Set(

[Microsoft.SqlServer.Management.IntegrationServices.ParameterInfo+ParameterValueType]::Referenc
ed,
    $SSISEnvVar)
$package.Alter()

# retrieving environment reference
$environmentReference = $project.References.Item($SSISEnv, $folder.Name)
$environmentReference.Refresh()

# executing with environment reference - Note: if you don't have any env reference,
# then you specify null as the second argument
$package.Execute("false", $environmentReference)

Write-Host "Package Execution ID: " $executionId
```

PowerShell and SSIS Using T-SQL

Earlier, you learned that PowerShell can be used to issue queries to a database. As you saw in Chapter 12, SSIS can be easily managed with the T-SQL API available. This opens up tremendous possibilities to just manage SSIS objects using the PowerShell over the T-SQL API available.

You can see an example of use of T-SQL using PowerShell in Listing 13-12, where the *operation_messages* view has been queried to find the state of the operations.

LISTING 13-12 Use of SSIS T-SQL API using PowerShell

```
#Create a new sql connection
$newSQLConn = New-Object System.Data.SqlClient.SqlConnection
$newSQLConn.ConnectionString = "Data Source=.;Database=AdventureWorks2012;Integrated
Security='True'"

#Create a new sqlcmd
$cmdText = "SELECT [operation_message_id]
      ,[operation_id]
      ,[message_time]
      ,[message_type]
      ,[message_source_type]
      ,[message]
      ,[extended_info_id]
  FROM [SSISDB].[internal].[operation_messages]"
$sqlCmd = New-Object System.Data.SqlClient.SqlCommand($cmdText,$newSQLConn)
```

```
#Open the connection and execute the command
$newSQLConn.Open()
$dataReader = $sqlCmd.ExecuteReader()

#Read the content of the data reader
while($dataReader.Read())
{
$ID = $dataReader["operation_message_id"].ToString()
Write-Host "$ID"
}
$newSQLConn.Close()
```

In Listing 13-13, you can see how PowerShell can be used to deploy a project using the SSIS T-SQL API.

LISTING 13-13 Creating package execution using PowerShell over SSIS T-SQL API

```
#Create a new sql connection
$newSQLConn = New-Object System.Data.SqlClient.SqlConnection
$newSQLConn.ConnectionString = "Data Source=.;Database=SSISDB;Integrated Security='True'"

#Create a new execution
$cmdText = "catalog.create_execution"
$sqlCmd = New-Object System.Data.SqlClient.SqlCommand($cmdText,$newSQLConn)

#Open the connection and execute the command
$newSQLConn.Open()

Write-Host "Create a TSQL Call for creating execution..."

#Setup the parameters
$sqlCmd.CommandType = [System.Data.CommandType]'StoredProcedure'
$sqlCmd.Parameters.Add("@folder_name","Folder")
$sqlCmd.Parameters.Add("@project_name","Integration Services Project1")
$sqlCmd.Parameters.Add("@package_name","ParentPackage.dtsx")
$paramOut = $sqlCmd.Parameters.Add("@execution_id",[System.Data.SqlDbType]'BigInt')
$paramOut.Direction = [System.Data.ParameterDirection]'Output'

#Execute the command
$dataReader = $sqlCmd.ExecuteReader()
$dataReader.Close()

Write-Host "Create a TSQL Call for starting execution..."

#Issue new command for starting execution
$cmdText = "catalog.start_execution @execution_id=" + $paramOut.Value
$sqlCmdNew = New-Object System.Data.SqlClient.SqlCommand($cmdText,$newSQLConn)

#Execute the command
$dataReaderNew = $sqlCmdNew.ExecuteReader()

$dataReaderNew.Close()
$newSQLConn.Close()
```

Advantages of Using PowerShell with SSIS

Working with PowerShell for managing SSIS has many advantages, including the following:

- The script environment allows it to be created and executed in any type of Windows environment.
- Because PowerShell can be used to manage any other Windows entity, you can effectively write scripts to manage SSIS and do other Windows or SQL Server administrative tasks in a seamless manner, creating a common management paradigm.
- PowerShell has tight integration with .NET libraries, enabling you to possible perform any task that you can perform with a managed API.
- PowerShell has a vibrant developer community. You will find an ever growing list of cmdlets and blog articles for solving complex administrative issues.

See Also *PowerShell scripts can be found on various PowerShell forums. TechNet has a very good repository to start with at* http://gallery.technet.microsoft.com/scriptcenter/site/search/?f%5B0%5D.Type=ScriptLanguage&f%5B0%5D.Value=PowerShell&f%5B0%5D.Text=PowerShell.

Summary

In this chapter, you learned about using PowerShell to administer SSIS objects. You were introduced to the basics of PowerShell and use of PowerShell with SQL Server. You learned how you can use the SSIS Management Object Model with PowerShell. You then saw how you can complete complex administrative tasks such as creating a catalog or a folder. You learned about deploying a project and configuring it, and how you can create parameters and environment references before executing a package on an SSIS Catalog.

CHAPTER 14

SSIS Reports

In This Chapter

Getting Started with SSIS Reports

SSIS 2012 introduces new capabilities that capture the incredibly rich set of information that is produced during the execution of SSIS packages that have been deployed to the SSIS Catalog. This information is exposed via public views, and provides administrators with insights into the execution of SSIS packages. Using the information provided, you can develop your own custom reports using SQL Server Reporting Services or the standard SSIS reports that are included in SSIS 2012.

In SQL Server Management Studio, you will be able to make use of the standard reports provided to find detailed information about SQL Server, including disk usage, blocking transactions, index usage statistics, and user statistics. If you are familiar with the SQL Server Management Studio standard reports, you will be familiar with the SSIS reports. These reports are launched from SQL Server Management Studio. In SSIS 2012, five SSIS reports are provided out-of-the box when SSIS is installed. Table 14-1 shows the list of reports and the information contained in each one. The reports can be launched from one of the following nodes in SQL Server Management Studio:

- SSISDB
- Each project
- Each package

TABLE 14-1 List of SSIS reports.

Report	What's in the report
Integration Services Dashboard	SSIS package executions in the last 24 hours; macro view of all the connections that have failed in the last 24 hours.
All Executions	Shows information about SSIS package executions.
All Validations	Shows information about SSIS package validations.
All Operations	Shows information about operations that are executed. When an SSIS package gets validated, gets executed, or when a package execution is stopped, this is logged as an operation. Other operations include project deployment and making changes to the SSIS Catalog properties.
All Connections	Shows information about the configurations that have failed. Each configuration is represented by a connection string.

The set of SSIS reports that are available at each of the SQL Server Management Studio nodes depends on its relevance to the content from the node. For example, the Integration Services Dashboard report is available only from the SSISDB node, and not at the other nodes. Figure 14-1 shows an example of reports that can be launched from the SSISDB node.

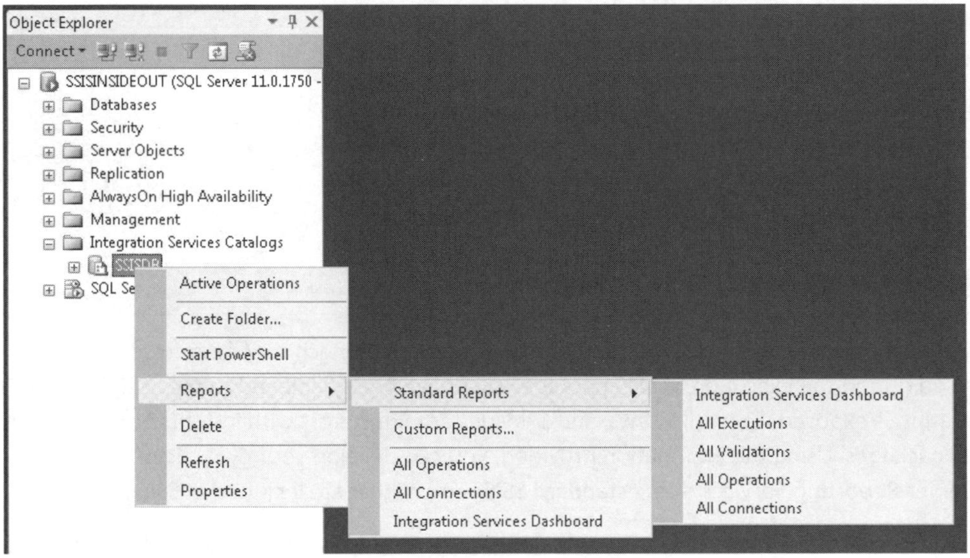

FIGURE 14-1 SSIS reports.

To launch a specific report, follow these steps:

1. Right-click the node.
2. Select Standard Reports.
3. Select one of the reports shown in the list of standard reports.

The SSIS reports are available only in SQL Server Management Studio. If you need to show the information presented in the SSIS reports in a SharePoint portal, or Reporting Services, you will need to develop custom Reporting Services reports, which query the public views that are available in SSISDB.

In this chapter, you'll learn how you can use the SSIS reports to find out about the operations that have been performed, monitor executions of SSIS packages, and troubleshoot common issues in executions.

Data Preparation

You can prepare the database, tables, and data needed to try the different examples in the chapters. To start the preparation, download the AdventureWorksDW2012 database from *http://msftdbprodsamples.codeplex.com/releases/view/55330*, and attach it to a SQL Server instance.

After the AdventureWorksDW2012 database has been attached, perform the following steps:

1. Deploy the SSIS project, Chapter14Project.ispac, found in *C:\InsideOut\Chapter 14\Code*, to the *SSISInsideout* folder in the SSIS Catalog.
2. After the SSIS Catalog has been deployed successfully, execute the package "0. PrepData.dtsx" using SQL Server Management Studio, by right-clicking the package "0. PrepData.dtsx" and choosing Execute Package. This will help you create the CSV files used in the package, and create the EnterpriseDW database.
3. By default, the data preparation step creates the EnterpriseDW database on the default SQL instance. If you are using a named instance or deploying it to a remote server, you will need to configure the project parameter *ServerName* with the correct ServerName. You might need to drop the EnterpriseDW database if the preparation step is failing.
4. Verify that the package executes successfully, and the database has been created successfully. When prompted whether you would like to open the Overview Report, click Yes. This will show you the overview report for the package execution. In the report, the status for the execution should be "Succeeded." If it is not, you can make use of the information provided in the report to troubleshoot. You can also continue reading the rest of this chapter to learn essential Transact-SQL (T-SQL) skills to troubleshoot SSIS package executions.

Monitoring SSIS Package Execution

Integration Services Dashboard

The Integration Services Dashboard report provides an insightful high-level view of all the SSIS package executions that have happened in the past 24 hours. A database administrator can make use of this to quickly figure out whether the SSIS packages that have been executed are successful or have failed. Figure 14-2 shows how to launch the Integration Services Dashboard, by using the following steps:

1. Right-click the SSISDB node.
2. Select Reports, then choose Standard Reports.
3. Select Integration Services Dashboard.

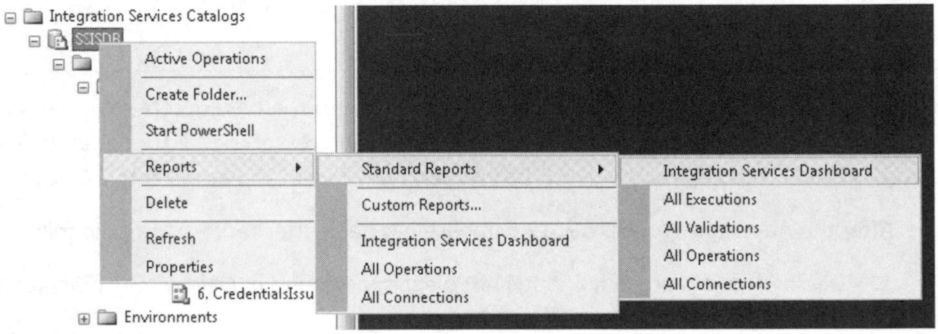

FIGURE 14-2 Launching the Integration Services Dashboard.

The dashboard provides an administrator with at-a-glance information on the reason(s) for failure of SSIS package executions. Figure 14-3 shows a screenshot of the dashboard after it is launched. The Integration Services Dashboard consists of three sections that show different information about the SSIS packages that have been executed in the past 24 hours. You can click the links provided (blue underline) to drill down to more detailed information for each of the executions.

- **Execution Information** Shows the total number of SSIS package executions that are in various states (Failed, Running, Succeeded, and Others).
- **Connection Information** Shows the connections that have been used in SSIS package executions that have failed.
- **Packages Detailed Information** Shows detailed information for SSIS package executions that have executed.

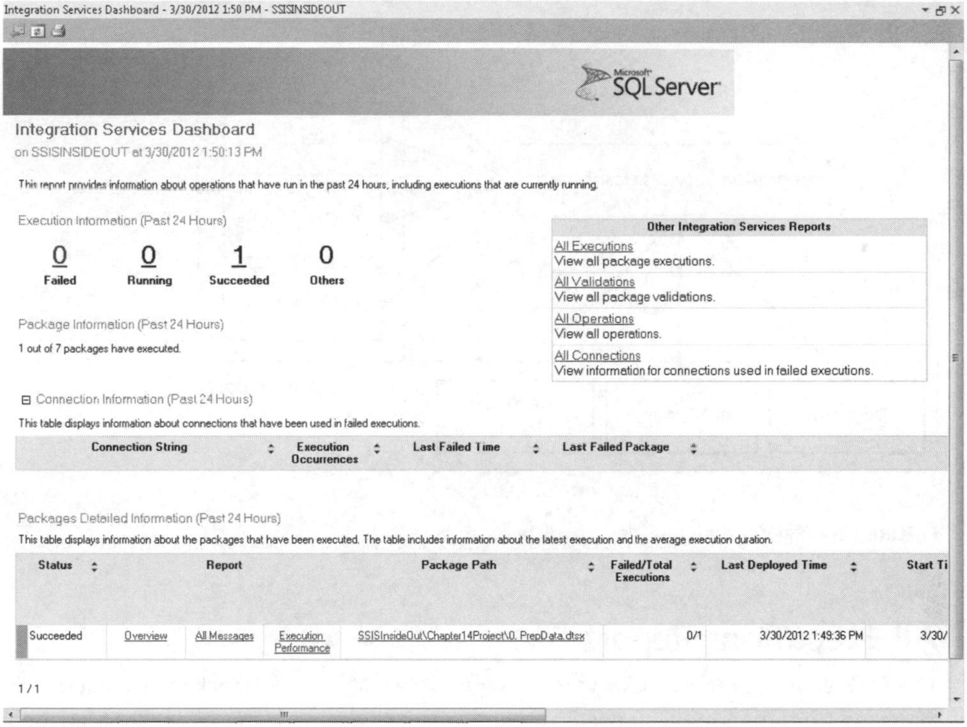

FIGURE 14-3 Integration Services Dashboard.

The Integration Services Dashboard can be used as the initial launch pad for the other SSIS reports that are provided in SQL Server Management Studio. Figure 14-4 shows the relationship between the dashboard and the other SSIS reports. From Figure 14-4, you can see that the Integration Services Dashboards allow you to navigate the to the SSIS reports (All Connections, All Executions, All Operations, and All Validations). In addition, you can use it to go directly to execution-specific reports by clicking the link for a specific execution.

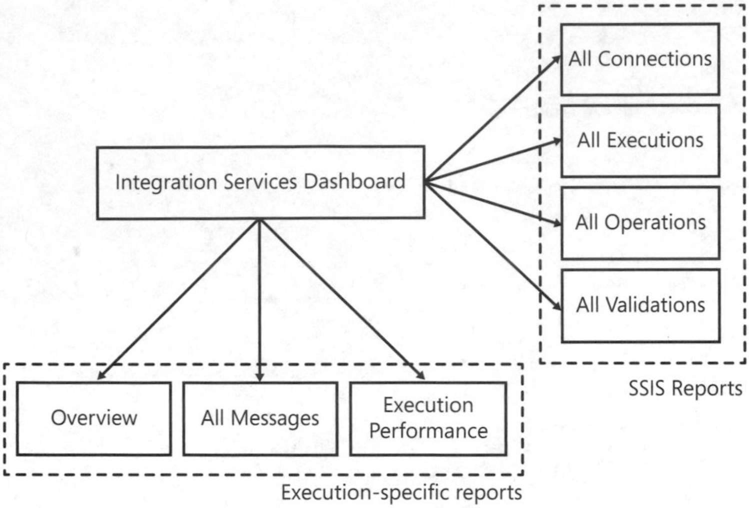

FIGURE 14-4 Relationship between the different SSIS reports.

All Executions Report

The All Executions report allows you to monitor the status of SSIS package executions. It can be launched from the SSISDB, a specific project, or a package node in SQL Server Management Studio. Depending on where the All Executions report is launched, the filter applied on the report will differ. For example, if you launch the report from the SSISDB node, all SSIS package executions that you have started will be shown. If you launch the report from the Projects node, only the SSIS package executions corresponding to the SSIS packages that are in the project will be shown. Figure 14-5 shows the All Executions report launched from the project node for the project, Chapter14Project.

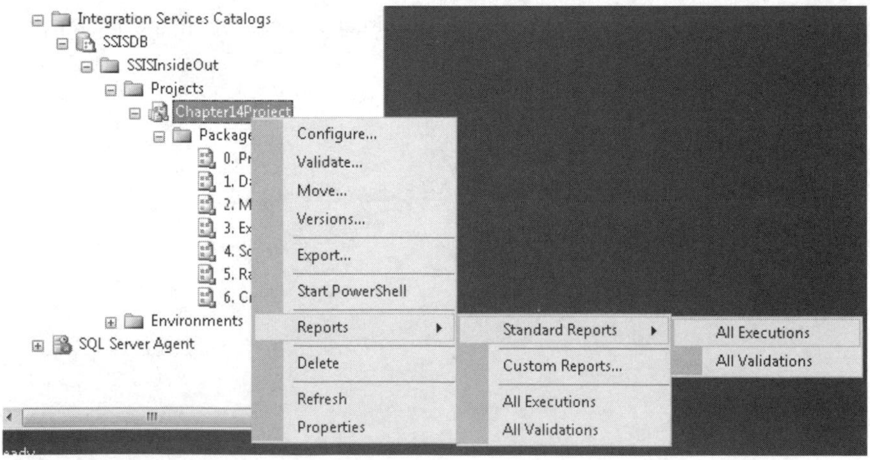

FIGURE 14-5 Launching the All Executions report.

Figure 14-6 shows the All Executions report that is launched. From the report, you can see clearly that three SSIS package executions have failed, and one SSIS package execution completed successfully. By default, the All Executions report will show all the SSIS package executions that have occurred in the past seven days (inclusive of the current date and time). To see SSIS package executions for a specific date, you can click the Filter to specify the criterions that apply to the report.

There are three action columns in the report, which you can click to find more information for each of the SSIS package executions, as follows:

- **Overview** Shows the status of all tasks and containers used in the SSIS package. In addition, it shows the values used for the parameters when the SSIS package is executed.
- **All Messages** Shows detailed messages that are logged during the SSIS package execution.
- **Execution Performance** Allows you to compare the execution duration for all successful executions. In addition, if Performance or Verbose logging is enabled, the Execution Performance report will also show the time spent at each phase for the components. This is useful for performance troubleshooting.

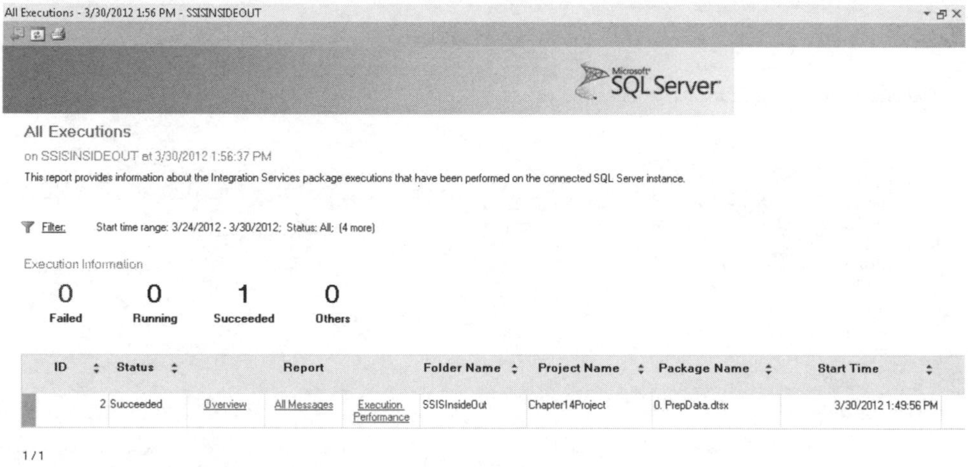

FIGURE 14-6 All Executions report.

All Validations and All Operations Reports

The All Validations and All Operations reports show information for all validations that are performed and all the operations that are executed on the server, respectively. You can also launch the All Validations report from the SSISDB, a specific project, or package SQL Server Management Studio nodes. The All Operations report can be launched only from the SSISDB node. Figures 14-7 and 14-8 show the All Validations and All Operations reports, respectively.

Tip In each of the reports, report filters are provided. The report filters allow you to find the information that you want quickly. The criteria provided in each of the SSIS reports might differ.

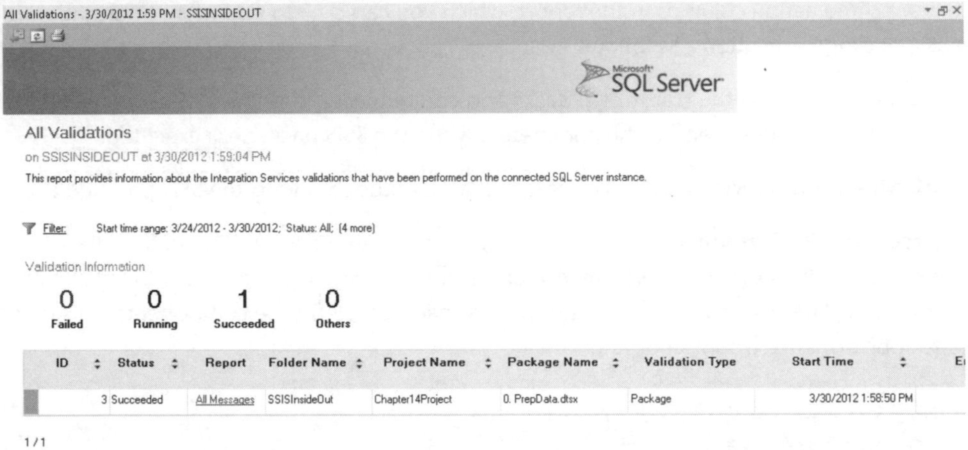

FIGURE 14-7 All Validations report.

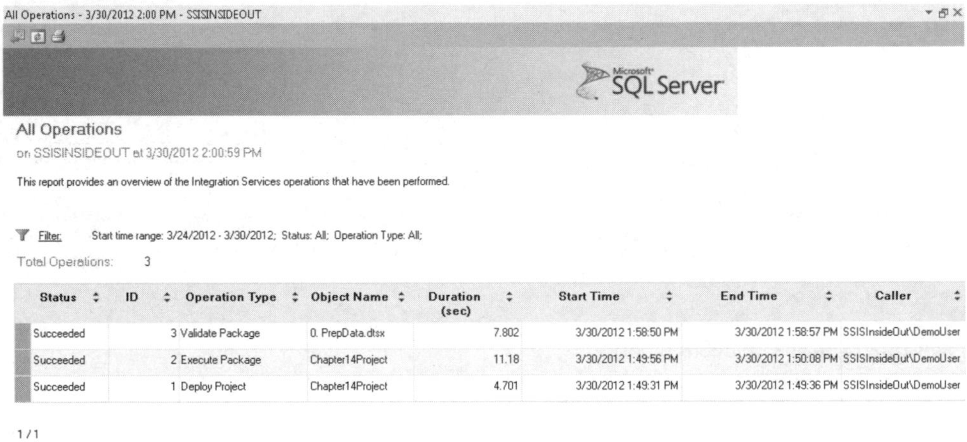

FIGURE 14-8 All Operations report.

Using SSIS Reports to Troubleshoot SSIS Package Execution

In this section, you'll learn how to use the SSIS reports introduced in SSIS 2012 to troubleshoot different types of failures.

The examples given in this section assume that you have completed the data preparation steps, and have successfully executed the SSIS package for data preparation. Next, perform the following steps to run the package "1. DataIssues.dtsx."

1. Using SQL Server Management Studio, navigate to the folder *SSISInsideOut*.
2. Expand the packages under *Chapter14Project*.
3. Right-click "1. DataIssues.dtsx" and choose Execute Package.
4. Figure 14-9 shows how you can navigate to Chapter14Project. Click OK.
5. Click Yes to open the Overview report, shown in Figure 14-10.

When the report is initially launched, it might show that the SSIS package execution is either in the Pending Execution or Running state. You might need to refresh the report several times. You will observe that the SSIS package execution will fail.

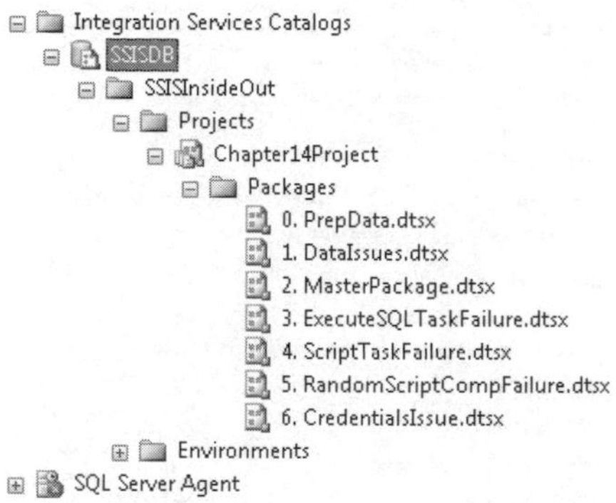

FIGURE 14-9 Navigate to Chapter14Project.

In the Overview report shown in Figure 14-10, you will see that the SSIS package execution has failed. From the Execution Overview, you will be able to see the parts of the SSIS package execution that caused the failure. In this SSIS package execution, the execution failed in the third iteration of the Foreach loop. The Overview report includes two sections. In the first section, the errors that caused the SSIS package execution are shown. In the second section, you will see all the messages that are logged during SSIS package execution. When you click the filter, you will see that a filter has been applied on the Execution Path criterion, with a value of \1 DataIssues\Foreach Loop Container[3]\Data Flow Task. This execution path specifies that the report will show all messages that are logged by the data flow, which is executed within the third iteration of the Foreach Loop container. The Foreach Loop container is contained in the Control Flow for the package "1. DataIssues".

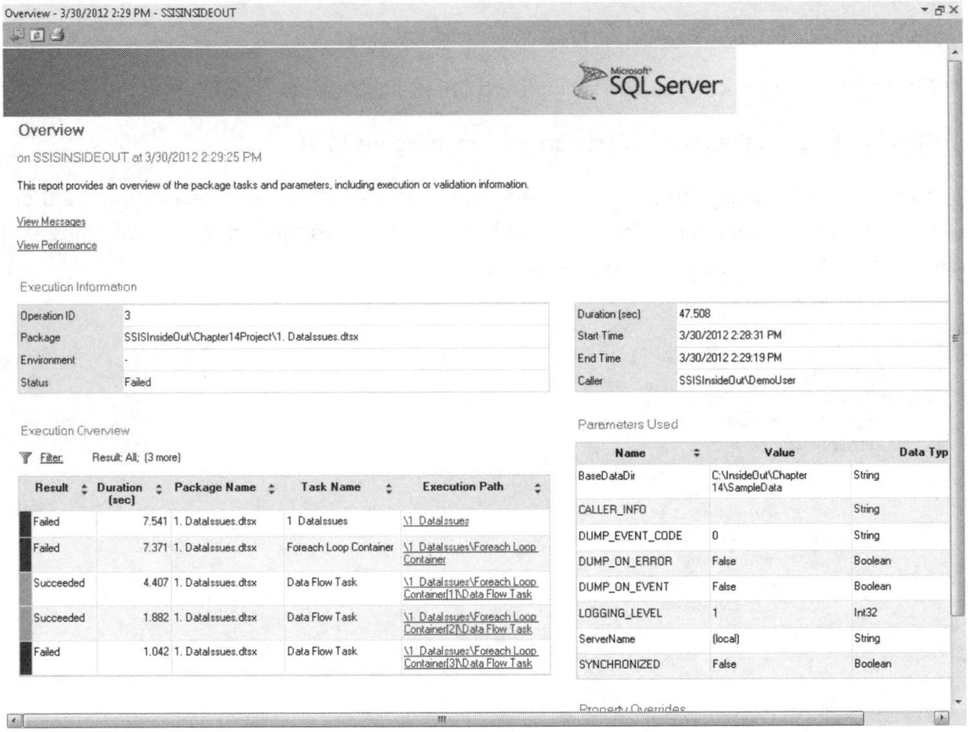

FIGURE 14-10 Overview report.

You can click the link shown in the Execution Path column, in the last row of the Execution Overview, to obtain more details about the failure. Figure 14-11 shows the All Messages report with a filter applied on the execution path.

Whenever an error occurs during the execution of an SSIS package, the context for the error is logged. From the All Messages report, you can click the View Context action to see the context for each of the errors. Figure 14-12 shows an example of the Context report, with a filter applied to limit the information shown to be a context depth of 2. The point at which an error occurred is often referred to as a context depth of 1. Hence, information shown at a context depth of 2 refers to errors that are one level before the point at which the error occurred. In the All Context Information section, you can see that the error is caused by the type cast of DT_I4 on the column HouseOwnerFlag. In addition, you can also observe that this is a property for a derived column in the Data Flow task.

Note By default, when you click the View Context link, a default context depth of 1 is used. Depending on the nature of errors that are logged, context depth 1 might not have context information that is logged. You will need to try the different context depths.

FIGURE 14-11 All Messages report.

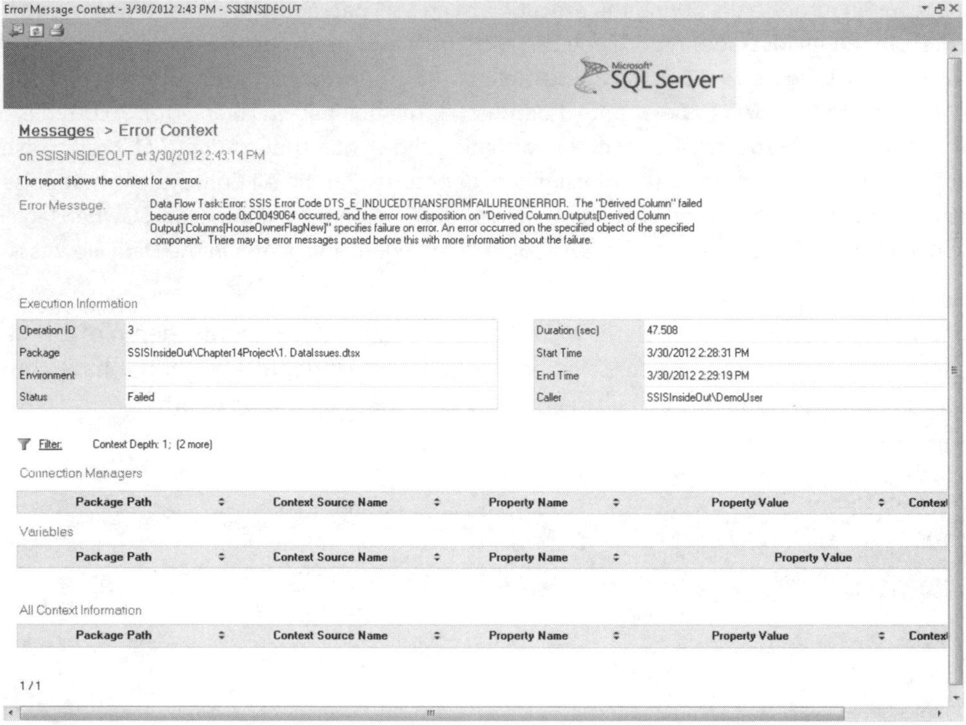

FIGURE 14-12 Error Message Context report.

From this exercise, you learned how to make use of the following SSIS reports to troubleshoot the failure of SSIS package executions:

- Overview report
- All Messages report
- Context report

Often, troubleshooting is an iterative process. You start with a high-level overview of the tasks and containers in the SSIS package that have failed, and drill down to more detailed information to find the root cause of the failure. SSIS 2012 introduces the ability to find out the property values for components that have led to the failure. This provides additional contextual information that can be useful in figuring out the root cause.

See Also *See Chapter 20, "Troubleshooting SSIS Package Failures," to learn how to use T-SQL for troubleshooting failures of SSIS package executions.*

In this next example, you will learn how to troubleshoot SSIS package executions that consist of child packages. To do this, perform the following steps:

1. Using SQL Server Management Studio, navigate to the folder *SSISInsideOut*.
2. Expand the packages under Chapter14Project.
3. Right-click "2. MasterPackage.dtsx" and choose Execute Package.
4. Click OK.
5. Click Yes to open the Overview report.

Figure 14-13 shows the Overview report. On the report, you can see the detailed execution information for both the parent and child packages. In the Execution Overview section, you can see the Foreach Loop container failed. In the Execution Path column, you will be able to see that the Foreach Loop container is in the child package. The child package is launched from the Execute Package task, called ExecuteDataIssues Package, which is in the master package.

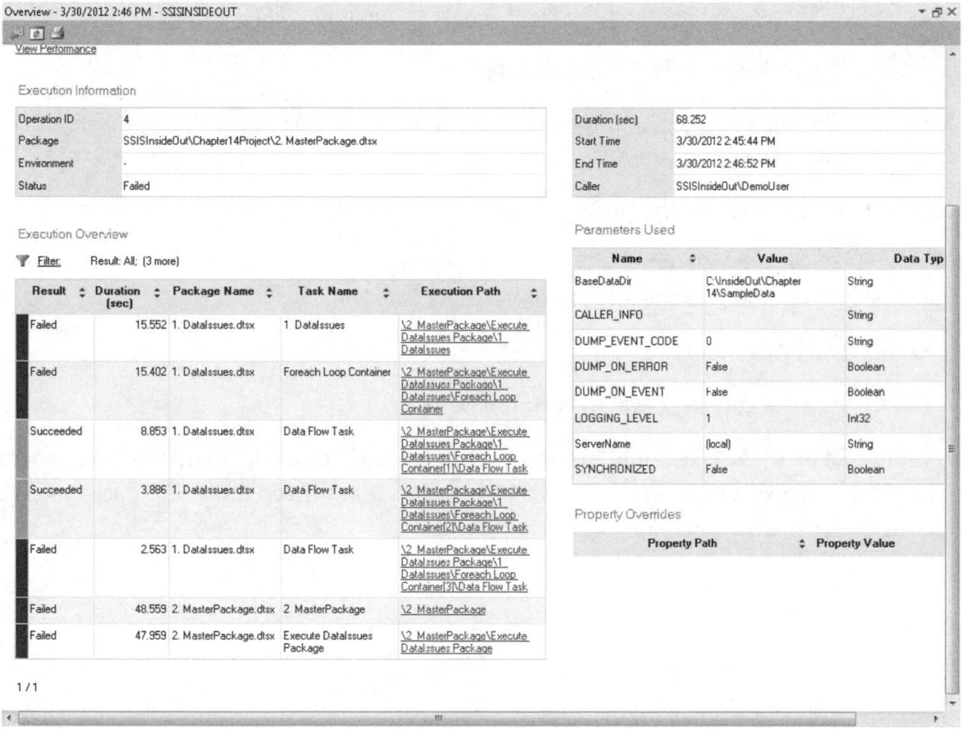

FIGURE 14-13 Overview report (with child packages).

Using the Execution Performance Report to Identify Performance Trends

In this section, you'll learn how to use the SSIS reports introduced in SSIS 2012 to identify performance trends. To prepare for this exercise, you need to perform the following steps:

1. Delete the file File3.csv from *C:\InsideOut\Chapter 14\SampleData*.

> **Note** Earlier, you found that the root cause of the failure of the SSIS package execution for "1. DataIssues.dtsx" is due to the type cast of DT_I4 performed on the HouseOwnerFlag column. In addition, you also found that this happens in the third iteration of the loop. By removing File3.csv from *C:\InsideOut\Chapter 14\SampleData*, we are removing the erroneous file that is causing the SSIS package execution to fail.

2. Using SQL Server Management Studio, navigate to the folder *SSISInsideOut*.
3. Expand the packages under Chapter14Project.
4. Execute the SSIS package "1. DataIssues.dtsx" twice. Each time, right-click the SSIS package and choose Execute Package.
5. Execute the package for the third time, with Performance Logging Level. To do this, follow these steps:
    a. Right-click the package and choose Execute Package.
    b. Click the Advanced tab.
    c. Change the Logging Level to Performance.
6. Verify that all the SSIS package executions completed successfully. To do this, you can make use of the All Executions report. Figure 14-14 shows that the top three SSIS package executions completed successfully.

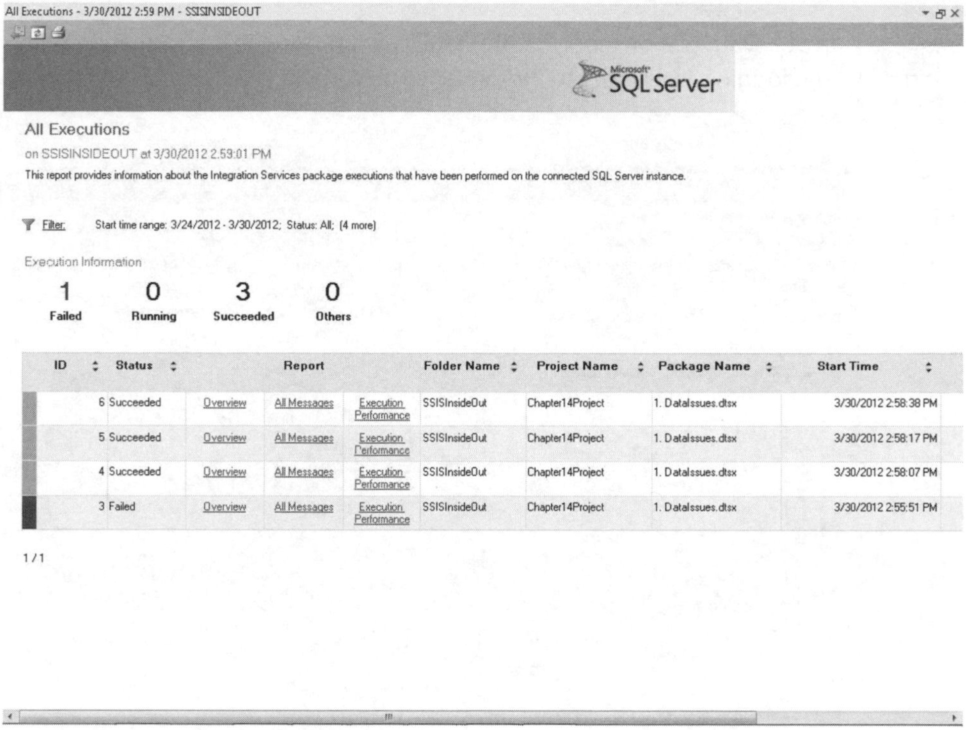

FIGURE 14-14 Successful completion of the "1. Data Issues.dtsx" package.

To identify the performance trends in SSIS package executions, click the Execution Performance report corresponding to the last SSIS package execution (that is, ID = 6). This launches the Execution Performance report shown in Figure 14-15, which consists of three sections:

- **Execution Information** Shows the status of the SSIS package execution, and when the SSIS package is executed.
- **Past Execution(s) Information** Shows statistics (average and standard deviation) for the SSIS package executions that have completed successfully and the execution duration. This allows you to quickly identify the SSIS package execution that might have potential performance issues.
- **Data Flow Components Information** Shows the active and total time spent in each phase of the Data Flow component. This section helps you identify the bottlenecks in the package.

Note Data is shown only in the Data Flow Components Information section when the logging level is set to Performance or Verbose.

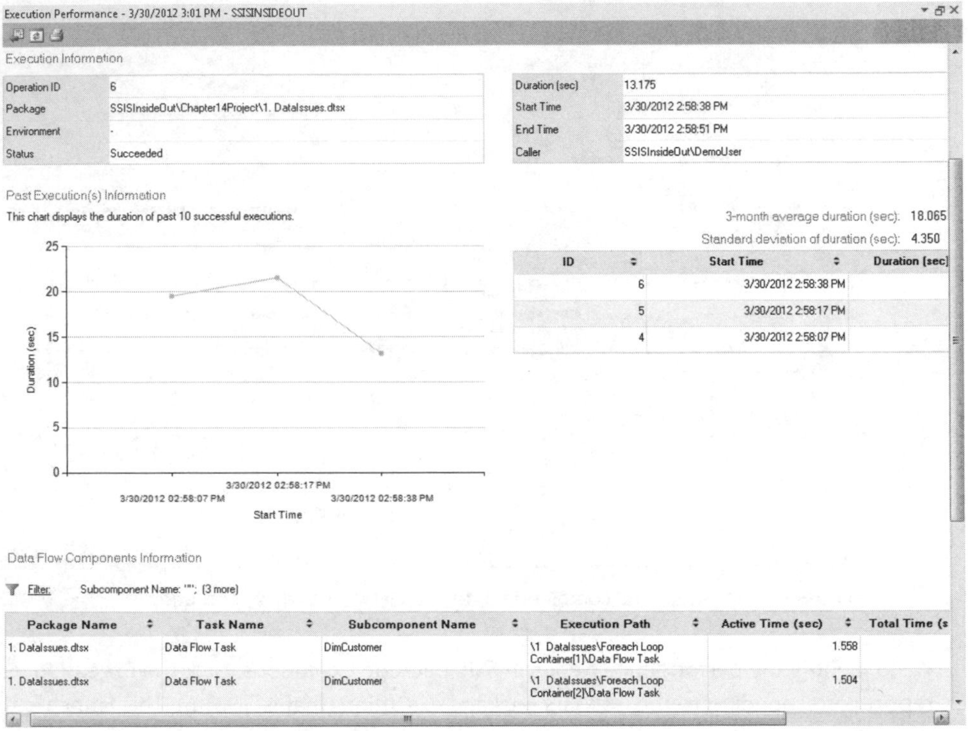

FIGURE 14-15 Execution Performance report.

The Execution Performance report provides you with information that can help you perform a preliminary analysis of performance issues and identify the bottlenecks in the SSIS package. It is important to note that the Data Flow Components Information shows only the time spent at each phase of Data Flow components (Source, Destination, and Transform) used in all the Data Flow tasks. Besides the Data Flow tasks, performance bottlenecks can exist in the other tasks that are in the Control Flow. For example, you might want to know the time spent in the Execute SQL tasks. To identify bottlenecks in tasks, you will need to make use of the Overview report, which shows the duration of each task. Hence, you will need to use the Execution Performance and the Overview report to holistically identify performance issues.

Summary

In SSIS 2012, a collection of standard SSIS reports are provided to empower you to gain insights into the execution of SSIS packages that are deployed to the SSIS Catalog. In this chapter, you learned how to use the SSIS reports introduced in SSIS 2012 to monitor package executions. You learned how to navigate between the different SSIS reports and how to launch the various SSIS reports in SQL Server Management Studio. You also learned how to make use of the reports to troubleshoot common issues that can cause the failure of SSIS package executions.

PART IV

Deep-Dive

CHAPTER 15

SSIS Engine Deep Dive

In This Chapter

Lots of people consider the engine to be the most important part of a car. After all, it's the engine that ultimately provides the ability for the car to move. Similarly, the SSIS package execution is driven by software components referred to as *engines*. Understanding how SSIS engines work and how to configure them is the key to getting optimal performance from your SSIS package design.

There are two main parts in SSIS: the Control Flow and the Data Flow. Correspondingly, there are two separate engines. The Control Flow engine (also referred to as the *runtime*) is responsible for orchestrating task execution. The Data Flow engine (also referred to as the *pipeline*) is used by the Data Flow task, and is used to move data between data sources.

The Control Flow Engine

Overview

The Control Flow acts as the "brain" for the execution of an SSIS package. At run time, it is responsible for loading the package and orchestrating the validation and execution of the tasks and containers it contains. The Control Flow engine has a number of responsibilities, including the following:

- Loading the package XML file and initializing tasks
- Applying parameter and configuration values
- Validating the package hierarchy
- Maintaining and retrieving connection managers
- Orchestrating task execution

- Dispatching log entries to corresponding log providers
- Coordinating execution of event handlers
- Evaluating variables and expression values

> **Note** The majority of the SSIS runtime engine is contained within a single native COM dynamic-link library (DLL)—*DTS.dll*. This functionality is also exposed through a managed .NET layer in *Microsoft.SqlServer.ManagedDTS.dll*.

A package goes through three main phases during execution (load, validate, and execute) with a fourth phase (apply parameters) that is used with the Project Deployment Model (shown in Figure 15-1). Each phase is triggered by the application running the package calling different Control Flow engine methods exposed by the SSIS object model.

FIGURE 15-1 Control Flow phases during package execution.

Load

Before an SSIS package can be validated or executed, it must be loaded by the SSIS runtime. The loading process involves reading the XML package definition, instantiating all of the objects it defines, and applying configuration values. Figure 15-2 shows a flowchart of the loading phase.

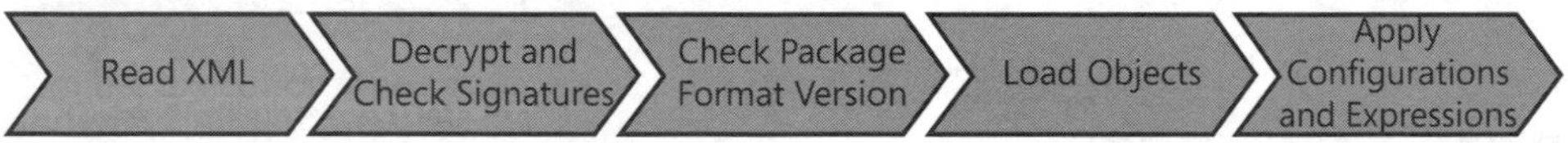

FIGURE 15-2 Phases of loading an SSIS package.

Read XML

The runtime reads the entire package document into an XML DOM format in memory. Any errors caused by malformed XML will be thrown at this phase.

Decrypt and Check Signature

SSIS provides a mechanism to ensure that sensitive values are not saved in clear text when a package is saved. SSIS is able to encrypt an entire package when it is saved, or just encrypt sensitive property values. This functionality is controlled using the package's *ProtectionLevel* property. Table 15-1 shows the possible *ProtectionLevel* values, and describes how each setting affects the way a package is persisted.

TABLE 15-1 *ProtectionLevel* values

Protection Level	Description
Do not save sensitive (DontSaveSensitive)	Sensitive values will be stripped from the package when it is saved to XML.
Encrypt all with password (EncryptAllWithPassword)	A password will be used to encrypt the entire package. When this protection level is used, the contents of the package are placed into a single encrypted block of text inside of the file.
Encrypt all with user key (EncryptAllWithUserKey)	A key from the current user profile is used to encrypt the entire package. Like EncryptAllWithPassword, when this protection level is used, the contents of the package are placed in an encrypted block of text. The package can be read only by the user who originally saved the package.
Encrypt sensitive with password (EncryptSensitiveWithPassword)	Sensitive values within the package are encrypted using a password. If the package is opened with an incorrect password, it can still be loaded, but any sensitive data will be stripped from the package.
Encrypt sensitive with user key (EncryptSensitiveWithUserKey)	A key from the current user profile is used to encrypt only the sensitive fields within the package. If a different user opens the package, the sensitive information will need to be reentered. This is the default protection level for SSIS packages.
Rely on server storage for encryption (ServerStorage)	This protection level can only be used when the package is saved to a SQL Server database (through the SSIS Catalog, or when saving to msdb). In this mode, the package XML contains unencrypted values.

> **Note** More information on how SSIS makes use of user key encryption can be found in the Windows Data Protection article in Books Online at *http://msdn.microsoft.com/en-us/library/ms995355.aspx.*

SSIS supports the use of cryptographic signatures to confirm the validity of a package. This feature can be used to ensure that a package is from a trusted source.

Check Package Format Version

The package XML contains a property that allows the runtime to determine what version of SSIS created the package. If an older version was used, the runtime will automatically upgrade the package XML to the latest version format. If SSIS encounters a higher version number than expected (for example, if the package was created with SQL Server 2012, and run in SQL Server 2008), an error will be thrown. The SSIS runtime is tied to a specific version, and is currently not forward compatible.

Load Objects

Once the XML is in the expected format, the runtime loads and instantiates the objects defined within the package. This includes variables, event handlers, tasks, containers, and connection managers. If a task fails to load, a replacement task will be substituted so that the package can still be loaded and viewed within the SSIS designer. A missing task is displayed on the design surface as an empty box. Other types of load failures could prevent the package from loading at all.

Apply Configurations and Expressions

If your package is using configurations, all types—except parent package variable configurations—will be applied once all of the package objects have been loaded. This phase does not apply when you are using the Project Deployment Model.

> **Note** Configurations are applied a second time during the validation phase. This was a change in behavior in SQL Server 2008 that also applies to SQL Server 2012. Parent package variable configurations are only applied once, during the validation phase, after all other configurations have been applied. For more information about package configuration, see Chapter 10, "Configuring SSIS Projects."

The final phase when loading a package is to compute all expressions within the package. This includes expressions that set values for task properties and variable values.

Apply Parameters

When using the Project Deployment Model, the application running the package will set package parameter values during this phase. Once a package parameter value is set, it cannot be changed during execution.

Validate

A package can be thought of as a tree-like hierarchy. The root of the tree is the package itself, the intermediate nodes are containers, and under each container are the individual tasks. To validate a package runtime engine tells all the top-level containers to validate themselves. Each container then tells its children to validate themselves, and so on. Sibling nodes in the tree are validated sequentially. Each task controls its own validation logic, and will return a validation status indicating failure or success. If a task fails to validate, it will not execute.

Validation is triggered in two ways: when a package is run, or by an explicit call to *Package.Validate()* through the SSIS object model. The validation phase can be delayed (see the next section), but cannot be skipped. The For Loop and For Each Loop containers will revalidate all of their children on each iteration of the loop.

A package will apply any package configurations and compute expressions prior to validating its children. Parent package variable configurations are applied after any other configurations (allowing them to override any value set by another configuration). Configurations are not reapplied during iterations of a loop container.

Delaying Validation

Although validation is required, it is possible to postpone validation using the *DelayValidation* property. Most SSIS package objects have this property, which has a default value of *False* (shown in Figure 15-3).

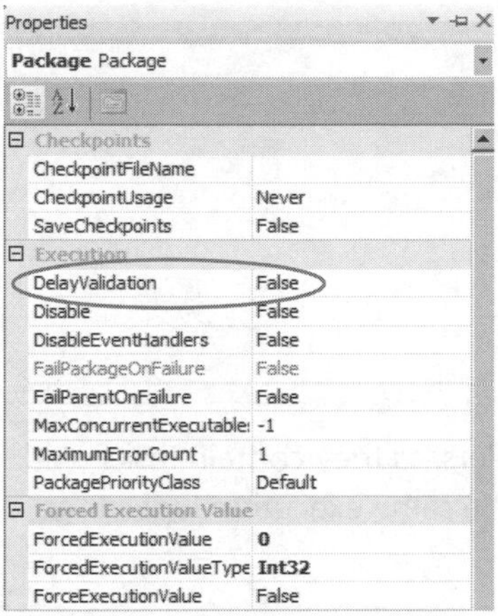

FIGURE 15-3 The *DelayValidation* property.

If *DelayValidation* is set to *True*, the task or container will not be validated until just before it is going to be run. This property should be set to *True* in situations where successful validation depends on the execution of a previous task in the Control Flow. For example, a package might contain a Data Flow task that loads data from a flat file that is copied from a remote machine using an FTP task. Because the file is created only after the FTP task is executed, the Data Flow task will fail to validate until after it runs. Setting *DelayValidation* to *True* postpones validation until after the FTP task has created the file, allowing the validation step to succeed.

Connection Manager Validation

An important performance improvement was made in SQL Server 2012 to the way connection managers are validated at design time (that is, within the SQL Server Data Tools designer). After a package has been loaded, but prior to validation, each connection manager in the package is validated separately. If a connection manager fails to establish a connection (for example, if the data source cannot be accessed), it is put in an *offline* state. When a connection manager is offline, subsequent calls to establish connections will be short-circuited and return immediately. This avoids the long delays that can occur while waiting for a connection to timeout.

Execute

The Control Flow engine is responsible for orchestrating the *executables* contained within a package. An *executable* is a package entity that exposes validate and execute methods, such as the following:

- Tasks
- Containers
  - Sequence
  - For Each Loop
  - For Loop
- Event handlers

> **Note** The package itself is a container, as are event handlers, as they contain tasks (and other containers) within them. Internally, a package has the same execution logic as a Sequence container.

An *executable* returns a *DTSExecResult* value after it is run. This value is used by the runtime to determine the flow of execution. It is possible to force this result to a specific value using the *ForceExecutionResult* property. For example, setting *ForceExecutionResult* to *Failure* on a task will cause it to fail, regardless of its actual execution result. Although there is limited use for this functionality in a production system, this can be useful when doing unit testing of your package. Table 15-2 shows a list of the possible *DTSExecResult* values.

TABLE 15-2 *DTSExecResult* enumeration values

Member	Numeric Value	Description
Success	0	The task or container succeeded.
Failure	1	The task or container failed.
Completion	2	The task or container completed, but did not indicate a success or failure status.
Canceled	3	The task or container execution was cancelled.

Compared to validation, package execution is a more dynamic process. Tasks cannot simply be run sequentially, as they can be connected by *precedence constraints* that indicate the condition(s) on which they should be run. The Control Flow engine will also make use of multiple threads during execution, allowing multiple executables to be run in parallel.

To illustrate the scheduling algorithm used by the Control Flow engine, let's take a look at a sample package Control Flow, as shown in Figure 15-4. This Control Flow has tasks that run sequentially and tasks that run in parallel. First, an Execute SQL task (Init Logs) will create initial log entries into a database. Then an FTP task (Download File) will download a data file from a remote FTP server. There are two different execution flows according to the outcome of the FTP task. If the FTP task fails, a Send

Mail task (Send Notifications) will be invoked to send a notification message to the administrator. If it succeeds, two different Data Flow tasks (Process Contacts and Process Orders) will load data from the downloaded file in parallel. Finally, another Execute SQL task (Update Auditing Table) will write auditing logs after both Data Flow tasks finish successfully.

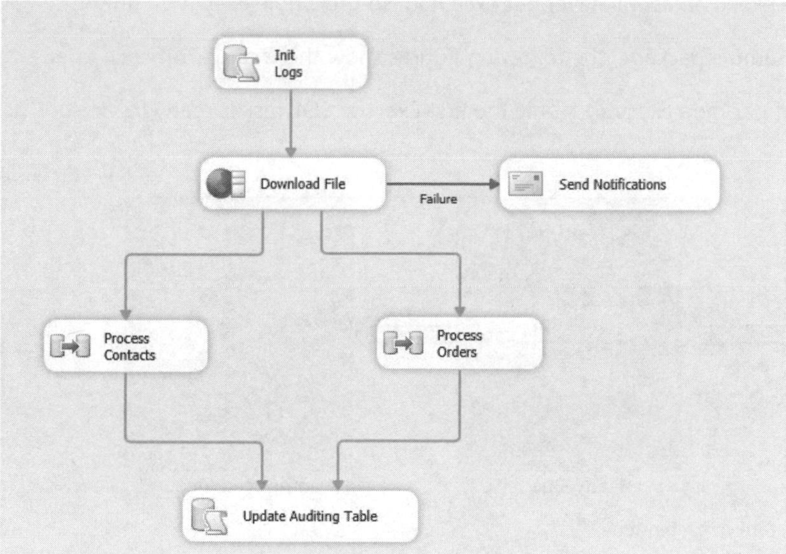

FIGURE 15-4 A sample Control Flow.

Scheduling Algorithm

The scheduling algorithm of the Control Flow engine is based on the precedence constraints and complete state of each executable. Conceptually the engine maintains three executable queues:

- **Ready queue** Executables in this queue are able to be started any time. The executable will be executed when there is an available thread.
- **Pending queue** Executables in this queue are not ready to be executed yet.
- **Completed queue** Executables in this queue have finished execution. Each executable already has its complete state.

At the beginning, all top-level executables are put into the pending queue. The other two queues are empty. Then the runtime engine will evaluate all executables in the pending queue to see whether their precedence constraints are met. If all the associated constraints are met on one executable, this executable will be put into the ready queue.

In a Control Flow there are always some initial tasks that do not have prior tasks. Internally those tasks have a precedence constraint that is always met, so those tasks will be put into the ready queue first. After they are started, the runtime engine will keep watching their status. Once an executable finishes, it brings a new complete state. Then runtime engine will reevaluate all remaining executables in the pending queue to see whether new executables become ready. If so, it puts those executables into the ready queue again.

The runtime engine continues do this work until all running executables have finished. It means there will be no new completion state changes. If there are still some executables remaining in the pending queue, those executables will never get executed, so the whole execution finishes.

For the preceding sample package, the following figures show the changes on each queue.

At the beginning of package execution, only the first Execute SQL task is ready to execute, as shown in Figure 15-5.

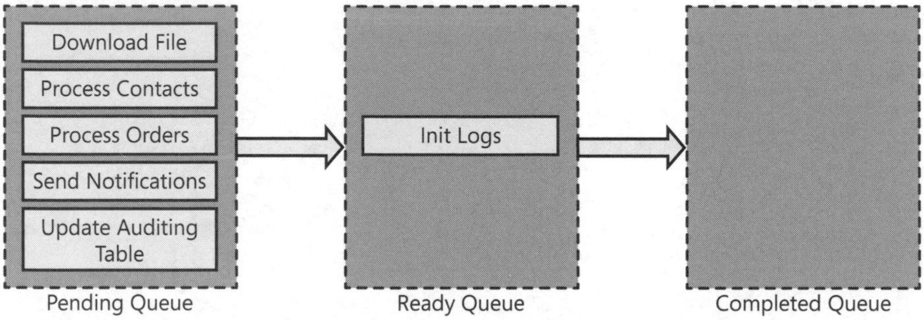

FIGURE 15-5 The initial state of each queue.

After the task finishes runtime, the engine will reevaluate all pending executables. What will happen if the Execute SQL task finished with a *failure* state? No remaining executables become ready, so the package execution stops: No tasks are executing and no new tasks become ready. That's exactly what we expected according to the Control Flow layout. If the task finished with a *success* state, the FTP task (Download File) will be moved to the ready queue because its precedence constraint has been met. The new state is shown in Figure 15-6.

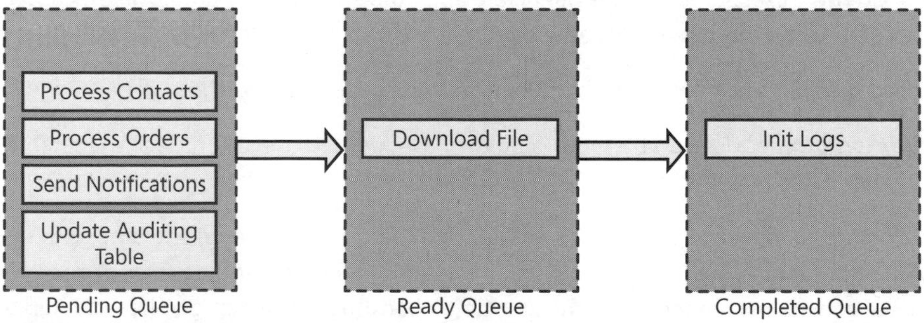

FIGURE 15-6 The queue state after the first task finishes successfully.

If the FTP task also finishes with a *success* state, the next two tasks will become ready at the same time, as shown in Figure 15-7.

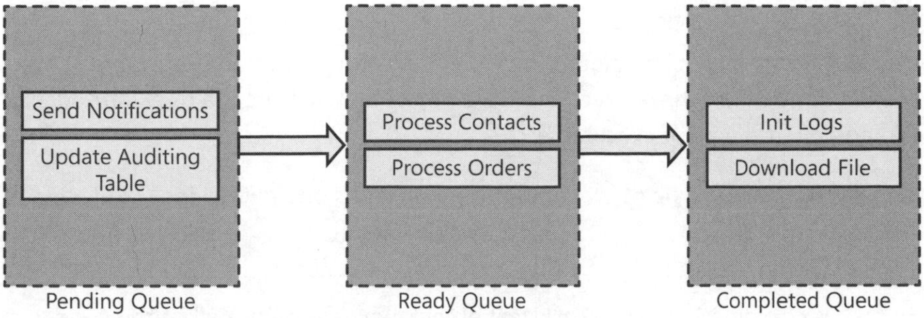

FIGURE 15-7 The queue state after the FTP task finishes successfully.

If both of them finish with a *Success* state, the last Execute SQL task, Update Auditing Table, will become ready as shown in Figure 15-8.

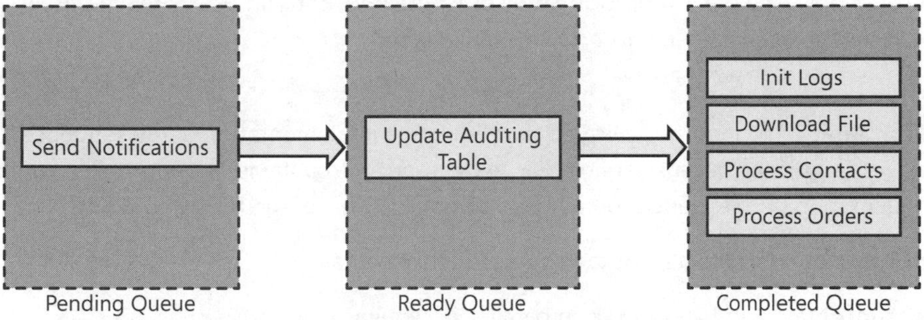

FIGURE 15-8 The queue state after data flow tasks finish successfully.

After the task finishes, the runtime engine could not find any new ready executables no matter the task succeeded or failed. The package execution thus finishes and the final state of the queues is shown in Figure 15-9.

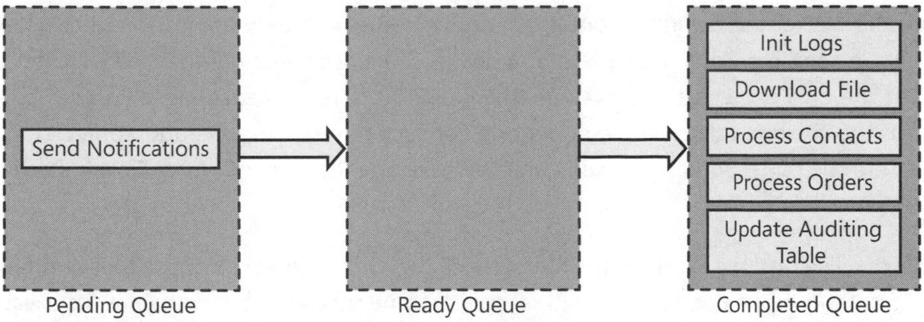

FIGURE 15-9 The queue state when the package execution finishes.

The Send Mail task is still in the pending queue because its precedence constraint was never met for every task complete state changes.

Executable Types

After the discussions of the scheduling algorithm, you have learned when an executable will be launched. The next thing is how those executables are implemented. Here is a brief introduction to the implementation of each type of executable.

Tasks A task is the most basic type of executable. It performs its operational logic and has a result status.

> **Note** Each task is contained within a *TaskHost* object, which provides all of the common functionality needed to integrate with the SSIS runtime, such as event handlers, and transaction handling logic. When a task is scheduled, the SSIS runtime is actually interacting with the *TaskHost,* but for the purposes of understanding the Control Flow engine, you can think of the task and *TaskHost* as being the same thing. For more information about the *TaskHost,* see the Integration Services Containers entry in Books Online at *http://msdn.microsoft.com/en-us/library/ms137728.aspx.*

Sequence Container The most complicated part lies in the implementation of the sequence container. It's very surprising because at first glance the sequence container is the simplest container. Why is implementation of a sequence container so complex? Think of the following points:

- There could be subcontainers or tasks in a sequence container.
- Those subcontainer or tasks can be in parallel, in sequence, or both.
- Those subcontainers or tasks could have their own event handlers.

It's easy to realize that a sequence container has the exactly same scheduling requirements with an entire package, so the sequence container shares the same scheduling algorithm with a package object. It also maintains its own executable queues and calculates the precedence constraint.

Loop Containers After the sequence container is implemented, it's easy to implement two loop containers. A loop container could be viewed as a special sequence container that will execute multiple times. The only extra cost is to evaluate the looping criteria. For example, a Foreach Loop container loads the corresponding loop enumerator. For each returned enumeration object, it will map the object to the corresponding variable and then execute the whole Control Flow in itself as a sequence container.

Event Handlers The last one is the implementation of the event handler. Because an event handler actually is a stand-alone Control Flow with access to some special system variables, its execution mechanism is also similar to the package execution mechanism. When an event is raised on a container, the container will check whether there is a corresponding event handler defined. If there is one, that event handler will be put into the ready queue as a new executable. The container continues to find matched event handlers upward until it hits the top-level container.

Threading

SSIS does not expose too many options for runtime execution scheduling. The main thing you have control of is the number of threads that can operate in parallel. The runtime engine maintains a thread pool to execute ready executables. When there are multiple executables in the ready queue, you need enough threads to execute them. It's possible to set a number quota on the thread pool. Figure 15-10 shows the property on the package object.

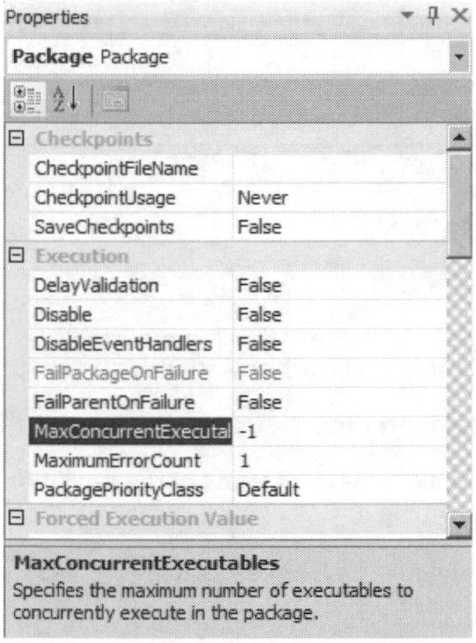

FIGURE 15-10 The *MaxConcurrentExecutables* property.

As its name suggests, this property decides the maximum concurrent executables that are allowed to run in parallel. Its default value is –1. It means the runtime engine will automatically decide the thread number based on your hardware configuration. Currently the number is set to the number of CPUs on the machine plus 2.

The default value is usually fine, but you might consider setting a new value in the following scenarios:

- **Limiting resource usage** If the machine running the SSIS package is also running other applications, you might want to lower the value to reduce the amount of system resources being used.
- **Debugging** It is sometimes difficult to debug an issue if there are multiple tasks running in parallel. Setting the *MaxConcurrentExecutables* value to 1 ensures that only one task is running at a time.
- **Low CPU usage** If you have a large number of long-running tasks that don't consume local CPU resources (such as an FTP file transfer from a slow system, or an Execute SQL task), you might want to increase the value to do more in parallel.

Events

A number of events are raised for each executable while a package is running. Events have two main side effects: The runtime will notify any loggers attached to the package that the event has occurred, and any event handlers for this event will be triggered. Events occur *synchronously;* this means that execution of the package does not continue until the event completes (that is, all logging and event handlers have finished running). Table 15-3 shows the list of standard runtime events. Executables can also register their own custom events that can be logged, but they cannot have their own event handlers.

TABLE 15-3 Control Flow events

Event Name	Description
OnError	This event is raised when an error message is posted.
OnWarning	This event is raised when a warning message is posted.
OnInformation	This event is raised every time an executable posts an information log message. Information messages typically provide details only, no errors or warnings.
OnPreExecute	This event is raised immediately before an executable runs.
OnPostExecute	This event is raised immediately after an executable runs (regardless of the execution status).
OnPreValidate	This event is raised immediately before an executable is validated. Note there is no *OnPostValidate* event.
OnProgress	This event is used by an executable to indicate its progress. This event is typically raised only by tasks that can measure their progress. When the event is raised, the task includes a numeric value indicating the percentage of completion.
OnQueryCancel	This event is raised by certain tasks that expect to perform long-running queries, such as the Execute SQL task. This event allows the package author to provide additional logic to determine if the task operation should be cancelled.
OnExecStatusChanged	This event is raised when an executable changes its execution status.
OnTaskFailed	This event is raised when a task fails. It is typically accompanied by one or more *OnError* events.
OnVariableValueChanged	This event is raised when a value of an SSIS package variable is changed.

An important thing to note about SSIS events is that they *propagate* ("bubble up") to their parent containers. For example, after an event occurs on a task, the event will also occur on the task's container and the container's container (and so on), until it gets to the package level. This means that you can capture all events occurring within a package by placing event handlers on the package itself. To prevent an event from bubbling up to its parent(s), an event handler can set its *@[System::Propagate]* variable to *False.*

> **Note** Events also propagate between packages when using the Execute Package task.

The Data Flow Engine

The Data Flow engine plays a key role in SSIS driving the execution of data flows. Earlier you were introduced to how the SSIS runtime engine drives the execution of Control Flows. You might wonder how the Data Flow engine is hooked into this work flow and how it is activated. Actually, the Data Flow task is a normal task only from the perspective of the Control Flow engine. When the Control Flow engine starts the Data Flow task according to precedence constraints, the Data Flow engine inside the task gets activated. That's it. There is nothing special on the Data Flow task. The runtime engine is even not aware of the concept of Data Flows.

> **Note** The SSIS Data Flow engine is contained within a single native COM DLL, *DTSPipeline.dll*. This functionality is also exposed through a managed .NET wrapper layer in *Microsoft.SqlServer.DTSPipelineWrap.dll*.

After the Data Flow engine is activated, it first analyzes the Data Flow layout and makes an execution plan for it. The execution plan includes the ordered instructions, such as allocating a memory block, sending the memory block to a component, or releasing the memory block. Then the engine starts the Data Flow execution following the plan strictly.

In this section, you'll learn the internal structure of the Data Flow engine and how it executes a Data Flow. Figure 15-11 shows a sample data flow that we'll use to illustrate how the Data Flow engine works.

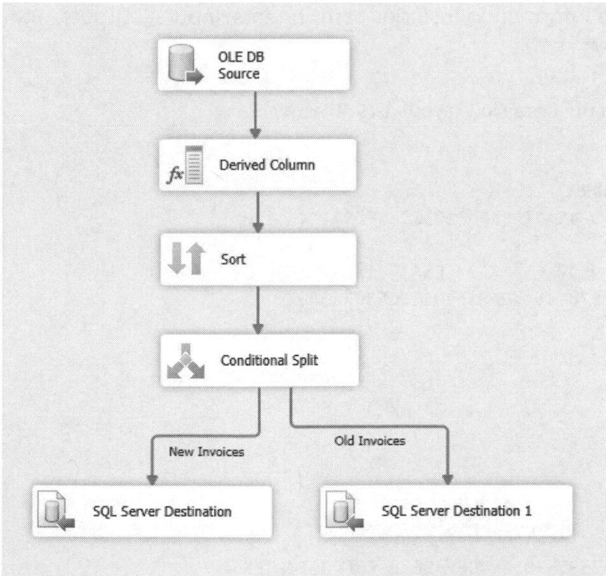

FIGURE 15-11 A sample Data Flow.

This sample Data Flow is for processing business invoices. It first uses an OLE DB Source component to load all raw records from a source database. For each record, a Derived Column component will calculate a new column to indicate whether this is a new invoice or an existing old invoice. Then all data rows are sorted by date. Finally they are divided into two flows by a Conditional Split component and inserted into two different SQL Server tables, respectively.

Overview

There are three primary parts in a Data Flow engine, including *layout management*, *buffer manager*, and *execution control*. Among those three parts, the execution control subsystem is the most complicated. It analyzes the Data Flow layout, makes the execution plan, and maintains the thread pool. The other two subsystems are relatively simple because they are just static repositories. The layout management subsystem maintains the Data Flow layout information, and the buffer manager maintains the buffer information. This section goes through these three parts briefly and then focuses on execution control.

Layout Management

The layout of a Data Flow means the internal structure or relationship among all components in this Data Flow. After users finish package designing, all information is saved to the package XML file. The Data Flow engine needs to rebuild the Data Flow layout in memory before execution. The first question is where the Data Flow layout is stored. Every SSIS task node has a subnode named *<DTS:ObjectData>* in the package XML file, where it could save some additional information for its own usage. The Data Flow task takes advantage of this feature and saves all of the Data Flow layout information under that node. The saved information includes components, inputs, outputs, and paths. Listing 15-1 shows a fragment of the XML.

LISTING 15-1 The XML fragment that stores the Data Flow layout`<DTS:Executables>`

```
  <DTS:Executable
    DTS:refId="Package\Data Flow Task"
    DTS:CreationName="{5918251B-2970-45A4-AB5F-01C3C588FE5A}"
    DTS:Description="Data Flow Task"
    DTS:DTSID="{32D39765-09B1-4662-9B07-C5AC35B75C5A}"
    DTS:ExecutableType="{5918251B-2970-45A4-AB5F-01C3C588FE5A}"
    DTS:LocaleID="-1"
    DTS:ObjectName="Data Flow Task">
    <DTS:Variables />
    <DTS:ObjectData>
      <pipeline
        version="1">
        <components>
          <component
            refId="Package\Data Flow Task\ADO NET Source"
            componentClassID="{874F7595-FB5F-40FF-96AF-FBFF8250E3EF}"
            contactInfo="Consumes data from SQL Server, OLE DB, ODBC, or Oracle, using the
corresponding .NET Framework data provider. Use a Transact-SQL statement to define the result
set. For example, extract data from SQL Server with the .NET Framework data provider for
SQL Server.;Microsoft Corporation; Microsoft SQL Server; © Microsoft Corporation; All Rights
Reserved; http://www.microsoft.com/sql/support;4"
```

```
              description="Consumes data from SQL Server, OLE DB, ODBC, or Oracle, using the
corresponding .NET Framework data provider. Use a Transact-SQL statement to define the result
set. For example, extract data from SQL Server with the .NET Framework data provider for SQL
Server."
              name="ADO NET Source"
              usesDispositions="true"
              version="4">
```

When the Data Flow task is started, the layout management subsystem will load the preceding XML fragment and reconstruct the entire Data Flow layout in memory. After this work is done, it will be able to do the following:

- Enumerate all components in current Data Flow.
- Given one input or output, determine which component it belongs to.
- List all data columns in an input or output.
- Detect cycles in the current Data Flow layout.

As you can see, the layout subsystem is only a passive repository. It doesn't include any active services or threads.

Buffer Manager

Inside a Data Flow task the data is always manipulated within a *buffer.* A buffer is a physical memory chunk that contains a collection of data rows. Each data row has an ordered list of data columns, and every data column has a given data type. A sample illustration is shown in Figure 15-12.

	Column 1	Column 2	Column 3	Column 4	Column 5	. . .	Column n
Row 1	<data>	<data>	<data>	<data>	<data>	<data>	<data>
Row 2	<data>	<data>	<data>	<data>	<data>	<data>	<data>
Row 3	<data>	<data>	<data>	<data>	<data>	<data>	<data>
. . .	<data>	<data>	<data>	<data>	<data>	<data>	<data>
Row n	<data>	<data>	<data>	<data>	<data>	<data>	<data>

FIGURE 15-12 A physical buffer.

The data cells in a buffer always have a fixed width. For instance, the cell will be 4 bytes in width if the data type is *DT_I4.* If the data type is *DT_WSTR[50],* it will be 100 bytes wide. For Binary Large Object (BLOB) data types (*DT_IMAGE, DT_TEXT, and DT_NTEXT*) the data size can vary and it's impossible to specify a fixed size for all those types of data. In this case, the BLOB data itself is not saved into the cell directly. Instead, a descriptor is put into the cell that describes the actual data location. The data itself could be saved in another memory location, or it could be stored to an external disk file if the data is too large to fit into an in-memory buffer. The location of BLOB storage files is specified by the property *BLOBTempStoragePath*. The environment variables *TMP* and *TEMP* will be used if that property is not specified by users.

> **Note** *VARCHAR(MAX)* and *NVARCHAR(MAX)* SQL Server types are treated as BLOBs, because they don't have a specific data length.

Those buffers are also called *physical buffers* because each buffer has a physical memory location. Because each buffer has a unique data type shape, the buffer manager maintains all different shapes and allocates a buffer type ID for each one. Thus the buffer manager could quickly allocate a physical buffer instance given the type ID during execution.

One or more *virtual buffers* could be defined on a physical buffer, and a virtual buffer could be based on column views or row views. Why do you need the concept of virtual buffers? A component usually needs to see only partial data in a physical buffer. It could be a subset of columns, a subset of rows, or both. For instance:

- A Derived Column component could create a new column in the physical buffer. For performance reasons, this column is actually allocated at the beginning instead of added later. The components before the Derived Column component should not see this hidden column, however, so each input has its own column view.

- A Conditional Split component will split the incoming physical buffer into several different buffers. Also for performance reasons, the pipeline engine will not physically split the buffer memory. It just uses some mark bits to indicate which component should see which rows, which presents the concept of row views. Each output will have its own row view.

Figure 15-13 illustrates the relationship between a physical buffer and its various views.

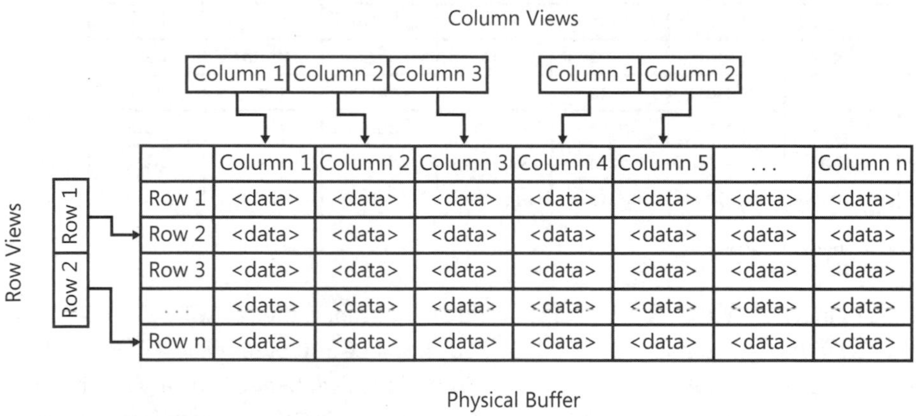

FIGURE 15-13 Row views and column views.

The buffer manager maintains all buffer-related information and serves the following typical requests from other subsystems:

- Create a new physical buffer type with a given data type.

- Create a new virtual buffer type on the given physical buffer type.

- Allocate a buffer instance according to the given buffer type.
- Release a buffer instance.
- Spool the buffer memory when the memory pressure is high.

Similar to the layout management subsystem, the buffer manager is also a passive repository. It doesn't have any active service or threads.

Execution Control

This section introduces you to the execution control subsystem, which is the most complicated of the three subsystems. To understand how execution control works, you first need to start with some basic concepts.

Component Interfaces

During the package execution phase, the pipeline engine interacts with Data Flow components through the *IDTSRuntimeComponent100* interface. This interface is defined under the *Microsoft.SqlServer.Dts.Pipeline.Wrapper* namespace and in the *Microsoft.SqlServer.DTSPipelineWrap.dll* assembly. Every Data Flow component needs to implement this interface. It's a contract between the pipeline engine and components. A clear understanding of this interface is necessary for both understanding how the pipeline engine works and writing your own Data Flow component. You can refer to MSDN (*http://msdn.microsoft.com/en-us/library/microsoft.sqlserver.dts.pipeline.wrapper.aspx*) for a detailed explanation of that interface. Here you need to pay attention to only two methods—*PrimeOutput* and *ProcessInput*. Any asynchronous component has to implement the *PrimeOutput* method. The component could be a source component or an asynchronous transformation component. If the component is a source component, this method is supposed to produce data rows and it will continue until the end of the row set. If the component is a transformation component, this method is only supposed to do some initialization work. After data rows are generated from the source component, the pipeline engine sends buffers to downstream components by calling the *ProcessInput* method on those components. They could be transformation components or destination components.

> **Note** The pipeline engine will execute *PrimeOutput* methods on all asynchronous transformation components in the current Data Flow before it starts source components, so do not block this method if you are writing a custom asynchronous transformation component. If you do, the whole Data Flow execution will be blocked.

Output Types

Chapter 2, "Understanding SSIS Concepts," includes a brief discussion on synchronous components and asynchronous components. Actually the introduction to the concept is not very detailed. Strictly speaking, there are only synchronous outputs and asynchronous outputs. Depending on the type of Data Flow components, it could have zero or more outputs. Usually we refer to a component as an asynchronous component if it contains at least one asynchronous output. Otherwise the component is a synchronous component.

An output is either synchronous to an input or not. If it's synchronous to an input, we call it a synchronous output, otherwise it is asynchronous output. Internally, an asynchronous output has its own physical buffer types, whereas a synchronous output shares the physical buffer type with its associated input.

In the package designer, you can check whether an output is associated with an input. Right-clicking the component and selecting Show Advanced Editor opens a dialog box that shows all information for that component, including component properties, inputs, outputs, and all data columns. This editor is a handy tool to help us to check some interesting knowledge about the pipeline engine. On the last tab, Input and Output Properties, you can check the output type after selecting the output in the list, where it shows whether an output is synchronous to an input. Figures 15-14 and 15-15 show two different output types in our sample Data Flow.

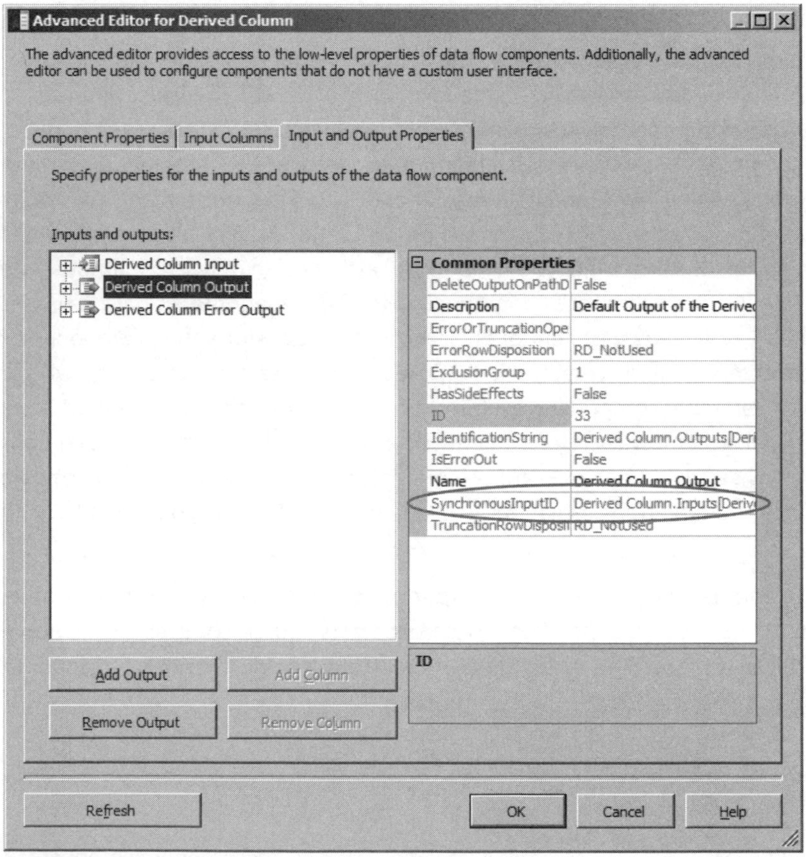

FIGURE 15-14 The output on a Derived Column transform.

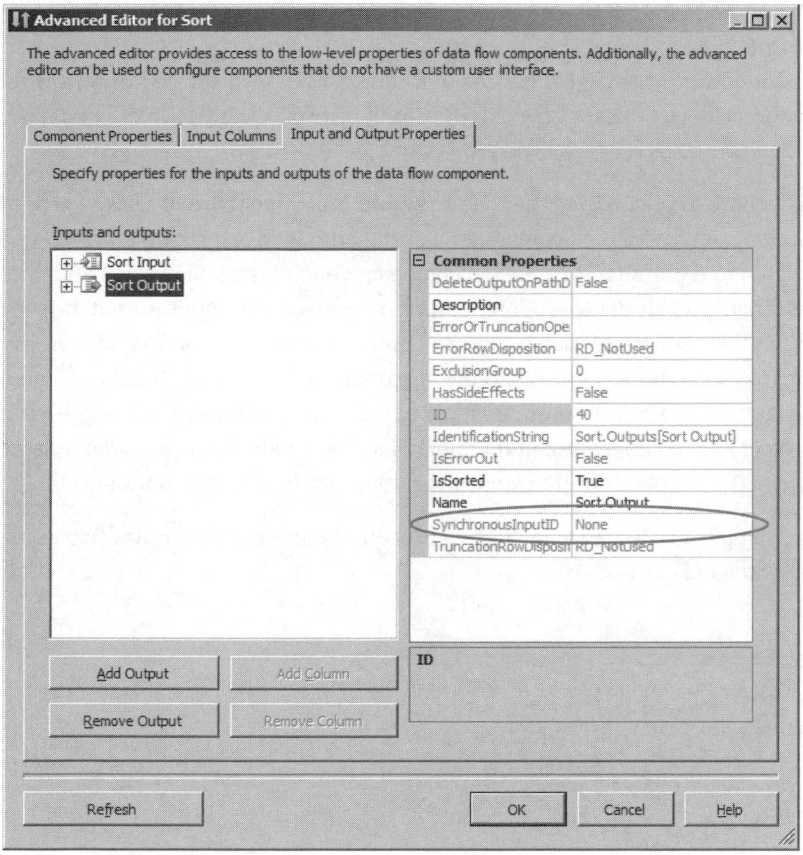

FIGURE 15-15 The output on a Sort transform.

Look at the highlighted entries in these two figures and notice they have different values. The entry on the Derived Column component shows that the output has a valid synchronous input ID, which means it's a synchronous output, whereas the corresponding entry in the Sort component shows None, which means it's an asynchronous output.

There are two points you should know. First, the output type is determined by the component writer instead of the package designer. In other words, you cannot specify whether an output is synchronous or not during package design time. Second, all outputs in a source component are asynchronous components. This is obvious because there is no input on a source component.

Execution Paths

Now that you have been introduced to the various output types, here comes the concept of an *execution path*, probably the most important concept you need to know to understand how the Data Flow engine works.

An execution path is a sequence of outputs or inputs starting from an output. Every output in the path is synchronous to the previous input, so its root node is always an asynchronous output, otherwise it should belong to another execution tree. A Data Flow instance consists of one or more execution paths. The engine does not care how many paths; it just splits the Data Flow into execution paths and performs the same steps on each execution path.

The first step in planning is to break down the Data Flow into execution paths. It's easy to identify the root of each execution path. There is a very simple rule: The number of execution paths is equal to the number of asynchronous outputs. The pipeline engine first enumerates all outputs and finds all asynchronous outputs. Then it builds the execution paths from each asynchronous output. It follows the associated path and adds the associated input. If there are outputs on that component that are synchronous to this input, it will add those outputs into the execution path, too. Then the same algorithm is performed on those outputs again. If there are multiple outputs synchronous to one single input, the execution path will be split into multiple paths at that point. Each split path is called a *subpath* and that point is called a *fork point*. The whole algorithm stops when it cannot find synchronous outputs.

For example, in the sample Data Flow there are two execution paths because it has two asynchronous outputs as highlighted in Figure 15-16.

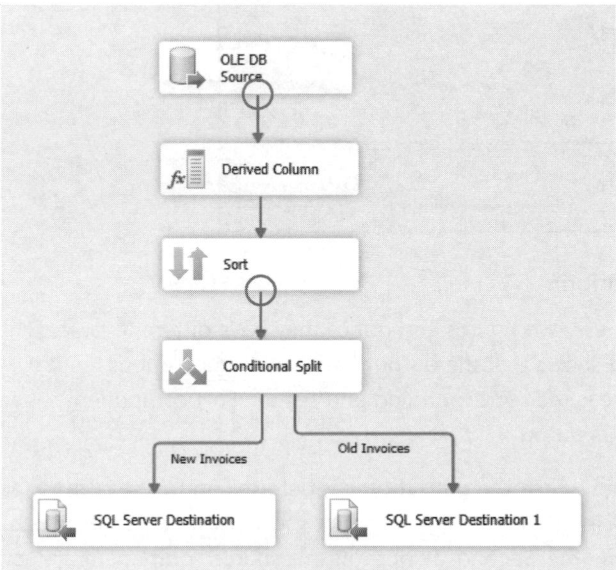

FIGURE 15-16 The execution paths of the sample Data Flow.

The first execution path starts from the output *[OLE DB Source].[Output]*, which is the first asynchronous output. Then it follows the paths to add all inputs and associated synchronous outputs. The path ends in the input *[Sort].[Input]*, where it could not find any output that is synchronous to this input. The second path starts from the output *[Sort].[Output]*, the second asynchronous output in the Data Flow. It has a fork point because the two outputs on the Conditional Split component are both synchronous to the input on that component. So at that point two subpaths will be created, and they end in input *[SQL Server Destination].[Input]* and *[SQL Server Destination1].[Input]*, respectively.

Actually you can view the execution paths of a Data Flow task in SSIS logging. The pipeline engine will print all execution paths in the logs to help diagnose if the *PipelineExecutionTrees* item is selected in the package logging options (see Figure 15-17).

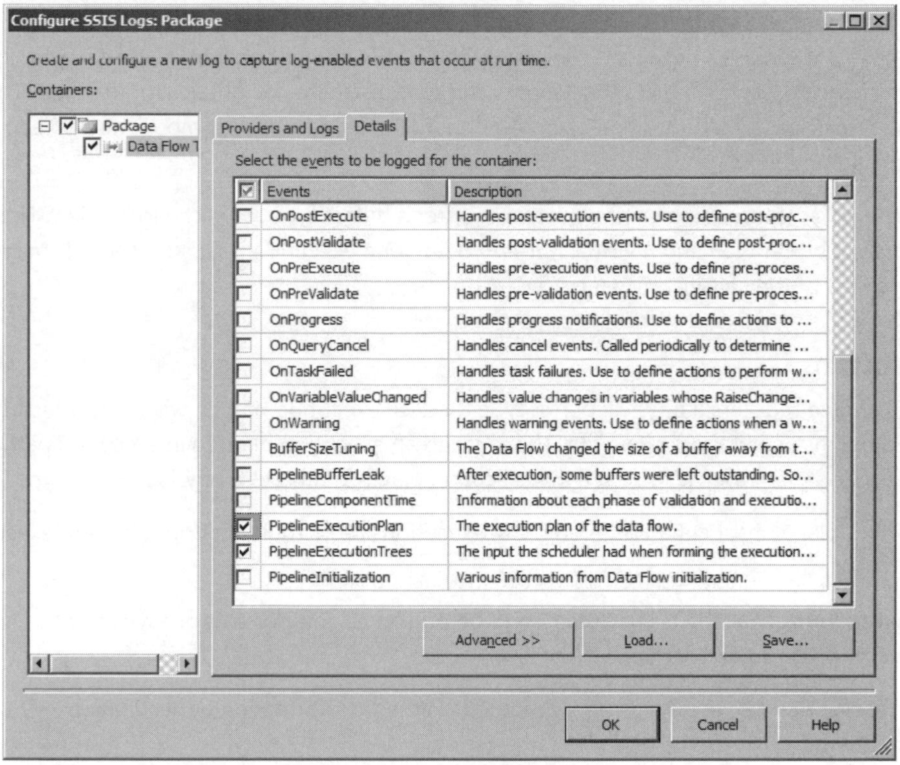

FIGURE 15-17 Configure logging options to log execution paths.

Listing 15-2 shows the generated execution paths.

LISTING 15-2 The logged execution paths

```
Begin Path 0
   OLE DB Source.Outputs[OLE DB Source Output]; OLE DB Source
   Derived Column.Inputs[Derived Column Input]; Derived Column
   Derived Column.Outputs[Derived Column Output]; Derived Column
   Sort.Inputs[Sort Input]; Sort
End Path 0Begin Path 1
   Sort.Outputs[Sort Output]; Sort
   Conditional Split.Inputs[Conditional Split Input]; Conditional Split
   Begin Subpath 0
      Conditional Split.Outputs[Old Invoices]; Conditional Split
      SQL Server Destination 1.Inputs[SQL Server Destination Input]; SQL Server Destination 1
   End Subpath 0
   Begin Subpath 1
      Conditional Split.Outputs[New Invoices]; Conditional Split
      SQL Server Destination.Inputs[SQL Server Destination Input]; SQL Server Destination
   End Subpath 1
End Path 1
```

The reason the Data Flow engine needs to identify execution paths is because it needs to register physical buffer types. Each execution path has one and only one physical buffer type. As mentioned earlier, an execution path is built from one asynchronous output. It ends before the first asynchronous output. Therefore, in the whole execution path, all the outputs are synchronous outputs. You probably still remember how a synchronous output works. It just performs in-place modifications on the buffer and does not require a new buffer. Therefore the pipeline needs only to create one physical buffer type for each execution path and all inputs and outputs share this physical buffer type. This physical buffer includes all columns that each component needs, and each component is able to see only its own columns.

To ease the work, the pipeline engine will also register a buffer type for each virtual view. There is thus one physical buffer type and *n* virtual buffer types in one execution path, and each virtual buffer type is only a part of the physical virtual buffer.

Execution Plans

The pipeline engine registers a physical buffer type for each execution path. It will check which steps need to be done inside this execution path. This is called an execution plan. Each execution path has only one execution plan. You can also see the execution plan is bound to a physical buffer type.

An execution plan consists of an ordered set of execution steps. There are four different execution steps:

- ***PrimeOutput*** Call the *PrimeOutput* method on source components or asynchronous transformation components.
- ***ProcessInput*** Call the *ProcessInput* method on the transformation or destination component.
- ***NewRowView*** Build a new virtual buffer for an output based on row view.
- ***NewExecutionItem*** Create a new execution item at the fork point. A work item is a single execution step with an associated buffer.

SSIS could also dump the whole execution plan if users select *PipelineExecutionPlan* in the package logging options. Listing 15-3 shows the execution plans for the sample Data Flow.

LISTING 15-3 The logged execution plan

```
Begin output plan
   Begin transform plan
     Call PrimeOutput on Sort
          for Sort.Outputs[Sort Output]
   End transform plan   Begin source plan
     Call PrimeOutput on OLE DB Source
          for OLE DB Source.Outputs[OLE DB Source Output]
   End source plan
End output planBegin path plan
   Begin Path Plan 0
      Call ProcessInput on Derived Column for Derived Column.Inputs[Derived Column Input]
      Create new row view for Derived Column.Outputs[Derived Column Output]
```

```
      Call ProcessInput on Sort for Sort.Inputs[Sort Input]
   End Path Plan 0   Begin Path Plan 1
      Call ProcessInput on Conditional Split for Conditional Split.Inputs[Conditional Split
Input]
      Create new execution item for subpath 0
      Create new execution item for subpath 1
      Begin Subpath Plan 0
         Create new row view for Conditional Split.Outputs[Old Invoices]
         Call ProcessInput on SQL Server Destination 1 for SQL Server Destination 1.Inputs[SQL
Server Destination Input]
      End Subpath Plan 0
      Begin Subpath Plan 1
         Create new row view for Conditional Split.Outputs[New Invoices]
         Call ProcessInput on SQL Server Destination for SQL Server Destination.Inputs[SQL
Server Destination Input]
      End Subpath Plan 1
   End Path Plan 1
End path plan
```

As we can see from this code, the pipeline engine first calls *PrimeOutput* on the two asynchronous outputs. Then there are two execution plans: path plan 0 and path plan 1 for the two execution paths, respectively. Path plan 0 is relatively simple; it just contains a linear sequence of steps on the Derived Column component and Sort component. Path plan 1 is more complex. It has two subpath plans, so it will create two execution items when the execution arrives at the fork point. Each execution item will execute different subpath plans in parallel.

Execution

Actually the work becomes relatively easy for the pipeline engine after it finishes the planning phase. Everything has been decided. In the execution phase, it just needs to execute the plan. There are basically three steps:

- Start all source components and keep producing physical buffers.
- For each physical buffer, find the associated execution plan and assign a thread to execute the plan.
- Release the physical buffer if all steps have been executed.

The pipeline engine will start all source components by calling its *PrimeOutput* method. Each source component will occupy a thread that runs the source component and produces data until it hits the last row. Then it reports an end of row set so the engine knows all data have been pulled.

The source component uses a buffer pointer to add rows. When a physical buffer is full, the pipeline engine will allocate a new physical buffer and pass a new pointer to the source component. From the perspective of source components, it looks like there is an infinite buffer, but actually it's already a different physical buffer. It's like using a basket to hold the apples falling from a tree. You switch to a new basket whenever the current basket is full.

For each generated physical buffer, the pipeline engine will look up the associated execution plan from the corresponding output and execution path. Then it needs to ensure the associated execution plan is executed on this buffer in an orderly way. To do that, it uses two data structures: the work item queue and the thread pool. Whenever there is a free thread in the thread pool, it will try to get a ready work item from the work item queue. However, the required component might be occupied by another buffer. In that case, this work item or buffer will be put into a pending queue until the required component becomes available. The whole execution stops when all existing physical buffers have been released and all source components have reported an end of row set.

Note SQL Server 2008 changed the planning and execution mechanism for the Data Flow. In SQL Server 2005, the Data Flow was limited to using a single thread per execution path. The changes made in SQL Server 2008 had a big impact on performance for existing packages, as the introduction of multiple threads per execution path allows more work to be done in parallel. SQL Server 2012 has the same Data Flow execution logic as SQL Server 2008.

Backpressure

Backpressure is an important mechanism during the Data Flow execution. Its intention is to reduce memory usage without decreasing performance. The idea is very intuitive: You don't have to load more data into memory if you already have plenty of data in memory waiting for processing.

There are two backpressure mechanisms implemented in the Data Flow engine—the basic backpressure mechanism and the enhanced backpressure mechanism. The latter is introduced in SSIS 2012.

Basic Backpressure

The basic backpressure mechanism tries to reduce memory usage when the downstream component is not as fast as the upstream component. In some cases a source component is pretty fast, for example, a source component that loads data from a local text file. If the downstream component is complex and time-consuming, there will be lots of physical buffers on the execution path waiting for it to do the data transformation.

The SSIS engine adopts a straightforward way to deal with this problem. Before a new physical buffer is allocated to a source component, the pipeline engine will check the existing physical buffer number on the target execution path. If there are already *n* physical buffers on that execution path, the engine will block the AddRow request until the buffer number becomes less than *n*. Therefore the source component will stop pulling data until the downstream components have consumed one buffer. This process is totally transparent to the source component. It only seems that the AddRow invocation calls a longer time than usual.

> **Note** In the current version, the value of *n* is set to 5. This value is based on suggestions from performance experts. It's an internal setting and cannot be configured by users.

Notice the basic backpressure mechanism works not only on source components, but it also applies to any component that has an asynchronous output. A component will fail to add rows into the output if there are already five buffers on the associated execution path. Thus the *ProcessInput* invocation on this component is blocked, which causes its upstream component to be blocked, and so on. Finally the source component will be suspended, so no new rows will be pulled into memory until the existing ones have been processed.

Enhanced Backpressure

The basic backpressure mechanism looks good enough for most scenarios. It's the only flow control mechanism in the SSIS Data Flow engine for SQL Server 2005 and SQL Server 2008.

Enhanced backpressure is an important feature introduced with SQL Server 2012. It is used to resolve the data rate mismatch issue. In many scenarios you will have two independent data sources, and then merge or merge join them in one component, as illustrated in Figure 15-18.

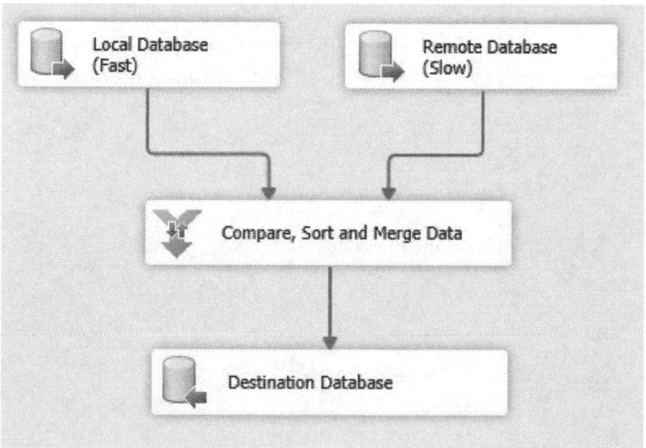

FIGURE 15-18 A Data Flow component has two inputs.

The incoming data rate of two sources could be different. In some cases the difference could be very large. For example, one source is from a local file and another one is from a remote database. The problem is that the Merge component has to cache all incoming rows before it can find the matched rows in another input. The memory usage is therefore increasing without limit until it finds the matched row. This issue can cause problems if the data volume is very large.

The solution is to allow components to temporarily suspend an input if it already has enough rows on that input. Note that suspending one input does not decrease any performance because the bottleneck is on another input. A new interface (*IDTSMultiInputComponent100*) shown in Listing 15-4 was introduced in SQL Server 2012 to handle the issue.

LISTING 15-4 The interface of IDTSMULTIINPUTCOMPONENT100

```
IDTSMultiInputComponent100
{
  void CanProcess (int[] inputIDs, [ref] bool[] canProcess);
  void GetDependencies(int inputID, [out] int[] dependentInputIDs);
 }
```

There are two methods in this interface. The first method, *CanProcess,* returns the status of each input on this component. If the method returns *false* for one input, it means that input has been suspended and is not intended to accept new buffers for now. At the beginning of execution, the pipeline engine will check each component to see whether it has implemented that interface. If a component implements the interface, the pipeline engine will call the method *CanProcess* before any *ProcessInput* invocation (in other words, sending a buffer to that input). The buffer will not be sent to the input until the input is resumed.

It looks like a simple and reliable mechanism to resolve the problem, but it could cause some unexpected problems (see Figure 15-19).

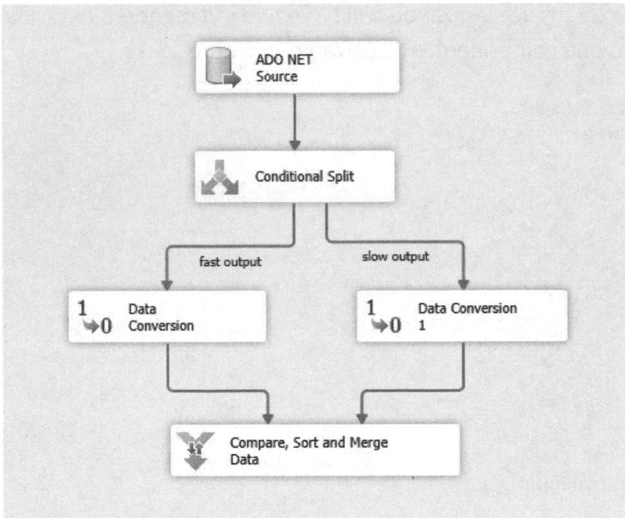

FIGURE 15-19 A deadlock example.

In Figure 15-19, the incoming data streams are divided into two streams by a Conditional Split component. Based on the data characteristics, the left stream might be much faster than the right stream. The two streams are synchronized by a Merge component after some data conversions. Because the left stream is faster than the right stream, the Merge component needs to suspend the left input and expects more buffers on the right input. Because the Conditional Split component is a synchronous component, the left input and right input are in the same execution path. After the buffers on the left path number greater than five, the Conditional Split component will be blocked by the basic backpressure mechanism. Now we have a very interesting deadlock situation:

1. To resume the left input, you need more buffers on the right input.
2. To get more buffers on the right input, you need to unblock the Conditional Split component.
3. To unblock the Conditional Split component, you need to resume the left input on the Merge component to consume the existing buffers.

Obviously deadlocks are not allowed in Data Flow execution. To handle the situation, the pipeline engine adopts a complex algorithm to detect and fix such deadlocks. Essentially it maintains a global dependency graph and monitors the blocking information before adding buffers into an execution path. In the example scenario, it will smartly unblock the Conditional Split component temporarily. In other words, in a short time it will override the basic backpressure mechanism and allow more than five physical buffers on the same execution path.

To do that, though, it needs the component to provide the dependency information among all of its inputs. That's why another method, *GetDependencies,* is needed in the *IDTSMultipleInputComponent100* interface. The method returns a dependent inputs list for each different input, and the list can vary depending on the data received. The pipeline engine will call this method to update the dependency graph every time it sends a buffer to an input. Also, when the engine detects possible deadlocks, it will print a warning message to remind you, so you can change the layout if it's possible.

Currently among all the built-in Data Flow components, only the Merge and Merge Join components implement the *IDTSMultiInputComponent100* interface. If you are going to develop a custom component that has multiple inputs, you need to consider whether there are synchronization issues among your multiple inputs. If so, you could implement the *IDTSMultiInputComponent100* interface and leverage the enhanced backpressure mechanism to ensure the memory usage is under control.

Engine Tuning

This section introduces some Data Flow engine properties and practices you can utilize when you try to tune the Data Flow performance.

Buffer Size

There are two properties that decide how many rows a physical buffer should contain: *DefaultBufferMaxRows* and *DefaultBufferSize*. Those two properties have the default values of 10,000 (rows) and 10,485,760 bytes (10 MB), respectively. In other words, one physical buffer could contain either 10,000 rows or 10 MB of data, whichever is less.

The buffer size affects execution efficiency because most engine operations are executed buffer by buffer. There will be many small buffers if the value is too small, which will decrease performance. Usually getting more rows into one buffer will benefit performance, but the risk of memory allocation failure will increase if the value is too large. In that case, some buffers will be written out to disk and that will greatly reduce performance. Also, internally, the SSIS Data Flow engine has a threshold of 100M and no buffer will exceed that size.

You can turn on the *BufferSizeTuning* logging item on the Data Flow task. This log entry will provide you some additional information if the pipeline engine adjusted the buffer size during execution.

EngineThreads

The *EngineThreads* property determines how many threads the pipeline engine should use. Obviously the value should not be too small, otherwise your CPU cores will not be fully utilized. More threads does not always mean better performance, however, because there will be more context switching on the CPU. In SSIS 2012 the default value is set to 10.

You can change the value depending on your hardware configuration or your special requirements. However, the pipeline engine only takes the value as a suggestion. It does not guarantee the value will be adopted if it is too small. The reason is that the pipeline needs enough threads to make sure there are no deadlocks in the execution.

For instance, there are *n* source components in your Data Flow and you set the property value to *n*. From the previous discussion you know that each source component occupies a dedicated thread during the execution, so there will be no other threads to serve downstream components. As a result, the produced buffers will never get a chance to be consumed. Finally, the source components will be blocked by our backpressure mechanism. It's a deadlock if there are no new threads.

RunInOptimizedMode

This property is set to *true* by default. It determines whether the pipeline engine should trim unused components during the planning stage. If the output of a component is not referenced by downstream components and the corresponding input is not marked as *hasSideEffect*, the pipeline will regard it as an unused component.

If input or output has side effects, that means it could do some extra work besides the normal data reading or writing. For instance, an input could update some variables in the background before it starts processing data. Therefore the pipeline engine should never try to trim the component out based only on the Data Flow topology. Whether an input or output has side effects is decided by the component author. For example, the input of a Derived Column component does not have side effects. In Figure 15-20, the Derived Column component will be trimmed if the property is set to *true*.

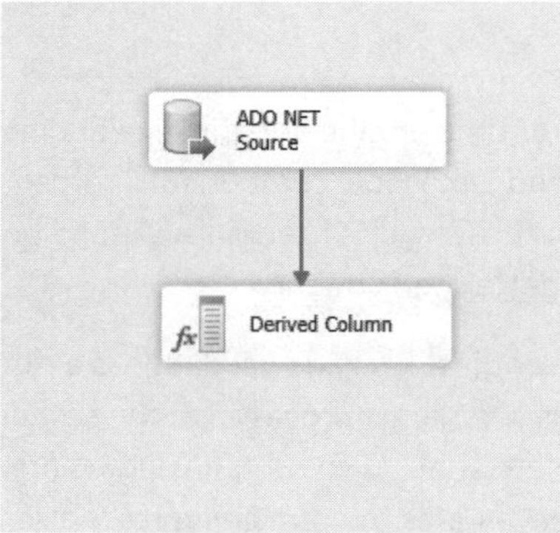

FIGURE 15-20 An unused Data Flow component.

If your package has unused components, you will notice the Data Flow behave differently between running inside the package designer and running by dtexec.exe because the pipeline engine never trims Data Flows if you debug the package inside the package designer. In other words, the property is always taken as false in the designer environment to help you do the debugging. To make sure the components are executed even with dtexec.exe, set the property to *false*.

Split Complex Components

The SSIS pipeline engine always calls the *ProcessInput* method of components in a single-thread manner. The invocations are sequential for components with one input. If a component has multiple inputs, the pipeline engine will lock the component when it calls *ProcessInput* on one of those inputs. When there are buffers arriving at other inputs, they have to wait until the previous *ProcessInput* invocation finishes and releases the component. In this way, component development is greatly simplified. Otherwise the component author has to ensure the implementation of the *ProcessInput* method is reentrant.

In some cases, though, this approach could decrease performance. For example, suppose you have a Derived Column component that has numerous complex conversions. Due to the single-threaded nature, those conversions will only be executed by one thread at any time. Because those conversions are usually CPU-bound, obviously the performance could be better if they are executed with multiple threads.

Some smart users found a way to optimize the scenario. They split the component into multiple Derived Column components, and each component only performs part of the conversions. As you know, the components inside an execution path can be executed in parallel. In this way those conversions are executed by multiple threads!

Summary

This chapter introduced the internal architecture of the SSIS runtime engine and pipeline engine. You learned how those two engines drive the execution of tasks and Data Flow components, respectively. You also learned some important properties and practices on those two SSIS engines. A solid understanding of SSIS engines will help you design packages with better performance.

An SSIS package is validated and executed by the runtime engine. Package validation is a simple process based on the package hierarchy. Package execution is a dynamic process and the scheduling algorithm is based on precedence constraints and task complete states. The runtime engine first starts those tasks that don't have precedence constraints. It then reevaluates the remaining tasks after each task finishes to see if there are any new tasks that have become ready. It repeats this behavior until no task is in execution and no new task is ready.

When a Data Flow task is started by the runtime engine, the Data Flow engine embedded in the task gets kicked in. It rebuilds the Data Flow layout from the package XML file, and then plans the execution of the Data Flow. First it breaks down the Data Flow into different execution paths. For each execution path it will register a physical buffer type and some virtual buffer types. Then for each physical buffer type the pipeline engine will create an execution step list. During runtime, it starts all source components and processes the generated buffers according to the associated steps list. The execution ends when all physical buffers have been consumed and no more new buffers are generated from source components.

CHAPTER 16

SSIS Catalog Deep Dive

In This Chapter

SSIS Catalog Deep Dive

SSIS 2012 introduces new capabilities that make it easier to deploy, configure, and manage SSIS packages in the enterprise. SSIS packages are deployed to the SSIS Catalog. On each SQL Server instance with SSIS installed, this corresponds to the user database, called SSISDB. SSISDB consists of a set of internal and public stored procedures (both T-SQL and CLR stored procedures), scalar-value functions and table-value functions (TVFs). Collectively, these provide the capabilities for SSIS 2012.

SSIS 2012 uses SQLCLR functionality. It requires CLR to be enabled on the SQL Server instance before you start using SSIS 2012. This can be done when you first create the SSIS catalog or using T-SQL. In addition, during SSIS Catalog creation, you can enable the autoexecution of SSIS startup procedures. The SSIS startup procedures are executed whenever the SQL Server instance is started. In this chapter, you'll learn the role of the SSIS startup procedure.

Creating the SSIS Catalog

To start using SSIS 2012, you will need to make use of SQL Server Management Studio to create the SSIS Catalog. You can also make use of a SQL Server PowerShell script to create the catalog. When the SSIS Catalog is first created, you will need to perform the following steps:

1. Enable SQLCLR on the SQL Server instance.

2. Provide a password for the database master key. The password is used to encrypt the master key in the database, and must adhere to Windows password policy requirements for the computer on which SQL Server is installed.

3. Enable the SSIS startup stored procedure to autoexecute (optional). This is discussed in more detail later in this chapter.

After the SSIS Catalog is created, you should back up the database master key to a file, and store the backup file in a secure location. Figure 16-1 shows how you can create the SSIS Catalog on a new SQL Server instance. After the SSIS Catalog is created, you will see a new user database called SSISDB, which is the physical instantiation of the SSIS Catalog. As SSISDB is a user database, a database administrator can manage SSISDB, similar to how other SQL Server databases are managed.

> **Note** In versions earlier than SSIS 2012, stored procedures corresponding to SSIS functionalities can be found in the msdb database. These stored procedures are mainly used by SSIS tools, and are not directly invoked by the user.

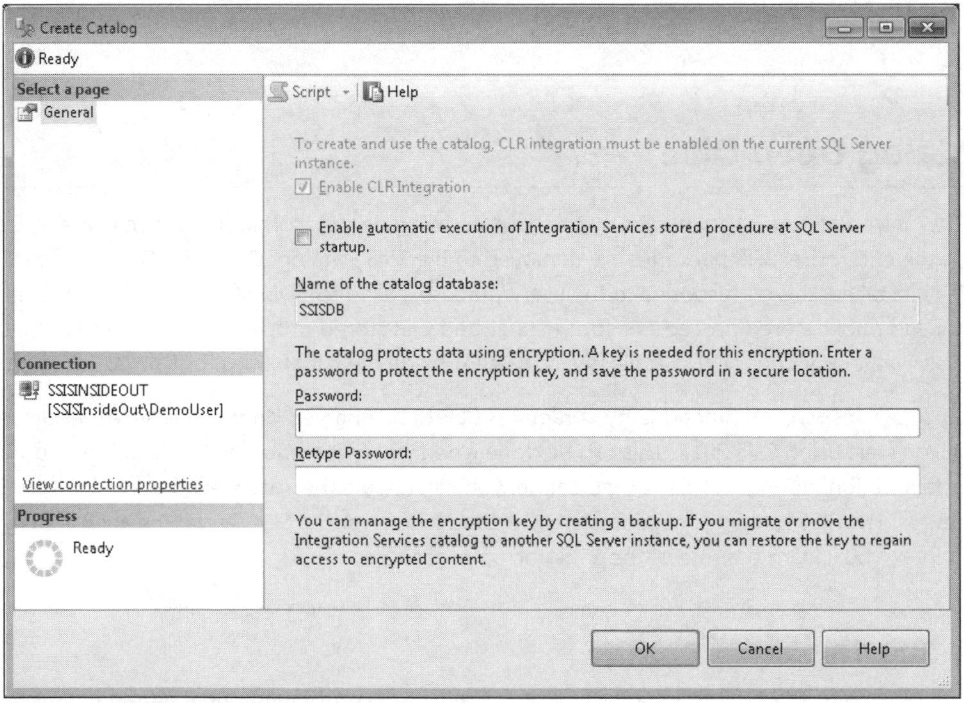

FIGURE 16-1 SSIS Catalog creation.

Unit of Deployment to the SSIS Catalog

The unit of deployment to the SSIS Catalog is the Integration Services Project Deployment file (with an .ispac extension). Each .ispac file consists of SSIS packages and a manifest file. The manifest contains the metadata for all the packages and the SSIS project. When the .ispac file is deployed to the SSIS Catalog, the binary for the file is encrypted and stored in internal SSISDB tables. In addition, the content of the manifest file is extracted and stored in internal SSISDB tables, too. To ensure that the sensitive content in the SSIS Catalog is protected, that content is encrypted before being stored in SSISDB. To perform encryption and decryption, you need to provide a database master key during SSIS Catalog creation. Figure 16-2 shows the logical flow of what happens when a package is deployed. In addition, the data stored in the SSIS Catalog is protected by row-level security. When you access the SSIS Catalog, you will see the SSIS securables that you have been granted the permission to access. Members of sysadmin and ssis_admin are able to access all securables.

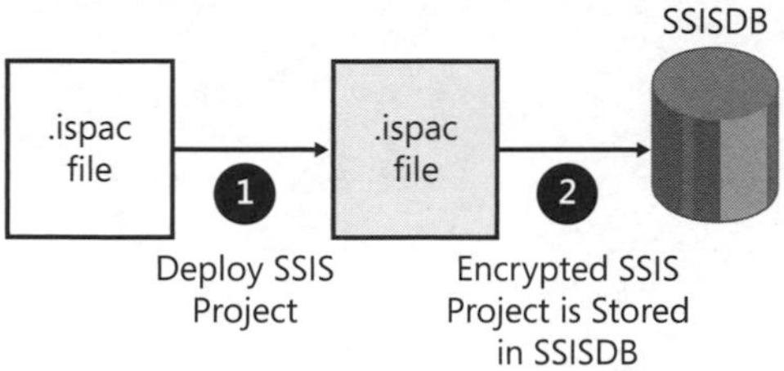

FIGURE 16-2 Deployment of an SSIS project.

In each of the folders in the SSIS Catalog, a project is uniquely identified by the project name. During deployment of a project, the project metadata is extracted and stored in the SSIS Catalog. This includes the parameters of the project and the packages in the project. In addition, the SSIS Catalog maintains multiple versions of the project internally. This allows you to restore the project to a previous known good state when it is required. The number of project versions that are maintained per project depends on the value of the SSIS Catalog property *MAX_PROJECT_VERSIONS*. A SQL Agent job is responsible for removing the older versions of the project. This is covered later in this chapter.

What Is Inside SSISDB?

SSIS 2012 uses stored procedures, TVFs, and scalar-value functions in SSISDB to provide SSIS capabilities. These capabilities include deployment, configuration, and management of SSIS objects that are in SSISDB. In addition, the stored procedures provide the ability for you to validate and start and stop SSIS package executions. Information for the SSIS objects is exposed through a set of views. Figures 16-3 and 16-4 show the stored procedures and views that are available in SSISDB.

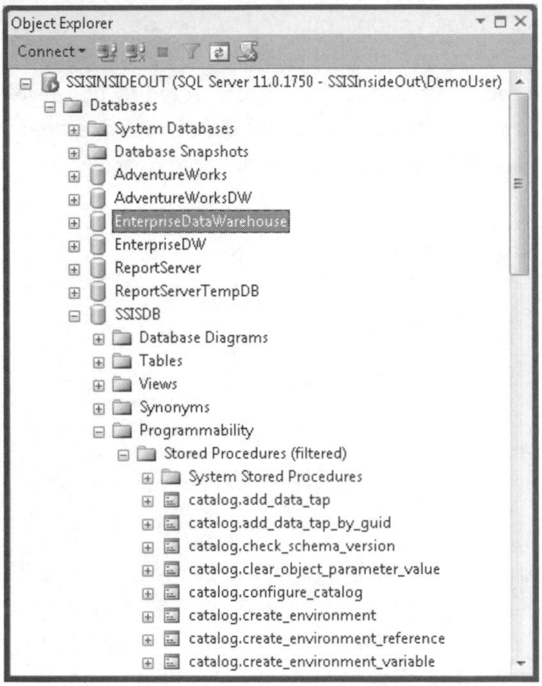

FIGURE 16-3 SSIS stored procedures in SSISDB.

Note As you explore SSISDB, you will notice that SSISDB objects (stored procedures, TVFs, scalar-value functions, tables, and views) belong to either the *internal* or the *catalog* schema. The *internal* schema is used by SSIS internally, and should not be invoked directly. The *catalog* schema provides the publicly accessible SSIS functionalities. Documentation for the public views can be found at *http://msdn.microsoft.com/en-us/library/ff878135(v=sql.110).aspx*, and documentation for the public stored procedures and functions can be found at *http://msdn.microsoft.com/en-us/library/ ff878099(v=sql.110).aspx.*

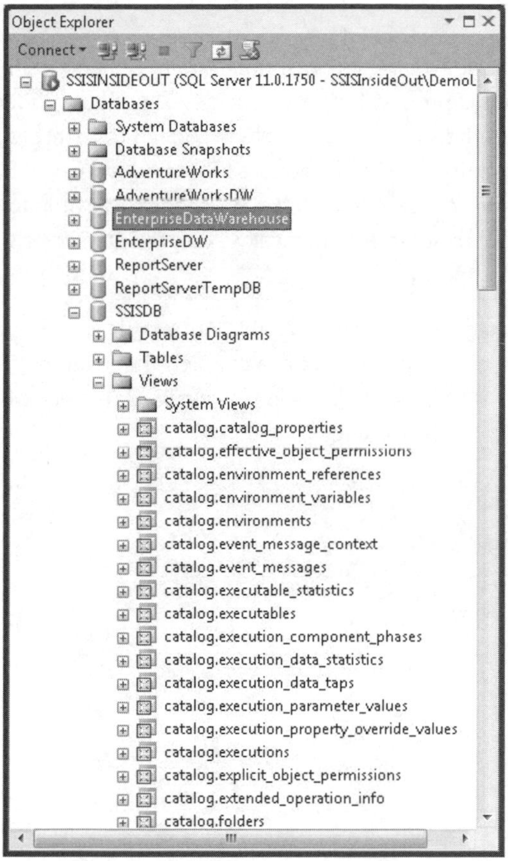

FIGURE 16-4 SSIS public views in SSISDB.

Access to the stored procedures, functions, and views are provisioned using SQL Server security statements. After the SSIS Catalog has been created, you can add database users to the SSISDB to provision these users to use SSIS. You can also designate some of these users as members of the SSISDB database role *ssis_admin* to allow them to manage the SSIS Catalog.

See Also *Chapter 10, "Configuration in SSIS," delves into the details of SSIS Catalog security, and shows how you can use it to manage access to the different SSIS securables in SSISDB.*

Many SSIS operations, such as deployment, validation, and execution, create an external process (called ISServerExec) in the context of the caller of the stored procedure. This requires a Windows authenticated user to create this external process successfully. Consequently, most of the stored procedures and functions in SSISDB require a SQL Server login that uses Windows Authentication. If you invoke the stored procedures or functions using a login that uses SQL Server Authentication, you will see the error message given in Listing 16-1.

LISTING 16-1 Error message shown when using a SQL Server authenticated login

```
The operation cannot be started by an account that uses SQL Server Authentication. Start the
operation with an account that uses Windows Authentication.
```

SQL Server Instance Starts Up

The SQL Server instance where SSIS is installed might experience downtime due to restart or shutdown of the server. As SSIS 2012 relies on an external process for SSIS package execution, sudden downtime for the SQL Server instance might cause the state of operations in SSISDB to revert to an earlier state. For example, an SSIS package execution might be shown as Running when the SQL Server instance is shut down. After the SQL Server instance is restarted, SSIS needs to be able to resolve this earlier state. SSIS relies on SQL Server capability to automatically execute SQL Server stored procedures at startup and help perform cleanup of the state.

During the creation of the SSIS Catalog, you are given the option Enable Automatic Execution Of Integration Services Stored Procedure At SQL Server Startup. If you have enabled that option, the Integration Services stored procedure, called *sp_ssis_startup*, which is in the master database, will be executed. Figure 16-5 shows the *sp_ssis_startup* stored procedure.

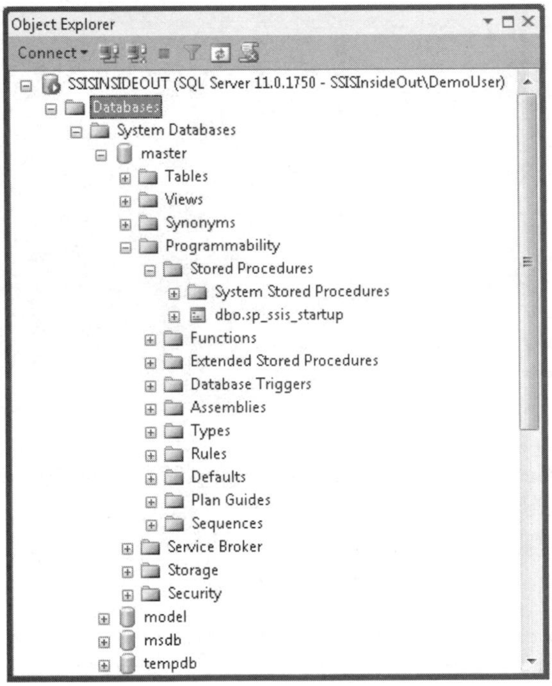

FIGURE 16-5 sp_ssis_startup stored procedure.

During execution, the *sp_ssis_startup* stored procedure calls the *catalog.startup* stored procedure in SSSIDB, which performs the following functions:

- For all running operations, *catalog.startup* checks whether the corresponding process with the relevant process identifier exists. If the corresponding process does not exist, the state of the operation is marked as unexpected termination (with a value of 6).

- This stored procedure cleans up intermediate project data. Deployment of SSIS projects is handled by the *ISServerExec* process. A deployment might be in progress the SQL Server instance goes down. Consequently, the intermediate project data needs to be cleaned up because it is no longer in use.

> **Note** In a strict production environment, where IT policies do not allow the enabling of automatic execution of stored procedures at SQL Server startup, the database administrator might not enable this option during SSIS Catalog creation. If it has been enabled earlier, and needs to be disabled, refer to *http://msdn.microsoft.com/en-us/library/ms189915(v=sql.110).aspx* on how you can disable the automatic execution of the SSIS stored procedure.

> **Tip** You can run *catalog.startup* directly, without waiting for the next SQL Server startup. In addition, you can also schedule the execution of *catalog.startup* using a SQL Server Agent job.

To check whether the SSIS startup stored procedure is executed at SQL Server startup, you can use the SSIS All Operation report, following these steps:

1. Under Integration Services Catalogs, right-click the SSISDB node.
2. Choose All Reports, then select All Operations.

Figure 16-6 shows an example of the All Operations report. From the report, you can see the rows where the operation type is Server Start Up.

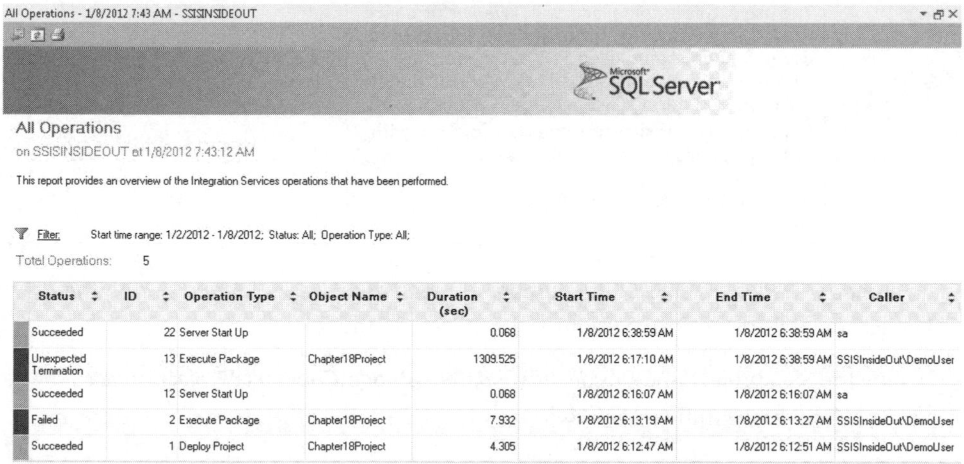

Status	ID	Operation Type	Object Name	Duration (sec)	Start Time	End Time	Caller
Succeeded	22	Server Start Up		0.068	1/8/2012 6:38:59 AM	1/8/2012 6:38:59 AM	sa
Unexpected Termination	13	Execute Package	Chapter18Project	1309.525	1/8/2012 6:17:10 AM	1/8/2012 6:38:59 AM	SSISInsideOut\DemoUser
Succeeded	12	Server Start Up		0.068	1/8/2012 6:16:07 AM	1/8/2012 6:16:07 AM	sa
Failed	2	Execute Package	Chapter18Project	7.932	1/8/2012 6:13:19 AM	1/8/2012 6:13:27 AM	SSISInsideOut\DemoUser
Succeeded	1	Deploy Project	Chapter18Project	4.305	1/8/2012 6:12:47 AM	1/8/2012 6:12:51 AM	SSISInsideOut\DemoUser

FIGURE 16-6 All Operations report and Server Start Up.

SSIS Catalog and Logging Levels

SSIS 2012 introduces new capabilities that logs information produced during SSIS package executions to the SSIS Catalog. The amount of execution information that is logged is determined by the logging level of the execution. The default logging level for the SSIS catalog is determined by the SSIS Catalog property *SERVER_LOGGING_LEVEL*. During SSIS package executions, if the logging level is not specified, the server logging level is used. Table 16-1 shows the logging levels that are supported in SSIS 2012, and the common events that are captured.

See Also *Chapter 14, "SSIS Reports," shows how you can set the SSIS Catalog properties.*

TABLE 16-1 SSIS 2012 logging levels

Logging level	Description	SSIS events logged
None	No SSIS events are logged to the SSIS Catalog. High-level information for the execution is captured in *catalog.excecutions* and *catalog.executable_statistics.*	None
Basic (Default)	This logging level introduces minimal performance impact on the SSIS package execution. A set of SSIS events that are useful for troubleshooting common SSIS package execution failures is logged to the SSIS Catalog.	*OnError, OnInformation, OnPostExecute, OnPostValidate, OnPreExecute, OnPreValidate, OnWarning*
Performance	This logging level introduces minimal performance impact on the SSIS package execution. A minimal set of SSIS events is logged to the SSIS Catalog. Performance information is logged to *catalog.[execution_component_phases*	*OnError, OnWarning*
Verbose	This logging level logs all the events that are produced during SSIS package execution. The use of this logging level will have performance impact on the package execution and should be useful for debugging deep SSIS package issues where you need to analyze all the SSIS events that are produced during SSIS package execution. Conceptually, it is similar to the /ConsoleLog (without any options specified) option used in dtexec. Performance information is logged to *catalog.[execution_component_phases]*	All SSIS events are logged

To gain a deeper understanding of the number of messages that are logged during the execution of an SSIS package and the performance impact, you can do the following:

1. Deploy the SSIS project in *C:\InsideOut\Chapter 16\code\Chapter18Project.ispac* to the *SSISInsideOut* folder in the SSIS Catalog.
2. Run the SSIS package "0. PrepData.dtsx" to set up the database and files.

> **Note** This requires the use of the AdventureWorksDW2012 database. To start the preparation, download the AdventureWorksDW2012 database from *http://msftdbprodsamples.codeplex.com/releases/view/55330*, and attach it to a SQL Server instance.

3. Run the SSIS package "2.MasterPackage.dtsx" using the four different logging levels: None, Basic, Performance, and Verbose.
4. Compare the number of messages that are logged and the execution times.

Figure 16-7 shows the number of messages that are logged to the SSIS Catalog when the "2.MasterPackage.dtsx" package is executed using the different logging levels. Specifically, the messages are logged to *catalog.event_messages*. Depending on the complexity of the SSIS package that is run, the execution duration for an SSIS package that is executed using the Verbose logging level can be 1.5 times or more. When the logging level is set to None, no SSIS events are logged to *catalog.event_messages*.

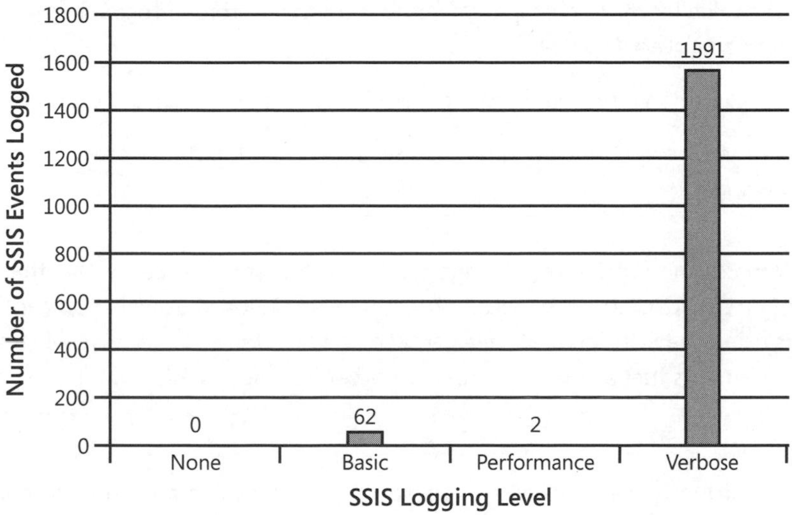

FIGURE 16-7 Number of SSIS events that are logged (different logging levels).

Understanding the SSIS Package Execution Life Cycle

SSIS 2012 provides powerful new capabilities for managing the entire life cycle for execution of SSIS packages. During SSIS package executions, an execution log is automatically written back to SSISDB. The amount of information that is captured in the log depends on the logging level that is set by the user for the SSIS Catalog or for the specific execution. The execution log provides rich information for troubleshooting issues that can occur during SSIS package executions.

An SSIS package is executed on the SQL Server instance where the SSIS Catalog is provisioned. When you use SQL Server Management Studio to connect to the SQL Server instance and use the SQL Server Management Studio user interface to start SSIS package execution, the SSIS package is executed on the remote SQL Server instance. Similarly, if you make use of T-SQL to start package execution, it all happens on the machine where the SQL Server instance is provisioned. In contrast, when you execute a package in earlier versions of SSIS (SSIS 2005, SSIS 2008, and SSIS 2008 R2), the SSIS package execution happens locally on the machine where dtexec is invoked.

In SSIS 2012, the following steps are invoked when you start the execution of an SSIS package:

1. An SSIS package execution is created using the stored procedure *catalog.create_execution*. A unique execution identifier (ID) is returned after the SSIS execution is created. When the execution is created, a corresponding set of certificate and symmetric keys is created and managed by SSIS. This certificate and symmetric key pair is used when encrypting the sensitive values that are logged during SSIS execution.
2. (Optional) Set the parameters for the execution using the stored procedure *catalog.set_execution_parameter_value*.
3. (Optional) Set the value for the SSIS property overrides using the stored procedure *set_execution_property_override_value*.
4. The SSIS package execution is started using the stored procedure *catalog.start_execution*.
5. During SSIS package execution, you can stop the execution using the stored procedure *catalog.stop_operation*.

> **Tip** When you use the SQL Server Management Studio user interface to start the execution of an SSIS package, the stored procedures are invoked as well. You can observe this using the SQL Server Profiler or SQL Server extended events to observe the T-SQL statements that are sent to the SQL Server instance.

> **Note** You use property overrides when you want to set the value for a specific component property in the package. When specifying the property override, you specify the *property_path*. The property path is similar to the paths that are defined in an SSIS configuration file. This is useful when the relevant set of parameters that have been defined during the design of the SSIS package does not include the property that you want to set.

When an SSIS package execution is started, an external process, called *ISServerExec*, is created in the context of the user who started the package execution. *ISServerExec* is used as the host for the SSIS package execution. The process identifier for the external process is logged in *catalog.executions*. During SSIS package execution, the use of Execute Package tasks within the parent package causes execution of child packages. SSIS 2012 tracks the parent package and the child package using a single execution ID.

> **Tip** The amount of physical and virtual memory that is available when the process started is logged in SSISDB. This allows you to determine the amount of resources available when the SSIS package execution started.

When the external process is started, it loads the project (and all the packages in the project) from SSISDB into memory. When the project is loaded, the execution remains in a pending state. If the package specified uses SSIS configurations, the SSIS configurations that are defined are applied when the package is loaded. After the package has been successfully loaded, each of the parameters is applied to the package. When the SSIS package starts execution, the execution is in a running state.

After the SSIS package starts execution, it continuously writes the execution log back into SSISDB. The number of SSIS events that are logged depends on the logging level that is used. During SSIS package execution, if the *ISServerExec* process is unable to connect to the SQL Server instance to insert the execution log entries, the process writes a message to the Windows Application event log and terminates gracefully.

Figure 16-8 shows the logical flow for SSIS package execution.

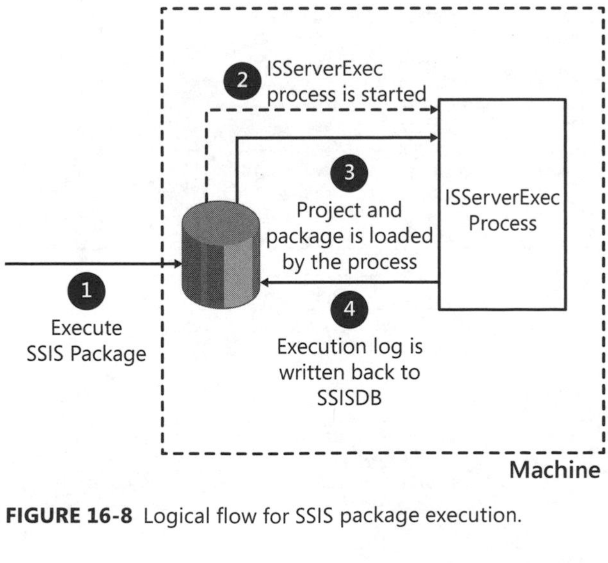

FIGURE 16-8 Logical flow for SSIS package execution.

Stopping SSIS Package Executions

To stop SSIS package execution, you can invoke the stored procedure *catalog.stop_operation*, and provide the execution identifier. As the *catalog.stop_operation* can be invoked by multiple users concurrently, the first invocation of *catalog.stop_operation* causes the state to be set to Stopping (with a value of 8). Subsequent invocation of *catalog.stop_operation* on the same execution will result in and error message indicating that the Integration Services server cannot stop the operation because it is already in the Stopping state. When the SSIS package execution is stopped, the *ISServerExec* process is stopped, and the state of the execution becomes Canceled (with a value of 3).

Using the Windows Application Event Log

When the SSIS package is executed and the SQL Server instance is shut down unexpectedly or restarted, it will cause the external process that is executing the SSIS package to terminate, because it is unable to write the execution log back to the SSISDB database. An error message is written to the Windows Application event log. You can view this using the Windows Event Viewer. Figure 16-9 shows the application event that is logged, and Figure 16-10 shows the detail of the error message.

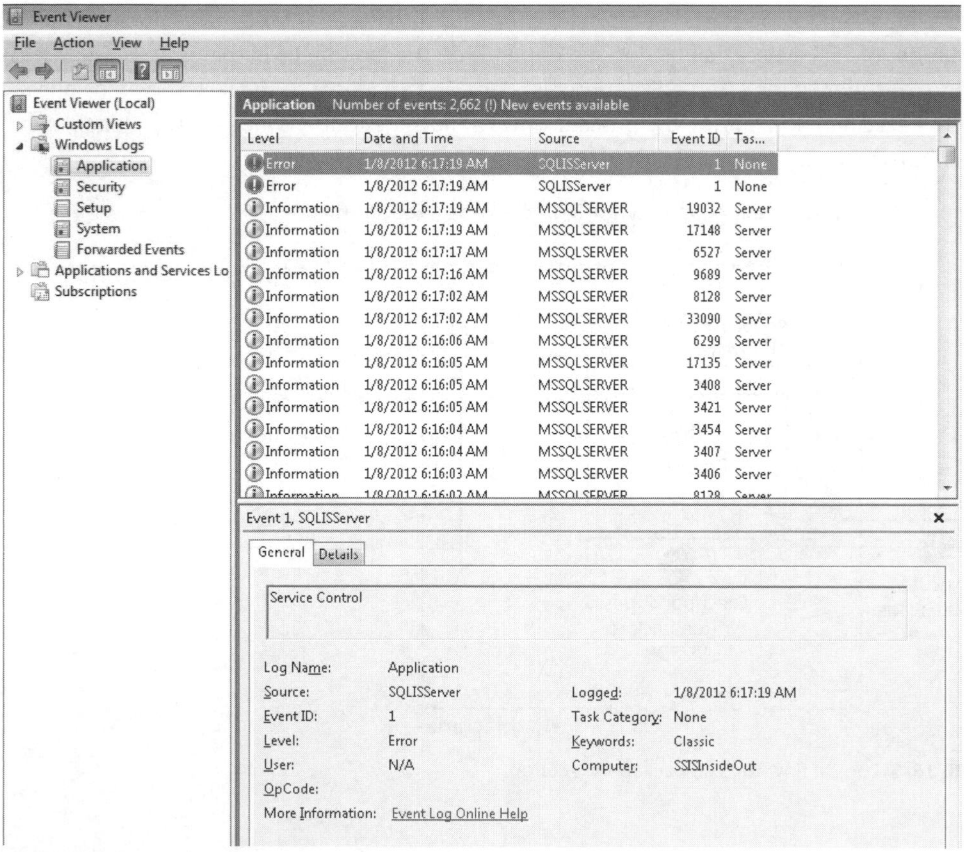

FIGURE 16-9 Application event entry for SSIS.

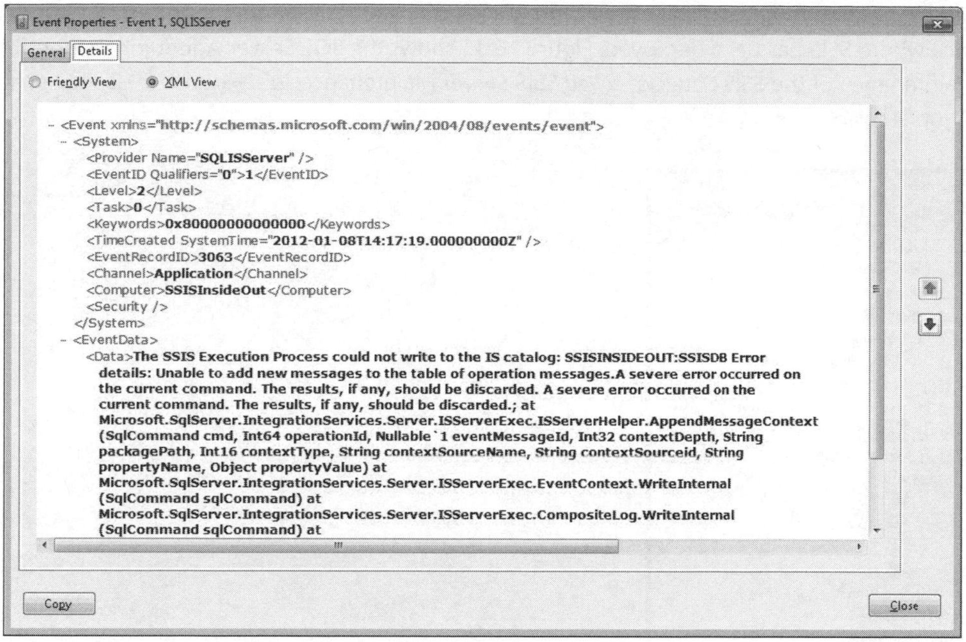

FIGURE 16-10 Event text for the SSIS error.

SSIS Catalog Maintenance and SQL Server Agent Jobs

SSIS 2012 relies on a SQL Server Agent job to perform maintenance tasks on the SSIS Catalog. The maintenance tasks include the following:

- **Operation records maintenance** This ensures that the operation logs that are in the SSIS Catalog are within a user-specified retention window. All operation logs that fall outside the retention window period are purged from the SSIS Catalog. By default, the retention window is 365 days.
- **Maximum versions per project maintenance** The SSIS Catalog maintains multiple versions of the same project. This allows you to restore to an earlier version (if needed). To ensure that the SSIS Catalog contains only the required number of versions for a project, this maintenance job removes older versions of a project. By default, the maximum number of versions maintained per project is 10.

You can use SQL Server Management Studio to change these properties by right-clicking on the SSISDB node.

See Also *Chapter 14 shows you how you can make use of T-SQL to change the SSIS Catalog properties.*

For SSIS Catalog maintenance to work, you will need to start SQL Server Agent on the SQL Server instance where SSIS has been deployed. Figure 16-11 shows the SQL Server Agent job responsible for the maintenance of the SSIS Catalog, *called* SSIS Server Maintenance Job. Figure 16-12 shows the two T-SQL job steps.

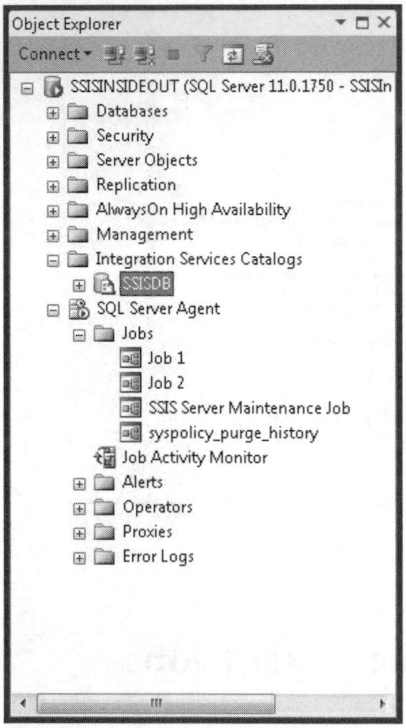

FIGURE 16-11 SQL Server Agent job for SSIS Catalog maintenance.

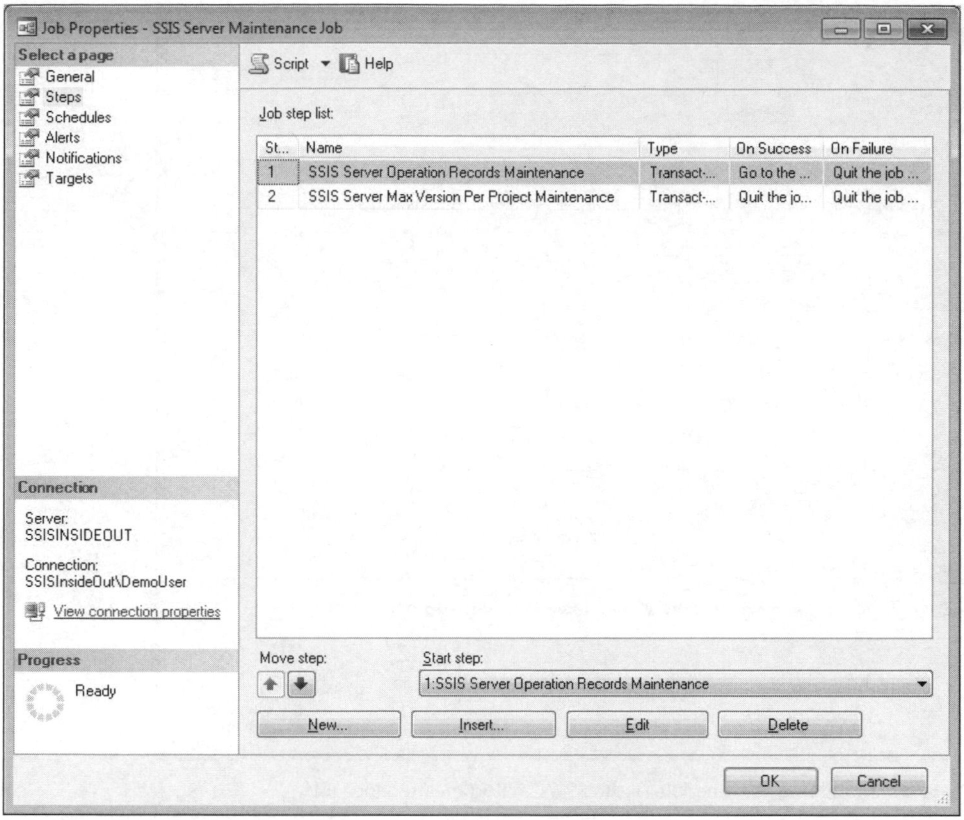

FIGURE 16-12 T-SQL job steps in the SQL Server Agent job.

By default, the SQL Server Agent job is scheduled to run every day at 12:00:00 AM. Figure 16-13 shows how you can make changes to the schedule in which the maintenance job is run, by doing the following:

1. Click Schedules.
2. Click Edit.
3. Change the Schedule Type and Frequency to suit the desired schedule.
4. Click OK.

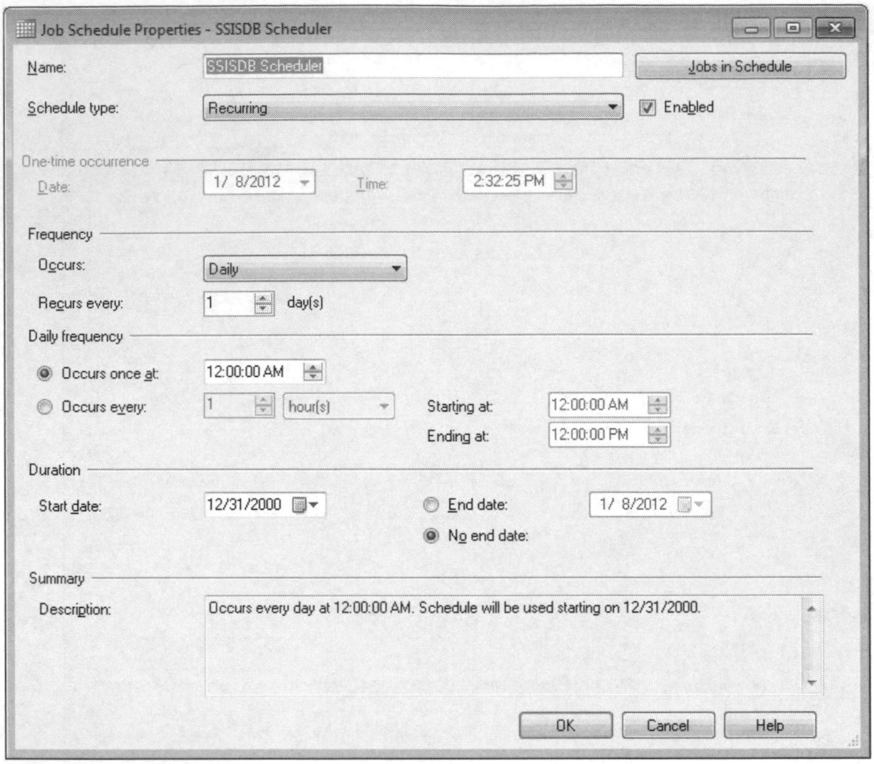

FIGURE 16-13 Modifying the schedule of the SSIS Catalog maintenance job.

The SSIS Catalog maintenance job runs in the security context of the owner of the job. The owner of the SSIS Catalog maintenance job is ##MS_SSISServerCleanupJobLogin##. This login is provisioned when the SSIS Catalog is created and should not be changed.

Backup and Restore of the SSIS Catalog

The SSIS Catalog is a user database, so SQL Server backup and restore functionalities can be used to minimize the risk of data loss in SSISDB caused by media or hardware failures and user errors. Deprecating an SSIS server and migrating to another server is also made possible by backup and restore functionalities. Backing up and restoring on the same server is a fairly straightforward process if encryption options in the database are changed between a backup and restore.

Standard SQL Server approaches to backup and restore are employed in single-machine scenarios. Moving an SSIS Catalog across machines requires some extra steps due to the way SSIS uses encryption mechanisms in SQL Server. Let's look at the steps involved in making a backup of the SSIS Catalog and restoring it to another SQL Server instance.

> **Note** To complete all the following steps for backup and restore, you need to have system administrator privileges for the source and target SQL servers.

Back Up SSISDB

1. As best practice, back up the database master key once it is created. Sensitive data in SSISDB is protected using encryption. Such database-level cryptographic features in SQL Server rely on the database master key. The copy of the master key for the SSISDB database that will be stored in the database is encrypted using a password provided by the user when creating SSISDB. The script in Listing 16-1 can be used to make the backup of the database master key.

   LISTING 16-1 Backing up the database master key for SSISDB

   ```
   USE SSISDB
   BACKUP MASTER KEY TO FILE = 'c:\DMK\SSISDB\key'
   YPTION BY PASSWORD = 'SS1SInside@ut'
   ```

   You need to perform this only once as long as you keep the master key file and the encryption password. You have to repeat this procedure if you lose the file or the password or if you change the master key of the SSISDB database. The password used to protect the file containing the backup must meet the Windows password policy requirements of the computer that is running the instance of SQL Server.

2. Back up the SSISDB database. The data in the SSIS Catalog is copied to a backup device using SQL Server Management Studio or the BACKUP DATABASE statement in T-SQL. Refer to *http://msdn.microsoft.com/en-us/library/ms187048(v=sql.110).aspx* for details on backup strategies and approaches.

3. Generate a script for stored procedure *sp_ssis_startup*. This stored procedure is created in the master database automatically when the SSIS Catalog is created in a server. When moving the catalog to another server, this stored procedure needs to be created on the new server if it is not already available there. The script is generated using SQL Server Management Studio. Right-click the stored procedure in the master database in SQL Server Management Studio Object Explorer, select Script Stored Procedure As, then CREATE TO, and then File to save the script to a file (for example, Ssisstartup.sql).

4. Generate the SSIS Server maintenance job. This job is created in SQL Server Agent automatically when SSIS Catalog is created on a server. When moving the catalog to another server, this job needs to be created on the new server if it is not already available there from creation of the SSIS Catalog. The script is generated using SQL Server Management Studio. Right-click the Agent job in SQL Server Management Studio Object Explorer, select Script Job As, CREATE TO, and then File to save the job to a file (for example, Ssisdbmaintenance.sql).

Restore SSISDB

1. First, you must enable CLR. SSIS 2012 and SSISDB depend on SQL CLR functionality. It has to be enabled on the SQL Server instance hosting the SSIS Catalog. When moving the catalog to another server, SQL CLR needs to be enabled on the new server if it is not already available there. The T-SQL script in Listing 16-2 is used for that.

   LISTING 16-2 Enabling SQL CLR functionality

   ```
   USE MASTER
   EXEC sp_configure 'clr enabled', 1
   RECONFIGURE
   ```

   SSISDB depends on an unsafe assembly loading functionality in SQL CLR. To grant that permission, a login needs to be created using the asymmetric key created using the public key from one of the SSIS assemblies. The login is used only for granting permission and does not have to be mapped to a database user. The T-SQL script shown in Listing 16-3 can be used to create the key and the login if they do not already exist in the new SQL Server instance to which SSISDB is restored.

   LISTING 16-3 Creating the asymmetric key and security principal

   ```
   USE MASTER

   CREATE ASYMMETRIC KEY MS_SQLEnableSystemAssemblyLoadingKey
   FROM EXECUTABLE FILE = 'C:\Program Files\Microsoft SQL Server\110\DTS\Binn\ISServerExec.
   exe'

   CREATE LOGIN MS_SQLEnableSystemAssemblyLoadingUser
   FROM ASYMMETRIC KEY MS_SQLEnableSystemAssemblyLoadingKey

   GRANT UNSAFE ASSEMBLY TO MS_SQLEnableSystemAssemblyLoadingUser
   ```

   You need to replace the value of the *Executable File* parameter in Listing 16-3 using the actual SSIS install location in your machine.

2. Next you restore SSISDB. The data in the SSIS Catalog that is copied to a backup device is restored using SQL Server Manager Studio or the RESTORE DATABASE statement in T-SQL. Refer to *http://msdn.microsoft.com/en-us/library/ms187048(v=sql.110).aspx* for details on restore strategies and approaches.

3. Create the login [##MS_SSISServerCleanupJobLogin##]. This login is created in the SQL Server instance automatically when the SSIS Catalog is created. When moving the catalog, this login has to be created in the master database on the new server if it does not already exist there. The CREATE LOGIN T-SQL statement is used to create the login. Because it is an internal server principal used only for SSISDB maintenance, a random password can be used and no one will ever have to log in to the server using it. See *http://msdn.microsoft.com/en-us/library/ms189751(v=sql.110).aspx* for details on creating a login in SQL Server.

4. Map SSISDB user ##MS_SSISServerCleanupJobUser## to server login ##MS_SSISServer-CleanupJobLogin##. The logic created in the previous step has to be mapped to the ##MS_SSISServerCleanupJobUser## user in the SSISDB database. The T-SQL script for doing so is given in Listing 16-4.

   LISTING 16-4 Mapping the SSISDB database user to the login

```
USE SSISDB
ALTER USER [##MS_SSISServerCleanupJobUser##] with LOGIN = [##MS_
SSISServerCleanupJobLogin##]
```

5. Execute scripts in the master database. The scripts created in steps 3 and 4 earlier in the back-up process need to be executed in the master database on the new server to which SSISDB is moved to create the startup stored procedure and Agent job used for the maintenance of the SSIS Catalog. You need to update the *@servername* parameter for the *sp_add_jobserver* step in *Ssisdbmaintenance.sql* to use the name of the new server, replacing the old server name.

6. Restore the master key. To restore SSISDB in an instance of SQL Server using the backup from another instance, you will need the backup of the database master key along with the password used to protect the key backup.

An alternative approach is to use the backup of the database master key and the T-SQL script in Listing 16-5 to restore the key in the new server.

LISTING 16-5 Restoring the database master key using key backup

```
USE SSISDB

RESTORE MASTER KEY FROM FILE = 'D:\MasterKeyBackup\SSISDB-Server1234\key'
DECRYPTION BY PASSWORD = 'SS1SInside@ut'
ENCRYPTION BY PASSWORD = 'NewC@talogPassw0rd'
FORCE
```

In this script, SS1SInside@ut is the password used to protect the file containing the backup of the master key and "NewC@talogPassw0rd" is the new password to encrypt the database master key. The warning reported during the execution of this script can be ignored and the master key will be restored successfully. When the master key is restored, SQL Server decrypts all the keys that are encrypted with the currently active master key, and then encrypts these keys with the restored master key. This resource-intensive operation should be scheduled during a period of low demand.

An alternative approach to restoring the master key is to use the password originally used to encrypt the database master key during the creation of the SSIS Catalog that was backed up. The following T-SQL script is used to restore the database master key in SSISDB if the password used during creation of SSISDB is available.

LISTING 16-6 Restoring the database master key using its password

```
USE SSISDB
OPEN MASTER KEY DECRYPTION BY PASSWORD = 'SS1SC@talog'
ALTER MASTER KEY ADD ENCRYPTION BY PASSWORD = 'NewC@talogPassw0rd'
```

In this script, SS1SC@talog is the password originally used during creation of the SSIS Catalog and NewC@talogPassw0rd is the new password to encrypt the database master key.

After SSISDB is restored using the steps just described, it will be fully functional. Projects, packages, environments, execution and validation history, and everything persisted to SSISDB will be available in the new server. If SQL Server Agent jobs were created in the old server, they have to be explicitly copied over to the new server.

Summary

In this chapter, you learned about the architecture of SSIS 2012 and how SSIS packages deployed to the SSIS Catalog are executed. SSIS 2012 provides capabilities to automatically log the details of the execution. The amount of information that is logged is dependent on the specified logging level. You learned the logging levels that are provided and the type of information that is captured at each level, how scheduled maintenance of the SSIS Catalog works, and how to modify the schedule. You also learned how to perform a backup and restore of the SSIS Catalog.

CHAPTER 17

SSIS Security

In This Chapter

Security is always a critical topic for a software product, especially when the product involves enterprise data. Before SQL Server 2012, most of the security considerations involve how to protect package access and the sensitive data in SSIS packages. SQL Server 2012 introduces the SSIS Catalog. As an enterprise server it supports multiple users to deploy, execute, and manage their SSIS solutions concurrently. In SSIS 2012, the SSIS Catalog provides powerful new ways in which you can control access to SSIS projects and executions.

Protect Your Package

Control Package Access

The first topic in SSIS security is how to control access to packages. In the new Project Deployment Model, all project files should be deployed to an SSIS Catalog, where they will be protected well by the Catalog server (you will be introduced to its security mechanism in later sections). But for those projects with legacy package deployment models, you still need to manage access permissions manually.

The legacy packages can be stored in the following package locations:

- File system
- msdb database
- Package store

File System

When a package is stored on a file system, it's nothing more than a regular file from the security perspective, so you need to utilize the built-in file system security mechanism to protect your packages. Most Windows machines now use the NTFS file system (you are not using FAT32, right?). It provides an excellent security system to allow you to customize the permissions on each file and folder.

To manage the security settings on a file, just right-click the file and select Properties from the shortcut menu. Click the Security tab in the Properties dialog box, shown in Figure 17-1.

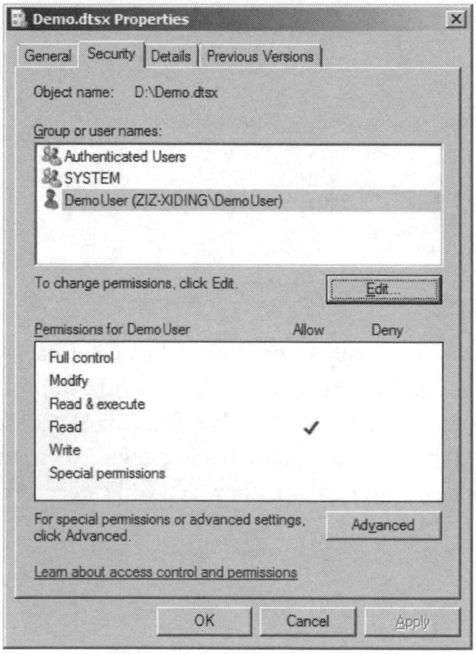

FIGURE 17-1 Security settings in NTFS file system.

In Figure 17-1, there are two lists. The first list shows which user has permissions on the current file and the second list shows which permission items that user has. Click Edit to add or remove user or groups. Although NTFS defines lots of permission items, we care only about two fundamental ones: Read and Modify. Figure 17-1 shows a demo user who has been granted the Read permission on the current package file. Thus that user could run the package with dtexec or other tools.

MSDB Database

MSDB is a system database in SQL Server to store management objects, such as SQL Agent job definitions or SSIS packages for server maintenance. All SSIS-related objects are saved in three system tables: *dbo.sysssispackages*, *dbo.sysssispackagefolders*, and *dbo.sysssislog*. To help you manage access to those three tables, three built-in database roles are provided, as shown in Table 17-1.

TABLE 17-1 SSIS-related database roles in the msdb database

Role Name	Read Permission	Write Permission
db_dtsoperator	Enumerate all packages. View all packages. Execute all packages. Export all packages. Execute all packages in SQL Server Agent.	None
db_dtsltduser	Enumerate all packages. View own packages. Execute own packages. Export own packages.	Import packages. Delete own packages. Change own package roles.
db_dtsadmin	Enumerate all packages. View all packages. Execute all packages. Export all packages. Execute all packages in SQL Server Agent.	Import packages. Delete all packages. Change all package roles.

You just need to assign users to an appropriate database role. It's much simpler than setting permissions for each database user.

Besides those three fixed database roles, you can also specify a user-defined database role to have Read or Modify permissions on a single package. The schema of table *dbo.sysssispackages* contains two interesting columns, *readerrolesid* and *writerrolesid*, that save the security identifier (SID) of the corresponding database role. To edit the roles, you can use SQL Server Management Studio to connect to Integration Services, find the package node, and select Package Roles from the shortcut menu shown in Figure 17-2.

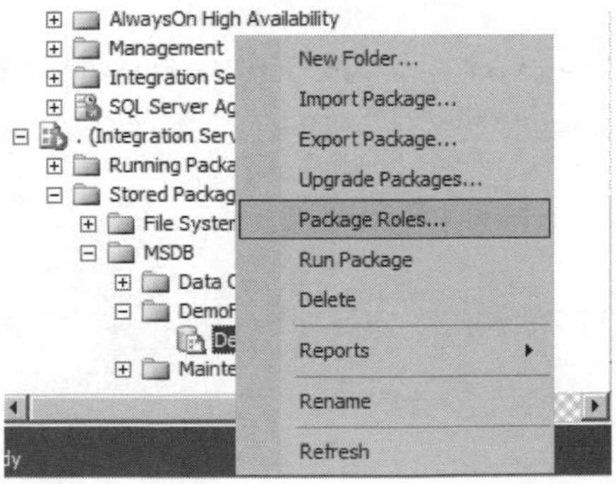

FIGURE 17-2 Edit the package roles in SQL Server Management Studio.

The Package Roles dialog box opens (see Figure 17-3), allowing you to pick an existing database role for reader and writer. After you change the roles, SQL Server Management Studio will convert them to an SID string and then save to the column *readerrolesid or writerrolesid.*

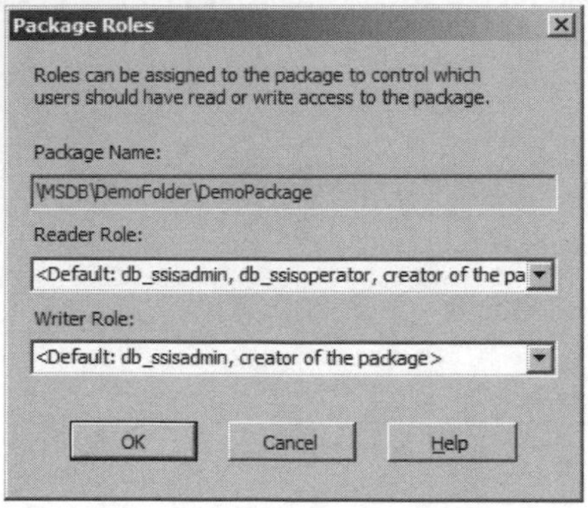

FIGURE 17-3 Edit the package roles of a package.

Package Store

The package store is a central place managed by Integration Services. You can create folders, remove folders, import packages, or remove packages with SQL Server Management Studio. Figure 17-4 shows a demo package in the package store.

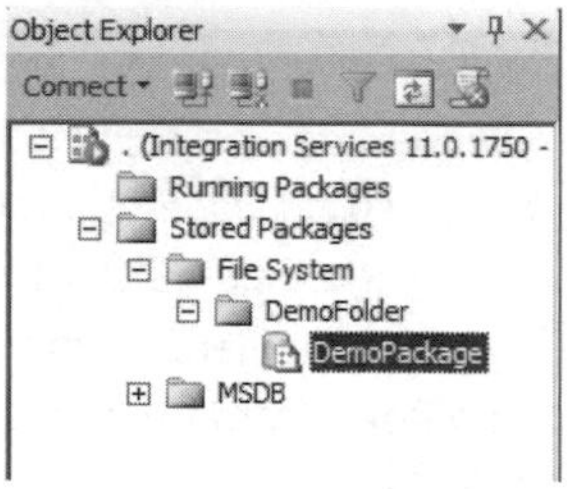

FIGURE 17-4 A demo package in the package store.

As discussed in Chapter 11, "Running SSIS Packages," those packages are actually stored in a fixed file system location. The location is defined in the configuration file *%Program Files%\Microsoft SQL Server\110\DTS\Binn\MsDtsSrvr.ini.xml.*

The package store provides a straightforward security mechanism based on the current user's Windows identity. If you create a folder in the package store, then you are the owner of that folder. You have full permissions on that folder, including importing packages or creating subfolders. Other users don't have any permission on that folder, except for users in the computer administrators group. Similarly, you are the owner of an individual package if you import that package. You have full permissions. Other users don't have any permission on that package, except for users in the computer administrators group.

Tip Because all packages in the package store are stored in a file system, you can open the file system location to check the default security settings on each folder and package file.

Package Encryption

There might be some sensitive properties in your SSIS package. For example, the connection string property of a connection manager might contain your password. People cannot see the plain text in the package designer because it will be shown as password masks, but you definitely don't want people to get the password by opening the package XML file with a text editor.

To prevent malicious users from getting sensitive information from the package XML file, all sensitive properties are encrypted before saving. An SSIS task needs to declare whether its properties are sensitive. If the property is not sensitive, its value is saved to XML in plain text. Otherwise it will be encrypted and saved. The encryption policy is determined by a package property called *ProtectionLevel.* See the screen shot in Figure 17-5.

There are five different protection levels. If you specify the protection level as *EncryptSensitiveWithPassword* or *EncryptAllWithPassword*, you also need to specify the password in another package property, *PackagePassword.*

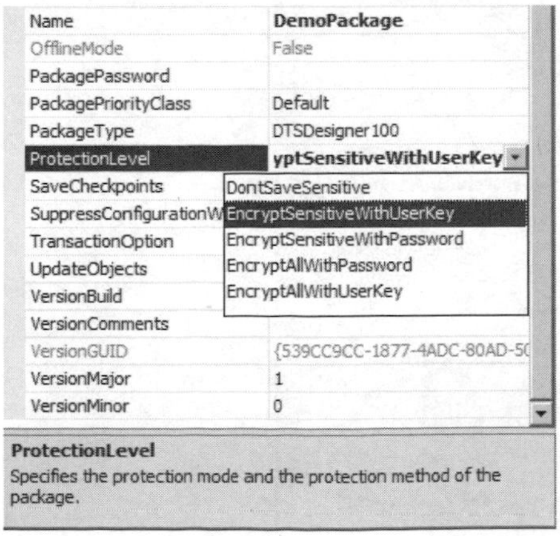

FIGURE 17-5 Package protection level.

Table 17-2 shows the detailed descriptions of each protection level.

TABLE 17-2 Protection levels and descriptions

Protection Level	Description
Do not save sensitive (DontSaveSensitive)	Sensitive values will be stripped from the package when it is saved to XML.
Encrypt all with password (EncryptAllWithPassword)	A password will be used to encrypt the entire package. When this protection level is used, the contents of the package are placed into a single encrypted block of text inside of the file.
Encrypt all with user key (EncryptAllWithUserKey)	A key from the current user profile is used to encrypt the entire package. Like EncryptAllWithPassword, when this protection level is used, the contents of the package are placed in an encrypted block of text. The package can be read only by the user who originally saved the package.
Encrypt sensitive with password (EncryptSensitiveWithPassword)	Sensitive values within the package are encrypted using a password. If the package is opened with an incorrect password, it can still be loaded, but any sensitive data will be stripped from the package.
Encrypt sensitive with user key (EncryptSensitiveWithUserKey)	A key from the current user profile is used to encrypt only the sensitive fields within the package. If a different user opens the package, the sensitive information will need to be reentered. This is the default protection level for SSIS packages.

SSIS 2012 introduces the Project Deployment Model, which is also the default deployment model. The project becomes a larger container unit than packages. Correspondingly, we also need a protection level on the project to protect shared project elements, such as project parameters or project connection managers. To set the protection level on an SSIS project, right-click the project node in Visual Studio Solution Explorer and select Properties from the shortcut menu. In the Property Pages dialog box (see Figure 17-6), there is a setting allowing you to specify both protection level and password (if required).

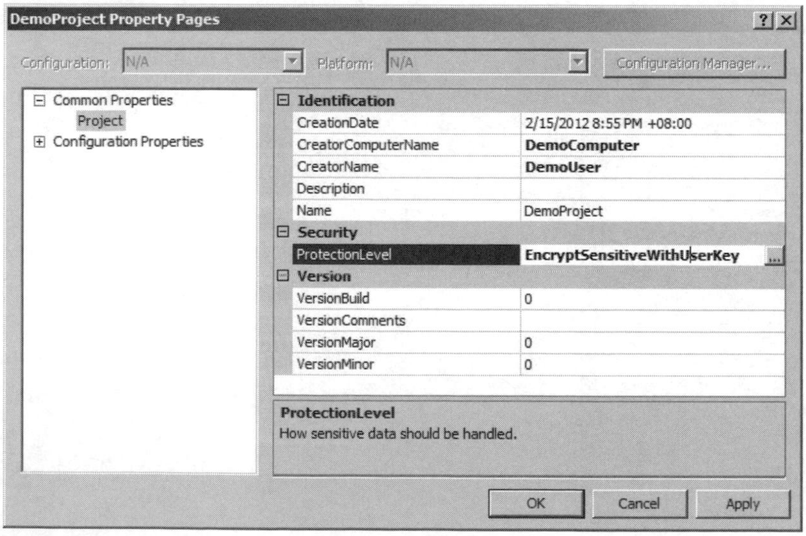

FIGURE 17-6 Set the protection level on an SSIS project.

> **Tip** Make sure you use the same protection level on the project and each individual package, otherwise you will get an error when you build the project.

Sensitive Variables and Parameters

Besides sensitive properties, there also could be information disclosure due to some variables or parameters. For example, suppose you have a package designed to process company payments. In the package there are some variables containing the employee names and salaries. One day your package execution encounters an error and a dump file is generated. Usually the dump file contains context information, including the variable values. The dump file is sent to the IT support department so the information is exposed.

To protect such information, every variable has a property named *IncludeInDebugDump*. When set to *false,* this variable would not be included in debug dumps. Similarly, it would not be included in view *catalog.event_message_context* when it's running on an SSIS Catalog server.

To set the property, first select the variable in the variable list window. Then select View | Properties Window from the menu (see Figure 17-7).

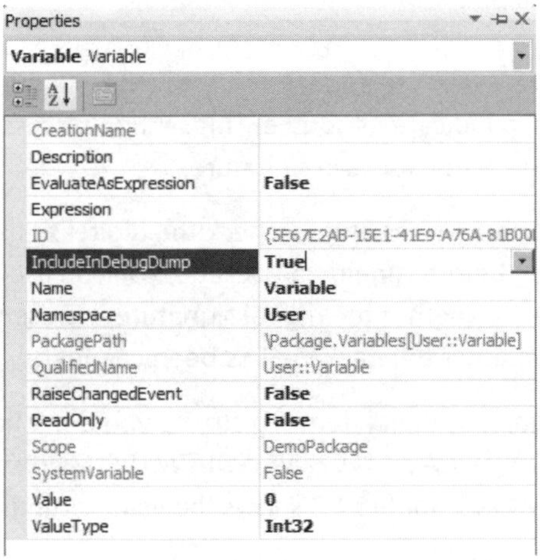

FIGURE 17-7 *IncludeInDebugDump* property.

Similarly, every parameter has a property named *IsSensitive*. If this property is set to *true*, the default value of the parameter will be shown as password masks in the editor window. Also its value will be saved to the package XML file according to the protection level settings (see Figure 17-8).

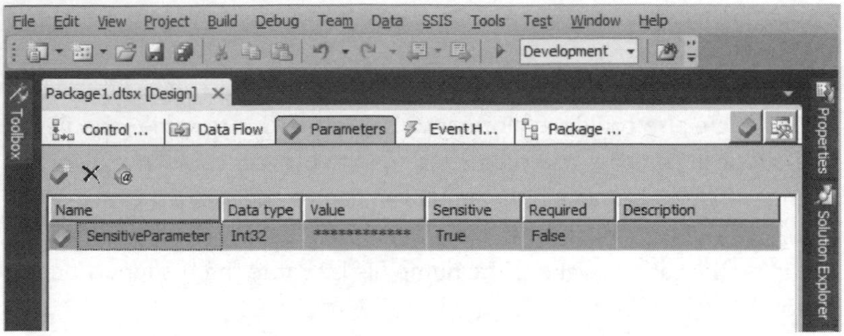

FIGURE 17-8 Set *IsSensitive* property on a package parameter.

Whether a parameter is sensitive also has some impacts on package logging. SSIS 2012 introduces a new log entry, *DiagnosticEx*. This new entry logs the initial values of all parameters during package startup. When a parameter is marked as *IsSensitive*, however, its value will be saved as empty in the log file.

Package Signing

An SSIS package can be signed with a digital signature to indicate its source. This section discusses how to check the signature and how to sign the package with your own signature.

You must explicitly set the option to let the Integration Services engine check the digital signature before running a package. To enable signature checking before running a package, you can use the dtexec option*/VerifyS[igned]*. Notice that SSIS only checks whether the digital signature is present, is valid, or is from a trusted source. SSIS does not check whether the package has been changed.

You can also create a key named *BlockedSignatureStates* in the system registry so you don't have to specify the option every time. Its registry path is HKEY_LOCAL_MACHINE\SOFTWARE\Microsoft\Microsoft SQL Server\110\SSIS and the value type is DWORD. Table 17-3 shows the valid settings and a description for each setting.

TABLE 17-3 Valid settings for *BlockedSignatureStates*

Value	Description
0	No administrative restriction.
1	Block invalid signatures. This setting does not block unsigned packages.
2	Block invalid and untrusted signatures. This setting does not block unsigned packages, but blocks self-generated signatures.
3	Block invalid and untrusted signatures and unsigned packages. This setting also blocks self-generated signatures.

In this list, an invalid signature is one for which the decrypted checksum does not match the decrypted checksum that is calculated as part of the process of loading SSIS packages. A trusted signature is one that is created by using a digital certificate signed by a trusted root certification authority. An untrusted signature is one that cannot be verified as issued by a trusted root certification authority, or a signature that is not current.

> **Tip** To learn more about digital signatures and package signing, visit the TechNet article at *http://technet.microsoft.com/en-us/library/ms137947(v=sql.90).aspx.*

SSIS also provides the Digital Signing dialog box to help you sign the package. To sign a package, you first need a digital certificate issued by a trusted certificate authority. You can use only certificates that were created for the purpose of code signing. To sign a package, click SSIS | Digital Signing. In the Digital Signing dialog box shown in Figure 17-9, click Signing and choose the certificate you want to use.

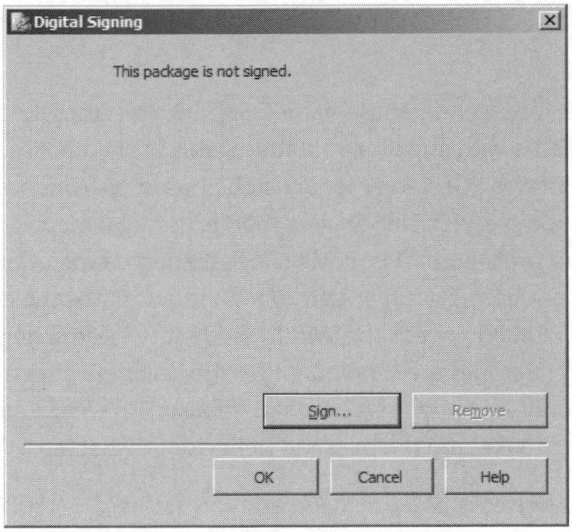

FIGURE 17-9 Sign your package.

Security in the SSIS Catalog

In SSIS 2012, the concept of the SSIS Catalog is introduced. As a back-end server, it supports multiple users to deploy, execute, and manage their SSIS solutions concurrently. Thus you are able to make use of a combination of SQL Server and SSIS security to secure the SSIS packages that have been deployed to the SSIS Catalog. This section covers the security mechanism and practices in SSIS Catalog.

Security Overview

As a start to SSIS Catalog security, consider the following questions:

- Which resources should be protected? The resources are not only limited to projects or packages. Some other resources such as environments and logs also need to be protected.
- How should you manage security settings on each type of resource? Permission entries should be defined and application programming interfaces (APIs) should be provided to set those permissions.
- How can you enforce that every user has access only to the authorized resources? The scope should include all public surfaces such as views and stored procedures.

The SSIS Catalog Security model addresses those questions. In this section we first give an overview of the security model, including principals, schemas, securable types, and permission types. In the next section, you learn how to use SSIS security APIs to secure the objects that are deployed to the SSIS Catalog.

User and Roles

All objects in the SSIS Catalog are stored in a SQL Server database named SSISDB. To access the SSIS Catalog, you must be a database user in SSISDB. As with any other database, an SSIDB database user is mapped to a SQL Server login. As you know, a SQL Server login can be based on Windows Authentication or SQL Server Authentication. However, SSISDB requires that its users be mapped to a Windows Authentication login. In all its stored procedure APIs, it will check the login type of the current user. An error will be thrown if the current user is not mapped to a Windows Authenticated login. The reason for this design is that the SSIS Catalog needs the Windows identity information to control the package access during run time. All packages are running under the security context of the current user. A package needs security credentials to access external databases. The SSIS Catalog needs to provide a correct security credential to make sure the package behavior is expected.

There are two types of users in the SSIS Catalog: common users and administrators. Any regular SSISDB database user is a common SSIS Catalog user; that is, a user in the default *public* role. You don't need to add them to any other roles.

There is a special database role, *ssis_admin,* in SSISDB. Any database users belonging to this role are administrators in SSIS Catalog. At the same time, members of the sysadmin server role are also able to access all securables in SSISDB. Therefore they are also SSIS Catalog administrators. As we explain in the following sections, only administrators are eligible to perform some special jobs. Common users cannot do them, even they are granted permissions.

Schemas

There are two schemas defined in SSISDB. The first one is named *catalog,* and the second one is named *internal.* All the database objects in the catalog schema are public objects. Any common SSISDB database users have access to them. Of course, that does not mean the access will necessarily succeed. For example, there is a stored procedure *catalog.stop_execution* in the catalog schema that accepts an input parameter of execution ID. This stored procedure is visible to any database user and they can call the stored procedure. Whether the invocation will succeed, however, depends on whether the current user has required permissions on that execution.

As its name suggests, all objects in the internal schema are for internal purposes. They are invisible to common database users. Although sysadmin members could view and update the objects in this schema, it's strongly recommended not to do that. You should always use public APIs provided by the SSIS Catalog to perform jobs. Thus the integrity of the SSIS Catalog will not be broken.

Securables and Permissions

The resources listed in Tables 17-4 are identified and protected by the SSIS Catalog security system. They are called *securables*. Correspondingly, some permission types are defined. Every permission type only applies to a specific securable type. See Table 17-4 for the securable types and Table 17-5 for permission types.

TABLE 17-4 Securable types

Securable Type	Type Code	Description
Catalog	1	The overall catalog
Folder	2	A folder itself
Project	3	All internal objects, such as packages, parameters, or shared connection managers
Environment	4	Includes all its environment variables
Operation	5	Includes executions and deployment

TABLE 17-5 Permission types

Permission Name	Type Code	Description
Read	1	This permission enables you to see the existence of an object.
Modify	2	This permission allows you to modify an object, such as overwrite a project or stop an execution.
Execute	3	This permission enables you to execute an object. It applies only to projects.
Manage_Permissions	4	You need this permission to change the permission settings on an object, such as granting permissions.
Read_Objects	101	This applies only to folders. This permission allows you to read all objects under that folder.
Modify_Objects	102	This applies only to folders. This permission allows you to write all objects under that folder.
Execute_Objects	103	This applies only to folders. This permission allows you to execute all projects under that folder.
Manage_Object_Permissions	104	This applies only to folders. This permission allows you to manage the permissions of all projects under that folder.

You can see from Table 11-4 that the project is an atomic unit from a security perspective. All subparts inside a project share the same security setting, such as packages, project parameters, or project connection managers. It means you cannot set a special security setting for a single package.

The folder is a little special in SSIS Catalog. To simplify administrative work, only administrators are allowed to manipulate folders, including creating folders, removing folders, or modifying folder descriptions. Those works are performed by corresponding stored procedures, and those procedures will check whether the current user is an administrator. Even if administrators grant the Modify permission on a folder to a common user, that user still cannot manipulate folders.

A frequently asked question is this: What is the relationship between SSIS Catalog security and the security mechanism for SQL Server itself? It is a complementary relationship. Generally speaking, SQL Server decides which database object you can access, and the SSIS Catalog determines whether access to that object will succeed. For example:

1. SQL Server decides whether you can query the *catalog.projects* view, whereas SSIS Catalog security decides which rows will be shown.
2. SQL Server decides whether you can execute the *catalog.stop_execution* stored procedure, and SSIS Catalog security decides if the execution will succeed or fail.

You should always use the security APIs provided by SSIS Catalog to manage your SSIS Catalog security settings. The exceptions are adding users, removing users, and managing roles. SSIS Catalog does not provide APIs to perform those jobs, so you can just use the SQL Server security API to do them.

Manage Permissions

In this section, you will be introduced to SSIS Catalog security APIs that help you manage security settings using some examples. Let's start with creating objects.

Permission Initialization

To demonstrate the initial security settings on an object, let's first log on to SSIS Catalog with an administrator account (Debby). Debby creates a folder named DemoFolder and then deploys an SSIS project named DemoProject under that newly created folder.

When an object is created in the SSIS Catalog, it is assigned a default group of permission items. The rule is that the object creator should own full permissions. No additional permissions are granted. If other users need to access that object, they must get permission approval from someone who already has the permissions. Table 17-6 shows the initial permissions for each securable type.

TABLE 17-6 Initial permissions for each securable type

Permission Name	Description
Folder	N/A
Project	Read, Modify, Execute, Manage_Permissions
Environment	Read, Modify, Manage_Permissions
Operation	Read, Modify, Manage_Permissions

In our example, Debby is the creator of the project so she should have all permissions on this project by default. There are two ways to verify this. First, you can select the project node in SQL Server Management Studio, right-click, and select Properties from the shortcut menu. There are two pages in the dialog box. The General page shows some basic information, such as the name and creation time. Click the Permissions page. You will see the initial permissions assigned on this project, as shown in Figure 17-10.

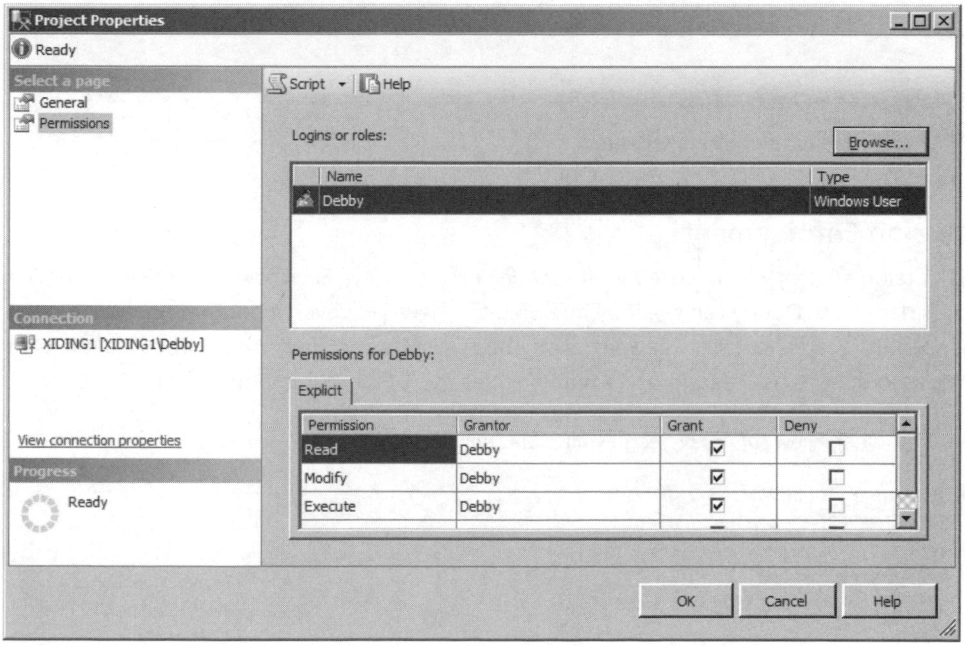

FIGURE 17-10 The initial permission settings on DemoProject.

As you can see, currently only one user has permissions on the project. It's Debby, and she has all the permission items.

Another way to check Debby's permission is to query *catalog.effective_object_permissions* view. This view lists all the permissions the current user has, so you need to query the view as user Debby. Listing 17-1 shows the T-SQL statement. This statement filters the view by object type (type code 2 for projects) and object ID (4 is the ID of DemoProject).

LISTING 17-1 Query *catalog.effective_object_permissions* view

```
SELECT * FROM [catalog].[effective_object_permissions]
WHERE object_type=2 AND object_id = 4
```

Figure 17-11 shows the query result. As you can see, Debby owns all permission items on DemoProject.

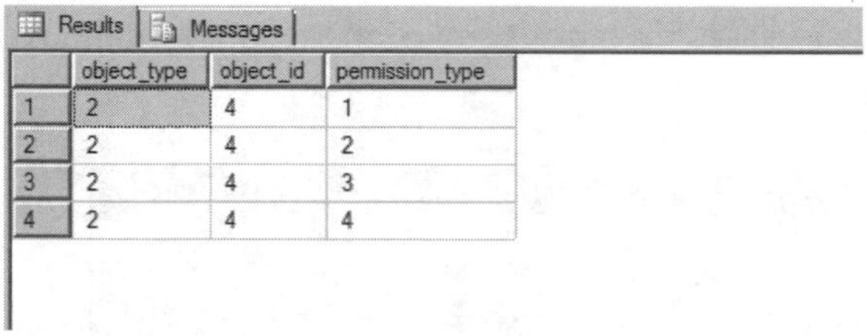

	object_type	object_id	permission_type
1	2	4	1
2	2	4	2
3	2	4	3
4	2	4	4

FIGURE 17-11 The initial permission settings.

Permission Enforcement

In SSIS Catalog all projects are listed in the *catalog.projects* view. Each row is a project. After Demo-Project is deployed, Debby can see it by querying the view. However, if another nonadmin user (let's call him Smith) queries the view, he will get an empty view, as no rows are returned. To make it clear, we make two queries as different users together. See the T-SQL statement in Listing 17-2.

LISTING 17-2 Query view *catalog.projects* by different user context

```
Execute As user='Debby'
      SELECT * FROM catalog.projects
   Revert
Execute As user='Smith'
      SELECT * FROM catalog.projects
   Revert
```

This T-SQL statement uses a feature called impersonation in SQL Server. To run the statement, you need to be the database owner, a member in server role *sysadmin,* or have the IMPERSONATION SQL Server permission on those two users.

The result is shown in Figure 17-12. As you can see, two different result sets returned on the same view. It means Debby and Smith will see different contents from the same view.

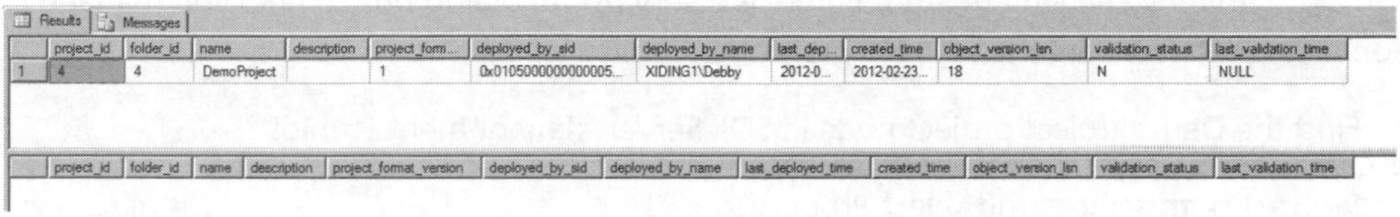

Results | Messages

	project_id	folder_id	name	description	project_form...	deployed_by_sid	deployed_by_name	last_dep...	created_time	object_version_lsn	validation_status	last_validation_time
1	4	4	DemoProject		1	0x0105000000000005...	XIDING1\Debby	2012-0...	2012-02-23...	18	N	NULL

project_id	folder_id	name	description	project_format_version	deployed_by_sid	deployed_by_name	last_deployed_time	created_time	object_version_lsn	validation_status	last_validation_time

FIGURE 17-12 Two different result sets returned on the same view.

You see different result sets returned on the same view because the SSIS Catalog enforces *row-level security* on all public views. When a user queries a view, that user's current identity will be used to join with internal base tables and object permission tables. Only those objects the user has Read permission on will be shown in the view. All other rows are silently filtered, so Smith isn't aware of DemoProject.

All stored procedures also will fail if you try to reference an object but do not have the Read permission. Suppose Smith somehow knows of the existence of DemoProject from other people and he tries to delete it by calling the stored procedure *catalog.delete_project*, as shown in Listing 17-3.

LISTING 17-3 Delete a project

```
EXEC [catalog].[delete_project] @folder_name = N'Demo', @project_name = N'DemoProject'
```

He will get the error message shown in Listing 17-4, which does not confirm or deny the existence of this project.

LISTING 17-4 The returned error message

```
Msg 27109, Level 16, State 1, Procedure delete_project, Line 88
Cannot find the project 'DemoProject' because it does not exist or you do not have
sufficient permissions.
```

To sum up, an SSIS Catalog object is totally invisible to you if you do not have the Read permission on it. Users query the same view but get different result rows. Every user can see only his or her own projects.

> **Tip** Sometimes you can guess the existence of an object. For example, each environment must have a unique name under the same folder. If you cannot find an environment name "foo" under a given folder from the *catalog.environments* view, but you always get an error when you try to create an environment named "foo," then the error likely means there is already such an environment, and it's just invisible to you!

Grant and Revoke Permissions

To enable user Smith to manipulate the newly deployed project, Debby must grant him some permissions. In SQL Server Management Studio there is a very useful dialog box to help you manage permissions on an object. Here are the steps to grant the permission:

1. Find the DemoProject project node in SQL Server Management Studio.
2. Right-click the node, and select Properties.
3. Click the Permissions page link on the left side.
4. Click Browse.
5. In the user list window, select Smith, and then click OK.
6. Click Smith in the list window to make sure he is selected.
7. Select the Read and Execute check boxes in the Grant column.
8. Click OK.

The resulting dialog box is shown in Figure 17-13.

This Project Properties dialog box is very useful for managing the permissions on an object. It first lists all users that have permissions on the current object. Then it shows all permissions granted or denied for the current user. To revoke permissions from the user, just clear the relevant check box.

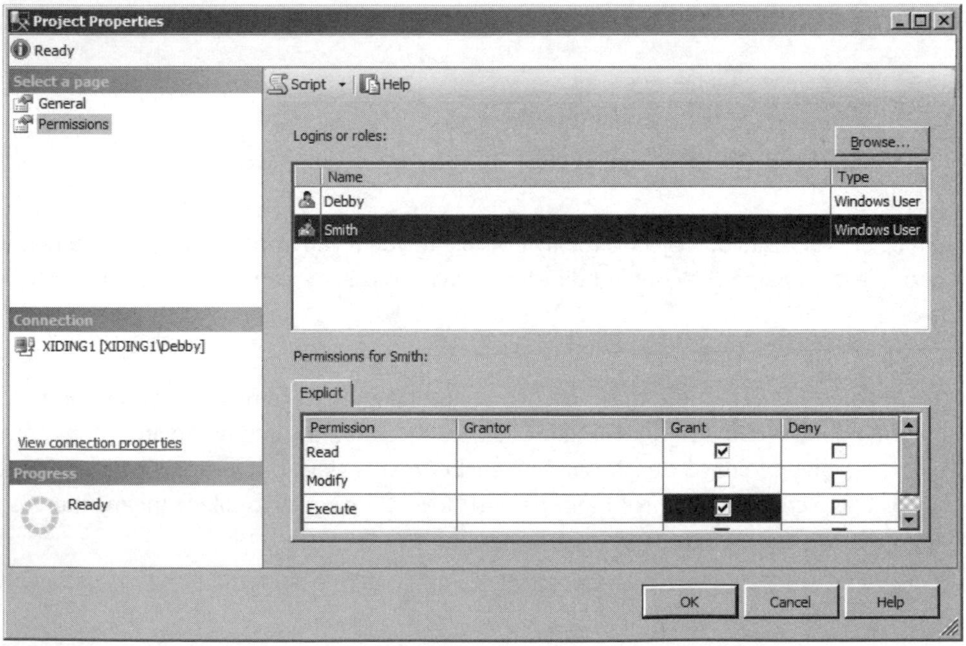

FIGURE 17-13 The Project Properties Permissions dialog box makes it easy to grant or remove permissions.

You can also grant or revoke permissions using the T-SQL stored procedures *catalog.grant_permission* and *catalog.revoke_permission,* respectively. Listing 17-5 shows a T-SQL statement that grants Read and Execute permissions to Smith:

LISTING 17-5 Grant Read and Execute permission to Smith

```
EXEC    [catalog].[grant_permission] @object_type = 2, @object_id = 4,
   @principal_id = 5, @permission_type = 1

EXEC    [catalog].[grant_permission] @object_type = 2,@object_id = 4,
   @principal_id = 5, @permission_type = 3
```

In the preceding T-SQL statement, the type code of object type and permission type is listed in Tables 17-4 and 17-5, respectively. The input parameter *object_id* is the identifier of the target object for which you want change permissions. In our case it should be the project ID. As to the parameter *principal_id,* it's an integer identifier of the target principal that you can get from the *sys.principals* view. The target principal can be a single database user or a database role.

At first only SSIS Catalog administrators and Debby could invoke the given T-SQL statements because they are the only users with the Manage_Permissions permission item on the object.

After Smith is granted the permission, he can see the project in the view. Figure 17-14 shows the new result of the same query in Listing 17-2.

Results | Messages

	project_id	folder_id	name	description	project_forma...	deployed_...	deployed_by_name	last_deployed_time	created_time	object_version_lsn	validation_status	last_validation_time
1	4	4	DemoProject		1	0x010500...	XIDING1\Debby	2012-02-23 22:3...	2012-02-23 22:3...	18	N	NULL

	project_id	folder_id	name	description	project_form...	deployed_...	deployed_by_name	last_deployed_time	created_time	object_version_lsn	validation_status	last_validation_time
1	4	4	DemoProject		1	0x010500...	XIDING1\Debby	2012-02-23 22:33...	2012-02-23 22:3...	18	N	NULL

FIGURE 17-14 The new result after Smith is granted permissions.

But if Smith tries to delete the project, he will still get a failure because he does not have the Modify permission.

Permission Inheritance

SSIS Catalog supports permission inheritance. One user will get the following permission items automatically:

- All permissions granted on the roles to which the current user belongs
- All permissions granted on the folder in which the current object resides

There are two dimensions. The first dimension is about roles. A user can belong to a role, and that role can also belong to another role. If you grant permissions to a role, all the direct or indirect role members get the same permission automatically.

Another dimension involves folders. In Table 17-5 there are some permission types with an "_objects" suffix, such as Read_Objects and Modify_Objects. Those permission types can be applied only to folders. For example, when you grant the Read_Objects permission to a user, it means that user gets Read permission on all objects inside that folder.

In any of the following cases, Smith could read DemoProject:

- You grant Smith Read permission directly.
- You grant one role the Read permission and Smith belongs to that role, directly or indirectly.
- You grant Smith or his role the Read_Objects permission on the folder.

If you combine all these factors (inheritance from roles, inheritance from folders, granted permissions, and denied permissions, which are introduced soon), it can become quite complex to determine whether a user has specified permissions on a given object. To simplify the administrative work, for permissions, the SSIS Catalog provides two different views for permissions.

The first view is *Catalog.object_permissions*. This view shows all the "raw" records of permissions. When you grant or deny a permission, a new record is inserted into the view. Revoking a permission removes the row from the view if it exists. The record also shows who granted or denied the permission. Using this view, you can track who made the current permission settings. The tricky part is that this view is itself protected by row-level security, so you cannot see the permission records of an object if you do not have Read permission for that object.

The second view is *catalog.effective_object_permissions*. This view is basically calculated from the first view. It's the final result instead of raw records. Every row in the view indicates one of the permissions on an object that the current user has.

Deny Permissions

Deny is a special kind of permission, invented for easier management of permissions. It also ensures a user will not be granted permissions mistakenly. When a user is granted a permission and denied the same permission at the same time, Deny always wins: The user cannot access the object.

To help you understand how Deny works, consider the following scenario. Suppose you have a database role "developer team" that has ten members. You want all of them to be able to read DemoProject except Smith. How can you do it? One way is to grant permissions to each team member except Smith. It's tedious, as you need to repeat the same operation nine times. This approach definitely won't work if the team has hundreds of members. After the Deny permissions are introduced, you can simply grant Read permission to the whole role and then deny the Read permission for Smith. It's much easier, right?

Another scenario is making sure a user cannot get permissions mistakenly. Suppose there are many roles in your database, including developer team, managers, senior group, and more. You have granted corresponding permissions to each role, and Smith could belong to lots of roles. Because one role can be the member of another role, the relationship can be very complex. Smith can inherit permissions from one or more of those roles. To make sure Smith does not have the Read permission on DemoProject, you have to clear the Read permission on Smith himself and remove him from all roles that have Read permission. With Deny permissions, it's much easier. You simply deny the Read permission on Smith. He cannot access the project even if he inherits the permissions from some roles.

To sum up, you can ensure one user does not have the permission as long as you have denied the permission on that user, no matter if he gets the permission from himself, from folder inheritance, or from role inheritance.

You can use the SQL Server Management Studio dialog box to deny or revoke permissions, or you can use the stored procedure API *catalog.deny_permission* to do it. Its usage is the same as the *catalog.grant_permission*. Listing 17-6 shows the T-SQL statements to deny Read permission for DemoProject on user Smith.

LISTING 17-6 Deny Read permission to Smith

```
Execute    [catalog].[deny_permission] @object_type = 2,@object_id = 4,
   @principal_id = 5, @permission_type = 1
```

To remove a denied permission item you also use the *catalog.revoke_permission* stored procedure, as shown in Listing 17-7.

LISTING 17-7 Revoke Read permission from Smith

```
Execute   [catalog].[revoke_permission] @object_type = 2,@object_id = 4,
   @principal_id = 5, @permission_type = 1
```

With this revoke command, both granted or denied Read permission are cleared on Smith.

DDL Trigger

All the permission items are saved in some internal tables. The SSIS Catalog needs to clean up those tables when a user is removed from SSISDB. To do that work automatically, it defines a database level Data Manipulation Definition (DDL) trigger named *ddl_cleanup_object_permissions*. This trigger is fired every time a user or a role is removed. Do not disable this trigger. Otherwise the permission records in internal tables could be inconsistent.

Following the conventions in SQL Server, this trigger will also prevent you from removing a user if that user has granted permissions to other users. For example, now user Debby has granted Read permission to user Smith. You can remove Smith from the database but you cannot remove Debby due to the cleanup work on permission tables. To remove Smith, it simply deletes the permission records and everything is fine. However, it cannot delete the record when removing user Debby, otherwise Smith's permission will be changed. That does not make sense, so Debby cannot be removed as the permission grantor. You have to revoke that permission before trying to remove user Debby.

Running SSIS with SQL Agent

SQL Agent is a service provided by SQL Server to run jobs on schedule or on certain events. As a data integration platform, SSIS has good integration with SQL Agent. Usually database administrators are very familiar with SQL Agent. One common scenario is using SQL Agent to run an SSIS package every night to update the data warehouse incrementally.

A SQL Agent job consists of several job steps, and each job step is running under a given security context. This security context determines which resources are accessible to this package. It's not related to the user who creates this job. Usually this credential is different than the credential of the user who creates this job. Lots of users do not have a clear understanding of it. They simply create a SQL Agent job and find the SSIS package throws an error during run time, such as access denied on a database connection establishment.

To make sure your SSIS Agent job works correctly, this section explains how SQL Agent security works and how to manage it to run SSIS packages under appropriate credentials.

Requirements

To create a SQL Agent job you must have the required privileges. Currently only the following role members can create SQL Agent jobs:

- Server role sysadmin
- Database role SQLAgentUserRole, SQLAgentReaderRole, and SQLAgentOperatorRole in the msdb database

There are three steps to creating a SQL Agent job:

1. Create a *credential* that specifies the security context.
2. Create a *proxy account* that is associated with this credential.
3. Create the job, and each job step can reference different proxy accounts.

It looks a little complicated. The good news is that you don't have to repeat these steps every time when you try to create a SQL Agent job. After the required proxy accounts are set up, you can reference them in different SQL Agent jobs. In this section you are guided through those steps one by one.

Create Credentials

Before creating a SQL Agent proxy account, you first need to create a credential in SQL Server. A credential is usually a Windows account that has the specified security context. A credential could be associated with multiple SQL Agent proxy accounts.

To create a credential, in SQL Server Management Studio, right-click the Credential node and select New Credential from the shortcut menu, as shown in Figure 17-15.

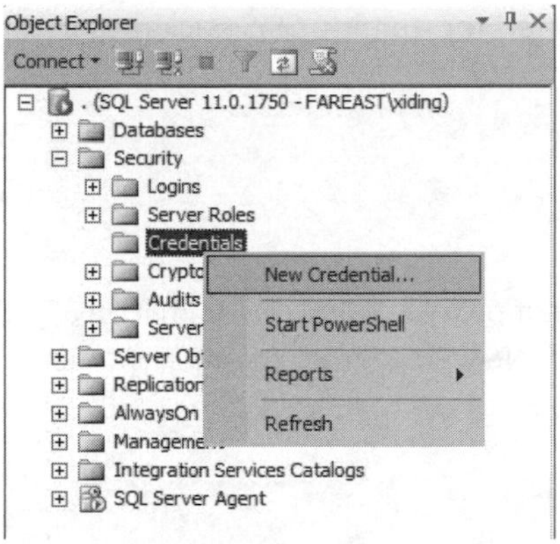

FIGURE 17-15 Create a new credential.

The New Credential dialog box (see Figure 17-16) opens, which allows you to name the credential and associate it with an existing Windows identity.

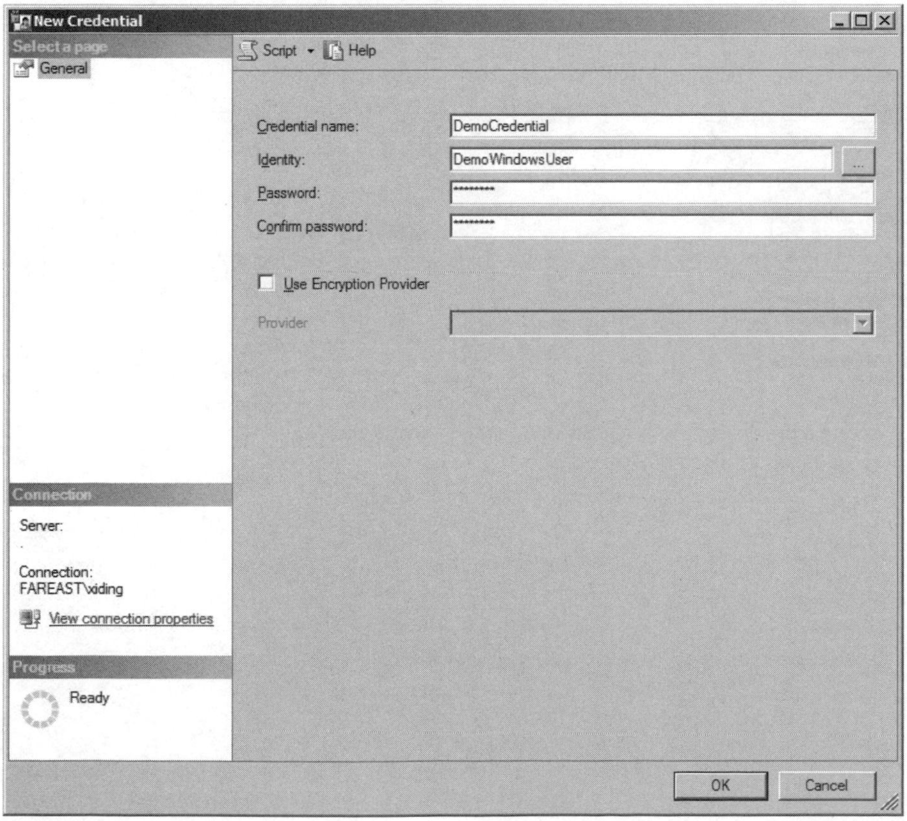

FIGURE 17-16 Create a new credential.

> **Tip** Do not simply use an administrator account as the credential. To protect against malicious attacks, you should always use a Windows identity with the lowest level of privileges. Consider creating accounts that are dedicated for running SSIS packages in SQL Agent.

Create Proxy Accounts

After you create a SQL credential you can create a SQL Agent proxy account. To do that, in SQL Server Management Studio, right-click the Proxies node and select New Proxy from the shortcut menu, as shown in Figure 17-17.

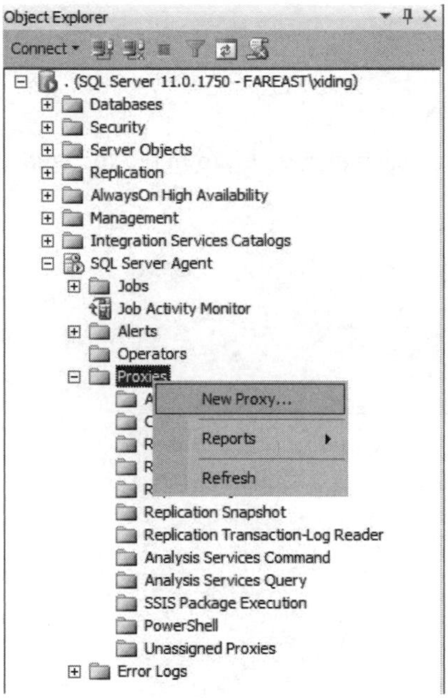

FIGURE 17-17 Create a proxy account in SQL Server Management Studio.

In the dialog box type in the proxy name and associate it with the new credential you just created, as shown in Figure 17-18. Remember you must select the SQL Server Integration Services Package check box in the list so this proxy account has access to SSIS jobs. Otherwise this proxy account will be not shown in the available proxy account list when you create an SSIS job step.

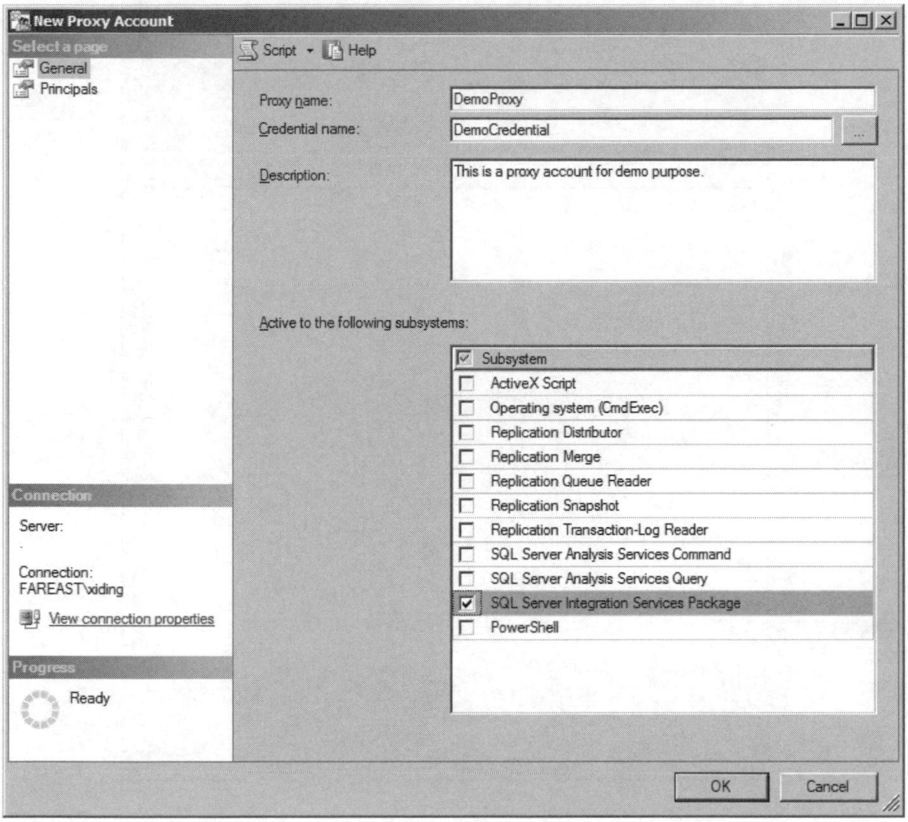

FIGURE 17-18 Associate the proxy account with credentials.

Like any other resources in SQL Server, you can manage the permissions on this newly created SQL Agent proxy account. Click Principals in the left pane. The resulting dialog box (see Figure 17-19) will show a list allowing you to specify who can use this proxy account.

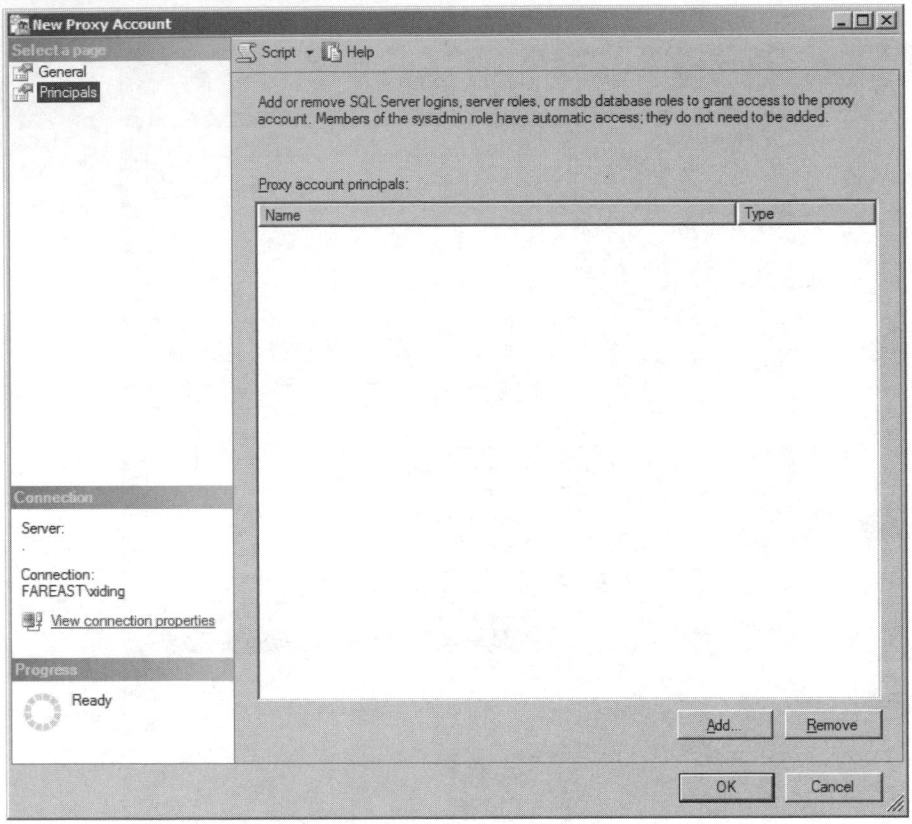

FIGURE 17-19 Manage the permissions on proxy accounts.

By default, only sysadmin server role members have access to this proxy account. In other words, this proxy account is invisible to other users when they create their own SQL Agent jobs. You can click Add to grant permissions to other users.

SQL Server Management Studio organizes all proxy accounts according to their categories. In Figure 17-17 you can see there are several subnodes under the Proxies node. These are called proxy subsystems. For your newly created proxy account, SQL Server Management Studio will show it under the SSIS Package Executions subsystem. If a proxy account has access to multiple subsystems, it will be shown under all those subnodes.

Create SQL Agent Jobs

Now everything you need has been created. You can create your own SQL Agent job that will execute under that proxy account. Here are the steps to create a SQL Agent job that consists of an SSIS job step:

1. Right-click the Jobs node under the SQL Server Agent node.
2. Select New Job.
3. Specify the job name in the first page.
4. Click the Steps tab.
5. Click New in the steps list.
6. Type the step name and choose the SQL Server Integration Services Package type in the drop-down box.
7. Choose your proxy account in the Run As drop-down box.
8. Specify other SSIS-related information.
9. Click OK.
10. Specify the job schedule or other steps that you want.
11. Click OK to save the job.

Figure 17-20 shows the editor window of the SSIS job step. By default there is only one account, SQL Server Agent Service Account, which is the Windows account you used to run the SQL Agent service itself. Normally this account does not have privileges to access SSIS Catalog objects unless you run the SQL Agent service with an administrator account. Now your proxy account appears in the list. This job step will be executed as this proxy account as if this account logs on to the server machine and runs the SSIS package.

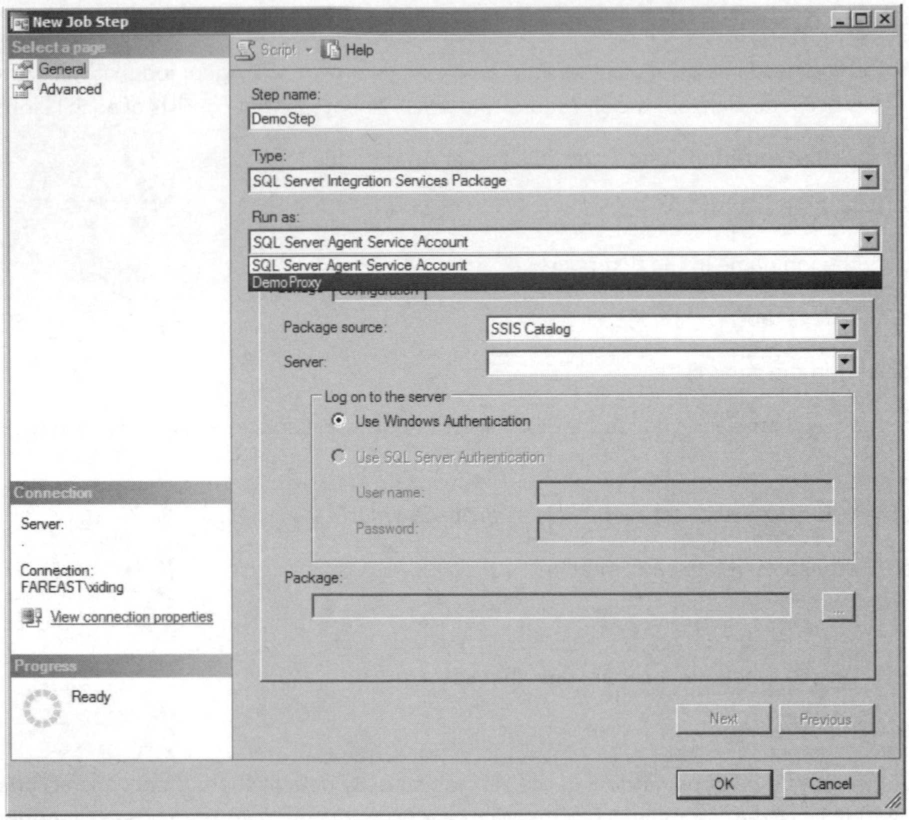

FIGURE 17-20 Editor window of the SSIS job step.

Summary

This chapter discussed various topics related to SSIS security in three parts. The first part focused on how to protect packages outside of the SSIS Catalog. The chapter showed how to control access to packages in different locations, how to set the protection level, and how to manage sensitive variables and parameters.

The second part focused on the new SSIS Catalog in SQL Server 2012, which brings lots of new security challenges. The SSIS Catalog defines a clear security model and a set of security APIs, including database views and stored procures. The security model contains the principal types, securable types, and permission types. The security APIs allow you to control the permissions defined on different securables, including granting permissions, revoking permissions, and denying permissions.

The last part explored how to integrate SQL Server Agent with SSIS. SQL Agent uses its own security mechanism to control the security context of each running package. It's very important for you to clearly understand the mechanism so your packages are running under the correct security credentials. The key concept is the proxy account. Every job step references a proxy account, and runs under the security credential of that proxy account instead of the job creator account.

CHAPTER 18

Understanding SSIS Logging

In This Chapter

Logging is an important feature provided by SSIS to help users work more efficiently. By analyzing the generated log entries, experienced users can quickly narrow down the problem scope or find a good way to optimize package performance. In some cases, logging is the only way to troubleshoot issues with the execution of SSIS packages. Logging is also used for auditing specific operations performed at different stages of data loading in some organizations. This chapter is useful for both the developer and database administrator who need to work with SSIS.

Configure Logging Options

By default, an SSIS package does not produce any logs, so you incur no performance cost. Often, logging is a balance between having the right information needed when there are issues during SSIS package execution and the potential performance overheads. To turn on the logging behavior, you need to explicitly configure the logging options in an SSIS package. Basically there are three steps:

- Choose containers that should emit logs.
- Choose interested events on selected containers.
- Add log providers to persist those generated logs.

Let's illustrate those steps one by one with a sample package.

Choose Containers

In an SSIS package there are multiple containers and tasks. Each container or task could emit its logs. The first step is therefore to choose the containers that should emit logs. Because a task is also a container (named *task host container*), we use the term *container* to represent both of them in the following text.

To show how to pick a container in log options, let's start with a sample package, shown in Figure 18-1.

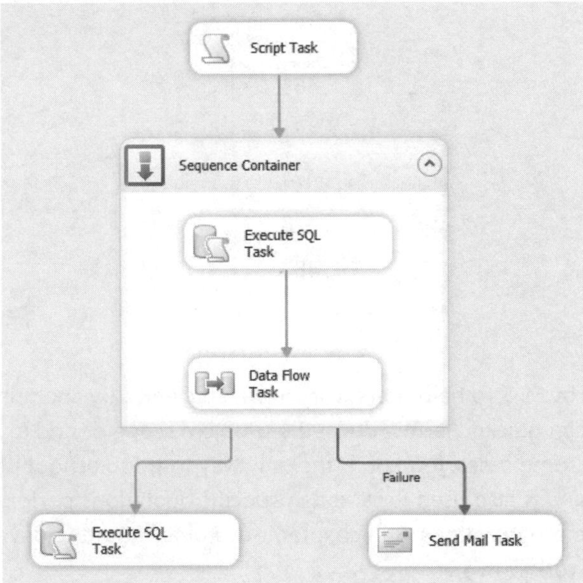

FIGURE 18-1 A sample package.

This sample package demonstrates a typical extract–transform–load (ETL) process. It first does some initialization work in a Script task and an Execute SQL task, and then performs the data transformation in a Data Flow task. All the database manipulation work is included in a sequence container, which includes the Execute SQL task and Data Flow task. Depending on the outcome of the sequence container, a success log is inserted into the database or a failure email notification is sent.

Suppose we are only interested in the log items on the Data Flow task and package itself. What shall we do to define the logging options?

Select the SSIS | Logging menu item. You will see the Configure SSIS Logs: Package dialog box. On the left, there is a tree view pane that shows all containers and tasks according to the package hierarchy. Figure 18-2 shows the initial state of that view.

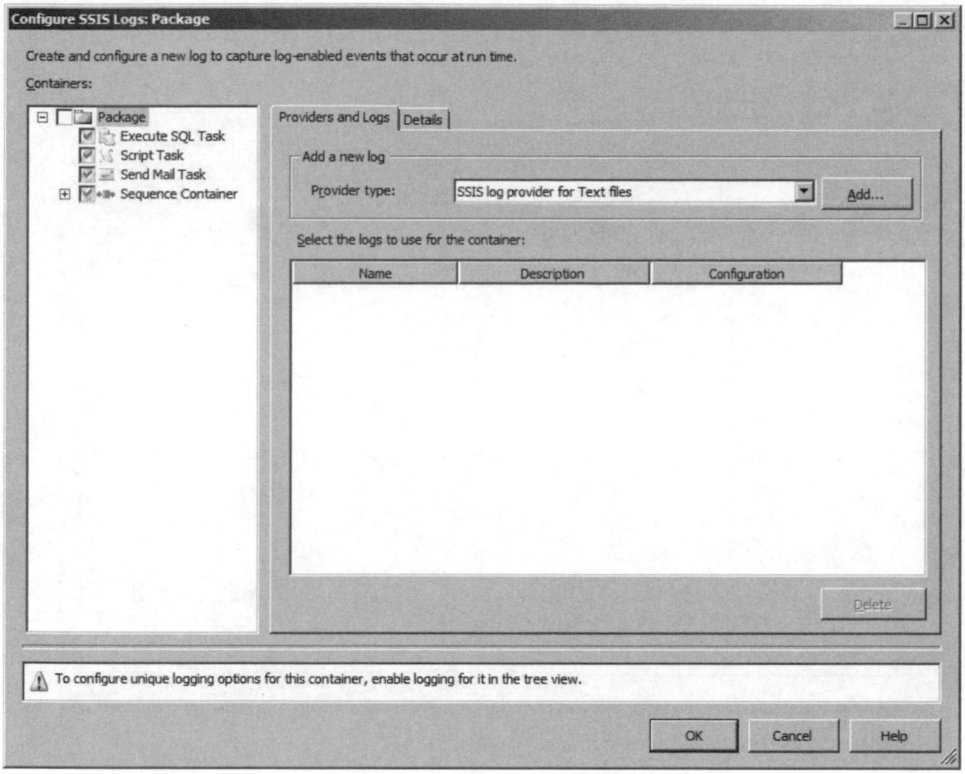

FIGURE 18-2 The initial selected status of each container.

As you can see, there is a check box before each container or task. This check box has three states with the following meanings:

- **Selected** This means explicit yes: This container will always produce logs.
- **Cleared** This means explicit no: This container will never produce logs.
- **Unavailable** This means "inherit options from its parent container." If its parent container produces logs, it also will. Likewise it will not produce logs if its parent does not produce logs.

By default the top-level container (package itself) is not selected and all other containers inherit options from it, so in the default situation no logs will be produced. To get our desired behavior, we should explicitly select the package container and the Data Flow task, and clear all other containers. Figure 18-3 shows the new state.

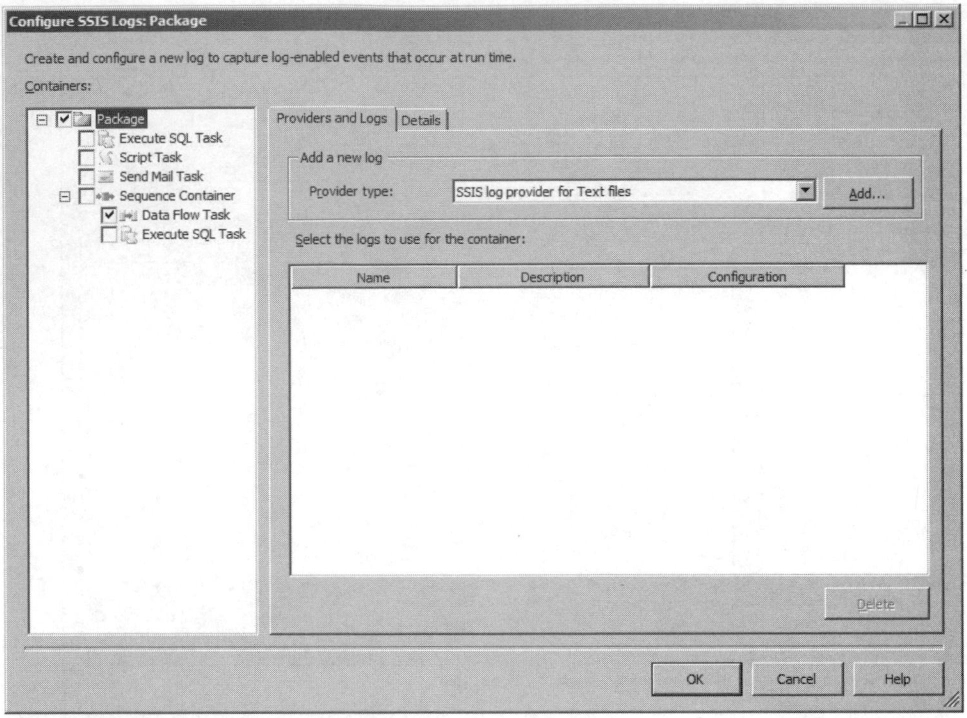

FIGURE 18-3 Choose containers that should produce logs.

Select Events

After you decide which containers should emit logs, the next question is which events should be logged on those containers. Every container has its own event list. This list is fixed and determined by the SSIS engine or the task developer. You cannot change it, but you can pick only the desired ones from the list. You will find the event list after you select a container in the left list. For example, Figure 18-4 shows all available events on the Data Flow task.

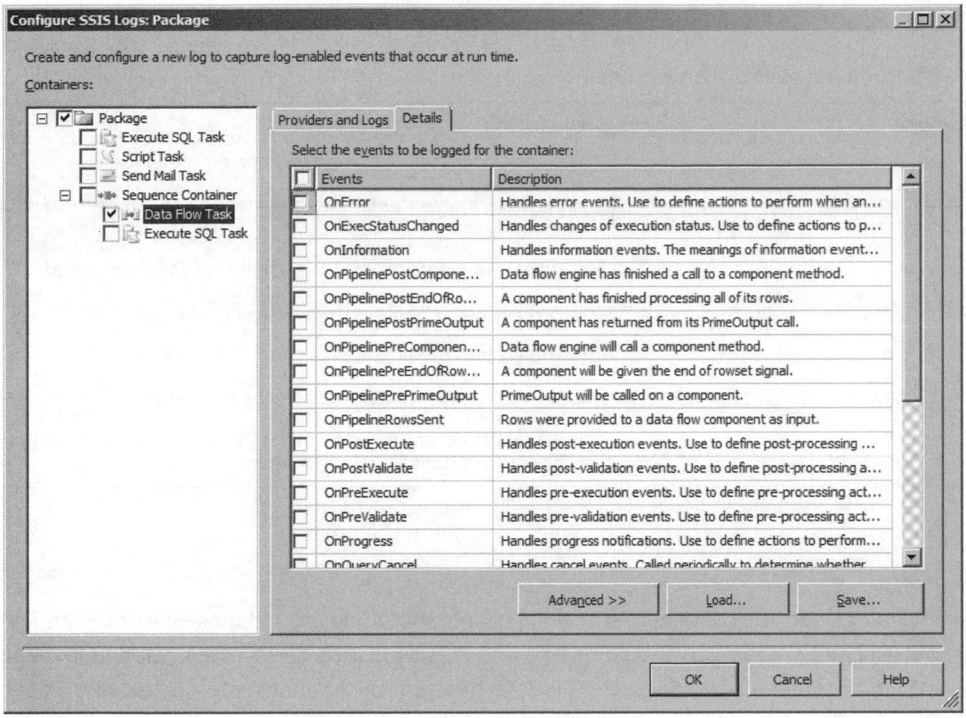

FIGURE 18-4 All available events on the Data Flow task.

From Figure 18-4 you can see that some events are standard items that you can find on other containers, such as *OnError, OnInformation,* or *OnPreExecute*. However, there are also lots of events that are specific to the Data Flow task, such as *OnPipelineRowsSent* or *OnPipelinePrePrimeOutput*. In the list there are short descriptions for each event. To finish our demo, let's just select the header check box in the Events column to select all events.

Table 18-1 shows some common events and their descriptions.

TABLE 18-1 Common events and descriptions

Event Name	Description
OnError	This event is triggered when an execution error happens.
OnInformation	This event is triggered when the container wants to show some informational messages.
OnPreExecute	This event is triggered before the current container is executed.
OnPostExecute	This event is triggered after the current container is executed.
OnPreValidate	This event is triggered before the current container is validated.
OnPostValidate	This event is triggered after the current container is validated.
OnQueryCancel	This is a callback event raised from the SSIS engine to check whether the user has cancelled the current execution.

Add Log Providers

Now we have decided the container list and the events should be logged on each container. The last step is to specify where the logs should be written to. SSIS encapsulates this information into a log provider. Each different log provider writes logs to different destinations, such as text files or SQL Server. The log provider is also responsible for formatting logs. You can add multiple log providers in a package, and each container could reference a different set of log providers. In a simple scenario you can only define one log provider and all containers write their logs to that provider. In a complicated scenario you can define multiple providers and each container writes logs into a different set of log providers.

In our case we only define one log provider to write logs into text files. Here are the steps to do it:

1. In the Configure SSIS Logs: Package dialog box, click the root node, Package.
2. In the Provider Type drop-down list, select SSIS Log Provider For Text Files and click Add.
3. A new row will appear in the Log Providers list. Select the row.
4. Click the Configuration cell in the selected row, and click <New Connection>.
5. In the Connection Manager dialog box, select Create File and input a valid file name.
6. Click OK.
7. Click the Data Flow task in the list and select the new log provider.

Figure 18-5 shows the screen shot of creating a new log provider for text files, and Figure 18-6 shows the configuration of the corresponding flat file connection manager.

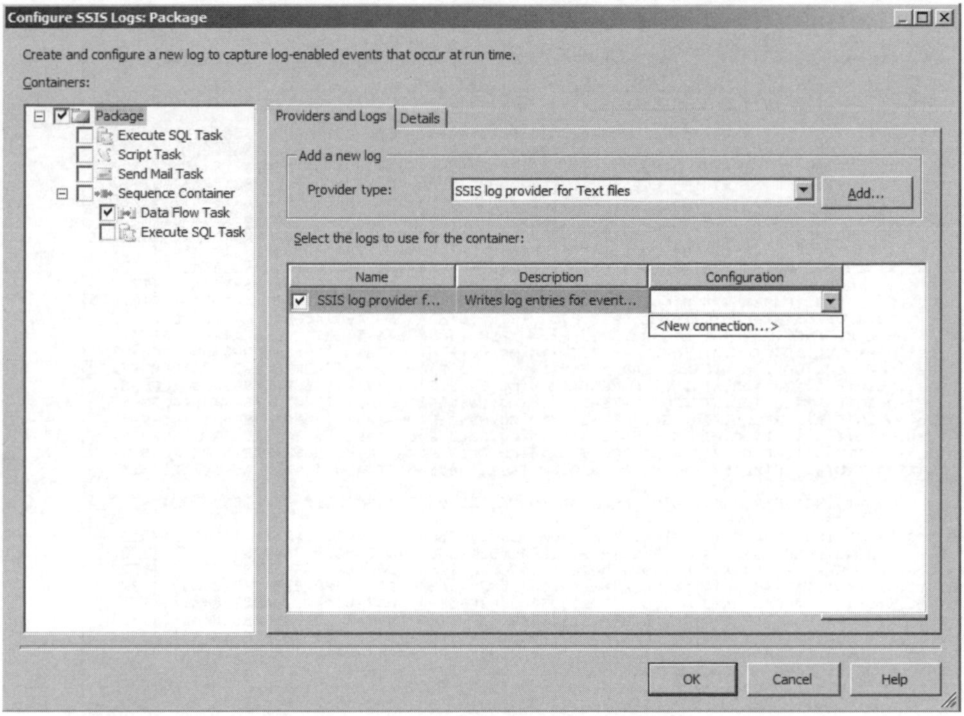

FIGURE 18-5 Add an SSIS log provider for text files.

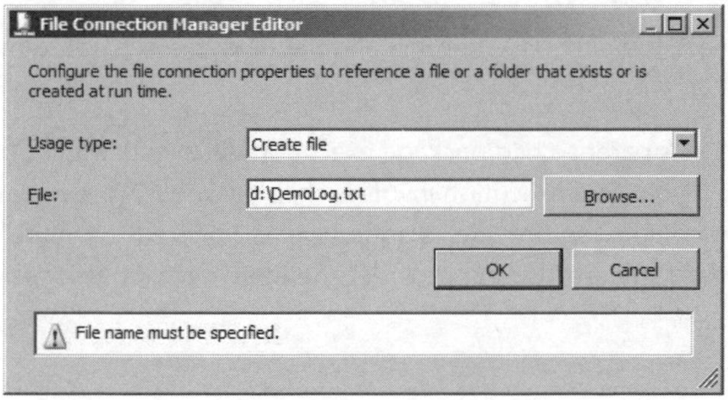

FIGURE 18-6 Configure the flat file connection manager.

After the preceding steps, you define a log provider and the selected two containers will write their logs into that provider. Now run the package in the package designer. After the execution finishes, you will see a new file, DemoLog.txt, is created. Figure 18-7 shows the generated log file.

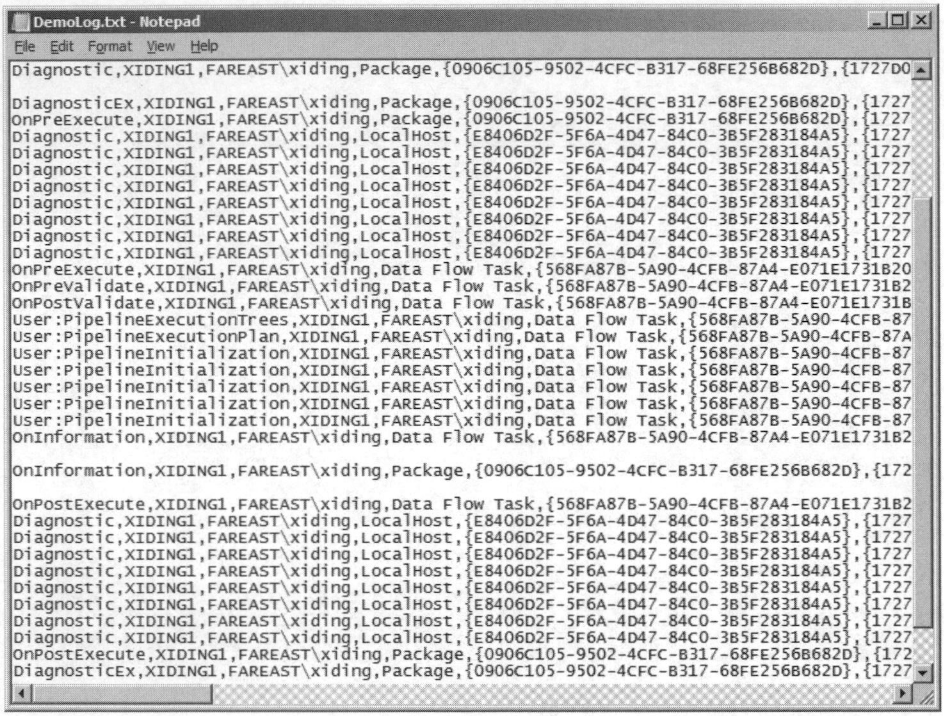
DemoLog.txt - Notepad

File Edit Format View Help

```
Diagnostic,XIDING1,FAREAST\xiding,Package,{0906C105-9502-4CFC-B317-68FE256B682D},{1727D0

DiagnosticEx,XIDING1,FAREAST\xiding,Package,{0906C105-9502-4CFC-B317-68FE256B682D},{1727
OnPreExecute,XIDING1,FAREAST\xiding,Package,{0906C105-9502-4CFC-B317-68FE256B682D},{1727
Diagnostic,XIDING1,FAREAST\xiding,LocalHost,{E8406D2F-5F6A-4D47-84C0-3B5F283184A5},{1727
Diagnostic,XIDING1,FAREAST\xiding,LocalHost,{E8406D2F-5F6A-4D47-84C0-3B5F283184A5},{1727
Diagnostic,XIDING1,FAREAST\xiding,LocalHost,{E8406D2F-5F6A-4D47-84C0-3B5F283184A5},{1727
Diagnostic,XIDING1,FAREAST\xiding,LocalHost,{E8406D2F-5F6A-4D47-84C0-3B5F283184A5},{1727
Diagnostic,XIDING1,FAREAST\xiding,LocalHost,{E8406D2F-5F6A-4D47-84C0-3B5F283184A5},{1727
Diagnostic,XIDING1,FAREAST\xiding,LocalHost,{E8406D2F-5F6A-4D47-84C0-3B5F283184A5},{1727
Diagnostic,XIDING1,FAREAST\xiding,LocalHost,{E8406D2F-5F6A-4D47-84C0-3B5F283184A5},{1727
Diagnostic,XIDING1,FAREAST\xiding,LocalHost,{E8406D2F-5F6A-4D47-84C0-3B5F283184A5},{1727
OnPreExecute,XIDING1,FAREAST\xiding,Data Flow Task,{568FA87B-5A90-4CFB-87A4-E071E1731B20
OnPreValidate,XIDING1,FAREAST\xiding,Data Flow Task,{568FA87B-5A90-4CFB-87A4-E071E1731B2
OnPostValidate,XIDING1,FAREAST\xiding,Data Flow Task,{568FA87B-5A90-4CFB-87A4-E071E1731B
User:PipelineExecutionTrees,XIDING1,FAREAST\xiding,Data Flow Task,{568FA87B-5A90-4CFB-87
User:PipelineExecutionPlan,XIDING1,FAREAST\xiding,Data Flow Task,{568FA87B-5A90-4CFB-87A
User:PipelineInitialization,XIDING1,FAREAST\xiding,Data Flow Task,{568FA87B-5A90-4CFB-87
User:PipelineInitialization,XIDING1,FAREAST\xiding,Data Flow Task,{568FA87B-5A90-4CFB-87
User:PipelineInitialization,XIDING1,FAREAST\xiding,Data Flow Task,{568FA87B-5A90-4CFB-87
User:PipelineInitialization,XIDING1,FAREAST\xiding,Data Flow Task,{568FA87B-5A90-4CFB-87
User:PipelineInitialization,XIDING1,FAREAST\xiding,Data Flow Task,{568FA87B-5A90-4CFB-87
OnInformation,XIDING1,FAREAST\xiding,Data Flow Task,{568FA87B-5A90-4CFB-87A4-E071E1731B2

OnInformation,XIDING1,FAREAST\xiding,Package,{0906C105-9502-4CFC-B317-68FE256B682D},{172

OnPostExecute,XIDING1,FAREAST\xiding,Data Flow Task,{568FA87B-5A90-4CFB-87A4-E071E1731B2
Diagnostic,XIDING1,FAREAST\xiding,LocalHost,{E8406D2F-5F6A-4D47-84C0-3B5F283184A5},{1727
Diagnostic,XIDING1,FAREAST\xiding,LocalHost,{E8406D2F-5F6A-4D47-84C0-3B5F283184A5},{1727
Diagnostic,XIDING1,FAREAST\xiding,LocalHost,{E8406D2F-5F6A-4D47-84C0-3B5F283184A5},{1727
Diagnostic,XIDING1,FAREAST\xiding,LocalHost,{E8406D2F-5F6A-4D47-84C0-3B5F283184A5},{1727
Diagnostic,XIDING1,FAREAST\xiding,LocalHost,{E8406D2F-5F6A-4D47-84C0-3B5F283184A5},{1727
Diagnostic,XIDING1,FAREAST\xiding,LocalHost,{E8406D2F-5F6A-4D47-84C0-3B5F283184A5},{1727
Diagnostic,XIDING1,FAREAST\xiding,LocalHost,{E8406D2F-5F6A-4D47-84C0-3B5F283184A5},{1727
Diagnostic,XIDING1,FAREAST\xiding,LocalHost,{E8406D2F-5F6A-4D47-84C0-3B5F283184A5},{1727
OnPostExecute,XIDING1,FAREAST\xiding,Package,{0906C105-9502-4CFC-B317-68FE256B682D},{172
DiagnosticEx,XIDING1,FAREAST\xiding,Package,{0906C105-9502-4CFC-B317-68FE256B682D},{1727
```

FIGURE 18-7 The sample log file generated by log provider for text files.

As you can see, it's a plain text file. Each log entry is a new line and the fields are separated by a comma.

One case you need to pay attention to is parent–child package execution. All events will propagate from child packages to parent package if your SSIS execution involves child packages. Those events are still logged in the parent package even if no log provider is added in child packages. On the other hand, those events will be logged twice if there are also log providers defined in child packages.

Log Providers

In the previous section we demonstrated how to write logs into a text file. In that case we used the SSIS log provider for text files, which is very straightforward. Actually there are five different built-in log providers in SSIS. Each of them writes logs to a different destination with a different format. In this section we quickly go through those log providers and explain their use.

Text Files

The text files log provider writes log entries to ASCII text files in a comma-separated value (CSV) format. The default file name extension for this provider is .log. As you have seen in the example, this log provider requires a flat file connection manager. You can refer to Figure 18-7 for a sample text file log.

SQL Server

The SQL Server log provider writes log entries into the *sysssislog* table in a SQL Server database. This log provider requires an OLE DB connection manager. It will create the table *dbo.sysssislog* automatically if the table does not exist in the target database; otherwise, it just appends the logs to that table. Because that table is a system table, you need to expand the System Tables node in SQL Server Management Studio to find it. See Figure 18-8.

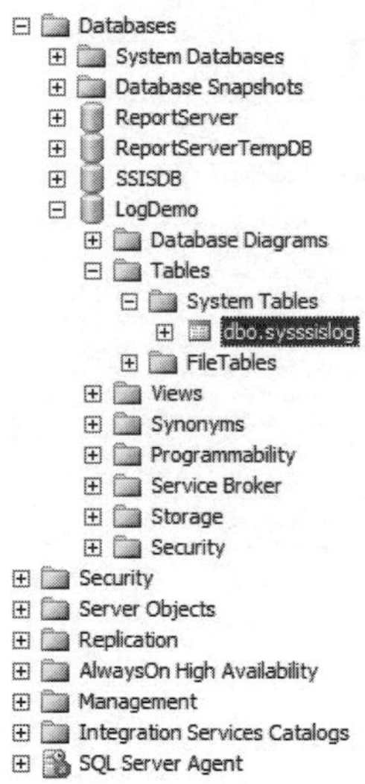

FIGURE 18-8 The *sysssislog* table in SQL Server.

The table schema contains all possible log fields, including event, computer, operator, and so forth. Figure 18-9 shows some sample data rows in the table.

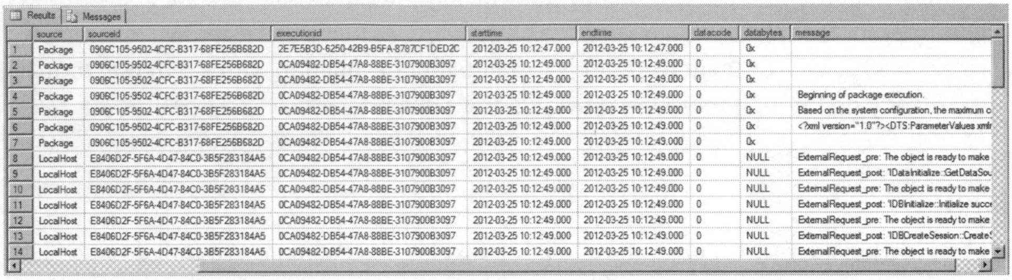

	source	sourceid	executionid	starttime	endtime	datacode	databytes	message
1	Package	0906C105-9502-4CFC-B317-68FE256B682D	2E7E5B3D-6250-42B9-B5FA-8787CF1DED2C	2012-03-25 10:12:47.000	2012-03-25 10:12:47.000	0	0x	
2	Package	0906C105-9502-4CFC-B317-68FE256B682D	0CA09482-DB54-47A8-88BE-3107900B3097	2012-03-25 10:12:49.000	2012-03-25 10:12:49.000	0	0x	
3	Package	0906C105-9502-4CFC-B317-68FE256B682D	0CA09482-DB54-47A8-88BE-3107900B3097	2012-03-25 10:12:49.000	2012-03-25 10:12:49.000	0	0x	
4	Package	0906C105-9502-4CFC-B317-68FE256B682D	0CA09482-DB54-47A8-88BE-3107900B3097	2012-03-25 10:12:49.000	2012-03-25 10:12:49.000	0	0x	Beginning of package execution.
5	Package	0906C105-9502-4CFC-B317-68FE256B682D	0CA09482-DB54-47A8-88BE-3107900B3097	2012-03-25 10:12:49.000	2012-03-25 10:12:49.000	0	0x	Based on the system configuration, the maximum c
6	Package	0906C105-9502-4CFC-B317-68FE256B682D	0CA09482-DB54-47A8-88BE-3107900B3097	2012-03-25 10:12:49.000	2012-03-25 10:12:49.000	0	0x	<?xml version="1.0"?><DTS:ParameterValues xml
7	Package	0906C105-9502-4CFC-B317-68FE256B682D	0CA09482-DB54-47A8-88BE-3107900B3097	2012-03-25 10:12:49.000	2012-03-25 10:12:49.000	0	0x	
8	LocalHost	E8406D2F-5F6A-4D47-84C0-3B5F283184A5	0CA09482-DB54-47A8-88BE-3107900B3097	2012-03-25 10:12:49.000	2012-03-25 10:12:49.000	0	NULL	ExternalRequest_pre: The object is ready to make
9	LocalHost	E8406D2F-5F6A-4D47-84C0-3B5F283184A5	0CA09482-DB54-47A8-88BE-3107900B3097	2012-03-25 10:12:49.000	2012-03-25 10:12:49.000	0	NULL	ExternalRequest_post: 'IDataInitialize::GetDataSou
10	LocalHost	E8406D2F-5F6A-4D47-84C0-3B5F283184A5	0CA09482-DB54-47A8-88BE-3107900B3097	2012-03-25 10:12:49.000	2012-03-25 10:12:49.000	0	NULL	ExternalRequest_pre: The object is ready to make
11	LocalHost	E8406D2F-5F6A-4D47-84C0-3B5F283184A5	0CA09482-DB54-47A8-88BE-3107900B3097	2012-03-25 10:12:49.000	2012-03-25 10:12:49.000	0	NULL	ExternalRequest_post: 'IDBInitialize::Initialize succe
12	LocalHost	E8406D2F-5F6A-4D47-84C0-3B5F283184A5	0CA09482-DB54-47A8-88BE-3107900B3097	2012-03-25 10:12:49.000	2012-03-25 10:12:49.000	0	NULL	ExternalRequest_pre: The object is ready to make
13	LocalHost	E8406D2F-5F6A-4D47-84C0-3B5F283184A5	0CA09482-DB54-47A8-88BE-3107900B3097	2012-03-25 10:12:49.000	2012-03-25 10:12:49.000	0	NULL	ExternalRequest_post: 'IDBCreateSession::Create
14	LocalHost	E8406D2F-5F6A-4D47-84C0-3B5F283184A5	0CA09482-DB54-47A8-88BE-3107900B3097	2012-03-25 10:12:49.000	2012-03-25 10:12:49.000	0	NULL	ExternalRequest_pre: The object is ready to make

FIGURE 18-9 Sample data rows in the *dbo.sysssislog* table.

SQL Server Profiler

SQL Server Profiler log provider writes logs into a trace file, so you can view them using SQL Server Profiler. This log provider also requires a flat file connection manager. After the specified file is generated, run SQL Server Profiler and click File | Open | Script File to open the trace file in the profiler. You will see all log entries, as shown in Figure 18-10.

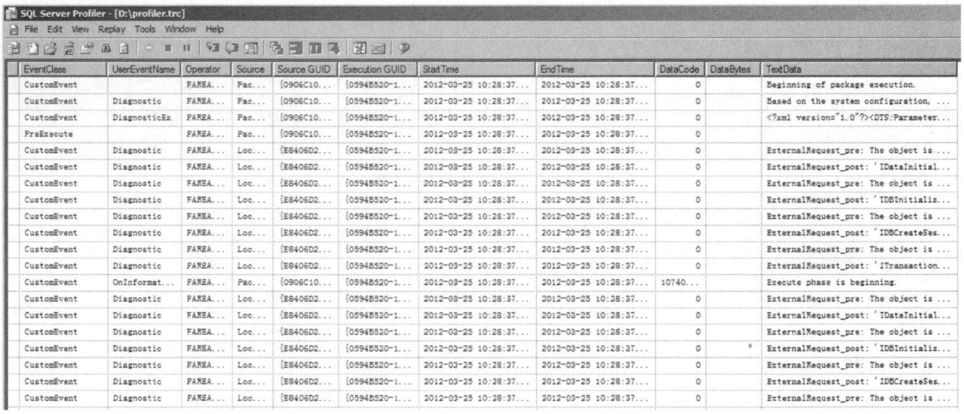

SQL Server Profiler - [D:\profiler.trc]

File Edit View Replay Tools Window Help

EventClass	UserEventName	Operator	Source	Source GUID	Execution GUID	StartTime	EndTime	DataCode	DataBytes	TextData
CustomEvent		FAREA...	Pac...	{0906C10...	{0594B520-1...	2012-03-25 10:28:37...	2012-03-25 10:28:37...	0		Beginning of package execution.
CustomEvent	Diagnostic	FAREA...	Pac...	{0906C10...	{0594B520-1...	2012-03-25 10:28:37...	2012-03-25 10:28:37...	0		Based on the system configuration, ...
CustomEvent	DiagnosticEx	FAREA...	Pac...	{0906C10...	{0594B520-1...	2012-03-25 10:28:37...	2012-03-25 10:28:37...	0		<?xml version="1.0"?><DTS:Parameter...
PreExecute		FAREA...	Pac...	{0906C10...	{0594B520-1...	2012-03-25 10:28:37...	2012-03-25 10:28:37...	0		
CustomEvent	Diagnostic	FAREA...	Loc...	{E8406D2...	{0594B520-1...	2012-03-25 10:28:37...	2012-03-25 10:28:37...	0		ExternalRequest_pre: The object is ...
CustomEvent	Diagnostic	FAREA...	Loc...	{E8406D2...	{0594B520-1...	2012-03-25 10:28:37...	2012-03-25 10:28:37...	0		ExternalRequest_post: 'IDataInitial...
CustomEvent	Diagnostic	FAREA...	Loc...	{E8406D2...	{0594B520-1...	2012-03-25 10:28:37...	2012-03-25 10:28:37...	0		ExternalRequest_pre: The object is ...
CustomEvent	Diagnostic	FAREA...	Loc...	{E8406D2...	{0594B520-1...	2012-03-25 10:28:37...	2012-03-25 10:28:37...	0		ExternalRequest_post: 'IDBInitializ...
CustomEvent	Diagnostic	FAREA...	Loc...	{E8406D2...	{0594B520-1...	2012-03-25 10:28:37...	2012-03-25 10:28:37...	0		ExternalRequest_pre: The object is ...
CustomEvent	Diagnostic	FAREA...	Loc...	{E8406D2...	{0594B520-1...	2012-03-25 10:28:37...	2012-03-25 10:28:37...	0		ExternalRequest_post: 'IDBCreateSes...
CustomEvent	Diagnostic	FAREA...	Loc...	{E8406D2...	{0594B520-1...	2012-03-25 10:28:37...	2012-03-25 10:28:37...	0		ExternalRequest_pre: The object is ...
CustomEvent	Diagnostic	FAREA...	Loc...	{E8406D2...	{0594B520-1...	2012-03-25 10:28:37...	2012-03-25 10:28:37...	0		ExternalRequest_post: 'ITransaction...
CustomEvent	OnInformat...	FAREA...	Pac...	{0906C10...	{0594B520-1...	2012-03-25 10:28:37...	2012-03-25 10:28:37...	10740...		Execute phase is beginning.
CustomEvent	Diagnostic	FAREA...	Loc...	{E8406D2...	{0594B520-1...	2012-03-25 10:28:37...	2012-03-25 10:28:37...	0		ExternalRequest_pre: The object is ...
CustomEvent	Diagnostic	FAREA...	Loc...	{E8406D2...	{0594B520-1...	2012-03-25 10:28:37...	2012-03-25 10:28:37...	0		ExternalRequest_post: 'IDataInitial...
CustomEvent	Diagnostic	FAREA...	Loc...	{E8406D2...	{0594B520-1...	2012-03-25 10:28:37...	2012-03-25 10:28:37...	0		ExternalRequest_pre: The object is ...
CustomEvent	Diagnostic	FAREA...	Loc...	{E8406D2...	{0594B520-1...	2012-03-25 10:28:37...	2012-03-25 10:28:37...	0		ExternalRequest_post: 'IDBInitializ...
CustomEvent	Diagnostic	FAREA...	Loc...	{E8406D2...	{0594B520-1...	2012-03-25 10:28:37...	2012-03-25 10:28:37...	0		ExternalRequest_pre: The object is ...
CustomEvent	Diagnostic	FAREA...	Loc...	{E8406D2...	{0594B520-1...	2012-03-25 10:28:37...	2012-03-25 10:28:37...	0		ExternalRequest_post: 'IDBCreateSes...
CustomEvent	Diagnostic	FAREA...	Loc...	{E8406D2...	{0594B520-1...	2012-03-25 10:28:37...	2012-03-25 10:28:37...	0		ExternalRequest_pre: The object is ...

FIGURE 18-10 A sample log file opened by SQL Server Profiler.

Windows Event Log

This log provider always writes entries to the Application log in the Windows Event log on the local computer. It is probably the simplest log provider because it does not require any configurations or connection managers.

To view the generated logs, from the Start menu, select Run and type **eventvwr.msc**. This command launches the Windows Event Viewer tool. Click the Application node in the left pane under the node Windows Logs. Now you can find the SSIS log items in the right list (see Figure 18-11).

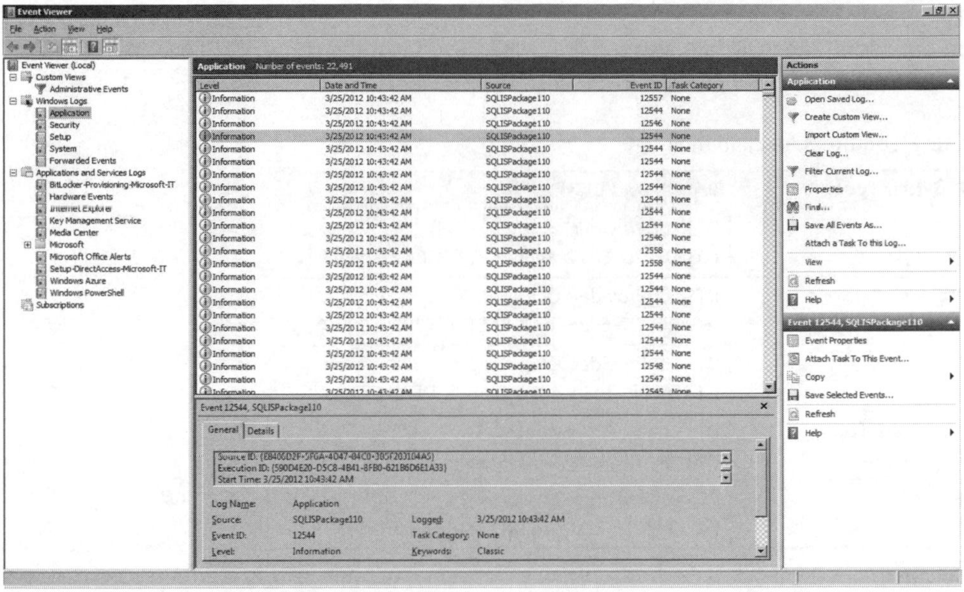

FIGURE 18-11 SSIS logs in Windows Event Viewer.

XML Files

This log provider is similar to the text files log provider. The only difference is that it formats log items in XML format instead of CSV format. See Figure 18-12 for a sample XML file generated by this log provider.

```
  <?xml version="1.0"?>
- <dtslogs>
  - <dtslog>
    - <record>
        <event>OnPreValidate</event>
        <message/>
        <computer>XIDING1</computer>
        <operator>FAREAST\xiding</operator>
        <source>Package</source>
        <sourceid>{0906C105-9502-4CFC-B317-68FE256B682D}</sourceid>
        <executionid>{2E7E5B3D-6250-42B9-B5FA-8787CF1DED2C}</executionid>
        <starttime>3/25/2012 10:43:40 AM</starttime>
        <endtime>3/25/2012 10:43:40 AM</endtime>
        <datacode>0</datacode>
        <databytes>0x</databytes>
      </record>
    - <record>
        <event>OnPreValidate</event>
        <message/>
        <computer>XIDING1</computer>
        <operator>FAREAST\xiding</operator>
        <source>Data Flow Task</source>
        <sourceid>{568FA87B-5A90-4CFB-87A4-E071E1731B20}</sourceid>
        <executionid>{2E7E5B3D-6250-42B9-B5FA-8787CF1DED2C}</executionid>
        <starttime>3/25/2012 10:43:40 AM</starttime>
        <endtime>3/25/2012 10:43:40 AM</endtime>
        <datacode>0</datacode>
        <databytes>0x</databytes>
      </record>
```

FIGURE 18-12 SSIS logs generated by XML log provider.

If you are creating packages via a programmatic method, you need to know the ID of those different log providers. Those IDs are also required when you set some command-line options related to log providers. Table 18-2 shows the ID for each log provider.

TABLE 18-2 Log providers and their IDs

Log Provider Type	ProgID and Class ID
Text file	DTS.LogProviderTextFile.3 { 03E07F2D-EA22-440B-8DE9-B56A22F0E9FF }
SQL Profiler	DTS.LogProviderSQLProfiler.3 {601D0CD1-672E-4F07-BA58-BFF7B5CE0060}
SQL Server	DTS.LogProviderSQLServer.3 {1E4F606D-382A-4812-8E08-C5D5A04FFE98}
Windows Event Log	DTS.LogProviderEventLog.3 {9BD4455F-7B98-4280-9AA9-932EC8B411D9}
XML File	DTS.LogProviderXMLFile.3 {9D1392C1-01C0-4148-A258-F20AF6E4EA3E }

Logging in the SSIS Catalog

In this section, you learn how logging is done for SSIS projects that have been deployed to the SSIS Catalog. SSIS Catalog provides some logging options so you can effectively do logging on the server. Besides the log providers defined in the package, logs are also captured into a view named *catalog.execution_events*.

When there are errors, the corresponding error context is also captured. An error context contains all property values on the current container and all its ancestor containers.

Logging Levels

Every execution instance on the SSIS Catalog has a property named *Logging Level*. You can find this property on the Advanced tab of the Execute Package dialog box, as shown in Figure 18-13.

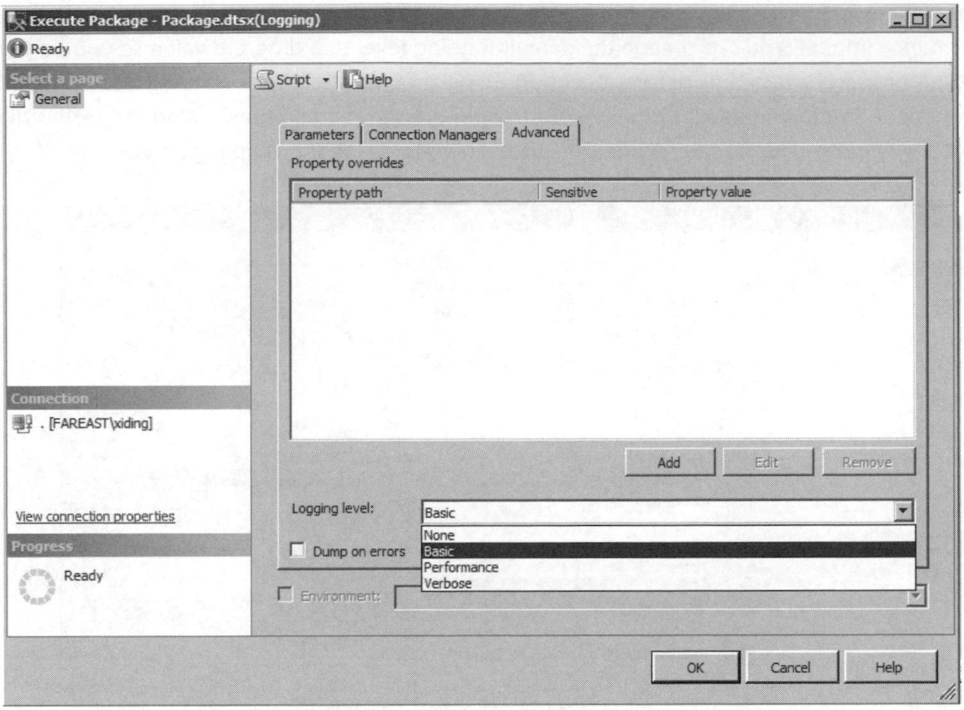

FIGURE 18-13 Configure the Logging Level of the execution.

In Figure 18-13 you can see there are four different logging levels available to this property. Different logging levels capture different sets of events, and as a consequence they have different performance impacts. Table 18-3 explains the scope of those four levels.

TABLE 18-3 Logging levels and descriptions

Logging Level	Description
None	No events will be captured.
Basic	All events are captured except *OnProgress* and *OnCustomEvent*.
Performance	*OnError* event is captured. Component phase information is captured.
Verbose	All events are captured. Component phase information is captured. Component data statistics information is captured.

From Table 18-3, we can learn some other functionalities (component phases and component data statistics) are also impacted by logging levels because those features are built based on corresponding system events. For example, the component phase information is actually derived from event *OnPipelineBeforeComponentCall* and *OnPipelineAfterComponentCall*.

The default logging level is set to Basic, which is a good balance between the functionality and performance impact. You can change the default logging level to a different value so you don't have to set the property every time before execution. To do that, right-click the Catalog node in SQL Server Management Studio and select Properties from the shortcut menu. In the Catalog Properties dialog box, you will find the item Server-Wide Default Logging Level, as shown in Figure 18-14.

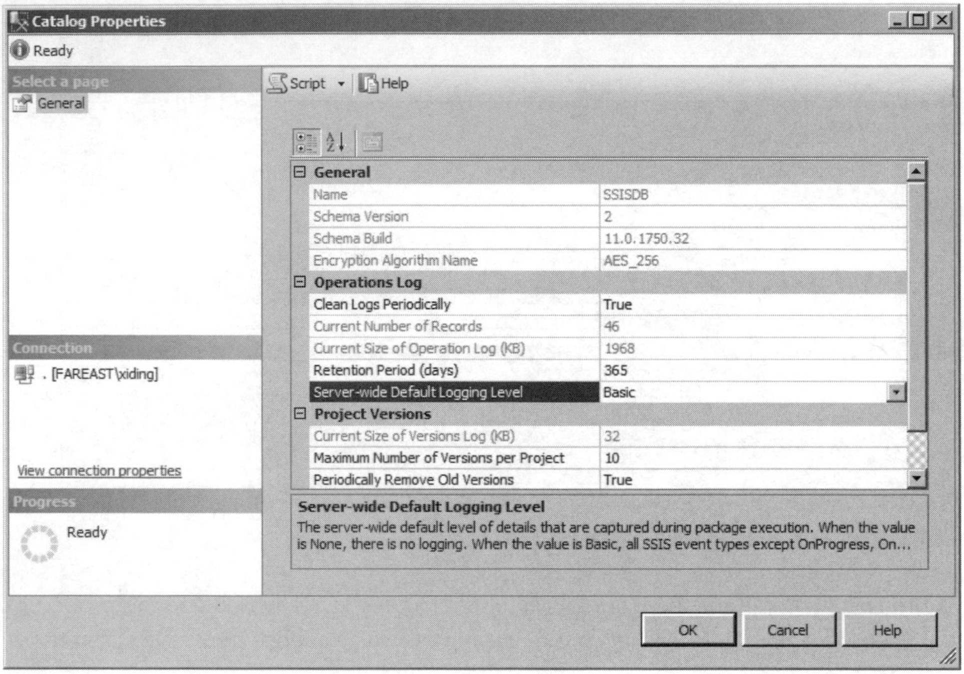

FIGURE 18-14 Configure the default logging level.

Event Logs

All the captured logs are exposed in this view by different filters such as execution ID or event name. See Figure 18-15 for a sample view.

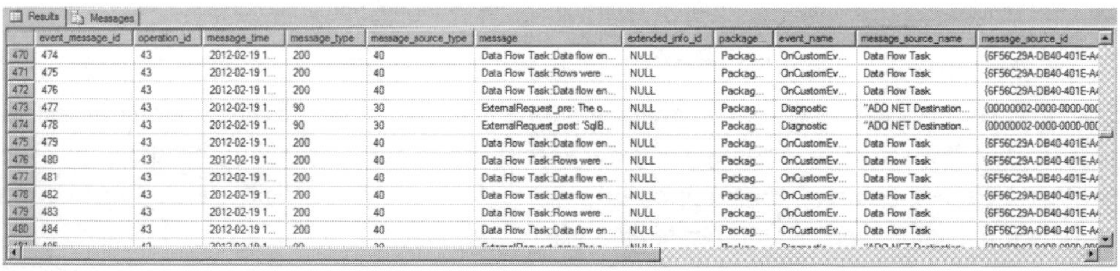

FIGURE 18-15 Captured event logs in view *catalog.event_messages*.

In this view, *operation_id* is actually the execution ID. The reason it's named *operation_id* instead of *execution_id* is because other operation types besides executions, such as validations or deployments, could produce logs. In this view you can also find some useful columns that are not available in package log providers. For example, the corresponding package path and execution path are shown for each log. Thus the event source is easily recognized even if the source container is inside a loop.

Event Context Information

An *OnError* event will be triggered if there are some errors during package execution. Usually we want to know more context information when an error happens. For example, suppose an Execute SQL task fires an *OnError* event and a database connection cannot be established. Usually we want to know its connection strings, variables, and so on.

To provide that feature, the SSIS Catalog saves additional context information when it receives an *OnError* event. It saves all properties of the current task or container as the context information. All context information is saved in the *catalog.event_message_context* view. See Figure 18-16 for a sample view.

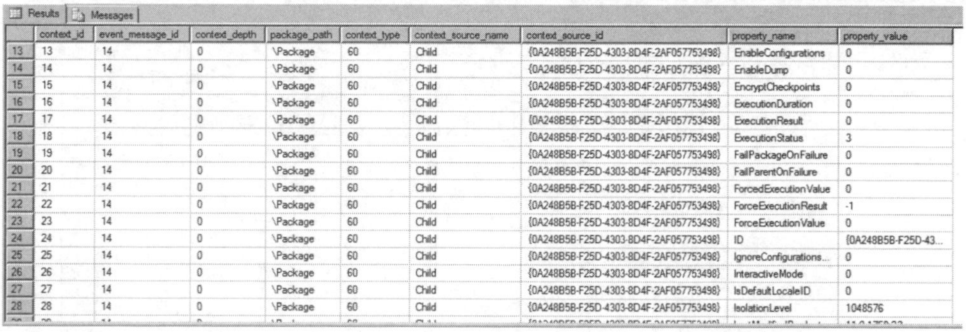
Results | Messages

	context_id	event_message_id	context_depth	package_path	context_type	context_source_name	context_source_id	property_name	property_value
13	13	14	0	\Package	60	Child	{0A248B5B-F25D-4303-8D4F-2AF057753498}	EnableConfigurations	0
14	14	14	0	\Package	60	Child	{0A248B5B-F25D-4303-8D4F-2AF057753498}	EnableDump	0
15	15	14	0	\Package	60	Child	{0A248B5B-F25D-4303-8D4F-2AF057753498}	EncryptCheckpoints	0
16	16	14	0	\Package	60	Child	{0A248B5B-F25D-4303-8D4F-2AF057753498}	ExecutionDuration	0
17	17	14	0	\Package	60	Child	{0A248B5B-F25D-4303-8D4F-2AF057753498}	ExecutionResult	0
18	18	14	0	\Package	60	Child	{0A248B5B-F25D-4303-8D4F-2AF057753498}	ExecutionStatus	3
19	19	14	0	\Package	60	Child	{0A248B5B-F25D-4303-8D4F-2AF057753498}	FailPackageOnFailure	0
20	20	14	0	\Package	60	Child	{0A248B5B-F25D-4303-8D4F-2AF057753498}	FailParentOnFailure	0
21	21	14	0	\Package	60	Child	{0A248B5B-F25D-4303-8D4F-2AF057753498}	ForcedExecutionValue	0
22	22	14	0	\Package	60	Child	{0A248B5B-F25D-4303-8D4F-2AF057753498}	ForceExecutionResult	-1
23	23	14	0	\Package	60	Child	{0A248B5B-F25D-4303-8D4F-2AF057753498}	ForceExecutionValue	0
24	24	14	0	\Package	60	Child	{0A248B5B-F25D-4303-8D4F-2AF057753498}	ID	{0A248B5B-F25D-43...
25	25	14	0	\Package	60	Child	{0A248B5B-F25D-4303-8D4F-2AF057753498}	IgnoreConfigurations...	0
26	26	14	0	\Package	60	Child	{0A248B5B-F25D-4303-8D4F-2AF057753498}	InteractiveMode	0
27	27	14	0	\Package	60	Child	{0A248B5B-F25D-4303-8D4F-2AF057753498}	IsDefaultLocaleID	0
28	28	14	0	\Package	60	Child	{0A248B5B-F25D-4303-8D4F-2AF057753498}	IsolationLevel	1048576

FIGURE 18-16 Event message context view.

The column *event_message_id* is the corresponding *OnError* event message ID in the *catalog.event_messages* view.

One interesting column is *context_depth,* which shows the context depth of the current message. When an error happens, the SSIS Catalog first saves all context information on the event source. It can be a task or a container. At that time the context depth is 0. Then the SSIS Catalog finds its parent container. All properties on the parent container are saved as context depth 1, and so on. Similar to a stack trace, SSIS will traverse up the execution stack until it reaches the top container (that is, the package).

Advanced Logging Topics

This section covers some advanced topics in SSIS logging, including customizing logging fields, behavior, and log providers.

Customizing Logging Fields

A log item has lots of fields to represent different information, such as machine, operator, and message text. By default all fields will be captured. However, sometimes you are only interested in a subset of those fields. For example, maybe the source name and message text is enough for you. In that case you can tailor the log fields to save some storage space.

You need to click Advanced in the Configure SSIS Logs dialog box to see the filtering view. In the Advanced view, there is a check box for each combination of event type and log field. Thus you can totally control which fields should be logged for each event type. See Figure 18-17 for a screenshot of the dialog box.

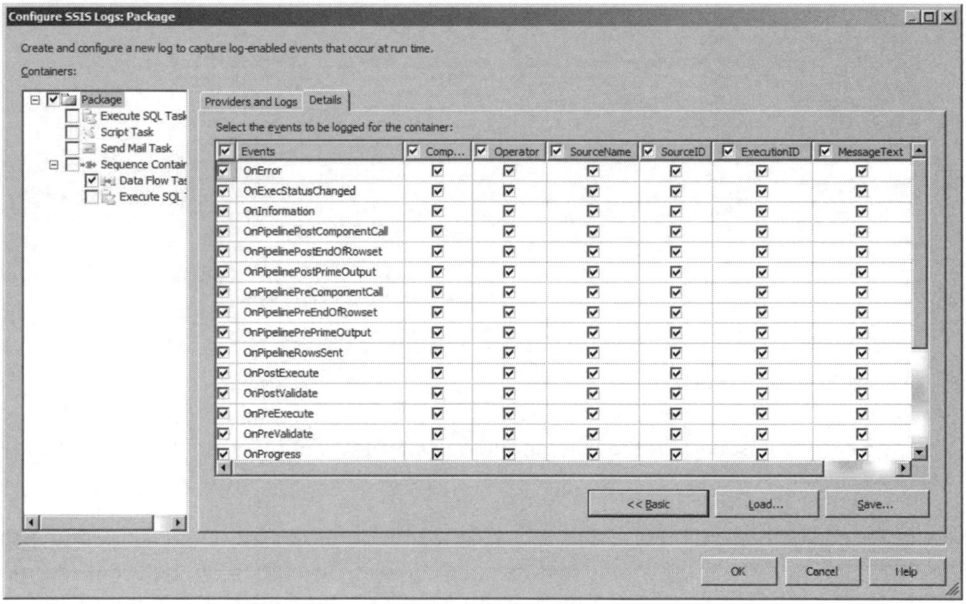

FIGURE 18-17 Customize the log fields for each different event.

Logging with dtexec Utility

Dtexec is the most frequently used utility to execute packages. Besides all those log options that have been specified in packages, dtexec also provides the ability to dynamically specify the logging options before execution. Three command-line arguments are provided:

- **ConsoleLog** This option could filter logs and print them in the command window.
- **Logger** This option could specify the given logger providers.
- **Vlog** Write all event logs to a dynamic log provider.

If you haven't defined any log providers in the package and want to temporarily log something, ConsoleLog is a good choice. The Logger option appends an extra log provider during package execution. The appended log provider is specified by its class ID or *ProgID*, which is listed in Table 18-2. VLog enables you to write all logs into a dynamic log provider specified on the command line, so it's helpful when you do quick troubleshooting.

Please refer to Chapter 11, "Running SSIS Packages," for detailed examples of these three command-line arguments.

Developing Custom Log Providers

SSIS provides good extensibility so you can create your own log providers if the built-in log providers cannot fulfill your requirements. With a custom log provider you can format the logs as you want and write them into any destination storage. For example, you can create a log provider that uses HTML to format all log fields and then save the logs as web pages.

Because many codes and steps are involved in creating a new log provider, we won't list all the detailed codes here. You can refer to MSDN at *http://msdn.microsoft.com/en-us/library/ms136010(v=sql.110).aspx* for a step-by-step tutorial. Here we just briefly summarize the main work in creating a custom log provider. It involves two main steps: building core functionality and registering the new provider.

Building Core Functionality

The core functionality of a log provider is implemented as a .NET class that inherits from the base class *Microsoft.SqlServer.Dts.Runtime.LogProviderBase*. You can write this class in any preferred .NET programming language. In this class you need to override the methods of the base class to implement your custom logging functionality.

One important property of that base class is *ConfigString*. This string represents the target location to which your log provider should write. This property is set during design time. Most of the log providers use this property to store the name of the connection manager that the provider uses to connect to an external data source.

Then you need to override some methods to do the logging. Listing 18-1 shows the code skeleton of your class.

LISTING 18-1 The code skeleton of a custom log provider

```
[DtsLogProvider(DisplayName = "CustomLogProvider", Description = "Sample log provider.",
   LogProviderType = "Custom")]
public class MyLogProvider : LogProviderBase
{
    public override DTSExecResult Validate(IDTSInfoEvents infoEvents)
    {
        //verify whether the ConfigString is set correctly if your provider
        //requires configuration
    }

    public override void OpenLog()
    {
        //This method is called at the start of package execution. In this
        //method you should establish a connection to the external data
        //source where you write logs to.
    }

    public override void Log(string logEntryName, string computerName, string operatorName,
string sourceName, string sourceID, string executionID, string messageText,
DateTime startTime, DateTime endTime, int dataCode, byte[] dataBytes)
    {
        //This method is called whenever there is a log emitted
        //Format the log and write it to your storage
    }

    public override void CloseLog()
    {
        //This method is called at the end of package execution. In this
        //method you should close the existing connection
    }
}
```

Registering the New Provider

Follow these steps to register your new log provider:

1. Compile the preceding code into a dynamic-link library (DLL) assembly.
2. Copy the assembly into directory *%Program Files%\Microsoft SQL Server\110\DTS\LogProviders* and also put the assembly into the Global Assembly Cache (GAC).
3. Restart SQL Server Data Tools if it's running, and then you will find your custom log provider appears in the providers list.

Summary

In this chapter we discussed various topics related to SSIS logging. First, you learned how to configure logging options in an SSIS package. These includes the following steps: enable a set of containers to produce logs, pick the event items on each container, and finally specify to which log provider those logs should be written.

All captured logs are formatted and saved to storage by different log providers. We reviewed the five built-in log providers to see their typical usage. Besides those built-in log providers, you can also write your own log providers.

After your projects are deployed to the SSIS Catalog, some additional server logging is provided. First you need to specify the logging level of your execution, which will determine the events that should be captured. Of course, different levels will have different performance impacts. You can query those captured logs in the *catalog.event_messages* view. If an *OnError* event is thrown, all context information will also be captured and exposed by the *catalog.event_message_context* view.

CHAPTER 19

Automating SSIS

In This Chapter

Introduction to SSIS Automation

The primary ways of using SSIS involve manual interaction; for example, creating packages in SQL Server Data Tools, running packages using DTEXEC and SQL Server Management Studio, or managing parameters in the SSIS Catalog. There are many scenarios where an automated approach is preferable. SSIS was designed with this in mind, and therefore any interaction with the product done through the SSIS tools is also possible through the SSIS application programming interfaces (APIs) and object model. Any time you find yourself doing the same SSIS tasks multiple times, you might want to consider automating the process.

There are two main forms of SSIS automation:

- Programmatic generation of SSIS packages
- Metadata-driven package execution

Programmatic Generation of SSIS Packages

Creating packages to transfer data from tables with many columns can be time consuming and repetitive. Although the Import And Export Data Wizard that comes with SQL Server is a good way to generate extract–transform–load (ETL) packages "in bulk," its functionality sometimes falls short of what you require. As you'll see later this chapter, packages can be generated programmatically using the SSIS object model. This .NET API allows you to load and modify existing packages, or dynamically create new ones. In fact, many aspects of the SQL Server product make use of this functionality today.

In additional to the Import and Export Data Wizard, the Copy Database Wizard, Data Collector, and Maintenance Plans all make use of the SSIS API to dynamically create new packages at runtime.

The two most common needs that drive customers toward a solution that programmatically creates or modifies packages are the following:

- Creating packages in bulk
- Applying consistent patterns across your solution

Creating Packages in Bulk

Consider the following scenario: A legacy database system, perhaps running on a different platform, needs to be migrated to SQL Server. This database is large, with more than 1,000 tables that need to be moved to the new system. Although many of the tables require minimal transformations for the new tables, consistent business logic (such as looking up keys in reference tables) and formatting needs to be applied in each Data Flow. Creating each of these SSIS packages by hand is a daunting task, and an ideal opportunity for automation.

To approach this problem, an ETL developer could create a package using the SSIS designer that acts as a *template*. This template contains common functionality that all packages in the solution will need, such as logging and error handling, and an empty Data Flow task. Using the SSIS object model, the developer can programmatically open the template and fill in the Data Flow logic needed for each table in the source system.

Applying Consistent Patterns

Another common reason to turn to automation is when you're looking to apply consistent ETL patterns across a solution. This could be done as part of your package generation process (as described in the previous section), or it might be done to modify a project after the fact. For example, many customers might find they need to add an auditing framework to their ETL processes to meet the latest compliance regulations. Using automation makes it easier to consistently reuse package logic, and reduces the likelihood of problems that arise from human error, such as forgetting to change certain task or connection manager properties.

> **Note** Although it is possible to create a fully automated solution, you might find scenarios where using the SQL Server Data Tools designer is still required. Many customers use a *hybrid* approach, where they use automation as an accelerator to generate the initial packages, and then make further modifications to them using the designer.

Metadata-Driven Package Execution

It is common to have packages running on a set schedule, but there are times where a more dynamic approach is required. Many customers will design a master package that orchestrates the rest of their ETL work, running one or more child packages. This approach provides some flexibility—as much as the ETL developer decided to implement—but changes to the execution logic or ordering of the child packages typically require modifications to the master package. To create a more dynamic solution, the list of packages to be run can be stored outside of the SSIS package (in a database table, for example). Instead of putting all of the child package execution logic in the master package, the master package simply reads this "execution metadata" at run time. This metadata will typically contain the name of the child package to be run, along with any parameter values it needs. With this approach you can change the order in which child packages will be run by modifying the metadata, and not modifying the packages themselves.

Dynamic Package Generation

Dynamic package generation can be done using the SSIS object model. The object model API is exposed through three main managed (.NET) assemblies. All activities supported by the SSIS tools (such as SQL Server Data Tools) can also be performed programmatically through the API. Table 19-1 lists the assemblies you'll need to reference for most applications that interact with the object model. Table 19-2 lists additional assemblies you will use when using or extending SSIS user interface classes (*Microsoft.SqlServer.Dts.Design*), or interacting with the SSIS Catalog (*Microsoft.SqlServer.Management.IntegrationServices*).

TABLE 19-1 Key assembly files for using the SSIS object model

Assembly	Description
Microsoft.SqlServer.ManagedDTS	This is the main SSIS object model assembly, which contains a managed (.NET) interface over the native COM runtime that is used by SSIS. This assembly is required when loading or creating SSIS packages.
Microsoft.SqlServer.DTSRuntimeWrap	This is the Primary Interop Assembly (PIA) for the native COM runtime. It mostly contains interface classes (all following the *IDTSxxx100* name pattern). Most of the interfaces found in this assembly are implemented by objects in the *ManagedDTS* assembly; you will rarely need to use any of these classes directly.
Microsoft.SqlServer.DTSPipelineWrap	This is the PIA for the native COM objects used by the SSIS Data Flow task (also referred to as the *pipeline*). Unlike the runtime, the SSIS pipeline does not have a managed layer like *ManagedDTS*. Most interaction with the SSIS Data Flow will require you to use the interfaces in this assembly.

TABLE 19-2 Other SSIS object model assemblies

Assembly	Description
Microsoft.SqlServer.Dts.Design	This assembly contains the base classes and interfaces required to implement custom user interfaces for your tasks and Data Flow components. We do not cover the classes in this assembly in this chapter.
Microsoft.SqlServer.PipelineHost	This assembly contains the classes you need when developing custom Data Flow components (sources, transforms, and destinations).
Microsoft.SqlServer.Management.IntegrationServices	Management Object Model (MOM) for the SSIS Catalog. The classes in this assembly are used to deploy, manage, and execute packages that have been deployed to the SSIS Catalog.

Note Most of these assembly files can be found in the *C:\Program Files (x86)\Microsoft SQL Server\110\SDK\Assemblies* directory, as well as the .NET 4.0 global assembly cache (GAC; *C:\Windows\Microsoft.NET\Assembly*). The SSIS Catalog management assembly can be found in the .NET 2.0/3.5 GAC (*C:\Windows\Assembly*).

Tip More information about the classes in the SSIS object model can be found in Books Online at *http://msdn.microsoft.com/en-us/library/ms136025(v=sql.110).aspx.*

Handling Design-Time Events

An important aspect of using the SSIS object model is handling events that are raised during package creation, execution, and persistence. To do this, you need to create an object that implements the *IDTSEvents* interface. This object (commonly referred to as an *event sink*) allows you to capture and report any events raised by the SSIS object model. This is useful for getting to the root cause of errors. The object used in this chapter, *PackageEvents*, is shown in Listing 19-1. It inherits from the *DefaultEvents* base class defined in the SSIS object model. The base class implements all of the methods defined in the interface, which means you only need to override the events you care about. In this sample, the *OnError* method is overridden, and simply outputs the event message to the console.

LISTING 19-1 The PackageEvents class will report errors that occur during package creation

```
internal class PackageEvents : DefaultEvents
{
    public override bool OnError(DtsObject source, int errorCode, string subComponent,
                                 string description, string helpFile, int helpContext,
                                 string idofInterfaceWithError)
    {
        Console.WriteLine("[Error] {0}", description);
        return base.OnError(source, errorCode, subComponent, description, helpFile,
                            helpContext, idofInterfaceWithError);
    }
}
```

To handle errors thrown while creating a Data Flow task, you need to create a second event sink class. This object, *PipelineEvents*, is shown in Listing 19-2. It implements the *IDTSComponentEvents* interface, and is similar to the *PackageEvents* class from Listing 19-1. Data Flow components will frequently throw COM exceptions whenever a problem is encountered. Debugging the cause of these errors can be quite difficult, as the exception message typically contains only the COM HRESULT numeric value. The most interesting method will be *FireError()*, as it allows you to capture detailed errors about the Data Flow components during package creation.

LISTING 19-2 The *IDTSComponentEvents* interface allows you to capture detailed error messages

```
class PipelineEvents : IDTSComponentEvents
{
    private void HandleEvent(string type, string subComponent, string description)
    {
        Console.WriteLine("[{0}] {1}: {2}", type, subComponent, description);
    }

    #region IDTSComponentEvents Members

    public void FireBreakpointHit(BreakpointTarget breakpointTarget)
    {
    }

    public void FireCustomEvent(string eventName, string eventText,
                                ref object[] arguments, string subComponent,
                                ref bool fireAgain)
    {
    }

    public bool FireError(int errorCode, string subComponent, string description,
                          string helpFile, int helpContext)
    {
        HandleEvent("Error", subComponent, description);
        return true;
    }

    public void FireInformation(int informationCode, string subComponent,
                                string description, string helpFile,
                                int helpContext, ref bool fireAgain)
    {
        HandleEvent("Information", subComponent, description);
    }

    public void FireProgress(string progressDescription, int percentComplete,
                             int progressCountLow, int progressCountHigh,
                             string subComponent, ref bool fireAgain)
    {
    }

    public bool FireQueryCancel()
    {
        return true;
    }

    public void FireWarning(int warningCode, string subComponent,
                            string description, string helpFile, int helpContext)
    {
        HandleEvent("Warning", subComponent, description);
    }

    #endregion
}
```

Note Although the SSIS object model refers to these objects as events and event handlers, they don't follow the same patterns used by the .NET event classes. The methods you override are closer to *callback* functions than true .NET events.

Samples

This section contains a number of package generation samples. The scenarios include the following:

- Creating, saving, and loading a package
- Working with projects
- Creating a Data Flow
- Inserting a task from another package
- Using an Execute Package task

Creating, Saving, and Loading a Package

The code sample in Listing 19-3 has three parts. It will do the following:

1. Create a new package and add a Data Flow task to it.
2. Save the package to disk in a location specified by the *PackagePath* variable.
3. Reload the package from the disk in two ways:
    a. Reading the XML data from disk, and loading it with the *Package.LoadFromXML()* method. Using this method is useful when loading a single package, as it allows you to set individual package properties that affect the way it is loaded, such as *Package.OfflineMode*, and *Package.IgnoreConfigurationsOnLoad*.
    b. Using the *Application.LoadPackage()* method. The *Application* class lets you set properties that will be used for all packages you open through this object, including a Password value that you can set if your packages are using a protection level that requires a password. You should use this method when opening a lot of packages, and when you are loading packages from the legacy SSIS service (*Application.LoadFromDtsServer()*), or MSDB storage locations (*Application.LoadFromSqlServer()*).

LISTING 19-3 Code sample for creating, saving, and loading a package

```
class Program
{
    const string PackagePath = @"c:\book\chapter19\package.dtsx";

    static void Main(string[] args)
    {
        PackageEvents events = new PackageEvents();

        //
        // Creating a package
        //
        Package package = new Package();
        package.DesignEvents = events;

        // Add Data Flow Task
        Executable dataFlowTask = package.Executables.Add("STOCK:PipelineTask");

        // Set the name (otherwise it will be a random GUID value)
        TaskHost taskHost = dataFlowTask as TaskHost;
        taskHost.Name = "Data Flow Task";

        // We need a reference to the InnerObject to add items to the data flow
        MainPipe pipeline = taskHost.InnerObject as MainPipe;

        //
        // Saving a package
        //
        string xml;
        package.SaveToXML(out xml, events);
        File.WriteAllText(PackagePath, xml);

        //
        // Loading a package-empty package object
        //
        string fileXml = File.ReadAllText(PackagePath);
        Package newPackage = new Package();
        newPackage.LoadFromXML(fileXml, events);

        //
        // Loading a package-using an Application object
        //
        Application app = new Application();
        Package anotherPackage = app.LoadPackage(PackagePath, events);
    }
}
```

Here are some notes about this code sample:

1. The *Package* class can be found in both the *Microsoft.SqlServer.Dts.Runtime* and *Microsoft.SqlServer.Dts.Runtime.Wrapper* namespaces. You will typically want to use the one in the *Microsoft.SqlServer.Dts.Runtime* namespace, as the other is a wrapper for the native COM object, which does not need to be accessed directly.

2. We use an instance of the *IDTSEvents* class defined in Listing 19-1, *PackageEvents*, to capture and report any errors that occur while saving and loading the package. Errors that occur during package creation (for example, while adding a new task) will throw an exception.

Working with Projects

The code sample in Listing 19-4 shows how to programmatically create and load an SSIS project. The code starts by creating a project with a file path specified by the *ProjectPath* variable. It adds a project-level parameter (*BatchSize*), a shared connection manager (*MyProjConnection*), and a single package (*Package1*). After saving the project to disk, it reloads it, sets a value for the *BatchSize* parameter, and then executes the package.

LISTING 19-4 Programmatically creating and loading an SSIS project file

```
static void Main(string[] args)

        {
            const string ProjectPath = @"c:\book\chapter19\Project.ispac";

            PackageEvents events = new PackageEvents();

            //
            // Create a new project with a default storage path
            //
            using (Project project = Project.CreateProject(ProjectPath))
            {
                // Set events
                project.Events = events;

                // Add a project parameter
                Parameter projectParam = project.Parameters.Add("BatchSize", TypeCode.Int32);
                projectParam.Value = 1000;

                // Add a shared connection manager
                var cm = project.ConnectionManagerItems.Add("OLEDB", "MyProjConnection.conMgr");
                cm.ConnectionManager.Name = "MyProjConnection";
                cm.ConnectionManager.ConnectionString = @"...";

                // Create a package with a parameter
                Package package = new Package();
                package.Name = "Package1";

                Parameter packageParam = package.Parameters.Add("InputFileName", TypeCode.
                String);
                packageParam.Value = @"\\data\inputfile.txt";
```

```
            // Add the new package to the project
            project.PackageItems.Add(package, "Package1.dtsx");

            // Save the project
            project.Save();
        }

        //
        // Reload the project, and run a package
        //
        using (Project project = Project.OpenProject(ProjectPath))
        {
            project.Events = events;

            // change the project parameter value for this run
            project.Parameters["BatchSize"].Value = 5000;

            // get a reference to the package we want to run
            var package = project.PackageItems["Package1.dtsx"].Package;

            package.Execute(null, null, events, null, null);

            if (package.Errors.Count > 0)
            {
                Console.WriteLine("Package failed!");
            }
        }
    }
}
```

Here are some notes about this code sample:

1. When creating a new project, you have a choice of how it will be stored. You can specify a file path, specify a .NET stream, or keep it solely in memory. If you do not specify a file path or stream, you will receive an exception when you call *Project.Save()*, because the project does not yet have a storage location. You can set a storage location by calling *Project.SaveAs()*.
2. You can only set the *IDTSEvents* object on the project after it has been loaded or created. Any errors that occur during load or create will result in an exception.
3. When adding items to a project, you must specify a value for the *streamName* parameter. This should be the name of the package or connection manager, and must have the correct file extension. For packages, this would be .dtsx. Connection managers have a .conmgr extension.

Creating a Data Flow

Working with the SSIS Control Flow (that is, adding tasks) is relatively straightforward. Unfortunately, working with the SSIS Data Flow is a bit more complex.

The first step is to create a new package with a Data Flow task, as shown in Listing 19-5.

LISTING 19-5 Creating a package with a Data Flow task

```
PackageEvents events = new PackageEvents();

Package package = new Package();
package.DesignEvents = events;

Executable dataFlowTask = package.Executables.Add("STOCK:PipelineTask");
TaskHost taskHost = dataFlowTask as TaskHost;
taskHost.Name = "Data Flow Task";

MainPipe pipeline = taskHost.InnerObject as MainPipe;
```

Once you have a reference to a Data Flow task object (a *MainPipe* instance), you can start adding components to it. Data Flows should be constructed the same way they are in the designer: You first add your source component(s), add transformations, connect them with paths, and end the flow with one or more destinations. Before you start adding components, however, you should add a component event handler to the Data Flow (an object that implements the *IDTSComponentEvents* interface).

To hook up the *IDTSComponentEvents* object, we create an instance of a class that implements the interface (*PipelineEvents*) and assign it to the *MainPipe.Events* property (as shown in Listing 19-6).

LISTING 19-6 Setting the *IDTSComponentEvents* object

```
// Set the IDTSComponentEvent handler to capture the details from any
// COMExceptions raised during package generation
PipelineEvents dataFlowEvents = new PipelineEvents();
pipeline.Events = DtsConvert.GetExtendedInterface(dataFlowEvents as IDTSComponentEvents);
```

Once the pipeline events are being captured, you can begin adding your source components. The code in Listing 19-7 adds a new OLE DB Source component to the Data Flow.

LISTING 19-7 Adding a new OLE DB Source component to the Data Flow

```
// Add OLEDB Source
IDTSComponentMetaData100 srcComponent = pipeline.ComponentMetaDataCollection.New();
srcComponent.ComponentClassID = "DTSAdapter.OleDbSource";
srcComponent.ValidateExternalMetadata = true;

IDTSDesigntimeComponent100 srcDesignTimeComponent = srcComponent.Instantiate();
srcDesignTimeComponent.ProvideComponentProperties();
srcComponent.Name = "OleDb Source";
```

Data Flow components need to be added in two phases:

1. An instance of *IDTSComponentMetaData100* is created by calling *MainPipe.ComponentMetaDataCollection.New()*. You can refer to this as the *metadata component*. This object contains all of the common Data Flow component properties, such as *Name*, *ValidateExternalMetadata*, and *ComponentClassID*. You will use this object whenever you are interacting with the rest of the Data Flow; for example, when connecting a path between components, or mapping input and output columns.

2. An instance of *IDTSDesigntimeComponent100* is created by calling *IDTSComponentMetaData100.Instantiate()*. You can refer to this as the *design-time component*. You will use this object to set component properties. It also contains the important methods for interacting with the Data Flow, such as *ProvideComponentProperties*() and *AcquireConnections()*. You must have set the *ComponentClassID* of the metadata class prior to calling *Instantiate()*, so that the Data Flow knows which SSIS transform to create.

Once the metadata and design-time components have been created, you can start configuring the component. This would be equivalent to the values you set through the component user interface in the designer. The code in Listing 19-8 sets the *AccessMode* property to 0 (Table/View), and the *OpenRowset* property to the name of the source table from which the package will read.

LISTING 19-8 Setting the *AccessMode* property

```
// Configure it to read from the given table
srcDesignTimeComponent.SetComponentProperty("AccessMode", 0);
srcDesignTimeComponent.SetComponentProperty("OpenRowset", "[DimCustomer]");
```

> **Tip** You can look at the package XML to determine the names and values of the component properties you want to set.

The next step is to create a connection manager, and assign it to the source component. This can be done through the *RuntimeConnectionCollection* property of the metadata component (Listing 19-9).

LISTING 19-9 Adding a connection manager

```
// Add connection manager
ConnectionManager con = package.Connections.Add("OLEDB");
con.Name = "localhost";
con.ConnectionString = @"Data Source=.;Initial
Catalog=AdventureWorks;Provider=SQLNCLI11.1;Integrated Security=SSPI;";

// Set the connection manager
srcComponent.RuntimeConnectionCollection[0].ConnectionManager =
DtsConvert.GetExtendedInterface(con);
srcComponent.RuntimeConnectionCollection[0].ConnectionManagerID = con.ID;
```

The final step to configuring the component is to retrieve its external metadata information from the source server. This can be done once its connection information has been set (Listing 19-10).

LISTING 19-10 Retrieving metadata for the source component

```
// Retrieve the column metadata
srcDesignTimeComponent.AcquireConnections(null);
srcDesignTimeComponent.ReinitializeMetaData();
srcDesignTimeComponent.ReleaseConnections();
```

The next section of code (Listing 19-11) creates an OLE DB Destination component. The code is very similar to creating the source; the main difference will be the values we use for the *ComponentClassID* and custom properties.

LISTING 19-11 Creating the OLE DB Destination component

```
    // Add OLEDB Destination
    IDTSComponentMetaData100 destComponent = pipeline.ComponentMetaDataCollection.New();
    destComponent.ComponentClassID = "DTSAdapter.OleDbDestination";
    destComponent.ValidateExternalMetadata = true;

    IDTSDesigntimeComponent100 destDesignTimeComponent = destComponent.Instantiate();
    destDesignTimeComponent.ProvideComponentProperties();
    destComponent.Name = "OleDb Destination";

    destDesignTimeComponent.SetComponentProperty("AccessMode", 3);
    destDesignTimeComponent.SetComponentProperty("OpenRowset", "[DimCustomer]");

    // set connection
    destComponent.RuntimeConnectionCollection[0].ConnectionManager =
DtsConvert.GetExtendedInterface(con);
    destComponent.RuntimeConnectionCollection[0].ConnectionManagerID = con.ID;

    // get metadata
    destDesignTimeComponent.AcquireConnections(null);
    destDesignTimeComponent.ReinitializeMetaData();
    destDesignTimeComponent.ReleaseConnections();
```

We can connect the source and destination components with an *IDTSPath100* object. A new path is created by adding to the Data Flow's *PathCollection*, and attached by calling *AttachPathAndPropagateNotifications*(). The code in Listing 19-12 attaches the output of the source component to the input of the destination.

LISTING 19-12 Attaching the Data Flow path

```
    // Connect source and destination
    IDTSPath100 path = pipeline.PathCollection.New();
    path.AttachPathAndPropagateNotifications(srcComponent.OutputCollection[0], destComponent.
InputCollection[0]);
```

The final step is to configure the column mapping for the destination. The code in Listing 19-13 maps the virtual input columns of the destination to its external metadata columns.

LISTING 19-13 Configure column mapping for the destination

```
    // Configure the destination
    var destInput = destComponent.InputCollection[0];
    var destVirInput = destInput.GetVirtualInput();
    var destInputCols = destInput.InputColumnCollection;
    var destExtCols = destInput.ExternalMetadataColumnCollection;
    var sourceColumns = srcComponent.OutputCollection[0].OutputColumnCollection;
```

```
// The OLEDB destination requires you to hook up the external columns
foreach (IDTSOutputColumn100 outputCol in sourceColumns)
{
    // Get the external column id
    var extCol = (IDTSExternalMetadataColumn100)destExtCols[outputCol.Name];
    if (extCol != null)
    {
        // Create an input column from an output col of previous component.
        destVirInput.SetUsageType(outputCol.ID, DTSUsageType.UT_READONLY);
        IDTSInputColumn100 inputCol = destInputCols.GetInputColumnByLineageID(outputCol.ID);
        if (inputCol != null)
        {
            // map the input column with an external metadata column
            destDesignTimeComponent.MapInputColumn(destInput.ID, inputCol.ID, extCol.ID);
        }
    }
}
```

Inserting a Task from Another Package

The code sample in Listing 19-14 copies an Execute SQL task and the connection manager it uses from one package to another. This operation is useful as a quick way to add to a package from a template, or quickly duplicate and reuse package functionality.

LISTING 19-14 Copying a task from one package to another

```
const string SourcePackagePath = @"c:\book\chapter19\SourcePackage.dtsx";
const string DestinationPackagePath = @"C:\book\chapter19\DestinationPackage.dtsx";

PackageEvents events = new PackageEvents();
Application app = new Application();

// Load the source package
Package source = app.LoadPackage(SourcePackagePath, events);

// Load the destination package
Package destination = app.LoadPackage(DestinationPackagePath, events);

// Get a reference to the task you want to copy, and remove it from the original
package.
// The source package won't be modified if you don't save it.
Executable task = source.Executables["Execute SQL Task"];
source.Executables.Remove(task);

// get a reference to the connection manager you want to copy
ConnectionManager cm = source.Connections["SourceConnection"];
source.Connections.Remove(cm);

// add both objects to the destination package
destination.Connections.Join(cm);
destination.Executables.Join(task);

// save the destination package to preserve the changes
app.SaveToXml(DestinationPackagePath, destination, events);
```

Using an Execute Package Task

The code in Listing 19-15 creates an SSIS project with two packages (Parent and Child). It adds a parameter on the child package (*InputFilePath*) and an Execute Package task on the parent package.

LISTING 19-15 Using an Execute Package task

```
PackageEvents events = new PackageEvents();

// Create a project
Project project = Project.CreateProject();

// Create the Child package
Package childPackage = new Package();
childPackage.DesignEvents = events;
childPackage.Name = "Child";

// Define a parameter
var param = childPackage.Parameters.Add("InputFilePath", TypeCode.String);
param.Required = true;
param.Value = @"c:\book\chapter19\inputfile.txt";

// Create a connection manager with an expression that uses the InputFilePath parameter
var cm = childPackage.Connections.Add("FILE");
cm.Name = "Input File";
cm.SetExpression("ConnectionString", "@[$Package::InputFilePath]");

// add the child package to the project
project.PackageItems.Add(childPackage, "Child.dtsx");

// Create the Parent package
Package parentPackage = new Package();
parentPackage.DesignEvents = events;
parentPackage.Name = "Parent";

// Add the Parent package to the project
project.PackageItems.Add(parentPackage, "Parent.dtsx");

// Add a variable to store the value we'll use in the Execute Package task binding
parentPackage.Variables.Add("FilePath", false, "User", @"C:\ParentFilePath.txt");

// Add the Execute Package task
var taskHost = parentPackage.Executables.Add("STOCK:ExecutePackageTask") as TaskHost;
var execPkgTask = taskHost.InnerObject as ExecutePackageTask;

// configure the task
execPkgTask.UseProjectReference = true;
var assignment = execPkgTask.ParameterAssignments.Add();
assignment.BindedVariableOrParameterName = "FilePath";  // variable in parent
assignment.ParameterName = "InputFilePath";             // parameter in child
```

Note To use the *ExecutePackageTask* class, you need to add a reference to the *Microsoft.SqlServer.ExecPackageTaskWrap* assembly, which can be found in .NET 4.0 GAC (C:\Windows\Microsoft.NET\assembly\GAC_MSIL).

Metadata-Based Execution

There are different ways to design a metadata-based execution solution. As requirements for such a system will vary depending on the type of ETL work being done, most solutions need to be custom made. This section describes two example solutions that you can customize to meet your needs. The first solution uses a simple command-line application that loads and runs one or more SSIS packages from a project file (.ispac). The second solution uses a PowerShell script to dynamically create and schedule a series of SQL Agent jobs.

Both of these solutions will read from a SQL Server table. This table, which we'll call *WorkItems*, is described in Listing 19-16. It contains all of the metadata needed to run the SSIS packages contained within the solution. Each row in the table is a package that needs to be run (specified by the *PackageName* column). The package used in this example (*ImportData.dtsx*) receives a single parameter value, which is specified by the *InputFileName* column.

LISTING 19-16 Work Item table definition

```
--
-- Create the WorkItems table
--
CREATE TABLE [dbo].[WorkItems] (
   [WorkItemID] [bigint] IDENTITY(1,1) NOT NULL,
   [PackageName] [nvarchar](50) NOT NULL,
   [WorkItemState] [nvarchar](50) NOT NULL,
   [InputFileName] [nvarchar](1024) NULL,
   [DateCreated] [datetime] NOT NULL,
   [LastUpdate] [datetime] NULL,
         CONSTRAINT [PK_WorkItems] PRIMARY KEY CLUSTERED
   (
            [WorkItemID] ASC
   )
)

--
-- Add default values
--
ALTER TABLE [dbo].[WorkItems]
     ADD CONSTRAINT [DF_WorkItems_DateCreated] DEFAULT (getdate()) FOR [DateCreated]

ALTER TABLE [dbo].[WorkItems]
     ADD CONSTRAINT [DF_WorkItems_WorkItemState] DEFAULT (N'Queued') FOR [WorkItemState]
```

Each work item has a *WorkItemState* value that is used to determine whether it is ready to be run. Table 19-3 shows the list of possible values for this column.

TABLE 19-3 Work item states

State	Description
Queued	The state of the work item when it is first created. Work items in this state are ready to be executed.
Running	The work item is currently running.
Failed	The work item was run, but failed.
Succeeded	The work item completed successfully.

For the purposes of the demo, we prime the table with four sample work items (shown in Listing 19-17).

LISTING 19-17 Sample work items

```
INSERT INTO [dbo].[WorkItems]
         ([PackageName], [InputFileName])
      VALUES
            (N'ImportData.dtsx', N'\\datafiles\File1.csv'),
     (N'ImportData.dtsx', N'\\datafiles\File2.csv'),
     (N'ImportData.dtsx', N'\\datafiles\File3.csv'),
     (N'ImportData.dtsx', N'\\datafiles\File4.csv')
```

Custom Package Runner

In this solution we use a custom application to load and execute packages contained within an SSIS project deployment file (.ispac). The application will use the SQL Client libraries to read the list of work items from the local SQL Server instance, and use the SSIS object model to programmatically load, configure, and execute an SSIS package.

First, you create a local class (*WorkItemExecution*) to hold the information that defines an execution of a package (shown in Listing 19-18).

LISTING 19-18 *WorkItemExecution* class

```
        class WorkItemExecution
        {
            public Int64 WorkItemId { get; set; }
            public string PackageName { get; set; }
            public string InputFileName { get; set; }
        }
```

The packages run by this code sample come out of a single SSIS project file (.ispac). Open the project using the *Project.OpenProject* method, passing in the path to the project file, and your event sink. The *Project* object implements *IDisposable*, so it is important to wrap it in a using block, or ensure you call *Project.Close()* once you have finished with the object. If you don't, the underlying .ispac file will remain open (and perhaps locked) until the object gets disposed by the .NET garbage collector.

```
var project = Project.OpenProject(ProjectPath, Project.AccessMode.Read, null, events)
```

The next block of code (Listing 19-19) executes a SQL query to retrieve the work item details from the WorkItems table. It creates a new *WorkItemExecution* object for each entry in the table.

LISTING 19-19 Loading the work item details from the WorkItems table

```
var workItems = new Collection<WorkItemExecution>();
var cmd = new SqlCommand("SELECT WorkItemID, PackageName, InputFileName " +
                         "FROM   WorkItems " +
                         "WHERE  WorkItemState = N'Queued'", connection);
using (var reader = cmd.ExecuteReader())
{
    while (reader.Read())
    {
        var item = new WorkItemExecution()
        {
            WorkItemId = reader.GetInt64(0),
            PackageName = reader.GetString(1),
            InputFileName = reader.GetString(2)
        };

        workItems.Add(item);
    }
}
```

After you have a list of work items, you can start executing the packages. For each item, you will get a reference to the Package object from the project by accessing it by name. Once you have the package, you set the *InputFileName* parameter using the value retrieved from the WorkItems table. Before running the package, update the WorkItems table to indicate that this work item is currently running. The package is run using the *Package.Execute()* method. Here you use the event sink object again so you can capture and report errors as they occur. This procedure is shown in Listing 19-20.

LISTING 19-20 Retrieving and executing the package

```
// Get package
var packageItem = project.PackageItems[item.PackageName];
var package = packageItem.Package;

// Set parameter value
package.Parameters["InputFileName"].Value = item.InputFileName;

// Change row state
var updateCmd = new SqlCommand("UPDATE WorkItems " +
                               "SET WorkItemState = N'Running', " +
                               "    LastUpdate = GETDATE() " +
                               "WHERE WorkItemID = @workItemId", connection);
updateCmd.Parameters.AddWithValue("workItemId", item.WorkItemId);
updateCmd.ExecuteNonQuery();

// Run package
package.Execute(null, null, events, null, null);
```

The final block of code updates the WorkItems table based on the result of the package execution. Listing 19-21 contains the full code for this sample.

LISTING 19-21 Package execution sample using C#

```
using System;
using System.Collections.Generic;
using System.Linq;
using System.Text;
using Microsoft.SqlServer.Dts.Runtime;
using System.Data.SqlClient;
using System.Collections.ObjectModel;

namespace PackageRunner
{
    class PackageRunner
    {
        const string ProjectPath = @"c:\book\chapter19\SimpleProject.ispac";
        const string ConnectionString = @"Data Source=localhost;Initial
Catalog=Chapter19;Integrated Security=SSPI;";

        class WorkItemExecution
        {
            public Int64 WorkItemId { get; set; }
            public string PackageName { get; set; }
            public string InputFileName { get; set; }
        }

        static void Main(string[] args)
        {
            var events = new PackageEvents();

            // Load project
            using (var project = Project.OpenProject(ProjectPath, Project.AccessMode.Read, null,
events))
            {
                // Get list of work items
                using (var connection = new SqlConnection(ConnectionString))
                {
                    connection.Open();

                    var workItems = new Collection<WorkItemExecution>();

                    var cmd = new SqlCommand("SELECT WorkItemID, PackageName, InputFileName " +
                                             "FROM WorkItems " +
                                             "WHERE WorkItemState = N'Queued'", connection);
                    using (var reader = cmd.ExecuteReader())
                    {
                        while (reader.Read())
                        {
                            var item = new WorkItemExecution()
                            {
                                WorkItemId = reader.GetInt64(0),
                                PackageName = reader.GetString(1),
                                InputFileName = reader.GetString(2)
                            };
```

```
                    workItems.Add(item);
                }
            }

            foreach (var item in workItems)
            {
                // Get package
                var packageItem = project.PackageItems[item.PackageName];
                var package = packageItem.Package;

                // Set parameter value
                package.Parameters["InputFileName"].Value = item.InputFileName;

                // Change row state
                var updateCmd = new SqlCommand("UPDATE WorkItems " +
                                               "SET WorkItemState = N'Running', " +
                                               "     LastUpdate = GETDATE() " +
                                               "WHERE WorkItemID = @workItemId",
                                               connection);
                updateCmd.Parameters.AddWithValue("workItemId", item.WorkItemId);
                updateCmd.ExecuteNonQuery();

                // Run package
                package.Execute(null, null, events, null, null);

                // Check for errors
                if (package.Errors.Count > 0)
                {
                    var failedCmd = new SqlCommand("UPDATE WorkItems " +
                                                   "SET WorkItemState = N'Failed', " +
                                                   "     LastUpdate = GETDATE() " +
                                                   "WHERE WorkItemID = @workItemId",
                                                   connection);
                    failedCmd.Parameters.AddWithValue("workItemId", item.WorkItemId);
                    failedCmd.ExecuteNonQuery();
                }
                else
                {
                    var successCmd = new SqlCommand("UPDATE WorkItems " +
                                                    "SET WorkItemState = N'Succeeded',
                                                    " +
                                                    "     LastUpdate = GETDATE() " +
                                                    "WHERE WorkItemID = @workItemId",
                                                    connection);
                    successCmd.Parameters.AddWithValue("workItemId", item.WorkItemId);
                    successCmd.ExecuteNonQuery();
                }
            }
        }
    }
}

internal class PackageEvents : DefaultEvents
{
    public override bool OnError(DtsObject source, int errorCode, string subComponent,
```

```
                                                string description, string helpFile, int helpContext,
                                                string idofInterfaceWithError)
            {
                Console.WriteLine("[Error] {0}", description);
                return base.OnError(source, errorCode, subComponent, description, helpFile,
                                helpContext, idofInterfaceWithError);
            }
        }
    }
}
```

Using PowerShell with the SSIS Management Object Model

In this solution, you use a PowerShell script (shown in Listing 19-22) to read the list of queued work items. For each work item found in the table, the script creates and runs a new package execution through the SSIS Catalog. The script makes use of the Invoke-SqlCmd cmdlet to issue SQL statements against the local SQL Server instance, and uses the SSIS Management Object Model (MOM) to interact with the SSIS Catalog. Listing 19-22 shows the output of running the script.

LISTING 19-22 PowerShell script that runs SSIS packages through the SSIS MOM

```
# Load SQL
Import-Module SqlPs

# Load SMO and SSIS MOM extensions
[System.Reflection.Assembly]::LoadWithPartialName("Microsoft.SqlServer.Smo") | Out-Null;
[System.Reflection.Assembly]::LoadWithPartialName("Microsoft.SqlServer.Management.
IntegrationServices") | Out-Null;

# Set the SQL instance name and database
$sqlServer = "localhost"
$database = "Chapter19"
$catalogName = "SSISDB"
$folderName = "Chapter19"
$projectName = "SimpleProject"

# package execution parameters
$use32BitRuntime = "false"

# Changes work item state
Function UpdateWorkItemStatus([string]$workItemId, [string]$status)
{
    $sql = "UPDATE WorkItems SET WorkItemState = N'{0}', LastUpdate = GETDATE() WHERE WorkItemID
= {1}" -f $status, $workItemId

    invoke-sqlcmd -database $database -serverinstance $sqlServer -query $sql
}

Function IsStillRunning($status)
{
    $enum = [Microsoft.SqlServer.Management.IntegrationServices.Operation+ServerOperationStatus]

    if ($status -eq $enum::Created -or $status -eq $enum::Running -or $status -eq
$enum::Pending)
```

```
    {
        1;
    }
    else
    {
        0;
    }
}

$typeSource = @"
public class WorkItem
{
    public int Id;
    public int WorkItemId;
}
"@

Add-Type -TypeDefinition $typeSource

# Create an SMO Server object
$srv = New-Object "Microsoft.SqlServer.Management.Smo.Server" $sqlserver;

# Create the Integration Services object
$ssis = New-Object "Microsoft.SqlServer.Management.IntegrationServices.IntegrationServices" $srv

# Get a reference to the project in SSISDB.
# This code assumes that the project has already been deployed.
$catalog = $ssis.Catalogs[$catalogName]
$folder = $catalog.Folders[$folderName]
$project = $folder.Projects[$projectName]

$listOfExecutions = @()

# Look for new work items
foreach ($item in invoke-sqlcmd -database $database -serverinstance $sqlServer -query "
                                        SELECT WorkItemID,
                                               PackageName,
                                               InputFileName
                                        FROM   [WorkItems]
                                        WHERE  WorkItemState = N'Queued'"  )
{

    # print execution info: package name, input file name
    Write-Host "WorkItemId   :" $item["WorkItemID"]
    Write-Host "PackageName  :" $item["PackageName"]
    Write-Host "InputFileName:" $item["InputFileName"]

    # get a reference to the package
    $package = $project.Packages[$item["PackageName"]]

    # setup parameter
    $param = New-Object "Microsoft.SqlServer.Management.IntegrationServices.PackageInfo+Execution
ValueParameterSet"
    $param.ParameterName = "InputFileName"
    $param.ParameterValue = $item["InputFileName"]
    $param.ObjectType = 30 # string
```

```
    $collection = New-Object
"System.Collections.ObjectModel.Collection[Microsoft.SqlServer.Management.IntegrationServices.Pa
ckageInfo+ExecutionValueParameterSet]"
    $collection.Add($param)

    Write-Host "Running package " $package.Name

    # Execute the package
    # The first parameter indicates whether we want to use 32bit or 64bit runtimes
    # The second parameter is a reference to a server environment
    # The final parameter is a collection of parameters
    $executionId = $package.Execute($use32BitRuntime, $null, $collection)

    UpdateWorkItemStatus $item["WorkItemID"] "Running"

    # store the execution id
    $exec = New-Object WorkItem
    $exec.Id = $executionId
    $exec.WorkItemId = $item["WorkItemID"]

    $listOfExecutions += $exec

    Write-Host "[Exec ID]: " $executionId

}

# Check on the status of each job
foreach ($workItem in $listOfExecutions)
{
    $exec = $catalog.Executions[$workItem.Id]

    # Loop until the package has completed
    while (IsStillRunning $exec.Status)
    {
        Write-Host "[Exec" $exec.Id "] Status:" $exec.Status
        Start-Sleep -s 2
        $exec.Refresh()
    }

    $status = 'Failed'
    if ($exec.Status -eq [Microsoft.SqlServer.Management.IntegrationServices.Operation+
ServerOperationStatus]::Passed)
    {
        $status = 'Succeeded'
    }

    Write-Host "[Exec" $workItem.Id"] Status:" $exec.Status

    # Change work item state
    UpdateWorkItemStatus $workItem.WorkItemId $status
}
```

LISTING 19-23 Results of running the PowerShell script that uses the SSIS MOM to run packages

```
PS SQLSERVER:\> C:\book\Chapter19\listing19-3.ps1
WorkItemId   : 25
PackageName  : ImportData.dtsx
InputFileName: \\datafiles\File1.csv
Running package  ImportData.dtsx
[Exec ID]:  30111
WorkItemId   : 26
PackageName  : ImportData.dtsx
InputFileName: \\datafiles\File2.csv
Running package  ImportData.dtsx
[Exec ID]:  30112
WorkItemId   : 27
PackageName  : ImportData.dtsx
InputFileName: \\datafiles\File3.csv
Running package  ImportData.dtsx
[Exec ID]:  30113
WorkItemId   : 28
PackageName  : ImportData.dtsx
InputFileName: \\datafiles\File4.csv
Running package  ImportData.dtsx
[Exec ID]:  30114
[Exec 30111 ] Status: Success
[Exec 30112 ] Status: Running
[Exec 30112 ] Status: Success
[Exec 30113 ] Status: Running
[Exec 30113 ] Status: Success
[Exec 30114 ] Status: Pending
[Exec 30114 ] Status: Success
```

Using PowerShell with SQL Agent

An alternative to running the SSIS package directly through the MOM is to use SQL Agent. This approach allows you to run the package using different user credentials through a SQL Agent feature called Proxy Accounts. Listing 19-24 provides a sample PowerShell script that iterates the WorkItems table (just like in Listing 19-22), and uses the SQL Management Objects (SMO) classes to create an run a SQL Agent for each queued work item. Listing 19-25 shows the output of running the script.

LISTING 19-24 PowerShell script that runs SSIS packages with SQL Agent

```
# Load SQL
Import-Module SqlPs
# Load SMO extension
[System.Reflection.Assembly]::LoadWithPartialName("Microsoft.SqlServer.Smo") | Out-Null;
# Set the SQL instance name and database
$sqlServer = "localhost"
$database = "Chapter19"
$projectPath = "\SSISDB\Chapter19\SimpleProject\"

# Changes work item state
Function UpdateWorkItemStatus([string]$workItemId, [string]$status)
{
    $sql = "UPDATE WorkItems SET WorkItemState = N'{0}', LastUpdate = GETDATE() WHERE
```

```
WorkItemID = {1}" -f $status, $workItemId
    invoke-sqlcmd -database $database -serverinstance $sqlServer -query $sql
}
# Create an SMO Server object
$srv = New-Object "Microsoft.SqlServer.Management.Smo.Server" $sqlserver;

$listOfJobs = @()

# Look for new work items
foreach ($item in invoke-sqlcmd -database $database -serverinstance $sqlServer -query "
                                        SELECT WorkItemID,
                                               PackageName,
                                               InputFileName
                                        FROM   [WorkItems]
                                        WHERE  WorkItemState = N'Queued'"  )
{

    # print execution info: package name, input file name
    Write-Host "WorkItemID   :" $item["WorkItemID"]
    Write-Host "PackageName  :" $item["PackageName"]
    Write-Host "InputFileName:" $item["InputFileName"]

    # create agent job
    $jobName = "Run_" + $item["PackageName"] + "_" + $item["WorkItemID"]
    $job = New-Object "Microsoft.SqlServer.Management.Smo.Agent.Job" ($srv.JobServer, $jobName)
    $job.IsEnabled = $TRUE

    # store the WorkItemId in the job's description field—we'll need it later
    $job.Description = $item["WorkItemID"]

    $job.Create()

    # Add SSIS job step

    $step = new-object Microsoft.SqlServer.Management.Smo.Agent.JobStep($job, "Run SSIS
package")
    $step.SubSystem = [Microsoft.SqlServer.Management.Smo.Agent.AgentSubSystem]::Ssis
    $step.Command = '/ISSERVER "' + $projectPath + $item["PackageName"] + '" ' +
                    '/SERVER "' + $sqlServer + '" ' +
                    '/Par "InputFileName";"' + $item["InputFileName"] + '" ' +
                    '/Par "$ServerOption::SYNCHRONIZED(Boolean)";True ' +
                    '/CALLERINFO SQLAGENT'

    # OPTIONAL: Set proxy account name
    # $step.ProxyName = "SSIS"

    $step.Create()

    # Run the job
    Write-Host "Running job:" $job.Name
    $job.ApplyToTargetServer($srv.Name)
    $job.Start()

    # Change work item state
    UpdateWorkItemStatus $item["WorkItemID"] "Running"

    # add execution ID to  list
```

```
    $listOfJobs += $job
}

# Check on the status of each job
foreach ($job in $listOfJobs)
{
    # Refresh the job to pick up its latest status
    $job.Refresh()

    # Loop until the job has stopped
    while ($job.CurrentRunStatus -ne
[Microsoft.SqlServer.Management.Smo.Agent.JobExecutionStatus]::Idle)
    {
        Write-Host "[Job " $job.Name "] Status: " $Job.CurrentRunStatus
        Start-Sleep -s 2
        $job.Refresh()
    }

    Write-Host "[Job " $job.Name "] Outcome: " $Job.LastRunOutcome

    $status = 'Failed'
    if ($job.LastRunOutcome -eq
[Microsoft.SqlServer.Management.Smo.Agent.CompletionResult]::Succeeded)
    {
        $status = 'Succeeded'
    }

    # Change work item state
    UpdateWorkItemStatus $job.Description $status
}
```

LISTING 19-25 Results of running the PowerShell script that uses SQL Agent to run packages

```
PS> C:\book\Chapter19\listing19-5.ps1

WorkItemID   : 17
PackageName  : ImportData.dtsx
InputFileName: \\datafiles\File1.csv
Running job: Run_ImportData.dtsx_17
WorkItemID   : 18
PackageName  : ImportData.dtsx
InputFileName: \\datafiles\File2.csv
Running job: Run_ImportData.dtsx_18
WorkItemID   : 19
PackageName  : ImportData.dtsx
InputFileName: \\datafiles\File3.csv
Running job: Run_ImportData.dtsx_19
WorkItemID   : 20
PackageName  : ImportData.dtsx
InputFileName: \\datafiles\File4.csv
Running job: Run_ImportData.dtsx_20
[Job  Run_ImportData.dtsx_17 ] Status:  Executing
[Job  Run_ImportData.dtsx_17 ] Status:  Executing
[Job  Run_ImportData.dtsx_17 ] Outcome:  Succeeded
[Job  Run_ImportData.dtsx_18 ] Outcome:  Succeeded
[Job  Run_ImportData.dtsx_19 ] Outcome:  Succeeded
[Job  Run_ImportData.dtsx_20 ] Outcome:  Succeeded
```

Alternative Solutions and Samples

This section describes some of the third-party alternatives to creating your own SSIS automation solutions, and code samples that you can use as starting points for your projects.

Samples on Codeplex

The following projects can be found on Codeplex (*http://www.codeplex.com*), Microsoft's open source project hosting web site.

EzAPI

EzAPI is an alternative way to create SSIS packages. It acts as a higher level API over the SSIS object model, and provides an easy-to-use interface for creating packages. It especially simplifies the creation of Data Flows, as it is able to automatically map columns based on name and data type. The library was originally developed by the SSIS test team to simplify the creation of automated tests. It is now available on Codeplex, and is actively updated by the product team.

The library and code can be found at *http://sqlsrvintegrationsrv.codeplex.com/.*

Package Generation Sample

The SSIS development team published a simple package generation sample as part of the Microsoft SQL Server Community Samples: Integration Services project. This sample provides a stand-alone executable that generates an SSIS package with a Data Flow. It supports CSV, SQL, and Excel formats as a source or destination. The code provides a good example of how to dynamically create a Data Flow from column metadata.

The sample code can be found at *http://sqlsrvintegrationsrv.codeplex.com/.*

MDDE Studio

The MetaData Driven ETL (MDDE) Studio project is a tool developed by an internal group at Microsoft. The tool takes a template-based approach: You design your packages using the SSIS designer, load them in MDDE Studio, and generate multiple copies based on metadata input. Although the tool isn't meant for production (it only supports a subset of SSIS tasks and transforms), it can provide a good starting point for anyone looking to create a user-interface–based automation tool.

The code can be found at *http://sqlservermddestudio.codeplex.com/.*

Vulcan

Vulcan provides an XML-based language for describing SSIS packages (similar to Biml, described later in this chapter). It allows you to model your data and the transformations you wish to perform in XML. It then uses a compiler to generate one or more SSIS packages (as well as the SQL table definitions, if you so choose).

The Codeplex project can be found at *http://vulcan.codeplex.com/*.

Third-Party Solutions

BIDS Helper

BIDS Helper is an open-source extension for Visual Studio that adds a lot of useful functionality for SSIS and SQL Server Analysis Services developers. One of the newer feature additions allows for dynamic package generation using the Business Intelligence Markup Language (Biml). Biml allows you to model your ETL work using XML, and dynamically generate a set of packages based on defined metadata. Figure 19-1 shows the Solution Explorer options that are added by BIDS Helper, and Figure 19-2 shows a code snippet of the Biml language.

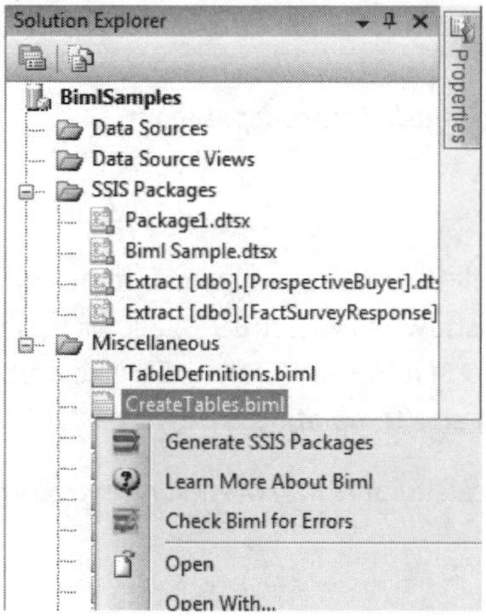

FIGURE 19-1 Accessing Biml files from the Solution Explorer.

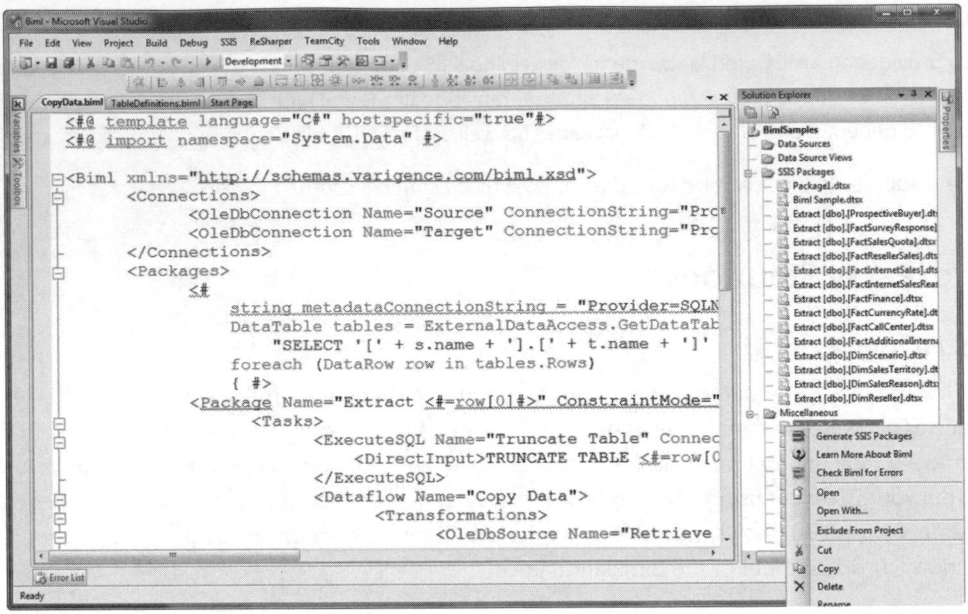

FIGURE 19-2 Biml is defined using XML and embedded scripts.

The BIDS Helper project can be found on Codeplex at *http://bidshelper.codeplex.com/*.

Varigence Mist

BIDS Helper supports the community (free) version of BIML. Full Biml functionality can be found in the Mist application, created by Varigence. The Mist designer (shown in Figure 19-3) allows you to create a unified data model to generate your ETL packages and SQL Server Analysis Services cubes. It supports a .NET-based scripting language for easy automation and templating.

More information about Biml can be found on the Varigence site at *http://www.varigence.com/*.

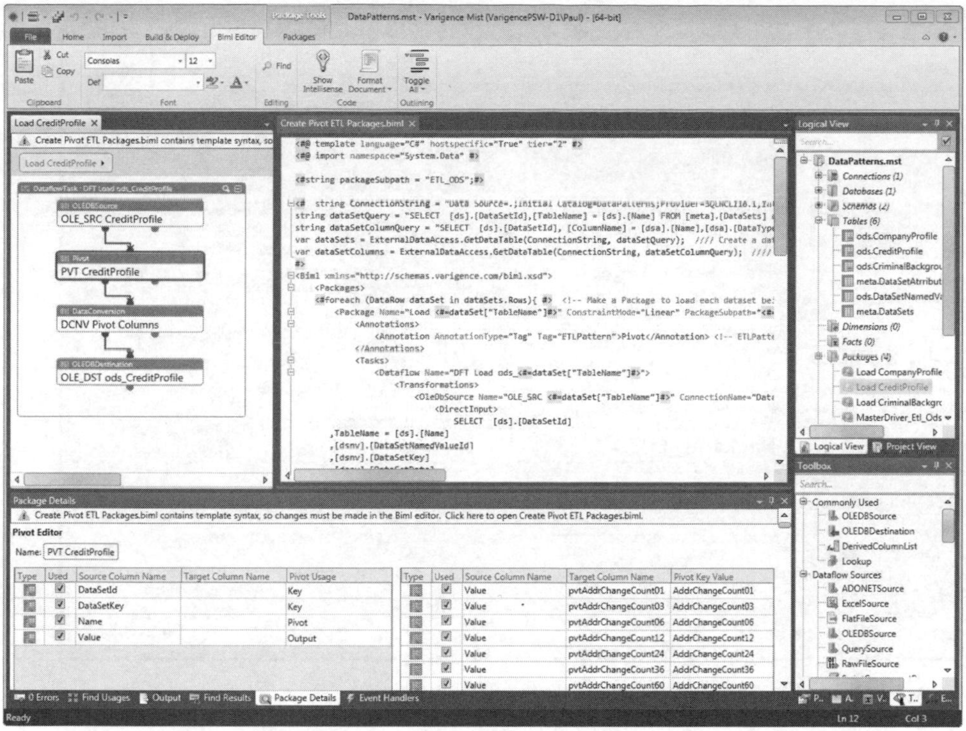

FIGURE 19-3 Varigence Mist provides full Biml functionality.

Pragmatic Works BI xPress

BI xPress from Pragmatic Works (*http://www.pragmaticworks.com/*) is an add-on for Visual Studio with useful productivity enhancements for SSIS. The tool allows you to create reusable package templates (shown in Figure 19-4), and provides automation features, like a "one-click" package auditing framework.

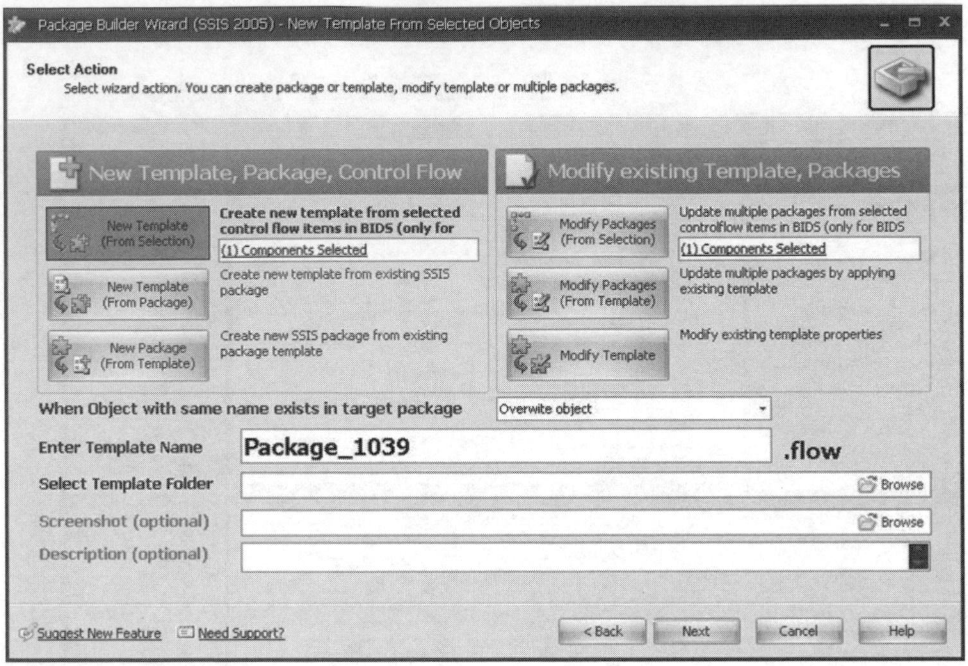

FIGURE 19-4 Package templating in Pragmatic Work's BI xPress tool.

CozyRoc

For those mostly interested in reuse functionality, CozyRoc provides the Script Task Plus, Script Component Plus, and Data Flow Plus components. These custom extensions allow you to reuse scripts and Data Flow logic across packages.

More information about these components can be found at *http://cozyroc.com/*.

Summary

This chapter covered the technologies required to implement your own SSIS automation solutions. It provided a look at the SSIS object model, and code samples for package execution and generation. It described various approaches to creating a metadata-based package execution solution, and useful third-party alternatives to creating everything by yourself. More code samples can be found on Codeplex and other SSIS-related blogs on the Internet.

PART V

Troubleshooting

CHAPTER 20

Troubleshooting SSIS Package Failures

In This Chapter

Getting Started with Troubleshooting

After you have designed the SSIS packages and deployed them to either the development, staging, or production environment, you will need to learn skills that are essential to finding out why a specific execution fails. An SSIS package execution can fail for many reasons. Some common failure scenarios include the following:

- **Failure to acquire connection to a remote data source or destination** This can be due to different credentials being used when connecting to different servers. The credentials used to connect to a production server can be different from development settings.
- **Mismatch in data types** During development, SSIS developers might be using a set of test data, and the SSIS packages are executing successfully. However, when the packages have been deployed to the production environment, the new data might have data type mismatch in specific records, which might not have been handled by the SSIS package. In addition, the changes to metadata in the different deployment environment might also cause packages to fail.

- **Script task and Script component errors** Custom code that is written in Script task and Script component might not have been designed to deal with some conditions, which triggers exception in the code. Consequently, this causes the package to fail.
- **Missing components** An SSIS package might rely on custom log providers, connectivity components that might not have been installed in the production servers.
- **Scheduled SQL Agent SSIS job step issues** Often, the service account used to execute the SSIS packages might not have the right permissions to connect to the remote data source and destinations. In addition, the service account might not have the permissions to access resources used during the execution.

When using SQL Server Data Tools, you can make use of the progress reporting or execution report to obtain high-level details on why a package execution failed. After the SSIS packages are deployed to the production environment, SSIS developers often make use of the logging capabilities to troubleshoot package execution issues. In previous versions of Integration Services (SQL Server 2005, SQL Server 2008, and SQL Server 2008 R2), SSIS developers enable SSIS logging capabilities during package execution to have sufficient useful information available when the package execution fails. During package failures, SSIS developers sift through the information that is logged to make sense of what went wrong, and to identify the root cause of failure. In addition, the SSIS event handlers are often used to implement custom logic whenever specific SSIS events are detected during package execution.

In some production environments, the SSIS packages need to undergo significant reviews before they get deployed. This can sometimes cause problems for operators or administrators who are responsible for the daily scheduled package executions, when they realize that the packages are not logging a sufficient level of information that can help them troubleshoot package failures. For example, the relevant collection of SSIS events that relates to the error might not be logged. At the other extreme, too much unstructured event information could get logged, which makes it hard for operators or database administrators to pinpoint the exact point of failure, as it requires them to sift through huge amounts of unstructured information. Many SSIS developers and software vendors have developed custom SSIS logging frameworks to simplify the task of logging the right set of information.

> **Note** This SQL Server 2008 R2 Books Online (BOL) article provides a good discussion on troubleshooting SSIS package execution for SSIS 2005, SSIS 2008, and SSIS 2008 R2: *http://technet.microsoft.com/en-us/library/aa337088.aspx*.

SSIS 2012 introduces new capabilities that make it easier for SSIS developers and database administrators to monitor package executions, to quickly identify the root cause of package failures, and to obtain detailed contextual information about a failed component. In addition, it provides database administrators with the ability to obtain a macro view of connection failures for package executions. This allows database administrators to quickly address the connection failures, which solves the issues with the failed execution. In earlier SSIS versions, you might have to go to each of the SSIS packages and determine what went wrong. In most cases, as you go through each individual SSIS package, you might realize that it is because of some connection issues.

Most important, logging of the events during package execution is enabled automatically in SQL Server 2012. You no longer have to fiddle with log providers, or have to make choices on the right events that are logged. In SSIS 2012, whenever you execute an SSIS package that has been deployed to the SSIS Catalog, logging happens automatically. You can control the amount of information logged by modifying the server-wide default logging level, or by changing the logging level before the SSIS package starts execution. Four logging levels are provided: None, Basic (default), Performance, and Verbose. The Basic logging level ensures that when package failures occur, you have sufficient execution information that is logged and can be used for troubleshooting.

SSIS 2012 provides a set of standard reports that can be launched within SQL Server Management Studio to help you jumpstart the troubleshooting of package failures. (Refer to Chapter 14, "SSIS Reports," where you learned about these SSIS standard reports.) In this chapter, we focus on using Transact-SQL (T-SQL) in troubleshooting of package failures.

Data Preparation

In this section, you prepare the database, tables, and data needed to try the different examples in the chapter. To start the preparation, download the AdventureWorksDW2012 database from *http://msftdbprodsamples.codeplex.com/releases/view/55330*, and attach it to a SQL Server instance.

After the AdventureWorksDW2012 database has been attached, perform the following steps:

1. Deploy the SSIS project, Chapter20Project.ispac, found in *C:\InsideOut\Chapter 20\Code* to the *SSISInsideOut* folder in SSIS Catalog.
2. By default, the data preparation step will create the database EnterpriseDW on the default SQL instance. If you are using a named instance or deploying it to a remote server, you will need to configure the project parameter *ServerName* with the correct ServerName value.
3. After the SSIS Catalog has been deployed successfully, execute the package "0. PrepData.dtsx" using SQL Server Management Studio, by right-clicking the package "0. PrepData.dtsx" and choose Execute Package.
4. Verify that the package executes successfully, and the database has been created successfully.
5. When prompted whether you would like to open the Overview report, click Yes. This will show you the Overview report for the package execution. In this report, the status for the execution should be Succeeded. If it is not, you can make use of the information provided in the report to troubleshoot. You can also continue reading the rest of this chapter, where you will learn essential T-SQL skills to troubleshoot SSIS package executions.

Troubleshooting Failures of SSIS Package Executions

In this section, you learn how to use the new capabilities introduced in SSIS 2012 to troubleshoot different types of failures. You learn how to make use of the information that is captured in the public views shown in Table 20-1.

TABLE 20-1 Public views in SSISDB that are useful for troubleshooting

Name of view	Description	Available logging level
catalog.executions	Provides information about the execution, including: Status of the execution Amount of physical and virtual memory Name of the SQL Server instance Name of the machine Number of CPUs available in the server	All
catalog.execution_parameter_values	Shows the value specified for each parameter of the project and package when the package execution started	All
catalog.event_messages	Provides information about the SSIS events that are logged during package execution. Depending on the logging level used for the execution, the events that are logged can differ.	Basic Performance Verbose
catalog.event_message_context	Provides information about the properties of a component whenever an error occurs during package execution.	Basic Performance Verbose
catalog.executables	Shows the SSIS executables that are used during package execution. These SSIS executables include SSIS tasks and containers	Basic Performance Verbose
catalog.executable_statistics	Shows the execution duration of each SSIS task, the execution result, and execution value returned. A value of 1 indicates that the executable failed, and 0 indicates that it executes successfully.	Basic Performance Verbose
catalog.execution_component_phases	Shows the time spent at each phase of a Data Flow component during package execution.	Performance Verbose

The examples given in this section assume that you have completed the data preparation steps, and have successfully executed the SSIS package for data preparation. Next, perform the following steps to run the package "1. DataIssues.dtsx":

1. Using SQL Server Management Studio, navigate to the folder *SSISInsideOut*.
2. Expand the packages under Chapter20Project.
3. Right-click "1. DataIssues.dtsx" and choose Execute Package.
4. Navigate to the folder *SSISInsideOut* (see Figure 20-1).

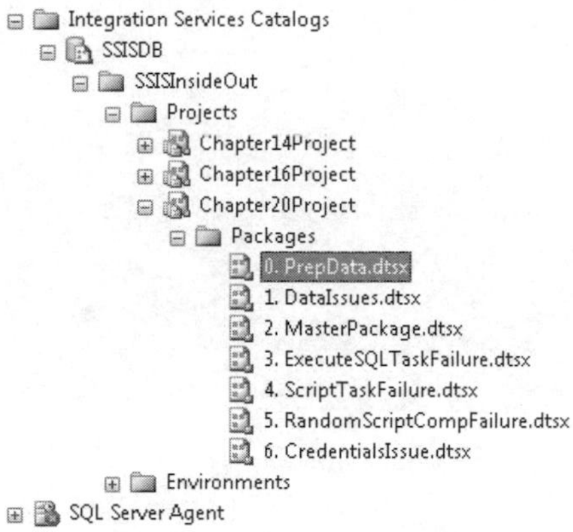

FIGURE 20-1 Navigate to Chapter20Project.

5. Click OK.
6. Take note of the operation ID for the execution.
7. The Microsoft SQL Server Management Studio dialog box (Figure 20-2) shows that the package execution (with operation ID 14) has started.

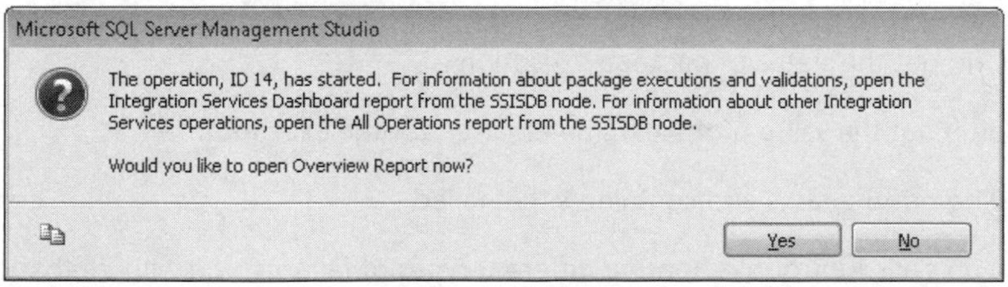

FIGURE 20-2 Microsoft SQL Server Management Studio dialog box showing the operation ID.

8. Click No to close the dialog box.

Note When you start a package execution in SSIS 2012, a unique identifier, known as an execution ID, is used to track the execution. Another name for the execution ID is the operation ID. You will see this term of reference in the SQL Server Management Studio user interface, as well as the column names for some of the views.

Tip You can also leverage the T-SQL skills that you acquired in Chapter 12, "SSIS T-SQL Magic," to start the package execution using T-SQL. In this case, you will need to print out the execution ID to start the investigation. Listing 20-1 shows how to start the package execution using T-SQL.

LISTING 20-1 Starting package execution

```
USE SSISDB

DECLARE @execution_id bigint
EXEC catalog.create_execution
   @package_name=N'1. DataIssues.dtsx',
   @execution_id=@execution_id OUTPUT,
   @folder_name=N'SSISInsideOut',
   @project_name=N'Chapter20Project',
   @use32bitruntime=False,
   @reference_id=Null

EXEC catalog.start_execution @execution_id
SELECT @execution_id AS execution_id
```

Three Key Steps Toward Troubleshooting Failures of SSIS Package Executions

In this section, you learn the key steps that can be used to gain insights into why a package failed. You can remember these steps as the SVT steps:

- **S** Finding out the status of package execution
- **V** Finding out the value of the parameters used for the execution
- **T** Finding out the tasks and containers that failed

As you build up skills for troubleshooting different types of failures, you will see that these three steps are important precursor activities toward a deeper dive into pinpointing the exact cause of failure.

See Also *See Chapter 14 on how you can make use of the SSIS reports to troubleshoot failures.*

Step S: Finding Out the Status of Package Execution

The *catalog.executions* view provides high-level information about the package execution. The status column in this view shows whether the package execution is successful. The values for the status column are as follows:

- **Created (1)** The package execution is in this state when it has been created using *catalog.create_execution* and has not started.
- **Running (2)** The package execution is currently running. Using the *catalog.executions* view, you will be able to obtain the ProcessID for the process that corresponds to this package execution.
- **Canceled or Stopped (3)** The package execution has been stopped by the user.
- **Failed (4)** The package execution failed. In this chapter, you learn how to troubleshoot failed executions.
- **Pending (5)** This is an internal status for a package execution. When you see a package execution with this status, it usually means that the package execution somehow failed to load properly, or the SQL Server instance shut down unexpectedly. To clean up this intermediate state, execute the stored procedure *catalog.startup*.
- **Terminated unexpectedly (6)** All package executions have this status when a relevant process for the package execution cannot be found. This is triggered during SQL Server startup or when the stored procedure *catalog.startup* is executed.
- **Successful (7)** This indicates that the package execution is successful.
- **Stopping (8)** When the stored procedure *catalog.stop_operation* is first executed, it will mark the package execution with a stopping status. Subsequent invocation of *catalog.stop_operation* will fail until the package execution has been stopped successfully.
- **Completed (9)** This indicates that the package execution has completed. It is important to note that this can mean that the package execution is successful or failed. To obtain more information about package execution that is in this state, you should examine the view *catalog.executable_statistics*.

Listing 20-2 shows the T-SQL used to find information about the execution (with execution ID 14). Besides obtaining the status of the package execution, the T-SQL also obtains other useful information about the execution.

LISTING 20-2 Obtaining information for package execution, with execution ID 14

```
USE SSISDB

SELECT status, execution_id,
   folder_name,project_name,package_name, project_lsn,
   use32bitruntime, executed_as_name, process_id
FROM catalog.executions
WHERE execution_id = 14
```

Figure 20-3 shows the results that are returned. From the results, you can observe that the package execution failed (that is, status = 4), and its corresponding ProcessID *is* 5836. In addition, the package is executed by the Windows account *SSISInsideOut\DemoUser*, and uses the 32-bit runtime. There is other useful information that can be obtained from the *catalog.executions* view, including the number of CPUs, the amount of available and free physical memory, and the amount of available and free virtual memory.

	status	execution_id	folder_name	project_name	package_name	project_lsn	use32bitruntime	executed_as_name	process_id
1	4	14	SSISInsideOut	Chapter20Project	1. DataIssues.dtsx	12	1	SSISInsideOut\DemoUser	1544

FIGURE 20-3 Results returned from executing the query in Listing 20-2.

Step V: Finding Out the Values Specified for the Parameters

Package failures can be due to the wrong values specified for an execution. The *catalog.execution_parameter_values* view provides information about the values that are specified when package execution started. Listing 20-3 shows how you can find out about the values of the parameters for the execution. In the T-SQL snippet, *OBJECT_TYPE = 50* is not included in the results. The object type provides information on the type of parameters (package, project, or execution-scope parameters). This is because the parameters, with *OBJECT_TYPE = 50*, refer to execution-scoped parameters, and are not immediately useful in the initial investigation. In addition, you will also notice that parameters, with names that contain the CM. prefix are filtered out, too (except when they contain the connection string). These CM. prefix parameters refers to the properties for the connection managers used in the package. In most cases, only the connection string is immediately useful for investigation purposes. The results are ordered by *OBJECT_TYPE* to make sure we can clearly differentiate between project and package parameters.

LISTING 20-3 Finding out the values of the parameters

```
USE SSISDB

SELECT object_type, parameter_name, parameter_value, parameter_data_type
FROM catalog.execution_parameter_values
WHERE execution_id = 14
AND (PATINDEX('CM.%',parameter_name)= 0 OR
 PATINDEX('CM.%.ConnectionString',parameter_name) > 0)
AND object_type <> 50
ORDER BY object_type
```

Figure 20-4 shows the result from executing the query. After the query is executed, you can do a quick review of the values used for the parameters to see whether they are correct. Parameters with *object_type = 20* and *30* refer to project and package parameters, respectively. When a package is executed, it can contain SSIS expressions that make use of both project-scoped and package-scoped parameters. Hence, it is useful to include them in the query for investigation purposes.

	object_type	parameter_name	parameter_value	parameter_data_type
1	20	BaseDataDir	C:\InsideOut\Chapter 20\SampleData	String
2	20	ServerName	(local)	String
3	20	CM.LocalHost.master.ConnectionString	Data Source=.;Initial Catalog=master;Provider=SQLNC...	String
4	20	CM.LocalHost.EnterpriseDW.ConnectionString	Data Source=(local);Initial Catalog=EnterpriseDW;Pro...	String
5	20	CM.LocalHost.AdventureWorksDW2012.ConnectionString	Data Source=.;Initial Catalog=AdventureWorksDW20...	String

FIGURE 20-4 Results from executing the query given in Listing 20-3.

Step T: Finding Out the Tasks and Containers That Failed

In Steps 1 and 2, you make use of the *catalog.executions* view to find out the status of the package execution, and the *catalog.execution_parameter_values* view to find out the value specified for each of the project and package parameters. In this section, you learn how you can find information about the tasks and containers in the package that caused the failure.

The *catalog.executable_statistics* view provides high-level run-time information about the executables that are in the SSIS package. The *catalog.executables* view provides the name of all the executables used in the package. The executables that are in the SSIS package include all the tasks and containers that are used in the package.

Listing 20-4 shows the T-SQL query that can be used to find the executables that have failed. In Figure 20-5, you can see the execution result for each of the executables. A value of 1 indicates that the executable failed during execution, and 0 indicates that the executable completed execution successfully. From the results, you can see that the package failed (row 1), caused by the Foreach Loop container (row 2). As you investigate further, you can see from the execution path that the Foreach Loop container contains a Data Flow task that executes for three iterations (rows 3–5). The first two iterations (rows 3 and 4) executed successfully; the execution failed at the third iteration.

LISTING 20-4 Finding the executables that failed

```
USE SSISDB

SELECT s.execution_result, e.executable_name,s.execution_path,
s.execution_duration AS duration,

CONVERT(nvarchar(30), s.end_time , 109) as end_time
FROM catalog.executable_statistics s, catalog.executables e
WHERE s.execution_id = 14
AND s.executable_id = e.executable_id
AND s.execution_id = e.execution_id
ORDER BY s.execution_path
```

	execution_result	executable_name	execution_path	duration	end_time
1	1	1 DataIssues	\1 DataIssues	3796	Mar 30 2012 5:00:18.5816016PM
2	1	Foreach Loop Container	\1 DataIssues\Foreach Loop Container	3725	Mar 30 2012 5:00:18.5805984PM
3	0	Data Flow Task	\1 DataIssues\Foreach Loop Container[1]\Data Flo...	1392	Mar 30 2012 5:00:16.2612000PM
4	0	Data Flow Task	\1 DataIssues\Foreach Loop Container[2]\Data Flo...	1271	Mar 30 2012 5:00:17.5533216PM
5	1	Data Flow Task	\1 DataIssues\Foreach Loop Container[3]\Data Flo...	1022	Mar 30 2012 5:00:18.5785920PM

FIGURE 20-5 Results from executing the query given in Listing 20-4.

Execution Path

The concept of an execution path is introduced in SSIS 2012, and is used to provide information on the exact point in a package at which an executable executes. When tasks are executed in different iterations of containers, such as the For and Foreach loops, the iteration index is captured in the execution path. In addition, if the package is executed as part of a child package invocation, the execution path will also capture the point in the parent package at which the child package is invoked. We will see this later in this chapter.

At this point, we have figured out that the package failed because the Data Flow task in the third iteration of the Foreach Loop container failed. Next, we dive deeper to find the root cause.

Finding the Root Cause of Failure

The *catalog.event_messages* view provides the detailed execution log that can be used to find the root cause. Listing 20-5 shows how you can query for all the *OnError* events that are logged during package execution.

LISTING 20-5 Finding the *OnError* events

```
USE SSISDB

SELECT m.message,m.subcomponent_name, m.execution_path
FROM catalog.event_messages m
WHERE m.operation_id = 14
AND m.event_name = 'OnError'
ORDER by subcomponent_name
```

In Figure 20-6, you can see clearly that there are three *OnError* events that contributed to the error. Specifically, the error is caused by the Data Flow component Derived Column [2], when it is trying to perform a type cast. The square bracket [2] indicates the identifier for the component is 2.

	message	subcomponent_name	execution_path
1	Data Flow Task:Error: An error occurred while attempting to perform a type cast.	Derived Column [2]	\1 DataIssues\Foreach Loop Container[3]\Data Flow Task
2	Data Flow Task:Error: SSIS Error Code DTS_E_INDUCEDTRANSFORMFAILUR...	Derived Column [2]	\1 DataIssues\Foreach Loop Container[3]\Data Flow Task
3	Data Flow Task:Error: SSIS Error Code DTS_E_PROCESSINPUTFAILED. The ...	SSIS.Pipeline	\1 DataIssues\Foreach Loop Container[3]\Data Flow Task

FIGURE 20-6 Results from executing the query given in Listing 20-5.

If you collate all the results from the failure investigation, you will realize that the Data Flow task has been successful in executing the Data Flow task for two iterations. It failed at the third iteration due to a type cast error. This is likely caused by the data that is in the file. In Chapter 23, "Troubleshooting Data Issues," you will learn how to make use of new capabilities in SSIS 2012 to troubleshoot data issues for packages that are deployed to the SSIS Catalog.

Context of an Error

Whenever an error occurs during package execution, the context for the component that caused the error will be logged. The context of an error refers to the value of the properties for the component that failed. In addition, the properties of all tasks and containers that are in the execution path of the Data Flow component are captured. This is similar to the stack trace for an application program, except that it is the SSIS runtime stack trace.

To allow users to figure out the ordering for the entries in the stack trace, the concept of a *context depth* is introduced. The point at which the error occurred is referred to as having a context depth of 1. The context depth is incremented by one when the component or container is further from the error. In this example, to dig deeper, you need to look at the following:

1. The properties for the component when the error occurred at context 1.
2. The value of the connection strings used when the error occurred. The connection strings are part of the properties of connection managers, and the collection of connection managers occur at the package level. Consequently, the context depth is greater than or equal to 1.

In Figure 20-7, you can see the Derived Column transformation in the Data Flow task failed. The context depth for the Data Flow task is 1. As the Data Flow task is in the Foreach Loop container, the value of the properties for the Foreach Loop container is also captured, as part of the context of the error. The context depth for the Foreach Loop container is 2.

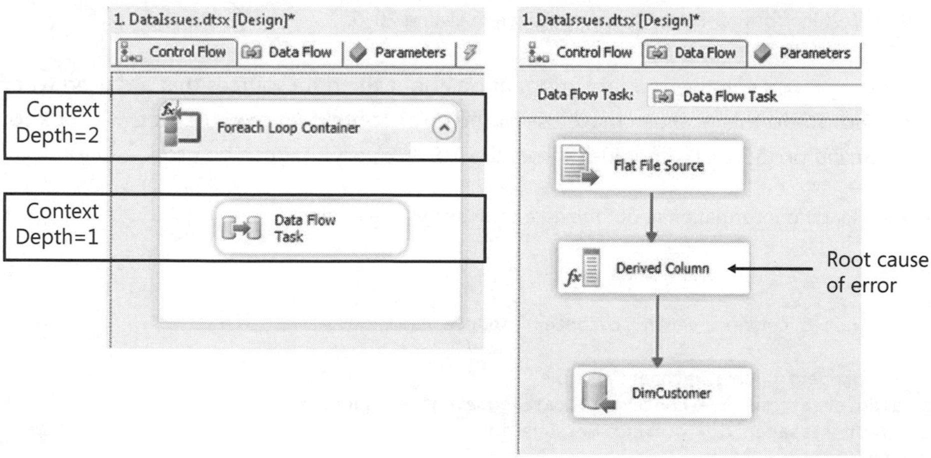

FIGURE 20-7 Context depth.

> **Tip** When a package is started, the properties of the package and all the connection managers in the package are captured, with a context depth of 0.

Listing 20-6 shows how you can obtain the immediate context of an error, the properties of the component when the error occurred.

LISTING 20-6 Immediate context of an error

```
USE SSISDB

SELECT distinct c.context_depth, c.context_source_name,property_name, property_value
FROM catalog.event_message_context c, catalog.event_messages m
WHERE m.event_message_id = c.event_message_id
AND m.operation_id = 14
AND c.context_depth = 1
```

Figure 20-8 shows the results of executing the query given in Listing 20-6. In this example, you can see a type cast to DT_I4 is performed on the *HouseOwnerFlag*. This might be a likely cause of error.

	context_depth	context_source_name	property_name	property_value
1	1	Data Flow Task	[Derived Column].[Derived Column Output].[HouseOwnerFlagNew].[FriendlyExpression]	(DT_I4)HouseOwnerFlag
2	1	Data Flow Task	AutoGenerateIDForNewObjects	1
3	1	Data Flow Task	CreationName	SSIS.Pipeline.3
4	1	Data Flow Task	DefaultBufferMaxRows	10000
5	1	Data Flow Task	DefaultBufferSize	10485760
6	1	Data Flow Task	DelayValidation	0
7	1	Data Flow Task	Description	Data Flow Task
8	1	Data Flow Task	Disable	0
9	1	Data Flow Task	DisableEventHandlers	0
10	1	Data Flow Task	EnableCacheUpdate	1
11	1	Data Flow Task	EnableDisconnectedColumns	0
12	1	Data Flow Task	EngineThreads	10

FIGURE 20-8 Results from executing the query given in Listing 20-6.

To dig deeper, you will need to find information about the data sources that are used when the error occurred. To do this, you can make use of the error context. In this case, you will look for the *ConnectionString* property. Listing 20-7 shows the T-SQL query that can be used.

LISTING 20-7 Finding information about the data sources that are loaded

```
USE SSISDB

SELECT distinct c.context_depth, c.context_source_name,

           property_name, property_value
FROM catalog.event_message_context c, catalog.event_messages m
WHERE m.event_message_id = c.event_message_id
AND m.operation_id = 14
AND m.subcomponent_name = 'Derived Column [2]'
AND c.property_name = 'ConnectionString'
ORDER BY context_depth ASC
```

Figure 20-9 shows the results of executing the query. From the results that are returned, you can observe that four data sources might be used when the error occurred. In this example, the input to the Derived column is a provided by a Flat File source, called CSV Data File. Hence, you can infer that the file that contains the data is *C:\InsideOut\Chapter20\SampleData\File3.csv* (row 1).

Results | Messages

	context_depth	context_source_name	property_name	property_value
1	4	CSV Data File	ConnectionString	C:\InsideOut\Chapter 20\SampleData\File3.csv
2	4	LocalHost.AdventureWorksDW2012	ConnectionString	Data Source=.;Initial Catalog=AdventureWorksDW2012;Provider=SQLNCLI11.1;Inte...
3	4	LocalHost.EnterpriseDW	ConnectionString	Data Source=(local);Initial Catalog=EnterpriseDW;Provider=SQLNCLI11.1;Integrated ...
4	4	LocalHost.master	ConnectionString	Data Source=.;Initial Catalog=master;Provider=SQLNCLI11.1;Integrated Security=SS...

FIGURE 20-9 Results from executing the query given in Listing 20-7.

In many production deployments, it might not be possible to have deep knowledge of the internals of a package. In this case, you will have to export the SSIS project, load the project in SQL Server Data Tools to view the package, and understand how the different tasks and Data Flow components are used in the package. Alternatively, you can make use of the column *package_path* in the *catalog.executables* view to infer the structure of the package.

Troubleshooting the Execute Package Task and Child Package Executions

So far, you have learned how to make use of the different public views to iteratively dig deeper, until the root cause of failure of the package execution is identified. In most production deployments of SSIS packages, SSIS developers use the Execute Package task as a means for coordinating the execution of several child packages. In this section, you learn how to troubleshoot package executions that contain one or more Execute Package tasks (EPTs).

The examples given in this section assume that you have completed the data preparation steps, and have successfully executed the SSIS package for data preparation. Next, perform the following steps to run the package "2. MasterPackage.dtsx":

1. Using SQL Server Management Studio, navigate to the folder *SSISInsideOut*.
2. Expand the packages under Chapter20Project.
3. Right-click "2. MasterPackage.dtsx" and choose Execute Package.
4. Click Advanced, and for Logging Level, select Verbose (Figure 20-10).
5. Click OK.
6. Take note of the operation ID for the execution. In this example, assume that the operation ID for the execution is 16.
7. Click No to close the dialog box.

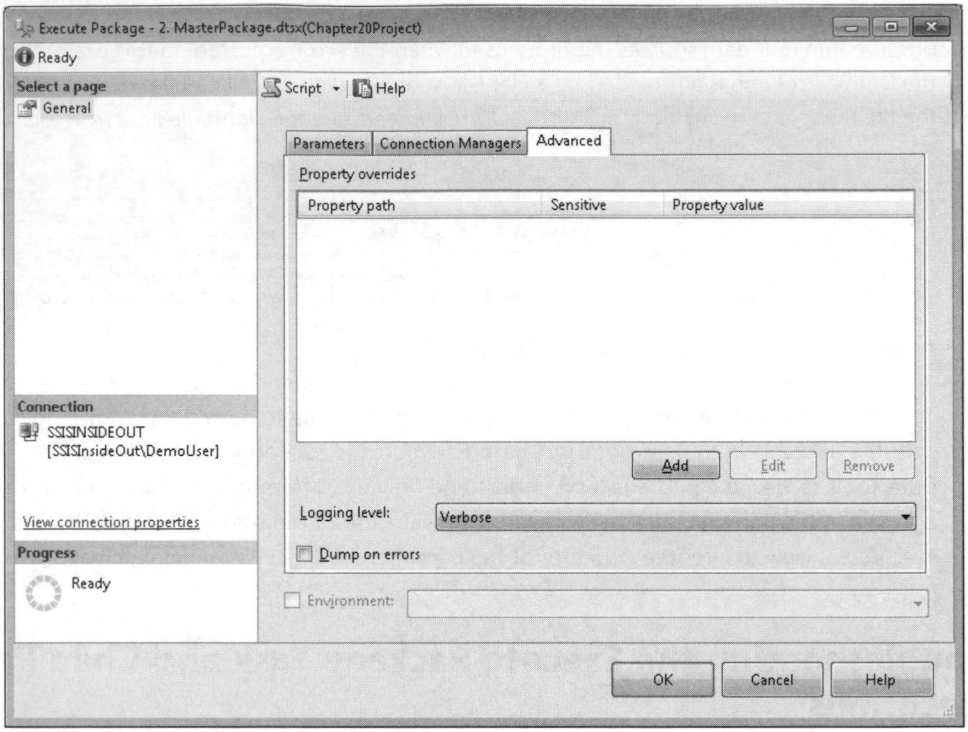

FIGURE 20-10 Setting the Logging Level to Verbose.

Using the SVT steps that you learned in the previous section, check the status of the execution of the SSIS package. You will notice that the package execution has failed (that is, Status = 4). Next, issue the T-SQL query given in Listing 20-8. The query obtains the unique set of events that are produced from the execution. The results of the query are shown in Figure 20-11, in which you will notice 23 distinct event names that are logged during the package execution because you are executing the package using the Verbose logging level. Consequently, this leads to more events being logged.

LISTING 20-8 Obtaining the distinct set of event names

```
USE SSISDB

SELECT distinct event_name
FROM catalog.event_messages m
WHERE m.operation_id = 16
ORDER BY event_name
```

Results | Messages

	event_name
1	BufferSizeTuning
2	Diagnostic
3	DiagnosticEx
4	OnCustomEvent
5	OnError
6	OnInformation
7	OnPipelinePostEndOfRowset
8	OnPipelinePostPrimeOutput
9	OnPipelinePreEndOfRowset
10	OnPipelinePrePrimeOutput
11	OnPostExecute
12	OnPostValidate
13	OnPreExecute
14	OnPreValidate
15	OnProgress
16	OnTaskFailed
17	OnWarning
18	PackageEnd
19	PackageStart
20	PipelineComponentTime
21	PipelineExecutionPlan
22	PipelineExecutionTrees
23	PipelineInitialization

FIGURE 20-11 Results from executing the query in Listing 20-8.

DiagnosticEx Events

You will also notice a new event name, DiagnosticEx. This event is new in SSIS 2012, and is available in the Verbose logging level. DiagnosticEx provides detailed information that is useful for diagnostic purposes. The value of the message column that is logged for DiagnosticEx is different from the other SSIS events, and consists of XML text. Whenever an EPT executes a child package, it will log DiagnosticEx, which consists of the parameter values passed to the child package. This can be useful in investigating child package failures, when you want to find out the value of the parameters specified for the child package.

Figure 20-12 shows examples of the XML text for this event. In Figure 20-12, you can see that the value used for the *BaseDataDir* parameter is *C:\InsideOut\Chapter20\SampleData*. If you query the *catalog.event_messages* for operation ID = 16, you will notice that there are three rows with DiagnosticEx events. You can make use of an XML T-SQL query to flatten the results from the XML text. Listing 20-9 shows how you can do this. Figure 20-13 shows the results from executing the XML T-SQL query, in which you can see that when the child package is invoked, the parent package set the value of the parameter *BaseDataDir* to be *c:\InsideOut\Chapter20\SampleData*.


```
<DTS:ParameterValues xmlns:DTS="www.microsoft.com/SqlServer/Dts">
  <DTS:PackageParameter DTS:DataType="8" DTS:ObjectName="BaseDataDir"
                        DTS:DTSID="{8C359D86-D9D6-41BE-940F-0EEF345039A1}" DTS:CreationName="">
    <DTS:Property DTS:Name="ParameterValue" DTS:DataType="8">C:\InsideOut\Chapter 20\SampleData</DTS:Property>
  </DTS:PackageParameter>
</DTS:ParameterValues>
```


FIGURE 20-12 Example of XML text that is captured for the DiagnosticEx event.

LISTING 20-9 XML T-SQL query to flatten the message text for the DiagnosticEx events

```
WITH DiagnosticExTable
(EventMessageID, EventName, MessageSourceName, XmlData)
AS (
SELECT event_message_id,
event_name,message_source_name,
cast( message as xml)
FROM catalog.event_messages m
WHERE m.operation_id = 16
AND m.event_name = ‘DiagnosticEx’
)
SELECT EventMessageID,Eventname,MessageSourceName,
           parameter.value(
           ‘declare namespace DTS=”www.microsoft.com/SqlServer/Dts”;
(@DTS:ObjectName)[1]’,
           ‘nvarchar(260)’) as ParameterName,
           parameter.value(
           ‘declare namespace DTS=”www.microsoft.com/SqlServer/Dts”;
(DTS:Property/text())[1]’,
           ‘nvarchar(256)’) as ParameterValue
FROM DiagnosticExTable
CROSS APPLY XmlData.nodes(
   ‘declare namespace DTS=”www.microsoft.com/SqlServer/Dts”;
   (/DTS:ParameterValues/DTS:PackageParameter)’) as PackageParameter(parameter)
```

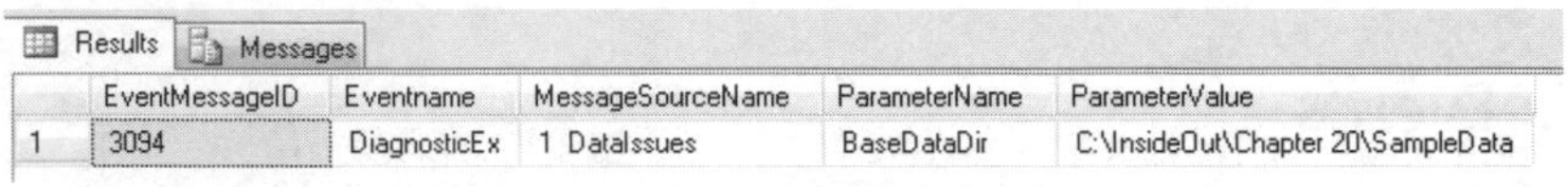

	EventMessageID	Eventname	MessageSourceName	ParameterName	ParameterValue
1	3094	DiagnosticEx	1 DataIssues	BaseDataDir	C:\InsideOut\Chapter 20\SampleData

FIGURE 20-13 Results from executing the query given in Listing 20-9.

Execute Package Task and Execution Path

The concept of an execution path is introduced in SSIS 2012, and plays an important role in helping to pinpoint the exact point of failure. Most important, if a child package is executed, the execution path captured will indicate the point in the parent package at which it is invoked.

In this section, we use the execution that has the execution ID equal to 16 to illustrate how the execution path can help you pinpoint the exact point of failure. Listing 20-10 shows the T-SQL query to obtain the distinct execution paths that led to errors in the package. It is important to note that the execution IDs on your computer will differ. You should note the execution ID for your execution, and replace the *<value>* portion of the line with your *execution_id* (for example, *m.operation_id = <value>*).

LISTING 20-10 Obtaining the distinct execution paths where errors occurred

```
USE SSISDB

SELECT DISTINCT execution_path
FROM catalog.event_messages m
WHERE m.operation_id = 16
AND m.event_name = 'OnError'
```

When you execute the query it returns the following execution path: *\2 MasterPackage\Execute DataIssues Package\1 DataIssues\Foreach Loop Container[3]\Data Flow Task*. From the execution path, you can derive the following information:

- The errors occurred in the Foreach Loop container. Specifically, the errors occurred during the third iteration of the loop.
- The names of the parent and child packages are 2 MasterPackage and 1 Data Issues. The .dtsx extension has been removed from the package name.
- The child package is invoked from the EPT, which is called Execute DataIssues Package.

Using techniques you saw earlier in Step T, you can query the *catalog.executable_statistics* view to get a good understanding of how the errors caused the failures of the different executables. Listing 20-11 shows the T-SQL query. Figure 20-14 shows the results of executing the query. From the results, you can see that the parent package "2. MasterPackage" failed. This is caused by the EPT "Execute DataIssues Package", which executed the child package "1. DataIssues.dtsx". In the child package, a Data Flow task is contained within a Foreach Loop container. The Data Flow task executed successfully in the first two iterations and failed in the third iteration. Hence, you have constrained the possible cause of failures to the Data Flow task in the child package. Knowing that it executed twice successfully helps narrow the investigation surface area.

LISTING 20-11 Finding out how an error occurred

```
USE SSISDB

SELECT execution_result, execution_path
FROM catalog.executable_statistics
WHERE execution_id = 16
ORDER BY execution_path
```

Results | Messages

	execution_result	execution_path
1	1	\2 MasterPackage
2	1	\2 MasterPackage\Execute DataIssues Package
3	1	\2 MasterPackage\Execute DataIssues Package\1 DataIssues
4	1	\2 MasterPackage\Execute DataIssues Package\1 DataIssues\Foreach Loop Container
5	0	\2 MasterPackage\Execute DataIssues Package\1 DataIssues\Foreach Loop Container[1]\Data Flow Task
6	0	\2 MasterPackage\Execute DataIssues Package\1 DataIssues\Foreach Loop Container[2]\Data Flow Task
7	1	\2 MasterPackage\Execute DataIssues Package\1 DataIssues\Foreach Loop Container[3]\Data Flow Task

FIGURE 20-14 Results of executing the query in Listing 20-11.

Troubleshooting SSIS Package Execution Failures Scheduled with SQL Agent

In many production environments, SSIS packages are often scheduled for execution using SQL Agent. In this section, you learn how you can correlate the errors captured in the SQL Agent log with the execution log in SSISDB.

Using the T-SQL given in Listing 20-12, create the SQL Agent job with an SSIS job step that executes one of the packages. After the query has executed, verify that the SQL Agent job called SSISChapter21Job has been created. You should replace the value for *@owner_login_name* with the name of a Windows Authenticated login that you are using to run the packages. Figure 20-15 shows the SQL Agent job that is created.

LISTING 20-12 Creating a SQL Agent job

```
USE [msdb]
GO
DECLARE @jobId BINARY(16)
EXEC msdb.dbo.sp_add_job @job_name=N'SSISChapter20Job',
            @enabled=1,
            @notify_level_eventlog=0,
            @notify_level_email=2,
            @notify_level_netsend=2,
            @notify_level_page=2,
            @delete_level=0,
            @category_name=N'[Uncategorized (Local)]',
            @owner_login_name=N'SSISInsideOut\DemoUser', @job_id = @jobId OUTPUT
select @jobId
GO
EXEC msdb.dbo.sp_add_jobserver @job_name=N'SSISChapter20Job', @server_name = N'SSISINSIDEOUT'
GO


USE [msdb]
GO
EXEC msdb.dbo.sp_add_jobstep @job_name=N'SSISChapter20Job', @step_name=N'Step1',
            @step_id=1,
            @cmdexec_success_code=0,
            @on_success_action=1,
            @on_fail_action=2,
            @retry_attempts=0,
            @retry_interval=0,
            @os_run_priority=0, @subsystem=N'SSIS',
            @command=N'/ISSERVER "\"\SSISDB\SSISInsideOut\Chapter20Project\1. DataIssues.dtsx\""
/SERVER "\".\"" /Par "\"$ServerOption::LOGGING_LEVEL(Int16)\"";1 /Par "\"$ServerOption::SYNCHRON
IZED(Boolean)\"";True /REPORTING E /CALLERINFO SQLAGENT',
            @database_name=N'master',
            @flags=0
GO


USE [msdb]
GO
```

```
EXEC msdb.dbo.sp_update_job @job_name=N'SSISChapter20Job',
          @enabled=1,
          @start_step_id=1,
          @notify_level_eventlog=0,
          @notify_level_email=2,
          @notify_level_netsend=2,
          @notify_level_page=2,
          @delete_level=0,
          @description=N'',
          @category_name=N'[Uncategorized (Local)]',
          @owner_login_name=N'SSISInsideOut\DemoUser',
          @notify_email_operator_name=N'',
          @notify_netsend_operator_name=N'',
          @notify_page_operator_name=N''
GO
```

FIGURE 20-15 SQL Agent job: SSISChapter20Job.

After creating the SQL Agent job, do the following:

1. Right-click the job, and select Start Job At Step....
2. After the SQL Agent job is started, you will notice that it failed. Figure 20-16 shows the screenshot for the failed job.

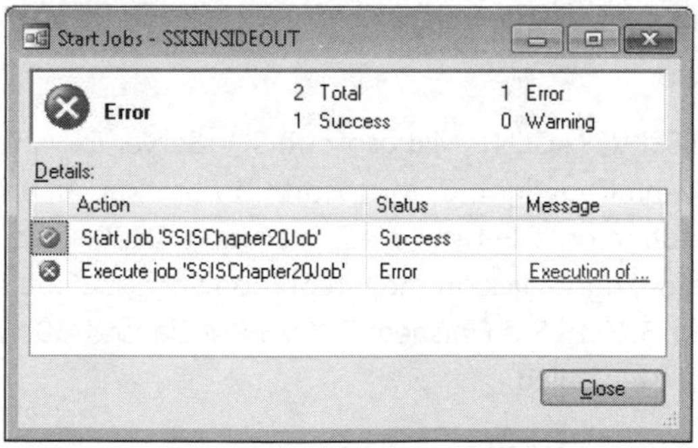

FIGURE 20-16 Failure of the SQL Agent job.

3. If you click the link given in the Message column, you will see the following error message: "Execution of job 'SSISChapter21Job' failed. See the history log for details."
4. Right-click the job, and select View History.

5. In the Log File Viewer, select the most recent job that executed. Figure 20-17 shows the Log File Viewer window.

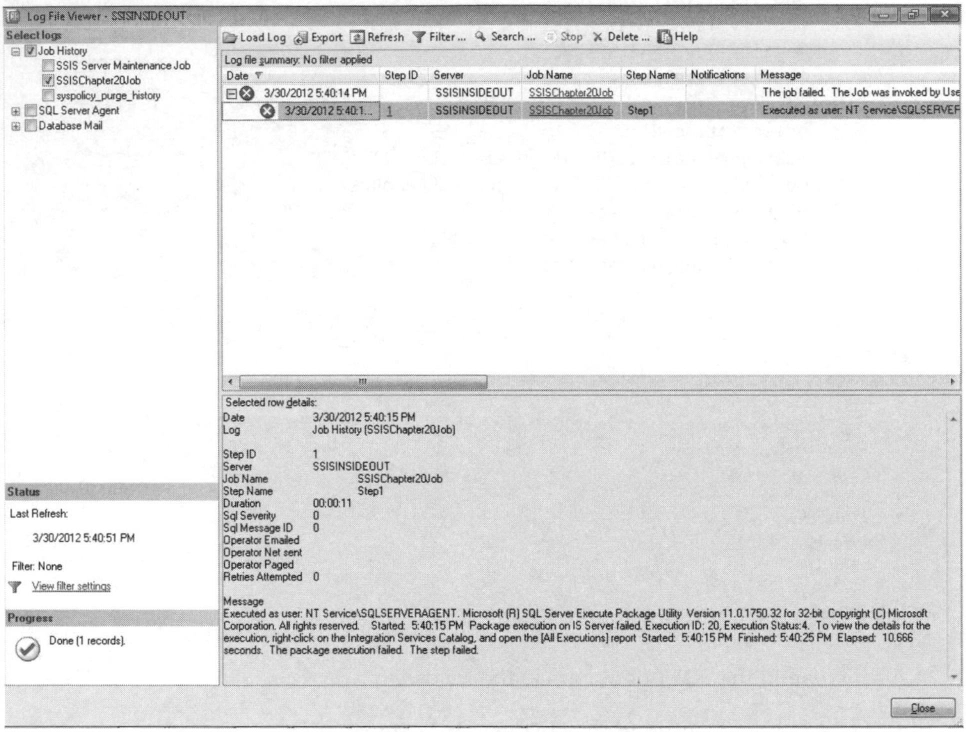

FIGURE 20-17 Log File Viewer and failed job.

6. In the Selected Row Details pane, you will see a detailed message on why the job failed. In Figure 20-17, the message reads as follows:

   Message

   Executed as user: NT Service\SQLSERVERAGENT. Microsoft (R) SQL Server Execute Package Utility Version 11.0.1750.32 for 32-bit Copyright (C) Microsoft Corporation. All rights reserved. Started: 5:40:15 PM Package execution on IS Server failed. Execution ID: 20, Execution Status:4. To view the details for the execution, right-click on the Integration Services Catalog, and open the [All Executions] report Started: 5:40:15 PM Finished: 5:40:25 PM Elapsed: 10.666 seconds. The package execution failed. The step failed.

7. You can see that the execution ID for the failed execution is 20.

8. Using the execution ID, you can apply the SVT steps reviewed earlier to troubleshoot the failed SSIS package execution.

In most production environments, the SSIS packages run based on the schedule specified by the administrator. Hence, you might not see the dialog box shown in Figure 20-16, which is shown when you manually start the SQL Agent job. In SSIS 2012, you can make use of the SSIS Dashboard to monitor all the SSIS package executions that have been started in the past 24 hours (refer to Chapter 14 on how to make use of the different SSIS reports provided in SSIS 2012).

In the next two sections, you will learn two methods for using T-SQL to quickly identify the SSIS package executions that have failed.

Using CallerInfo to Determine SSIS Package Executions That Are Executed by SQL Agent

Another method that can be used for troubleshooting SQL Agent job failures is to make us of the *catalog.execution_parameter_values* view. In SSIS 2012, whenever an SSIS package is executed using SQL Server Agent, the execution will be marked as a SQL Agent execution. This is specified using the execution parameter, *CALLER_INFO*, with a value of SQLAGENT.

Listing 20-13 shows the T-SQL query that is used for viewing the status for all SSIS package executions that are started by SQL Agent. If you want to know all the SSIS package executions that are started by SQL Agent within some time range, you can modify the query given in Listing 20-13 by specifying the relevant time range.

LISTING 20-13 Obtaining the status of all SSIS package executions that are started by SQL Agent

```
USE SSISDB

SELECT e.status,
          e.execution_id,
          e.folder_name,
          e.project_name,
          e.package_name,
          CONVERT(nvarchar(30), e.start_time, 109) as start_time
FROM catalog.execution_parameter_values v, catalog.executions e
WHERE v.parameter_name = 'CALLER_INFO'
AND v.parameter_value = 'SQLAGENT'
AND e.execution_id = v.execution_id
```

Using SQL Agent History Tables to Determine the SSIS Job Steps That Failed

Instead of using Log File Viewer to scan through all the jobs, you can also use the SQL Agent history tables to determine the SSIS job steps that failed. Listing 20-14 shows how you can make use of the SQL Agent related tables to obtain the job status. A job status of 0 indicates that the job has failed. In the query, the execution ID is derived from the text in the message column. This is further cast to be a bigint. You can use this derived execution ID and perform a join with the *catalog.executions* and *catalog.event_messages* views to correlate the SQL Agent job execution with SSISDB views.

LISTING 20-14 Using SQL Agent related tables to obtain the job status for a SQL Agent job that has a SSIS job step

```
SELECT h.run_date,
   h.run_status,
   j.[name],
   CAST(
            SUBSTRING(h.message,
            PATINDEX('%Execution ID:%', h.message)+13,
            PATINDEX('%To view%', h.message)-
            PATINDEX('%Execution ID:%', h.message)-16) AS bigint
) as execution_id
FROM

   msdb.dbo.sysjobs j,
   msdb.dbo.sysjobsteps js,
   msdb.dbo.sysjobhistory h
WHERE  j.job_id = h.job_id
AND   js.job_id = j.job_id
AND js.subsystem = 'SSIS'
AND PATINDEX('%Execution ID:%',h.message ) > 0
   ORDER BY h.run_date DESC
```

Summary

In this chapter, you learned how to make use of the public views and stored procedures that are introduced in SSIS 2012 to troubleshoot SSIS package executions. You learned about the concept of the execution path and how it can help you pinpoint the exact failure point in an SSIS package execution. In addition, you learned how to obtain more contextual information for the failed components, and how this contextual information can be used to figure out common causes of failures that span multiple packages. When SSIS packages are scheduled using SQL Agent, you learned how to correlate SQL Agent job failures with the execution log.

CHAPTER 21

SSIS Performance Best Practices

In This Chapter

As you have seen in earlier chapters, SSIS has become the de facto platform for performing extract–transform–load (ETL), data warehousing, and other data movement-related activities. It is capable of scaling to handle data loads ranging from small departmental databases sized in gigabytes to massive multiterabyte data warehousing systems. To optimize performance of SSIS while handling larger data loads might require some tuning. One of the primary advantages of SSIS is its simplicity, so a new developer can quickly start creating and executing packages to handle small data loads. However, it also supports advanced tuning and configuration features that, when tuned according to the infrastructure, data, and processing requirements, can attain high performance in handling massive amounts of data.

After reading this chapter, you will understand the following advanced tuning and configuration features:

- Creating a performance strategy
- Measuring performance
- Common designing for performance techniques
- Advanced tuning of packages

Creating a Performance Strategy

Optimizing the performance of an SSIS environment can be a quite complex and daunting task if you don't know where to start. Thus, it is imperative that you have a strategy to improve the performance of your environment. As with any good strategy, yours could have the following steps:

- **Measuring your current performance and creating a baseline** Before deciding on optimizing a package or an environment, you have to understand the current performance. This involves executing the packages in the current setup and measuring various metrics, which are discussed in later sections.
- **Create performance goals** After measuring the performance, you should have a rough estimate of your final performance goals. You might or might not achieve these goals after the tuning exercise but the goals will help you to understand the areas where you might want to concentrate your efforts.
- **Hypothesize various alternatives and tuning options** After exploring the various facets of your current package design and infrastructure, you will have a fair understanding of your tuning options. Note that this chapter helps you understand several such facets of your package and infrastructure designs, which will help you identify tuning options.
- **Apply the tuning options, execute, and remeasure** You can now apply the various options you enlisted in the previous step. You can then execute each of these tuning options and remeasure your execution metrics. The cycle of hypothesizing and applying the tuning options can continue until you achieve your performance goals or satisfactory results.

In the final step where you measure your execution metrics with the new tuning options, it is useful to note the following considerations:

- The modified environment and the baseline environment should be as identical as possible with the exception of the application of the tuning option. This will make sure that you don't inadvertently change the aspect of the environment that can create erroneous measurements.
- Use similar data profiles between the modified and the baseline environment. Data is a major factor in overall performance measurements. SSIS packages under different environments can behave very differently with difference in data profiles.

OVAL Technique

SSIS performance tuning strategies often are initiated with the OVAL technique. The OVAL technique, which has been described in a Microsoft whitepaper, describes a strategy to initiate a performance tuning exercise for SSIS solutions.

See Also *For the original whitepaper on OVAL technique, refer to* http://technet.microsoft.com/en-us/library/cc966530.aspx.

The following steps from the OVAL technique will help you accurately diagnose the bottlenecks in your setup and help you hypothesize any alternatives and tuning options.

Your analysis of your setup can be broken down into the following steps:

- **Operations** In this step, you will have to break up your scenario into individual operations. For instance, in an overall data loading scenario, you might be performing multiple individual operations. Operations such as data loading from different sources, different transformations, and different data formats can each constitute an individual operation. You might be staging intermediate data and inserting data into different destinations. These can also be considered individual operations. Because SSIS would be processing each individual operation separately, each individual operation can be subject to its own tuning actions.
- **Volume** Now, it is important to understand what volume of data you would be processing in each of these individual operations. You would want to understand the profile of the data that is currently being processed and estimate the data growth. The operations that process the most data are usually the ones that have the longest execution duration and would benefit the most from a performance tuning exercise. Package designs are often governed by optimizing the slowest performing individual operation. Hence, understanding the volume of data being processed is a very important step in the process.
- **Application** There is usually more than a single way to load or process data. SSIS is one such alternative. SSIS is flexible and has good performance over most cases. However, there might be scenarios where you can utilize different tools available in the SQL Server ecosystem that might be more efficient. We cover such a scenario later in the chapter. SSIS itself is highly flexible. You can thus modify an SSIS package to do the same individual operation in more than a single way. Hence, choosing the right way to perform the individual operation is important.
- **Location** The infrastructure on which the individual operations occur is important. There are multiple ways that you could design your infrastructure to execute SSIS packages. For instance, you could have your SQL Server service containing the SSIS Catalog on the same machine as your data warehouse databases. In such a case, SSIS processes would be competing for resources with the data warehouse processes. You also could have the SSIS Catalog residing on a different machine, which can increase your infrastructure costs but would give you a dedicated SSIS environment. You also need to think about various I/O considerations when locating your SSIS environment. Ideally the processing environment should be as close as possible to the data sources and destinations to minimize I/O latency. You will learn more about such infrastructural aspects in the following sections.

Measuring SSIS Performance

As you saw in the previous sections, one of the primary operations that you would perform to formulate your tuning strategy would be measuring existing and tuned SSIS performance. There are various aspects of an individual operation that you will need to monitor to improve its performance, as follows:

- **Environment** You would want to know how the individual operation is performing with respect to the environment. You would want to know how much of the resources it is utilizing and whether there is scope for better utilization.
- **Performance of individual components** You would also want to measure how individual SSIS components in the operation are performing. You could use initial metrics as a baseline when you apply various tuning options available for each component. You could then remeasure to evaluate the benefits of a given tuning option.
- **Performance of external systems** Sometimes performance bottlenecks can be caused by external sources or a destination. For instance, you might have an incorrect indexing strategy on a destination table that could be slowing down your inserts. Identification of such components will help you narrow down the problem to the component you would want to tune.

> **Note** Optimization of various external components is not discussed in this chapter. For more information refer to the TechNet whitepaper about optimizing SQL Server query performance at *http://technet.microsoft.com/en-us/magazine/2007.11.sqlquery.aspx*.

Measuring System Performance

SSIS packages are stored on the Catalog. However, during execution they are executed by an external process called the *ISServerExec*. This process works with the resources available on the Windows operating systems to perform its operations. Thus, you can make use of several SSIS-based Windows performance counters to monitor the resources used during the execution of a package.

Let us first look at an overview of how you can use Windows performance counters to monitor SSIS execution.

Performance counters can be viewed on the Windows Performance Monitor (*perfmon.exe*). By default the performance monitor shows the *% processor time* used by all the processes running on the system. SSIS has two specific counter groups, SQL Server:SSIS Pipeline 11.0 and SQL Server:SSIS Service 11.0. Whereas the former group has various counters monitoring the activities in the Data Flow engine, the latter group has a single counter denoting the number of active package execution instances in progress. A sample preview is shown in Figure 21-1.

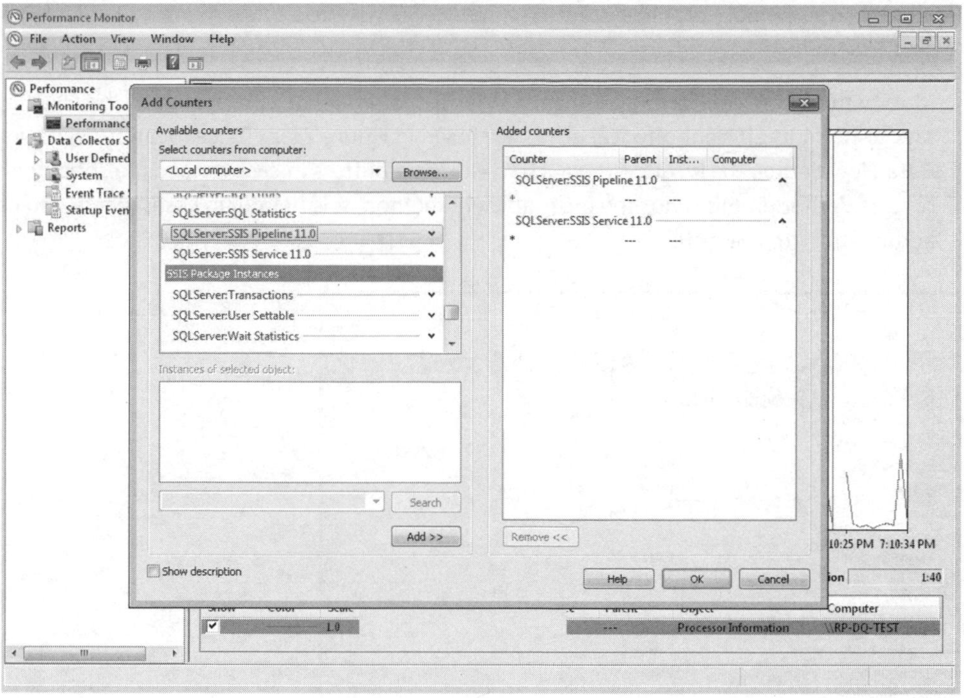

FIGURE 21-1 SSIS Pipeline performance counters.

> **Tip** For a description of all the counters, check out the MSDN page at *http://msdn.microsoft.com/en-us/library/ms137622.aspx.*

As you can see Figure 21-1, there are quite a few counters available. The following section covers some of the most interesting counters from the SSIS Pipeline group as well as other generic Windows performance counters that can help you diagnose your performance issues.

Buffers Spooled

This counter from the SQL Server:SSIS Pipeline 11.0 denotes the number of buffers SSIS has spooled to disk during execution. Ideally the value should always be 0, which denotes that the Data Flow engine has enough memory available to have all the buffers under processing in the memory. This will result in efficient processing as the Data Flow engine doesn't have to perform I/O operations, which can be expensive. However, in some cases the value might not be 0 and will denote the number of buffers that the Data Flow engine is writing to disk as it didn't have the required memory available. There can be two solutions for this problem.

1. Increase the memory on the system. As a result SSIS will have more memory available to process the buffers.

2. Modify the *BLOBTempStoragePath* and *BufferTempStoragePath* properties of the Data Flow task to point to efficient physical drives as shown in Figure 21-2. These locations will tell the Data Flow engine the location to which to write the buffers in case it needs to spool the buffers. Although this is not the most efficient method, it is helpful in cases where you cannot add memory to the system.

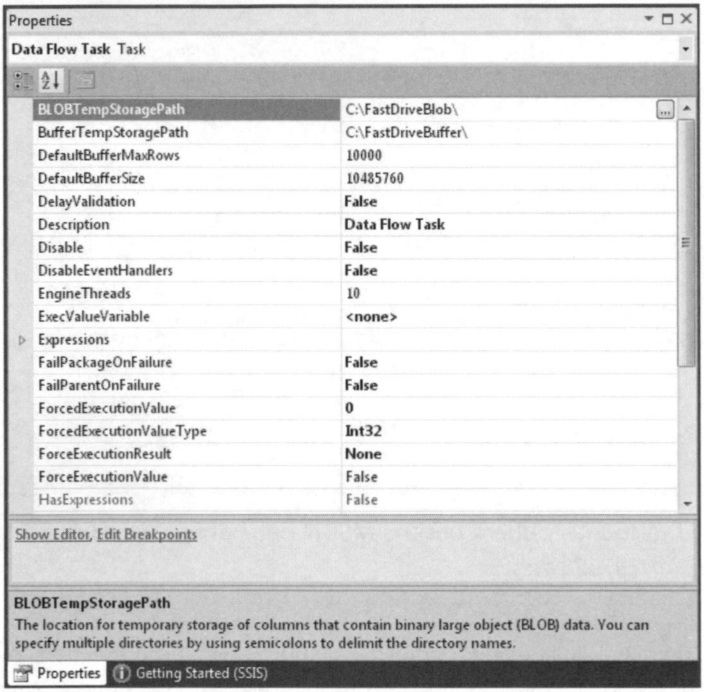

FIGURE 21-2 *BlobTempStoragePath* property of a Data Flow task.

Tip A good article about setting temporary blob storages can be found at *http://blogs.msdn.com/b/sqlperf/archive/2007/05/01/set-blobtempstoragepath-and-buffertempstorage-path-to-fast-drives.aspx.*

Other Useful Counters

There are several other generic counters that are useful for monitoring the activity on the system when the packages are being executed.

- Processor
    - % Processor Time

    While executing your packages, you can monitor the % processor time used by your processors on the system. If you see your counter consistently being above 70 percent while the package is executing, it is a good indicator that the package execution is utilizing all of the CPU available. If the system peaks at 100 percent, it signifies that the package execution is being throttled due to unavailable CPU resources. One of the possible solutions to this problem would be to increase the number or capacity of the CPUs on the system.

- LogicalDisk
    - Avg. Disk sec/Transfer
    - Read Bytes/Sec
    - Write Bytes/Sec

    Another important counter is the average disk transfer rate. In packages that involve reading and writing to disks as well as in cases where the package has to spool buffers to the disk, the disk I/O rate becomes very important. In most cases where we have a slow physical storage system, the disk I/O proves to be the bottleneck in package execution. It is therefore useful to understand how your disk transfers are performing and if they can be replaced with faster disks.

> **Tip** See the TechNet article about detecting disk bottlenecks at *http://technet.microsoft.com/en-us/library/cc722466.aspx.*

- Network
    - Current Bandwidth
    - Bytes Total/Sec

    These counters indicate the current network bandwidth that your package execution could be utilizing. If the total bytes per second value is more than 50 percent of the total capacity, then your server might be having network I/O saturation during the package execution. This could become a bottleneck while importing or exporting data into remote sources and destinations, respectively.

> **Tip** See the TechNet article about monitoring network bottlenecks at *http://technet.microsoft.com/en-us/magazine/dd722745.aspx*.

- Memory
    - Working Set (DTExec.exe/ISServerExec)
    - Private Bytes (DTExec.exe/ISServerExec)

  The memory performance counters are indicators of the system memory available to SSIS during execution. As you know already, SSIS requires memory for storing intermediate temporary buffers as well as allocating buffers as needed in a Data Flow task's execution tree. If the Data Flow engine doesn't find enough memory to hold the buffers, it will start writing to the disk, which can cause performance bottlenecks.

SSIS Catalog Counters

The new SSIS Catalog has several provisions for you to can monitor metrics about your package when executing on the Catalog. You can monitor metrics like rows read and written per second, number of buffers allocated, and so on. This can be monitored while the package is executed using dynamic table valued functions in the Catalog. You will learn more about this in Chapter 22, "Troubleshooting SSIS Performance Issues."

Measuring Performance of Data Flow Tasks

In this section, you'll learn about measuring the performance of individual components of a Data Flow task.

Most Data Flow tasks can be simplified into a source, transformation, and destination-based structure. Thus, the overall performance of a Data Flow task can be considered as the sum total of these individual components. You can baseline the performance of each component and target your optimization efforts on it. Hence, by optimizing the individual components, you would be able to optimize the overall performance of the Data Flow task.

You would be measuring factors such as the following:

- Overall time spent
- CPU utilization (using counters)
- Memory utilization (using counters)
- Any I/O or network bottlenecks (using counters)

To understand the process, we take the example of a simple Data Flow task shown in Figure 21-3.

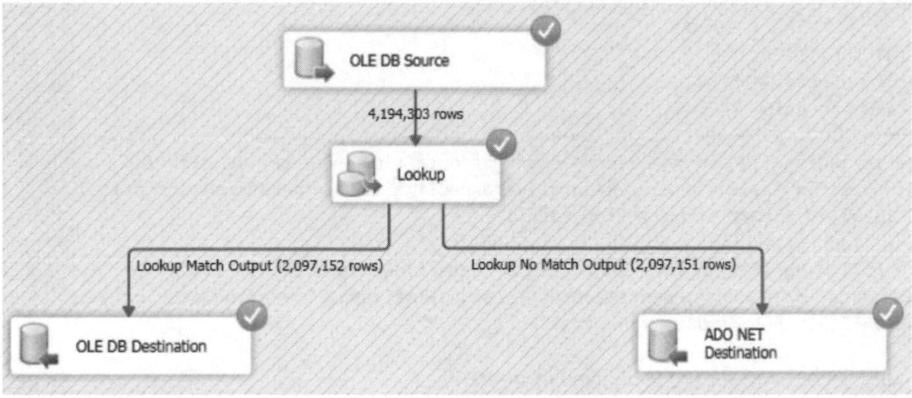

FIGURE 21-3 Sample Data Flow task.

In the preceding example, we have the following components:

- **Source: OLE DB Source** This is an OLE DB Source that is importing data from fact tables from a SQL Server database.
- **Transformation: Lookup** This is a lookup component looking up a dimension table from another SQL Server database.
- Destinations
  - **OLE DB Destination** This OLE DB destination will insert the rows that had a match in the lookup transformation.
  - **ADO.NET Destination** This ADO.NET destination will insert rows that did not have a match in the lookup transformation.

In the following sections you learn how to individually measure the performance of all three components.

Instrumenting the Package

Before we break the Data Flow task into individual components, it will be useful to add some tasks just to record the start and end of the Data Flow and record the metrics. These can be simple Execute SQL tasks that can record the start and end timestamp, which can be used to calculate the time taken by the task. The table can be inserted in their trace record as shown in Listing 21-1.

LISTING 21-1 Instrumenting package with trace start and end

```
CREATE TABLE DataFlowTaskPerformanceRecords
(
   IDCol INT IDENTITY(1,1),
   RecordedTimeStamp DATETIME,
   OperationDescription VARCHAR(100)
)
/* Use the following TSQL in the Record start of data flow execute SQL task*/
INSERT INTO DataFlowTaskPerformanceRecords(RecordedTimeStamp, OperationDescription)
VALUES (GETDATE(), 'Start of data flow task')

/* Use the following TSQL in the Record end of data flow execute SQL task*/
INSERT INTO DataFlowTaskPerformanceRecords(RecordedTimeStamp, OperationDescription)
VALUES (GETDATE(), 'End of data flow task')
```

The resultant package should look like Figure 21-4.

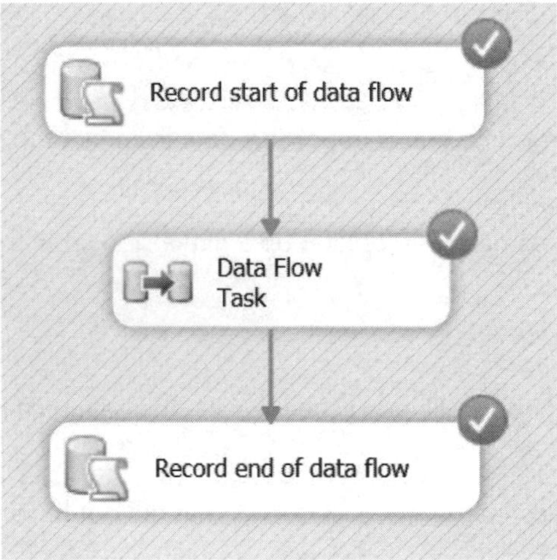

FIGURE 21-4 Instrumented Data Flow task.

> **Note** SSIS Catalog now records the performance of each component. It is described in Chapter 22. Hence, if you are using SQL Server 2012, you might not be required to instrument individual components.

Measuring Performance of the Source Component

The main task that we target in the Source component would be the actual source task. A Data Flow task with just the source is going to become your benchmark for measurement. This is because the package without any other transformations or destinations doesn't have the performance overhead of the extra components. Hence, with just the Source component the Data Flow task will be at its fastest execution time and hence will give you a good baseline to start with. The easiest way to get a baseline for only the source task is to replace the rest of the body of the task with a simple transformation. A dumb transformation will not add any processing overheads of its own and we can assume that the total processing time taken by the task would be the source task itself. You can use the following steps to create the Data Flow task:

1. Create a Data Flow task.
2. Use the same source as the Data Flow task in Figure 21-4.
3. Replace the transformation and destination components by a *Row count* transformation.

This example is shown in Figure 21-5.

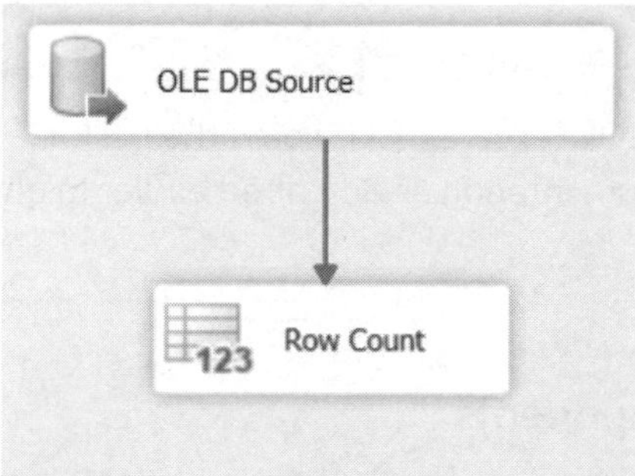

FIGURE 21-5 Measuring performance of the Source component.

Measuring Performance of the Transformation Component

Measuring the Transformation component is a little trickier, as you will need an identical source as the original source components. This is because you will want to maintain a similar data profile that the Transformation component processes in the complete and the standalone scenarios. You can follow these steps to create the transformation component:

1. To replicate an identical source, you will use the same source as in Figure 21-4 but store the output in a flat file destination.
2. You would then use the flat file created in the previous step as a source for the transformation as shown in Figure 21-6.
3. You can also note that you would only be measuring time spent for the Data Flow task containing the Transformation component and not the Source component.

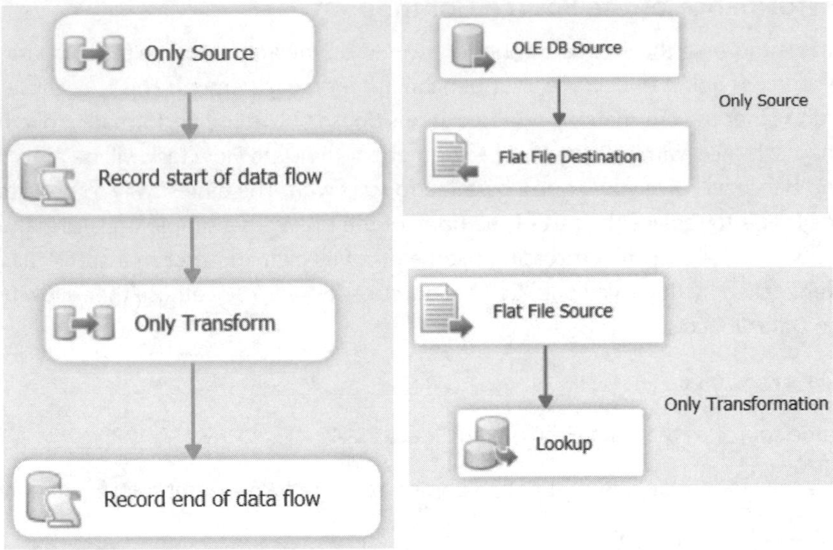

FIGURE 21-6 Measuring performance of transformation.

> **Note** As mentioned in Chapter 22, SSIS Catalog in SQL Server 2012 records the performance of individual components. Hence, extra instrumentation as described earlier might not be required.

Measuring Performance of Destination Components

Measuring the performance of the Destination components is similar to the method we employed to measure the Transformation component. You can follow these steps to measure the performance of the Destination component:

1. You would now have the same source and the transformation from Figure 21-4 in one Data Flow task.
2. You can store the outputs of the transformation into two separate flat files.
3. You can then use the flat files as sources for the destinations in two different Data Flow tasks where each task uses one flat file source to export data to the respective destination.

The process is shown in Figures 21-7 and 21-8.

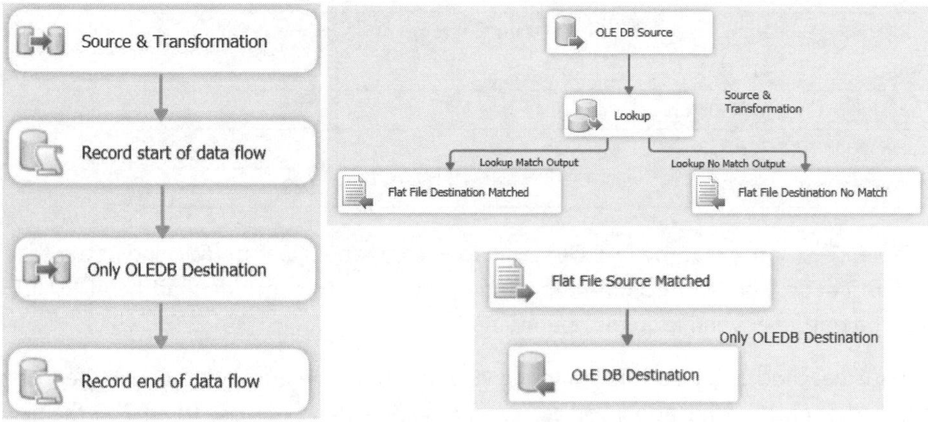

FIGURE 21-7 Measuring performance of the OLE DB destination.

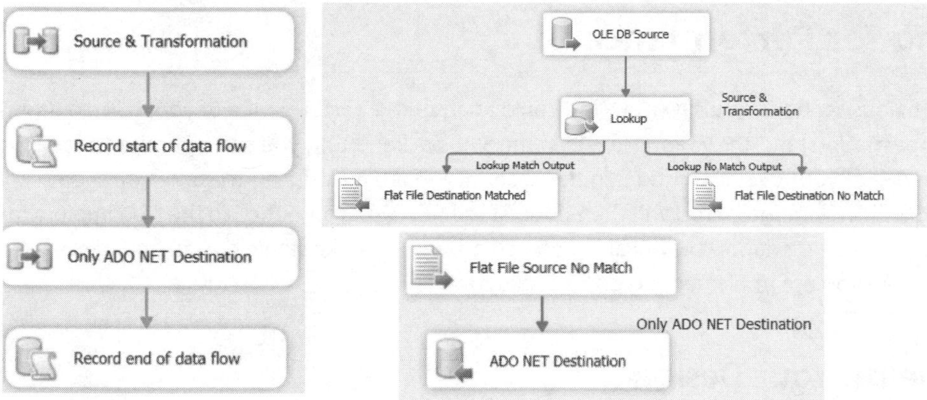

FIGURE 21-8 Measuring performance of the ADO.NET destination.

Analysis of a Data Flow Task

Using the previously described technique, you will be able to record the execution duration (by using the timestamp table) of each task as well as the other environmental metrics such as CPU, memory, I/O, and network bandwidth usage. Because you can get the row count of each operation by either looking at the package execution on SQL Server Data Tools or directly querying the destination tables, you will even be able to calculate the row throughput of each component. A result can be described in a tabular format such as the sample shown in Table 21-1.

TABLE 21-1 Performance analysis for a data flow

Component	Number of Rows Input to the Component	Time Taken (Sec.)
OLE DB Source	4194303	121
Lookup Transform	4194303	356
OLE DB Destination	2097152	674
ADO.NET Destination	2097153	1039

From Table 21-1, notice that the OLE DB destination component was performing better than the ADO.NET destination. For the preceding experiment, you can thus conclude that the ADO.NET destination was the bottleneck and requires optimization.

You can further modify each of the components using the techniques described in the following sections. After each optimization, you can repeat the preceding exercise to analyze the new performance. Thus, through statistical analysis, you can optimize any targeted component in your Data Flow task.

Designing for Performance

In the previous sections, you saw how you could analyze the performance of your SSIS solutions. You should now understand the various facets of the SSIS package that you can optimize to improve the performance of your overall solution. In this section, you are introduced to some common scenarios where SSIS is implemented. You will then understand how you can optimize the SSIS implementation in each respective scenario. You will also understand how to make smart design and infrastructural choices when you are implementing an SSIS solution.

Parallelize Your Design

In most SSIS solutions, there is more than a single operation happening in a workflow. In several of them operations might be mutually exclusive and don't have any dependencies among each other. These operations can easily be parallelized. The trend in computing has resulted in an increasing number of cores on a single machine. Thus parallelizing your design can efficiently use the available cores on your machine.

As you learned in Chapter 15, "SSIS Engine Deep Dive," the SSIS Data Flow engine can execute multiple operations in different threads and scale up with the number of available threads on a system. Thus, to maximize the utilization of the resources on your system, you should use parallelism in your solution design, where each operation can be executed in parallel if it's mutually exclusive to an operation that is currently under execution.

Parallelize Solution Architecture

In various solution implementations, sets of operations can be encapsulated into independent execution siloes. In doing so, you enable your solution design to use the parallelization capabilities of SSIS. If your solution design involves concurrent parallel execution on multiple packages, the available multiprocessing capabilities and memory on the system will be efficiently used to execute those packages. If your solution design involves a single master package with Data Flow tasks that have concurrent parallel execution trees, SSIS can schedule those execution trees to be executed in parallel.

For instance, think of the following data mart loading solution.

In your data mart loading, you have to load five tables into the *Purchasing* schema and another six tables into the *Sales* schema. There is no dependency between both these schemas. In other words, you can load any one of these schema without any dependency on loading the other schema. Imagine having a multicore machine available for executing this solution.

There are two ways you can use parallelization to optimize the design. Let's look at how we can use parallelization outside SSIS to optimize your design.

In the preceding problem, because you have two distinct operations that can be executed in parallel, you can make two different packages to execute the data mart loading and execute these packages in parallel. Because there is no process flow dependency between the two schemas, the schemas can be independently loaded without any data discrepancy. An example is shown in Figure 21-9.

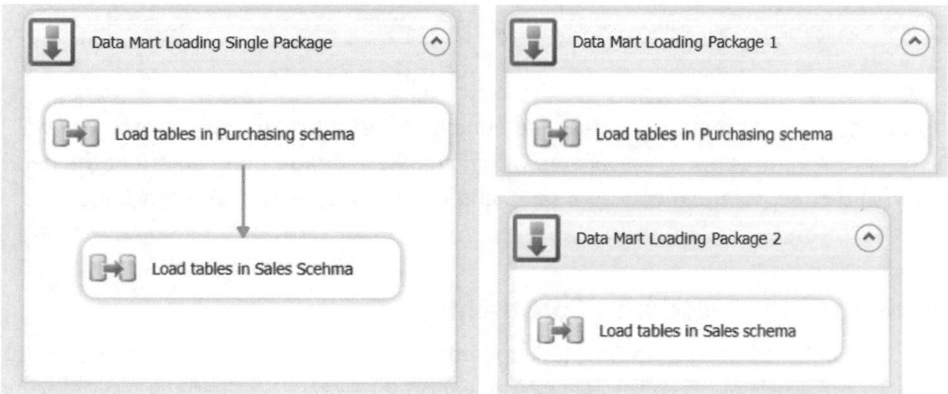

Single package execution

Execution broken up into two packages executing in parallel

FIGURE 21-9 Parallelizing a single package into multiple packages.

Now let's look at how you can use SSIS parallelization to achieve a similar result by executing within a single package.

Within the same package, because the two Data Flow tasks don't have any logical data dependency between each other, you shouldn't force any design limitation by introducing a precedence constraint in their data loading sequence. Hence, if you can just remove the precedence constraint, then the SSIS engine will treat them as two different execution tasks. In Chapter 15, you learned how during package execution, an execution plan is created. This execution plan created will treat the two preceding Data Flow tasks as independent tasks in the absence of a precedence constraint between them and schedule them to be executed as soon as required resources (execution threads, memory, and so on) are available. Thus, the overall package execution duration would decrease as both these tasks can be executed in parallel. The process is shown in Figure 21-10.

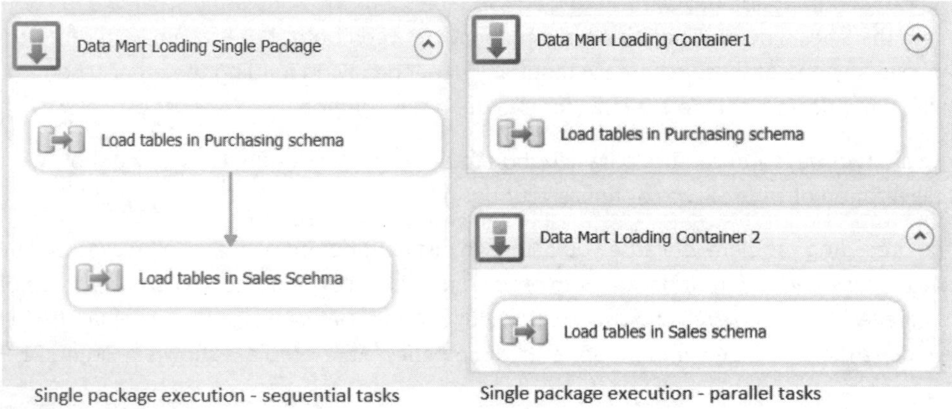

FIGURE 21-10 Parallelizing within a single SSIS package.

> **Tip** In one of the next sections, "Advanced Tuning of Packages," in this chapter, you will understand the various options available within an SSIS package that can affect the parallelization and concurrent execution of tasks and components within your package.

Parallelizing Using Precedence Constraints

As you saw in Chapter 15, each Data Flow task undergoes a process where an execution plan is created for a package. Precedence constraints play an important role in the creation of this execution plan. You already know that tasks are connected through precedence constraints. These precedence constraints determine the order of execution of the tasks. Any unconnected tasks would be executed in parallel. Hence, you should have a precedence constraint between any two tasks only if you have a processing dependency between them.

Precedence constraints can also be distinguished between various types. Understanding each type of the precedence constraint will help you understand how the execution plan would be created for your package. A precedence constraint primarily has these two attributes:

- **Evaluation operation** This defines what needs to be evaluated for the constraint to be passed. It can be just the execution value of the preceding task or an expression based on a variable or even with a combination of both.
- **Multiple constraints evaluation logic** If a given task is preceded by more than a single task, you will use multiple constraints. In such a case, you will also have to define the behavior of these multiple constraints. You can mention that all the precedence constraints should evaluate to *true* or just one of them is enough for the subsequent task to execute.

See Also *For more about SSIS precedence constraints, see* http://msdn.microsoft.com/en-us/library/ms141261.aspx.

Now, let's look at how the preceding configuration will affect your package design with respect to parallelization.

If your package workflow permits it, always make sure that you are not using unnecessary *AND*-based multiple constraints. The execution of a task is blocked until all the *AND* precedence constraints are evaluated. If such an *AND* multiple constraint is converted into an *OR* constraint, the subsequent task will execute even if one preceding task has completed. For instance let's look at Figure 21-11.

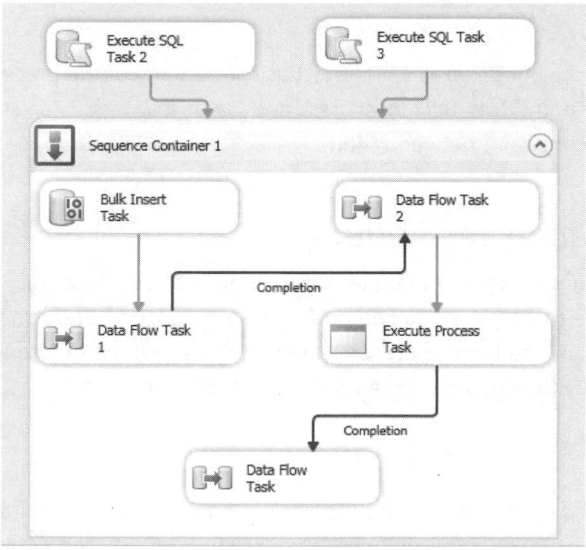

FIGURE 21-11 Package with multiple constraints.

The package depicted in Figure 21-11 is an example of a sequential design. Now, let's say that you had the option of optimizing the package. You realize several optimization scenarios based on your understanding of the package workflow such as these:

1. The Sequence container 1 can start even if one preceding Execute SQL task completes successfully.
2. The Data Flow task 2 can start without waiting for any other task to complete in the Sequence container 1.

Based on these findings, you can now optimize your package design to the one shown in Figure 21-12.

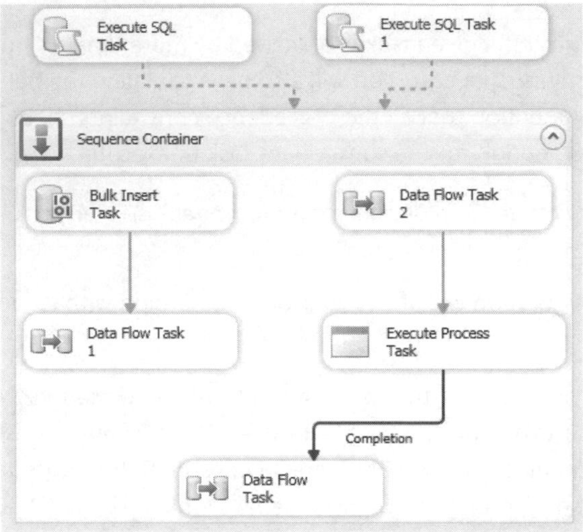

FIGURE 21-12 Optimized package design.

In the new package design, the Sequence container will now start as soon as any of the preceding Execute SQL tasks have completed successfully. Both Bulk Insert task and Data Flow task 2 can start parallel as they don't have a precedence constraint between them.

Using SQL Server Optimization Techniques

In most scenarios, you would be using a SQL Server database in conjunction with SSIS for your operations. There are a few scenarios where using the SQL Server database instance to perform your operations will benefit your overall solution. These mostly rely on the SQL Server infrastructure to perform certain operations more optimally than you can on an SSIS-based solution.

Staging Data

The first step of most operations where the operation is being performed on SQL Server is to stage data in the same SQL Server instance. Staging the data is defined by querying the required dataset and storing it in a table. This will ensure that all the operations are completely performed on the same SQL Server and there is no I/O or network overhead of querying data from multiple sources.

Once the data has been staged using a simple Data Flow task, you can perform the next set of operations using Execute SQL tasks where all the T-SQL operations are performed on the same SQL Server as shown in Figure 21-13.

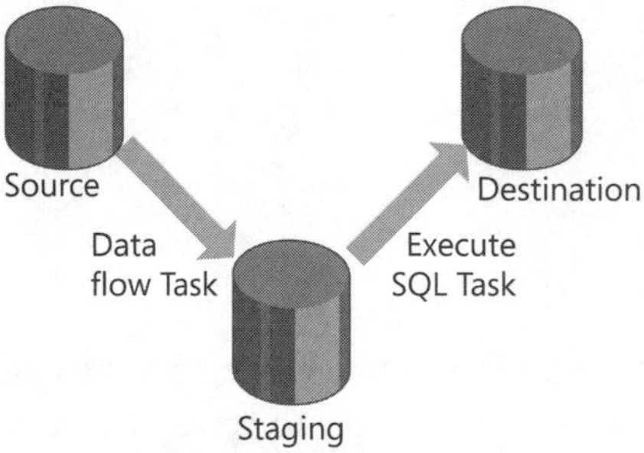

FIGURE 21-13 Staging data on SQL Server.

Now, let's look at some of those scenarios.

Replacing OLE DB Commands with Staging on SQL Server

OLE DB command is a useful component that can be used for executing a SQL command in a Data Flow task. However, it has its own shortcomings. OLE DB command, as other similar pipeline components, processes commands row by row. This operation results in a dataset that is processed in a Data Flow task being bottlenecked as instead of processing the data set as a batch, the OLE DB command will lead to the Data Flow task processing the data set row by row. This can significantly hurt the overall performance of the Data Flow task. Instead, in such a scenario, where you are actually looking for a batch operation on your data set instead of row by row, you should use the following techniques:

1. Stage the data set that you need to process into SQL Server.
2. Use an Execute SQL task to execute a stored procedure or a T-SQL statement that can then process the data set efficiently.

Replacing Suboptimal Aggregation SSIS Operations

In several data-intensive cases, the aggregate operations such as *SORT* and *AGGREGATE* available in SSIS can prove very costly primarily because they are *fully blocking* operations. A fully blocking operation is described as an operation that blocked until all of its input buffers are completely available to it. It will only be processed when the transform performing the operations can access the complete input buffers.

Thus, you need to optimize those operations whenever possible. One of the most efficient ways to optimize data-intensive operations is to perform them on SQL Server. You can use the SQL Server native processing capabilities to perform such an operation. You can look at Table 21-2 to understand which operations map to their respective operations on SQL Server.

TABLE 21-2 SSIS operations and equivalent T-SQL operations

SSIS Component	Equivalent T-SQL Operation
Sort component	Use T-SQL ORDER BY clause
Aggregate component	Use T-SQL GROUP BY clause

To use the T-SQL components, you will have to stage the data into SQL Server before the operation as described in the previous sections. Because SQL Server would be able to perform these operations in a batch, it will have better performance than doing the same operation on SSIS.

Using SQL Server Partitioning

SQL Server partitioning is a powerful technique where data in a table is stored into well-defined partitions based on a differentiating key. If such a table is queried using that partitioning key, then SQL Server doesn't do entire table scans, as it knows the specific partition to look up data or insert data into. Hence, a query or an insert statement's performance increases tremendously as the overhead of entire table scans or index seeks is avoided.

This optimization technique is true in general for any kind of SQL Server solution implementation where you are performing Create, Read, Update, and Delete (CRUD) operations on a significantly large table. You should also look at the PARTITION SWITCH technique to move data between partitions. This way, you can avoid expensive data movement operations using SSIS or T-SQL.

See Also *To learn more about SQL Server partition switching, refer to* http://technet.microsoft.com/en-us/library/ms191160(SQL.105).aspx.

Bulk Loading Your Data

One of the most efficient ways to load data into various destinations is using the Bulk Loading option. Bulk insert is a native SQL Server data loading optimization technique for loading data from flat files, where SQL Server minimizes a lot of operations that it performs on the incoming data, resulting in better performance when loading data according to the bulk insert guidelines.

See Also *To learn more about bulk insert refer to* http://msdn.microsoft.com/en-us/library/ms187042.aspx.

SSIS has a task called the Bulk Insert task. SSIS ADO.NET destination also has an option to notify it to use Bulk Insert while inserting data into SQL Server. With SQL Server 2012, you have that option displayed as a property when you are using the ADO.NET destination as shown in Figure 21-14.

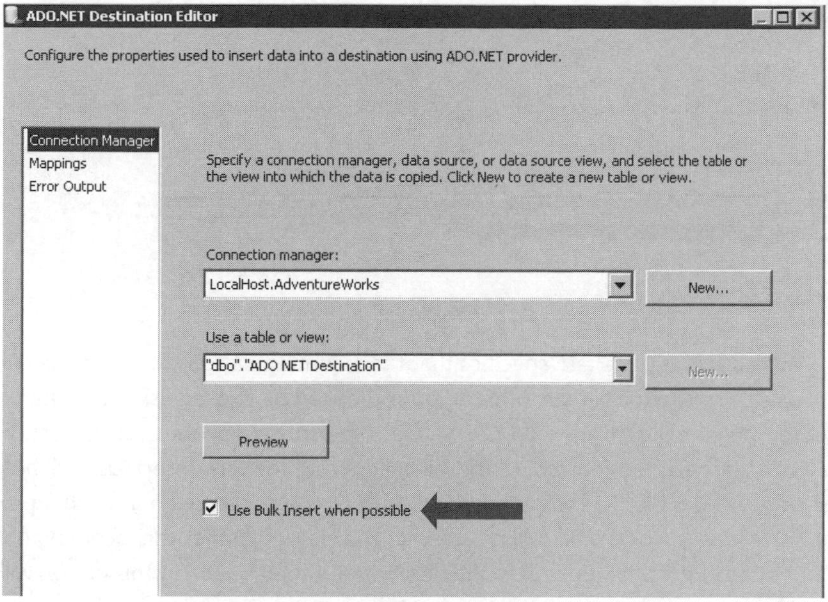

FIGURE 21-14 Bulk loading option for ADO.NET destination.

You can optimize the standard Bulk Insert task further by using the available options. You learn some of these techniques in the following section.

> **Tip** For a list of complete options and their description on the Bulk Insert task, refer to *http://msdn.microsoft.com/en-us/library/ms141239.aspx.*

You can use table and query hints along with the Bulk Insert task to create an optimal query to insert your data. The most efficient bulk loading scenarios occur when you are loading into an empty table with no indexes or constraints. In such a case, SQL Server doesn't perform any *CHECK* or *Indexing* operations on the incoming data, resulting in better performance. However, in many cases, you would load into a table with existing data with constraints and indexes. In such a case, providing hints to the task will ensure that SQL Server uses those hints while loading the data. For instance, you can use the ORDER hint to signify that your data is ordered when you are loading into an indexed table. SQL Server will then not perform the extra action of ordering the incoming data. You can provide hints as shown in Figure 21-15.

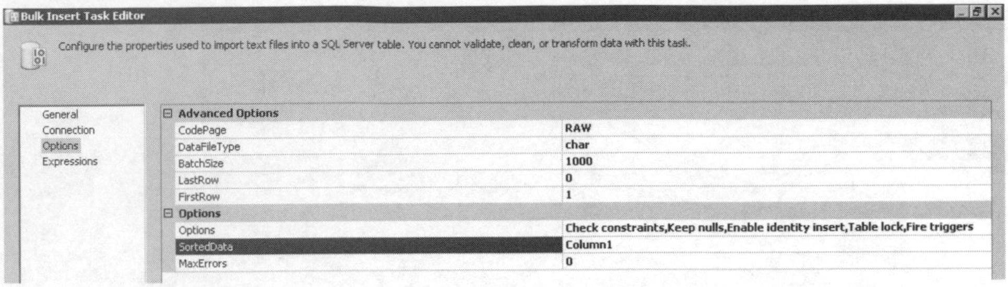

FIGURE 21-15 Query hints on the Bulk Insert task.

In Figure 21-15, you can see that the task specifies that the incoming data is sorted on the column named *Column1*. You can also see the various other options that can be chosen using the Options property group. These options will similarly lead SQL Server to perform or avoid a specific action on the incoming data. For instance, choosing *Table Lock* will ensure that the Bulk Insert task will hold an exclusive *TABLOCK* lock on the table. This will ensure that it is not contending with any other process to get a lock on the table. *Check Constraints* will ensure that SQL Server verifies the incoming data according to the *Check Constraints* mentioned on the destination table. Selecting this option will slow down an insert but will maintain data integrity in the destination table.

Bulk Loading Using Partitions

You will realize that the more constraints that you have on your table, the slower the data loading scenario you will have. You can thus improve performance by circumventing these constraints. However, these constraints help maintain data integrity on the destination table and hence are necessary. In some scenarios, you have the knowledge that the data you are inserting is clean and will not violate the data integrity constraints, so you can avoid all the data integrity constraint checks. To solve this issue you can follow the work flow described in Figure 21-16.

1. Create a partitioned destination table.
2. Create a staging table with no constraints.
3. Bulk insert data into the staging table.
4. If you are not sure that the data adheres to the data integrity constraints on the destination, then perform checks and cleaning operations on the staging table.
5. Enable check constraints on the staging table.
6. Switch the staging table into a partition on the destination table.

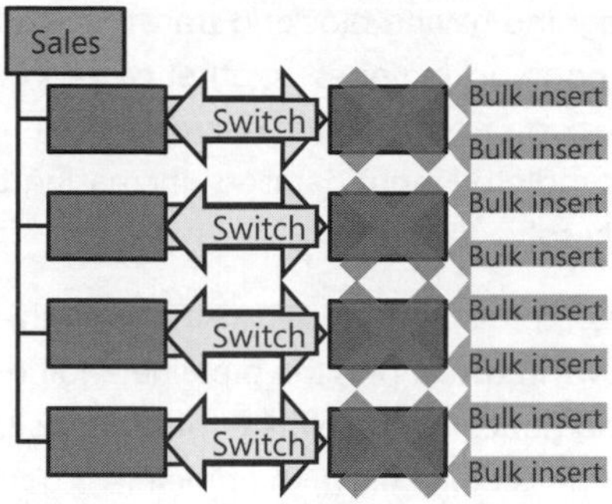

FIGURE 21-16 Using partitioning techniques to perform data loading operations.

You can use a similar technique to perform updates on existing data as well.

See Also *Learn more about using partitioning to perform data loading on SQL Server at* http://msdn.microsoft.com/en-US/library/ms345146(v=SQL.90).aspx.

Keeping SSIS Operations in Memory

In Chapter 15, you learned how SSIS uses memory in the form of buffers during execution within the pipeline engine. The performance of the pipeline task thus is dependent on how efficiently SSIS can access memory locations to create and use these buffers.

One of the most common bottlenecks in performance of the SSIS pipeline engine is when SSIS doesn't have enough memory available to it to allocate buffers. In such a case, SSIS has to write buffers to disk. Writing buffers to disk involves I/O operations, which are relatively very expensive. Hence, the overall package performance degrades. Thus, you have to understand why and when SSIS runs out of memory to allocate new buffers and employ strategies to avoid such scenarios. Some of the scenarios are as follows:

- **Running out of memory** The pipeline engine can simply run out of new memory to allocate to new buffers. This can happen due to multiple factors. Lookup caches are one such component that can hog memory and will not release it for the pipeline engine to consume. Note that the lookup component itself doesn't swap to disk and throws an error. However, it can hog enough memory for the rest of the pipeline component to swap to disk.

  To solve this issue, one can run such SSIS packages on systems with large amounts of memory available. One can also redesign the lookup caches such as writing the cache to disk, slimming down the cache, and so on.

- **Blocking transforms** Blocking transforms lead to stacking up of buffers until the complete set of buffers for the input data set is available for processing. This will result in too many active buffers being held in memory without available memory for new buffers.

To solve this issue, one needs to rethink the design behind having blocking transforms. Blocking transforms in some cases can be substituted for nonblocking ones. In other cases, you should try to trim down the input datasets to the blocking transforms to decrease the time spent by the transforms being blocked waiting for completed input datasets. Increasing the available memory on the system can also temporarily solve the issue.

- **BLOB columns** BLOB columns will be usually written to disk. This is because even if they are small, and there are empty spaces available in the rows in the buffer, the pipeline engine will fit them in. However, they are usually not so small and hence the pipeline engine writes them to the disk. Thus, in most cases where a BLOB data type is being used, the pipeline is going to write to the disk.

As you saw, in some cases, it might become unavoidable to keep buffers in memory. In such cases you can ensure that whenever the pipeline engine is writing to the disk, it will write to a fast drive. This will reduce some of the I/O performance overhead.

You have already learned in the previous section how to monitor if your buffers are getting spooled to the disk. Thus, you can also use the SSIS properties such as *BLOBTempStoragePath* and *BufferTempStoragePath* to point to fast drives that can reduce I/O performance overhead.

Optimizing SSIS Lookup Caching

Using the Lookup Cache transform is a common practice in SSIS packages, where you will want to look up dimensional values. However, it is also a common cause of a performance bottleneck due to imperfect design of the package containing the transform. In this section, you learn about the various nuances involved in designing a Cache transform and how you can design it for performance.

Lookup and Cache Transforms Primer

The Lookup transform is used to perform lookups by using joins between the input data set and a given referenced lookup data set. The reference data can be sourced from cache file, a table, a view, or even a SQL query. If you require a cache file to contain the reference data set, you must create a cache file using the Cache transform manager. You can even use an OLE DB connection manager to query a database table or view storing your cached reference dataset.

Figure 21-17 shows the General tab of the Lookup Transformation Editor where you can see the most important properties of a Lookup transformation as noted by the arrows.

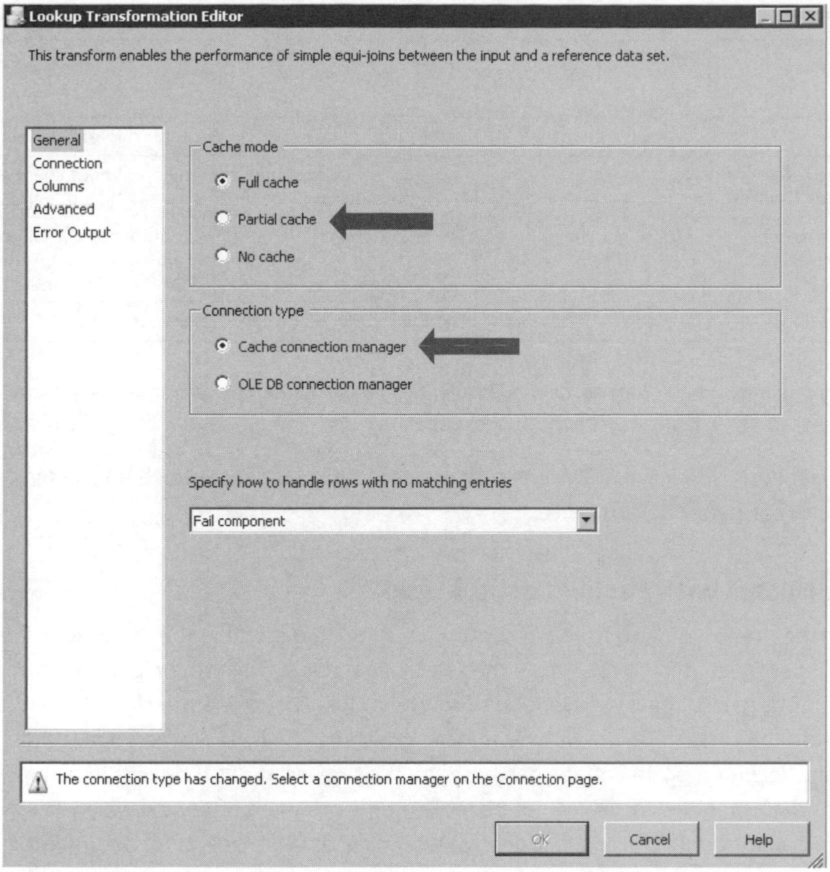

FIGURE 21-17 Important properties of a Lookup transformation.

The cache mode of a Lookup transform determines the way the cache is being stored in memory. For a full cache, the entire reference dataset is queried and stored in memory. After being stored once, the cache is not modified by the transform. In the partial cache mode, the transform starts with an empty cache. As the input rows arrive, it performs a lookup. If no matching lookup entries are found in the references dataset, it queries the database. If a matching row is found, it is then stored in the cache. The third mode is called the No Cache mode. In this mode, the transform doesn't store any rows in its cache and would be querying the database of all input rows.

Cache Mode Comparisons

Table 21-3 shows the comparisons between various cache modes. This will give you an idea of which cache mode will best suit your particular scenario when using a Lookup transformation.

TABLE 21-3 Cache mode comparisons

Cache Mode	Full	Partial	No
Memory available	High	Medium	Low
Reference table size	Small reference table	Larger reference table	Larger reference table
No. of changes in the reference table (Inserts/Updates/Deletes)	No changes	Any number of changes but limited to inserts only	Any number of changes with any type of change
Estimated number of matches between input and reference dataset in cache	A lot of matches	Fewer matches	Not applicable as all rows will be looked up from the database
C6onnection type options	Cached file or database	Database only	Database only

See Also *For a complete description of the cache modes refer to the SSIS team blog at* http://blogs.msdn.com/b/mattm/archive/2008/10/18/lookup-cache-modes.aspx.

In the next few sections, you learn how some of these cache modes can be further tuned in appropriate scenarios for better performance.

Storing Cache Misses with Partial Cache Mode

With the partial cache mode, you also have a provision for allocating space in the cache specifically for rows with no respective matching rows from the reference dataset. This can help in cases when you anticipate the input dataset having repetition of rows that will not have a match in the reference dataset. If you enable the cache for rows with no matching entries, the Data Flow engine will store these rows in the cache with the label of no-match, so the next row that has the same ID as a row from this *no-match* dataset in the cache will not be looked up from the reference dataset. This will thus result in a performance gain where the repetitive reference dataset lookup for an unmatched row is avoided. This process is shown in Figure 21-18.

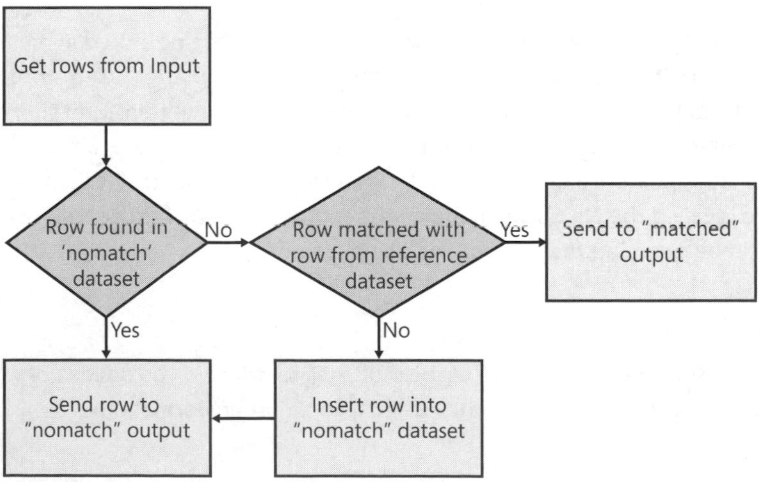

FIGURE 21-18 Using the cache for rows with no matching entries feature of partial cache.

See Also *For a complete description of the unmatched rows caching feature refer to MSDN at* http://msdn.microsoft.com/en-us/library/ms189962.aspx.

Sharing a Cache

In many situations, you will find that several Data Flow tasks would be looking up on the same dataset. For instance, if you are processing multiple fact tables using the same dimension like Customer or Employee from the AdventureWorks table, then storing the Customer or Employee dataset in a cache that can be shared across Data Flow tasks is useful. This means you will not have to create and insert rows into a reference cache for each individual data flow, reducing the overall number of database queries for the reference dataset and resulting in improved overall performance of the package. This process is explained in Figure 21-19.

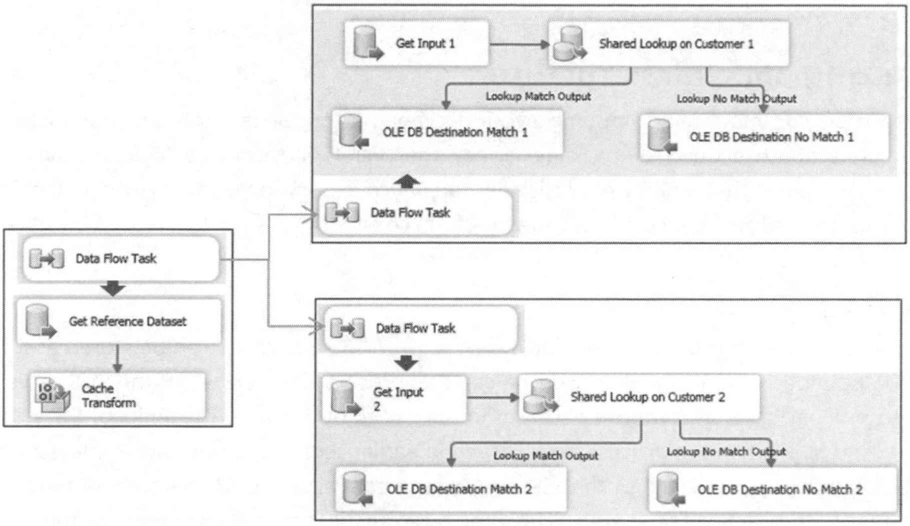

FIGURE 21-19 Use of shared cache in a package.

A shared cache can be created using one of the following methods:

1. Create a temporary database table containing your reference values. Use the OLE DB connection manager to connect to the same table from each Lookup task.
2. Use the cache connection manager to save a cache file (.caw).

As shown in Figure 21-19, we can use a cache connection manager to save the cache into a file. The file then saves to disk and is loaded into memory every time a Lookup transform queries it for using it as reference data for a lookup. Because the cache file is persisted to disk, you can also use it across package executions.

> **Note** The cache connection manager uses the RAW file format. It also stores data in clear text so you shouldn't use it for storing sensitive data. To learn more about the SSIS RAW file format, refer to the description in the RAW file destination at *http://msdn.microsoft.com/en-us/library/ms141661.aspx.*

When the cache connection manager is also used as a shared connection manager, you can effectively share the cache between package executions within the same project. Thus, you can create a cache connection manager in a parent package and use it in all respective child packages. As soon as the first child package uses the connection manager, it will be kept in memory and used in subsequent operations. Thus, you can effectively share the cache across package boundaries using the cache connection manager.

Optimizing SSIS Infrastructure

One of the most common ways to optimize your package performance is to understand how the infrastructure that is executing the packages affects the overall performance. SSIS 2012 has many infrastructural aspects that, when well-designed, can improve package performance. In the following sections, you learn about some of these infrastructural considerations.

SSIS Catalog

As you have seen in earlier chapters, with SQL Server 2012, SSIS packages can be stored and executed on the SSIS Catalog. The SSIS Catalog uses the external process *ISServerExec* or the SSIS server process to execute SSIS packages. It therefore becomes important to understand the limits of the system that would be used to execute this process. You learned in earlier sections about how to measure and optimize the various parameters for the SSIS server, such as available CPU, memory, I/O, and network performance. In this section you learn about some best practices that might help you improve the performance of your package execution.

- **Standalone SQL Server instance with SSIS** A standalone SSIS Server ensures that all the available CPU and memory on a server is reserved for SSIS. It might have other databases, but it should primarily be used for SSIS operations. This is useful in scenarios where you find the SSIS is contending with other SQL Server–based solutions like Reporting or Analysis services or even large Online Transaction Processing (OLTP) workload processing on the same SQL Server as the SSIS Catalog. You should think of offloading such expensive operations onto a different server.

- **Avoid network transfers: Locate sources and destinations close to the processing server** One of the most expensive operations that SSIS performs is transferring data over networks, so having a fast network subsystem between sources/destinations and the SSIS Catalog will help you minimize this overhead. The optimal scenario is one in which you can have the sources or destinations on the same server as the SSIS Catalog. However, you should note as mentioned earlier, the source or the destination databases should not have expensive OLTP processing requirements.

Choosing the Right Connectors

SSIS has multiple ways you can connect to data sources and destinations. They vary in terms of connection technologies as well as custom connectors being developed by the SSIS community as well as database vendors. The key to choosing the right connector is based on your database type as well as your requirements.

Various providers will have different strengths, such as bulk loading technologies. Some of these technologies will offload processing to the server, which might or might not help your scenario based on how much processing overhead your server can handle. There can also be providers that can handle certain complex data types, which might aid in your scenario. However, they might have a processing overhead compared to other providers available. Choosing the right connector therefore depends on multiple factors that might override the performance criteria. Hence, experimenting with various available connectors and measuring their performance using the measuring techniques explained in previous sections will help you choose the right connector for your scenario.

See Also *Chapter 7, "Understanding SSIS Connectivity" includes an in-depth explanation of various connectivity options in SSIS Tuning options for packages.*

The Data Flow task has various options that can be tuned to improve performance. These options allow the Data Flow engine to optimally assign the resources required for execution of the Data Flow. The properties for tuning a Data Flow task are as follows:

- **Buffer size (*DefaultBufferMaxRows*) and Rows per buffer (*DefaultBufferMaxSize*)** You can control the buffer size and the maximum number of rows per buffer for a Data Flow engine. The default for *Buffer size* is 10 MB and the maximum size for it is 100 MB. The default value for maximum number of rows per buffer is 10,000. This signifies that one buffer would either contain 10,000 rows or have 10 MB of data (whichever limit is reached first). Setting the buffer size to a higher value could result in higher resource usage, as large buffers would be created and fitted into memory. This can result in better performance as you would be able to fit the required buffers in memory and the engine doesn't have to write buffers to the disk. However, it could also result in the Data Flow task sitting idle waiting for the source components to fill up the large buffers.
- **Engine threads (*EngineThreads*)** In Chapter 15, you learned how the Data Flow engine uses CPU threads for execution. The Data Flow engine also exposes a property that lets you suggest to the engine the number of threads it should allocate. In SQL Server Data Tools, the default value of this property is set to 10. However, the engine calculates the number of threads it requires during execution. The engine adopts the formula as the number of execution trees including the sources plus two. Thus if you have three execution trees within a Data Flow, five engine threads would be utilized for the Data Flow task. If you end up setting the *EngineThreads* property to anything below that number, the number is ignored when the engine performs the calculation.

Summary

In this chapter, you learned about how you can measure and optimize the performance of your SSIS packages. You learned how you can monitor the properties of the package execution, which can help you determine the bottlenecks. You also learned about the various design patterns that can help you optimize the performance of your packages. This chapter also talked about the common causes of bottlenecks in SSIS solutions. You can use the framework and suggestions mentioned in the chapter to take an analytical approach toward optimizing the performance of your packages.

In Chapter 22, you will learn how you can troubleshoot similar performance issues using the new reporting capabilities available in SSIS 2012.

CHAPTER 22

Troubleshooting SSIS Performance Issues

In This Chapter

Performance Profiling

When working with SSIS, there are different performance-related questions that you might have to deal with, such as the following:

- **SSIS package that is taking longer than usual to complete execution** Usually, the normal execution time for an SSIS package that is performing the loading of a fact table is approximately one hour. The SSIS package, which has been scheduled for nightly execution, has been running well for the past six months. One day, you realize that one of the SSIS package executions that has been scheduled to run through the night is taking almost six hours, and has just completed execution. You want to find out what caused the execution to take longer than usual.
- **Need to identify performance bottleneck in the package** You suspect that the SSIS package is not performing optimally, and that one of the tasks or Data Flow components (source, transform, and destination) might be a performance bottleneck. You want to identify the performance bottleneck.

- **Establishing a performance baseline** You want to be able to monitor the executions of an SSIS package over an extended period of time. Using the information from the historical executions, you want to establish a performance baseline. You want to be able to make use of the performance baseline to make comparisons and identify "abnormal" executions and be alerted when it happens. You might also want to make use of the performance baseline to aid you in performance tuning of the SSIS package so that it runs optimally.

Understanding the performance profile of SSIS package execution plays an important role in helping you tune the performance of the SSIS packages, identify performance bottlenecks, and establish a performance baseline for SSIS package executions. This is similar to how you will make use of a performance profiler to gain a deeper understanding of an application program in Microsoft Visual Studio. During the execution of the SSIS package, a performance bottleneck can occur within the Control Flow (for example, use of an Execute SQL task) or can be caused by a Data Flow component (source, transformation, destination) at one of its processing phases.

Prior to SSIS 2012, you could make use of SSIS performance counters, or log the right information to understand the performance profile of your SSIS packages. SSIS 2012 introduces new capabilities that make it easier for you to gain a deep understanding of the performance profile of SSIS package executions. In addition, these capabilities make it easier for you to leverage historical execution information to proactively monitor SSIS package executions, and alert you when the SSIS package execution timing differs from the SISS package execution baseline.

See Also *See Chapter 21, "SSIS Performance Best Practices," where you learned best practices for SSIS performance tuning.*

Troubleshooting Performance Issues

Before SSIS 2012, methods for monitoring the performance of a SSIS package execution included the following:

- Using logging to capture the SSIS events that can help you compute the execution times of different phases of an SSIS component execution. Among the various SSIS events that are captured, the *PipelineComponent* event is most commonly used to gain an understanding of the processing time (in milliseconds) for each phase of a Data Flow component execution. These phases include *PreExecute, PostExecute, PostExecute, ProcessInput, PrimeOutput, and Validate*. For example, a package that is taking a long lime in the *PreExecute* phase might require investigations into the lookup cache modes that are used. Most existing custom SSIS logging frameworks parse the log entry to extract the time spent at each phase of the running Data Flow component.
- Using performance counters to understand the different statistics (Blob read/write, amount of buffer memory used by flat and private buffers, and the numbers of rows read/write). On the machine where SSIS packages are executed, these performance counters present aggregated statistics of all the running packages.

Note Refer to *http://msdn.microsoft.com/en-us/library/ms138020.aspx* for a good discussion on the different SSIS events and *http://msdn.microsoft.com/en-us/library/ms141031.aspx* to find out more about the use of the *PipelineComponent* time.

Besides the existing performance monitoring methods, SSIS 2012 introduces new methods for monitoring the performance of an SSIS package execution. These methods include the following:

- **Table-value function (TVF) for runtime performance counters information** The TVF *catalog.dm_execution_performance_counters* can be used to obtain per-execution performance counter information for a running SSIS package.

  This runtime performance counter information is not logged to the SSIS Catalog. Hence, when the SSIS package execution has completed, you will not get any more performance counter information.

  If you need to log this performance counter information for subsequent investigations, you can consider writing a Transact-SQL (T-SQL) script that logs this runtime performance information at regular sampling intervals.

- **Views providing detailed performance information** The detailed performance information is logged to the SSIS Catalog during SSIS package execution, when the Performance or Verbose logging level is used. These views include *catalog.executable_statistics* and *catalog.execution_component_phases*.

In addition, SSIS 2012 logs additional phases of a Data Flow component. The phases that are logged during execution using the Performance or Verbose logging level include *AcquireConnections, Cleanup, PostExecute, PreExecute, PrepareForExecute, PrimeOutput, ProcessInput, ReleaseConnections, and Validate.*

Data Preparation

In this section, you prepare the database, tables, and data needed to try the different examples in this chapter. To start the preparation, download the AdventureWorksDW2012 database from *http://msftdbprodsamples.codeplex.com/releases/view/55330*, and attach it to a SQL Server instance.

After the AdventureWorksDW2012database has been attached, perform the following steps:

1. Deploy the SSIS Project, Chapter22.ispac, found in *C:\InsideOut\Chapter 22\Code* to *the SSISInsideOut* folder in the SSIS Catalog.
2. By default, the data preparation step will create the database *EnterpriseDW* on the default SQL instance. If you are using a named instance or deploying it to a remote server, you will need to configure the project parameter *ServerName* with the correct server name.

3. After the SSIS Catalog has been deployed successfully, execute the package "0. PrepData.dtsx" using SQL Server Management Studio by right-clicking the SSIS package ("0. PrepData.dtsx") and choosing Execute Package.
4. Verify that the package executes successfully, and the database has been created successfully.
5. Right-click the SSIS package "2. MasterPackage.dtsx" and choose Execute Package.
6. In the Execute Package dialog box, click the Advanced tab.
7. Set the logging level to Verbose.
8. Click OK to execute the SSIS package.

   Take note of the operation ID that is given. You will need this in the later exercise. It is important to note that all the T-SQL snippets given in this chapter assume an operation ID (that is, *execution_id*) with a value of 49. You should replace this with the operation ID that you observe when you complete step 8.

Understanding SSIS Package Execution Performance

In this section, you learn how to investigate the performance of an SSIS package execution.

SSIS Package Execution Duration

To start this exercise, you first query the view *catalog.executions* to find out the execution duration for the SSIS package "1. LoadData.dtsx" that has been deployed to the *SSISInsideOut* folder. Listing 22-1 shows the T-SQL query that can be used to compute the execution duration of the SSIS package. This is given in the *duration_secs* column.

LISTING 22-1 Duration of an SSIS package execution

```
USE SSISDB

SELECT execution_id,
   folder_name,
   project_name,
   package_name,
   status,
   DATEDIFF(second, start_time, end_time) as duration_secs,
   CONVERT(nvarchar(100),start_time,20) as start_time,
   CONVERT(nvarchar(100),end_time,20) as end_time
FROM catalog.executions
WHERE folder_name = 'SSISInsideOut'
AND project_name = 'Chapter22Project'
AND package_name = '2. MasterPackage.dtsx'
```

Time Spent at Each Task in the SSIS Package

SSIS tasks and containers (sequence, ForEach, For) are also referred to as executables. After you have obtained the overall duration of the SSIS package, you can drill down further and obtain the time spent at each of the tasks and containers. To do this, you can query the *catalog.executable_statistics* view. Listing 22-2 shows the T-SQL query that can be used to find the time spent at each of the executables in the SSIS package.

LISTING 22-2 Duration of executables

```
USE SSISDB

SELECT es.execution_path,
   e.executable_name,
   es.execution_duration,
   es.execution_result
FROM catalog.executable_statistics es, catalog.executables e
WHERE es.execution_id = <your operation id value>
AND es.execution_id = e.execution_id
AND es.executable_id = e.executable_id
ORDER by es.execution_duration DESC
```

Figure 22-1 shows the results of the query, from which you can identify the executables in the package where most of the execution time is spent. From Figure 22-1, you can see that the Data Flow task in the "1 LoadData" package is executed twice. This can be inferred by looking at the execution path. You can dig further to find out the time spent at the phase of the Data Flow components that are in the Data Flow task for the first iteration, given by the execution path *\2 MasterPackage\Execute DataIssues Package\1 LoadData\Foreach Loop Container[1]\Data Flow Task*.

Results | Messages

	execution_path	executable_name	execution_duration	execution_result
1	\2 MasterPackage	2 MasterPackage	4066	0
2	\2 MasterPackage\Execute DataIssues Package	Execute DataIssues Package	4046	0
3	\2 MasterPackage\Execute DataIssues Package\1 LoadData	1 LoadData	2514	0
4	\2 MasterPackage\Execute DataIssues Package\1 LoadData\Foreach Loop Container	Foreach Loop Container	2504	0
5	\2 MasterPackage\Execute DataIssues Package\1 LoadData\Foreach Loop Container[1]\Data Flow Task	Data Flow Task	1502	0
6	\2 MasterPackage\Execute DataIssues Package\1 LoadData\Foreach Loop Container[2]\Data Flow Task	Data Flow Task	982	0

FIGURE 22-1 Time spent at each of the executables in the SSIS package.

Time Spent at Each Phase of the Data Flow Component

To find out the time spent at each phase of the Data Flow component, you will need to query the view *catalog.execution_component_phases*. Listing 22-3 shows the T-SQL query used.

LISTING 22-3 Time spent at each phase of the Data Flow component

```
USE SSISDB

SELECT subcomponent_name,
   phase,
   DATEDIFF(second, start_time, end_time) as duration_secs
FROM catalog.execution_component_phases ecp
WHERE ecp.execution_id = 49
AND execution_path = '\2  MasterPackage\Execute DataIssues Package\1  LoadData\Foreach Loop
Container[1]\Data Flow Task'
ORDER BY duration_secs DESC
```

Elapsed Time for Data Flow Component Phases (Active Time vs. Total Time)

Prior to SSIS 2012, the total time captured for each component phase contains wall clock time, from when the Data Flow starts to when it processes its last buffer. It includes all time spent idle, sleeping, or waiting on upstream or downstream components.

SSIS 2012 introduces the ability to obtain the active time spent at each phase of a Data Flow component during execution. For real performance analysis, active time is the only thing that matters. This would be the amount of time actually doing work. Components with a high active time should be the first place you look to try and resolve bottlenecks.

This allows you to find out the time in which the Data Flow component is doing actual work. This improves on the coarser grained *PipelineComponentTime*, which captures the total time spent in each phase. To illustrate this, do the following:

1. Navigate to the *SSISInsideOut* folder.
2. Right-click the package *"2. MasterPackage.dtsx"*.
3. Click Execute.
4. Click the Advanced tab, and change the Logging Level to Performance.
5. Click OK to start the execution.
6. Take note of the operation ID.

After the SSIS package has completed execution, execute the T-SQL query given in Listing 22-4. The result from executing the query is shown in Figure 22-2. The total time spent in all the *ProcessInput* invocations is 3.169 seconds. Similarly, if you look at the *PipelineComponentTime* that is captured, it will be close to the total time reported here. However, the actual time spent is only 1.430 seconds. This is obtained by summing all the timings given in the *phase_duration_secs* column.

You should replace the *execution_id* with the value 50 below with the operation ID that you observe after you have completed step 5.

LISTING 22-4 Active vs. total time

```
USE SSISDB

SELECT phase,
   cast (start_time as time) start_time,
   cast (end_time as time) end_time,
   datediff(millisecond, start_time, end_time) / 1000.0 as phase_duration_secs
FROM catalog.execution_component_phases ecp
WHERE ecp.execution_id = <your operation id value>
AND phase = 'ProcessInput'
ORDER BY start_time
```

Results | Messages

	phase	start_time	end_time	phase_duration_secs
1	ProcessInput	20:26:17.0935200	20:26:17.1055584	0.012000
2	ProcessInput	20:26:17.1135840	20:26:17.4667104	0.353000
3	ProcessInput	20:26:17.1155904	20:26:17.1155904	0.000000
4	ProcessInput	20:26:17.4717264	20:26:17.4747360	0.003000
5	ProcessInput	20:26:19.1711472	20:26:19.1861952	0.015000
6	ProcessInput	20:26:19.1942208	20:26:20.2385520	1.044000
7	ProcessInput	20:26:19.1962272	20:26:19.1962272	0.000000
8	ProcessInput	20:26:20.2596192	20:26:20.2626288	0.003000

FIGURE 22-2 Start, end, and execution duration for the *ProcessInput* phase.

From this example, you can see the distinct differences between the actual time and total time. You can make use of this to gain deeper insights into the execution performance of Data Flow components. Listing 22-5 shows how to obtain the active and total time in a T-SQL query. The result from executing the query is shown in Figure 22-3.

LISTING 22-5 Computing the active and total time spent in each phase

```
SELECT task_name + '.' + subcomponent_name TaskSubComponent, phase,
  SUM(DATEDIFF(millisecond,start_time,end_time)) /1000.0 as active_time_secs,
  DATEDIFF(MILLISECOND,min(start_time), max(end_time))/1000.0 as total_time_secs
FROM catalog.execution_component_phases
WHERE execution_id = <your operation id value>
GROUP BY task_name, subcomponent_name, phase
ORDER BY active_time_secs desc
```

Results | Messages

	TaskSubComponent	phase	active_time_secs	total_time_secs
1	Data Flow Task.DimCustomer	ProcessInput	1.403000	3.149000
2	Data Flow Task.DimCustomer	Validate	1.144000	2.640000
3	Data Flow Task.DimCustomer	PreExecute	0.586000	2.144000
4	Data Flow Task.Flat File Source	PrimeOutput	0.520000	2.239000
5	Data Flow Task.DimCustomer	AcquireConnections	0.162000	2.801000
6	Data Flow Task.Derived Column	ProcessInput	0.027000	2.103000
7	Data Flow Task.Flat File Source	AcquireConnections	0.021000	3.110000
8	Data Flow Task.DimCustomer	ReleaseConnections	0.016000	4.955000
9	Data Flow Task.Flat File Source	PreExecute	0.011000	1.883000
10	Data Flow Task.Flat File Source	Validate	0.005000	2.633000
11	Data Flow Task.Flat File Source	PostExecute	0.003000	2.801000
12	Data Flow Task.Derived Column	PrepareForExecute	0.002000	1.529000
13	Data Flow Task.Flat File Source	Cleanup	0.000000	2.790000
14	Data Flow Task.DimCustomer	PrepareForExecute	0.000000	1.522000
15	Data Flow Task.Derived Column	ReleaseConnections	0.000000	5.013000
16	Data Flow Task.Derived Column	Validate	0.000000	2.279000
17	Data Flow Task.DimCustomer	Cleanup	0.000000	2.790000
18	Data Flow Task.DimCustomer	PostExecute	0.000000	2.788000
19	Data Flow Task.Derived Column	AcquireConnections	0.000000	2.779000
20	Data Flow Task.Derived Column	Cleanup	0.000000	2.791000
21	Data Flow Task.Derived Column	PostExecute	0.000000	2.789000
22	Data Flow Task.Derived Column	PreExecute	0.000000	1.829000
23	Data Flow Task.Flat File Source	PrepareForExecute	0.000000	1.515000
24	Data Flow Task.Flat File Source	ReleaseConnections	0.000000	4.963000

FIGURE 22-3 Active and total time spent at each phase (Results).

Monitoring SSIS Package Execution Performance

Often, you might want to proactively monitor the execution of SSIS packages to identify packages that are running slower than usual. In this example, you will make use of the average execution duration as a measure of packages that are slower than usual. You start off by using a common table expression (CTE) to obtain the average execution duration for all the packages that have been deployed to the SSIS Catalog. Specifically, you compute the average execution duration for packages that have executed successfully. Next, you identify SSIS package executions that are running slower than the average execution duration. Listing 22-6 shows the T-SQL that can be used to perform the task.

LISTING 22-6 Find executions that are slower than usual

```
With ExecutionStats AS (
   SELECT exe.object_id,
exe.folder_name,
exe.project_name,
exe.package_name,
           avg(datediff(millisecond , start_time, end_time)) as avg_duration_ms
   FROM  [SSISDB].catalog.executions exe
   WHERE exe.status = 7
   GROUP BY exe.object_id,
exe.folder_name, exe.project_name, exe.package_name
)
SELECT exe.folder_name,
   exe.project_name,
```

```
    exe.package_name,
    (datediff(millisecond , start_time, end_time) /1000.0)
    as execution_duration_secs,
    (exeStats.avg_duration_ms / 1000.0) as avg_duration_Secs
FROM [SSISDB].catalog.executions exe,
ExecutionStats exeStats
WHERE exe.folder_name = exeStats.folder_name
AND exe.project_name = exeStats.project_name
AND exe.package_name = exeStats.package_name
AND exe.status = 7
AND datediff(millisecond , start_time, end_time) > exeStats.avg_duration_ms
```

You might also want to proactively monitor the tasks and components in the SSIS package that are performing slower than usual. Using the performance information captured in the views, you can use the T-SQL query given in Listing 22-7 to find the executables that are slower than the average execution duration. In this example, you drill down the investigation to a specific package, which is identified by the folder name, project name, and package name. You can consider relaxing the constraints, and identify tasks and components in all the packages.

LISTING 22-7 Monitoring the performance of SSIS package executions

```
With ExecutionStats AS (
SELECT e.executable_id, e.executable_name,
    avg(es.execution_duration) as avg_duration
    FROM  [SSISDB].catalog.executable_statistics es,
                    catalog.executables e,
                    catalog.executions exe
    WHERE es.executable_id = e.executable_id
    AND   es.execution_id = e.execution_id
    AND   es.execution_id = exe.execution_id
    AND exe.folder_name = 'SSISInsideOut'
    AND exe.project_name = 'Chapter22Project'
    AND exe.package_name = '2. MasterPackage.dtsx'
    AND exe.status = 7
    GROUP BY e.executable_id, e.executable_name
)
SELECT es.execution_id,
    e.executable_name,
    es.execution_duration,
    exeStats.avg_duration,
    es.execution_path
FROM  [SSISDB].catalog.executable_statistics es,
    [SSISDB].catalog.executables e,
    [SSISDB].catalog.executions exe,
ExecutionStats exeStats
where es.executable_id = e.executable_id
    AND es.execution_id = e.execution_id
    AND   es.execution_id = exe.execution_id
    AND exe.folder_name = 'SSISInsideOut'
    AND exe.project_name = 'Chapter22Project'
    AND exe.package_name = '2. MasterPackage.dtsx'
    AND exe.status = 7
    AND e.executable_id = exeStats.executable_id
    AND es.execution_duration >   exeStats.avg_duration
ORDER BY es.execution_duration DESC
```

Tip A custom SQL Server Reporting Services report can be built that leverages the T-SQL query.

See Also *Chapter 14, "SSIS Reports," shows you how to make use of the SSIS reports that are available in SQL Server Management Studio.*

When investigating performance issues for SSIS package execution, it is important to note after you have identified the executions, tasks and components that are slower than usual, there might be different causes for the performance issues. Many SSIS performance issues can be caused by external factors. Hence, it is important to look beyond SSIS. For example, the servers where the SSIS packages are executed, the data source, and destinations can be potential areas to widen the investigation.

To identify the root cause, ask yourself the following questions:

- Have there been any scheduled maintenance tasks on the servers hosting the data sources or destinations?
- Are there any intensive queries that are running on the databases where the SSIS packages are reading from or writing to?
- Have the SSIS packages been modified recently?
- Are there any scheduled network maintenance or network issues?

Per-Execution Performance Counters

SSIS introduces the ability to obtain per-execution performance counters for an SSIS package execution. This is similar to how you will make use of SQL Server Dynamic Management Views (DMVs) to obtain server state information to diagnose problems and perform performance tuning. The performance counter information for an SSIS package execution is not persisted once the execution completes.

To obtain per-execution performance counters, you can make use of the TVF, *catalog.dm_execution_performance_counters*. The TVF can be used with all logging levels. To use the TVF, you should pass in the execution identifier as the argument to the TVF.

To illustrate this, do the following:

1. Navigate to the *SSISInsideOut* folder.
2. Right-click Chapter22Project, and the package "3. LoadDataSlow.dtsx".

Note This SSIS package has been designed to ensure that the execution time is relatively long so that you see the effects from running the TVF.

3. Click Execute.

4. Click the Advanced tab, and change the Logging Level to Performance.

5. Click OK to start the execution.

6. Take note of the operation ID. Suppose the operation ID is 60.

Listing 22-8 shows the T-SQL query used to obtain per-execution performance counters. Figure 22-4 shows the results from executing the query.

LISTING 22-8 Using *catalog.dm_execution_performance_counters*

```
SELECT *

FROM catalog.dm_execution_performance_counters(<your operation ID value>)
```

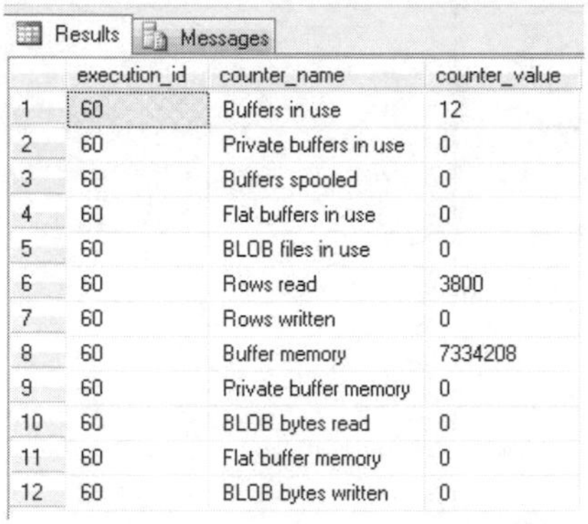

	execution_id	counter_name	counter_value
1	60	Buffers in use	12
2	60	Private buffers in use	0
3	60	Buffers spooled	0
4	60	Flat buffers in use	0
5	60	BLOB files in use	0
6	60	Rows read	3800
7	60	Rows written	0
8	60	Buffer memory	7334208
9	60	Private buffer memory	0
10	60	BLOB bytes read	0
11	60	Flat buffer memory	0
12	60	BLOB bytes written	0

FIGURE 22-4 Performance counters for execution, with ID = 60.

Interactive Analysis of Performance Data

Similar to the SQL Server management data warehouse, the execution details that are automatically logged to the SSIS Catalog constitute useful data that can be used for analyzing the usage of SSIS packages and their performance over time. SSIS 2012 provides a set of SSIS reports that can be launched from within SQL Server Management Studio for gaining insights into the execution of SSIS packages.

In this section, you learn how to interactively analyze the performance data that is in the SSIS Catalog using PowerPivot for Microsoft Excel. PowerPivot for Excel is a self-service, business intelligence tool for authoring PowerPivot data in an Excel workbook. If you have not downloaded PowerPivot, you can download it from *http://www.microsoft.com/en-us/bi/powerpivot.aspx*.

After you have downloaded and installed PowerPivot, you can do the following to get started:

1. Start Excel.
2. Click PowerPivot, and then click PowerPivot Window to launch PowerPivot.
3. Click From Database | From SQL Server.
4. In the Table Import Wizard (see Figure 22-5):
   a. Specify the SQL Server instance where SSIS is installed.
   b. Specify SSISDB as the database.

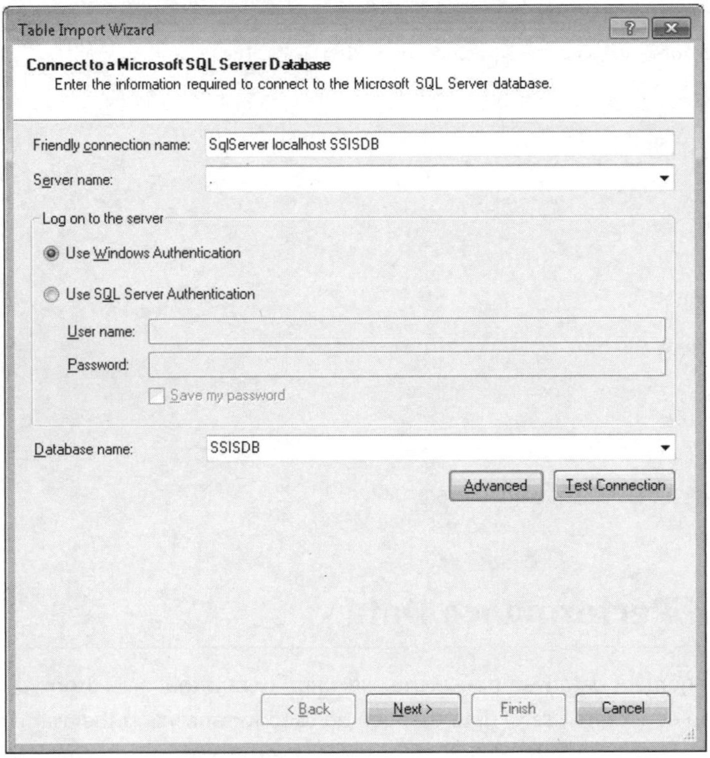

FIGURE 22-5 PowerPivot Table Import Wizard.

5. Click Next, and select Select From A List Of Tables And Views To Choose The Data to Import.
6. Click Next, and select the following views under the catalog schema:
   a. executions
   b. executable_statistics
   c. executables

Figure 22-6 shows the views that are selected.

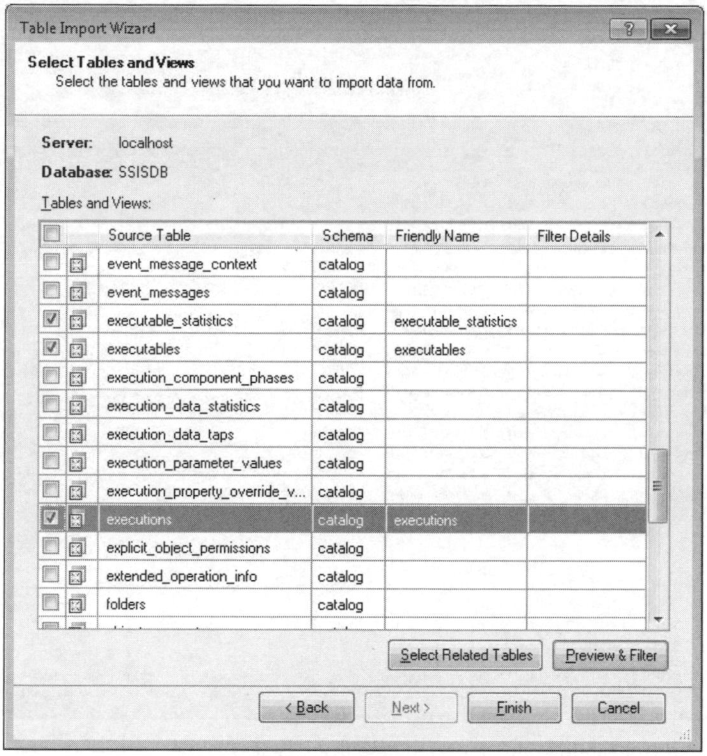

FIGURE 22-6 Selecting the views used for analysis.

7. Select the check box for executions in the Source Table column, and click Preview & Filter.
8. Clear the check boxes for the following columns:
   a. reference_id
   b. reference_type
   c. executed_as_sid
   d. caller_sid
   e. stopped_by_sid
   f. dump_id
9. Click OK. You will notice that the executions source table has the Applied Filters text shown in the Filter Details column.
10. Click Finish.
11. You should see that all the rows are successfully imported.

The PowerPivot should be similar to what is shown in Figure 22-7.

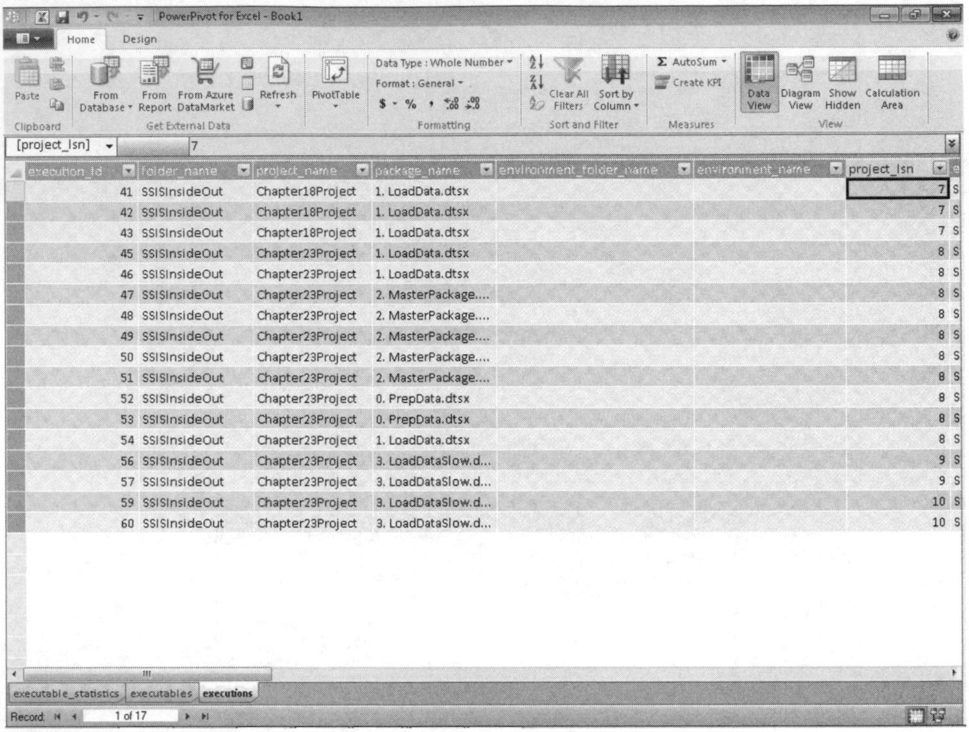

FIGURE 22-7 PowerPivot window with imported data from SSISDB.

12. After this is done, you are ready to interactively analyze the data in Excel. In the top left corner of the window, click the Excel icon to close the PowerPivot window.
13. In the PowerPivot Ribbon, select PivotTable | Four Charts.
14. Click the Top Left Chart, and perform the following steps:
    a. In the PowerPivot Field List, select execution_id and then package_name.
    b. Make sure that *package_name* is under Axis Fields.
    c. Under Values, check the Sum of *execution_id* to Count of *execution_id*. You can do this by clicking the arrow, and selecting Count, as shown in Figure 22-8.

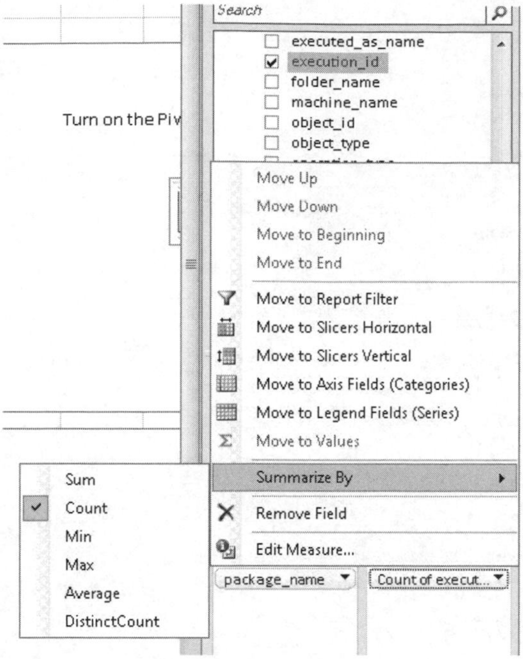

FIGURE 22-8 Count of Execution IDs.

15. Click Change Chart Type, and change the top left chart to be a bar chart.
16. Under Pivot Chart Tools, choose Layout.
17. Under Axis Titles, choose Primary Horizontal Axis Title.
18. Modify the horizontal axis title to **# Occurrences**.
19. Modify the chart title to **# Executions SSIS Package.**
20. After all this is done, you will be able to see a similar chart, as shown in Figure 22-9.

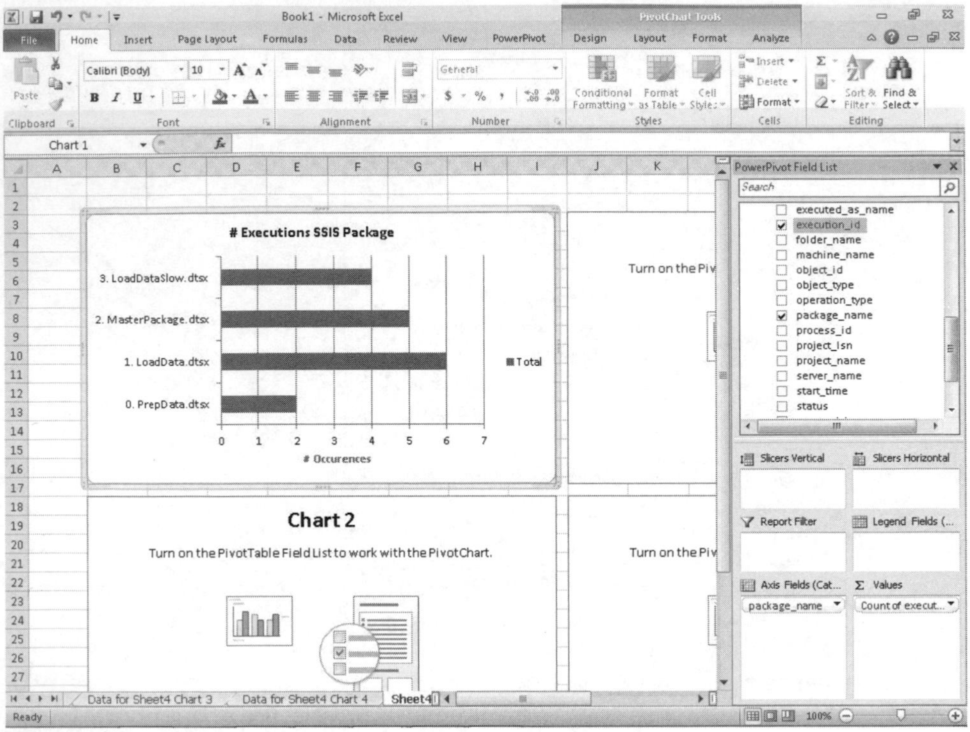

FIGURE 22-9 Chart showing number of executions of SSIS packages.

21. Go back to the PowerPivot window.

22. For the *executables* worksheet, add a new column called *executable_newid*, and provide the following formula: *=CONCATENATE(CONCATENATE([executable_id],"."),[execution_id])* as shown in Figure 22-10.

23. For the executable_statistics worksheet, add a new column, called *executable_newid* and provide the same formula: *=CONCATENATE(CONCATENATE([executable_id],"."),[execution_id]).*

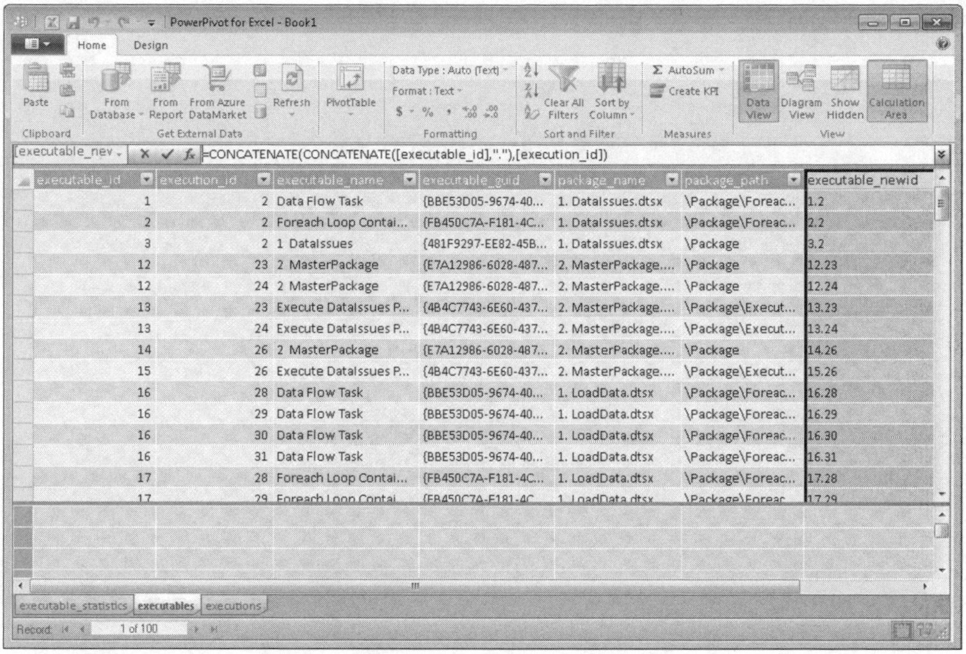

FIGURE 22-10 Add new column: executable_newid.

24. Click the Diagram view, and create the following relationships:

a. For executable_statistics:

- Drag the column *executable_newid* to point to the *executable_newid* column in the executables table.
- Drag the column *execution_id* to point to the *execution_id* column in the executions table.

b. For executables:

- Drag the column *execution_id* to point to the *execution_id* column in the executions table.

After this is done, you should see a diagram similar to Figure 22-11.

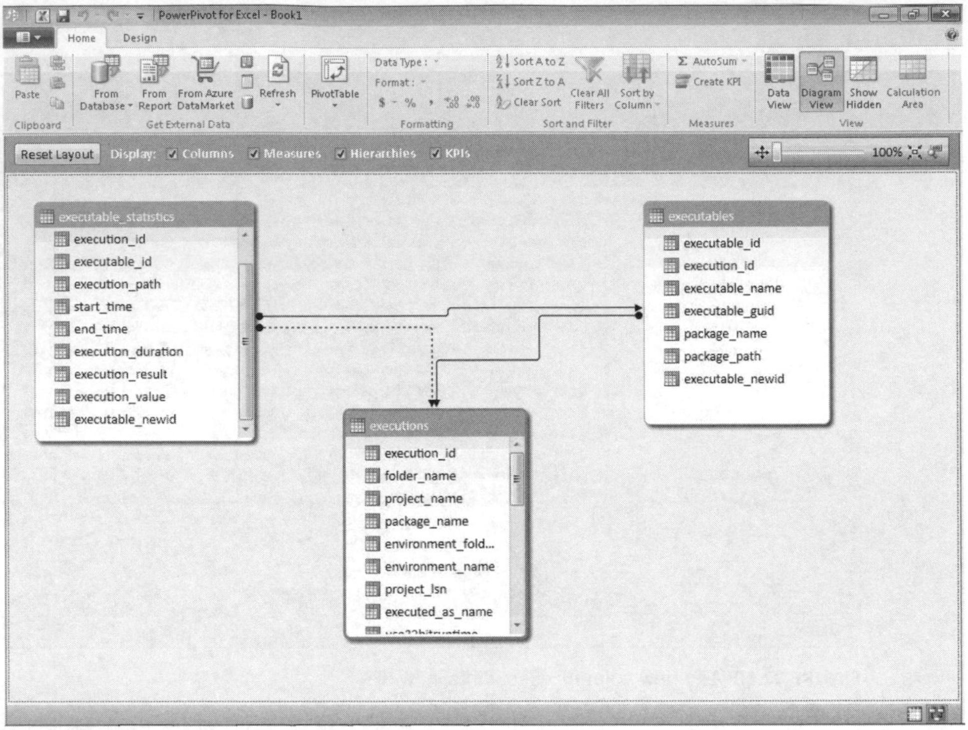

FIGURE 22-11 Diagram view of relationships between the two tables.

25. Switch back to the Excel view by clicking the Excel icon in the top left corner.

26. Under executions (from the PowerPivot Field List), add the following to the horizontal slicer:

- **a.** folder_name
- **b.** project_name
- **c.** package_name

27. Under Values, compute the min, max, and average value for execution_duration.

28. Figure 22-12 shows the PowerPivot Field List and selections.

29. Change the Chart Title for the upper right chart to **Min, Max & Average Execution Duration**.

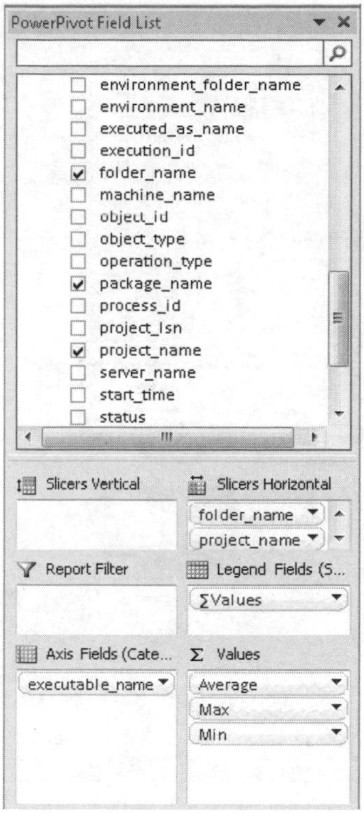

FIGURE 22-12 PowerPivot Field List for Min, Max & Average Execution Duration chart.

30. Change the Chart Type to Bar Chart.
31. Using the horizontal slicer, select the following:
    a. Folder: SSISInsideOut
    b. Project: Chapter22Project
    c. Package: 1. LoadData.dtsx
32. Figure 22-13 shows the completed charts.

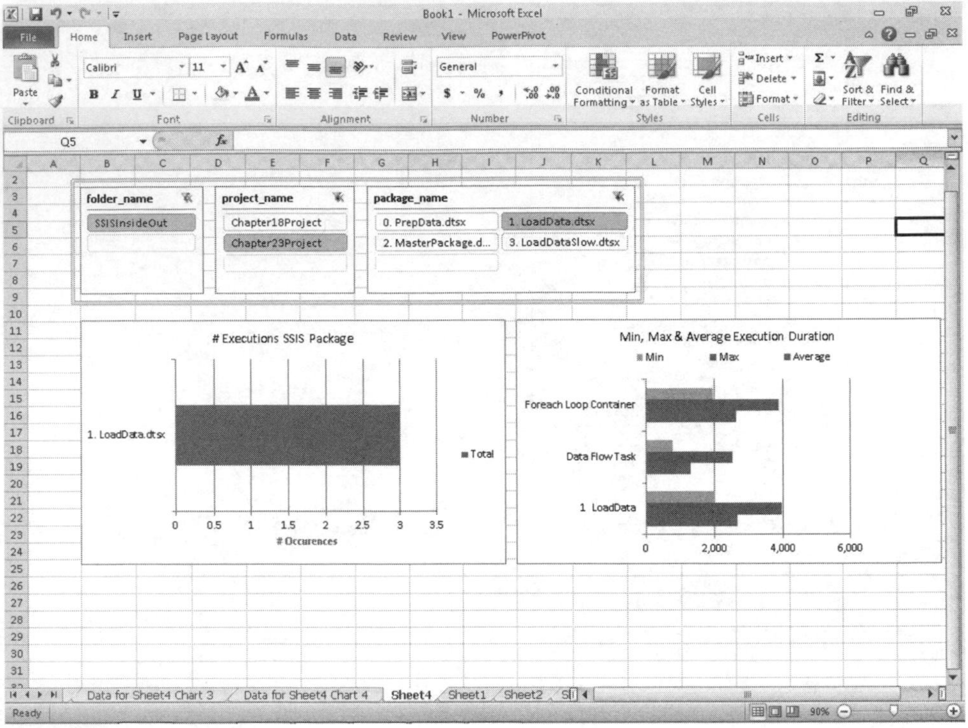

FIGURE 22-13 Completed charts.

Summary

In this chapter, you saw how to make use of the new capabilities in SSIS 2012 to investigate performance issues for SSIS packages. You learned how to make use of the views provided in the SSIS Catalog to obtain the duration of all SSIS package executions. Next, you learned how to drill down deeper to obtain the execution duration of all tasks and containers for an SSIS package. Finally, you learned how to drill down to gain a deeper understanding of the different phases of the Data Flow components. You also learned the difference between active and total time spent at each phase. In the later part of the chapter, you learned how to proactively monitor the SSIS package executions, and be alerted when abnormal package durations occur. Finally, you learned how to make use of PowerPivot to interactively analyze the performance of packages that have been deployed to the SSIS Catalog.

CHAPTER 23

Troubleshooting Data Issues

In This Chapter

An important feature of any mission-critical system is to provide the ability to identify failure or error in an operation, investigate the reasons, and allow users to take actions. Data integration projects often deal with important data and any error in data reading, processing, or writing can potentially lead to serious mistakes in business decisions. Hence troubleshooting data issues is an essential feature of data integration software. SSIS, as an enterprise-class data integration platform, has the capabilities to help with troubleshooting issues such as wrong data or incorrect number of rows loaded by SSIS packages. In this chapter, we look into the details of the features related to troubleshooting data issues.

Troubleshooting in the Design Environment

SQL Server Data Tools is the design environment for SSIS-based integration projects. It has features to deal with data issues during the design of SSIS packages. Copies of packages that fail in production environments can also be opened in SQL Server Data Tools for troubleshooting purposes. Let's review the features that could help in troubleshooting data issues in SQL Server Data Tools.

Row Count Values

When packages are designed, you often need to validate the Data Flow logic on given test data. SQL Server Data Tools provides an easy way to validate the logic using the number of rows that flow through each path in the package. This is especially useful if the data flowing through different paths is not the same due to the data flow routing and processing logic in the task. When a package with a Data Flow task is executed in SQL Server Data Tools in Debug mode, the number of rows that flow through each data path is displayed next to the paths in the design surface. As the execution progresses and more data flows through each path in the flow, the row count for each path is updated.

When the package execution finishes, the final row count numbers for each path are displayed until the debugging is stopped. Figure 23-1 shows the row count numbers on a Data Flow task.

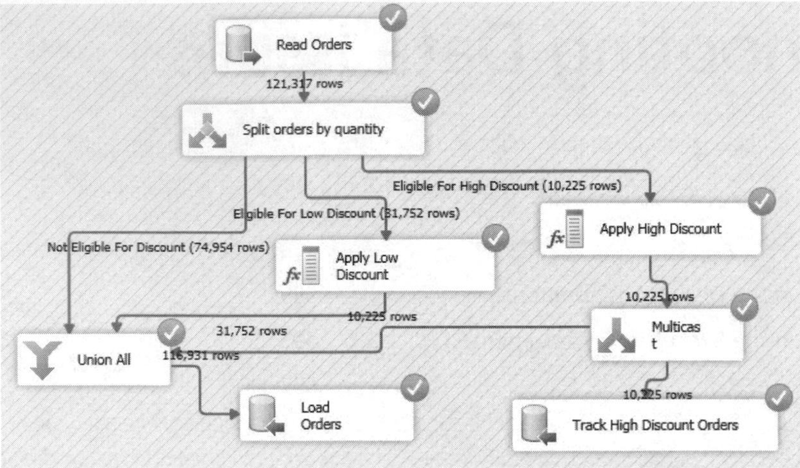

FIGURE 23-1 Row count numbers on a Data Flow task.

A common approach to SSIS package design that could help with troubleshooting data issues is to instrument packages using Row Count transformation and verify data integrity in the Data Flow paths as a part of the package execution. With such instrumentation, the number of rows flowing through some key Data Flow paths are captured and used to validate the execution time behavior. For example, in a data loading scenario, it is important to make sure that rows read from sources are either loaded to destinations or routed to the appropriate path of the Data Flow task. So, row count transformation can be inserted into the output columns of source components to track the number of rows read into the Data Flow pipeline and other Row Count transformations are inserted in the paths flowing into destination components. In the Control Flow of the package, the variables used in Row Count transformations can be processed after the Data Flow task to ensure that all rows were accounted for in the data processing and kick off additional steps in the control if needed. Such a proactive approach to dealing with data issues can be quite useful when dealing with business-critical data or meeting corporate compliance standards. Counts of rows flowing through different Data Flow paths are automatically recorded to the SSIS Catalog in SSIS 2012 without the need for explicit instrumentation if appropriate settings are used. Because special security permissions and logging settings are required, using execution statistics to verify data integrity might not be as easy or efficient as the row count instrumentation approach.

Data Viewers

Data viewers are used to view data flowing between any two components in a Data Flow task. They are quite useful to understand data in any path of an SSIS data flow. They are often used as the simplest way to validate data processing logic in a Data Flow task as packages are built. For example, data viewers could be added to the path between a source component and a transformation to verify the data that is extracted from the data source and a data viewer between two transformations can be used to validate the result of transformation logic. With data viewers, it is easy to identify unexpected data values, view transformation changes on data, or narrow in on to invalid data that is causing failure of a Data Flow component. SSIS 2012 supports displaying data in tabular format as rows and columns. A data viewer is added to a Data Flow path using the Enable Data Viewer option on the shortcut menu of the path in SQL Server Data Tools as shown in Figure 23-2.

> **Note** SSIS versions prior to SSIS 2012 supported viewing data in different formats. In SSIS 2012, only tabular format is supported and other viewers are discontinued.

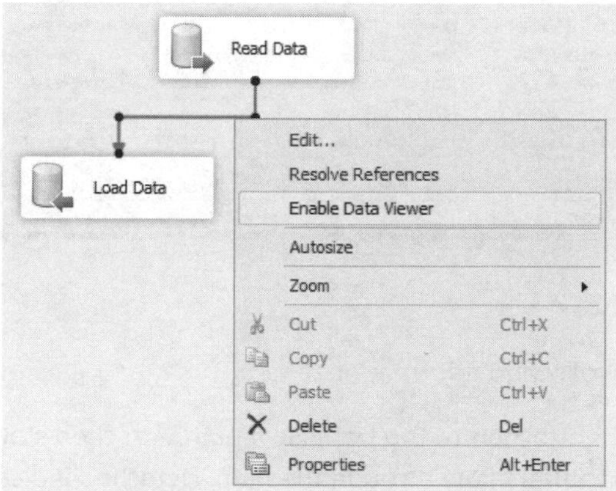

FIGURE 23-2 Adding a data viewer to a path.

When a data viewer is added to a path in a Data Flow, an icon indicating the data viewer is added to the path in the design surface. When the package is executed in Debug mode in SQL Server Data Tools, the data flowing through the path containing the viewer is displayed. Every data buffer that is sent through the Data Flow path is displayed in the data viewer window (see Figure 23-3). As data in each Data Flow buffer is displayed by the viewer, execution of Data Flow in the path containing the viewer is paused. The viewer window has the following controls:

- **Resume** Execution of the Data Flow in the path that contains the viewer is paused every time the data in the buffer is displayed in the viewer. The green arrow (or continue button) is used to resume the execution and display data in the next buffer.
- **Copy data** Data in the current buffer displayed in the viewer can be copied to the Clipboard using the Copy Data button in the viewer.
- **Detach** This button is used to skip displaying buffer data as buffers pass through the path in the Data Flow. It does not delete the data viewer from the package. It only disables display of buffer data for that particular execution of the package.

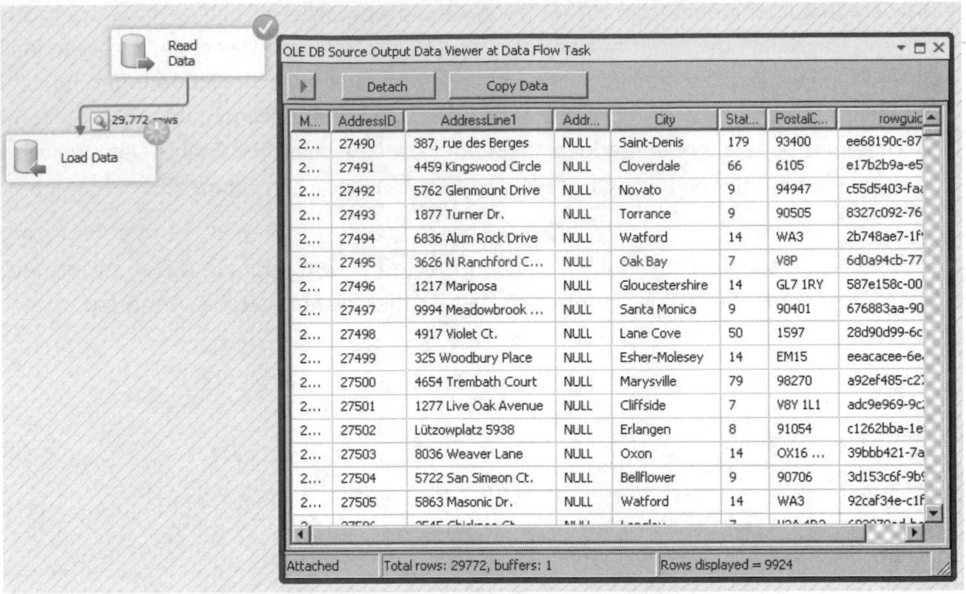

FIGURE 23-3 Buffer data displayed in viewer.

The status bar of the data viewer displays the following information:

- **Status** This indicates if the data viewer is attached to the Data Flow path. Attached status means the data viewer will be updated as buffers flow through the path. Detached indicates the viewer is not attached to the execution of the Data Flow in the path.
- **Total rows** This shows the number of rows that have passed through the path during the current execution of the Data Flow task.
- **Total buffers** This is the number of active Data Flow buffers associated with the path.
- **Rows displayed** This is the number of rows currently displayed in the viewer.

Data viewer functionality is enabled only if a package with a data viewer is executed in SQL Server Data Tools in Debug mode. If the package is executed in Business Intelligence Development Studio using the Ctrl+F5 option in SQL Server Data Tools, debugging will not be enabled and hence the data viewer will not be available. Data viewers will not have any effect on packages executed outside of SQL Server Data Tools. Figure 23-3 shows a Data Flow viewer in a package. There are some limitations in displaying data in the viewer. For example, BLOB or TEXT data cannot be displayed in the viewer and a placeholder text is displayed instead.

Data in Error Output

Error in a Data Flow can be caused by data truncation, unexpected data values, or issues in data conversion, expression evaluation, or lookup. Error output is available in several Data Flow components to deal with row-level errors in the data processed. A common reason for issues in SSIS-based data processing is ignoring the error outputs. Although component failure is the default option on error, it is possible to set property of a Data Flow component to ignore error, which can lead to data issues. The recommended approach is to redirect error rows to the error output of the components. During package design time, data viewers or a Row Count transformation in the error outputs can be used to understand the erroneous data in a Data Flow task. A popular package design-time approach to troubleshooting issues caused by data errors is using a Raw Destination on error output to persist the error data and later using the raw file generated in another package to profile the data and determine necessary actions that need to be taken to update the Data Flow with preprocessing steps before applying business logic to the data.

Breakpoints and Debug Windows

Variable and parameters values in a package can influence the execution-time logic of the package. Often the reason for data issues can be traced back to variables and parameters. In SQL Server Data Tools, values for variables and parameters can be inspected when packages are run in Debug mode using breakpoints and debug windows. Several types of breakpoints are available that are used to suspend the execution of packages for debugging purposes. Debug windows in SQL Server Data Tools like Locals or Watch can be used in conjunction with breakpoints for inspection. For example, the value of a date variable like *Last Load Date* that is used in a Data Flow task can be inspected by enabling a breakpoint on the *OnPreExecute* event of the task. This will suspend the execution of the package in Debug mode before the execution of the task begins. Locals windows can be used when the breakpoint is hit to inspect the value of the *Last Load Date* variable.

Troubleshooting in the Execution Environment

Earlier, you saw how to perform troubleshooting of data issues using SQL Server Data Tools, and the data visualizations that can be used to understand the data passing through the various Data Flow paths.

In this section, you learn about new capabilities introduced in SSIS 2012 that allow you to perform troubleshooting of data issues for packages that have been deployed to the SSIS Catalog. You will learn how to make use of Transact-SQL (T-SQL) stored procedures and views for troubleshooting.

Execution Data Statistics

It's great to get the real-time execution progress when you are debugging packages in the SSIS package designer. On every Data Flow path, there is a changing row count number that indicates how many rows have been processed on this path. This feature is very intuitive and helpful. After the package is deployed into the SSIS Catalog server, though, how can you get the execution progress information when the package is executed? You cannot get it through the package designer, as it does not support debugging executions on a remote server.

To solve this problem, SSIS Catalog provides a *catalog.execution_data_statistics* view that presents the detailed execution progress information. It tells you how many rows have been sent from one component to another component at the current time. Those statistics are updated in real time and they will be frozen after the execution finishes.

Listing 23-1 shows how to query this view to get the execution progress of an execution with ID 43.

LISTING 23-1 Query view *data.execution_data_statistics*

```
SELECT * FROM Catalog.execution_data_statistics WHERE execution_id = 43
```

To execute the preceding T-SQL query, you should have Read permission on the execution ID 43. Figure 23-4 shows the result of this query. Of course, the query result depends on the package executed.

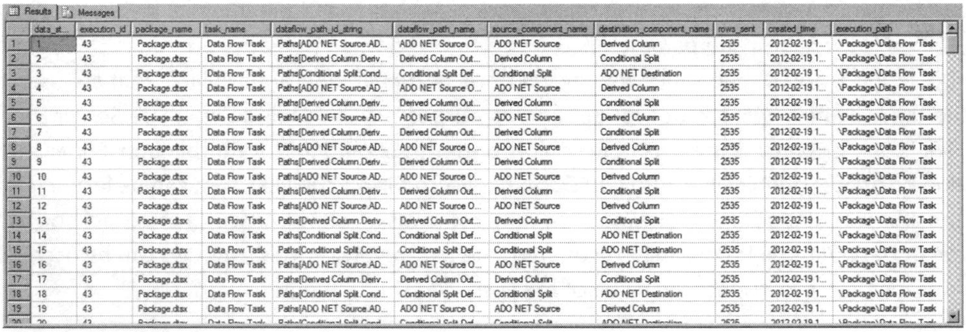

	data_st...	execution_id	package_name	task_name	dataflow_path_id_string	dataflow_path_name	source_component_name	destination_component_name	rows_sent	created_time	execution_path
1	1	43	Package.dtsx	Data Flow Task	Paths[ADO NET Source.AD...	ADO NET Source O...	ADO NET Source	Derived Column	2535	2012-02-19 1...	\Package\Data Flow Task
2	2	43	Package.dtsx	Data Flow Task	Paths[Derived Column.Deriv...	Derived Column Out...	Derived Column	Conditional Split	2535	2012-02-19 1...	\Package\Data Flow Task
3	3	43	Package.dtsx	Data Flow Task	Paths[Conditional Split.Cond...	Conditional Split Def...	Conditional Split	ADO NET Destination	2535	2012-02-19 1...	\Package\Data Flow Task
4	4	43	Package.dtsx	Data Flow Task	Paths[ADO NET Source.AD...	ADO NET Source O...	ADO NET Source	Derived Column	2535	2012-02-19 1...	\Package\Data Flow Task
5	5	43	Package.dtsx	Data Flow Task	Paths[Derived Column.Deriv...	Derived Column Out...	Derived Column	Conditional Split	2535	2012-02-19 1...	\Package\Data Flow Task
6	6	43	Package.dtsx	Data Flow Task	Paths[ADO NET Source.AD...	ADO NET Source O...	ADO NET Source	Derived Column	2535	2012-02-19 1...	\Package\Data Flow Task
7	7	43	Package.dtsx	Data Flow Task	Paths[Derived Column.Deriv...	Derived Column Out...	Derived Column	Conditional Split	2535	2012-02-19 1...	\Package\Data Flow Task
8	8	43	Package.dtsx	Data Flow Task	Paths[ADO NET Source.AD...	ADO NET Source O...	ADO NET Source	Derived Column	2535	2012-02-19 1...	\Package\Data Flow Task
9	9	43	Package.dtsx	Data Flow Task	Paths[Derived Column.Deriv...	Derived Column Out...	Derived Column	Conditional Split	2535	2012-02-19 1...	\Package\Data Flow Task
10	10	43	Package.dtsx	Data Flow Task	Paths[ADO NET Source.AD...	ADO NET Source O...	ADO NET Source	Derived Column	2535	2012-02-19 1...	\Package\Data Flow Task
11	11	43	Package.dtsx	Data Flow Task	Paths[Derived Column.Deriv...	Derived Column Out...	Derived Column	Conditional Split	2535	2012-02-19 1...	\Package\Data Flow Task
12	12	43	Package.dtsx	Data Flow Task	Paths[ADO NET Source.AD...	ADO NET Source O...	ADO NET Source	Derived Column	2535	2012-02-19 1...	\Package\Data Flow Task
13	13	43	Package.dtsx	Data Flow Task	Paths[Derived Column.Deriv...	Derived Column Out...	Derived Column	Conditional Split	2535	2012-02-19 1...	\Package\Data Flow Task
14	14	43	Package.dtsx	Data Flow Task	Paths[Conditional Split.Cond...	Conditional Split Def...	Conditional Split	ADO NET Destination	2535	2012-02-19 1...	\Package\Data Flow Task
15	15	43	Package.dtsx	Data Flow Task	Paths[Conditional Split.Cond...	Conditional Split Def...	Conditional Split	ADO NET Destination	2535	2012-02-19 1...	\Package\Data Flow Task
16	16	43	Package.dtsx	Data Flow Task	Paths[ADO NET Source.AD...	ADO NET Source O...	ADO NET Source	Derived Column	2535	2012-02-19 1...	\Package\Data Flow Task
17	17	43	Package.dtsx	Data Flow Task	Paths[Derived Column.Deriv...	Derived Column Out...	Derived Column	Conditional Split	2535	2012-02-19 1...	\Package\Data Flow Task
18	18	43	Package.dtsx	Data Flow Task	Paths[Conditional Split.Cond...	Conditional Split Def...	Conditional Split	ADO NET Destination	2535	2012-02-19 1...	\Package\Data Flow Task
19	19	43	Package.dtsx	Data Flow Task	Paths[ADO NET Source.AD...	ADO NET Source O...	ADO NET Source	Derived Column	2535	2012-02-19 1...	\Package\Data Flow Task
20	20	43	Package.dtsx	Data Flow Task	Paths[Conditional Split.Cond...	Conditional Split Def...	Conditional Split	ADO NET Destination	2535	2012-02-19 1...	\Package\Data Flow Task

FIGURE 23-4 Data displayed in view *catalog.execution_data_statistics.*

Some important columns in the view are *dataflow_path_name*, *source_component_name*, *destination_component_name*, and *rows_sent*. Those column names clearly explain their contents. The only column you might not be familiar with is *execution_path*. An execution path is the same as the package path if your package object is not under a loop; otherwise it will append a number index to the package path to help you differentiate each run, such as *\Package\For Each Loop\Data Flow task[3]*. The reason you need this column is because your Data Flow task might be executed multiple times during an execution.

A more exciting view is *catalog.execution_component_phases*. When a package is running unexpectedly slow, you need to figure out the root cause. Which phase cost most of the time during the execution, an abnormal initialization, or a slow database connection establishment? This view shows you each invocation of the Data Flow component; thus, you can clearly see how time is spent on each phase.

Listing 23-2 shows how to query all component phases on a given execution.

LISTING 23-2 Query view *catalog.execution_component_phases*

```
SELECT * FROM catalog.execution_component_phases WHERE execution_id=43
```

Similarly, you also need Read permission on the execution. Figure 23-5 shows the query result.

	phase_stats_id	execution_id	package_name	task_name	subcomponent_name	phase	start_time	end_time	execution_path
628	1252	43	Package.dtsx	Data Flow Task	ADO NET Destination	ProcessInput	2012-02-19 11:23:06.6228009 +08:00	2012-02-19 11:23:06.7008054 +08:00	\Package\Data Flow Task
629	1254	43	Package.dtsx	Data Flow Task	Conditional Split	ProcessInput	2012-02-19 11:23:06.8388132 +08:00	2012-02-19 11:23:06.8388132 +08:00	\Package\Data Flow Task
630	1256	43	Package.dtsx	Data Flow Task	Conditional Split	ProcessInput	2012-02-19 11:23:06.8538141 +08:00	2012-02-19 11:23:06.8538141 +08:00	\Package\Data Flow Task
631	1258	43	Package.dtsx	Data Flow Task	ADO NET Destination	ProcessInput	2012-02-19 11:23:07.1028283 +08:00	2012-02-19 11:23:07.1548313 +08:00	\Package\Data Flow Task
632	1260	43	Package.dtsx	Data Flow Task	ADO NET Destination	ProcessInput	2012-02-19 11:23:06.8408134 +08:00	2012-02-19 11:23:06.9098173 +08:00	\Package\Data Flow Task
633	1262	43	Package.dtsx	Data Flow Task	Derived Column	ProcessInput	2012-02-19 11:23:06.9718209 +08:00	2012-02-19 11:23:06.9718209 +08:00	\Package\Data Flow Task
634	1264	43	Package.dtsx	Data Flow Task	Conditional Split	ProcessInput	2012-02-19 11:23:06.9748210 +08:00	2012-02-19 11:23:06.9748210 +08:00	\Package\Data Flow Task
635	1267	43	Package.dtsx	Data Flow Task	ADO NET Destination	ProcessInput	2012-02-19 11:23:07.1578315 +08:00	2012-02-19 11:23:07.2068343 +08:00	\Package\Data Flow Task
636	1269	43	Package.dtsx	Data Flow Task	ADO NET Destination	PostExecute	2012-02-19 11:23:07.2828386 +08:00	2012-02-19 11:23:07.2828386 +08:00	\Package\Data Flow Task
637	1271	43	Package.dtsx	Data Flow Task	ADO NET Destination	ReleaseConnections	2012-02-19 11:23:07.2848388 +08:00	2012-02-19 11:23:07.2858388 +08:00	\Package\Data Flow Task
638	1273	43	Package.dtsx	Data Flow Task	ADO NET Source	PostExecute	2012-02-19 11:23:07.2868389 +08:00	2012-02-19 11:23:07.2868389 +08:00	\Package\Data Flow Task
639	1276	43	Package.dtsx	Data Flow Task	ADO NET Destination	ProcessInput	2012-02-19 11:23:07.0438250 +08:00	2012-02-19 11:23:07.0998282 +08:00	\Package\Data Flow Task
640	1279	43	Package.dtsx	Data Flow Task	ADO NET Destination	ProcessInput	2012-02-19 11:23:07.2098345 +08:00	2012-02-19 11:23:07.2748382 +08:00	\Package\Data Flow Task
641	1281	43	Package.dtsx	Data Flow Task	ADO NET Destination	ProcessInput	2012-02-19 11:23:07.2778384 +08:00	2012-02-19 11:23:07.2778384 +08:00	\Package\Data Flow Task
642	1283	43	Package.dtsx	Data Flow Task	ADO NET Source	ReleaseConnections	2012-02-19 11:23:07.4928507 +08:00	2012-02-19 11:23:07.4938507 +08:00	\Package\Data Flow Task
643	1285	43	Package.dtsx	Data Flow Task	Conditional Split	PostExecute	2012-02-19 11:23:07.4958508 +08:00	2012-02-19 11:23:07.4958508 +08:00	\Package\Data Flow Task
644	1287	43	Package.dtsx	Data Flow Task	Conditional Split	ReleaseConnections	2012-02-19 11:23:07.4978509 +08:00	2012-02-19 11:23:07.4978509 +08:00	\Package\Data Flow Task
645	1289	43	Package.dtsx	Data Flow Task	Derived Column	PostExecute	2012-02-19 11:23:07.4998511 +08:00	2012-02-19 11:23:07.4998511 +08:00	\Package\Data Flow Task
646	1291	43	Package.dtsx	Data Flow Task	Derived Column	ReleaseConnections	2012-02-19 11:23:07.5018512 +08:00	2012-02-19 11:23:07.5018512 +08:00	\Package\Data Flow Task
647	1293	43	Package.dtsx	Data Flow Task	ADO NET Destination	Cleanup	2012-02-19 11:23:07.6728610 +08:00	2012-02-19 11:23:07.6728610 +08:00	\Package\Data Flow Task

FIGURE 23-5 Data displayed in view *catalog.execution_component_phase.*

You can also perform some aggregations on this view to get some more useful statistics. For example, Listing 23-3 shows the T-SQL statement that sums up the invocation count and total time spent on each phase and then groups by each subcomponent and Figure 23-6 shows the result.

LISTING 23-3 Aggregate the information from view *catalog.execution_component_phases*

```
SELECT subcomponent_name, phase, count(phase_stats_id) AS InvocationCount,
SUM (DATEDIFF(second, CAST(start_time AS datetime2(7)), CAST(end_time AS datetime2(7)))) AS
TotalTime
FROM catalog.execution_component_phases
WHERE execution_id=43
GROUP BY subcomponent_name, phase
ORDER BY subcomponent_name, phase
```

	subcomponent_name	phase	InvocationCount	TotalTime
1	ADO NET Destination	AcquireConnections	3	0
2	ADO NET Destination	Cleanup	1	0
3	ADO NET Destination	PostExecute	1	0
4	ADO NET Destination	PreExecute	1	0
5	ADO NET Destination	PrepareForExecute	1	0
6	ADO NET Destination	ProcessInput	92	10
7	ADO NET Destination	ReleaseConnections	3	0
8	ADO NET Destination	Validate	2	0
9	ADO NET Source	AcquireConnections	3	0
10	ADO NET Source	Cleanup	1	0
11	ADO NET Source	PostExecute	1	0
12	ADO NET Source	PreExecute	1	0

FIGURE 23-6 An aggregation result on view *catalog.execution_component_phases.*

As expected, there would be some performance cost to update the preceding two views in real time during package execution. By default, an execution does not generate the statistics data. You must change the logging level of the execution to produce the data just shown.

- For the *catalog.execution_component_phases* view, the logging level must be set to *Performance* or *Verbose.*
- For the *catalog.execution_data_statistics* view, the logging level must be set to *Verbose.*

To set the logging level, just open the Advanced tab of the Execute Packages dialog box in SQL Server Management Studio and choose your logging level, as shown in Figure 23-7.

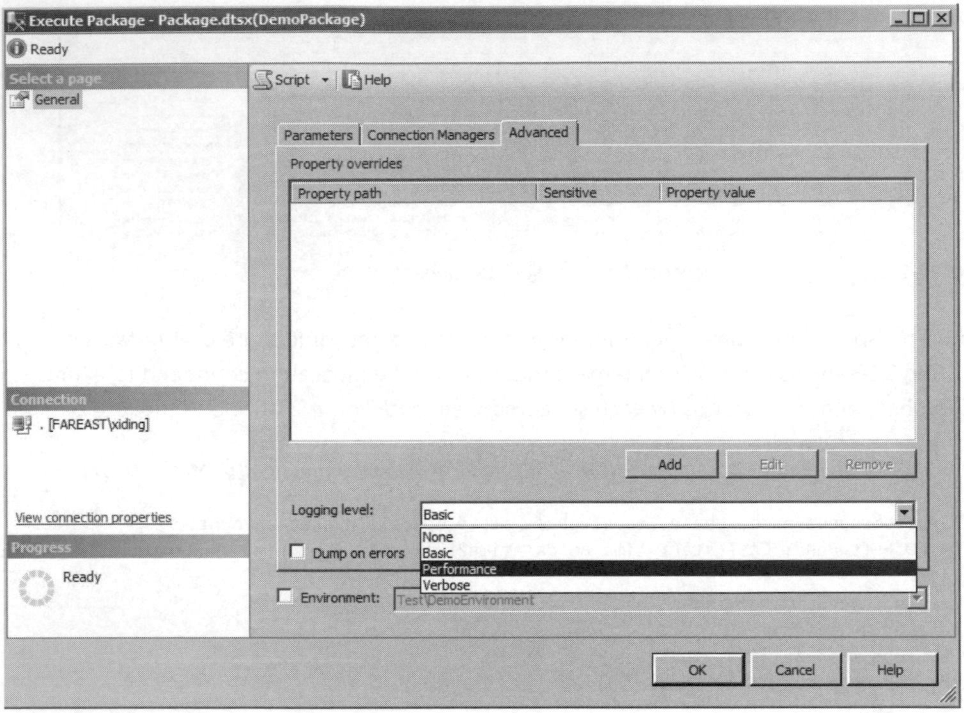

FIGURE 23-7 Set the logging level to produce statistics data.

Data Tap

The ability to perform data taps on SSIS packages during execution is new in SSIS 2012. It helps package developers to troubleshoot the Data Flow issues in a production environment. You might remember how we handle Data Flow issues under the package designer environment. For example, usually we will attach some data viewers into different data paths if the output data content is not expected. By checking the data in different viewers, we could quickly figure out where the data is wrongly converted.

But what can a package developer do if the package has been deployed into the SSIS Catalog server? As you learned earlier, the package is executed in a non-interactive way on a remote production server. In most enterprises, there are strict policies governing modifications of SSIS packages that have been deployed to a production environment.

Data tap is introduced for this problem. Essentially it is a simulation of the data viewer in the package designer environment. After you create an execution you can set some "tap points" on some Data Flow paths. All data that passes this point during execution will be captured and saved to a file. Thus you can analyze those data after the package execution finishes. Data tap does not affect the original package behavior. What has been saved is a just a copy of the data.

There is no visualization help in SQL Server Management Studio to set up data taps on an execution. You have to use T-SQL to make data tap settings. SSIS Catalog provides the stored procedures and views for data tap listed in Table 23-1.

TABLE 23-1 Data tap related stored procedures and views

Object Name	Object Type	Description
Catalog.add_data_tap	Stored Procedure	Add a data tap into the package. SSIS Catalog will check whether the Data Flow task and Data Flow component path is valid. This application programming interface (API) locates the target Data Flow task by its package path.
Catalog.add_data_tap_by_guid	Stored Procedure	Add data tap into any parent or child packages. No checking on the Data Flow task globally unique identifier (GUID) or Data Flow component path. This API locates the target Data Flow task by its task GUID.
Catalog.remove_data_tap	Stored Procedure	Remove an existing data tap by ID.
Catalog.execution_data_taps	View	This view lists all defined data taps.

Add Data Taps by Name

Let's start with *catalog.add_data_tap*, which is the most frequently used one. To add a data tap, you first need to create an execution. Listing 23-4 shows how to use this stored procedure to add a data tap on an existing execution with ID 44.

LISTING 23-4 Add a data tap

```
EXEC [catalog].[add_data_tap]
@execution_id = 44,
@task_package_path = N'\Package\Data Flow Task',
@dataflow_path_id_string = N'Paths[Derived Column.Derived Column Output]',
@data_filename = N'Data.csv',
@max_rows = 100
```

This T-SQL statement first specifies the target execution ID, and then the package path of the target Data Flow task, because there could be multiple Data Flow tasks in a package. Then it specifies the identification string of a Data Flow component path, which is the location to which the data should be tapped. The last two parameters tell the engine how many rows should be tapped and the file name to which the tapped data should be saved.

The package path of a given Data Flow task is shown as a read-only property in the package designer, as shown in Figure 23-8.

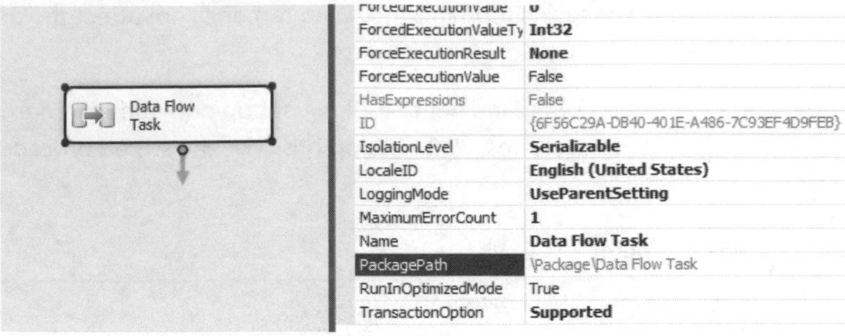

FIGURE 23-8 Get the package path of a Data Flow task.

To get the identification string of a given Data Flow path, you need to open the Data Flow design view and select the path. The identification string is also shown as a read-only property in the Properties window, as shown in Figure 23-9.

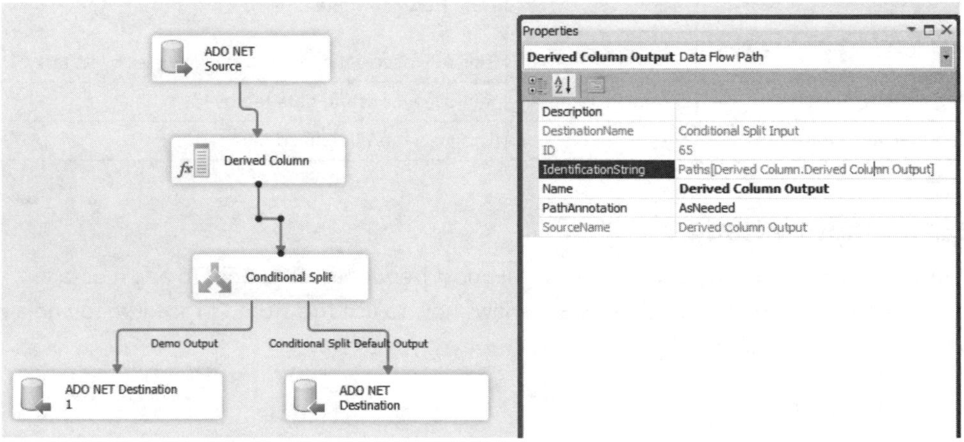

FIGURE 23-9 Get the identification string of a given Data Flow path.

All the data tap files are saved in the folder *%Program Files%\Microsoft SQL Server\110\DTS\DataDumps*. This is the only place that the SSIS Catalog will produce data tap files. In the preceding query, you only need to specify the file name instead of the full path. If you specify the full file path, it will return an error. One interesting issue is how to name the file if the Data Flow task is executed under a loop. In that case different data tap files will be generated for different loops. Because only one file name is specified in the stored procedure, a number such as "[1]" or "[2]" will be appended to the file name.

The data tap file is a standard .csv file with column names in the header line. You can open the file with Microsoft Excel or any regular text editor. Figure 23-10 shows the generated data tap file opened by Windows Notepad.

FIGURE 23-10 A data tap file opened by Windows Notepad.

To set a data tap you must have Modify permission on the target execution. Also all data taps must be set before the execution starts. You could set multiple data taps on a single execution. To protect the package data information, by default only the execution owner and machine administrator group have access to the generated data tap files.

The SSIS Catalog provides a *catalog.data_taps* view, so it's very easy to query all data taps that have been defined on an execution. The T-SQL statement in Listing 23-5 shows how to get the data tap lists defined on execution ID 44. Figure 23-11 shows the query result.

LISTING 23-5 Query all data taps defined on an execution

```
SELECT * FROM catalog.execution_data_taps where execution_id=44
```

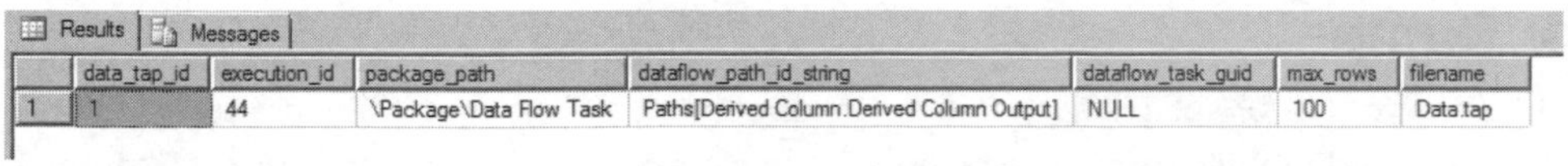

Results | Messages

	data_tap_id	execution_id	package_path	dataflow_path_id_string	dataflow_task_guid	max_rows	filename
1	1	44	\Package\Data Flow Task	Paths[Derived Column.Derived Column Output]	NULL	100	Data.tap

FIGURE 23-11 Data taps defined on a given execution.

Add Data Taps by GUID

Another stored procedure to set data tap is *catalog.add_data_tap_by_guid*, an advanced version of the stored procedure *catalog.add_data_tap*. We need an advanced version because there could be a complex parent–child invocation chain during package execution. For example, package A could call package B and package B could call package C depending on dynamic conditions. The former stored procedure *catalog.add_data_tap* specifies the Data Flow task by its package path. It is very user friendly, and the SSIS Catalog could verify its correctness before package execution. That does not apply to child packages, however. The SSIS Catalog cannot find the package path or Data Flow path if the data tap is targeted to a child package.

To resolve this problem, the stored procedure *catalog.add_data_tap_by_guid* is introduced. As its name suggests, this procedure uses GUID instead of package path to specify the target Data Flow task. During package execution, the SSIS engine will check data tap settings before executing any Data Flow task. If its GUID matches one of the given GUIDs, the corresponding data tap setting will be applied to this Data Flow task.

To get the GUID of a Data Flow task, just select the task in the package designer, and then copy the value of ID property in the Properties window, shown in Figure 23-12.

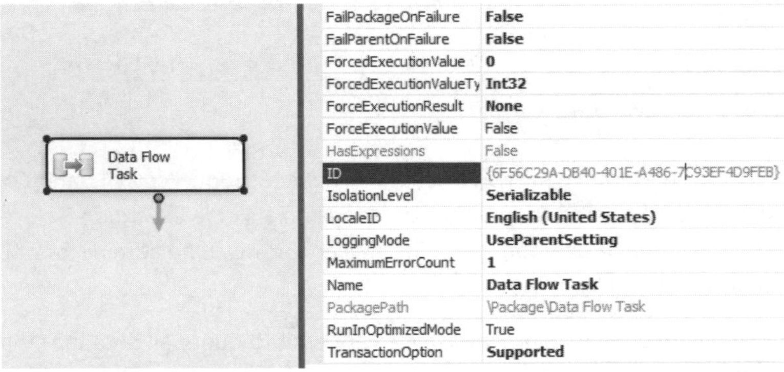

FIGURE 23-12 Get the GUID of a Data Flow task.

Because a child package can be executed conditionally, the SSIS Catalog does not require all provided GUIDs to be matched. If a GUID is never matched during execution, it is just silently ignored.

Error Dumps

One important of feature of SSIS is that it can generate dump files when there are some errors during execution. Those dump files provide a comprehensive context for troubleshooting. In Chapter 11, "Running SSIS Packages," we discussed how to configure error dump options when running packages with the dtexec utility. Let's do a quick recap:

- Use the command-line argument */Dump ErrorCode* to declare that a dump file should be generated for a specific error.

- Use the command-line argument */DumpOnError* to declare that a dump file should be generated for any errors.
- You can set the options in the system registry so that you don't need to set the arguments on dtexec every time.

The same problem also exists when the packages are running on the SSIS Catalog, which also provides the functionalities already discussed. The only difference is that you need to specify them as execution parameters instead of command-line arguments. Table 23-2 shows all execution parameters related to error dumps.

TABLE 23-2 Execution parameters related to error dumps

Parameter Name	Data Type	Description
DUMP_ON_EVENT	Boolean	Whether SSIS Catalog should generate dump files.
DUMP_EVENT_CODE	String	A comma-separated event code list that SSIS Catalog should generate dump files for.
DUMP_ON_ERROR	Boolean	Create dump files for any errors.

To assign a value to an execution parameter you need to call the stored procedure *catalog.set_execution_parameter_value*. Listing 23-6 shows how to set the *DumpOnError* option on an execution with execution ID 45.

LISTING 23-6 Set the value of execution parameter

```
EXEC        [catalog].[set_execution_parameter_value]
            @execution_id = 45,
            @object_type = 50,
            @parameter_name = N'DUMP_ON_ERROR',
            @parameter_value = 1
```

In that T-SQL statement, you need to specify the target execution ID, parameter name, and parameter value. Those parameters are pretty straightforward. The only mysterious parameter is @*object_type*, which indicates the category ID of the target parameter. The category could be project parameters, package parameters, or system execution parameters. By assigning a unique ID to each type, you can avoid the possible coincidence that someone also defined a package parameter named *DUMP_ON_ERROR*. In this case it should be 50 because it is a system execution parameter.

The SSIS Catalog also provides a *catalog.execution_parameter_values* view so you can view the value of each parameter. You can query the view to make sure your settings are correct, as shown in Listing 23-7.

LISTING 23-7 Query the values of all execution parameters

```
SELECT * FROM Catalog.execution_parameter_values WHERE execution_id=45
```

As the query result shows in Figure 23-13, the value of execution parameter *DUMP_ON_ERROR* has been set to 1.

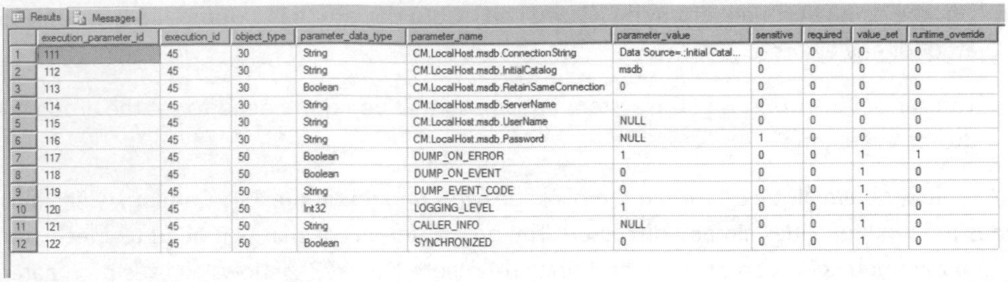

	execution_parameter_id	execution_id	object_type	parameter_data_type	parameter_name	parameter_value	sensitive	required	value_set	runtime_override
1	111	45	30	String	CM.LocalHost.msdb.ConnectionString	Data Source=.;Initial Catal...	0	0	0	0
2	112	45	30	String	CM.LocalHost.msdb.InitialCatalog	msdb	0	0	0	0
3	113	45	30	Boolean	CM.LocalHost.msdb.RetainSameConnection	0	0	0	0	0
4	114	45	30	String	CM.LocalHost.msdb.ServerName	.	0	0	0	0
5	115	45	30	String	CM.LocalHost.msdb.UserName	NULL	0	0	0	0
6	116	45	30	String	CM.LocalHost.msdb.Password	NULL	1	0	0	0
7	117	45	50	Boolean	DUMP_ON_ERROR	1	0	0	1	1
8	118	45	50	Boolean	DUMP_ON_EVENT	0	0	0	1	0
9	119	45	50	String	DUMP_EVENT_CODE	0	0	0	1	0
10	120	45	50	Int32	LOGGING_LEVEL	1	0	0	1	0
11	121	45	50	String	CALLER_INFO	NULL	0	0	1	0
12	122	45	50	Boolean	SYNCHRONIZED	0	0	0	1	0

FIGURE 23-13 The execution parameter values.

Because *DumpOnError* is a very frequently used option, the SQL Server Management Studio user interface provides a shortcut for it. In the Execute Package dialog box in SQL Server Management Studio, click the Advanced tab and you will see there is a Dump On Errors check box (see Figure 23-14).

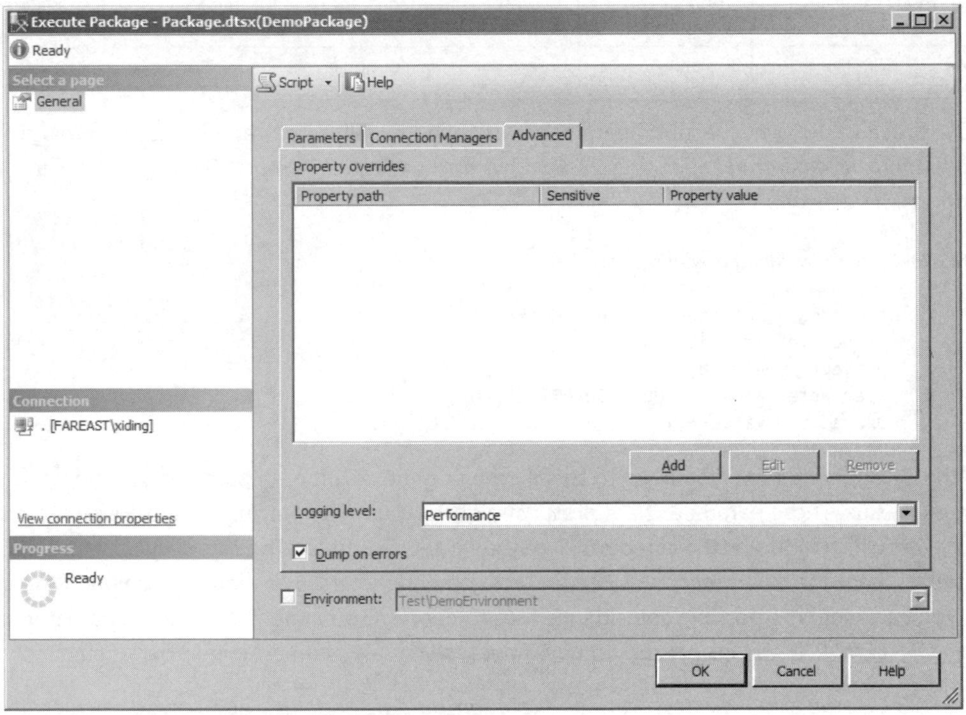

FIGURE 23-14 Set the dump on error options in SQL Server Management Studio.

As mentioned in Chapter 11, the dumped files are put into the folder *%Program Files%\Microsoft SQL Server\110\Shared\ErrorDumps*. Every dump actually contains two files. The file with the .mdmp extension is a binary file that contains the memory snapshot and requires some special tool such as WinDBG to view the file contents. The other file with extension .tmp is a plain text file and you can open it with a regular text reader such as Windows Notepad. It saves the values of some important class members when the error happens.

The SSIS Catalog also provides a stored procedure *catalog.create_execution_dump* to generate dynamic dump files on the fly. Its functionality is the same as the traditional dtutil tool with the option */Dump*. The stored procedure generates a dump file to save the current context and it does not affect the package execution. Listing 23-8 shows such a T-SQL statement to generate a dynamic dump file.

LISTING 23-8 Create a dynamic execution dump

```
EXEC [catalog].[create_execution_dump] @execution_id = 1
```

Notice you need Modify permission on the target execution to create the dynamic dump.

Summary

In this chapter, you learned different options available in SSIS for troubleshooting data issues. Although the troubleshooting capabilities available in the SSIS package design environment help in identifying and fixing data issues, it is essentially inevitable to need to deal with similar issues in a production environment. That's where troubleshooting capabilities in the execution environment help. SSIS packs together these powerful functionalities and enables you to carry out investigations on data-related issues.

Index

B

C

D

E

F

G

H

I

J

K

L

M

N

O

P

S

T

U

V

About the Authors

DR. WEE HYONG TOK is a Program Manager on the SQL Server Integration Services team. Since joining the team in 2008, he has worked on many aspects of the product. Prior to joining Microsoft, Wee Hyong is a Microsoft Most Valuable Professional (MVP), and frequently presents at various technology conferences.

RAKESH PARIDA is a Software Development Engineer on the SQL Server Integration Services team. Rakesh joined the team during the development of SQL Server 2012 and has worked on many new features of this release. He has been working with SSIS since SQL Server 2005 and has extensively worked with ETL frameworks, data warehousing and SSIS based solutions.

MATT MASSON is a Senior Program Manager on the SQL Server Integration Services team. Matt joined the team shortly after the SQL Server 2005 release, and has worked on many aspects of the product. A frequent presenter at Microsoft conferences, he is heavily involved with the SSIS community, and maintains the SSIS Team Blog (*http://blogs.msdn.com/b/mattm/*).

DR. XIAONING DING is a Software Development Engineer on the SQL Server Integration Services team. Xiaoning joined the team in 2007 shortly before the release of SQL Server 2008. After spending some time on the development of SSIS Connector for SAP BW, he started working on SQL Server 2012. Xiaoning has worked on many aspects of the product.

KAARTHIK SIVASHANMUGAM is a Lead Software Engineer in SQL Server Data Curation team. Kaarthik joined the Integration Services team during the development of SQL Server 2005 SP1 and involved in several feature improvements in SSIS until SQL Server 2012.